Black Drama
Anthology

EDITED BY

Woodie King and Ron Milner

———

Columbia University Press

New York and London   1972

Contents

INTRODUCTION: EVOLUTION OF A PEOPLE'S THEATER
Woodie King and Ron Milner   vii

JUNKIES ARE FULL OF (SHHH . . . .)
by Imamu Amiri Baraka (LeRoi Jones)   11

BLOODRITES
by Imamu Amiri Baraka (LeRoi Jones)   25

JUNEBUG GRADUATES TONIGHT
by Archie Shepp   33

THE CORNER
by Ed Bullins   77

WHO'S GOT HIS OWN
by Ron Milner   89

CHARADES ON EAST FOURTH STREET
by Lonne Elder   147

GABRIEL
by Clifford Mason   167

BROTHERHOOD
by Douglas Turner Ward   229

THE ONE
by Oliver Pitcher   243

THE MARRIAGE
by Donald Greaves   253

THE OWL KILLER
by Philip Hayes Dean   301

REQUIEM FOR BROTHER X
by William Wellington Mackey   325

ODODO
by Joseph A. Walker   349

CONTENTS

ALL WHITE CASTE
by Ben Caldwell   389

MOTHER AND CHILD
by Langston Hughes   399

THE BREAKOUT
by Charles (Oyamo) Gordon   407

THREE X LOVE
by Ron Zuber   429

A MEDAL FOR WILLIE
by William Branch   439

LADIES IN WAITING
by Peter DeAnda   475

BLACK CYCLE
by Martie Charles   525

STRICTLY MATRIMONY
by Errol Hill   553

STAR OF THE MORNING
by Loften Mitchell   575

TOE JAM
by Elaine Jackson   641

Evolution of a People's Theater

UNTIL QUITE RECENTLY, so-called Negro plays were plays about Negroes written by whites to be viewed by a white audience. No attempt to change this pattern occurred until the mid-fifties after the demise of the "Negro theaters" in Harlem when the fashionable "night out" in Harlem became unfashionable. It was about then that it was discovered, in a series of small community projects, that survival meant developing within the community. Actors who had worked with the white groups were instrumental in developing black community groups. Gradually the plays being produced changed from revivals of white plays with all-black casts to original dramas written by writers familiar with the black life-style. The plays no longer were written for white acceptance, since no white people would see them. In schools, YMCA's, and churches across the country, from Los Angeles' Watts to New York's Harlem, plays started trying to communicate to those nearest, those next door. This was done out of necessity, out of a need to survive. Those in the audiences were few, but those few responded. More blacks tried their hand at playwriting.

In the thirties and forties, the Communists tried to use theater to propagandize blacks; in the fifties, it was the politicians who tried to use theater, and in the sixties, the social workers. Theater communicated directly and quickly. There was no easier or cheaper way to reach black people. In the late fifties, Lorraine Hansberry's *Raisin in the Sun* reaffirmed in blacks the necessity for more involvement in black theater. As a matter of fact, Lonne Elder III, Robert Hooks, Douglas Turner Ward, and Ossie Davis all appeared in *Raisin in the Sun*. This marked a turning point, for until this time no black writer, black actor, black director, or technician had benefited financially from any of the plays about black people that had been presented. It had always been a white producer or white writer who had profited. Phillip Yordan's *Anna Lucasta* is a case in point. Marc Connelly's *Green Pastures, Porgy and Bess, In Abraham's Bosom*—on down the line—are all cases in point.

In the early sixties, poverty programs came into existence around the country. Social workers tried to use theater, and young people who had only dreamed of participating in the theater arts now had the opportunity to participate through so-called cultural enrichment programs. Toward the mid-sixties these projects became more professional. The message became the medium. Serious black writers who had been unable to get

their plays done in the mainstream theaters submitted their work to the programs. The underground flocked to see productions of these writers' plays. And the writers began to receive major attention from the critics who reviewed plays on Off-Broadway.

But because the critics and the programs' administrators still sought to define black theater and to place restrictions on them, these young writers were forced to move out of the poverty program structure and set up their own thing.

And so it came to pass—the day black artists realized they would never be accepted in the mainstream of American theater life. It came very early for black theater. American theater was (and still is) the nut that few blacks are able to crack. This is due to the directness and immediacy of the image projected. LeRoi Jones called it "revolutionary theater": "The plays that will split the heavens for us will be called 'the destruction of America.' The heroes will be Crazy Horse, Denmark Vesey, Patrice Lumumba, but not history, not memory, not sad sentimental groping for a warmth in our despair." It was an art that had to express in beautiful and artistic form the life-styles of its black participants. Black participants had to create their own Othellos, their own Willy Lomans. This realization came when the country was (as it still is) going through terrible changes, political and social. After 360 years, blacks could no longer believe anything white people said, and they were, indeed, making them face up to their lies.

Black theater is, in fact, about the destruction of tradition, the traditional role of Negroes in white theater. Listen to Ron Milner, playwright and director of Spirit of Shango Theater in Detroit, run it down: "It will be a theater having to do with love of one's self, and one's personal, national, and international family; with wariness and hatred of one's personal, national, and international enemies; with, ideally, points as to how to break their grip and splatter their power."

Black theater—go home! If a new black theater is to be born, sustain itself, and justify its own being, it must go home. Go home psychically, mentally, aesthetically, and, we think, physically.

Now what does all this mean? First off, what do we mean by a new black theater? We mean the ritualized reflection and projection of a unique and particular way of being, born of the unique and particular conditioning of black people leasing time on this planet which is controlled by white men; it has something to do with the breaking of that "leasing-syndrome." A theater emerging from artists who realize that for the black

viii

people of this world, and, specifically, this country, every "universal" human malady, dilemma, desire, or wonder is, by the heat of the pressure of white racism, compounded and enlarged, agitated and aggravated, accented and distilled to make that omni-suffusing, grinding sense of being we once called the blues but might now just term: *blackness*. From this peculiar and particular extra dimension of being, of experiences, of conditioning, will come the kind of theater we are looking for. And neither Shaw nor O'Neill nor any of those other great ones, could write it. Not within this level of blackness we are talking about.

We say that if this theater is to be, it must—psychically, mentally, aesthetically, and physically—go home. We are sure you know now what we mean by going home psychically and mentally. But just in case there is still any confusion, let us try to run a short, quick summary. By *psychically* we mean coming away from your dues-paying to all those "outside— i.e., white—influences" and going into the real, black, YOU by way of those places, people, and experiences which began and had the most to do with the shaping of what is now yourself; we mean making works, theater, out of that and, in doing it, extending and validating that particular psyche. By *mentally* we mean understanding that you and your experiences are, in time and history, collective repetitions, have been repeated and multiplied many times. So, as artists, you are to try to find the terms and the pictures which will most simply clarify those experiences and that knowledge for the *you's* who do not, or could not, understand what is, or was, happening to them, and to future *you's* who will need to be warned and directed in terms from inside that level we call *blackness*.

Going home *aesthetically* will follow naturally after those first two steps—since your aesthetics come out of your mental and psychic environment. So we won't go into the demand for new dynamics, for a new intensity of language and form that the material and the desired atmosphere will make on you, except to say that the further you go home, the more startlingly new and black the techniques become. Musicians are pointing that out to us.

Now, going home *physically* with the new theater means just that. Probably we should have started here. For this new theater must be housed in, sustained and judged by, and be a usable projection of and to a black community!

Blacks will never have a theater, an art, a life really representative of them and their kind until they and their kind have come together and pooled their desires, plans, resources, and

capabilities to throw off the jailers. (Yes, there are aesthetic and psychic jailers!)

Broadway does not want our blackness, wasn't designed or intended for it, definitely doesn't want any strange new forms inspired by that very blackness. She is a contented fat white cow. If you can slip in and milk her for a minute—well, then, more black power to you, brother. But we're telling you—it's a weird price she's asking. She wants you to be a singing hyena, dancing on the graves of yourself and everyone you know. (Serious plays, dramas, are things that come from some other country, some other century, and even then are best set in a madhouse. And "Black Comedy" has nothing to do with Afro-Americans!)

And dig it closely, brothers—*There is no longer any such thing as Off-Broadway:* it, like all recognized New York theater, is in the *Great White Way.*

Recognizing all of this, and understanding that if we blacks are to have a theater in our own image, according to our own views, then we blacks will have to say which plays are in those images and of those views, we have here compiled an anthology of works by twenty-two of the best black playwrights. There is no generation gap. The plays deal in time with both the historical past and the soon-to-come future. (There is no great distance between LeRoi Jones and Langston Hughes—the times that produced them are the same.) William Mackey, Joe Walker, and Ron Zuber may well become names familiar to every classroom. Douglas Turner Ward uses a laugh, while Ben Caldwell uses a blunt blade, but they are out to break down the same doors. You may be familiar with some of the writers such as Ed Bullins and Lonne Elder III; others such as Philip Hayes Dean, Charles (Oyamo) Gordon, and Elaine Jackson will be new names, but all command equal respect.

Twenty-three selections from an immensely rich field of talented black artists forging new, unique, and viable theater. Yes, new, unique, viable. It will eventually happen to theater in this country, this world, just as it happened to this world's music when black musicians set out to artistically express their own sense of reality.

WOODIE KING and RON MILNER

New York City
May 1970

Junkies Are Full of (SHHH . . .)*

by IMAMU AMIRI BARAKA (LeRoi Jones)

Imamu Amiri Baraka (LeRoi Jones), poet, playwright, novelist, and essayist, was born in Newark, New Jersey, in 1934. He graduated from high school in Newark, and from Howard University when he was nineteen. He has been both a John Hay Whitney and a Guggenheim Fellow. He was awarded the Obie for Best American Play of the 1963–64 season for *Dutchman,* and is a scholar of the Yoruba Academy. Mr. Jones is the founder of the Black Arts Theater in Harlem, and is presently director of the Spirit House in Newark. Among his published works are: *Preface to a Twenty-Volume Suicide Note, Blues People, Dutchman* and *The Slave, The Dead Lecturer, The System of Dante's Hell, The Baptism* and *The Toilet, Black Art, Black Music, Arm Yourself or Harm Yourself.* He is the editor, with Larry Neal, of *Black Fire,* an anthology of Afro-American writing. *In Our Terribleness,* a poetic-photographic work on black people, was published in 1970. He is also the author of the highly acclaimed ritual drama *Slave Ship* and a full-length play entitled *A Recent Killing.*

CAST

CONFETTI
FIRST ITALIAN (FRANKIE)
SECOND ITALIAN (SAMMY)
FIRST JEW (IZZY)
SECOND JEW (IRVING)
BIGTIME
DAMU (BLK MAN)
CHUMA (BLK MAN)
VOICE
SAM
YOUNG BOY
DOODOO
WOMAN
SIMBAS

[*In this and the following play, the idiosyncratic punctuation and spelling have been retained according to the author's wishes.—Eds.]

Scene 1

ITALIAN (*in white hat, noticing audience*): What? A buncha niggers! (*Approaches edge of stage with mock-ginnie tone.*)

11

I'se a cosa nostra. Means "our thing." Like niggers sez "our thang," we say "cosa nostra" means our Italian, Siciliano, in old days thing. In old days because now we have to hire a few niggerinos to take the place of the Sicilianos, you know you can't get many Italian kids to do the hard stuff no more. They all wanna go the fuck to Cornell or someplace. What the hell, how can you blame 'em.

VOICE: Hey, phone call from Hughie.

ITALIAN: What? I just talked to that creep. What's he want now?

VOICE: Niggers actin' up again. He needs you to get the dust over to the south ward area right on.

ITALIAN: Right: OK, lemme me have the phone . . . Hughie . . . Yeh . . . Yeh . . . Hey . . . Look, who the hell you talkin' to? . . . Thass right . . . Thass right . . . You'll get the stuff . . . Who the hell got you elected in the first place, no-neck??? Thass right. Thass right. When I say I'll get the powder there, I mean it. Powder and the goofballs. The pills. Thass right. I got a meet with the nigger in a few secs! Thass right! Just cool off, Hughie. Yeh, yeh, I heard about the grand jury. What the hell, they ain't gonna do nothing, it's just a lot of talk to front off . . . Yeh, I told you don't worry, didn't I, so shadup about it . . . Go cool off . . . (*Hangs up.*) (*To audience.*) Jeez, what a creep. How the hell that bum got elected . . .

(BIGTIME *trying to be hip nigger, semi-high, lapses into nod from time to time, but trying to make believe he ain't high, but businesslike.*)

ITALIAN: Howsit going, Bigtime? (*Puts out hand.*)

BIGTIME: How's everything, Mr. Confetti? Things OK with me. You know. Everything's together. You know.

ITALIAN: How much ya buyin' this time, Bigtime?

BIGTIME: Uh, gimme a halfa load . . . and about a hundred torpedoes.

ITALIAN: Thass all? What's going on? You usin' all the stuff yrself??

BIGTIME: What? (*Tries to straighten up.*) What? Naw, Mr. Confetti, you know I don't use that stuff. Strictly takin' care a bizness. You know that, Mr. Confetti. Only suckers use hops . . . I look like a sucker to you? . . . and the rest a that jive is for shorties. I just had a bad week. I got beat a couple times. Couple a jive niggers . . .

ITALIAN: Look, Bigtime, don't shit me! The south ward ain't high as it shd be. Too much activity going on up there. A guy called me just before you come in. Too much runnin' around, political jazz going on over there, same in central

ward. (*Begins to get more intense.*) Now, you told me you cd get people high and make the bux . . . you didn't tell me you wanted to stick it in yr own arm . . . whatta you think, I'm a nut?

BIGTIME: Naw, Mr. Confetti. I can get people high. I can get the bux too. I ain't shootin' up. I just got burnt by some turkeys.

ITALIAN (*advances*): You betta get the money you owe me . . . or I get another boy . . . Get me the money . . . and you betta get that dope out in the community, where it belongs.

BIGTIME: Yas, sir . . . yas, sir . . . I'm gonna do it, Mr. Confetti, gimme another chance . . . I'ma get the dust right off, straight on back to you, you know me and you tight.

ITALIAN (*steps back*): Don't touch me. You get the bux or you get lead for breakfast! And get them niggers high, you hear me . . . get'em high!!! (*Whips out package of glassine envelopes . . . bag of bills.*) OK, now where's the dough?

(BIGTIME *comes out with money.*)

ITALIAN: What? That's all you got? Goddamit, shine, you betta get outta my face or I'll blow yr cottonpickin' brains out. Get me my money, boy . . . I'm not playin' with you . . . I want my money . . .

BIGTIME: I'm gonna get it . . . I just need another load, Mr. Confetti, I'll get the dough for this load and the other . . . I'll just cut it some more, plus I know where those chumps live that burnt me . . . I'll get it back . . . just please lemme have the load . . .

(ITALIAN *looks at him a long time, holds load out, then slowly pulls hand back as if he's going to put load in inside pocket again.*)

BIGTIME (*hits pavement on knees*): Mr. Confetti, please, I never begged nobody before.

ITALIAN: Shit, you begged me last week, shine . . . remember . . . almost the same story.

BIGTIME: But not like this . . . I never cried before, I know that . . . I never cried. (*Weeps.*) Please, please . . .

ITALIAN: If I didn't need to keep you niggers high all the time . . . I wouldn't do it, but since you know how to beg . . . ain't that what that song sez . . . (*Sings.*) We ain't too proud to beg . . . hahahaha. (*Throws load at him.*) Get up and get outta my sight, creep, and you betta not come back without the dough and there better not be all that activity over in them wards no more after this either . . . none a that political voting stuff . . . you hear.

BIGTIME: Oh, no . . . Mr. Confetti . . . none a that . . .

13

no more . . . we'll see to that . . . yes. (*He splits on the run.*)

ITALIAN (*calls on phone*): Hughie? Yeh, I got it out . . . I think things'll be a little cooler now . . . Yeh, I'm pretty sure . . . You check it out . . . Why's the grand jury tryin' to get you? Hughie, are you for real? Hang up, for cryin' out loud! (*Slams phone down.*) The Only Good Nigger Is A High Nigger! (*Laughs.*)

(*Lights.*)

Scene 2

(BIGTIME *comin' down street in blood neighborhood, walkin' his cool walk, stuff in his slide. People slidin' up to him, he doin' his bizness on the slow cool stroll. To* A: "Yeh, givin' up the smack." *To* B: "Man, yeh, it's good.")

SAM: Hey, man. You carrying?

BIGTIME: Yeh, where's the dough you owe me, jim? You gonna get your head tightened.

SAM: Aw, man, we cool. Here's the bread.

BIGTIME: Yeh, OK . . . (*Slaps hops on him. Stands at corner dispensing dope in different way-out ways to people with carriages. Hipsters, dipsters, young kids get the pills.*)

YOUNG BOY: Torpedo, man.

BIGTIME: Yeh, how many you want, little man?

YOUNG BOY: I got two cents.

BIGTIME: You can do it. Here you go.

YOUNG BOY: Bi-ness . . . (*Hopadops away.*)

BIGTIME (*wheels around, slides over behind something, goes thru his own act. With his belt, taps in, goes into hightime*): Yehhhhh!

(NIGGER DOODOO *coming down the street with television set he just copped from someone's house.*)

DOODOO: Hey, BT, man, you want the set or some dust? I need to cop, man. I'm sick.

(*Screams in the background. Woman whose set it is, in the chase. She screaming,* "Hey, nigger, come back with my mammytappin' TV . . .")

BIGTIME: Dust or rust . . . my man. I must have gold . . . no uncold TV will suffice, you dig?

DOODOO (*pauses for second to talk*): Hey, man . . . you don't want the set, huh??

BIGTIME: Naw, DooDoo, yo' creditors too close up on ya . . . the gol' mole . . .

DOODOO: Don't split, man. (*He starts gettin' up.*) I Shall Return. (*He gets up.*)

14

WOMAN (*running by with paring knife in her hand*): I'll kill that nigger-ass junkie. I done worked all year for that television. (*Screams.*) *Why Don't You Steal From The White Folks? Go Rob A Bank. Why You Got To Come In This Neighborhood And Steal From Poor Folks, Nigger Fool?* (*Stops in front of* BIGTIME.) And you, nigger, you the cause of it, you the sick thing sells 'em all that stuff. (*She tries to stab him.*)

BIGTIME: What? Woman you betta cool yrself. (*He side-steps, and gets right on up.*)

WOMAN (*takes off after other dude*): Niggaaaa, I bet' not catch yo' ass. . . .

(*Lights.*)

(BLK MAN *talking to young boy on pills.*)

DAMU: Young brother, what's wrong with you? Why you acting like that?

YOUNG BOY: Ain't nuthin' wrong with me . . . man. (*Droops.*)

DAMU: Man? What? Aw, nigger, you high . . . little as you is . . . Who been givin' you this jive?

(*Other brother comes out.*)

DAMU: Hey, Chuma, man, this young brother is noddin' . . . he's high off somethin'.

CHUMA: Them pills probably, these niggers sellin' 'em in stores all over town, the Glitter Club, on South Orange Avenue . . . in front of the Jackson Lounge, Hawthorne and Bergen, all over . . . man, this stuff is getting to be too much now . . .

DAMU: Wow, brother, we got to do something about this stuff . . . the cops ain't gonna do nuthin' but bust the junkies . . . we got to get to them mu'fuckin' pushers.

CHUMA: Yeh, but more than that . . . we got to get to the ones who givin' it to the pushers . . . the ones who livin' good on the money they make killin' our people . . . the ones with the boats bringing it in from 'cross the sea.

DAMU: Teach! (*To* YOUNG BOY.) Hey, little man, where'd you get t'em pills from, huh?

YOUNG BOY: Aw man . . . what you wanna know for?

DAMU: You 'sposed to be my man . . . you want me to teach you martial arts, karate and all that, and here you are drag-ging around the streets lookin' like a junkie. I wouldn't teach you nothin', my man. Not till you clean up and try to be black.

YOUNG BOY: I'm gonna clean up tomorrow, man . . . really, brother . . . (*Stuffin'.*) You know, man . . . I really mean it

15

. . . this ain't me, man, this is just for tonight, ya know?

DAMU (*lifts him up off the ground*): Boy, if you turn into a nigger junkie I'ma throw you through a window. (*Shakes him.*) Now tell me who sold you that stuff or I'll throw you through one, anyway.

YOUNG BOY: OK, OK, man . . . It was Bigtime 'round on Howard Street.

CHUMA: Oh, that nigger, that sideways walkin' nigger . . . nigger turnin' gray.

DAMU: Yeh, I figured who it was. Man, we got to tighten that nigger's head up.

CHUMA: Yeh, for real. But I got a better idea. (*To kid.*) Look, man. You get off the streets. Next time I see you, if you high, I'm gonna knock all your teeth out, *una fahamu?* Tha's "dig" in Swahili.

YOUNG BOY: OK, OK. (*They push him up the stairs.*)

DAMU: Yeh, what's happenin', man?

CHUMA: We get Bigtime, but more than that we get Bigtime to take us to Mr. Real Bigtime. *Una fahamu?*

DAMU: Yeh, I dig.

CHUMA: Get some more brothers together and let's clean this mammyjammer right on up. (*Holds out hand. Brother slaps it.*)

DAMU: Get it together. (*Shouts, toward doorway.*) SIMBAS . . . NDONI . . . SIMBAS . . .

(*Brothers come falling out of house, get together, and they begin to get their plan uptight.*)

(*Lights.*)

Scene 3

(BIGTIME *is in his spot wheeling and just handing off to the TV thief.* CHUMA *and* DAMU *approach.* BIGTIME *looks up, tries to size them up. He's seen them before in the neighborhood. Them political cats, he thinks.*)

CHUMA: *Habari Gani,* brother, what's going on?

BIGTIME: *Salmon Laikum,* hey babareebop, and all that. What's happenin', babee?

DAMU: Everything's happenin' from here on out. (*With edge.*) *Brother.* I hear you the dope king of Howard Street . . . South Orange Avenue . . . Hawthorne and Bergen and parts south, west, and central.

BIGTIME: What? Dope? Aw, man, I don't know why you wanna take me there, brother. I'm just out here, you know, baby, on the street, down with the people, you dig?

CHUMA (*collars him*): I dig, I'm gonna break yr jive nigger neck.

BIGTIME (*reaches for blade.* CHUMA *takes it from him, cuts his belt with it, so his pants droop*): Hey, man . . . what's happenin'?

DAMU: You, baby, that's what's happenin' . . . just you. We wanna know first, where you get this garbage. (*Opens his clutching hand, takes out decks, lights match to them. Goes in his pocket.*)

BIGTIME (*panicking about losing dope*): Heyyyy, man, what the fuck's wrong with you nutty dudes? What'd I do to you cats? You studs fucked up, man. You givin' me a bum rap, man, a bum rap.

(CHUMA *holds* BIGTIME, DAMU *empties all dope out of his pockets, sets fire to it, throws rest down sewer hole. Takes pills, throw them down sewer hole.*)

BIGTIME (*screams*): Oooooooooohhhhhh, man, ooo, maaaaaaan, you cats are finishin' me . . . man, you might as well kill me, you fuckin' punks . . . why the fuck you bother me? I never did nuthin' to you creeps. Why don't you just do that shit you do and stop messin' with me? You messed me completely up. You might as well kill me . . . (*Repeats.*)

DAMU: Hey, don't give us no ideas, punk. We might!

CHUMA: Now where you get this shit from, man? Come on. We might save yr life.

BIGTIME: Don't do me no favors, jive——

(DAMU *punches him in stomach.* BIGTIME *doubles up and throws up.*)

CHUMA: Damu!

DAMU: Man, I'll kill this nigger if he don't talk. (*Winks at* CHUMA.)

BIGTIME: Waitaminute, man . . . waitaminute . . . You know where I get it . . . man . . . what all that about?

CHUMA: Where. Just tell us, thass all.

BIGTIME: I don't know what difference it makes.

DAMU: It makes this difference, nigger. We tired of dope in this neighborhood. We tired a sick chumps like you poisoning our little brothers. We even tired a you poisoning yourself . . . 'cept you probably too sick to even dig that.

CHUMA: Now, let us hear the name of the devil you get the shit from, man, thass all, otherwise you might not survive.

DAMU: He might not anyway . . .

BIGTIME: OK, bad . . . I get it from Confetti, over on First Avenue. What's that mean? What you gonna do about that??

CHUMA: What we gonna do? Nuthin' but follow you over

17

there. You gonna get a whole big 'nother order and we gonna go with you. Thass all.

BIGTIME: Man, you mad . . . you out to lunch. Let me the fuck go. You crazy. Them ginnies'll wash you out for good, dig it??

DAMU: Let us worry about that, pusher. You just take us there.

BIGTIME: No.

(DAMU *draws back to hit him.*)

BIGTIME (*changes his mind just as the punch comes toward him*): OK OK . . . oooooffff. (*Changed it a little too late; it caves in his stomach and he throws up for a couple of minutes.*) Oooooooooooooo, man, oooooo, why don't you just kill me, goddam all this' beatin', you worse than the cops.

DAMU: Thass right . . . not worse than the cops, brother, the way you mean, but we damn sure hit harder!!!

CHUMA: Now you call and tell this devil you sold all yr stock, got all the bux, and you gotta get some more. A record, or something. Tell him the whole south and central wards are high. Everybody's staggering. Tell'm even them political dudes in the Committee for Unified Newark are staggering around. You done cleaned up all the bloods in Newark blind. Dig it? (*Gets idea, changes up.*)

DAMU (*with recognition*): Yeh, teach, brother.

CHUMA: Yeh, tell him that you got some young guys that wanna push too.

BIGTIME: Oh, thass your game! Shit, you didn't have to beat my ass if you wanted to push. Just say so. I'll take you over there. I thought you was thinking of some ol' other off-the-wall shit.

, CHUMA: What? Naw, man. Thass all we wanna do is push. Just push. We gonna get every nigger in Newark high. But we really wanna do some bizness. Some big bizness. And we need to see the higher-ups about it. We gotta see yo boy Confetti's boss, to be sure we gettin' the best deal. We want some good shit, and not none a this cut-down jive you sellin' the chumps, dig it.

DAMU: Thass right, the big boys.

CHUMA: Yeh, you tell him, you got two of the key guys to gettin' all the real tough nationalist niggers in town on stuff.

BIGTIME: Nationalist?

DAMU: Yeh, tell him. He'll know.

CHUMA: A nationalist man is somebody who's trying to build up his people. That's why the Italians call their organiza-

18

tion the cosa nostra. It's their thing. Pure nationalism. You understand?

DAMU: Yeh, only thing, we talking black nationalism. 'Cause we black people.

BIGTIME: Aw, man, into that political shit . . . Confetti ain't interested in all that. He just wants the bux.

CHUMA: Just tell im what I said. Tell him we can get all the militants high. Dig it?

BIGTIME (*threatened into understanding*): Yeh. I dig it. A whole new market, huh?

DAMU: Dig it.

BIGTIME: Yeh. (*Extends hand for slap.*) I'm down with it now, brother. Thass hip.

CHUMA: Yeh, we gonna take care of all them rallies and picket lines. You know all them cats that dig Malcolm X and them dudes. We gonna get them high, you know. It's a hip thing, if you dig it. Tell Confetti that.

BIGTIME: Yeh, thass hip, man . . . thass real hip . . . yeh . . . look, man, if I make the connection will you say somethin' for me, you know, or throw me out somethin', you know, something, baby, you know, I'm just out here tryin' to make it like everybody else.

CHUMA: Yeh. Aw man, dig it, you know we'll take care'a you, man . . . right on . . .

(BIGTIME *goes over to the public telephone, makes call. While he is occupied,* CHUMA *signals to other Simbas. They off in shadows getting their stuff together.*)

BIGTIME: Yeh, Mr. Confetti, really, the real thing . . . it's big . . . yeh . . . Would I lie to you?
(*Lights.*)

Scene 4

(CONFETTI *in room, knock on door, two other Italians come in in black hats.*)

CONFETTI: Hey, Frankie, what's new?

FIRST ITALIAN: Hey, I come right over. Big thing, huh?

CONFETTI: Yeh, I think so, the shine wouldn't lie after the goin' over I give 'im. (*Laughs.*)

FIRST ITALIAN: Ya boxed him around, huh?

CONFETTI: Yeh, look, what can I do, the nigger keeps shootin' my stuff up, in his own scabby arm.

FIRST ITALIAN: Jeees . . . they're filthy, ain't they??

SECOND ITALIAN: Hiya, Frankie . . . yeh . . . yeh, I donna how you handle 'em . . . Frankie . . .

CONFETTI: Look, Sammy, business, like they say, is business . . . I see these shines once a week, I make a couple million a year clear . . . what can I say . . . You gotta better bizness?

SECOND ITALIAN: Yeh.

CONFETTI: OK, OK, you mean the digits . . . what the hell, I got some a that tied up, too, through you, right? (*They punch each other, friendly, yet maybe not so friendly.*)

SECOND ITALIAN: You know it, Frankie babe!

CONFETTI: Is Izzy comin'?

FIRST ITALIAN: Yeh. Iz shd be here with Irv in a minute. I called him. You sounded big over the phone.

CONFETTI: Hey, yeh. This cd be the openin' we need. The feds'll back us, kid. We can get the whole black power crowd outta their heads blind. The country's at peace again. Remember how we did it to the gangs in the fifties? Huh?

FIRST ITALIAN: Do I. It's how I made my first million. (*All laugh.*)

(*Knock at the door.* IZZY *and* IRVING, *gang accountants.*)

IZZY: Hiya, fellas, what's up?

(*All greet.*)

CONFETTI: Our bank account we hope . . . (*All laugh.*)

IRVING: Sammy babe, how's tricks. How's the wife?

SECOND ITALIAN: Great. How's by you, kid? You still spending other people's cash?

IZZY: Hey, that's below the belt, kid. (*All laugh.*)

IRVING: Hey, how cd I spend it if it was somebody else's, huh? (*All laugh.*)

CONFETTI: Yeh, yeh . . . Look, let's get a couple things straight before them jigs arrive, hey?

IZZIE: Yeh, what's up? Is what I heard true? You got a way to get the militants junked up? It's worth a million in goodwill from the feds. They'll probably even let us run a couple of the other rackets without a lotta static, as tribute to us. (*All laugh.*)

FIRST ITALIAN: Let's hope. Anyway, what's the scoop, Frankie?

CONFETTI: The way I got it, they wanta get in on the pushin' set, to their own people. We'll get our regular price, but they wanna do big volumes. Peddle it as part of the admission at the next black power conference. Yeh, all the ————

IRVING: What?

FRANKIE: Yeh, all the leaders are in it. You know those guys, they all like to get high.

SAMMY: That's why they all wear those dark glasses. (*Laughter.*)

FRANKIE: Yeh.

(*Buzzer rings. Hoods look at each other in expectation.*)

CONFETTI (*calls over intercom*): Who is it?

INTERCOM: BT, Mr. Confetti, and friends.

CONFETTI (*looks up at closed-circuit TV set*): Yeh. There here couple a political lookin' shines. (*Rubs hands together.*) Two of 'em.

(*Hoods look at their pieces, see that they're in good shape, etc.*)

CONFETTI: OK, BT, come on up . . .

FIRST ITALIAN: It's them, huh?

CONFETTI: Yeh, right on time. I tell you, men, tonight we're gonna make a real killing.

(*Laughter, punch each other, half-friendly, etc. Door buzzer rings.* CONFETTI *gets up, looks thru peephole in door. Nods to his boy. Opens door.* BIGTIME *comes in.*)

BIGTIME: Hiya, Mr. Confetti. (*Nods to other dudes.*) Hiya do . . . See, I'm right on time . . . I want you to meet my two friends. (*Turns to door, and nuthin' but bullets come thru door. Brothers shooting. About eight brothers come in door.* BIGTIME *still alive. He is duckin' and dodgin', now he goggled-eyed, lookin' around at dead gangsters.*) Wow, hey, brothers, hey, man, wow, you guys, wow, you really, wow, you took care a business. (*Knees wobble.*) Hey, you think you can get away with this?

CHUMA: Why not. We just a community sanitation committee out cleaning up the garbage the city fathers won't take care of.

DAMU: Yeh, and now what about this piece of garbage here? (*Refers to* BIGTIME.)

BIGTIME (*begs*): Please don' kill me, please, don' kill me, please, please, please, don't do that to me . . .

CHUMA: Naw, we ain't gonna do that to you, BT, we got a job for you. We want you to go out in the community with us. Right now. We want you to walk thru the community and talk to the people, and tell 'em what's happening. Tell those brothers and sisters right here, what's happening with the dope thing, Bigtime. Go ahead. (CHUMA *gestures to* DAMU *to fix something up.*) Go ahead, Bigtime, tell our brothers and sisters all about the dope thing . . .

BIGTIME: It's bad . . . it's terrible . . . don't take no dope . . . please don't take no dope . . . the devil just sell it to you

21

so you can't do nuthin' for yrself, it's why he don't care if you shoot up all you want, long as you don't ask for no better schools or no hospitals or no home or no land, long as you just be high and be cool, it's awright . . . please don't take no dope. (CHUMA *puts gun to his head, he starts weeping and pleading.*) Please don't take no dope, please, leave dope alone, it'll kill you, it's destroying our whole people. (*Screaming at top of his lungs.*) It ain't no good, it's shit, that's all it is, is shit, and junkies are full of it . . . please, they just want to kill, to kill us all off with it. Don't take it. Please don't take no dope. (*Whining, crawling.*) Please don't take no dope, please don't take no dope, please, please . . .

DAMU: Ready, brother? (DAMU *comes over with bag of smack and bent spoon.*)

CHUMA: Yeh, we ready. My man, you so dedicated to scag, we gonna get you high 'cause you done such a good job for us with yr speech. (CHUMA *begins to dump one bag after another in spoon, dumps four nickel bags in spoon.*) Yeh, baby, we gonna get you high.

BIGTIME (*calms a bit*): Yeh? Wow. Yeh? Man, you cats really hip. After all. We betta get outta here, huh, all these dead (*gets word together*) honkies!

CHUMA: Don't worry, we'll be outta here in a minute. Just gotta get you high first.

DAMU: Nice and high. (*Pours another nickel bag, and another in spoon.*)

BIGTIME: Wow, ya'll gon' take off with me, huh? I knew ya'll was down. (*Grins.*) Thass a buncha hops man, whewee!!!

CHUMA: Naw, babee, this all for you, every little bit of it. (*Pours yet another bag in spoon, begins melting it down in cooker.*) All for you, BT, you can get high as you wanna get.

BIGTIME: Huh? Hey, man, you guys are kiddin'. (*Grins.*) I know you must gon' get some a this dope. There's . . . too much for (*Gets point, tries to pull away.*) Noo, noo, noooooo.

DAMU (*grabbing him*): Naw, man, you gon' get real high this time, baby, you gon' get right off the planet.

BIGTIME: Thass too much, man . . . you'll make me OD, thass too much, man . . . nooo, please.

CHUMA: OD? What you, OD? Come on, BT, we know you can't OD, thass impossible. (*He dumps another nickel bag into the melted smack.*)

BIGTIME: Nooooooo, please, please, *brothers,* please . . . nooooo, it ain't right . . . noo . . .

DAMU: Shutup, nigger. (*He grabs his arm, and brothers tie him up with belt, make his vein pop up.*)

22

BIGTIME: Nooo, please . . .

CHUMA: Nigger, you an example. We gonna put you in the middle of Hawthorne and Bergen with a big sign say, JUNKIES ARE FULL OF SHIT, and let all them pushers and junkies look at you. You see, BT, you gonna be a martyr, and a true help to the race. You gonna do some good with yr sick ass before it's carried away from here by the worms. You gonna be a nationalist symbol.

BIGTIME: Nooooo, please, please . . . I don't want it, I don't want none, I don't want none, please.

CHUMA: Yes, you do . . . get high, nigger. (*Jabs it in his veins, pinches dropper.*) GET HIGH!

BIGTIME (*eyes stretched wide as he can get them, mouth open, screaming, screaming*): Noooooooooo, noooooooooo, noooooooo. (*His eyes bat open and closed, he stiffens, his tongue shoots out of his mouth.* DAMU *lets him spin around the room. He almost leaps off the floor, screaming.*) Shiiiiiiiiiiiiii . . . (*Dies.*)

CHUMA (*pencils sign and pins it on* BIGTIME's *body*): Get this dude, let's put him in the street.

DAMU: Yeh, BT gonna do some heavy teachin' in Newark tonight, and for days to come.

(*All laugh.*)

CHUMA: Yeh, and let's put one of these pimplefaces pizza gobblers out there with him. Master and slave.

DAMU: Yeh. (*All laugh.*) Teach devil, teach nigger. Teach righteousness!

(*Lights go down.*)

(*Lights go up again, and the bodies are in place, the two of them hanging from a light pole. Signs read "Master" and on* BIGTIME *"slave,"* BIGTIME *with needle still sticking out his arm. Bloods walk by looking, stopping, whispering, cutting out.*)

BLACK

Bloodrites

by IMAMU AMIRI BARAKA (LeRoi Jones)

Brother comes out. Looks, spins around. Looks, spins around. Spins around. Silence. Head bowed, mumbles, head comes up.

"Life I want to live." (Ducks.) "Life . . . I want life. The sunrise."

Woman comes out . . . shuffles, slips, and falls.
Man slips and falls.
(Lights go out.)
Drums beat.

Brother comes out, gets a chicken, cuts head off, scatters blood into audience.

"I want life. I want to live."
Woman comes out. "I want life. I want to live."

They grapple with each other, but it is really a dance, it speeds up. She rolls on floor, gets up. He traps her, then wiggles, then speeds off corner, back corner, *humming.* "No matter how hard you try . . ."

Groups of three ("Poets and pseudo activists") come out. Catercorned. Recite poems all at same time. Man and woman are seated on stage, go to sleep, after rolling around.

Group come out. *One at a time.* Reciting. Another picks it up.

Man stands up, wakes. *Walks in sleep. Wakes. Pulls at woman.* She wakes. She runs to edge of stage. "Black Black Black Black Black." Man circles. Her. Man runs to edge of stage. "Black Black Black Black Black." Woman circles. They circle each other.

People ("Poets") in background are slapping palms. "Yeh. Yeh. Aww." *Slapping* palms.

They retreat catercornered. Saying "Yeh," tryin' to slap palms as they are drawn away.

They come out again. Man and woman still running to edge of stage screaming "Black Black" in pantomime, with each circling the other.

While they do this, devils march by. With guns and uniforms. Build a "nation" out of blocks. March around it. Brothers and sisters (poets) come out catercornered. Blown like. Swaying from side to side. Screaming "Yeh," hands trying to slap each other. "Yeh, Yeh."

Devils march back and forth saying, "No, No," building with blocks. Constructing roads. Devils in slow-motion march across the stage. Devils in fast-motion march across the stage.

Brother and sister at edge of stage in slow motion. Then brother and sister at edge of stage in slow motion, they go through same changes, start giggling under hands. Start getting mannered.

Brothers and sisters (poets) still come out. They scream in slow motion. Do buck step. Come out screaming and writhing. Twisting. From swaying gentlingly they see bro and sis at edge lull'd slow in grim lyric sink to floor. They slide and skitter. Try to stop, bump into bro and sist. They in motion into middle of circle heads bow in gigantic moving circle, heads in middle, then out.

Devil marches across back of stage. "Hup hup no no hup no hup no three foo."

Raises gun points at brothers' backs sisters' backs, brothers at edge of stage deftly move around snakelike, in behind devils, howlin' "Whoo whooo whoo whoo whoo whoo whoo whoo whoo whoo," devils turn, race; brother and sister they run hide behind blocks. Saying, "Who whooo whoo whoo whoo."

Devil takes blocks away, shoots, runs in.
> Devil runs in
> Lights
> Devil runs in
> Lights
> Devil runs in

Brother locked in death struggle. Woman locked in death struggle with man at same time. Deathdevils all around, struggling with them, they trying to struggle with devils at same time.

Brothers and sisters (poets) all around, slapping each other's hands.

"Yeh—Yeh."

They move around in slow drunken circle. "Yeh, Yeh."

Devil struggling with brothers hissing, "Naw, Naw, Naw, Nigger, Naw."

Some devils disengage themselves from main struggle, start singing, "Eat of the host, eat of the host. Yes, love is the answer, eat of the host."

They sing, occasionally sticking their hands in to be

slapped. One devil has on a beret, he has paintbrushes stuck in his pockets, he has an instrument case out of which he takes a horn. (Welk rock music plays.)

Devil woman and man sing, serenade all brothers and sisters. One brother and sister begin dancing with them. Singing "Eat of the host." They in turn begin to serenade the bros and sisters:

> Loudspeaker: "A culture provides Identity, Purpose, and Direction. If you know who you are, you will know who your enemy is. You will also know what to do. What is your purpose?
> A culture provides Identity, Purpose, and Direction. If you know who you are, you will know who your enemy is, and also what you must do.
> What is your purpose??"

Some bros and sisters still slapping hands, and being "blown" back off, and they giggle and sway and return to watch the death struggle going on now in slow motion. First struggle in slow and bros and sister in uptempo, then reverse struggle in uptempo, brothers and sisters in slow.

"Black People

Black People

Black People" . . . spread out, ("Poets") run off all directions, blown, sway, giggle, try to slap hands, point at the struggle. Strugglers: "Black People, Black People, Black People"

Bros and sisters kneel and pray. Devils march back and forth.

Two devils twirl with the drum.

Another brother spins into struggle, starts to help, the devils try to woo him, leaving them spinning spinning. Spinning and spineless, drooping.

Devils are goosestepping. "I'm Jack Armstrong, I'm John Wayne, I'm FDR, I'm MacArthur, I'm Zeus, I'm the dudes that be with Sly." (As they march they come to sudden halt and call out these identifications.)

Devils put hands on shoulders with dancing ones, do goose-step chorus-girl line: "We're Devils, We're Devils, OOOOO We're Devils, OOO You know it, you knew it, you knew it, we knew it, we knew it, we knew it toooo. We're Devils, etc."

Siren devils jump in line when nigger ain't lookin'.

One bro checks, moves to help with struggle.

Siren devil tries to stop him, but he sidesteps.

Brother does battle, helps bro, bro and sis begin moving together, bro's slapping hands moves too as blown away, return, get in on struggle, sidestepping wheeling wheezing devils.

Women devils they move: "Our Gal Sunday—I'm Trixie Lowlife—I'm Cyrisse Breathgo—I'm Lorna Bean—I'm Raquel Welch."

Nigger screams, twisting toward her, "I'm Jim Brown, I'm big bad bebobdiddlybad ass jim jb bad nigger brown" (Voice high.) "in hollywood."

Women devils (Identifying themselves.) "Eleanor Roosevelt, Mollie Goldberg, Jackie Kennedy," (Bowing slightly, vulgar curtsy, as they croon their sours IDs.) "Rainbow Honeycunt."

Bros and sisters still cruising around now shuffle "Emo" (Running 1-2 stomp 3.) step, doing hands like boot dance, first one side as they stomp their feet, then other. "What can we do . . . what can we do . . . what can we do . . . what can we do?"

Voice: "Identity . . . Purpose . . . and Direction . . . our purpose must be the building and maintaining of our own communities, and restoring our people to their traditional greatness."

"What can we do . . . who are we?" (They alternate . . . struggle still goes on, blood talking furiously to woman.)

"What can we do . . . who are we?"

"Do you know . . . do you know?"

"What is the purpose of your life, what is the purpose, what is the purpose, what is the purpose purpose?"

"What will you do with your energy, what will you do with your energy, what will you do with your energy?"

"In what direction, in what direction?"

They stop. Come out, one at a time to edge of stage, struggle goes on in slow motion, bro talking furiously to sister.

Loudspeaker: "Black Art must be Collective, Committed, and Functional."

They move, couples in meeting, and embrace.

They talk, they move in slow blood ways, and point as they move, they laugh, and hold each other. They might walk through the audience holding each other close, in a way of close high love, holding each other close, and walking. "We all need each other. We all need each other. If we are to survive. We all need to love each other. How does that sound?

It sound good. We all need to sound this good, forever. What about you, sister? What about you, brother, you love somebody? . . ." *What Does It Take?*—Jr. Walker.

Brother, sister seeing this, react, move to imitate it . . . Brothers start running at high speed. Every brother starts running, except ones still dallying with crackers. They move slower and slower, clutch crackers, other brothers moving top speed, devils trying to keep up, all brothers moving top speed begin to move around devils,

OOOOOOOOOOOOOOOOOOOOOO   UMOJA (Alternating.)
                                             Unity

KUJICHAGULIA	UJIMA	UJAMAA	NIA
Self-Determination	Collective	Cooperative	Purpose

KUUMBA   IMANI
Creativity   Faith   (Alternating speaker + in English.)

Alternating around the stage, running at top speed, moving everywhich way, from corner to corner, from point to point, they greet devils sometimes, as devil is trying to catch up with them. They are seen to do bizness with devil. They are running, blocks are coming out, a site seems to come into being, moving devils' blocks, devil comes over, but too late, brothers and sisters are everywhere moving, all over the stage, now here, now somewhere else, they move, move, and the devil tries to catch up but he can't, it's too late, they are already building, children are there, they are teaching and the children are moving even faster.

The devils gettin' slower, nigger on the floor looks like he's gonna move, is he gonna move . . .

"RAISE THE DEAD RAISE THE DEAD NIGGER RAISE THE COME BACK RAISE THE RACE" Poem is read: "RAISE THE RACE RAISE THE RAYS THE RAZE RAISE IT RACE RAISE ITSELF RAISE THE RAYS OF THE SUN'S RACE TO RAISE IN THE RAZE OF THIS TIME AND THIS PLACE FOR THE NEXT, AND THE NEXT RACE OURSELVES TO EMERGE BURNING ALL INERT GASES GASSED AT THE GOD OF GUARDING THE GUARDIANS OF GOD WHO WE ARE GOD IS WHO WE RAISE OURSELVES WHO WE HOVER IN AND ARE RAISED ABOVE OUR BODIES AND MACHINES THOSE WHO ARE WITHOUT GOD WHO HAVE LOST THE SPIRITUAL PRINCIPLE OF THEIR LIVES ARE

29

NOT RAISED AND THEIR RACE IS TO THEIR NAT-
URAL DEATHS NO MATTER HOW UNNATURAL,
WITHOUT SPIRIT WITHOUT THE CLIMB THROUGH
SPACE TO THE SEVENTH PRINCIPLE WITHOUT THE
PURE AND PURITY OF, THE SPIRIT, TO RAISE THE
EYES TO RAISE THE RACE AND THE RAYS OF OUR
HOT SAVAGE GODS WHO DISAPPEARED TO REAP-
PEAR IN THE BODY IN THE ARM MOVE THROUGH
THE GOD OF THE HEAVEN OF GOD WHERE WE
RAISE AND THE RAYS OF THE RACE WILL RETURN
THROUGH ALL SPACE TO GOD TO GOD TO GOD TO
GOD TO GOD TO GOD, GOD GOD GOD GOD GOD
GOD GOD GOD GOD GOD GOD GOD GOD GOD GOD
GOD GOD GOD GOD GOD GOD GOD GODGODGOD
GOD GOD GOD GOD GOD GOD GOD GOD GOD GOD GOD
GOD GOD GOD GOD GOD GOD GOD GOD GOD GOD GOD
GOD GOD GOD GOD GOD GOD GOD GOD GOD GOD GOD
GODGOD. To Sun's raise, to raise the sons and the old heat
of our truth and passage through the secret doctrinaire uni-
verse. Through God. We are raised and the race is a sun son's
sun's son's burst out of heaven to be god in the race of our
raise through perfection."

Until the end it is chanted by whole group as they move.
Nigger coming off the floor. Devil running, trying to defend,
can't stay in struggle. Blk couple embracing, still moving, sit
children down to watch. ALL MOVING ALL MOVING at
a fantastic rate of speed.

UMOJA   KUJICHAGULIA   UJIMA   UJAMAA
NIA   KUUMBA   IMANI   (Alternating chant.)

Devil wearying, Devil getting tired, trying to struggle with
brother, telling brother to slow down, brothers, some doing
wild steps while they building, black blocks, backdrop being
put up, other gray cold set coming down, lights coming up and
backdrop of futuristic black swift design, a city dancing against
the sun, gold towers beat our eyes with sensuous natural har-
monies.

Devil slowing and withering, Devil wild and crazy, choking,
dying of the speed.

Emo dance, Emodance, with the chant of the Nguzo Saba,
then as crackers wither all strung out across the stage with the
Emo dance, and the Nguzo Saba . . . we say:

JULIE: Men make love for fun.

JESSIE (*sings*):

> Well, now, Mama. That ain't no way
> To treat a man. I mean, if he
> Don't wanna do a song and dance
> You gotta to ake it like it is.
> Yeh, yeh, yeh.

CELIA: Hey, Billy, where you been?

BILLY: I gotta pocketful of money, and the world to spend.

CELIA: What is that, Jessie. What is that?

BILLY: Hey, where's Junebug?

JESSIE: Yes, where is my son? Tonight's his night. He's gonna turn the banker out, all God's victims gather 'bout.

(*Sings.*)

> Just as he prophesee'd
> Rich man pays, mellow days

JULIE: What are you doing here?

(*Music.*)

AMERICA: He's Uncle Sam. I'm America. (SAM *feels her thigh.*) He's a dirty old man.

UNCLE SAM: She's a dried-up twat.

(*Music.*)

ACT 1

Scene 1

(*As the curtain opens, we see a kitchen table covered with an old piece of oil cloth.* CELIA, JESSIE, *and* JULIE *are seated around the table.*)

CELIA: Sour milk. Jessie, there's sour milk on your breath. You're lactating.

JESSIE (*squeezes her breast with her hands*): Where?

CELIA: It stinks in here. It distinctly stinks. I don't mind that you ain't got no money. But you stink.

JULIE (*squeezing an imaginary insect between her fingers*): When you squeeze a bug in your hands it's like having a man, don't you think? But after all, when a man's gone he's gone, eh, hun? You're not listening.

JESSIE: Shh!

CELIA: I will not!

JULIE: She's listening for her man. My, there's such a marvelous breeze coming in at the window.

JESSIE: If you don't like it here you can leave. After all, this is the Lord's house. The idea! It stinks in here. Have you ever been inside the White House?

Junebug Graduates Tonight

A JAZZ ALLEGORY

by ARCHIE SHEPP

Archie Shepp is a leading figure in the new jazz, the music jazz men developed in the 1960's. He is also a playwright. In addition to *Junebug* he has another drama, *Revolution,* that played for two weeks in 1969 at Brooklyn College, plus other plays that have not yet been produced. He also collaborated recently with Gilbert Moses on the music for LeRoi Jones' ritual drama *Slave Ship.*

Shepp has had concomitant interests in music and drama since the 1950's, but he did not begin to think seriously of writing until 1962. He had only written sporadically since he graduated in 1959 from Goddard College, where his literary talents were encouraged by a drama professor.

Shepp is currently teaching at the University of Buffalo.

PROLOGUE

(*A bombed-out church.* MUSLIM, JESSIE, JULIE, SONJA, CELIA, AMERICA, UNCLE SAM, BILLY.)

(*Music.*)
MUSLIM:
>A nigger's ass is like a tree,
>Dispensable.
>He's only safe when he's like me,
>Invincible.
>Toodleloo, you've placed your bet
>That Christian jive is all you'll get.
>Unschemable, irredeemable,
>Deemockrable, hypockriful.
>I leave you wanting from afar
>Your sweet love that always will be near to me
>But I must go off to fight a war,
>For freedom's price is in a knife.

(*Music.*)
JESSIE: Honey, wait a minute. Sonja, you're his daughter. Tell him how much we need him.

JULIE: Let that nigger split, Jessie. He ain't never treated you like a wife, nor me as your sister.

JESSIE (*sings*): I don't want him to go.
JULIE (*sings*): Better let that nigger go.
JESSIE: I don't care what he's done.

33

"CAN YOU DO IT CAN YOU DO IT CAN YOU DO IT CAN YOU DO IT" (Cool Jerk melody.)

(Camel walk around devil pointing to the new city, and back to the edge of stage, then into audience with song . . .)

"CAN YOU DO IT CAN YOU DO IT CAN YOU DO IT CAN YOU DO IT"

LIGHTS

CELIA: No. Have you?

JESSIE: That's beside the point. But I can imagine the odor. There's nothing like the smell of money and musty old antiques kicking around.

CELIA: I would like for once, just for once, to own an antique.

JULIE: Your home is an antique. Your man is an antique. Your very life is an antique. By now, my dear, you should be priceless. For sale! For sale! A musky Negress with fat breasts and a plump butt! She eats, she sleeps, she starves when you don't feed her. She bloats up when you pump her, ha ha. Look at that gentleman there. See how his eyes light up. He's taking out his wallet. A thousand-dollar bill. Oh no, sir. Her child was sold for two. And a girl at that.

CELIA: I don't like your sense of humor.

JULIE (*laughs*): No?

CELIA: No.

JULIE: Get your feet off mine or I'll kill you.

CELIA: You wouldn't dare!

JULIE: Is it Saturday?

JESSIE: No. It's Friday.

(*Dreamily sings: "Junie Graduates Tonight."*)

> Junie graduates tonight,
> Junie makes his speech tonight.
> He's gonna tell 'em like it is:
> My chillun starve,
> The landlord carves,
> On Judgment Day
> There'll be a mighty price to pay.
> White she-devils roam the land
> Will the Devil tempt my lamb?
>
> Heaven help him be
> A Christian man,
> The man of God,
> A man,
> And free.

CELIA: Your pumpkin turns into a prince.

JESSIE: Yes, oh yes! My Junebug graduates tonight.

CELIA (*to* JULIE): You pinched me.

JESSIE: What can I give him? It ain't right Junebug should graduates school without a present. After all, he's the very first member of this family to . . .

CELIA: It's gonna rain. I can feel it in my corn.

JULIE: I'd give him a gun or a Molotov cocktail.

CELIA: Why do Negroes love the color red?

JULIE: It's for the blood that flows in torrens inside us, beneath your dress, everywhere.

CELIA (*looks down into her bosom*): I don't see anything.

JULIE: It's there in your eyes. You, your baby, you're both covered with blood!

CELIA: Oh no! Please don't say that. My baby must be born strong and healthy.

JULIE: What will you feed it, roaches?

CELIA: Yes, roaches at first. But later when his father finds a job there will be food—lots of it. Tuna.

JULIE (*laughing*): Tuna?

CELIA: Yes, I love tuna. At night, I dream about whole tunas swimming about in the ocean, live. Spawning, loving, little tunas, big tunas . . . little tunas, big tunas, tunas that suck my liver from a spoon. (*Sucking the air pruriently.*) Sssssssss. GREEN TUNAS! RED TUNAS! PURPLE TUNAS! SOCK-IT-TO-ME TUNAS! (*A mirage.*) LOOK AT THAT GREAT BIG ONE OVER THERE! . . . BABY . . . DON'T THROW THAT ONE BACK! MAN HE'S A BIG BLACK HIP TUNA! Just like that wonderful television commercial . . .

JULIE: Why don't you sell your television?

CELIA: Sell my television? I don't know. I never thought of that. It cost four thousand dollars, you know.

JULIE: Four thousand dollars? Where would you *get* four thousand dollars!?

CELIA: WE'VE ONLY PAID . . . WELL, FIVE DOL-LARS. That's what the ad said, you see. A dollar down, a lifetime to repay. I couldn't resist. My Marcus was working then. He brought me home a beautiful cat and a diaper for the baby and a television so I wouldn't be lonely when he went to the latrines. Now there are no more latrines. There are only his work clothes, those smelly old clothes that stink like Jessie. Sometimes, late at night, when the baby kicks me hard, I get up and I take the clothes out of the closet and I smell them.

JULIE: You smell them?

CELIA: Yes, and I have beautiful visions of money . . . Oh, it's too painful to think.

JESSIE: I've only had my prayers to offer. Tonight I'm say-ing the biggest prayer ever. I want a home for him, and a future somewhere out of this dirty hole forever.

JULIE: Don't you know that nobody hears you when you pray.

JESSIE: Maybe not anymore, but once they did.

JULIE: No one ever heard you.

JESSIE: But maybe my boy will be a president. Yes, maybe my boy will be a president or something even finer. Maybe he'll be a . . .

(JULIE *is almost dreamlike.*)

JESSIE: Yes, yes. Late at night I see him reading. (*She gets up quickly. They sit puzzled.* JESSIE *gets a large book.* JULIE *snatches it from her hand.*)

JULIE (*examines book*): MALCOLM X! Nigger ain't got no last name. This book frightens me.

JESSIE: There's a miracle in that book.

JULIE: A miracle?

JESSIE: That's when somebody tells the truth, and nobody else believes it.

JULIE: Ah!

JESSIE: No, it's true! At night he reads it and I see him light up with a fire. It can only be the truth. What else could it be?

CELIA: Well, maybe he drinks.

JULIE: She's mad. Our mother died of the same disease.

CELIA: Truth?

JULIE: As long as there's a song, niggers will sing it. As long as there are lies, niggers will believe them.

JESSIE: No, no, look here, see . . . (*Points frantically at a passage in the book.*)

CELIA: Once I had a beautiful dress the color of mud. It had spangles and tassles. Sometimes I used to walk from Fifth Avenue over by St. Patrick's Cathedral . . . clear to the river where the United Nations delegates hang out. I could feel their eyes boring through me like a tick in a bitch's flesh. I'd set on the park bench and feed arsenic to the white pigeons before they crawled up my black thighs to die. Then the ju-ju man he come and set next to me one day, and he say . . . Celia . . . Celia, come and set with me to the auction block. Git away, I say to the old devil man, and kept on a switching down that big silver street . . . (*with a touch of nostalgia*) but then I was raped and my Marcus wouldn't let me wear that dress anymore.

JULIE: Maybe he thinks it ain't his baby.

JESSIE (*enjoying it just a little*): Julie!

JULIE: Hell, all that promenadin' 'roun' the church and sumthin's gotta give.

CELIA: I'll have you know it wusn't me that gave it up.

JULIE: If you ask me, that husband of yours has got a "proplem."

CELIA (*indignantly*): What do you mean Marcus got a

37

"proplem"? Just because he ain't always in your ugly face talkin' trash and putting on airs like that brokendown friend o' yours, Billy.

JULIE: Don't you worry 'bout Billy.

CELIA (*carrying on*): . . . and furthermore when he introduces Junie.

JULIE: Who?

CELIA: Marcus. He's going to introduce Junie for his speech tonight.

JULIE: For what?

CELIA: Tonight before Junebug makes his valedictorian speech.

JULIE: Who asked him?

CELIA: Junie did, of course.

JULIE (*slowly*): *Kiss my ass.* Whut I'm wondering is who the hell's gone introduce Marcus. You know when that boy shoots that white powder in his veins he don't know Saturday from Sund'y. Why he's OD'd more times in this kitchen . . .

CELIA: He done no such a thing.

JULIE: Then what the hell would you call it when a man lays out flat on his back hollerin' how the moon's gonna turn him into a wolf that feeds him death?

CELIA: He has . . . fits . . . spells, you might say.

JULIE: SHEEEIT! Stop feelin' sorry for the nigga. I wonder where that Billy is!

CELIA: He be fefawned!

JULIE: How you know?

CELIA: I didn't mean he is, I mean he felt like it!

JULIE: You've got your nerve, chile.

CELIA: Then ask your niece.

JULIE: Sonja!? That's a lie! A bold-faced mothafuckin' lie! Jessie, make her say so.

JESSIE: I wouldn't make that chile say nothin' like that.

JULIE: Where did I put that nigger anyway? (*Calls out.*) Billy! Billy!

CELIA: He's outside waiting for you.

JULIE: That's right. Let him wait. A man can start to take a woman for granted, you know. Besides, I hate him. He's a cripple. A man who can't serve in the army is embarrassing to have around, especially at parties when all the others are showing their wounds. I want a man with a hollow chest or a plate in his head or a gaping hole that bleeds when people are around. Then there's the GI Bill, that always helps. I tell you, it's absolutely disgusting. Who ever heard of a crooked spine?

JESSIE (*moves as in a dream*): GOOD EVENING, JES-
SIE. MY, WHAT A WONDERFUL SON YOU HAVE,
WHY I'VE NEVER SEEN A SMARTER BOY. REALLY?
DO YOU THINK SO? REALLY, MRS. MOORE? (*Sings.*)
> Could I steal a brighter sun?
> No more than two worlds can equal one.
> Junie turns hollow days to mellow.

> My Junebug, my son
> Is a valedictorian.

(*A loud noise is heard outside as if a bomb were being
exploded.*)

JESSIE: What was that?

JULIE: They're testing. Or maybe it was a Negro church.
Or maybe it was a grenade on Lenox Avenue, announcing the
war of the races.

JESSIE: Really, Julie!

JULIE: Yes, that's what it was. It's that because I want it to
be that.

JESSIE: But why? Junie belongs to you too. He belongs to
all of us.

JULIE: Oh, go to hell! I don't need no little boys. I can get
a man any time I want.

JESSIE: You should have had a child. I always said that.
Look at Celia.

(JULIE *glares contemptuously at* CELIA *who is fast asleep.*)

JULIE (*at* CELIA): A woman oughta smell like hyacinth and
vanilla flavor in a close room. Look at me, I've still got my
shape. When the wind lifts my skirts the corner blows real
hot, baby!

(*Enter* SONJA, *a young fool.*)

SONJA (*clapping, singing, doing the twist*): Who's making
love to your sweet baby, when you are out making love?

JULIE: Miss young fool.

SONJA: Mind your beeswax.

JULIE (*sticks out her tongue*): You'd clean your mammy's
dirty kitchen.

SONJA: Mose is cute, but I dig bread.

JESSIE: You're beautiful. Your brother will be proud.

SONJA: It's ugly and the house stinks. When I go to school,
the white girls laugh at me.

JULIE (*cynically*): Maybe you've got a chip on your shoulder.

SONJA: So big, baby, it spills over into continents and
worlds.

JULIE: But can you put your finger on it? Would you know the rascal if he bit you between your legs?

SONJA: I see him curled around my mammy's throat.

JULIE: Your mammy's been dead for a long time.

JESSIE: Julie! What a thing to tell a child.

JULIE: She's got to grow up sometime.

JESSIE: There's a beautiful man, a beautiful man some-where, somewhere waitin' for my Sonja. One day, she'll make love to him and then . . .

JULIE: He'll send her back.

SONJA: Mama, what happened when the pie was cut? Why didn't you get your share? Why does Papa cry these days and sleep with other women?

JESSIE: Your father's a good man, girl. I never seen him wrong, exceptin' maybe once or twice and I understood. If I was a man I would have done the same.

SONJA: Oh yeah.

JESSIE: You ask me that, when your mouth would go hungry without a mother?

SONJA: Then let this mouth go hungry.

JESSIE: I don't understand you.

SONJA: You never have. But you'll see one day. One day I'll take a big tall cracker in a white hat who's got millions to burn. My babies will drive Rolls Royces for wagons. I'll never go hungry again.

JESSIE: You're so young to be bitter.

JULIE: Let her be. May God make a good whore of her.

JESSIE: Your humor makes me want to spit up flies.

JULIE: You'd better save them. It's all you've got!

JESSIE: If there's an honest man, it's your father.

SONJA: But he beats you. I've seen him.

JESSIE: He was beaten. They'll beat him for the rest of his life, unless your brother can save us all.

JULIE: A black man needs savin'.

JESSIE: America needs savin'!

JULIE: My country 'tis of these. America I do love you. America? My, what a white word that is. Even on paper it seems white. It smells white, tastes white. It stinks white.

JESSIE: There's no white or black in a word. There is only power and corruption and dirt which takes us all in the end if we ain't careful. Every day my man used to go out into the ditch through all seasons and when he came home there would be substance in his eyes from the wind. His hands would be bleedin' from the pickaxe and his teeth started to drop out. When he beat me I cried not out of anger at him, but at that

thing that made him beat me. The ignorance of a lifetime. The hatred that is kept alive through ignorance.

SONJA: I saw him with that woman. That woman who wears torn stockings and green eye shadow. She's not even a good-looking trick.

JESSIE: You saw no such thing!

JULIE (*laughs uproariously*): Get your foot off mine. (CELIA *is asleep.* JULIE *kicks her.*) Wake up. I say, get your foot off mine, you lazy bitch!

SONJA: And he cries. I've seen him cry. Do you know how repulsive it is to see a man cry?

JESSIE: Shut up!

JULIE: You fool. Keep your feet to yourself.

CELIA (*drowsily*): Oh, I was just having the most beautiful dream. I dreamt about a huge tuna . . .

JULIE: Who cares about your stupid dreams?

JESSIE: If you knew the feel of the shovel in your hand, if you lived through a terrible day without no letup, if you . . .

SONJA: Mama, I know only that my dress is torn and the white girls laugh. What fixes a dress? It takes bread, you eat bread, you spend it, you roll it into a ball and you sleep with it. Who cares if it doesn't talk. It acts. That's the thing. Give me action. (*She does a furious twist.*)

Enter BILLY, *a dancer with a curved spine. He starts to twist with* SONJA. *They become almost obscene.*)

JULIE: Ah, Billy, my love, I've been waiting for you. Give me a drink. (*He doesn't hear her, she is visibly annoyed.*)

> He was a gimp
> With a limp
> And he danced
> Like a monkey.

BILLY (*stops suddenly*): My name is Billy, baby, not Gimpy. Don't ever say that again!

JULIE (*screaming*): Gimp! Roach Gimp! Monkey Gimp! Mickey Mouse Gimp!

SONJA: Kill her, Billy. She wants to die.

JULIE: Go on, murder me. Kill me if you dare!

(BILLY *walks away.*)

> You know what, Billy
> You could've been a big-time pimp.
> Instead the whores all call you "Gimp."
> The draft makes you exempt
> Nobody wants a spade who limps.
>
> You could've been a numbers' man

A wealthy bloke what deals in coke
But you're anonymous.
Where can I find a man with nuts?

Old Desdemona tricked her gentle Othello,
He at least wasn't yellow,
When "Miss Ann," broke
He cut her throat!

By now I've given up the thirst,
You'll never be a Negro "first."
All of the lamp shades
Made from Gimps.

(*to* SONJA) Okay, baby, move out. Poor Billy, did I hurt your feelings? Come here. (BILLY *whispers something in her ear.*) Oh, go on, you fool! You know I detest the feel of you in bed. Besides, we ain't got no bed. The finance company repossessed it.

BILLY: I might as well become a faggot!

JULIE: Or a politician. But you have no money.

BILLY: A man can die from loneliness and poverty. Which is worse I don't know. I'd masturbate but it only makes me hungrier. I would steal, but I'm a coward.

(*Music.*)

Is there an answer to this kind of problem? (*Sings.*)

I'm a virgin. Thirty years.
I've been hurtin'. Thirty years.
I need a gal
Someone to lie with me
Never had a chance
To know romance
Guess nobody likes
My monkey dance.
But with you at my side
I'll make you proud
To lie down with a man
Just as proud as I can be
To lay down with a man like me!

JULIE (*throws him the book*): Here, take this and live with it for a year.

BILLY (*to audience, clutching the book to his chest with mysterious passion*): Do you think if I learned this book, that a woman could like me? I mean lay down with me honest to God like people are supposed to? I mean, would you . . .

(BILLY *drops to his knees, kisses and strokes her thighs frantically, passionately.*)

JULIE: That ought to hold me for another hour.

BILLY: I love you, Julie. I mean neither of us is gettin' any younger . . .

JULIE: Shut up! You foul-mouthed little cripple! Get away from me! Now! You hear? Now!

(SONJA *offers* BILLY *a knife, he refuses it.*)

BILLY (*slow, intense*): If I didn't love you so much, didn't need you so, I'd . . . (*Softening.*) Julie, I didn't mean no harm. I mean about you gettin' old and all that. I'll see you after Junie makes his big speech, huh? Just like we planned.

JULIE: Get away from me! You make me feel like I wasn't no woman at all.

JESSIE: You'd better go, Billy. Take that book with you. There's a miracle in it—I swear—that'll make her love you.

BILLY: Yeah, yeah, you've gotta be right. (*He exits.*)

SONJA (*while closing knife*): One day I'll cut her myself.

JULIE: Don't be too sure, honey. I'm a tough titty. I've been through war and calamity. Seen my father hung, my mother violated, watched blood flow in streets like great rivers.

SONJA: Then I'll beat you at your own game.

JESSIE: When will Junebug be here? What's taking him so long? We'll be late. A boy only graduates once in a life, you know. I've heard it said it's the greatest moment in a person's life.

JULIE: In Carolina, the niggers got their schooling on rainy days. On good days they worked the fields.

SONJA: Oh I detest them people with all their airs.

JESSIE: Hush! You're talking about the principal and the school officials.

JULIE: Well, your Junebug could have the decency to be on time.

JESSIE: Yes, where is Junebug?

JULIE: Probably getting drunk or taking heroin. That wouldn't be novel.

JESSIE: Oh no, not my Junie.

JULIE: I mean your husband, you fool.

JESSIE: Yes, perhaps so. I've always wanted to try heroin myself.

SONJA: Suppose he was to refuse?

JULIE: Refuse what?

SONJA: His diploma. Suppose he was to say, I'll have nothing to do with this annual sacrifice. Suppose he was to say in his vanedictorian address . . .

(*Music. The lights go out quickly.*)

Scene 2

(*The lights come up on the other side of the stage where* JUNEBUG *and* AMERICA, *a white girl, are seated on the grass beside a pond in a park.*)

JUNEBUG: I'll raise an army of niggers and tell America the truth. I'll tell them to visit my hovel and take water for a meal. I'll tell them that my anger has turned from bitterness to rage at this shit of a system which murders me and mine.

AMERICA (*with a heavy southern drawl*): Ha, ha. Oh, June-bug, you are such an idealist.

JUNEBUG (*throws a pebble into the pond*): See the way that pebble sinks. That's how far the truth goes in this land.

AMERICA: Will you undress me again and tell me how beautiful I am?

JUNEBUG: No. In fact, that was the last time.

AMERICA: But once more so that I can see the water and the trees reflected in your eyes.

JUNEBUG: It's getting dark. A black man is invisible in the dark. But then he's invisible in the light too, ain't he?

AMERICA: You know, loving you is like being held by the night. I feel its arms gripping me ever so tightly. With you I die a sweet death.

JUNEBUG: Give me some money if you want me to love you.

AMERICA: Don't be silly, darling. You can't buy love.

JUNEBUG: Oh yeah, yeah. It can be bought and sold. Lives are bought and sold.

AMERICA: How much would you charge?

JUNEBUG: Enough to bring my entire race out of bondage.

AMERICA: Well, I'll think about it, but I don't believe Daddy has got that much money.

JUNEBUG: He can raise it. Tell him to cut out smoking cigars for a week. Tell him to stay home with his wife once in a while. Tell him to auction off a factory for charity—no, not for charity . . . for love.

AMERICA: Yes, love is wonderful, isn't it?

JUNEBUG: You know if you didn't pay me, I'd beat you up.

AMERICA: Would you really beat me, darling? Here and here, so that it hurt. Then would you kiss me and we'd start all over again?

JUNEBUG: You're clouding the issues. You always do. Why, right now I should be at home preparing my speech. Instead I'm goosing you by a silly pond. And all for free. In a few years when you're out of college you'll look back on me as your nigger fling. You'll marry a banker and turn liberal.

AMERICA: Oh, Junebug, do you really think so little of me? Are you angry with me? Will you beat me? Please. Oh, Junebug, darling. My groin's on fire. Take me. (*She throws back her head in exaggerated frenzy.*)

JUNEBUG (*oblivious of her passion*): One day, one day America will have to answer and what will you say?

AMERICA: Hand me my skirt.

JUNEBUG: I mean what else?

AMERICA: I'm cold and hungry too.

JUNEBUG: Yes, yes. What else will you say?

AMERICA: Oh, stop this silly talk and hand me my clothes.

JUNEBUG: Why do you wear that silly hat?

AMERICA: I'm fascinated by its color.

JUNEBUG: There ain't no black stripes in it.

AMERICA: Oh, Junebug, you're such a dunce. Who ever heard of black stripes. Why, that's like green marmalade, or purple bombs. Yes, that's it exactly, a purple bomb. Ha, ha, ha.

JUNEBUG: Your throat is beautiful in the moonlight.

AMERICA: Am I really?

JUNEBUG: Just your throat. I want to rape it. I want to make an incision in it. I'm a black Dracula and you are a tender lonely white throat.

AMERICA: But where's the rest of me?

JUNEBUG: Hiding. (*He kisses her.*)

AMERICA: That was good-bye, wasn't it?

JUNEBUG: No, not yet.

AMERICA: But there is someone else, isn't there?

JUNEBUG: Yes, that face there in the pond.

AMERICA: Oh, darling, what's in a face?

JUNEBUG: My sister's eyes.

AMERICA: I detest your sister.

JUNEBUG: But you've never seen her.

AMERICA: I don't like her name.

JUNEBUG: You don't know her name.

AMERICA: I've heard about her. She's a whore.

JUNEBUG: She only takes enough to pay for food.

AMERICA: Then that's worse because she's a sentimentalist.

JUNEBUG: When she was fifteen I found her with a frosh behind the bushes.

AMERICA: I know that place.

JUNEBUG: Yes, the place where the busts of Plato and Socrates are standing.

AMERICA: Did you try to stop them?

JUNEBUG: No, she seemed to be enjoying herself. Besides, I helped to eat the food she brought home.

AMERICA: And you blame me for that?

JUNEBUG: Should I blame it on the busts of Socrates and Plato? or should I go back to the library to pray?

AMERICA: You know what I think?

JUNEBUG: No.

AMERICA: Don't be nasty. (*Pause.*) You're in love with me.

JUNEBUG: I walk the streets looking for love and I take it where I find it. From a bitch, from a queer. It don't matter. I'd steal it from the earth if it would give me an orgasm.

AMERICA: You still haven't answered my question.

JUNEBUG: Maybe I do love you. So what?

AMERICA: Last night, last night I had a wet dream.

JUNEBUG: You mean you cried in your sleep?

AMERICA: You never take me seriously, do you?

JUNEBUG: I dreamed I pissed blood in my bed and soaked it up with your tissue-paper skin . . . stuffed you down the toilet with your head above water-level so I could see your eyes.

AMERICA: You don't take me seriously at all!

(*Music.*)

JUNEBUG:

> The weather forecast stays the same
> You never say, "Let freedom reign"
> I know the score,
> My lot's with the poor.
> Gendarmes are lurking
> to steal in
> and kill more.
>
> Not a word
> Or else the turnkey's stirred.
> Easy does it.
> Play his funeral dirge.
>
> The Lord knows
> I'm gonna make a place for me and mine
> Sunshine all the time.
>
> I'll make the earth proclaim.
> Let freedom reign!

Now you're supposed to ask me if I'm bitter.

AMERICA: Give me your love and I'll make you a rich nigger.

JUNEBUG: I have you. (*He turns away.*)

AMERICA: Then why do you turn away from me?

JUNEBUG: One day I'll come back to kill you.

AMERICA: Yes, but right now, put your head here, right here

between my thighs and there you'll find the scene of America. Of fish and roaches, of syphilis and money; of power and corruption. My groin is a judge's jaw and it will chomp you up and spit you out like pork chops and fat dripping, boy.

JUNEBUG: I haven't read enough.

AMERICA: You ain't lived enough! You can be had at a price!

JUNEBUG: I can't be had at any price!

AMERICA: I could take you home, put you in a nice warm bed at the back of the house. Fill your belly. Why, you could be borough president. Wear a black patch over one eye and hang signs on unnamed streets. You could take a church, any church. Use it any way you liked. Have sex with the sisters, corrupt the deacons. Oh, can't you see it, Reverend Junebug. A sign! Yes, a sign! "Come unto me all ye that labor and are heavy-laden" and I will give you the wind . . . at a price.

JUNEBUG: You shut up! Shut up! You're talking to a black man.

AMERICA: A nigger and a Christian, too?

JUNEBUG: Baby, my religion is nigger! Go down to Cuba and find me an atheist. But I'll show you a revolution.

AMERICA: Poor, foolish, frightened boy.

JUNEBUG: I ain't afraid. Not really.

AMERICA: Have you thought about death? You know what happens to violent people here.

JUNEBUG: I'm not violent. If I'm angry it's at power. Not men. I hate no man. But you see sometimes the truth is black. I don't know . . . somebody has to have the courage to tell the simple truth.

AMERICA: Oh! You can hate me a little. I don't mind. It's all so beautifully complicated, isn't it? When a thing is neither itself or another. Neither black nor white. Only shades of yellow. A little cross-section of truth!

JUNEBUG: America, you are insane!

AMERICA: Then save me. It must be you.

JUNEBUG: But I have to save you on my terms. Not yours.

AMERICA: Oh, don't be a fool. I could swallow you up in a minute. You're like a little black minnow in a swamp full of snakes and crocodiles and man-sized turtles.

JUNEBUG: Don't try to scare me off.

AMERICA: You're already scared. Go out into the world armed with your unabridged copies of Marx and Lenin and I'll bring you back a corpse picked clean by the worms. You saw what happened to your Lumumba, even the Secretary-General. Go back further.

JUNEBUG: Don't go back. Go ahead if you dare!

AMERICA: Oh, I'm sick of talking. Sick of ideas and idea men. If I had balls I'd rape myself. Why must you be so difficult. Why can't you be like you were? You know, a pig foot and a bottle o' beer, that sort of thing. You don't even like fried chicken and watermelon. What kind of a Moor are you? You're not worth a wet dream. You aren't romantic. Karl Marx was a white man! He wasn't no nigger. Don't you know that?

JUNEBUG: It's gettin' late. I gotta go meet my old man.

AMERICA: Do you really believe all that stuff your daddy tells you?

JUNEBUG: I'm taking him some food.

AMERICA: How come you never take me there with you?

JUNEBUG: He don't like white folks.

AMERICA: What does he do all by himself every day? Pretendin' to be prayin'. I'll bet he's really jerkin' off or readin' dirty books.

JUNEBUG: Sometimes he don't say nothin' for hours, and we leave each other like two ghosts in the night. Then there are times when he shouts and won't let me go till the morning.

AMERICA: But what does he say?

JUNEBUG: I gotta go.

AMERICA: You know sump'n? I'll bet you can't even get it up there anymore. (*He ignores her.*) . . . Your daddy's one of them there nigger A-rabs ain't he? (*He bristles.*)

JUNEBUG: Lay offa my family!

AMERICA: Ha, ha. A nigger "revolutionary" and a nigger A-rab. You bastards'll get strung up for sure.

JUNEBUG: I told you, lay off. Why you ain't fittin' to wash my mama's dirty drawers. Oh, I don't know why I waste the time. You ain't worth it. (*Turns to go.*)

AMERICA (*as only a white woman can*): You come back here, nigger! You hear me! Who are you? Junebug! Nigger! I took you off the streets and fed you! I made you!

JUNEBUG: You're tryin' to make somethin' I'm not. I'm a black man, not a white man. You see this shirt. Well my name's painted there, baby! Junebug Gibbons, it says, ex-cannibal-turned-Christian. Son of Jessie the maid and Sam the janitor. Sam's got nothin' and Junebug's got nothin'. Hunger is my name. Kill! is my name. Do you think I can't see past your tricks? I taught you how to swing your ass to jungle music, baby. But I don't need you no more for cheap thrills. One of these days soon now I'm gonna take this shirt offa my back and . . .

AMERICA: You're gonna make me wear it! You want to make me a slave now, is that it?

JUNEBUG: I thought about that a lot of times . . . a lot of times. Yeah it's a season for choice. I don't know, one minute I'm talkin' like my father, the next I'm (*Suddenly, beseechingly.*) DON'T YOU SEE, AMERICA, THERE AIN'T MUCH TIME LEFT TO DECIDE?

(*Enter* UNCLE SAM *with a pointed beard, wearing an undershirt and red, white and blue shorts. He is hatless and he wanders on the stage oblivious of the two lovers. He seems to be looking for something.*)

AMERICA: He looks familiar.

JUNEBUG: What are you doing here?

UNCLE SAM (*bewildered*): I . . . I lost my clothes. And my hat. I can't find my hat. What's a man without his hat? Do you have any war bonds?

JUNEBUG: Who did this to you?

UNCLE SAM: Freddie Douglass, Johnny Brown, and a young buck they called Bird. I remember I was alone. And the sound of the night kind of frightened me. (*Music.*) It was like a sound of a bird but harsher. Then they leaped on me and beat me and cursed me and spat at me. It was terrible. When they left, I was naked and my bonds were . . . (*weeps*) my bonds were gone. Do you know what that's like? No, you don't, do you? Bread . . . (*music*) it's like . . . you can feel it, man, touch it, roll it into a ball . . . it's like . . . action, man.

> I dig action.
> Real satisfaction
> Harlem riots,
> Watchin' the cops kill kids
> Is kicks!
>
> When the billionaires make war
> I stay calm.
> Nothin' thrills me
> Like the flow of napalm.
>
> Burning flesh
> Is a unique aesthetic
> Prurient
> Kinetic
>
> It's a bitch
> to match 'em
> Death in action.

AMERICA: Haven't I seen your photograph somewhere?

UNCLE SAM (*perking up*): Why yes. Yes. That was me. A

49

cocky hat and a turned-up nose always accompanied by a jaded bitch.

AMERICA: Your figure is disgusting.

UNCLE SAM: I've balled a few chicks in my day.

AMERICA: Ha, ha, ha.

UNCLE SAM: You find me amusing?

AMERICA: Your knees . . .

UNCLE SAM: What about my knees?

AMERICA: They're like door knobs. (*She wrenches his knees like door knobs.*)

UNCLE SAM: Ha, ha, ha. Oh stop it, I'm ticklish.

JUNEBUG: How can you laugh when he's lost his dignity?

AMERICA: His dignity? His dignity? Ha, ha, ha.

JUNEBUG: Shut up!

(*They both stop laughing abruptly.*)

UNCLE SAM: Yes, I've spoiled it, haven't I? I mean you were about it . . . about to . . . lay her, weren't you?

JUNEBUG: No such thing. I'm going to raise an army of communists. I'm going to turn white into black. Rich into poor. Evil into good.

UNCLE SAM: That's a neat trick.

JUNEBUG: Yes. Exactly what I told her. Her mother was a whore.

UNCLE SAM: Do you really find my figure disgusting?

AMERICA: I'm only bored with you. Bored with your lies. Who would ever think that I'm a product of your knobby sperm? Do you realize . . . here, feel my breasts. (UNCLE SAM *touches her breasts and snickers to the audience.*) Feel my thigh. (UNCLE SAM *tries to run his hand up her slip. She slaps him.*)

UNCLE SAM: I was only trying to carry out your request, my dear.

AMERICA: I want a hard-on! A real live honest-to-john hard-on. Not you.

UNCLE SAM: I've lost my clothes . . . and my bonds . . . where are my bonds?

AMERICA: I want life forced up me with a fireman's pump. I want it to come out squealing *America!* Let it be red, let it be black, let it be Technicolor, but let it shout *America!*

JUNEBUG: Let it be free.

UNCLE SAM: Free? I can't imagine a man without capital. The marketplace. Let there be a marketplace and stocks and bonds, and action. (*Pops his fingers.*) I dig action . . . Lots of . . . The one they called Bird . . . I can't forget him. His eyes. He kicked me in the face. But I couldn't take my eyes off his.

Do you play the saxophone by any chance?

JUNEBUG: No.

UNCLE SAM: Oh come, you must play something. I've never known a nigger who didn't.

JUNEBUG: Have you ever been lynched?

UNCLE SAM: Give me back my hat. You stole my hat! (*Sings.*)

> I'm a yankee doodle pansy
> A yankee . . .
> No, that's not it . . . I've forgotten the words.
> It was so long ago.

AMERICA: You'd better leave, you're embarrassing me. What about Guantanamo.

UNCLE SAM: Remember the *Maine.*

AMERICA: The War of 1812.

UNCLE SAM: Tippecanoe.

AMERICA: The Monroe Doctrine, *"UNCLE SAM NEEDS YOU!"*

UNCLE SAM: Yes, yes. That's it!

JUNEBUG: I'm your son, but you don't recognize me . . . (*He reaches out to the old man beseechingly.*)

UNCLE SAM (*with utter disgust*): Please.

AMERICA: Sing me an old song.

(*She sings "America the Beautiful" and continues singing it quietly under* UNCLE SAM'*s speech.*)

UNCLE SAM: I had a son. But he's dead now. Leaped from a roof. That's the way to go, a poet's death. Byron. Yes. Byron was his name, or was it Charlie? What was I saying? Oh yes, the Bird. He kicked me in the face but I couldn't take my eyes off his. And there's nothing homosexual about me. Oh no. There, feel that muscle . . . go on, feel it. (AMERICA *touches his arms and recoils in disgust.*) I used to pose for a painter. That's where I got my uniform. We need a hero!

JUNEBUG: Did I tell you that story?

AMERICA: What story?

JUNEBUG: About the library. I found Malcolm, bound in a smelly dew-rag.

UNCLE SAM: Sounds like a public library!

JUNEBUG: Couldn't afford to buy the book. I once saw my mother cry from gas pain.

UNCLE SAM: Why, that's absolutely obscene! Didn't you learn from Ben Franklin, our poet laureate? A penny saved is a . . . what . . . help me, I've lost my line. Well, *prompt me, goddamn you!*

JUNEBUG: If I weren't a pacifist, I'd murder you.

UNCLE SAM: Well, then do it and finish me off. I'm sick. Help me, I'm sick. America, you're a white woman. Play your role as you've done so well in the past.

AMERICA: I'm not a white woman, and I wish you'd stop spreading that silly rumor. I'm . . . well, I'm cobalt, uranium, copper, manganese, hydrogen, chlorine, florine, H_2, fire, water, the elements, that's me. But most of all I've got ego without balls.

UNCLE SAM: Well, you won't get any of that here. Help me, young man, I'm ill.

JUNEBUG: I wish I could.

UNCLE SAM: You can, God damn you, give me back my trousers or I'll catch cold.

JUNEBUG: But I don't have your trousers.

UNCLE SAM: Then make me a new pair.

JUNEBUG: Without stripes?

UNCLE SAM: Without stripes, with stripes, God damn! (*Sneezes.*) There, you see, I'm catching cold.

JUNEBUG: I've got to go. I have a speech to write. My mother will be worried.

UNCLE SAM: Give me your clothing . . . please . . . give me your clothing . . . I'm cold.

JUNEBUG: I'm bashful. All these people.

UNCLE SAM: Are you a nigger or aren't you, damn it. (JUNEBUG *pauses, then takes off his shirt, goes to the old man and gently puts it around him.*) God bless you! God bless you, son! Have you got any bonds?

JUNEBUG: I've got to go.

UNCLE SAM (*with unaccustomed power*): No, wait! *UNCLE SAM NEEDS YOU!*

JUNEBUG: That's what you said a long time ago. But now, I don't need you.

UNCLE SAM: Why, that's silly. I only made that up just now.

JUNEBUG: I've got to go.

AMERICA: Junebug, come back.

JUNEBUG: I've got to tell my pop.

AMERICA: But Uncle Sam is right, he does need you.

JUNEBUG: I've gotta tell my pop that I gave away my shirt and I found new dignity.

(*Music.*)

AMERICA:
> Poor foolish frightened boy
> Leave well enough alone.
> Junebug is our summer play
> Take me before you've gone.

You think you gonna make a world
Where men are free and such
But if you don't give in
I'll make you bend
I'll kill you—
I love you that much
'Cause I'm just a girl who needs
You to herself alone.
You to herself alone.

ACT II

Scene 1

(*The place: anywhere.* Characters: MUSLIM, JUNEBUG, UNCLE
SAM, SONJA, COWBOY, OLD NEGRO MAN, OLD NEGRO WOMAN,
OLD WHITE WOMAN, BIRCHITE, SDS GIRL, PANTHER BOY, PAN-
THER GIRL, PIG, DAR, WHITE LIBERAL, RETARDED BLACK GIRL.
The MUSLIM *sits in a dark room. His head is bald. He is
wizened. He is Black. He sings.*)

MUSLIM:

ALLA
ALLA
AH-HA-LA
They stole my land and gave me the boot!
I have his God and he's got the loot!
The godamned white man ain't fit to shoot!
ALLA, AHLAA

(*Speaks, over background music.*)
Give up eatin' pork, fools. It's white man's flesh. Totally un-
clean, these knees of mine. I hate them. I'm always on them.
(*Sings.*) I've gotta get off my knees. It's painful even to pray
for that reason. Ohhh I almost had him, two, no, three days
ago . . . seems longer somehow. If I could have taken his
skinny head here I'd . . . Forgive me, Alla. Forgive me. I didn't
always want to hurt him, but I let him into my home and he
picked me clean, you know what that's like? Of course you
know what I mean. A wife I had, dead now. And sons, lots
of sons. Ohhh Alla, where are my pretty babies . . . gone . . .
to the ground. But I'm gonna meet that son of a bitch in the
promised land or hell, I don't know which, and when I get
him. (*He brings the sword down on the floor.*) Hah! Hah!

(*Enter* JUNEBUG . . . *the* MUSLIM *is startled. He lets out a
stifled sound.*)

MUSLIM: Ohhh, it's you.

JUNEBUG: You can't hate him that much.

MUSLIM: It gets worse. But anyway, what are you doing here? (*Gives him the once-over.*) You've been doing some thinking, haven't you?

JUNEBUG: That song, it frightened me.

MUSLIM: See this hand. Look at it. It's your father's hand.

JUNEBUG: When did he die?

MUSLIM: A long time ago.

JUNEBUG: Those stories you told. They weren't true.

MUSLIM: White men have stockpiles of the black anatomy. Sometimes they even murder their own. I see you brought some bread. (*He snatches the bread and devours it ravenously.*) But what about the rest of the family? Have they enough to eat?

JUNEBUG: I don't know, sometimes I forget. My sister brings home a little.

MUSLIM: Where does she get the money?

(JUNEBUG *turns away. The old man smiles cynically.*)

JUNEBUG (*intensely*): Papa, I gave away my shirt tonight.

MUSLIM: Get up off your knees, boy.

JUNEBUG: This old man was cold and he needed me!

MUSLIM: To make his bed; to wipe his ass!

JUNEBUG: I felt like . . .

MUSLIM: Get up off your knees, boy.

JUNEBUG: I do my best!

MUSLIM: My son can do better.

JUNEBUG: Mama's waiting, Papa. The stove is getting cold.

MUSLIM: Like an icebox. A ditch is only a grave and a grave's a ditch. But I won't go back to that. No, not that . . . ninety degrees in the shade, and I was in the sun. You know how that feels. No, you don't. And then the work stopped and the money, and your mama dreamin' a black could be anything at all, while the devil squeezed and squeezed.

JUNEBUG: I don't know.

MUSLIM: How could you know? Dry up . . . Oh, there were times. There were times. Ha, ha, Mr. Black Sam, in a panama hat and a funeral suit. So what if nigger wears a gold chain and a diamond ring . . . yah-ssm, ohhh Mr. Black Sam. I don't give a damn if I do die . . . Ain't nobody gonna carry me home. I'm gonna walk home.

JUNEBUG: You see, Papa, they want me to accept this award, but I can't.

MUSLIM: Of course, you can't, boy. They want to buy you out. Why, next they'll ask you to be a lawyer, then a judge.

JUNEBUG: I know all that.

MUSLIM: I've been waiting for you. Are you with us?

JUNEBUG: Sometimes I am. Sometimes I don't even understand myself. This evening, I met Uncle Sam. I slept with America.

MUSLIM: Oh? That Sam, that old man, that bastard. (*Sings.*) I know you of old, boy, I know you of old. You, Jack of Diamonds.

JUNEBUG: It's like they think I'm committing a crime or something.

MUSLIM: Your only crime was to be born black. They'll always hold that against you. It'll never change under this man. If you know how your mother suffered with you, and the others.

JUNEBUG: But you left us.

MUSLIM: I can't speak of love, it's been burned out of me. I can tell you about revenge and that's my love for you.

JUNEBUG: It's easy for you here in this room. Prayin' and swearin' oaths. Get out of the turf and you'll see it's a lot different.

MUSLIM: I told you I'd never go back.

JUNEBUG: Listen. You can hear the drums beatin' out there like a hammer slammin' into steel.

MUSLIM: So you're gettin' to be your own man now, are you. (*Approaches slowly, menacingly.*) But can you fend off a karate chop to the jaw? What if some ofay thug should hem you up one night with that white gal and stick a knife to your throat? (*He pulls knife from beneath his garment and holds it at* JUNEBUG's *throat.*) I got my own special treatment for niggers who sell out . . . (*Pushes him roughly but with a hint of affection.*) Scamp! Go fetch m'glasses.

(JUNEBUG *gets his glasses. He and the old man seat themselves. The* MUSLIM *reads silently from the Koran, every now and then commenting,* Yeah! Yeaeah! . . . er Amen! *Occasionally he breaks into wild laughter! Finally lapses into a deep silence. He begins to doze off to sleep.*)

JUNEBUG: Papa . . .

MUSLIM: Yeah, boy . . .

JUNEBUG: Papa . . .

MUSLIM: What is it, son . . .

JUNEBUG: I was thinkin' about gettin' me a suit of clothes for graduation. I mean I never owned a suit, or anything like that . . . (MUSLIM *dozes back off.*) I mean what do you think about that, Pa?

MUSLIM: A nigger in a tuxedo is still a nigger to me.

55

JUNEBUG (*flaring*): I didn't mean no tuxedo.

MUSLIM: NEW SUIT, eh? Heh. Heh. That's what we need in this family, another cleric.

JUNEBUG: Don't you never say anything nice to folks ever?

MUSLIM: You're soft like your ma. If your sister had been a boy, by the prophet, there'd be a revolution to suit a few . . . What are you gonna do with your new suit after twenty years of unemployment?

JUNEBUG (*defiantly*): I'm gonna show 'em.

MUSLIM: What?

JUNEBUG: That a black man's got dignity.

MUSLIM: And what's your dignity, boy? Can it make a woman love you? Can it stop Whitey from rippin' out your guts? Your dignity gonna make you free, boy?

JUNEBUG: When I took that shirt off tonight it was like handing that old man back all the lies he'd fed me all my life.

MUSLIM: Now you're naked for the second time.

JUNEBUG: Oh yeah? Well, I get down the best way I know how. In my whole life you never give me nothin', not even a toothpick.

MUSLIM: Why you young punk. I'm your daddy. Me! Sam!

JUNEBUG: But I'm gettin' to be a man now, Pa. I'm lookin' at the world my own way . . . Pa . . . I'd like it if you'd come tonight . . . to hear my speech . . . I know you don't like them folks much . . .

MUSLIM (*awake, rearing up slowly*): What did you say?

JUNEBUG: Well, if you won't do it for me, do it for Ma and them, huh?

MUSLIM: So they *sent* you here.

JUNEBUG (*hesitates*): I came because I wanted to. Because I . . .

MUSLIM: You what?

JUNEBUG: I want to know who I am, and you're the only one who can tell me.

MUSLIM (*laughing*): Ha, ha. Don't you know that, boy?

JUNEBUG (*insistently*): I learned something this evening . . . Are you listening to me?

MUSLIM (*ignoring him*): Well Whitey ain't gonna tell you, that's sure.

JUNEBUG: Goddamn! Are you listenin' to me? You walk out this door, one block past the ghetto, you'll see that your sword ain't nothin' against a tank or a plane. Just look up in the sky. You gotta live long enough to be free. You don't own the ground you're standing on. Even your prayers belong to the landlord.

MUSLIM: My prayers are between me and Allah.

JUNEBUG: Only because you've got your soul. That's what stands between you and enslavement. Look, they brought you here four hundred years ago with that other bible in your hand and now you're tryin' to put one to me.

MUSLIM: But that ain't no put-down!

JUNEBUG: Depends on who's putting it down. Some of them had black skins like you and me. But they weren't black. It's men's desires that makes them brothers, not the color of their skins. That's what I found out tonight.

MUSLIM: You're just a kid! You'd be raped in jail.

JUNEBUG: You got it all figured out, ain't ya?

MUSLIM: I told you to quit sassin' me, boy.

JUNEBUG: You're gonna do it all by yourself, ain't ya? Folks laugh at you in this room! They think you're crazy!

MUSLIM: Do you think so too . . . ? If you do, then get outta here and don't come back no more. I don't need nobody, you understand! Not you, your mama, not nobody! I been sold out too many times by you cop-out burr-headed niggers. This time I do it alone. Then you'll see.

JUNEBUG (*incredulous*): You can say that about her? (MUSLIM *turns away*.) We're your family! Papa, I wake up in the mornin' with this thing. If my sister turns another trick I can't say what I won't do.

MUSLIM (*motions toward scrim at right. Nude white girl and black man*): This is your family! Handkerchief heads and cunt-mongers. Sold out to the Man! (*Apparition disappears*.)

JUNEBUG: God! Won't you never wake up in a sane state? I'm talkin' about what's possible. The world can't ever be the same again. An African heart and a black skin scares the Man to death. Well, goddamn who do you think he's makin' all these bombs to kill anyway? I went to school with guys . . . we can't even look into each other's eyes anymore.

MUSLIM: Look! Yonder!

(*The lights fade and come up behind the scrim slowly.* SONJA *and the* TEXAS COWBOY *embrace wantonly*.)

COWBOY: Hey, Sonja, let's try something else.

SONJA: What? (*He whispers in her ear. She reacts violently*.) Are you crazy? I don't do that!

COWBOY: Come on. I'll give you a hundred dollars to do it.

SONJA: Let me see the money.

(COWBOY *reaches into his pockets, slowly pulls out a wad of bills. She laughs and embraces him. Lights fade*.)

JUNEBUG (*sinks to his knees, turns to* MUSLIM *slowly*): Has it come to that?

MUSLIM: Worse. They put her in a sweatshop sewing on men's zippers. Now she makes more taking them off.

JUNEBUG: I'd give my life for your freedom.

MUSLIM: You dare to patronize me. That liberals' trick!

TOGETHER (*at each other defiantly*): AMERICA IS ME AND I AM AMERICA!

JUNEBUG: NIGGERS OF THE WORLD, UNITE!

MUSLIM: It'll take a switchblade knife for that.

JUNEBUG: You don't scare me.

MUSLIM: You've got to kill the beast. There's no living with him.

JUNEBUG: Yes! Goddamn, kill him back when he murders you! But I mean . . .

MUSLIM: Murder begins and ends with him.

JUNEBUG: No. It's power. It's power that stops killin'. Power is the iceman's tongue. (*To the audience.*) Get on with it out there. I know you're waitin' for me! (*Holds out his arm.*) See that scar? That runs clear up to my eyeball. But I got a jackknife, see. I'm capable of murder! Don't you think that I ain't!

MUSLIM (*comes up from behind and slips a knife into his hand. He points to someone out in the audience*): Go on!

JUNEBUG (*drops knife*): This won't do me no good!

MUSLIM: Ha, ha, you're scared.

JUNEBUG: HOW MANY TIMES HAS YOUR BLOOD BEEN SPILLED FOR BULLSHIT?!

MUSLIM (*grabs him by shirt, starts to hit him, thinks better of it*): SHUT UP! . . . Oh, I'm sick to death of you intellectuals. You got a lot o' white ideas, boy, learned from white men who mean you no good. Nonviolence. Don't you know, cattle prods can kill. They can sterilize.

(*Enter* UNCLE SAM *on his knees.*)

UNCLE SAM: I'm cold.

MUSLIM: Go to hell or I'll slash you, boy. You know niggers carry knives.

UNCLE SAM: I'll do anything. I've got money.

JUNEBUG: I don't have any more to give you. You see, I'm poor and my sister's a whore.

(MUSLIM *kicks at* UNCLE SAM.)

MUSLIM: It's a new day, boy.

UNCLE SAM: Help me. I'm cold and America won't speak to me. I think she loves you.

MUSLIM: Don't listen to him. It's a trick . . . what about Cicero?

UNCLE SAM: My world is coming down around me. See

that. (*Produces crumpled dollar bill.*) There's blood in old George's eyes. Thank God we can't see his hands. But the sins are as much the son's as the father's. Don't treat me as I treated you, you know better.

MUSLIM: I'm a crazy nigger. I don't know no better. I want to see you bleed.

(MUSLIM *begins to beat* UNCLE SAM.)

JUNEBUG (*stops his arm*): Papa! . . . A poor white man and a poor black eat the same crumbs from the same table.

MUSLIM: I know that story and a few others. I know my enemy. I know that he owns Arkansas and ropes off streets in New York. I know he's a philanthropist and likes good paintings, but I've seen the mines and the thousands of miles of track, and mortar, and the holes dug in the ground by men who become less than men. Moles. I've seen the crooked hands of the old women, eating rancid fatback and moldy greens. But my white brother—the beast. He'll never learn. I leave him to this. (*Points to* UNCLE SAM.) This is his future. The lion who turned out a lamb.

UNCLE SAM: It's cold . . . cold as a bald eagle . . . ACHTUNG! . . . Are niggers the beasts locked in for the night? Give me a count of the dead and the living. This concentration camp is overcrowded as it is. It's cold . . . The walls of my rooms were done up in satin. Black cigars and virgins from Vassar. Young boys from the best prep schools. We've become a race of bigots and homosexuals. How did we allow that to happen? You know, once I had lunch with old JP right in this very spot. I = PP—interest equals principal, rate . . . ? Drat! I've forgotten the principles of profit . . . What are they . . . what are they now, quickly . . . Asia, you vast empire, you sun for my setting flag. Africa, you teeming jungle that I raped. America beneath me, Cuba, Venezuela, you starved, forgotten masses, my kinsmen, you ex-slaves, now men. We are ex-men, now slaves, I am . . . I am . . . I am ashamed. No, not ashamed. Not before you. Where's my money? This year I think I will give a million dollars to Latin America! What is that in pesoes? Sam? Who shed blood for the Glory of Empire! Dictators springing up around me. Communists, religious fanatics. They come out of the walls. Coup d'etats like springing spikes jabbing me in the back. Come back! Come back, America! Or were you ever there? Were you just something I dreamed one day with Madison and Paine and Lincoln and Douglass and Brown? Where are our heroes? Perhaps this boy is our hero. This innocent child who will surely die at my hands. This child who in his innocence speaks only the truth and gave me

his shirt. I'd join you, boy, I swear, but no . . . no . . . it's too late to turn back. More vigor in our Cuban policy. That's it. Keep the wetbacks down. Stone the niggers. Blow them up. We need bigger bombs and men who aren't afraid to use them. We need burly brainless men with guts. Rednecks, men out of the black manse. Our middle-income projects won't be safe, our suburbs, our ranches, our thousand-acre farms, our Rockefeller Centers must be kept safe for Democracy . . . Yes, Democracy. (*Looks at his hands and begins to cry.*) Democracy . . . Democracy . . .

JUNEBUG: I know that I must die in this thing, but can't we save America?

UNCLE SAM: I don't know. I don't know. We need a minimum wage! Jobs, food for the impoverished! A great society!

JUNEBUG: I have a book, but I haven't learned. I want to save my sister.

MUSLIM: It's too late for her. She knows. Three states is what I ask.

JUNEBUG: I ask for America. All of it.

(LIGHTS FADE SLOWLY. *The sound of a tambourine. Enter three women upstage left, two are Negro and one white, accompanied by a Negro man. These are the sit-ins. They are surrounded by white people on either side. In the extreme upstage rear is the figure of a cross.*)

PROTEST CHORUS:

Hey now! Hey now! (*Clapping hands.*)
We got the man by the balls!
But the money's ten feet tall
Hangin' mighty low. Hangin' mighty low.
Hey now. Hey now.

PANTHER CHORUS (*spoken*): Your shit don't cut no more cheese.

(*sung*):

Pleeze Mr. Chahlie. I'm off my knees
Nothin's hangin' down.

(*Protesters repeat song with* OLD NEGRO MAN *as leader.*)

DAR (*shouts over them*): It's obscene. That's what it is.

PIG: All niggers has got skinny legs and high asses! you ain't fittin' for a lampshade, nigger.

BIRCHITE (*with armband*): I don't know about that.

(SDS GIRL *starts to cry.*)

PANTHER (*trying to comfort her*): Hey now. Hey now. (*The others are silent and obviously frightened. He stops abruptly.*) Hey now. Hey . . .

60

BIRCHITE: Nigger, your head would look good on my wall.
(PANTHER *slaps him down in retaliation.*)

PIG: Shoot the bastard, don't just hit him. (*Then to the audience.*) You see, it's not that I'm against the Negroes' rights. It's just that they never had any.

DAR: I hate a buck with all my heart.

PANTHER: Drop dead, bitch, we've got the same daddy.

PIG (*to* OLD NEGRO WOMAN): Hey, you gotta lot o' spirit!

(*He pulls her to him by the buttocks and kisses her. She recoils in disgust. Suddenly she bursts into laughter. The PIG goes after her. She draws out a knife.*)

CHORUS (*in unison*): Kill the nigger. Kill the nigger. Kill the nigger. Kill the nigger.

WHITE LIBERAL (*to* OLD NEGRO MAN): Tom, stop it! These are ungracious people.

OLD NEGRO MAN: How long have we got to endure this?

WHITE LIBERAL: You think I don't want to kill him?

OLD BLACK WOMAN (*pulls out a razor*): Then do it!

WHITE LIBERAL (*shocked*): We took an oath. Stop! This is insanity, can't you see that? If you get us, there are others who'll take our place tomorrow. Why have we come through all this, being more human than you? Tomorrow there'll be a new president in this land.

CHORUS: Not in Mississippi. Kill the nigger! Kill the nigger!

SDS GIRL: No, wait! This is Chicago 1968—the people have the right to demonstrate peacefully.

BIRCHITE (*to* PIG, *as they advance on the sit-ins*): Say, don't I know you from Salem?

PIG: Well, maybe . . .

BIRCHITE: Nothing like the people exercising their democratic rights.

PANTHERS: My people will win this right, and if my people win, America will win.

OLD WHITE WOMAN (*with a basket of flowers, approaches the* RETARDED BLACK GIRL): That's odd! I like the things you say, young woman, young man. Here . . . take these. (*The girl turns to take the flowers. The* OLD WOMAN *takes out a gun and shoots her.*)

JUNEBUG (*from offstage*): I'll take your staff. Who'll join me? . . . Well? . . . Is there no one?

MUSLIM (*to* JUNEBUG): Now, you join me?

(JUNEBUG *hesitates.*)

MUSLIM: You wear my patience thin, boy. Oh, I know, you're depending on your white liberal friends to bail you out

of this thing. But there's got to be some blood shed, boy, don't you see that? A nigger's scared to die, that's his problem.

JUNEBUG: I'm less afraid of the liberal than the Gestapo.

MUSLIM: When you were a child, I wept for you because I knew the white man had stolen your dream, or worse, would never allow you your dream. I am a black man. Proud for the second time because I've found, beneath the centuries of Tarzan and Aunt Jemima, a culture older and richer than time itself. (*Pulls out sword.*) This is my brand of protest, not that I would be violent. No. But because men make me so. All-ah . . . Allah, save this child's mind.

JUNEBUG: My roots are as African as yours. You are my father. All I know is America.

MUSLIM: Your veins will run rich into the earth, into the sewers. Here, take this. (*Tries to force the sword on him.*)

JUNEBUG (*takes something from the inside of his undershirt—it is a Nationalist flag*): If you'll take this and join me. We'll do more than you ever dreamed to aid our African brothers. Oil for the Venezuelans. Liberty and Fraternity for the Americans.

UNCLE SAM: Now, there's a point.

(*Lights fade: lights come up slowly on stage left on* SONJA *and the* COWBOY.)

COWBOY: I never had it like that before, honest. Will you marry me?

SONJA: I . . . I can't . . . I'm busy.

COWBOY: You got somebody else?

SONJA: You might say that.

COWBOY: Christ, you coons are fickle. I just offered to marry you. You know what that means. You know, Edwin Walker's a personal friend o' mine.

SONJA: Who's he?

COWBOY: Why, just the greatest patriot America ever produced. And smart! Hates presidents. You know, you might say he hates mos' everybody ceptin' Mr. Hunt . . .

SONJA: I'm cold.

COWBOY: Here. (*Offers his short. He kisses her.*)

SONJA: Have you got any more money?

COWBOY: No, I spent it all. You know, New York sure is purty. I always heard it was a big nasty ol' town, full o' niggers carryin' syphilis, and Jew lawyers. Course, some Jews are all right. See we got a few in Dallas. You ever hear o' Jack Ruby? The town won't be the same without him.

SONJA: Man, your talkin' makes me sick. You're not even a good-looking trick.

COWBOY: I'm sorry. I tried, honest. See, I'm kind o' shy ever since I got that plate in my groin. A steer nicked me, you see.

SONJA: Are you an honest-to-God cowboy?

COWBOY: Sure.

SONJA: I mean, do you rustle cows and all that?

COWBOY: Oh, no, we ain't stole no cows since grandpap died. There's a legal way of doin' that kind of thing now.

SONJA: I always thought Tonto was kind o' a gas.

COWBOY: Sun's comin' up.

SONJA: Yeah. I gotta go. Mama will be worried.

COWBOY: You ain't gonna leave me now?

SONJA: I gotta buy groceries.

COWBOY: Well, what's the matter with the rest of your family?

SONJA: No work, and my aunt Julie's too old to trick.

COWBOY: Don't you ever think about the future? What about when you get old?

SONJA (*dreamlike*): The future? Yeah, I use to. Papa used to talk about schooling and pretty dresses, parties, and beaux, and food to eat and . . . oh . . . it's too late for me now.

COWBOY: But you're only sixteen.

SONJA: No, no, I'm a million years old. I could drop dead now from hardening of the arteries.

(*Music.*)

> Walkin' streets is borin'
> Trickin', runnin', scorin'
> Makes a girl seem old.

> All the fellas think that you are ninety-nine
> When you're just sixteen
> And livin' clean.

> Youth is wasted
> Once it's tasted
> Jitterbuggin' ain't forever.

> How's a girl like me to
> Meet a guy
> Who'd wanna
> Take her home to ma.

> A wretched thing
> Like me
> A tramp
> Who's sweet sixteen.

I drink a lot too. Mama would kill me if she knew. But then

Mama's funny. She knows a lot o' things. It's hearing them said out loud that hurts her.

COWBOY: My mama's like that too. (*He touches her.*) Baby, I want some more. (*Wantonly.*)

SONJA: You gonna pay me first, or I'll yell "rape" just like you said your mammy did when her houseboy wouldn't make it with her.

COWBOY: Now, I didn't exactly say that. I mean, Maw wouldn't want a thing like that to get out.

SONJA: You're like a big baby, you know that.

COWBOY: Then you do like me a little.

SONJA (*putting on her boots in a chair*): Just then I did. But mostly I hate you. Or better still, I hate what's been done to you and me. I mean we ain't people no more, Cowboy. We're legends and myths. But one day, my legend's gonna smash yours to bits. (*She knocks him to the ground.*)

COWBOY: I didn't do nothin'.

SONJA (*jabs at him as he lies on the floor with the bottle*): It's funny, on television you bastards look ten feet tall. But right now I pity you.

COWBOY: We won this land fair and square.

SONJA: Here. (*Takes a slug of whiskey from the bottle, hands it to the* COWBOY. *He tries to kiss her. She pushes him away.*)

COWBOY: Please, just a little bit. You got me crazy.

SONJA: You know what I'm thinkin' now?

COWBOY: No, what?

SONJA: I'm thinkin' I'd like me a pink Cadillac to ride up and down Harlem's streets with. This is me, Sonja. Who? What's my last name? I don't even know that. But a Cadillac has got meaning. It means you're somebody. You ever walked along 67th and Park Avenue, Cowboy? "Oh, it must be wonderful to live in New York!" I been in it all my life and I never seen it. Except maybe from the outside. I'd like one day to go inside Rockefeller Center and while everybody was lookin' smear shit on the walls. Just to let folks know that that was as much mine as it was his. I'd like for once in my life to take a busride through Carolina and Mississippi, dance in the rivers and streams. Alabama, let it run through my fingers and hair, let it course down my legs. I'm that river and that stream. It's mine. But I've never seen it. You ever been scared? I mean *really* scared? I been scared since my midwife slapped me on my ass. I been so scared so long that now I'm a killer inside. If I had a rusty nail, I'd jam it in your eyes, your mouth, into your testicle. I'd like to kill you slow, Cowboy. The way you

killed me. You know how you got the President. That's how I'd like to get you. Americans would forget. They wouldn't even want to know. Maybe they'd even put me on the investigating committee.

COWBOY: Now, you hold on a minute, there, Topsy. Don't you forget your place. You're talkin' to a white man.

SONJA: Ha, ha! A white man! You're no more than a redneck flunky. A status-seeker in denim breeches. Your daddy worked for the same man as mine, only he threw your daddy bigger crumbs.

COWBOY: Would you marry me, honey? I'll change, honest. Look, you said you wanted a pink Cadillac. I'll buy it for you and more. You name it. The sky's the limit.

SONJA: I changed my mind. You know what I want?

COWBOY: You just name it.

SONJA: I want me a hundred billion dollars in small bills.

COWBOY: Honey, I ain't got that kind o'money. Even Mr. Hunt ain't got that kind o'money.

SONJA: Then get it from the government. You know how.

COWBOY: They'd shoot me for treason. Call me a liberal.

SONJA: They call my folks "niggers." Could you live with that?

COWBOY: I can't. I'm a hundred percent American. Look at them veins.

SONJA: I'll settle for Park Avenue as a low-income housing development. Adam Clayton Powell as President.

COWBOY: A nigger for President? Man, you're really way out there.

SONJA: Take it or leave it.

COWBOY: A *nigger* for President. Bang! Bang! Bang! Boy, this little shootin' iron makes a great sound when she pops off. I love to play cowboys and Injuns! Bang! Bang! Just let me catch a nigger President with his bubble top down. I'm sorry. I guess I lost my head.

SONJA: You ain't brushed your teeth for a long time, have you?

COWBOY: Now you hold on a minute . . .

SONJA: Get outta here. I'm sick o'you. Your face turns white in the morning like your heart. (*She turns away.*)

COWBOY: What do you want from me! Name it!

SONJA: I want your death! You incredible son of a bitch! (*Starts as if to go.*)

COWBOY: Honey . . . wait a minute . . .

SONJA: I'm goin' home and I'm gonna pray that you die.

COWBOY: Come here, you black bitch. No nigger tramp is

gonna talk to me that way. (*He slaps her, wrestles with her to the bed.*)

SONJA: Die! Die! Die!

COWBOY: It'll be good this time. Better than last, I promise.

(MUSLIM *enters from wings carrying a short cord. He strangles the* COWBOY.)

SONJA: FATHER! (*She embraces him.*)

MUSLIM: My dearest. I'm sorry I arrived so late. (*Lights begin to dim very slowly.*)

(JUNEBUG *enters from wings. At first they are unable to make him out; upon seeing that it's him, they become more composed but still seem a little uneasy.*)

MUSLIM (*to* JUNEBUG): That's one down . . . (*He laughs hysterically, seems almost giddy with a strange power.*)

JUNEBUG: Where will you go?

MUSLIM (*more composed*): I've made plans for . . . (*Sounds of someone approaching. Lights are almost twilight. They try to hide themselves in the near darkness. The* MUSLIM *pulls out his sword threateningly.*) Now's the time to play his fun'ral dirge. (*He raises his sword as if to attack.* UNCLE SAM *is unaware of what's happening.* JUNEBUG *instinctively stays his hand, the* MUSLIM *slaps him. They confront each other for a hard implacable moment.* SONJA *appears confused, unwilling to choose between them.*)

JUNEBUG: Papa, just then you had that same look in your eyes that he has.

SONJA (*urgently, not looking at* JUNEBUG): Papa, there's not much time. We'd better go. (*They start walking off.*)

JUNEBUG: Where will you go?

MUSLIM: To hell perhaps, but then you may see us sooner than you think. (*They exeunt.* JUNEBUG *exits.*)

(UNCLE SAM *comes stage center in the darkness carrying a pistol. He has the air of a mock villain, but there is something more sinister about him now. He appears younger, harder. He starts to examine* COWBOY *lying on floor. Spot comes up suddenly. He feels unnatural, exposed in the naked light. He shivers. The pistol embarrasses him. He smuggles it inside his coat.*) Does anyone know who did this thing? . . . (*Smugly.*) Good . . . We'll blame a liberal. (*Music.*) Or perhaps a liberal with a pink pink past. They're always good for a hanging. Let's have a red bait!

A good old-fashioned red hate.

Just let them yell till they're blue in the head.

They're still red. Negroes' rights, civil strife.

A Cuban fracas, a Dallas shakeup, Zanzibar, Shangri La

Blame it, blame it on the reds.
Lil' Lee Oswald was catchin' a flick.
Took a rip 'et patrolman Tippat
The papers said the cop was dead
Who dunnit? A red! Ruby, Ruby Red!
If you've got problems
A strike or citation
School integration
A plastic bomb
Vietnam
A burning Birch
In front of a church
'Nuff said.
Blame it, blame it on the reds.

CURTAIN

Scene 2

(The church prior to the explosion. Large rectangular table on lowest platform. Scene suggests the Last Supper. UNCLE SAM *is seated in the center and will act as the principal. He is heavily made up . . . something like a transvestite, rouge, lipstick, etc.* JUNEBUG *is seated at his right hand and to the left of* UNCLE SAM *is* AMERICA. *Other arrangements of characters are designed by director. The three women,* JESSIE, JULIE, *and* CELIA, BILLY, MARCUS, *and some of the white characters from the earlier demonstration are all seated. From time to time* JESSIE *wipes her eyes with the back of her hand.* JULIE *chews vigorously on a wad of gum, while making certain that the better part of her legs are exposed under the table. The* MUSLIM *and* SONJA *are standing on the tier above, suggesting a certain Faustian mischievousness.)*

UNCLE SAM *(clears throat ceremoniously)*: Brrr . . . ladies and gentlemen . . . Quality integration is the goal of American education.

JULIE: Who'd wanna get anything together with that old bastard. No wonder he's an educator.

JESSIE: Julie!

UNCLE SAM: This year for the first time no fewer than thirty of our senior class are niggers . . . er . . . Negroes . . . er . . . black . . . er . . . what you color it . . . you get the picture. Indeed, we here at the Adam Smith School look forward to the day when cultural deprivation will be a thing of the past. Already we have added several new busses to the concentration . . . I mean, projects route. And a group of socially promi-

nent Philadelphia mothers have promised a thousand board erasers by the end of this fiscal year. Taxes, you understand. In addition to this, our school plant will be drastically enlarged so that the lunch program can continue serving hot from a super-duper sterno can. We will not tolerate starvation . . . on these premises. Oh, as I look out there into that multitude of smiling faces I am reminded of the words of that famous Victorian bard, Ben Jonson . . .

JUNEBUG (*whispers*): Elizabethan.

UNCLE SAM: What?

JUNEBUG (*whispers louder*): Elizabethan!

UNCLE SAM: Oh? . . . Yes, yes, quite so. (*Takes a swig from his hip flask.*) "Drink to me, Celia!"

CELIA (*who had been sleeping*): What a thoughtful thought from that Mr. Johnson.

JULIE: Not you, fool!

UNCLE SAM (*clearing throat*): My friends, I don't know how you're going to take this . . . but I won't be with you next year. Er . . . you can take that sitting down. So, for my last sacrificial gesture . . . (*gesturing toward* AMERICA) America-the-beautiful notwithstanding . . . overlooking her mountains and valleys . . . hmmm! . . . I have chosen JUNEBUG as our new valedictorian to offer the final eulogy!!! Now, how about a little applause? (*Everyone stands and applauds.*) But before we introduce Junebug to the service table, we will have a few words of encouragement from a . . . a . . . distant relative . . . Uncle . . . Uncle . . .

CELIA (*urging* MARCUS *forward*): Marcus! Go on, Marcus! Go on!

MARCUS (*rises: scratches nose, buttocks, etc. He nods occasionally without saying a word; mumbles to self*): Ahhhhh . . . hmmmm . . . yeahhhhh!

CELIA (*slight whisper; pulling* MARCUS' *coat*): Marcus! Honey, say something!

MARCUS: Yeah, where was I? Oh, yeah . . . I didn't go too far in school, you understand. I split. So I can dig what cuttin' this place loose means to a kid . . . yeah. I give Junie his first dictionary. Told him to look up the Bird . . . the Charlie Bird. He said he couldn't find the Bird. That was his first introduction to . . . life . . . to the world of . . . facts!

CELIA: Careful, Marcus. Don't you embarrass Jessie.

MARCUS: Yeah, Jessie. Sweet little Mama. I watched her raise them kids on nothin' . . . And they always give me respect. Know what I mean? I mean some people think 'cause a cat's got raggedy clothes he ain't worth knowing 'cause he ain't

got sense enough to keep a cent. They be assuming . . . (*Nods.*) . . . he's a junkie. Or some other stuff. Some kind of a cat who smells like shit no matter what company he keeps. But a man ain't nothin' but a man. When he takes his clothes off, his whole life is before him. Out there! And that's what a woman sees . . . finally . . . even if that man lays buck naked on his back at night . . . in a cold sweat for her and can't get the old boy up. Nights, lonely nights. When your belly's on fire. But you don't move . . . 'cause you be flyin', man. Over the sun, with the moon inside you . . . and clouds of hot white stars. Churning . . . your innards. And you wonder . . . does it take all that just to have a little space?

PIG: I bet the nigger steals.

MARCUS: How you know what I do? Did I tell you? I ain't here for your benefit, you know! Don't mess with me . . . you honkies staring at me like I got sif or somethin' . . .

JULIE: Set that damn fool down!

MARCUS: You pig! You stuck a needle in my brain and left me oozin' like a vegetable. Chicken soup oozes from my pores. You're staring at the junkman, fellers!

UNCLE SAM: Er . . . can we conduct this meeting with order?

MARCUS: Livin' with you bastards is an eternal race for my life. Sometimes I think I'm gonna have to have me a gun to rescue my mother's soul from her tomb. Now if y'awl will excuse me, I'll get my hat! (*To* CELIA *as he rubs his hands together nervously.*) Gimme the money!

CELIA: What money?

UNCLE SAM: Can we proceed, now?

MARCUS: The five, Mama, the five!

CELIA: You said I could use it for the baby's diapers.

MARCUS: We ain't got no baby!

UNCLE SAM (*annoyed*): Thank you very much Mr. . . . er . . . (*To whites.*) What's that boy's name, anyway?

CELIA: But the baby, Marcus.

MARCUS: I said we ain't got no child. No child . . . no house . . . no nothin'. That five dollars might take me some place I ain't been yet. Baby, I got to get high.

JESSIE: Marcus!

CELIA: What you talkin' 'bout?

MARCUS: You know what I'm talkin' 'bout.

UNCLE SAM (*shaking head*): Nigger shit!

JULIE: Give him the money!

MARCUS (*takes money from* CELIA): Later, y'awl!

UNCLE SAM (*begins applause*): Thank you, Mister Nigger.

69

CELIA (*as* MARCUS *exits*): Where you goin', honey?

JULIE (*restraining* CELIA *from leaving*): He's on his way to Canaan Land.

(*Everyone applauds.*)

UNCLE SAM: Please! Now can we go on. I don't see your name on the speaker's roster.

JULIE (*hand on hip*): You is a bossy ol' dude, ain't yah? You see, it's my nephew who is graduating tonight and I was just sittin' here thinkin' up a few words that might be appropriate . . . and stuff. You might say, on the case. I knew him when he was still wet behind the ears . . . a toddler. You see, it took us folks five hundred years to produce a graduate. So, quite naturally we're proud. Why, shit, Junie don't cuss, don't smoke. You know, when I used to sell numbers back of the house, Junie used to keep a lookout for the Man. He was the best little lookout you ever did see. Smart at figures too. By the time he was three he could tell the difference between 069 and 960. 069's my numbers. One year I hit three times runnin' on that 069. Only had a nickel to box it with, though . . . So it didn't amount to much.

JESSIE: JULIE!

JULIE: Huh?

JESSIE: I wish you'd stick to the point!

JULIE: Oh . . . well . . . hell I plays numbers and don't care who knows it. Besides, I seen a couple of policy slips on your dresser too.

JESSIE: No such thing. Well, at least I never played on the Lawd.

JULIE: Which brings me to another point . . . (*stops suddenly and looks at* UNCLE SAM *who stares at her curiously.*) Why you dressed so strange for this occasion? Is you a hippie or some other trash? My nephew tells me you're responsible for all this shit. Well, now, maybe he's got a chance. With a rich uncle like you, he can't miss, can he? I know you won't let him down and stuff. But if you do, just remember there'll be a whole lot of relatives after your ass. But before I close off here, just tell me one thing. With the whites sittin' on one side of this table and the blacks on the other, what kind of man do you want Junie to be? What kind of friend has he got in America?

BIRCHITE: Turn that nigger off and let's get down to business.

UNCLE SAM: Er . . . yes, let's do get on with it!

MUSLIM (*from upper tier*): Let the boy speak!

UNCLE SAM (*looks up as if surprised*): What?

MUSLIM: Get on with it, Sam, and don't spare the best parts.

SONJA: Yeah. Tell 'em about you and the biology teacher.

UNCLE SAM: I'll do no such thing. Besides, how did you get in here? (*Rebukes* SONJA.) Say, ain't you the tart who was caught readin' dirty books in the john? (*He advances toward her;* MUSLIM *intercedes; he returns disconcertedly to introduction of* JUNIE.) Well . . . er . . . ready or not . . . I give you this year's valedictorian . . . who has found a friend in America . . . Junebug. (*Applause.*)

JUNEBUG (*slowly*): For seventeen years I bought the American Dream and now there's nothin' else to sell. I find it sterile, a dull companion. (*To* BILLY.) Get up, brother, and run tell the others. You are the victim of a lie and we . . . will never be the same again. Who would believe that a nigger sold a nigger? I don't know you anymore, but I'm able to walk these cosmic floors right out into hell, mister, and come back. Stronger! I die at a rate six times more than you per second. That means I live six times faster than you. When I'm finally shifted outta this here dump into the incinerator, think that you might just as well have blown a Martian—one you never understood. I'm only capable of so much tragedy. Remember that. Then we'll begin to share our nightmares; my black body for the Vatican, my hands for the future of children. I ask you; what do you see when you look inside yourselves? POVERTY IS A WHORE!!

(*Negroes applaud. Whites sit stonyfaced, silent.*)

UNCLE SAM (*pushing* JUNEBUG *into his seat*): That ain't the speech I okayed. What're you trying to do, make me lose my pension?

JUNEBUG (*defiantly*): Is this or ain't it a free country?

UNCLE SAM (*confused*): Free . . . why . . . I . . .

AMERICA (*suddenly, as if just realizing it herself*): Yes . . . yes . . . , baby, it's FREE FOR ALL.

(*Everyone is suddenly still. Negroes seem more confident at this moment than whites.*)

JUNEBUG (*to* MUSLIM *and to* AMERICA *and* UNCLE SAM): Then I was right!

UNCLE SAM (*puts pistol to his head*): Set down, boy. Niggers with speeches are a dime a dozen! (JUNEBUG *sits down slowly, somewhat intimidated by pistol. He continues to fix on* AMERICA. UNCLE SAM *turns threateningly to* AMERICA.) REMEMBER YOUR IMAGE.

AMERICA: My image . . .

JUNEBUG (*to* UNCLE SAM): She doesn't have to be what you want her to be.

AMERICA: I'm Big Steel. I'm cobalt. I'm . . . no . . . I'm an idea . . . a dream about . . . freedom.

UNCLE SAM: You trollop! (*Forces a whiskey bottle into her hand.*) I won't let you forget your image! (*Everyone stares at him as though waiting to see what will happen next.*) As master of ceremonies . . . I . . . uh . . . would like to propose a toast. (*He forces* AMERICA *up onto the table.*) To the fighting men of the world! (*Whites applaud.* AMERICA *guzzles. She is confused and mimics* UNCLE SAM's *toast like a mannequin.*) To the prettiest blue-eyed girl!

CROWD: Yaaa!

UNCLE SAM: To policy-making, rum-running, belly-shaking, machine-gunning lovelies everywhere. (*Crowd cheers.*)

AMERICA (*slumping*): Something's gone wrong. I'm sick.

JUNEBUG (*to whites and* UNCLE SAM): Don't you care anything at all about her? About us?

UNCLE SAM: Go on, America. Show them what you really are!

AMERICA (*looks around embarrassed. Everyone seems to share her confusion*): I . . . don't know what I really am.

UNCLE SAM: Go on!

AMERICA (*pleading to* JUNEBUG): Help me, June, I'm ill.

JUNEBUG: Take my hand. (JUNEBUG *starts to help her.*)

MUSLIM: Oh, oh, watch that bullshit!

SONJA: Yeah, remember it's for the rest of your natural life.

UNCLE SAM: Go, America, show them your image. Where's the music? Somebody turn up the music.

(*Music.*)

AMERICA (*sings*):

> Poor foolish frightened boy
> Leave well enough alone.
> Junebug is our summer play
> Take me before you've gone.
>
> You think you gonna make a world
> Where the men are free and such
> But if you don't give in
> I'll make you bend
> I'll kill you—
> I love you that much
> 'Cause I'm just a girl who needs
> You to herself alone
> You to herself alone.

UNCLE SAM: Go on, go on.

JUNEBUG: What had you done to her?

AMERICA: I'm cold. Hand me my dress.

UNCLE SAM: You stay away from my daughter if you know what's good for you.

JUNEBUG: There's still time, America. I'm waiting for you.

MUSLIM: You've sold your birthright too cheap, boy. The girl brings no dowry. It ain't in the book. Every Negro is a nigger is a nigger in his and Junebug's heart, because niggers are made of blood, not books.

AMERICA: Save me, Junebug. It must be you.

JUNEBUG: Then come with me.

AMERICA: I want to.

UNCLE SAM: Shut up. (*Pulling gun on* JUNEBUG.)

(JUNEBUG *helps* AMERICA *down from table.*)

SONJA: Papa!

MUSLIM: He's made his choice.

UNCLE SAM (*as he takes aim*): I'll have your prick, you black bastard.

MUSLIM: Enough. Strike the scene.

(*Explosion and blackout. Hurls bomb. When the smoke clears the snare drum beats.* UNCLE SAM, *the* MUSLIM, *and* SONJA *are above.* JUNEBUG *and* AMERICA *are on the table. All others have left stage.*)

SONJA: Hallelujah! The Lord is my shepherd!

UNCLE SAM: Let freedom reign.

SONJA (*sings*):

> My man don't love me
> Treats me oh so mean.

AMERICA: I'll no longer live this ugly lie.

SONJA:

> My man don't love me
> Treats me oh so mean.

JUNEBUG: Revolutions call for life, not death.

UNCLE SAM: Let freedom reign.

SONJA:

> He is the meanest man
> That I have ever seen.

JUNEBUG: You don't know how I've tried not to love her. (*He dies.*)

AMERICA: My own son has become a stranger to me. (*She dies.*)

SONJA:

> He is the meanest man
> That I have ever seen.

MUSLIM: Did she die so soon?

UNCLE SAM: Let freedom reign.

SONJA:

> My man don't love me
> Treats me oh so mean.

MUSLIM: . . . and my son.

UNCLE SAM: Stone dead.

SONJA:

> He is the meanest man
> That I have ever seen.

MUSLIM: Tomorrow I'll come to get you, but today . . .

UNCLE SAM: Mah, sevens. Sevens.

SONJA:

> He took me to his bedroom
> Pulled my pants down low.

UNCLE SAM: Seven sends a nigger to heaven.

SONJA:

> I said stop it, daddy, stop it.
> I can't come. I've got to go.

UNCLE SAM: Let freedom reign.

SONJA:

> My man don't love me
> Treats me oh so mean.

MUSLIM: Every man's got a lump in his chest nowadays.

SONJA:

> He is the meanest man
> That I have ever seen.

UNCLE SAM: Let freedom reign.

MUSLIM: Time stopped. (*Beat.*) Never owned a watch nor a piece of bread for that matter. At hog-killing time I always got queasy. Was I less than a man for that? I've forgotten how . . . how to murder. You must be capable of love for that. But she don't bleed no more. Allah, I've prayed all my life. Can there be so little satisfaction in another's death. Oh your death was too easy, you blue-eyed devil. How can you love and hate. (*Beat.*) If it was ever possible, I would like to have shared my dream with you. But it's too late for that. I won't go back.

UNCLE SAM: Let freedom reign.

MUSLIM: Death to your freedom, you bastard. Do you see what's happened to my children?

UNCLE SAM: Yes, and to mine.

MUSLIM: But where is America? He needs her now.

UNCLE SAM: She's dead with her other lovers.

MUSLIM: Come back, America, my son has given his life for you.

UNCLE SAM: She's a long way off. So I guess we'd better call her in a loud voice.

UNCLE SAM and MUSLIM: America, America. AMERICA. AMERICA.

(*Lights fade.*)

The Corner

by ED BULLINS

Ed Bullins is the director of the Black Theater Workshop, Harlem, New York.

CAST

CLIFF DAWSON, Twenty-two years old, large, husky, a hint of subdued swagger and worldliness about him. He is light-complexioned, brown, not yellow.

BUMMIE, Nineteen years old, a bully but loyal; medium height and athletic build.

SLICK, Seventeen, small, wiry, and dark.

STELLA, Nineteen years old, good figure, on the heavy side. She wears her hair long and presses it daily with a hot comb, giving it a copper tone.

BLUE, Twenty-two years old, very dark, with eyes and smile shining whitely from his face.

SILLY WILLY CLARK, Twenty-four years old, a progressive alcoholic who has never mentally grown older than sixteen. Brown-skinned, moon-faced, clothes always five years out of fashion.

• TIME: *The 1950's.*

The people in this play are black.

1. SPENDS IT ON ME

(BUMMIE *and* SLICK *stand under the street lamp on "the corner," passing a bottle of wine between them. It is the early fifties and King Pleasure sings "Moody's Mood for Love." Throughout the scene, other music of the period plays.*)

SLICK (*drinks in gulps, takes a breath*): I sho' feel sorry for you when Cliff gets here, Bummie.

BUMMIE: C'mon, man, pass the jug. Stella's gone into the store now. 'N that mathafukkin' cop might pass by any minute.

SLICK: We'll save Stella some . . . 'n mathafuk the cop! . . . 'N his mama too. I drink mah wine where I want to.

All inquiries concerning production rights to this play should be addressed to Whitman Mayo, General Manager, The New Lafayette Theater, 2349 Seventh Avenue, New York, N.Y. 10030.

BUMMIE: You gonna save some for Cliff?

SLICK: Sheeet . . . Cliff can get his own. We got this, didn't we? And what chou worry'in 'bout Cliff for?

BUMMIE: I just got to look out for mah boy Cliff, that's all.

SLICK: Like you looked out for his brother, Steve?

BUMMIE (*drawing him out*): You mean you really ain't gonna save no wine for Cliff?

SLICK: Hell no! If you want him to have any, then save him yours . . . if I don't drink it up first.

BUMMIE: Man . . . you sho' are cold.

SLICK: That's right . . . Hey, man, pass the bottle.

BUMMIE: I'm gonna tell him when he gets here. And laugh when he kicks the cowboy shit out of you.

SLICK: He's gonna put his big foot up your ass before he does mine.

BUMMIE: Nawh . . . I doubt that . . . I just fucked with his brother . . . you're fuckin' with his wine.

SLICK: Sheeet . . . that big crazy mathafukker better not lay his hands on me.

BUMMIE: He's not gonna lay his hands on you . . . he's gonna lay his big foots on you . . . yeah, square in your ass.

SLICK: Hey, man, I thought you was my boy.

BUMMIE: I am. I'm your nigger if you gets no bigger . . . but I'm still gonna crack up seein' Cliff plant his big foots in your ass, man.

SLICK: Bummie . . . Bummie . . . you one of those humanitarian cocksuckers, man.

BUMMIE: What you call me, man? What kinda cocksucker is that?

SLICK: A humanitarian . . . you know . . . a do-gooder like . . . like Eleanor Roosevelt.

BUMMIE: Who?

SLICK: Roosevelt . . . Eleanor . . . well, look, man . . . You remember when you was a kid, don't cha?

BUMMIE: Yeah . . . but wha' . . .

SLICK: And you us'ta go to the movies every Saturday . . .

BUMMIE: Yeah . . . man . . . we all us'ta go.

SLICK: Well, you remember when the news us'ta come on?

BUMMIE: Nawh, man . . . I don't know nothin' 'bout no news. When that shit come on I'd have mah hand under some bitch's skirt or out gettin' some popcorn.

SLICK: But, man . . . you remember Eleanor Roosevelt . . . she was married to President Roosevelt.

BUMMIE (*enlightened*): Oh . . . Oh! . . . Yeah . . . like that

real black ole lady . . . Mary . . . Mary . . . what's-her-name . . . ya know, Mary somethin'-or-other.

SLICK: But she wasn't married to no President!

BUMMIE: Yeah, yeah . . . I know . . .

SLICK: Well, yeah . . . I know who you mean.

BUMMIE: Yeah . . . I know you do. *Her.*

SLICK: Yeah . . . like that broad who looks like your mama.

BUMMIE: Hey, man, I don't play that shit.

SLICK: Awww . . . man. You know I'm just jivin' . . . But she was at the White House and all that.

BUMMIE: I don't give a fuck where the old fat black bitch was . . . I don't know nothin' about it. (*Pause.*) Hey, man, what you mean I'm like her?

SLICK: I only said that you was kinda like a humanitarian . . . and she and President Roosevelt's old lady and that white cat out in the jungles wit' all them natives was the only ones I thought about.

BUMMIE: Well, man, I don't want to hear nothin' 'bout some fat ole-timey black bitch that I'm supposed to be like. Or some ole white man runnin' 'round the jungles with a bunch of savages. (*Takes* SLICK's *lapel.*) I'm a man and if you don't believe it I'll put my number twelve at you for what you done to Steve.

BUMMIE: Is dat any of your business?

SLICK: Awww . . . man, forget about it. Pass the bottle.

BUMMIE: Nawh.

SLICK: What you say?

BUMMIE: I said nawh.

SLICK: Hey, man, what's wrong with you? I went in on half for that jug.

(*The confectionary store door opens and* STELLA *steps out.*)

BUMMIE: I don't care what you went in on, nigger. You ain't gettin' no more. I'm savin' it for Cliff.

STELLA: Hey, give me a taste of your wine, Bummie.

SLICK: You just scared of Cliff . . . and want to kiss his ass because of Steve.

BUMMIE: Hi, Stell, how you doin', baby? (*He hugs her waist.*)

STELLA: Give me some of that wine, Bummie.

SLICK: You a chicknshit mathafukker, Bummie!

BUMMIE: If I didn't have hold of this girl I'd kick your ass, smart nigger.

SLICK (*furious*): You would! You would!

BUMMIE (*holds bottle in front of* STELLA): You want some of this stuff, baby?

STELLA: You know I do, man. You gonna keep it all for yourself?

BUMMIE: Nawh . . . baby. Here . . . (*Hands her the bottle.*)

SLICK: Hey, Bummie, man, what about me?

BUMMIE: You had yours, smart mouth.

SLICK (*whines*): Awww, man . . . I paid for that wine just like you and look at it . . . The way Stella swills it, won't be any left.

STELLA (*takes breath*): What you mean I swill? (*She takes another swallow.*)

SLICK: Ahhh, baby . . . not so fast.

(*She gives bottle to* BUMMIE.)

STELLA: That sure was good. Thanks.

BUMMIE (*kisses her cheek and pats her rear*): That's okay, baby. Anytime.

STELLA (*pulls away*): Go on, man . . . with that stuff.

SLICK: You gonna save the rest for Cliff, Bummie?

BUMMIE: Nawh.

SLICK: You gonna give me the rest?

BUMMIE: Nawh.

SLICK: You gonna drink it all up by yourself?

BUMMIE: Nawh.

STELLA: What you gonna do with it, Bummie?

BUMMIE (*pulls* STELLA *in by her waist*): Me and you's gonna drink it, Stella.

STELLA (*teases* SLICK): That's really nice of you, Bummie. Really it is.

SLICK: I put my money into it . . .

BUMMIE (*drinks*): Relax. (*Pause.*) Cliff'll get a jug when he gets here . . . always does.

STELLA: Ha, ha . . . all Cliff is gonna get is a piece of your butt, Bummie.

BUMMIE: Hey . . . baby . . . why you got to sound on me like that?

SLICK: But he might not can get any money off'a his ole lady.

STELLA: Because I dig you, honey.

SLICK (*whines*): But he might not can get any money off'a his ole lady.

STELLA: Who? That little broad of his named Lou? She'd give him her last quarter . . . silly as she is.

SLICK: She might not have it . . . and I paid my money for that jug.

BUMMIE: Shut up, lil' chump! You need to be learned a lesson.

STELLA: You teachin' Slick a lesson, Bummie? You always teachin' somebody somethin', man.

SLICK: Teachin' somethin' when he don't know shit.

BUMMIE (*to* STELLA): Yeah, baby. The lil' young blood's gettin' out of hand . . . thinks he's bad or somethin' . . . like Steve . . . (*Ironic.*) Got to show him his place, ya know?

STELLA (*teases*): Yeah, I know how it is with these youngsters. Don't even have any respect anymore. Pass the bottle, won't cha, hon?

BUMMIE: Sho, baby. (*Hands her the bottle.*)

SLICK: Awww . . . you shouldn't do nothin' like that.

STELLA (*breath*): These hare youngblood's bones ain't hard enough . . . right, Bummie?

BUMMIE: You said it, Stell. Little jive suckers . . . don't even know how to talk when they around ya.

SLICK (*angry*): I hope Cliff don't come. I hope Lil don't give him no fucken money to spend on you.

STELLA (*breath*): He'll come. He knows I'm here.

SLICK: You here? Sheeet . . . woman, he don't care if you here or on the moon.

STELLA (*drains bottle*): Yes, he does. He's only with that little bitch 'cause she works and gives him money. But he spends it on me.

SLICK (*coldly furious*): Spends it on you? You mean he buys you a bottle of wine to drink with him before he screws you? (*Mocking.*) Spends it on you . . . He don't even buy you a hotel room at night . . . ha, ha, ha . . . Spends it on you? . . . How many times you've spent in the back seat of Silly Willy's broke-down Buick that don't run no mo'? (*Names her.*) *Spends it on you* . . . you weak-minded bitch! How many times you been on *my* couch . . . in *my* front room . . . with him? (*Cruel.*) Spends it on you . . . Ha, ha, ha . . . (*To* BUMMIE.) Man . . . I can hear those old springs just a-squeakin' . . . "Squeaka . . . squeaka . . . squeaka" . . . Spends it on you. I can hear Stell here sayin' from through the wall in the other room: "Don't you love me, Cliff, baby? . . . Don't you care 'bout me some, Cliff, huh? . . . ha, ha . . . Spends it on you?

(*She throws the empty wine bottle at* SLICK; *it misses.*)

STELLA: Punk! Faggot!

SLICK: Hey, woman, stop that! (*Wry.*) You could hurt me and my pretty self.

BUMMIE (*laughing*): Hey, man. . . . lighten up on the pore broad.

(STELLA *tries to scratch* SLICK'*s face; he holds her arms.*)

SLICK: Hey, Bummie, help me. Help me, man, get this crazy bitch off'a me.

BUMMIE: I ain't in it . . . Ha, ha, ha . . . I ain't in it. I hope she kicks your little ass.

SLICK (*breathing hard*): Stella . . . you better stop foolin' 'round or I'm gonna knock you on your big ass.

STELLA (*angry*): You just do it, mathafukker! . . . You just do it.

(SILLY WILLY CLARK *and* BLUE *turn the corner and enter the light. They are drunk.*)

BLUE: Hey . . . mathafukkers . . . what's happenin'?

SILLY WILLY (*stumbles, giggles*): What you doin' to that girl . . . lil Slick nigger?

SLICK (*still holding her*): I ain't doin' nothin', man . . . Hey, Blue . . . Hey, Silly Willy . . . get this simple bitch off'a me.

SILLY WILLY: Awww . . . you simple niggers . . . Later for all that shit . . . have a drink.

(*He takes a bottle from his back pocket and lifts it.*)

BUMMIE: A drink?

BLUE: Yeah, man, a drink.,

(STELLA *quits her wrestling.*)

STELLA: I'm gonna git you, Slick.

SLICK (*pats her butt as they break*): Awww . . . Stell . . . you knows I loves you.

STELLA: Fuck you, punk!

BLUE: Oooeee, Slick . . . you gonna take that shit?

BUMMIE: You ain't signifyin' . . . is you Blue-Black, friend of mine.

(*They gather in a circle under the street lamp and pass the bottle around.*)

BUMMIE: Old Silly Willy Clark . . . I knew you were good for somethin' . . . You fat-head mathafukker.

SILLY WILLY: But you ain't gonna be when Cliff catches up with you.

BUMMIE (*apprehensive*): He's lookin' for me?

SILLY WILLY (*shrugs*): Uummmmm ummm . . . is he?

SLICK: What you go and punch his brother for and pull a .38 on him when he tried to fight back?

BLUE: You know how Cliff feels about his little brother.

STELLA: Is Cliff gonna get you, Bummie, huh?

BUMMIE (*scared*): Nawh, woman. (*Boasting.*) Ain't nobody gonna get me.

SLICK: If Cliff don't . . . Steve will. That's an evil little nigger.

BLUE: Yeah . . . that little nigger's mean . . . He'll sneak you if he can't get you any other way.

BUMMIE: Awww . . . why don't you people quit fuckin' with me?

BLUE: Hey, I got one . . . (*Pulls out another bottle.*)

STELLA: Let me drink out of yours, Blue, honey.

BLUE: Sho', baby.

STELLA: Silly Willy probably slobbers in his.

SILLY WILLY: Slobbers!

STELLA: I can't even kid with you, can I, sweetie pie?

SLICK: You better stop flirtin' wit' the fellas, Stella.

STELLA: You mind your business, man. Everybody knows I'm Cliff's girl.

SLICK: Then stop messin' wit' the fellas . . . you just gave ole Silly here a hard-on.

(BLUE *and* BUMMIE *laugh.* SILLY WILLY *half-turns, half-crouches, hand over groin, and takes another drink.*)

2. THE CORNER

(*Time passes. The Corner.* BLUE, STELLA, SILLY WILLY, *and* BUMMIE *drink.*)

BLUE: You can drink out of my bottle anytime you wants, Stella.

STELLA (*tipsy*): Thanks, baby.

SILLY WILLY: Where's Cliff Dawson?

BUMMIE: He ain't come up yet.

BLUE: I better save him some.

STELLA (*tilts head back and takes long drink*): Yeah . . . you do that.

BUMMIE: Wow . . . this broad sho' can put it away.

SLICK: Well, there's the sharks . . . and there's the fishes.

BLUE: Some fish are called suckers, man. You hip ta that?

SILLY WILLY (*to* STELLA, *still drinking*): Kill it, girl! (*Hysterically.*) Heeee, ha, ha, ha . . . let me see how ya do it!

3. THE TAKING

(*Later. The Corner.* CLIFF *and* STELLA *stand under the street lamp.*)

CLIFF: You niggers drank up everything, huh?

STELLA (*drunk*): I tole them . . . I tole 'em . . . I tole 'em not to . . .

CLIFF: Well, I don't give a fuck, see?

STELLA: . . . do it. Tole 'em not to do it or . . .

CLIFF: I can get a drink whenever I want.

STELLA: They over to Slick's, baby. They over there, Cliff.

CLIFF: Was it that little Slick nigger who drank up everything?

STELLA: Yeah . . . yeah . . . it was him. It was Slick. I tried to save you some but . . . hey, ain't you goin' over to Slick's, Cliff?

CLIFF: Nawh, I ain't goin' over there.

STELLA: You're not? . . . Awww, Cliff. They probably got another Big Man 'a wine and just waitin' for you C'mon, Cliff. Let's go. Please?

CLIFF: Nawh . . . let 'em keep it. And what the fuck you want some more to drink for? Ya can hardly stand now. C'mon . . . let's go.

STELLA: Where, Cliff?

CLIFF: C'mon, let's go sit in Silly Willy's car.

STELLA: Nawh, Cliff. Nawh . . . I don't want to do nothin' in there no mo':

CLIFF (*jerks her*): C'mon, woman . . . let's go!

STELLA: (*whines*): Awww . . . Cliff . . . nawh . . . I don't want to go.

CLIFF: What do ya mean ya don't want to go?

STELLA: (*drunk*): I'm not a tramp, Cliff . . . Ah'm not a tramp.

CLIFF: Don't argue with me, bitch! When I say come . . . I mean just that!

STELLA: Don't do this to me, Cliff.

CLIFF (*pulls her*): Come on!

STELLA: Don't, Cliff!

CLIFF: Now what you actin' like a fool for?

STELLA: You can take me somewheres besides that ole car. You can take me somewheres.

CLIFF: C'mon, we just gonna sit and talk.

STELLA: Oh, stop lyin', man. You know I want you, baby. But not in no back seat of some fuckin' broke-down car all the time.

CLIFF (*pushes her*): Shut up!

STELLA: Take me to a motel, Cliff.

CLIFF: What?

STELLA: Please . . . Cliff . . . please. Take me to a motel, Cliff . . . just once.

CLIFF: What's wrong with you, woman?

STELLA: Just this once, Cliff. Just this once.

CLIFF: I ain't got no money to be wastin' on that foolishness, woman!

STELLA: Yes, you have, Cliff. I know you have money . . . I know it! You keep money . . . you get it from that girl you live with . . . Lou.

CLIFF: It ain't none of your business what I get, bitch! You don't know nothin' 'bout mah business. You just keep your mouth shut, ya hear?

STELLA: Nawh, I ain't gonna keep mah mouf shut! I ain't no whore, Cliff. I'm a woman . . . I want to be your woman. I don't care none about Lou or Sue or Annie or any of the rest of your funky bitches . . . just as long as you treat me right. But this ain't right, man. This ain't right.

CLIFF: It ain't? It ain't right?

STELLA: Nawh, it ain't right, Cliff. I do anything for you . . . you know that. I do almost anything 'cept get out on these streets for you.

CLIFF: You gonna do that before it's all over with.

STELLA: Don't say that, Cliff. You don't mean that, do you? You wouldn't have me do that, would you? You don't have that bitch Lou on the street. She ain't on the block!

CLIFF: Nawh, because she's in the laundry. In the laundry bringing home that paycheck every week.

STELLA (crying): And you want me to go out on the street.

CLIFF: You out here already. All you got to do is make it pay.

STELLA: You sonna bitch . . . you know I ain't doin' nothin' like that!

CLIFF: C'mon, baby . . . let's go to the car.

STELLA: Ohhh . . . Cliff . . . please. Please, Cliff.

CLIFF: Let's go to the car, Stell.

STELLA: Tell me I don't have to go out on the block, Cliff. Tell me that.

CLIFF: Let's go to the car, Stell.

STELLA: Let me talk to you, baby.

CLIFF: The car.

STELLA: Please . . .

(They start off and CLIFF kisses her; she clutches him and he pulls away and she stumbles after him into the shadows.)

STELLA (from the shadows): I'm yours, baby . . . but don't treat me so bad. Just don't treat me so bad.

4. IT'S TOO LATE NOW

(Two hours after. The Corner. CLIFF, BUMMIE, SLICK, BLUE,

and SILLY WILLY CLARK *stand under the street lamp. All are drunk except* CLIFF.)

CLIFF: What a motley-ass bunch of cheap mathafukkers!

BUMMIE: We sorry, man. I tried to get them . . .

CLIFF: Awww . . . shut up! I'm through with you all. All of you.

SLICK: Cliff . . . don't be like that.

(CLIFF *slaps* SLICK.)

CLIFF: You . . . little nigger . . . I heard about you.

BLUE: Hey, Cliff . . . cool it.

SILLY WILLY: Everythin's gonna be all right, Cliff. C'mon, let's go up on the avenue.

SLICK: Man . . . you shouldn't ah done that. It wasn't just me.

CLIFF: Nawh . . . I ain't goin' nowhere. I'm through with you niggers.

BUMMIE: Ahhh . . . Cliff . . . we sorry.

BLUE: Forget it, man.

CLIFF: Nawh, I ain't gonna forget nothin'. I'm sick of you all . . . all of you. Just came from down the street in that broke-down car with Stella. Bitch so damn drunk she fell asleep on me . . . (*Offers car key.*) Here . . . here's the car key . . . you niggers can go down there and wake her up if you can.

BUMMIE (*incredulous*): Man . . . you don't care . . .

BLUE: Do you know what you sayin', Cliff?

SILLY WILLY: Give me that goddamn key. I always did want some of Stella . . . good as she looks.

(SILLY WILLY *takes key.*)

SLICK: Cliff . . . you ain't gonna be mad tomorrow, are ya?

CLIFF: Do you think I'm gonna be mad? What makes you think I care what you niggers do?

SILLY WILLY: C'mon . . . let's go.

BUMMIE: Hey, you guys . . . I'm not goin' . . . I'm not gonna do nothin' like that.

BLUE: But, man, if Cliff don't care . . .

SLICK: Now, Cliff . . . Cliff . . . if we do, you ain't gonna be mad, are ya? If you get mad at one of us, man . . . you got to get mad at us all.

CLIFF: Go on, man . . . enjoy yourself. She's yours. All of you deserve each other.

SILLY WILLY (*starts off*): I knew I had a good reason for buyin' that car.

BLUE (*following*): Shsssh . . . man. Somebody might hear us.

SLICK: Look, man . . . I'll get a jug tomorrow, hear? I'll bring it by your house.

SILLY WILLY (*singing*): Stella . . . Stella . . . our little fancy bella . . . we're comin' ta be your fellas.

CLIFF: Get the fuck out of my face . . . little Slick nigger.

BLUE (*from shadows*): Shhhh . . . quiet, man! Stop dat singin', Silly, man.

(SLICK *exits. Silence.* CLIFF *and* BUMMIE *stand on the corner.*)

BUMMIE: What's wrong, man? Huh? What's wrong?

CLIFF: You don't know?

(*Silence.*)

BUMMIE: Well . . . man . . . you know Steve don't like me none.

CLIFF: But you sneaked him, Bummie.

BUMMIE: But he was gonna do the same thing to me, man. I could see it comin', man.

CLIFF: You could see it comin', huh?

BUMMIE: Yeah . . . Cliff. I could.

(*Pause.*)

CLIFF: Well . . . that's between you and him. Steve can take care of himself.

BUMMIE (*relieved*): Well, thanks, man . . . I'm sorry about . . .

CLIFF: But you know he's not gonna forget it, Bummie. He's that way, man.

BUMMIE: Yeah, I know.

CLIFF: I'll talk to him. He's always listened to me.

BUMMIE: Cliff . . . is there anything really bothering you, man? You don't . . .

CLIFF (*annoyed*): Awww . . . man . . . it's just one of those goddamn days, I guess.

BUMMIE: But somethin' had to happen, man. This ain't like you, Cliff.

CLIFF: What's like me, huh? To be a bum? To drink wine and fuck bitches in junky cars? To stand half the night on some street corner that any fucken cop can come up and claim? . . . Is that like me?

BUMMIE: But, man, we've always done it. Even before you went into the Navy and got out.

CLIFF: But I ain't doin' it no more, Bummie . . . no more.

BUMMIE: Are you goin' away, man?

CLIFF: Nawh . . . nawh . . . not goin' away no more. Not anymore . . . I'll be here for a long time, man. I'm a family man now.

BUMMIE: You and Lou are gonna get hitched?

CLIFF: Hitched? Hummp . . . that's funny . . . I never thought about that.

BUMMIE: You gonna settle down, man?

CLIFF: Yeah, Bummie, yeah. Lou's gonna have a baby. I'm gonna be a father.

BUMMIE: Well . . . I'll be damned.

CLIFF: Yeah . . . you can start callin' me Daddy Cliff.

BUMMIE: Hey . . . man . . . that's great. C'mon up on the avenue . . . I'll buy ya a drink

CLIFF: Nawh, man. I'm not up to it. I'm goin' in.

BUMMIE: Hey, man, you changin' already.

CLIFF: Yeah, maybe I am. Well, I'll see ya, man.

(CLIFF *exits.* BUMMIE *stands a moment whistling, shuffling his feet with hands in his pockets and then exits in the direction of* SILLY WILLY'S *car.*)

BLACKNESS

Who's Got His Own

A PLAY IN THREE ACTS

by RON MILNER

Ron Milner was born on May 29, 1938, in Detroit. He graduated from high school and attended various colleges in Detroit.

He is the author of a novel, numerous plays, short stories, and essays.

Who's Got His Own was first presented at the American Place Theater in New York City; it then toured through New York state colleges under the auspices of the New York State Council of the Arts. It was also the premiere show at Harlem's New Lafayette Theatre. Milner's other New York productions include, most recently, *The Warning: A Theme for Linda,* which was presented as a part of *A Black Quartet,* four one-act plays produced by Woodie King Associates, Inc.

Recipient of both Rockefeller and John Hay Whitney fellowships, Milner attended Harvey Swados' writing workshop at Columbia University. For two years, 1966–67, he was writer-in-residence at Lincoln University, in Pennsylvania. Currently, Milner is conducting a cultural workshop at Michigan State University, and is director of his own theater company, Spirit of Shango, in Detroit.

Moving into a new form, film-writing, Milner is currently in the midst of several projects.

A gift in memory of my sister, Drenna Joy Milner
1939–1964

Papa may have
Mama may have
But God bless the child
Who's got his own.
B. HOLLIDAY

ACT 1

Scene 1

TIME: *1950's–60's.*

PLACE: *Midtown Detroit.*

SET:* BRONSON *family living room—a large, circular room with the doors to nearly all the other rooms of the flat leading*

* Nothing about the set, or specific design, need be followed to the letter. In the production of Harlem's New Lafayette Theatre, directed by Bob Macbeth, the concept was presentational; the idea being that it

to it; upstage left is the outside door; down from it, moving right, is the door to the corridor, leading to bathroom, closets, etc.; down farther right (circling the wall) not yet center, is the door to TIM JR.*'s old bedroom; farther right, center-stage rear, is the door to* CLARA*'s bedroom, and approaching stage right now, still rear, is parents' bedroom door; finally, upstage, is kitchen doorway.*

The large, aged couch, perfectly centers the set, with almost equal circular space all around it; there are end tables at each end of the couch, identical lamps sit atop the two, with magazines and/or a few books visible on the bottom ramps; one easy chair, the older one, sits upstage right, facing couch, a small table with lamp beside it; another more modern easy chair is opposite across the room upstage left, with a magazine rack (ancient and empty) next to it; just to left is small stand and telephone.

Stretching along the wall between CLARA*'s bedroom and parents', two tables have been pushed together; atop them is fried chicken, cakes, punch, etc. Between parents' bedroom door and kitchen doorway is another table, complete with tablecloth, seemingly in anticipation of more food and such.*

There is a cheap painting of a religious subject on the wall above the food-laden table.

TIM JR. *enters from kitchen, carrying open can of beer. He is youthful-looking, yet maturity shows in his bearing, his expression; when one looks closely to see that he is finished with his teens, one wonders if he is only twenty-two, or maybe twenty-four, or perhaps even a few years more. There is a tense, smoldering, smirking quality about him. The flavor of both college classrooms and coffee-jazz houses, of intimation with both the best of Western civilization's culture and the sharply mundane wisdom to be had on slum streets, is sensed in his gestures, postures, heard in his tone, and modes of speech.*

He moves about the room in extreme agitation: as a man trapped and waiting for either executioners or saviors.

He perhaps takes a pinch of cake or a piece of chicken from the table; various pieces of the furniture—especially the couch

---

—the play—was all taking place at, say, a wake at the funeral home, with the audience being included in all the goings-on—the monologues were presented as "evidence" to the audience—with even a woman playing traditional "church" funeral-type music to open the play. Many who saw this production and ones done as written preferred this more "theatrical" approach. The author leaves this decision to directors, as long as it is clearly understood that the lines themselves are not to be changed, but only the direction of them.

and the older easy chair with its footstool—cause him to pause involuntarily in bitter reflection. He makes a point of closing his parents' bedroom door. Then goes suddenly to the telephone, left near door, dials hurriedly; waits.

TIM: Hello? Is Al in?! Al! Al De Leo! Yeh—De Leo, room 14, that's right. Well, will you call him, or something, huh? (*Waits long moments.*) Huh? Naw, no message. Tell him Tim called. Thanks. Wait a minute—oh—Will you leave him this number? All right—Trinity 5-0119—Yeah—Thanks.

(*Comes away from phone, wiping face with handkerchief. He starts as the murmuring, demurring voices of* MOTHER *and* CLARA—*mingled with two, or three deep, patronizing male voices—are heard coming up the steps outside. He finishes beer in hurried gulps, then puts empty can atop the clear-topped table. Excitement and apprehension flare to his face for a moment; then he breathes and waits as a man expecting opposition.* CLARA *enters before* MOTHER, REVEREND CALDER, *and* TWO DEACONS. CLARA *is two years younger than* TIM JR., *and projects the same incongruous sense of age and maturity through an obvious youthfulness. She could be very attractive, as at first glance her face and body fetch approving attention, but the prim, black "funeral dress" she wears accents the wary, defensive withering quality in her personality which causes men to stare wonderingly—after the first glance of natural attraction—with the sense of something being awry, perverted in her, and then turn away feeling that they've seen something subtly disconcerting. She clutches and twists funeral program.*)

CLARA (*moving into room, looking around puzzledly*): Where is—? (*Looks warily, accusingly at* TIM JR.) Where are all the others?

TIM (*Smiles sardonically*): Expecting a big audience, huh, Clara? (*Loudly to all of them.*) I sent 'em home. All of 'em. (*To* CLARA, *smiling again.*) So I'll be the only one watching you sham and lie. Just me.

CLARA (*tensely, clenched whisper*): We don't need you here, Tim. Leave us alone.

TIM (*moving from her stare, watching* MOTHER, *and others*): Oh, yeh, clear field now, huh?

MOTHER (*glancing around, being unnecessarily helped toward couch by* REVEREND CALDER. *She hasn't heard* TIM JR. *and* CLARA): Oh—Nobody's come yet? I thought they were coming on with you, Tim Jr.

SECOND DEACON: Lord, Sister Hamilton, Brother Lambert, they all said they'd be here when we got back from the cemetery. What become of 'em?

FIRST DEACON (*going toward food-topped table*): That's my wife's bowl. Now where could she be?

CLARA (*standing before* TIM, *twisting funeral program*): What did you say to them?

TIM (*to others*): I sent 'em home. I told 'em my mother didn't need their condolences. She needed rest! Rest! I told 'em if they really felt for her they should go home and let her have some peace! Most of 'em left like good little children of the Lord. Some I had to put out.

MOTHER (*now seated on couch*): What is it, Clara? What's he saying?

CLARA (*sitting beside* MOTHER): He sent them home, Mother, Tim sent them all home.

REVEREND (*wonderingly*): You put them out, son? You sent them away?

TIM: Don't son me! Yeh, I put 'em out! They didn't know him! What were they hanging around like—like buzzards! for?

REVEREND: They weren't here for him, son. There's nothing more anyone can—

TIM: Save it, hear?! Save it! You might need it Sunday!

MOTHER: Tim Jr.—Tim Jr.

(*Closes eyes, as* CLARA *leans to assist her in whatever way she might be able to.* MOTHER *is an old acquaintance of both weariness and sorrow, they do not surprise and overwhelm her. It is only that she feels a void, a gap, more pronounced and lasting than any she has ever known before. And must now gather the resources to pull the thread-ends of her life together across this sudden chasm. She must pause before actions and answers for the moment. Her rhythm, sustained over many years, a thing like the flow of rivers, has been disturbed. She will move into it again, in a moment, day, or week.*)
Tim Jr.—Tim Jr.

REVEREND: Your mother doesn't need any irritation right now, son.

TIM: Damn right! So take that preachin' and prayin' on outta here! Got a mouthful of that at that church today. Yeh. You know, that was really somethin'; you all whoopin' and hollerin' over him. Ha.

CLARA: What do you want, Tim? Haven't you done enough?

MOTHER (*eyes still closed*): Tim Jr.—Clara—

TIM (*to* CLARA): Shut up, phony! (*To* REVEREND.) You know that was really funny: You all carryin' on over him, when what he thought about your whole business wouldn't make a good glob of spit! Yeh!

REVEREND: I told you, son, we weren't there for him.

TIM: Yeh! How many times had you seen this—this man, you were doing all that prayin' over? That those other phonies were doing all that crying about? Huh? How many times? I know you never saw him at that damned church!—

MOTHER (*opening eyes, seemingly about to rise*): You've said enough now, Tim Jr.—

FIRST DEACON: —Hold on now, boy!

SECOND DEACON: —Saddle that tongue, boy!

REVEREND (*holding reassuring hand out to* MOTHER *as* CLARA *restrains her*): We pray and preach, yes and cry, for ourselves, son. For our sinfulness, and our unworthiness to meet our Savior. Your father's departure is a dramatic reminder to us, son.

TIM (*has turned away, now whirls pointing*): You left your son at home! Daddy! You ain't got no son in here! Hear?! You better remember that, man.

FIRST DEACON (*moving toward* TIM): Now you just watch your tone, boy! You just better watch your tone there, now!

SECOND DEACON (*rushes up to* TIM, *shaking his finger in his face*): You go to college, don't you? Well, don't they teach you no better respect then this! Don't you know that Almighty God is seeing your disgraceful acts of disrespect, here today? He is weighing and judging your soul this very minute? He—

TIM (*coldly, tensely*): Man, get your damn finger outta my face. Get the hell away from me. Now! Damnit! Now!

(DEACON *recoils as* TIM *motions forward.*)

FIRST DEACON (*moving between* TIM *and* SECOND DEACON): Don't waste your breath on him, Deacon. My oldest one is just like this one. Knows everything! Too educated for us or the Lord! ! Just have to let the Devil teach him!—

MOTHER (*trying to rise, with* CLARA *and* REVEREND *restraining her*): I didn't raise you like this, Tim Jr.! You know I didn't. The Lord knows I didn't! I didn't raise you to be disrespectful! (*Her voice is strained, tremulous. Her tone makes* TIM *turn and move to kitchen doorway.*) Cussing in front of me—

CLARA (*an unwarranted franticness, as* MOTHER *merely rocks to and fro with eyes closed*): Mother, don't let him upset you! (*Bitterly to* TIM.) That's all he wants—to upset everything.

REVEREND (*laying a hand on each of them; as* DEACONS *come over with reassuring words*): No, Clara, now, now, we weren't going to get upset, now. No, dear, no. Your mother's all right now.

(CLARA *turns away from* REVEREND'S *hand.*)

MOTHER (*grips* REVEREND's *hand, looks up at him pleadingly*): I didn't raise him to be like this, Reverend. Before Our Lord I didn't. I didn't. I tried to bring him up in the church. I—

(TIM *squirms in kitchen doorway.*)

FIRST DEACON: We know you didn't, Sister Bronson. We know you didn't. Sure we do. Don't you worry about that. It's just these young ones who want to wear your shoes and theirs too.

SECOND DEACON: Sometimes they get away from home, runnin' wit' the Devil, and can't nobody do nothing with 'em. That's all.

REVEREND: Don't you think we know your heart, your sweet soul, Sister? And you know the Lord knows. When the pain settles a little and understanding dawns, you and your family are gonna be fine, just fine. (MOTHER *grips his hand in both of hers, and nods gratefully, smiling slightly.*) No, baby sister, you gotta keep that pretty chin up, if you want the sun shining around here. (*Gently turns* CLARA's *face from* MOTHER's *shoulder.* CLARA *politely moves her face free, gives slight smile, lowers head; her hands tight around funeral program.*)

MOTHER: I want you to thank them all for me, Reverend Calder. Sister Carter. Mother Tyree—every one of 'em. You've all been so wonderful. I don't know what I woulda'— When they called and said that—that he'd been hurt in that car, run into that wall, that he'd died, Jesus, before they could get him to the hospital—

FIRST DEACON: Lord, they say he was coming 'round that curve over eighty miles an hour.

SECOND DEACON: Went right on off the road right into that wall. Jesus take him in.

FIRST DEACON (*shaking his head*): Too old be driving that fast on a turn.

TIM (*involuntarily, to self*): He was coming from that factory, maybe he didn't really want to make that turn; maybe he'd had enough.

SECOND DEACON: What that you say, boy?

TIM (*startled*): Nothing—I didn't say nothing to you, man.

MOTHER: I didn't know what to—I told 'em thank you, that I'd be right over there. But then I just stood there—just—I had the baking pan in my hand and I looked at it and Lord, it was like I didn't even know what it was; I couldn't remember what I was doing with it. Somebody you don't even know just calls and tells you it's gone. All those years, and all the things

in 'em, just gone. I just stood there wondering—it was like I had dreamed something but couldn't remember what it was. (*Shaking head, fighting down tears*). If Clara hadn't called you all, and you all hadn't been so—just so wonderful to us all, I just don't know what— Now, you tell 'em all, that, Reverend, hear? You tell 'em I truly appreciate, and I'll never forget, never. Hear?

REVEREND: We did what we could, Sister Bronson.

SECOND DEACON: And when we see the others, we'll sure tell 'em what you said.

TIM: Miss Something-or-other—Louis, I think. Yeh, Miss Louis said they would move the game over to her house. They took the rest of the stuff over there. After all a feast celebrating the fact that you ain't the one dead is cool, no matter what the address. Right?

FIRST DEACON (*fed up, putting on hat, to* MOTHER): You just let us know if there's—

TIM: And Sister Something-else said she had to keep her good silver with her, Mama. She said you'd understand. They said you could call 'em if you needed anything. Then, very considerately (*looks at three men*) they left.

REVEREND: Perhaps your son here is right. Maybe a little rest and contemplation would be the best thing after all. You know how they say we Baptists overdo a funeral. Heh—

TIM (*in dry weary monotone*): Do tell. Ain't it the truth. Lord, Lord.

MOTHER (*takes* REVEREND'*s hand and that of* SECOND DEACON): I still can't thank you enough. You tell 'em I said that.

FIRST DEACON: Done no more than we should have. Christ couldn't carry his cross alone, Sister Bronson; Simon come to help. (*All nod and murmur amens.*) And in times like this when Calvary stretches before us long as a winter night and clear as a summer day—

TIM (*glances at others; looks at* MOTHER): All right. No hard feelings. I won't say anything. (*To* REVEREND *and* DEACONS.) You all stay. I'll leave. I'll just get out of here and let you two mourn him properly. You, Mama—and you, too, Clara. You, too. I'll bet you'll cry all night long, won't you, Clara?

CLARA: Go on if you're going, Tim. Just leave.

MOTHER (*pleadingly*): Tim Jr., don't go! Don't leave him for good, till you try to set your heart right with him! Till you try to touch him a little!

TIM (*stops suddenly, reflects, turns back, pain in his face*): I tried, Mama. You know? I sat at that funeral, listening to

the—the—eulogies! And the singing. And I really tried. I waited for something—anything to—to come and fill this—this —dead empty shell that used to be the hard knot of my hate for him!

SECOND DEACON: What're you saying, boy!

FIRST DEACON: Lord, Jesus forgive him.

MOTHER (*moaning*): Tim Jr.—Tim Jr.—

TIM (*with an almost vindictive resolution to say it*): I tried, Mama. I waited. I—but then I saw the truth! The truth, Mama. That for as long as I could remember, I'd felt only one thing when he was gone, he was outta this house—a sense of relief, Mama! A sigh of re——

CLARA: Who asked you how you feel?!

FIRST DEACON: Hush, boy!

REVEREND: Where's your respect, boy!?

SECOND DEACON: Respect the dead, boy!

MOTHER (*eyes closed, rocking to and fro, shaking head painfully*): Lord, touch his heart. Touch his heart.

TIM: Did you really expect me to feel different because he's gone for good now, Mama? Did you expect me to come back here after four years, screaming and crying for him? Did you, Mama? Well, I'm crying, Mama. Crying. Because I can't find any tears for a father I've cussed all my life!

MOTHER (*rocking, moaning*): Put forgiveness in him, Lord! Put forgiveness in him!

CLARA (*bitterly*): Well why did you come to the funeral, then! Why are you here now! Just go on and leave us alone. Go back where you come from!

TIM (*the question strikes him. He straightens; begins slowly*): I really don't know, dear baby sister. I've been asking myself that all day long, you know. Maybe I just came to see it for myself. Yeh. See what would happen when they put him in a dark, deep hole and covered him up forever.

REVEREND (*solemnly*): May Jesus see and understand.

TIM: And then I wanted to see your reaction, Clara. (*Picking up momentum, animation.*) I wanted to see how much truth would be in it. How much of the *real* would show. And baby sister, I have to say that your bit got 'em all. The sweet, Mother-loyal, church-loyal, Father-loyal daughter, grieving so correctly. 'Look at the poor daughter, sitting there with her head down. Lord, the po' thing can't even bring herself to look.' That's all it took, huh, Clara? Just a lowered head! That was so, so hip of you. That's what you did with the truth: just lowered your head on it.

CLARA (*same truculent whisper as before*): My truth is my business! Who asked you how you feel?! Who asked you to come here and try to stir up trouble?

TIM: Mama asked me to come, all right! And Mama—? I wanted to see you, too. See if I could maybe find out just what *is* the truth with you. (*Bends over, hands sliding to knees, to peer solemnly into* MOTHER's *face. Then with genuine awe.*) Mother enigma. Sweet, sad, spiritual enigma. (MOTHER *looks away, shaking head, closing eyes.*)

REVEREND (*putting on hat*): Son, you should be thoroughly ashamed.

SECOND DEACON (*in furious, whip-cracking accentuation*): ASHAMED! ASHAMED!

FIRST DEACON (*in dismissing tone*): Lord help him. Help him and forgive him.

TIM: Ashamed?! Yeh. I'm ashamed. I'm ashamed. But (*to* REVEREND *and* DEACONS) in a way that none of you could understand.

MOTHER: Lord, forgive him his son. Forgive him his son.

TIM: Forgive him! Me? Did he ever forgive me, Mama? For being born? Did he? Tell me, 'cause I never had a chance to ask him while he was still beating me. I didn't dare ask him while he was looking at me as if I was the curse of the whole human race!

MOTHER: He knowed you was made in his image. He knowed what this world is for a black boy. He was just trying to make sure you'd be strong enough, Tim Jr.; just trying to give you all he knew, the best he knew how.

TIM: Mama, when I left this house, four years ago, I had all he ever gave me: bruises and welts, Mama, bruises and welts—bruises so deep that people can just touch me with their eyes, and my soul aches, Mama, my soul aches—That's what he gave me, Mama, bruises and welts on my back and soul, my back and soul, Mama. (MOTHER *and* TIM *communicate deeply with eyes; he turns away. There is a long pause, as* TIM *moves upstage. Mutters.*) Strong enough, yeh. I remember one day I was out playing on the street, and the streetcar passed, and I looked up and saw him sitting in the back—I just forgot everything, and started running for that car stop. I was on the other side of the street, about to cross over, when the streetcar pulled away and I saw him—standing there in his dirty work clothes. I remember thinking that he didn't look as tall as he had seemed when he left that morning. He lit a cigarette, and I remember it was a warm summer day, but he hunched over

97

that cigarette as though we were in the middle of a blizzard, as if he were afraid that the wind would snatch it out of his hands—it was like he was stealing something in broad daylight!—And then he looked right at me, across the street, right at me. But I could see that his eyes were so tired, so beat, they couldn't even look that far. He didn't see me; didn't recognize me—I watched him start up the block; his head kinda' down; the cigarette smoking; his shoulders sagging like that lunch pail weighed four hundred pounds. I don't think I ever wanted anything as bad as I wanted to carry that lunch pail. But even as young as I was, I knew that it wouldn't be right for him to know that I had seen him like that: with his eyes and his shoulders like that. So I started running across to the alley. Down the alley—all wild inside with some weird, crazy-jumping joy. I wanted to get home before he did; tell you and Clara he was coming, get everything ready—hmmmmmh —But I fell down, and scarred my hands, and my chin, and my knees, I think. And—and—I was so excited, so all jumbled-up with this—this—anxiety, that I just sat there and cried for a while, trembling all over—sort of laughing and crying at the same time, you know. I just stayed there in that alley like that for a while, until it eased off, until I came down a little— Then I got up and started again, trying to beat him, trying to get there first. But the minute I hit the back steps I knew I was too late. I could hear him up there, hollering, shouting, banging things around! I knew what it was like before I opened that back door and saw you all huddled at the table, and heard Clara crying up front somewhere, and saw him waving that damn lunch pail around thundering about nothing like he was some damn god or something!

CLARA: It's all over now, leave it alone!

SECOND DEACON: Respect His Holy Name, boy!

TIM (*turns suddenly to stare at* DEACONS): His Holy Name? (*Slight chuckle.*) Oh, you mean the—the Lord, don't you? For a minute I thought you meant—meant him. Meant ol' Shit-house Tim! That was his holy name! Shit-house Tim! Yeh! He cleaned 'em, and he was scared to come out of 'em!

MOTHER (*apprehensive, admonishing*): Tim Jr.?!

TIM: You knew about that "holy name," didn't you, Mama? Well I——

CLARA: Vulgar, filthy dog!

REVEREND: Clara! Clara!

TIM: —Yeh—you didn't know about it, did you, Clara? I didn't either that day I saw him get off the bus. But I felt it. Somehow, I felt his other name. I was about thirteen. He had

an off-day. He took me out to that factory with him to get his check.

MOTHER: You don't know, Tim Jr. You just don't understand—

TIM: I understood, Mama. Yeh. Me and him was already on the outs, you know, but it isn't every day you get a chance to travel with your old man. Yeh, I felt good. I felt proud with him showing his badge, and me and him walking into all that noise, that power. That damned factory really flipped me! It seemed so huge, and powerful. Like I know better now, but then I even liked war movies, so that joint with all those men straining their lives away flipped me, seemed like a place where a cat could work and *know* he was a man. You know? Yeh. Well, like I said he didn't have to work that day. He left me outside the office and went to get his check. And a couple of hillbillies passed me and I heard one of 'em say that I was "ol' Shit-house Tim's boy." And they laughed, and the other one said: "Yeh, he cleans 'em and he's scared to come out of 'em." Now, I didn't really understand that, it didn't sit right with me. It didn't seem to go with all that thundering power. So when two black dudes came out of the office I asked 'em, why they called that man Shit-house Tim? That man who just went in the office? 'Cause that's his job, cleanin' 'em up, one of 'em said. The other one laughed and said it was because that man even eats his lunch in the shit house! He's a real live black rabbit, he said. You see, he's so scared of these white folks that he can't get too far from that toilet, less one of 'em might say boo, and make him have a accident in his pants!

FIRST DEACON: You don't know the first thing about what you talking about!

TIM: Yeh. They went off laughin'. And in a minute there he was. The same cat that was always gonna huff an' puff the walls down aroun' here. Standing with his head down, all shy and sheepish. With a big white arm around his shoulders. A big funky foreman of a white face grinning next to him. "This your boy, Tim? When you gonna bring him out and teach him your trade? Haw. Haw!"—Yeh, the same ol' human mountain stood there bent while that—that Chuck asked him to lend a hand with the mess they had in the south john. You see this— this—new boy wasn't worth much, and anyhow he was busy at the other end. Now Chuck knew it wasn't his work hours, but it would only take ol' Tim a minute to straighten the mess out. Yeh, you could see ol' Tim didn't wanta do it, but you couldn't hardly hear his argument. An' ol' Chuck started lookin' mean, and growling about lil' favors; so ol' Tim told

me to wait, and put on some overalls, and went to straighten out that mess.

MOTHER: That kind always knew. Wouldn't leave him alone.

TIM: Because he wouldn't make them leave him alone! He didn't make nothing happen nowhere but in here! Yeh! Then after he'd established hell in here, he'd sit in that chair watching us over the top of his newspaper, like—like he was guarding the fiery gates.

MOTHER: You don't understand, Tim Jr. You just don't understand—

TIM: Lotsa times after that I'd watch him get off the car and run to tell you two he was coming. But for a different reason: to warn you. I mean, I didn't really give a damn after that.

CLARA: Why can't you just let her have a little peace?! Just this once! Just for a little while!

REVEREND: Yes, Clara, I think—

TIM (*staring at* CLARA, *with both resentment and concern. Moving toward her with less tension than a moment before*): Peace. Oh yes, peace. That's all you want now, isn't it, Clara? A nice little cocoon of peace and quiet—You've built your own little convent right here, haven't you? (*Then stage-whispers wryly, malevolently.*) A convent? Naw—a tomb, baby. A tomb. And that's for dead folks, honey. You know? (*Winks. Then grins maliciously into* CLARA's *tense, bright-eyed glare. She is near eruption.*)

CLARA: I know that you're still the same. That nothing's right to you unless it's the way you want it. That you want everyone to wallow in your dirt.

MOTHER (*shaking her head in her moaning way, closing eyes*): He wasn't strong, Tim Jr. He wasn't real strong. That's why he was so hard. So hard, Lord.

TIM: Hard. Yeh, he was hard all right. Like leather. Like a leather belt. Yeh, boom goes the thundering voice of Shithouse Tim! And crack goes the belt! Crack! Crack! Crack! Oh he took it out on us, didn't he? Crack, don't do that, you bet not this! Crack, who the hell told you to do that! Oh, yeh, real leather—in this house! Well, I had enough and I got out! But he just about whipped you to death, didn't he, Mama! Huh! And now Clara is climbing in with you, and you both'll die happily ever after! Ain't that it!? Huh? That the story of the belt!? Huh?!

MOTHER (*a cry*): Tim! Tim!

CLARA (*coming to feet; entire body screaming*): Leave us alone! Leave us alone! You just came here to torture us! Make us miserable! That's all any of you want! You're all the same! Him! You! Wreyford! All of you! Mean! Vicious! Cruel! I'd rather die! Just shrivel up and die! Than let one of you touch me again! Ever again! I wish you were dead! I wish all of you were dead! Every last one of you! Dead! Dead! Dead! (*Sobbing, flailing self with funeral program.*)

REVEREND (*starting to her, reaching out*): Clara?!

(CLARA *recoils from* REVEREND, *giving slight shriek, throwing funeral program into his chest. Falls sobbing to couch.* REVEREND *moves back, having seen something that shocks him.*)

CLARA: Mama! Mama! Oh, Mama! (*Clutches* MOTHER's *skirt, sobbing, writhing, seemingly about to crawl into* MOTHER's *lap. Hides face in* MOTHER's *skirt.*) I wish I were dead. I wish I were dead!

MOTHER (*shocked, approaching franticness*): What is it, Clara baby? Honey, what is it? What've you done to her, Tim Jr.? You wish all of us were dead, baby? All of who, baby? All—?

(TIM *has watched* CLARA's *outburst with first startled, then sad, but always keen, interest; obviously curious to how far she will go, how much she will say. Now he slumps, his body almost as limp as the belt he now points at* CLARA. *Begins wearily.*)

TIM: Yeh, all who, Clara? All what? You wish all who were dead? Who is Wreyford, Clara? Huh? Who is Wreyford? Go on, tell your mother. Go on. Tell her. Come on, Clara? Tell all about it! Come on! Talk Talk!

CLARA (*shrieking*): Get that belt away from me! Don't touch me! Get away from me! Mama! (*Hides in* MOTHER's *arms.* MOTHER *has watched* TIM *and* CLARA *with fascinated, awed horror and perplexity, as stunned as the* REVEREND *and* DEACONS *who have become pillars of frozen astonishment. There is pained bewilderment in her tone now.*)

MOTHER: What're you doing to her, Tim Jr.? Why you want so to hurt her? Wreyford? Who is Wreyford? Clara baby, Clara baby, what's he doing to you—?

TIM: The belt—? This damn belt?! (*Flings it away.*) What does it, *he,* have to do with Wreyford? Huh, Clara? Huh. You mean because of that night? Naw—you trying to twist it up! Tell the truth, Clara! Tell the damn truth!!

CLARA (*desperately, leaving* MOTHER's *lap to fling herself to back of couch*): SHUT UP! SHUT UP!

MOTHER (*touching* TIM): What're you—why do you want so to hurt her?—Hurt us both.

(*He turns away.*)

REVEREND (*sense of intruding too much to bear now*): Uh —Sister Bronson, we're gonna have to leave you now. Uh—if there's anything—anything at all, we can do for you, you know we'd be more than glad to do it, now. (MOTHER *nods, with gratitude, and embarrassment.*) And Clara, little sister, now you've got to be strong, so you can help your mother, now you hear? (CLARA *keeps face away from him, doesn't acknowledge him. As* DEACONS *take leave from* MOTHER *and go to door,* REVEREND *looks at* TIM, *standing with back to them all. Goes near him.*) Son, and you too, Clara; now you can't lay in ambush for yesterday; it ain't ever coming down this road again. It's gone its way and you have to go yours. Now your father and mother have—

TIM (*turning to look at him, then*): Yeh, all right, I'll light a candle, first chance I get. Okay. 'Bye. Thanks.

MOTHER: Tim Jr.! Hush, boy! Now, you don't sass the Reverend! (*Starting to rise.*)

CLARA (*tearfully, grabbing* MOTHER, *stopping her*): Mama! Mama, don't——

SECOND DEACON (*coming from door to speed* REVEREND): We just trying to help, boy.

TIM (*staring coldly at the* REVEREND, *chuckles*): Help? All you old farmers can help is the hangups. Go on back to church and shout about Hell! (*Turns away.*)

REVEREND (*backing toward door, understandingly*): Just hold on to yourself, son. We're going. (*Reaches door.*) God is with you, Sister Bronson. (*Adjusts hat.*)

FIRST DEACON (*to* MOTHER): Don't you worry about a thing, sister. Everything's gonna be all right.

SECOND DEACON: And don't pay that one any mind, he'll get his measurement one day and soon.

MOTHER (*pleading for his understanding*): I'm so ashamed of my son, Reverend. Maybe it's that college. I didn't raise him to be like this. He didn't used to—

REVEREND: It's all right, I understand—Clara? See you Sunday?

(CLARA *first glares with a wary, defiant air. Then nods.* REVEREND *goes out with others.* TIM *slams door behind them. Moment of silence, as* MOTHER *stares at* TIM, *and* TIM *stares reflectively at* CLARA, *who nervously averts face from him.*)

MOTHER (*incredulous and concerned*): Tim Jr.?! What is it, Tim Jr.!? Why are you acting like this?

CLARA (*jumps to feet*): Because he's a dog! A filthy dog! (*Stands glaring at him, fist clenched.*) Animal!

TIM (*stares first curiously; then anger flares*): Yeh, I'm a dog! A black dog! And all black dogs are filthy! Right, Clara!? All black dogs! But a white dog is a whole different thing, huh?! Right?! Well, what about bitches, Clara!? What about black and white bitches!?

MOTHER (*slaps* TIM *strongly as he nears* CLARA): Enough, now, boy! That what they taught you in college! To talk like that to your sister?! Before your mother? In front of the Reverend! That what they teach you?!

(TIM *stunned, holds face, looking at* MOTHER *with disbelief; restrains angry impulses.*)

CLARA (*reacts to slap as if she had received it; holds face grimacing with emotional pain*): Good! Get out! Leave us alone! (*Breaks past* MOTHER *and* TIM; *heading, sobbing, for her bedroom door.* TIM *catches* CLARA *behind couch, some steps before her bedroom door. Grips her from behind by shoulders.*)

TIM: No, baby sister! Not yet! No more hiding.

CLARA (*desperately squirming, fighting to get free*): Let me go! Let me go!

MOTHER (*comes to pull at* TIM'*s arm. Incredulous*): Tim Jr.?! Tim Jr.!? Let her go! Leave her alone! What're you doing? What're you——?

CLARA: Tell him to leave me alone!

TIM (*gripping* CLARA *even tighter, but trying to reassure* MOTHER *with his tone*): I'm not going to hurt her, Mama! I swear—

(CLARA *frees one arm, turns and scratches the hand still holding her, and, free for a moment, tries to reach her bedroom.* TIM *recoils from scratch; recovers and, jumping out of* MOTHER'*s grasp, catches* CLARA *again, just at her bedroom door; pulls her back and steps in front of door, blocking it.*)

TIM: No, Clara! You're not going in——

CLARA: Get away from me! Get outta my way! (*Seemingly accepting the futileness of the attempt, she rushes forward with her hands down at her sides.* TIM *grabs her shoulders, holds her at arm's length. She shouts.*) Don't touch me! Don't touch me! (*Then shaking head from side to side, almost "chanting" in a pain-filled, hysterical tone just above a whisper.*) Get your hands off me—take your hands off me—take your hands off me—

TIM: I will, Clara! You hear me? I will let you go! When you tell your mother who Wreyford is! Tell her where we went

that night, me! your father! and you! Where we went and why we went! You hear me, Clara?! Huh!? (CLARA *stops to stare at him with bitter realization.*) Tell her where you went when you ran away! Who you lived with! And I'll take my hands off you!

(MOTHER *has at first stood bewildered and shocked where* TIM *left her; then slowly comes nearer the two of them, as if being drawn into some compelling, frightening mystery which she fears to become too involved with. Now is close enough to touch; puzzledly reaches out a tentative hand.*)

MOTHER: Tell me what, Tim Jr.? What happened when?

(CLARA *pushing self harder against* MOTHER; *attempting to cover* MOTHER's *ears with her hands; the desperate sound of tears in her voice.*)

CLARA: Don't listen to him, Mama! He's a liar. A filthy liar!

(MOTHER *gives reassuring sounds and pats.*)

TIM: Yes, listen, Mama! Listen to what she thinks about dogs! Black and white dogs! And bitches! Yeh, black and white bitches!

CLARA: Don't listen to him, Mama! Tell him to get out!

MOTHER: No, honey, now don't you worry. I ain't gon' listen to no more of that kind of talk in this house. Now, Tim Jr., you just leave her alone. Get out of the way now and—

TIM (*still blocking way; moving toward* MOTHER *slightly*): All right, Mama. When she ran away? Where did she go? Who with? Have you ever asked her? Do you know? Do you know why she ran away?

CLARA (*frantic*): You can't tell her anything about me, nothing!

MOTHER (*to* CLARA): Shhh, honey. Don't worry. Shhh. (*To* TIM.) All that was so long ago now, Tim. She's done nothin' like that no more. Now, just move. If she'd wanted to tell me about it she woulda by now. Just move, now— (*Putting arm around* CLARA; *pulling her on.*) We've had enough today.

TIM: Mama?!

MOTHER: You're talking crazy! Get outta her way now, Tim Jr.! She's going to her room, now!

(TIM *steps aside slightly after a moment, in which stares are exchanged, and watches* MOTHER *and* CLARA *approach; as they come alongside him, he touches* CLARA's *arm.*)

TIM: Clara?

MOTHER: Now, Tim—

CLARA: I'm going to my room and you can't stop me!

TIM: All right, Clara. Look— (*Opens* CLARA's *bedroom door slightly.*) I'll let you alone. You can go in and hide under

your pillow. But if you do, then I'm gonna tell her about it. Tell her about it all. My way! The way I saw it; see it, now, today. Now take your choice.

CLARA (*looking at him with something of both desperate and shrinking horror*): You can't tell her anything about me! You don't know anything but what's in your own sick filthy mind!

MOTHER: Stop this foolishness, now, Tim Jr.! You ain't gon' tell me no more! Not today! Maybe sometime when she feels like it— When we all feel—

TIM (*gesturing frantically; moving violently*): No! Today! Mama! Today! I didn't come here just to make it look right to your church members! I came to see if—if his old cracks were still in the walls! If he still had everything and everybody split and splintered to pieces! And it is, Mama! It's all the same! And I can't wait—till tomorrow or the next day! 'Cause I just might not never come back here again! That's why I got to do something before I go! Now! Today! I want to bury it all, Mama. Every bit of— But you've got to see it, or hear it, before you can kill it. You gotta put your—your finger, your hand, on it before you can do something about it.

CLARA: You just want to hurt! Just want to——

MOTHER: And you think this is something to do? To hurt your sister? Worry me?

TIM: Mama, I just want to do this: introduce you to your daughter; my mother to my sister.

MOTHER (*glancing from him to* CLARA): What're you saying, Tim Jr.? What're you telling me?

CLARA: You just want to destroy everything! That's all.

TIM: I'm saying you don't know no more about what's standing next to you than you do about what's standing over here. I want you to know what you're hugging! Who you're talking to! And then if the shamming and faking goes on, well, I tried. Because whether you know it or not, this thing between you and Clara is wrong, Mama! And sometimes I think you *know* it's wrong!

MOTHER: Wrong, Tim Jr.? Whatta you mean?

CLARA: Shut up! TIM!

TIM: Two years, Mama! She's been back, two years! And you think it's normal?! You think a young girl—supposed to be a *young woman*—is gonna stay up under her mother that long? and never want to be with anybody else?! Aw, naw, Mama. You know better than that. You know she's been asking you something. Begging you for something!

CLARA: Shut up!

TIM: Go, hide, little girl!—Am I right, Mama?! You know what she's been asking you, don't you?! How to be a woman! That's what!!

CLARA: I'm telling you to let her alone, TIM!!

TIM: I'm doing the telling! Remember!—That's what she's asking you, Mama! And you know what you're teaching her?— How to lie!!

MOTHER (*avoiding his eyes*): Lie, Tim Jr.? How can you—?

CLARA: Dog!!

TIM: How to take everything you really feel, think, and know, over to that—that—sublimation house! That all-purpose God! Then lie, to every human being you meet, just by not telling him nothing! Ain't that what you're teaching, Mama? Huh!?

CLARA: You'll say anything!! Do anything!!

MOTHER: Now, Tim Jr., I don't know what you—You don't have no right, now—You got to stop this now—

TIM: I am right! And you know why you're teaching her that, Mama?! Because you know if you get too deep into her, you'll find him in it somewhere, her father! Your husband! (MOTHER *tries to slap him: he catches her wrist.*) And you never could deal with him. Now could you?! I mean not really!

CLARA: Mean vicious dog!

TIM: —And the second reason, Mama?! You know that if she ever does become a woman, then she's got to get her own thing—own life—own family! Got to leave you! And you don't want to be alone. You're not gonna be alone if you can help it. You'll tie her life up so tight——

CLARA: God damn you! Leave her alone! I'll tell her!! I'll tell her! First him and now you! Just get out and leave her alone! I'll tell her! My way! With none of your filth! Your lies!

TIM (*stops, stares, emotions suspended; slumps exhausted; shaking head, goes to more modern chair*): Un-uh, Clara, ain't going for no fakes.

CLARA: God damn you, get out. I'll tell her.

(TIM *shakes head; watching them both.* TIM's *attack has had* MOTHER *holding on to the back of couch, bewildered, pained; now turns to* CLARA, *trying to come all the way back to her previous state.*)

MOTHER: Clara!?—Now, Clara, no, baby, now. We've had enough for today, now. You don't have to tell me anything now—

CLARA: No, Mother, he's right. I should tell you. So we can—bury it all. So that there'll be nothing left over from—from them. It'll be just us!—But you get out first.

TIM: Uh-uh, baby sister. You'll start to lying, and she'll start helping you by patting you on the head. I'll sit right here, real quiet-like.

CLARA: Filthy dog!

TIM: You got about one more time to call me that.

MOTHER (*coming to* CLARA): Clara, now you go on to your room. And Tim Jr.—I know you didn't mean all you said, and this is your home and you're welcome to stay, but we've had enough for one day, now——

CLARA: No, Mother, I want to.

MOTHER: Now, Clara—

CLARA: I want to, Mother. I want you to hear. I want you to see. To try to understand. Please, Mother. Sit down.

MOTHER: Baby—

CLARA: Please, Mother, sit down. Please, listen, please. And try to understand.

(MOTHER *and* TIM *exchange glances, then stare at* CLARA; MOTHER *apprehensively;* TIM *curious, wary.*)

CURTAIN

ACT II

A continuation of Act I, the set being the same. The action beginning some few minutes after closing sequence of Act I.

CLARA *still stands, stage right, facing kitchen.* MOTHER *is now seated at stage left end of couch, rigidly attentive to* CLARA. TIM *slouches in the more modern, stage left easy chair, watching* CLARA *with an expectant, almost wary curiosity.*)

CLARA (*a passionless, but strong voice now*): It is so much. How do I—say it all?

TIM: Just start talking and don't lie.

CLARA (*over and through* MOTHER; *glaring at them*): Start where? When I was born?! When I found out that he was my father? And all that that meant?! That where you want me to start?!

MOTHER (*shaking head with closed eyes*): We not gon talk about him no more today, Clara! We ain't gon say nothing about him.

CLARA: How can you say anything without talking about him!? He's in it everywhere! Isn't that right, Tim?! Isn't that what you were saying?!

TIM (*returns her glare, somewhat abashedly*): Start over there at that—Unity Church. Ha!—Unity is right!

CLARA (*whirling and moving off down center, involuntarily*): Unitarian—

MOTHER (*worriedly*): What did you say, honey?

CLARA (*irritatedly*): What?—Oh—Unitarian. Unitarian Church, Mama. That's its name. (*Looking pointedly.*) You do remember when I joined there, don't you?

MOTHER: Yes, baby, I remember. (CLARA *turns away.*) You left our church and went over there and joined that—that white church. It was the same year you went to college, wasn't it? I remember.

CLARA: Yes, that year. My freshman, my only year. Judy Jolaine took me. She was in two of my classes. Blond. Friendly. She took me. (*Pause.*) And Mama, it was the most beautiful thing I had ever seen.

TIM: Naturally—it was a white church, wasn't it?

CLARA (*whirling stage right*): It wasn't a "white church"! There were all kinds of people there! It's right on the campus, so there are European, and Asian and Oriental students; African students even. It's nondenominational, embracing all faiths.

MOTHER (*appeasingly*): Oh? I see, honey, I see.

(TIM *now leaning against the table with food, holding a pinch of cake, snorts derisively.*)

CLARA: And, Mama, when I saw how ordered, and—and—correct it was. How hushed and—and—reverent the services were. How everyone respected everyone else no matter how different their backgrounds were. I knew I just had to be a part of it; and to join. I— (*Turning to look at* MOTHER *with urgency, glaring at* TIM.) Mama, I couldn't stand——! (*Catches self; stops.*)

TIM (*coming off table; standing up straight*): *Couldn't stand what?* Huh?

CLARA (*defiantly to him*): I couldn't stand—! (*Stops again; turns to* MOTHER, *pleading for understanding.*) Mama, I never really liked our, your church!

MOTHER (*puzzledly*): What, honey?

CLARA: It was just more of that same horrible ripping! Ripping inside! You know what I mean, Mama? It was just so—so—

TIM: Black!

CLARA (*glaring at him*): —So full of him! He never went, but I felt him there!

MOTHER: Who, baby, who?

CLARA (*moving toward* TIM *slightly as she talks*): I could hear him screaming at the top of his lungs in all the singing and shouting! In all those twisted faces! I could see, could feel, that same terrible heat! I could feel that bitter, ugly something

about to burst open! It was a ritual! They were just dancing and singing to keep it controlled! Keep it from——

MOTHER: What, Clara? Who?

CLARA (*turning from* TIM; *losing some of her heat*): You know who, Mother! My father! Your husband! The church was just more of him! (*Folding arms; turning back to them.*) Yes. Instead of entering the body of Christ, I felt that I was inside the body of him! That same choking feeling. Some desperate, leashed-up something trying to break out! All my life I've been surrounded by that—that—turmoil! I was sick of it, Mama! Sick! (*Pauses expecting comment; goes on.*) And just as sick of your church's—other face, too. That hanging, humming face. Swaying so sadly, humming its—dirge; someone crying out every now and then. (*Sighs.*) The whole church like it was waiting for the—the—executioner. I couldn't ever really join that part of the church, either, Mama. Not then.

TIM (*disgustedly*): She means your face, Mama. She means she couldn't be like you.

CLARA (*ignoring him*): So, when Judy asked me to join there, I did. I did. (*Defiantly.*)

MOTHER: Well, Clara? If you felt like that about our church, why'd you come back to it? Why've you been so——

CLARA (*turning abruptly; going to* MOTHER): I didn't come back to the church. (*Sits opposite her on other end of couch.*) I come back to you. To you. (*Doing something tense with her hands.*) Because you're still and quiet, and good. And—I love you.

MOTHER: Clara?

CLARA: Isn't that what being good is, Mama? Being still and quiet? Well, I want to be good. Still and quiet. And you can show me. (*As* MOTHER *seems about to interrupt.*) And if church helps you be—what you are, then I'll go there too. Until I find it.

MOTHER: But, Clara? Don't you believe in—?

CLARA: I believe in you, Mama. I believe in what you believe in. Or try to. Isn't that all anyone can do in this world? Try to believe? To have faith in—something. Someone.

MOTHER: But, I—yes, I guess so, honey. I guess so. (*Shaking head, at a loss for expression.*) But I—

TIM (*coming to stand behind couch*): You know what she believes, Mama? She believes in being still and quiet around black folks. And real down-to-earth lively around those other folks. Yeh.

CLARA (*quietly*): Let me alone, Tim.

TIM: Mama, you know what the cats mean when they say: a whitey's tramp?!

CLARA (*turning to look at him*): Just shut up! I'm trying to tell it, now you just shut up!

(TIM, *seeming to be relenting, derisively, turns back and starts back toward food table.*)

MOTHER: A what, Tim Jr.? Tramp? (*Staring at* CLARA.)

TIM: A whitey's tramp, Mama. A black girl who don't get no closer to nothing black than she has to stand to a mirror to brush her teeth. But is a pushover (*snaps fingers*) for the first little *white* boy that comes along!

CLARA (*jumping to feet*): It wasn't like that!

MOTHER (*looking at* CLARA): A white boy, Clara?! You and a—a white boy?

(CLARA *nods; staring unbelievingly at the reaction on* MOTHER'*s face.*)

MOTHER: When, Clara? Where did you—? Oh, no, Clara? A white boy? And you knew about it, Tim Jr.?

TIM: Yeh, Mama, I knew. I had that ol' piece a car then, remember. Used to come by here on Sundays, remember? I took her to church a couple times, when she was running late for her rendezvous. I dug him, waiting outside the church for her. The last time he touched my car door and I told him to get the hell away, or I was gonna try to stomp his brains out. Then I drove her away and reminded her that she was my sister—my black sister. Yeh, Mama, I knew all right.

MOTHER: Tell me your daddy didn't know about it, Tim Jr. Please Lord, tell me Tim didn't know about it. (*Suddenly standing, face dreading as* CLARA *continues staring with disbelief.*) Did your daddy know about it? (*Turning to him.*) Tim Jr.?—Did he?

TIM (*lowers eyes guiltily*): He found out. (*Crosses hurriedly to kitchen; exits. There follows sound of refrigerator door: rattle of silverware; a can opening.*)

MOTHER (*face registering emphatic pain*): Clara? He knew? A white boy? A whi——

CLARA (*incredulously*): Yes, Mama, a white boy. A white boy. Why not? Mama, you sound like Tim! Or him! Mama, I didn't think you'd——

MOTHER: —But, Clara, don't you know what that must've done to him? (*Turning away, with perhaps, fingertips pressed to temples.*) Tim, Tim—

CLARA: Yes! I heard what it did to him! And Tim! I heard that! And I expected it! But now you, Mama! (*Bitterly.*) I thought you were a good, believing Christian, Mama. You

want to call me a whitey's tramp, too? Is that what you feel?

MOTHER: You don't understand, Clara. You don't—What did he say? Tell me, what did he say?

CLARA (*turning away*): You know what he said. What did his son say?!

MOTHER: Oh Clara, Clara. (*Forcefully.*) Is that where you went when you ran off?! To that white—?

CLARA: Wreyford, Mama! Wreyford Louis Tildon! That was his name! Not white boy! Wreyford, Mama, Wreyford!—No! (*Pause.*) No. (*Turning, moving down center.*) I didn't run off with Wreyford. Or to him.

(TIM *comes out of kitchen carrying can of beer; leans on wall near kitchen doorway.*)

MOTHER (*going back to couch; sitting with her body turned to one side*): You just don't know what that must've done to him, Clara. You and a white boy. (*Shaking head.*) Lord, a whi——

CLARA (*turning to her, moving toward her*): Isn't that just awful of me! Why couldn't I do the right thing and get a nice colored boy?! Huh, Mama? A nice colored boy with that—that —black thing leering in his eyes! Snarling in his throat! (*Tremulously.*) Serve him and that black thing, for six or seven years. And one day, full-grown, that black thing will leap out! And my little six- or seven-year-old daughter will come home from school, and find us at the kitchen sink! Yes! With his hands on my throat! Trying to kill me! Strangle me! (*Glares accusingly.*) Find a nice colored boy like that! Huh, Mama? Like him! Like all of 'em.

MOTHER (*shaking head*): You was just a baby, Clara. You didn't know what you was seeing! You didn't know.

CLARA: I know what I saw, Mama! Only seven years old or not! I know what I was looking at! And I saw something you couldn't see! I saw him reaching for the drain board! For that knife! Mama, if he hadn't seen me standing there he'd—he'd have killed you! (*Turning away, face in hands.*)

TIM (*as* MOTHER *again averts face. To* CLARA): Damn you! Lyin' bitch! Slap her, yeh! I've seen him! That's one of the reasons I got outta here! Hit her, and stand over her rarin' like a madman! Yeh! But you don't know what you talkin' about now! Lying—

CLARA: Oh, I'll bet you're shocked! I'll bet you are! You could stab me right now! Right this minute! All you need is a knife! (TIM *makes an aborted movement toward her, perhaps shifting beer can to other hand.*) The butcher knives are in the kitchen!

TIM (*quietly; sadly, after a moment in which their eyes lock*): White bitch.

MOTHER (*gesturing, shaking head*): Tim Jr.! Don't have to talk to her like that. She—she don't understand, but she ain't lyin' to you. She ain't lyin—

TIM (*only momentarily taken aback. To* MOTHER): I don't care! You hear! I don't care! (*Glaring at* CLARA.) She still ain't nothin' but a whitey-lovin'—— (*Stops.*)

CLARA (*turning, going downstage*): I know you don't care.

MOTHER (*staring at older easy chair*): He came in there and sat. And I could just feel him behind me, burnin' and hurtin'.

CLARA (*moving farther away from her*): Mama! (*Whine.*)

MOTHER: I told him what we was havin' for supper, he didn't say nothin'. Then I looked and saw him just sittin' there, lookin' down at the table, with, Lord, those veins in his forehead lookin' like the nex' minute they was jus' gone—split open. And—and—I didn't know what to say, what to do! I went to him, and—and—I touched his head and I—I said: "Tim, His eye is on the sparrow—"

TIM (*whirling*): What!? What, Mama? So what! His eye is on the—— (*Exasperation stops him.*)

MOTHER (*as* CLARA *glares at him*): I know, Tim Jr., I know. He felt just like you do. He looked at me, and for a minute I thought he was just gon' laugh. That little smile come over his face, like it used to those times before when— But it wasn't like that at all. He didn't laugh at all. He looked at me, and he said: "Cora, ain't you never gone open your eyes and look?" (*Pause.*) "Look-woman-open-yo' eyes-an'-look!" (*Closes eyes, fights for control.*) Then he jus' went crazy! Jus——

CLARA: Yes, crazy! They all go crazy! Thinking about "the white man!" "The white man's world!" Why'd you stay, Mama?! Why didn't you leave him?

TIM: I'll bet you think more about the white man and his world than he did! Baby sister! Yeh!

MOTHER (*shaking head regretfully*): Clara—Clara—

CLARA: All the sly young black cats, growling around the white man's world. I stop 'em cold. Yes, forever and ever! (*Moving downstage, reflecting.*) The jitterbugs are the easiest: heads piled with grease, shoulders going like seesaws, sliding up to you sideways, talking from the corners of their mouths. It's like shooting flies with them. One glance and they're gone. But you have to look close at the ones talking so politely, so correctly; hiding behind their fraternity pins! Or their church work! Have to look good to see it in their eyes! But it's always

there; way down in their dark, dark eyes. Sneering. Insane! All snarled and twisted up on itself, and wanting you to come in and strangle too! You look and see it, and your stomach warns you to stay away. Like looking off the edge of a cliff. Or down a long empty well.

MOTHER (*incredulous*): Clara? Clara baby.

CLARA (*a streak of vindictiveness in this leap for justification*): You want to tell me I'm wrong, Mama? That that black thing doesn't exist? Well, the first time I heard it I was probably inside you—and even then I probably trembled. But whenever the first time was that I saw him shouting that way, looking that way, something inside me just froze! Stopped dead! And I never took another step toward him! Or anything that looked like him!

TIM (*moving on* CLARA): What damn black thing!? Whatta you mean!? You little bitch! Whatta you mean?!

CLARA (*breathlessly, vindictively*): What do I mean?! Look in the mirror, right now! Right now!

TIM (*perhaps involuntarily touching his face*): Mad?! Anger?! That what you talkin' about?! Well, you goddamned right! I'm mad! Angry! All the goddamn time! You little white——! (*Bites off word; they glare in a charged moment.*)

MOTHER (*a strong shout*): Tim Jr.! You show me some respect, now! No more of that language, you hear!?

TIM (*his eyes on* CLARA, *murderous, his tone dull with the effort of his restraint*): All right, Mama. But you dig her. You dig your daughter, Mama? And what about that white thing? What was it like looking in your white boy's eyes? Huh?

CLARA (*glares suspiciously; then again with a malicious, vindictive air*): What was it like looking in his, Wreyford's eyes? I'll tell you! Like being on a hill looking down at a sweet green valley! How is that? (*Stands up to his glare a moment, he turns away; moves away.*) When I first met him I could stare in his eyes for hours. Days. Like sitting beside a clear green pool. They were so green, Mama. I wanted to walk right down to the bottom of them; just take off my shoes and stay there forever. Yes, beneath all that cool, clear green. (*Smirks sardonically.*) Hmmph!

TIM: You mean beneath all that snow!

CLARA (*closing eyes as if closing ears to* TIM. *Moderate pause; movement*): Mama, we'd go to the museum. Or just somewhere to talk. Yes, just listening to him was like—like taking good deep breaths of fresh air. Like standing up straight and stretching wide, wide! (*Glares at* TIM.) Yes! After having been bent over and choked up with fear for so long! Yes, fear!

Fear always in this house! Coming off the walls! Hanging from the ceiling! Like death!

TIM (*returning her glare*): Then Prince Charming came and kissed Snow White! And that ol' black apple just fell right outta her mouth!

MOTHER: Just let her be now, Tim Jr.

CLARA (*after a pause, smirks and turns away from* TIM): I guess you're right about that. Even I should have known it was too good to be true. But all I know was that—I was eighteen and finally I knew what it was to be a frilly, prickly, twirling little girl. Hmmph! Oh, it was too, too much! Just brand-new tingles everywhere! And it was me, me! Clara Wilma Bronson! No, it wasn't just me anymore. It was him and me! He and I! Wreyford and Clara! And I was all brand-new. Bright, shiny, never used! And just bursting with so many good things that I had never even known were there before! (*Smiles, staring.*) And I wanted him to know about it. What he had done. Wanted him to share it. Do whatever he wanted with it. Because it was his! His! (*Stops, pained perplexity on her face; shame.*) Do you understand, Mother! Have you ever felt like that? Like a dress made for just one person to wear? Like— (*Sudden bitterness.*) Do you know about that foolish, childish fairy tale? (*Turns away, fighting for self-control.*)

MOTHER (*softly, watching* CLARA *with deep concern*): Yes, baby. I wasn't even eighteen when I met your daddy.

CLARA (*composing self; suddenly smiling at thoughts*): For someone with no notion of what it was all about. Not even a clear idea of how to go about it. I sure had a lot of sex fantasies! (*Chuckles, falsely.*)

TIM (*gruffly, to cover embarrassment he feels for* MOTHER'*s sake*): I'll bet! Quit stalling!

CLARA (*turning to smile at his discomfort*): This is my way, remember? I was just terrible. (*Still smiling at him.*) Terrible. I guess you and—and everyone were right about that. (*Turns away from him; moves.*) We would be at one of his friends, or in a discussion group. And all I could think of was getting him alone somewhere. (*Sardonic smile.*) Covering his lips with mine, and feeling his eyelids fluttering, tickling my face. Hmmph. Low-down. Isn't that what you call women who think like that, Mama? Low-down and ripe for the Devil?

TIM (*barely audible*): Devil is right.

MOTHER (*evasively*): I guess it's a part of growing up, Clara. Thinking about some things. Wondering about them. But we don't have to talk about——

TIM: Oh, don't you? (*Looking away.*)

CLARA: Really, Mother? A part of growing up? Well, it didn't fit my good Baptist upbringing. I was ashamed of my— my preoccupation. I felt—well, low-down! (*Moving, reflecting.*) So I told myself I had to make myself better. Become worthy of those pure green eyes. Be cultured! Educated! That's what I had to do! I began reading like nobody ever read before. Oh, how I read, Mama. I didn't study very well at school. But the books he gave me: all those revolt books, revolutionary books! (*Pauses, then with at once sarcasm and fond remembrance.*) —Oh, you should have heard him, Mama! The rebel to top all rebels! In revolt against everything! The whole system! The whole world! Out to "Uproot the stifling status quo and make life livable!" end quote! (*Chuckles.*)

TIM (*getting out of easy chair; moving left toward door*): They're all going to uproot the system! All the right-thinking young paddy boys. And they always start by getting a black buddy, or a black girl. Symbol of their defiance, and all that. Yeh and it usually ends right there. In symbols, and all those books that never changed nothing unless they made somebody go out and bust somebody else in the head. Oh, I got me a white buddy, too. Al De Leo. A writer. Yeh, we've been picking each other's pockets for maybe two years now, almost; since I started this night school business. Yeh, with me getting hip to all those word smokescreens they throw up at you, those isms and schisms; so I can deal with 'em in their own terms when they start to try to deal me off the bottom of the deck! And I guess what ol' buddy Al is getting is something he calls (*poses subtly*) the Nakedness of Essence; or the Spontaneity of Being! (*Laughs.*) He's all right, though. Yeh, good buddy, Al.

MOTHER (*curiously, wonderingly*): You've got a white friend, Tim Jr.?

TIM (*forced flippancy; going back to easy chair*): Yeh, Mama, the curiosity kinda gets you, you know. It's like a part of the curriculum, you dig?

MOTHER (*gravely*): Good. That's good, Tim Jr. I'm glad to hear that. I really am.

CLARA: I am too, Tim. (*Laughs.*) That's really funny. Elija Muhammed Jr.!

TIM: Damn you. I ain't planning to marry him!

CLARA (*goes blank; moves away*): A part of the curriculum. No, words, ideas, weren't just smokescreens to Wreyford. They were everything. Yes, everything. (*Moves.*) He only came to Unitarian for the intellectual discussions after the services; never attended the services—"Religion is one of the

strongest links in the chain of ignorance binding mankind to its Promethean rock of childish fears and superstitions!" End quote. I remember that one all right. He used it whenever he had the chance.

TIM: Damn what he believed. Same old paddy-boy bull!

MOTHER (*unaware of what has been said*): He didn't believe in religion? In God? This—this—white friend of yours?

TIM: Who the hell cares?

CLARA: No, he didn't believe in your God, my white buddy. Or in honoring the "worn-out traditions of our parents." Yes, those were his special revolts. The church and his parents. His parents most of all—

TIM (*moving agitatedly in his seat*): So what? Big revolt! Come on, Clara. I'm getting——

CLARA: —Petty Episcopalian bourgeoisie, he called them! How he could spit that one out: bourgeois!

TIM: They've all got a thing for that word!

CLARA (*moving away from him*): He said that we were alike in that, he and I. In being in revolt against the traditions of our parents. Oh, we were among the forerunners of the new society! Haven't you heard of it, Mama? The one where there'll be no black and white. No rich and poor? (*Stops, sighs.*) Oh, Clara, how could you have been silly enough to listen to all that—that mess! (*Pauses; suddenly turns to* TIM.) We weren't really all that after all, were we? We weren't really alike at all, were we! I wasn't such a new thing, a forerunner, was I? Just a new cliché. A whitey's tramp!

MOTHER: Now, Clara—

CLARA: And he was a rebel, all right! But I knew all along that he was mostly just scared; had to keep talking to—to convince himself! (*Pause; calmer tone.*) I could feel it when we were around strangers, black or white, when they looked at us with those indignant! disgusted eyes! I could feel the sweat coming on his hands! His nerves jumping. And that would frighten me. (*Staring, straining.*) I didn't care about their looks. Until he squeezed my hand like that. Then I would feel like screaming for help and running! But yet— (*desperate to explain tangled emotions; reliving*) at the same time I would be glad, proud. Because there was something I could give him! I could help him, courage, determination, whatever it is, I had more of it than he did. And he would need it, wouldn't he? I mean he would have to—

TIM (*getting to his feet*): Ain't that a bitch! You could help *him!* *He* needed something! This white boy! You don't have nothing for the black cats! They don't need nothing!

They can make it or not! But you had to help this poor whitey! God damn! Look! I don't want to hear nothing else about that chump, hear! You get to the point, goddamnit!

MOTHER: Tim Jr.! I'm not gon' have no more of that language, now!

CLARA (*over and through* MOTHER): What does color have to do—!? (*Touching head.*) Why does color have to be all mixed into it all?! How can you know when it has something to do with it and when it doesn't?

TIM: That question wouldn't even come up between a cat and a broad, if they were both the same color, baby. Yeh. Now, you get to what's important, you hear me? I'm tired, damnit. I'm tired.

CLARA: Get to what's important! You mean the facts! The facts, man, the facts! The old black and white facts, huh, Tim? Well, I'll tell you something: the facts become black and white after the fact, dear brother! After! When they happen, they happen in reds and yellows—in—in—bright spots, and deep, deep dark spots. They're not black and white at all. At all!

TIM: So just tell it like it was. Dig? Like it was. That's all!

CLARA (*stares, moves*): Like it was. Like it was. You don't mean that at all. No. You mean say: first this happened and then that happened. That's what you mean. Well, all right. This is going to be your way anyhow, isn't it? Okay, let me see if I can tell it your way. Let's see now—

MOTHER: Let's just stop this right now! This could all just wait. Now, we could all just——

CLARA: No, it couldn't, Mother. Let's see now. Fact number one: we ended up alone at Fred's somehow that time, Wreyford and I. But, oh, that's unimportant. Just the simple facts, that's all. All the rest—hmmph! I mean, who cares! Who cares about all that pain and heat and, oh, yes, the blood, too, the blood too. I mean, who cares? Who cares about a silly little fool wanting to scream and wondering if she was at last really learning about life, or suddenly about to die? Oh, but being brave. Not wanting to scare him away—un—un—so—so—biting her lips—biting her lips and telling herself over and over; it always hurts the first time; they say, the first time it always hurts. Hmmph— (*Tries to laugh with tears in her eyes.*)

TIM (*coming toward her, angrily*): What the hell's the matter with you?! Talkin' that junk in fronta'—

MOTHER: Clara? What're you saying?

CLARA: —But there are facts, and then there are facts! You know what I mean? (*Seeing personal visions; caught in mo-*

mentum.) I mean like it's a fact that he was very concerned about me. Yes, oh, yes. "Clara? Did I hurt you? But you're bleeding! Oh God, you're bleeding! You're crying! Please don't!" (*Breaks this; whirls on* TIM.) All that's fact too, dear brother! All that's fact too!

TIM: Not the important one! You know what the important fact—facts—are!

MOTHER (*Dismayed, uncertain*): Clara? Clara?

CLARA: Oh, oh, now I see—give only the important facts! Right? (*Driving grimly on; a kind of masochism.*) It's not important that he said that one day—one day, when he had proven himself to himself, we'd get married. (*Snorts, chuckles.*) Oh, not in the conventional, bourgeois sense! With public oaths, legal enforcements, and all the other: "slavery insurance," he called it. But we would live together as man and wife. Yes, one day when he——

MOTHER (*who has been staring from one to the other, rising from seat now*): Live together as—? In common— Clara? What're you telling me!? Clara?!

(CLARA *keeps her back to her.*)

TIM (*going to* MOTHER; *driven by the same pain, seeking something that grips* CLARA): Quit lying to yourself, Mama! You know what she's saying! She's saying that her and that— whitey—went to bed together!

(*As words seem to make everything in* MOTHER *stand still and stare at him,* CLARA, *her back to them, seems to slump, perhaps lowers her head, also registering* TIM'*s words.*)

CLARA (*after a moment; in a sighing tone*): Yes, Mother, that's what I was saying. I was eighteen and—and I went to bed with a boy. (*Suddenly to* TIM.) Is that a simple enough fact for you? Is it really so terrible, Mama? Doesn't God forgive such—such weaknesses?

MOTHER (*after a moment; carefully*): Yes, baby, he forgives. If we—if we go and sin no more. But are you sure that that's what you want to tell me, baby?

TIM: Yeh. (*Advancing on* CLARA.) Are you sure it didn't get no worse than that? To tell the truth, after a while it wasn't so simple, now, was it? It started getting kind of complex! Didn't it, baby sister? Huh?

CLARA (*glares; struggles for control; then with calm maliciousness*): No, big brother. For me it got simpler and simpler, easier and easier.

TIM (*not what he expected*): Look. Clara!

CLARA (*smiling*): —better and better? I just—kept getting

taller and taller, wider and wider. I could feel the—the grass growing through my shoes. I understood why clouds drift the way they do. Oh, I could twirl the world and make the rivers run!

MOTHER (*incredulously*): Clara?

TIM (*stares, rooted by her expression, words; crushes beer can in his hands, tensely*): I just bet you could. I bet you just sent that white boy to heaven. (*Turning and moving away before he does something violent.*) You jive! I—

CLARA: No. You're wrong again, big brother. I—that heaven is an animal kingdom. And Wreyford wouldn't have anything to do with being an animal. Oh, he couldn't completely deny the little bit of one inside him. He—but it was always the same with him, each time the same. Yes—a fall. Yes, downhill. Yes, his love would come tumbling down, and the apologies would come stumbling after. Every time he touched me, kissed me, he would almost give a speech. Hmmph. The body and its pursuits below and separate from the mind and spirit and their pursuits! But, oh, how he did kiss me! How he would hold me! Like— like—(*Pauses; smiles, shrugs.*) But he was always ashamed afterwards. Always begging my forgiveness. He—and me playing coy and thinking. Sorry for what? I enjoyed myself, honey!

MOTHER (*disgustedly*): Now, Clara!

TIM: You hear her, Mama?! You hear her, braggin'? Braggin'! You were real good, huh, baby sister?! Real proud of yourself, huh?!

CLARA (*looks at him, moves away*): Proud? Yes, yes. I was proud. (*Tossing head, affecting again a subtle self-mockery.*) Because, honey, ol' Clara was a real, natural-born woman now! Oh, let me tell you, she had those, them, body pursuits and mind pursuits, down pat! All tied together, baby. She was on her man like white on rice, honey! And some ways she was way ahead of him! Of course, now, in some ways he wasn't really much of a man, yet; just a kid. But ol' Clara kinda' liked him, you know. She'd give the kid time. Why not. All the kid needed was time. Oh, sure, that's all! (*Pathetic self-mocking laugh.*)

MOTHER (*standing, a pitying tone*): Clara, you sound like a common street hussy. Just a common hussy.

CLARA: Hmmph. No. No, Mama, I wasn't common at all. I felt special, unique, inimitable! Hmmph. Until—(*stares, smirks*)—until that night I opened my eyes in that motel and saw his look—

TIM (*to* MOTHER): Will you listen to her?! (*Going a step*

or two toward CLARA). Heifer! This is your mother sitting here! What the hell're you trying—! Whatta you think you're—?

CLARA (*staring at him through his outburst, seeing her memory*): —And saw him looking at me—like—like I was something he had coughed up and spit out. (*Pauses.*)

MOTHER (*taking an instinctive step toward her*): What, baby—?

CLARA: Disgusted! I saw disgust lying there with me on that —that motel bed and I—I felt low-down then, Mama. I felt common then. (*Stops; stares.*)

TIM (*after a moment*): Uh-huh. And I'll bet you just couldn't understand it at all, could you. Yeh—(*Turning away with an irritation that might be empathy.*)

MOTHER (*watching* CLARA *carefully*): Just be quiet, Tim Jr. Hush now.

CLARA: Oh, I understood it immediately and it's not what you—at least I didn't think that had anything to do with— with anything between us. But there it was looking at me: disgust; disgust and—hate! (*Still incredulous, shocked.*) Yes, hate! Hate!

MOTHER: Now, Clara, you just can't say that that's all it——

CLARA: —I didn't want to believe it either, Mother! I grabbed it! I held his face and looked at it before he could turn it away; before he could change it! Wreyford? You hate me. You're disgusted with me. Sick of me, aren't you? Aren't you? (*A grim wryness.*) Oh, no, Clara. Oh, no. It's myself I'm disgusted with. It's me. I'm becoming an animal. Clara! An animal! What's happened to me!? To us! This isn't what we started out to be! I just wanted him to shut up! Stop making me feel filthy! Oh, but I didn't have enough sense to shut up myself. So I—oh, I really told him something, Mama! I said, "No, no, Wreyford, it's just that you won't enjoy yourself. Just let yourself go and enjoy yourself." Oh, that really got him! He couldn't even look at me when I said that! He looked sick! He really did! He said, "Let's get our clothes on and get out of this place." And oh did I want to put my clothes back on!

MOTHER (*going toward her*): But you were both so young, Clara. You had no business in the first——

TIM (*sarcastically*): They going to the moon, Mama. You have to hurry these days.

CLARA (*pointedly moving away from* MOTHER's *approach*): And I left him. I don't know if he knew it then. Because I

would still meet him in the same place. Come like I was walking in my sleep. Time was nowhere, no one else, to go to. But
I left him. I would be across from him, or beside him, while
he said the same things, looked the same way. But I couldn't
hear, couldn't see. I had left him. Maybe he did know—yes,
and I guess was glad, because I— I— stopped his falling. I
couldn't stand his hands on me anymore. I—but by then—by
then it was— (*Falters, tears coming, or coming stronger.*)

TIM (*whirling viciously*): By then it was too late! He had
already done his bit for integration!

(CLARA *slumps, closes eyes; then rigidly waits.*)

MOTHER (*from one to the other*): Tim Jr.! Clara!? What're
you saying!? Whatta you mean?!

TIM: I mean she was pregnant! I mean that whitey knocked
your daughter up, and then dropped her. Yes, like a burnt,
black potato! She can dress it up as much as she wants to, but
that's the fact! That's what happened!

MOTHER (*after stunned moment, going to her, touching
her*): Clara—? You were— When, Clara, when? (*Realizing*).
When you all, all three of you came back in here. All looking
at each other, not saying nothing. And you so sick, baby, oh
so sick. And none of you wouldn't tell me nothing; wouldn't
tell me—Oh Lord, my baby! Wouldn't let me know, wouldn't
let— (*Stops; eyes closed.*)

TIM: Did you really want to know, Mama? Did you really
try to find out? Huh? (*Turning toward kitchen.*)

MOTHER (*following her*): The baby, Clara? The baby? You
(CLARA *moves to couch; sits wearily.*)
—Tell me, Clara! You tell me now!

TIM (*agitatedly*): Naw, Mama! No baby! Abortion! An
abortion, Mama! You know what that is, don't you? Damn!
(*Stalks to kitchen for another beer.*)

MOTHER (*sitting beside her*): Clara baby? You had a—a—

CLARA (*quietly, but tearfully*): Oh, yes, Clara, there is a
modern way of looking at, of handling, these things. End
quote.

MOTHER (*tears, stroking her hair*): Oh baby. My poor baby.
You didn't have to—You could've—We could've— Oh, baby,
why? Why?

(TIM *comes out of the kitchen with fresh beer; stands watching them apprehensively. None of this has gone as he wanted.*)

CLARA (*tears coming, but grimly, quietly*): There's so much
ahead, Clara. How do we really know that you and I are right
for each other? You may not believe this, Clara, but—Hmmph,
that was funny—You may not believe this, Clara, but I had

121

never known any other kind of girl before you—before—
(*Pause.*)

TIM (*suddenly moving closer*): What?—what did he say?
Some other *kind* of girl?

CLARA (*looks up at him for a moment; then nods*): Yes.
Any other kind of girl before you. How do I know what I
would be like with someone else. Some other kind of girl.
(*Rocks on couch; tears coming.*)

MOTHER: Shhh. All right, honey. Shh, that's enough now.

CLARA (*rocking, fighting to keep a grip on herself*): Some
other kind of girl—

TIM (*looking around, moving, as though looking for someone to hit*): What kind do you think he was talking about,
Mama!? Any special color, you think? That mother—He didn't
even give her the money to have it done with! I— I—

CLARA (*bitterly*): I wouldn't let him. Wouldn't— (*Shaking
head, as she waits for breath.*)

MOTHER: All right, honey. All right. Don't—

CLARA: When he came with the money. I told him to get
away from me! Tried to tear his eyes out!

MOTHER: Shhh, Clara. Clara—

TIM (*glares at them a moment; then moves away*): I guess
he did go away. *I* got the money. *I* took care of the arrangements.

CLARA (*glaring pause; truculently*): Yes! Oh, yes! Get that
white baby out of this girl's belly! !

MOTHER (*utter shock*): CLARA!!

TIM (*defensive; frightened*): All right! Clara! All right!
Damnit! All right!

CLARA: Isn't that what he told her!?—Isn't that what he said
when—(*nearly overcome*)—when he threw me on the floor!
Get that white—!!

TIM: He didn't throw you on the floor, now! He didn't! He
—he pushed you! And—and—you fell! You fell!

MOTHER: What??!—Pushed her, Tim Jr.?! Who?! Who
pushed her?!

TIM (*turning away in exasperation*): Aw, Mama!!

CLARA: Tell her! Tell her!

TIM: Goddamnit, Clara! Goddamnit!

CLARA: TELL her! You tell her!!

TIM (*whirling to face her*): A witness! A witness. You had
to have a parent there! That woman wouldn't do it without a
parent there! She—she—

CLARA: Yes, a witness! A witness!

TIM: Yes! She didn't even believe I was your brother! Thought I—thought we—You had to have a parent there, all right!? (*Points to* MOTHER.) —Would you rather I brought her!! Huh?!

CLARA: Yes!—Yes!

TIM (*turning away*): Well, I didn't think so! Naw, I didn't think so!

MOTHER: Tim Jr.!—You mean when you took her to get this—this—Tim went with you? Your daddy was there?!

CLARA: Oh, yes! My big brother took care of all the arrangements! I had to ask him for help! Remember, big brother! Remember!!

MOTHER: Tim Jr.?! How could you?—Didn't you know—

TIM (*whirling*): Mama!—we had to have one of you, now! And I—I didn't want you to know. Figured you'd be cryin' and—and carryin' on. So I called him, and told him! But I didn't tell him all of it! (*Pause.*) So, when the time came, I told 'em both to meet me at this restaurant. She didn't know that he knew. I got him to come early, you dig?

CLARA: Yes, and the two of you got together on it. Didn't you!

TIM: I made a mistake! I just made a mistake, that's all!

CLARA: A mistake! A mistake!

MOTHER: Whatta you mean, a mistake, Tim Jr.?!

TIM: You see he wanted to know why she didn't want to have the baby! And who—who was the—the nigger. And where did he live! So, without thinking, I told him it wasn't a —a black cat, it was one of those whiteys at that church. And he—he—

CLARA: He what? Tell her! Tell her!

TIM (*remembering*): When I told him, he just stared at me, Mama. And—for once, Mama—for once, it was like we were really—really looking at each other. He and me—me and him.

CLARA: And then he went insane!

MOTHER: Clara—

TIM: You weren't there then, Clara, now!—He just sat down.

CLARA: He was insane! Grabbing me! Pushing me!

TIM: All right, now, Clara, damnit! All right!

CLARA: Calling me all those names! Cussing at me!

MOTHER: You shouldn't 've let him treat her bad out in the street, like that, Tim Jr.! You should've stopped him!

TIM: Naw, Mama, now, you don't know, now! I got 'em out to the car, but it kept on. It kept going around and around!

123

CLARA: Oh, but you stopped it, didn't you?! You had to take him over to the church! Didn't you!? Yes, to try to get Wreyford's address!

MOTHER: You didn't, Tim Jr.! I know you didn't! Tell me you didn't!

TIM: Hell! Did you want him to go by himself!? Huh!? He know where it was! He was talking about coming here and getting his gun! Hell! I figured I'd go along with him for a minute! Yeh, let him drive over there and find nobody there! come back to earth, cool off. Then we'd go on and do what we had to—

CLARA: Nobody there!

TIM: Damn, how the hell did I know those fools sit up and hold each other's hands all week long, every damn night?! I figured it would be empty—figured I'd just string him along, let him—

CLARA: Figured! You figured! Well it didn't work out that way at all, did it!? Did it!? The church wasn't empty at all, was it!? Was it!?

TIM (*pausing, sighing*): No, Clara, it wasn't empty. (*Turns away.*)

MOTHER (*apprehensively*): That boy wasn't there!? Tim Jr.? Clara? This boy wasn't there, was he?

TIM (*back to them*): Naw, he wasn't there.

CLARA (*bitterly, remorsefully*): No, Wreyford wasn't there. But everyone else was there. Everyone. Reverend Byron. Mrs. Carter. Miss Elliot. All of those people who had been so kind and understanding, and respectful toward me. Standing there on those steps, watching him, hearing him; looking at me as though they were seeing me for the first time. Oh, yes, the real me at last! It was finally coming out! The real truth! I was one of those three wild animals trying to force their way into the church! I was just another vulgar little colored girl after all! And pregnant! I can still see their faces—those looks— (*As though sick to her stomach, she crumbles back to the couch.*)

MOTHER (*going to her, patting and shushing*): It's all right now, baby, it's all right. (*Then to* TIM.) Tell me what he did to her, Tim Jr. What did he do?!

CLARA: Yes! Get it done! Get it done.

MOTHER: Is this what you wanted me to see, Tim Jr.? Is this what you were rarin' so to show me?

TIM (*pause, confusion*): Mama, I don't even know anymore. What he was doing, what I was doing.

CLARA: I know you don't know.

TIM (*angry reaction, back to motive*): But I knew what she

was doing—running. And I want you to see who she was running from and where her running took her.

CLARA: No, Mama, no, I was trying to find that woman. The blood. All the time. All over me. The sheets. Everywhere. It kept getting worse. I couldn't stop it.

MOTHER: You mean when you run off you went looking for this—this woman—Aw, baby, you shoulda told me! Shoulda—

CLARA: I couldn't let you know!—Don't you see? You were all I had left. I couldn't have you looking at me like the others at the church! No—no—

TIM: Others! She was running from you, Mama! From us! And from men too. All men!

MOTHER: What, boy!? From men?!

CLARA: I didn't know where to go! Mama, I had to find Tim.

TIM: Oh, I'll bet you looked real hard for me!

MOTHER: Running from men?

CLARA: I went up to the school, Mama, but I couldn't find him. I had to go in this coffee place—and there were people sitting all around—but I had to go in the bathroom, Mama, I had to, the blood, I had to—

MOTHER: What men?

CLARA: —Mama, my hands were shaking so—I couldn't get my purse open—I couldn't stand up straight. I—I fell down in the bathroom, I fell—and they picked me up.

MOTHER: Who, baby?

CLARA: Dee was a nurse. She could help me. Stop the bleeding! She was kind to me. They were good to me!

TIM: Anybody white looks kind to you, don't they!

CLARA: They got a cab and took me home! Dee stopped the blood. She made it stop!

MOTHER: Now who is this, baby?

TIM: Three white chicks! Some more of her people!

MOTHER: Oh?—They took care of you? That's where you were?

CLARA: Yes, Mama! Yes!

TIM: Yeh, they took care of her, all right. Hid her from we bad black folks! Two weeks, Mama, all the time you had it in the papers and everything. She was up there with them.

CLARA: Sick, Mama! I was sick!

TIM: Some cat I don't even know just walks up to me and asks me if my sister is still missing. Yeh, well, there's a girl staying with these three white chicks!

CLARA: Just go away—go away—

TIM: Yeh, go away. That's what you said then too, wasn't

it! Mama, I go up there and she tells me not to put my hands on her! That—no man, black or white, was ever going to put his hand on her again—as long as she lived. Hear that, Mama! No man! As long as she lived! Now, what does that mean? Huh!?

CLARA: No! No!

MOTHER: Tim Jr.?—What're you saying?

TIM: You tell me, Mama! Now she's up there with them two weeks. And now she's through with men.

MOTHER: Tim Jr.?—You mean— (*Turning to* CLARA.) Clara???—Tell Mama no—tell me you didn't, didn't—

CLARA (*moving to her*): I told you—told you. Stopped the blood. She took care of me, talked to me. Like you, Mama, like you. It was like I was home with you, Mama. I don't care if she was what Tim said she was. She was kind to me. Good. She didn't do anything wrong. She didn't do anything wrong. She didn't— (*In* MOTHER's *arms.*)

MOTHER: All right, baby, I believe you. Mama believes you. All right now, Tim Jr.! She said nothing happened now! That's all!

TIM: You can't see it, can you, Mama?

CLARA: He's wrong, Mama—He's wrong.

MOTHER: She's going to her room, Tim Jr. Just getta outta our way!

TIM: Mama? Don't you care?

CLARA: Leave us alone—Leave us alone—

MOTHER: It was just that so much had happened She was mixed up and scared and too ashamed to come home. That's all.

TIM: All this time she's just been hiding! Hiding in your shadow! When's it gonna stop, Mama, huh! Who's gonna stop it! Huh. (*Grabs* MOTHER's *arm.* CLARA *exits.*)

MOTHER: Get outta my way, Tim Jr. (*Pulls away.*)

TIM: You're just helping it go on, Mama.

MOTHER: And what about you, Tim Jr.? What about you? You come in here with your daddy—your daddy barely in the ground! Hollering about what a terrible man he was! And you—you want to strip your sister down to her soul, to find out what kind of woman she is! Or gon' be! But—

TIM: You know what it is, don't you!? She's scared to go back out there. (*Pointing toward door.*) 'Cause that's the mirror out there! And she's scared to really see herself!

MOTHER: Hush, Tim Jr.

TIM: Find out who she really is! What she really is! She doesn't even know if she wants a man or a woman!

MOTHER: Just shut your mouth now! All right—all right, you done showed us all our weaknesses. Showed me my blindness! My neglect! Made me look at what kind of woman, what kind of mother I am! But now you let me tell you something, Tim Jr. You say there's a mirror out there?! Well then, you go take a good long look in it. Take a real good look, and the next time you stand up to talk about somebody, let it be about you! That's something you need to hear yourself saying; what kind of man you can be! I say can be, 'cause you ain't one yet, by a long ways!

TIM: Can't you understand, Mama! If I'm a man I can't just stand and watch the same things going . . .

MOTHER: Don't say nothing else! I say can be 'cause before a man woulda brought up to me all that you did today, he woulda stopped and thought a minute! Thought about all the things I musta been through, musta seen all these years, and he would've thought that there must be some reason for me going on this way, being this way. He just woulda stopped and thought, Tim Jr., before he starting beating his chest so loud on today of all days. So you go on out to that mirror and find out what kind of man you can be! 'Cause, naw, you ain't one yet! And you done done all of what you been doing that you gonna' do around here today. So you just go on. Get outta my way and go on somewhere else. I'm tired now. Dead tired. (*Pushing past him.* CLARA *sobs in room.*) I'm coming, baby! I'm coming. (*Goes into room and closes door, as* TIM *stares after her.*)

TIM: Mama don't you see? I gotta grab things. Make 'em change. Make 'em— (*Pauses at* CLARA's *doorway; turns suddenly, starts out, stopped by telephone; goes to it, dials quickly; waits, staring at* CLARA's *doorway.*) What?—Hello—Huh?— (*Looks at phone as if just realizing he has it.*) What number is this?! Huh?? Oh, yeh! Al! Al De Leo, riom 14. Oh, naw, no message. (*Slams phone down. Paces.*) All right. I'll take a good look! A good long look! Damn you! Damn you!

(*Exits.*)

MOTHER (*comes out of room; concern and apprehension wild on her face*): Tim Jr.? Tim Jr.! (*Stops, looks down, stoops, picks up beer can. Holds it tenderly, shaking head at it.* CLARA *sobs.*) I'm coming, baby. I'm coming, Clara.

CURTAIN

ACT III

BRONSON *living room. Darkness, except for pale light coming from partially opened door of* MOTHER'*s bedroom, rear right; and a bluish light coming from kitchen doorway as if from something—a streetlight perhaps—outside. Clara's door, rear center, is shut; no light is seen there.*

There is the sound of voices, laughter, music; a party going on somewhere on the floor above them. It is near three o'clock in the morning.

There is the sound of someone coming slowly, heavily, up stairs and then along corridor. Slow, heavy knocks at the door, followed, after an interval, by harder ones, still widely spaced. MOTHER *comes apprehensively to bedroom door, carrying Bible. She wears sleeping gown; her hair is loose, untied. Looks toward door, as evenly spaced, hard knocks resume. Goes back into room; returns wearing robe, still clutching Bible. Goes toward door. As she passes it,* CLARA'*s door opens minutely.*

MOTHER (*at door*): Who is it? (*One hand at night lock, listening to muttered, muffled reply.*) Who?—Tim Jr.?—That you, Tim Jr.? (*Muffled reply convinces her; struggles with lock. Finally lays Bible on telephone stand; opens door.*) —Boy, where have you been?

TIM (*leaning inside with comically apologetic expression; yet asking seriously*): They come?

MOTHER (*moving back to let him in*): What?—Did who come? Where'd you go? I been worrying myself sick. (*Going to turn on lamp at left of couch.*)

TIM (*coming in, closing door*): They haven't been here, huh?—Funny. I thought—well, they didn't. (*He is dressed the same as before. And though the two top buttons of his suit coat are carefully fastened, his shirt collar and tie are more disarrayed than ever. The suit is rumpled, wrinkled. Around the knuckles of his right hand is wrapped his handkerchief. He carries a grocery bag. It becomes gradually clear that he is uncertain on his feet. Through the earlier portions of the scene, his manner and speech are hurried, forced.*)

MOTHER: Who didn't? (*Suspiciously.*) You been drinking, Tim Jr.?

TIM (*looking around tensely; staring at* CLARA'*s door*): Some old friends, Mama. Yeh, ol' friends. I—I owe 'em something. I thought they'd come here to try to—collect. But— (*Turning back to her with forced grin.*) They didn't. So, forget 'em, sweet Mama, forget 'em! (*Looking again at her door.*) Clara, Mama, is she asleep? I wanna' see her. Talk to her. Can you—

MOTHER (*suspicion mounting*): Owe 'em what, Tim Jr.? You mean some money? Somebody lookin' for you for some money?! Lord, you been gamblin'! And got that rag tied around your hand. Let me see. (*Going toward him.*) Ain't that blood? (*He moves away smiling.*) Lord, fightin.' Fightin', and drinkin', and gamblin'! Knowed I shouldna said what I did to you—

TIM (*moving away; shifting grocery bag*): You right, Mama. Fightin' and drinkin' and gamblin' and—and—whorin'. Just a no-good sinner. And I know the Lord's vengeance is at hand. So I come home to make my peace before—(*with wry chuckle*)—before I meet my Maker. Yeh. (*A tingle of his true urgency.*) Mama, call my sister, hear? Call her out, okay. She won't come if I—

MOTHER: You let me look at that hand, Tim Jr. Fightin'—

TIM (*moving away, irritatedly*): Naw, Mama, now. Call Clara now. Look, I haven't been fightin'. Honest to God I haven't—

MOTHER: Don't you swear now, Tim Jr.!

TIM: Naw, look—I fell down, okay. I was runnin', kinda high, you dig, and I fell and scarred my hand on the sidewalk. Right? Right. Looka here what I got—(*Pulls bottle of wine, and then small wrapped package from grocery bag.*)—Some groovy wine, and a real hip cheese. (*Striking pose.*) For the prodigal's last supper with his family! Hmmph. Yeh. (*Urgency suddenly returning.*) Mama, I ain't got much time.

MOTHER: What you mean, you ain't got much time, Tim Jr.? Your last supper? Coming in here with wine and cheese! Now, boy, you—

TIM: Aw, now, Mama, you can't say that wine is sinful. One of those "P" saints—Peter, or Paul, one of 'em—said something about coolin' your stomach out with wine. Didn't he? Well, this is the stomach-coolingest grapes you ever tasted. My—my—Al!—(*Backs up vaguely as he says the name; backs into couch; wavers, almost falls down onto it.*)

MOTHER (*coming to help him*): Tim Jr.?

TIM (*straightening up, putting wine down on table*):—I'm all right. Yeh, Al turned me on to this wine. It's a monster. And this funny-tasting cheese is like the whipped cream for it. (*Puts cheese on table.*)

MOTHER (*after watching him intently*): Now, Tim Jr., you my only son, and I know you in some kind of trouble. I can feel it. Now what is it?! What've you done?

TIM (*with irritation*): Aw, Mama, you just—just making things up. You see I'm—I'm going to California—Yeh—Yeh,

the schools there are cheaper. Free schools out there. Yeh. And a friend of mine's driving out there tomorrow, today, this morning. And I'm going with him. That's all I meant. (*Same urgency.*) Now you go get Clara out here, okay? And I'll go in the kitchen and get some—

MOTHER: Tim Jr., you're lying.

TIM (*guiltily, exasperatedly, banging fist down on arm of couch*): Mama, will you get Clara?! Huh?!—Look, everything's okay, Mama. I just want to talk to Clara. My sister. It's important. Understand? It's very important to me. Just— just—don't ask me nothin', Mama, please. Just do me this one last favor. I want to sit down with Clara, that's all. Please, Mama.

(MOTHER *looks at his sincere, pained, pleading face. Looks at* CLARA's *door; back to him. Moves few steps toward* CLARA's *room; her voice only slightly lifted.*)

MOTHER: Clara!?—Clara, I know you hear me. I know you're not asleep now, Clara.—Your—your brother wants to (*looks at* TIM)—to talk to you. I—I think he wants to—to apologize to you Clara. Clara?

(MOTHER *stands at one end of couch;* TIM *at the other.* CLARA *pulls door open and stands staring at* TIM; *wearing pajamas under robe, her hair down. Upstairs someone opens a door, laughs. The party sounds—music, etc.—heard earlier again come strongly, then fade with a slammed door.*)

CLARA (*stoically*): What is it, Tim? You don't need to apologize if that's what it is.

TIM (*seemingly off-balance for moment. Gestures vaguely toward table with wine and cheese*): Uh, naw—Well, yeh, that too. But I want us to—uh—uh—break bread together! Hell, why not? (*Laughs; it falls dead. So assumes theatrical pose of homage; jokingly.*) Enter Clara, last great black hope of the Bronsons! Hip sister of the dark sorrows! All bow and pay—

(CLARA *sighs in weary exasperation, starts back into room.*)

TIM (*rushing forward*): —Clara, don't go! Wait!

(CLARA *stops, her back to him.*)

MOTHER (*struck by* TIM's *plea; with empathy for him*): Now, Clara, couldn't you give him just a minute? Just—

CLARA (*half-turning to look at him*): What is it you want, Tim?

TIM (*faltering*): I just—just— (*Changing to bluffing, jovial, self-assuredness.*) Huh?—Nothing. Nothing. Looka' here— (*Taking her arm to lead her away from door and around couch.*) We got some wine and cheese! Gonna' have one of those foreign snacks! Continental, you dig?

CLARA: Wine?—Cheese?

TIM: Yeh. Didn't get none of that bread you have to cut with a knife, but that's all right. Now, Mama, (*Rubbing hands together.*) you go get three of those fancy glasses which you ain't never had occasion to use before. (*As she starts to speak.*) Get 'em from way up on that shelf where you think they're hid. No lip, now.

MOTHER (*almost smiling, despite herself*): Tim Jr., I still think you done went outta here an done—

TIM (*giving her a mock push*): Ol' woman, if you don't do like I said! (*She goes into kitchen, shaking her head and muttering.*) Now, let's see. Sit down, baby sister, sit down—

CLARA (*looking wryly askance at him*): Tim, are you sure you're—?

TIM: Sit down, girl. (*She sits on couch.*) Naw, this table won't do. (TIM *bends to move coffee table out of her way. Bent over, has to close eyes and steady himself a moment before lifting table up. Looks around for place to put it.*) Thing'll have us all bent over. Won't let us sit close enough. (*Decides on wall space near kitchen door where during first two acts food tables sat. Puts it down there.*) What we need is some kind of—(*Starts toward kitchen; stops, snapping fingers. Pointing at* CLARA.) The card table! Remember, Clara, that old card table!? Huh?!—Remember our little birthday parties an' shit! Huh? (CLARA, *speechless with wonder, nods, smiling at what she assumes is a drunken display. He turns to stare at* MOTHER's *bedroom; still pointing.*) It's in there, ain't it? On the wall near the closet. Right?

CLARA (*smiling, tongue-in-cheek*): There's about four card tables the deacon brought over this afternoon, out there in the kitchen.

TIM (*going somewhat hesitantly toward* MOTHER's *bedroom, rubbing sweat from face*): Naw, you know the one I mean. It's in here. Remember? Always kept it—Yeh— (*Goes in.*)

(MOTHER *comes out of kitchen with two thin cocktail glasses and two "china" saucers. Stops. Looks at open space before couch; coffee table on wall; then* CLARA.)

CLARA (*shrugs, smiles*): Said it wouldn't do. Had to get the old card table.

MOTHER (*going over to couch*): Lord, ain't no tellin' what he done went outta here an' done. California. I—

TIM (*from inside bedroom*): Got it!— (*Comes out snapping folding legs in place.*) Remember, Clara? Our little parties? When we'd get excused from the solemn kitchen, and eat out here, where we could show our behinds? (CLARA *nods*

Ron Milner

with a wistful smirk. MOTHER *watches him.*) Yeh, sit down next to Clara, there, Mama. Watch the bottle now. (*Sets table down.* CLARA *brings up bottle and cheese.* MOTHER *sets two glasses and saucers on table.*) Yeh, now I'll get me a— (*starts impulsively toward old armchair, down right; halts*) —chair— (*Rubbing forehead; taking an uncertain step backward.*)

MOTHER (*with concern*): Tim Jr., why don't you sit down an' rest yourself?

(CLARA *watches with amused smile.*)

TIM: I'll get this one here. (*Pulls over more modern armchair.*)

CLARA: Maybe you shouldn't drink anymore.

TIM: Hand me that bottle! (*Pours for himself and* CLARA.) Mama, you only brought two glasses. Come on now. One won't hurt.

MOTHER: Now, you know I ain't gon' fool with that stuff; nor that cheese either.

TIM: You missing something. (*Touching glasses with* CLARA.) The good ol' times at this table.

CLARA: At this table. (*Sips, while* TIM *downs one glass and pours another.*)

MOTHER: Tim Jr., now—!

TIM: Be cool, Mama. Yeh, Clara, we'd sit here and have all kinds of lil' games going. We were real tight then, wasn't we, Clara? (CLARA *nods; reflects.* TIM, *glancing at old armchair, raises glass to lips, then lowers it. Turning to* CLARA.) Remember those times I'd come in here and like I hoped you'd be by yourself—we was about fourteen, fifteen, then—and I'd get this table and get my ol' deck out from under my mattress—

MOTHER (*shocked*): Cards?!

TIM: Oh, yeh. Be needing show-fare, carfare, some kinda fare. (*Grinning at* CLARA, *slaps palm on table.*) High card for a dollar, Clara? (*Going along,* CLARA *shakes her head.*) Fifty-cents? Huh, you always had a little stash somewhere. Sometimes you wouldn't go for it. But sometimes you'd take pity on me—

CLARA: It sure was pity. If you won—zoom—you'd be gone! And when you lost you'd beg me for your money back and mine too!

TIM: Yeh, we was really close then, Clara. Wasn't we?

MOTHER (*as* CLARA *again nods*): Always was, from babies. Whip Clara, had to whip Tim Jr., too.

TIM: That's right. (*Stares into glass, infects others with a sudden sad reflectiveness. Then quickly downs glass. Begins pouring another, the words coming excitedly.*) Remember one

time I ran outta here so fast, my—my damn pro-phylactics fell outta my pocket in—in—the chair! I was scared sick Mama or him was gonna find—

MOTHER (*as* CLARA *gags on wine*): Tim Jr., you talkin' so fast, you liable to say anything! And look how you drinkin' that stuff! Like you in a hurry to get somewhere! Like you runnin' even while you sittin' there! Worryin' me, Tim Jr.! Now what is it, boy!? What is it?!

TIM (*glancing from her to* CLARA; *then wearily*): Didn't I tell you I was—was going to California? Yeh, with a—a— friend of mine. Yeh, going today. Pretty soon now. That's why I'm—rushing. (*Rubbing forehead irritatedly.*)

CLARA (*concerned*): Really, Tim? I mean, you're really leaving? Now? Today?

TIM (*avoiding her stare*): That's what I said. (*Then sighs.*) Yeh, Clara, I'm leaving.

CLARA: Oh—well, before you go, Tim, I—I guess I should tell you something. I was going to wait—But if you're leaving, I guess I—

MOTHER (*unable to restrain herself*): Are you sure you're going out there to go to school, Tim Jr.? Are you sure that's why you're going?

TIM (*in vexation*): I'm sure, Mama! Ain't that what I said! Huh?! (*His outburst silences the room. After glaring at her, he puts hands to face for moment; then suddenly looks at* CLARA, *remembering.*) What, Clara? You started to say something.

CLARA (*stares at him. Then takes plunge. Reaches across table to take his hand*): Tim, if you hadn't did what you did, today, I guess I never would have said anything about it. And that would have been—wrong just like you said. (*Takes hands away. Puts them in her lap.*) I—I—looked at myself over these last two years, and—and—I didn't even know that person. (*Pauses.*) I didn't even try to keep the baby. There's something terrible in that. I didn't even care. (*Stops, lowers head; then looks suddenly at* MOTHER.) But am I the one to punish me? Am I supposed to decide that? (MOTHER *shakes head and pats her hands.* CLARA *looks at* TIM.) Oh, you were right, Tim. I've just been—been— (*to* MOTHER) —going to church every day preparing my own funeral, Mama!—Mama, believe me, I don't—don't mean anything against the church. It's just that I've got to start trying again, Mama! Trying to be something! I'm not sure what. But some——

MOTHER (*patting* CLARA's *hands*): I know, baby, I know. I thought about it all too. And your brother's right in most of

what he said. It's just the way he goes about things! Lord, there ain't no tellin' what he might say! Might do!—

TIM (*has gone dead-still as* CLARA *talked; a slight, pleased smile fixed on his face. Now, ignores* MOTHER, *love clear in his eyes, his tone*): My pants kept sliding and my shoes felt too big, but maybe I was dancing all right anyway, huh, Clara?—

CLARA (*reaching to take his hand again*): Yes, Tim—it was —all right.

(MOTHER *looks at the two of them, as there is a still-smiling moment. Then a perceptible tremor passes over* TIM. *He suddenly grabs glass and lifts it to his lips. But doesn't drink.*)

TIM (*smiling strangely*): Good stuff, ain't it, Clara. What's the name of it? Always forget. Some foreign-ass— (CLARA, *giving* MOTHER *a glance, uncertainly turns bottle around to look at label. He suddenly bangs fist on arm of chair.*) Never mind! I don't wanna hear it! Al!—Al!—Goddamn! (*Bangs arm of chair.*)

CLARA (*dismayed*): Tim?

MOTHER: Al? What about him, Tim Jr.? He called here for you, right after you left. What—

TIM (*looks up as she says this. Reaches across and takes both of them by the hand; in a desperate, despairing tone*): We were so tight, Clara! So close! How'd it all come between us?! How'd— (*Words fail, shakes head.*)

CLARA: It's all right, Tim. It's all—

MOTHER: Tim Jr.? What're you trying to tell us?!

TIM: —How'd we let it all get mixed-in between us!? How'd—! (*Stops, eyes closed, head lowered; desperately clenching their hands, as up the steps outside come heavy, hurrying footsteps.*)

CLARA (*frightened*): Tim? You're trembling. Your hands are sweating. Are you all right?

(MOTHER *watches him with mounting suspicion, listening to the footsteps. They go on past the door; on up the stairs where there is knocking, then a door opening; the wild laughter and music, then relative silence.*)

TIM (*suddenly slumping; his head reeling*): Clara!— How'd we— (*Lolls in seat; terrible pain on face.*) Clara— (*Starts to go around table, falls.*)

CLARA (*coming to feet; shocked, bewildered*): Tim!—

MOTHER (*coming around table*): Tim Jr.!—Jesus!

TIM (*on knees, takes* CLARA'*s hand, presses it to forehead*): Don't die, Clara.—Don't you die.—Everybody's dead, but you —Don't you—

CLARA (*bending to help him*): What?!—Die—Oh, Tim, you're drunk! Come on, please! Get up and get in bed. You're all tired out. You need to rest.

MOTHER (*also trying to lift him*): Yes, now, Tim Jr., get up now. You need to sleep, now. It's been too much on you. Drinking on top of everything else. Come on now—

TIM (*fighting them off; struggling to his feet*): Who drunk? —I ain't drunk—Hell, naw. Just tripped. That's all. (*On feet, moves away.*) Too hot in here—

MOTHER (*incredulous, exasperated*): Boy, now you got to lay down! You hear!?

TIM (*pulling away from her; moving down center*): Who? —What?!—I gotta go, I tell you—Yeh, Californ—— (*Stops, seeing old armchair; points at it, his face twisting strangely.*) —Think I'm drunk. Show you I ain't drunk. That's his chair, there; Tim Bronson Sr. And I always wanted to—to—Hell, now—I ain't drunk—

CLARA: Tim, won't you lie down just for a—

TIM: For what?—Naw!—Just got to get outta here—Too hot! Too damned hot, that's all—

MOTHER: Now, boy!— (*Starts toward him and stops, as, unbuttoning suit coat and pushing it back and holding it in that position by putting his hands on his hips, he lolls in uncertain circle, then stands wide-legged before them, unconsciously letting them see the huge, smeared blood spots on his white shirt: it looks as though he has wiped his hand across the one spot many times.*)

CLARA (*freezing in apprehension; with horror*): Tim!!—

MOTHER (*ugly, curt, staccato shouts of reprobation and belated admonishment*): Boy!?—Tim Jr.!?

(TIM *turns at the strange pitch of their voices. Sees where, at what, they are looking; makes an awkward attempt to recover spot with coat. Then lets it go, and with strange, resigned smirk, goes to father's chair. Falls heavily into it; one hand half-hiding his face.*)

CLARA (*coming toward him*): Is it from your hand? Tim? You hurt your hand?

MOTHER (*coming also*): What you doin' with that blood on you!? What you done, boy!? Huh!? (TIM *shakes head, rubbing face.*) —Who have you hurt, Tim Jr.!? Who!?

CLARA (*hoping desperately*): It's not your blood, Tim? It isn't your blood?

MOTHER (*upon him now*): Who!? Who!?

TIM (*starting to rise from chair; painfully*): Al! Mama!

Al!— (*Falls back in chair; one hand over face, other pounding arm of chair.*) Al!—Goddamnit! Al!—Al!—

(MOTHER *stops; staring down at him.*)

CLARA: Al?!—Your—your friend?!—Oh, Tim, no! No! You didn't! You didn't—

MOTHER (*a sad fact becoming inevitably clear*): That white friend of yours. (TIM *nods in bobbing motion, his shoulders swaying from side to side.*) Dear sweet Jesus, (*Lowering her head.*) what have we done to offend thee?—What have we— (*Going with sudden weary resignation back to couch.*)

CLARA: Why?! You said he was your friend! Why did you have to go and—and—jump on him!? Why!?

(CLARA *is emptying bowl for him.* TIM *lowers head, and sits for moments—elbows on arm of chair, hands lying limply between knees, head hanging—as a man just revived from near-drowning. Finally, slowly raises head to look at her.*)

TIM (*in empty tone*): I don't know, Clara. I don't know why. Why did it have to be him, huh? Why didn't I call my girl first? Right? Or some black friend I've known all my life. Like Donald, right? But I've known him just two years and I call him first when my old man dies. Not Donald. Not Wilma. But him. Al. White Al De Leo.

MOTHER (*on couch, grimly*): How bad did you hurt him, Tim Jr.? How bad?

TIM (*avoiding* MOTHER's *question*): Clara? Listen. I remember twice before when I just had to see Al. Once when—

MOTHER (*same grimness*): Just tell us how bad, Tim Jr.

TIM: I mean like he was my safety valve, you know, Clara. Once I was thinking about putting school down. I mean why not. When you got a damn economics professor who looks at his watch and drums his fingers on the desk whenever one of us black students recite. A whole line of those cats just dying to instruct me to hell!

MOTHER: Just what did you do to that boy, Tim Jr.? Just what did you do?

TIM: And once when this cop with his gun and stick and white face knocked me down, and put his feet on my chest— (*Pressing for* CLARA's *attention, understanding.*) Because he felt like it! I was gonna get Don's gun and put an end to all that shit!—

MOTHER (*glancing over at him*): A gun, Tim Jr.? A gun?

TIM: But—but both times I just couldn't. Naw, couldn't just give up on an education. Naw, and couldn't just go out and kill a cop either! So both times I had to go see Al! Let him cool me out! Show me that they all didn't have a stick and

a gun out for me! Yeh! Al! Al, my—my safety valve!—

MOTHER: Yes, the police. That's who you thought had been here when you came in, wasn't it, Tim Jr.? Wasn't it?

CLARA (*backing to more modern armchair; glancing from her to him*): I—I understand, Tim. But then—but now you've —you've— (*Sits down, staring at him.*)

TIM: Yeh, Al would always cool me out. But I guess—I guess there's some things you just can't cool out.

MOTHER: You hurt that boy bad, didn't you, Tim Jr.?

TIM (*stands, moves right*): —All day long I've been walking and thinking; I didn't even know I was looking for anybody! But I always end up either calling Al! Or at Al's house! Always end up back to him. (*Pauses, staring again at armchair; wry snort of a chuckle.*) Becuse it's that way, ain't it? I mean when I think of him, I think of that—that funky Chuck at that factory! And when I think of you, Clara, I think of that— that Wreyford. Yeh, and those whiteys standing up on those church steps that night!

CLARA: Stop, Tim. Please, stop.

TIM: Hah. And when I think of you, Mama, I see gentle, snow-white Jesus with gold hair. Hmmph. See? Always back to white. You dig? (*Wavering; putting a hand to his eyes.*)

MOTHER (*shaken somewhat; the grimness of her tone lessened*): Just tell us about that boy, Tim Jr.! That's all.

TIM: Some things are so hot and deep inside you, you don't even feel 'em burnin' till they burn a hole right through you. Know what I mean, Mama? (*She looks at him curiously now.*) I guess not. (*To CLARA.*) Guess what I got, Clara? A picture of your father. Uh-huh— (*steadies self with one hand while with other reaches into his back pocket*) —the late Tim Bronson Sr. (*Takes out wallet.*) Yep. When you called me and told me, Clara, just like I had planned it or something, I went right upstairs to my dresser drawer and got it. In a box fulla junk I keep in there. Didn't even remember I had it. But here it is! After all this time: his picture. See— (*Leans to toss it before MOTHER on card table. She touches it and closes her eyes.*) —Something, ain't it? Now, why you suppose I got that, Mama? Huh? (*Moves down center.*) Why you think after all this time, all I've said, when I think of him, of him gone, I—I see this blinding red! and—and get this burning!—why? After all this—

MOTHER (*tears in her tone*): He was still your father! He was still your father!

TIM (*turning to her, a resurgence of energy*): Naw, Mama, father ain't just a word, you know. Some face that looks down

137

at you everyday in your damned crib! Naw! It's a whole lotta little things said and done! And I ain't had none! You dig? None to lose! None to miss! So what is this thing in my guts?! Huh! This thing I can't walk, talk, or drink away!? Huh?—I mean it's just another soldier gone! Another black soldier! I mean, I'm not even sure I knew him! You know?! So?—So what is this grinding me up inside!—Grinding me—

MOTHER (*with bitter anger*): You know what it is, boy! You know what it is!

TIM (*backing away*): Naw, Mama, naw. I even had to find a reason to come back here to the funeral. You dig? A reason!

MOTHER: Hush, boy—!

TIM: —Yeh, I thought about you two! The mess he had left here. So I came and huffed and puffed. But that didn't help! I sure didn't find no reason for this—this thing here! So I'm back out on the street with it. And it's growin' and burnin', burnin' and growin'.

CLARA (*in empathy with his pain and rage*): Tim, stop. Please stop—

TIM: —And I keep getting back to that day at that factory! That funky Chuck! Yeh, when we was leavin' he slapped ol' Tim on the back and laughed: "Good boy, Tim! Got that ol' shithouse in ship shape!" (*Bitter laugh.*) Yeh, funny man, with his funny little son.

MOTHER (*a whimpering return to the first act*): I told you those kind wouldn't ever leave him alone! They knew he got off the line and took that—that cleanup job so he could be off by himself! So they wouldn't be all the time standin' over him! Pickin' him! Jokin' him! They knew! They knew—

TIM: Knew he was scared of 'em! Scared!

MOTHER (*defiantly; pounding on arm of couch*): Of hisself, Tim Jr.! Scared of hisself! Not them! Hisself! Hisself!

CLARA (*on feet*): Let her alone, Tim! What difference does it make now what he was!? What he did?!

TIM: I'll tell you what difference! He didn't have to work! Understand!? I was standin' there! You understand! Me! His son! Standing there! Watching! Why couldn't he—he—damnit, just that once, stand up to 'em. Just that once! Why couldn't he—he— (*Straining, searching, filling up.*)

MOTHER (*plaintive strain*): Boy, you don't understand—!

TIM: —Why couldn't he leave me one thing! One thing to remember and respect! Respect! Respect! (*Stops in an embarrassed, pained bewilderment. Stunned,* MOTHER *and* CLARA *stare at him.*) —All this time that's all I've been lookin' for. Just one thing I could—just—that's all! That's all! That's all

I was trying to tell Al—! (*The name, the picture, brings pain.*) —Al!—Al! (*Hands to face, goes to old armchair, sits, muttering.*) —Al—

MOTHER: Yes. You come in here with blood on you, and you want to talk about his wrongs, his weaknesses. It's you and that boy you got to talk about. And right now! Right now!

TIM (*pleading*): But I'm trying to tell you why, Mama. Don't you wanna know why!?

MOTHER: No! If you gotta talk about your father again, no! Talk about yourself, Tim Jr.! What *you* done *tonight!*

TIM: All right!—All right. (*Takes hands from face; begins with head on back of chair staring at ceiling.*) Fightin' or fussin', beggin' or cussin', you always gotta go through Chuck. Ever heard that old Negro saying, Mama? Well that's what I kept thinking all the while I'm telling Al like everything I ever thought, felt, or saw in my whole life. Fightin' or fussin', beggin'—All the while I'm diggin' him sitting there noddin' to it all, so calm, so full of understanding. Like I was talkin' about—Rococo art, or Gothic architecture. But I can't stop telling him. It all comes rolling out like it's on film. With the same question bugging me all the time: Why? Why him? I didn't get no answer then, but maybe I know why now. Maybe it's because if you take it to another black face it's like saying: Here's a nickel, give me five pennies. Yeh. But taking it to a— a—white face, like his, like Al's, is like—like giving a cat a picture, a painting, of something, and all he's got to do is look at it, see it, and—and—if he's got any eyes at all he'll—see things different from then on. Yeh. Only, like they say on the corners: They ain't got no eyes for it.

CLARA (*whining protest*): But, Tim, he—

(MOTHER *motions her to silence.*)

TIM (*standing, moving right*): So I'm startin' to tell him about that day at that factory—ol' Tim. And I'm diggin' the way he's noddin' so understandingly, but keepin' his eye on the stove so his food don't burn. Listening so intelligently, so— objectively. And all of a sudden I was looking at every damned whitey in the whole fucking world. Sitting there, noddin' to me. How could I talk to him?! He didn't have ears to hear it! Eyes to see it! Lips to talk about it! No heart to feel it! He was just blank-white! Blank-white between me and my—my father! my sister! my mother! myself! I knocked him out of that chair! And he was on the wall, and it was like my fist was going right through it and still I couldn't hit him hard enough!

CLARA (*coming to feet in reaction to* TIM's *face, sickened*): Tim—

TIM: —He tried to get off that wall! Fought hard! Fought scared! But all my life my father couldn't talk to me 'cause white faces had choked his tongue out! (*As he talks he unconsciously rocks from the balls of his feet to his heels.*) He wasn't coming off that wall! 'cause he might be out there in that cemetery but it ain't over! It's still here! (*Hits chest.*) Achin'! Burnin'! And now I finally had one where I could make him feel it! Make 'em know! And, naw, I wasn't letting him get away! I—I—

CLARA: Stop it, Tim! Stop it!

MOTHER (*approaching him; tensely*): How bad did you hurt that boy, Tim Jr.? Tell me!

TIM (*looks at her; moves away in guilt and shame*): I don't know how it got in my hand, Mama. All at once it was just there. I just—had it.

MOTHER: What, boy?! What?!

TIM (*going to lean heavily on old armchair*): Bookend!— Heavy! Brass! I just had it all of a sudden! And—and—and I hit him and his head hit the wall. I hit him and his head hit the wall!

(*Door opens upstairs; laughter, shouts, music. The sound of footsteps going down hall; another door on same floor opening and closing.* MOTHER *stands near* TIM, *down right, at old armchair.* CLARA *is down left.*)

MOTHER: Tim Jr.?

TIM (*nodding*): He's dead, Mama. (*Moving away to sit heavily in* armchair.) He's dead. The way he fell. The way he laid there. So still. I know he was—I wanted to—to—see, bend down and see. But—but the blood, Mama. On that—thing. My hands. His head. On the floor. And him just laying there. (*Nodding.*) I knew. He was—I killed him. I—yeh. Yeh. God-damnit. Goddamnit. (*Face in hands, rocking to and fro; tremors seize him, clenching elbows to knees, buries face in arms and sways there to his pain and guilt.*)

CLARA (*starting in incredulous whisper*): Killed him? You killed him? Oh Tim, no! No—

MOTHER (*a deep stoicalness has come over her as* TIM *finishes. Starts wearily back to couch*): It's no use. It won't change. No use.

CLARA (*looking from her to him, shocked, bewildered*): But, Mama, he—he killed him! We have to do something! We— (*Going uncertainly toward him.*) They'll come for him! The police! We have to—

MOTHER: Let them come. They've been a long time coming.

Can't keep 'em away. Couldn't stop 'em no matter how hard I tried. Seems like it just had to happen. Just had to.

CLARA: But they'll—We'll—Mama?—Tim?—Tim! (*Goes to him; on knees to see his face, he squirms away, keeps it hidden. She hugs him.*) No!—I don't want them to!—Tim! Tim! Why? Why? (*Near sobs; puts face near his; hugging.*)

MOTHER: Can't do nothin'. Can't do nothin'. (*Deep sigh.*) No one knows his ways! All these years I struggled and prayed, cried and pleaded, Lord, to hold it down inside his daddy. And—and—when I couldn't keep it down, when he couldn't hold hisself no longer those times, then I'd—I'd—put myself in front of it; let him give it to me!

CLARA (*looking up at her, questioning*): Mama—?

(TIM *also raises his head and stares.*)

MOTHER: And, yes, Clara, sometimes, Jesus, he come just a breath from—from killing me—

CLARA: Mama—?

MOTHER (*tone rising to silence* CLARA): Just—just like he thought he'd have to kill one of them before he could have any peace! (*Deep sigh.*) But you fight it, stand against it, no matter how it comes, or how hard it is. Then, Jesus, you lay him in the cold dark ground, and you feel like somehow—somehow you done won a little; 'cause there ain't no blood on his hands—he never struck the life out a fellowman. No, he never done that! (*Almost losing self.*) Oh, Jesus! You think you done buried it! Beat it! (*Stops; composes herself.*) Then it comes in your house on the hands of your son.

CLARA (*in empathetic horror and pain; unconsciously clutching* TIM, *who stares at* MOTHER *intently*): Oh Mama! Mama!

MOTHER (*closing eyes a moment*): You can't stop it. It's just gon' on and on and on. You see, Tim Jr., it was your grand-daddy, your daddy's daddy that stood up to 'em for your grandmother down there in Barlow, Mississippi. It was him that knocked that man away from your grandmother and told 'em that if they come to his house he would shoot. And that night they did come, in their white robes, and he fought 'em. But he gave up to keep 'em from killin' everybody in the house—his wife, his sons. He gave up, and they took him out in the yard and made 'em all come out an' look, while they—they done to him something no eight-year-old boy should see done to anybody, much less, Lord, his own father! Yes, your daddy was only eight years old. He didn't see but a little of what they done, but that was too much. He heard his mother screaming, his big brother begging and crying. And when they

let 'em take him back in the house he heard the shot what killed his daddy, Lord, and his grandmama tried to keep him from seeing, but he saw that tree burnin' an' blazin' so till it lit up the front windows! He—

TIM (*strange, husky tone*): You mean even after they—they still—?

CLARA (*turning to hide face on* TIM'*s leg*): Oh, what kind of people—!?

MOTHER (*wiping eyes*): Oh, yes, they had to do it all to him, everything they could think of. Out there in the yard, hollerin' and laughin' like—like devils in a dream. (*Losing self a moment.*) Lord, he was eight years old! Only eight years old!

TIM (*tensely; painfully*): That's enough, Mama! That's enough!

MOTHER (*with heat*): No, you listen, Tim Jr.! Don't make no difference now. You done finished it. Only Clara now. So you carry this with you. You listen now. He was only eight years old when he saw all that. But that wasn't what—what put the poison in him. What it was was that week when him, his mother, and his grandmother had to go to town to make ready for the funeral. What it was, was that some of them same white men, his mother knew 'em, had seen 'em when they took them things off their heads to laugh and drink under —under that tree, and he knew 'em too, knew their voices, said he could hear 'em in his sleep, couldn't ever forget 'em; well, Jesus be my witness (*here an ironic yet bitter, sanity-defending chuckle comes to her voice*) some of them very same white men, nodded to 'em, spoke to 'em, telling his mother they were sorry to hear about all the trouble she'd had. And nodded to him, and spoke to him! That's what broke him, Tim Jr.! You talk about some professor lookin' at his watch! Well, he was just a baby, but ever since then he couldn't stand to look at no white faces. Couldn't look at one and believe it! He couldn't be around 'em, Tim Jr.! They made him sick! Made him feel like he was splittin' wide open! On, jus' job after job! after—Yes! He cleaned out their toilets! 'cause they let him alone there! They let him— (*hands to face*) —alone—

TIM (*grimacing, pounding fist on knee*): Mama, I didn't know! Hear!? I'm sorry! I'm sorry!

CLARA (*looks at him for a moment. Jumps to feet, wiping her eyes*): Maybe he isn't— (*Heading for telephone.*) Maybe, if we call the hospitals—

TIM (*tearful, angry tone*): Don't you hear her, Clara!? It ain't no use! Ain't no use!

(CLARA *shakes head against him. And during rest of* MOTHER's *speech has the three semi-pantomimes of which we now and then hear variations of the same words*): —Emergency receiving?—Yes. I'd like to—Al De Leo—De Leo—Tonight—We heard he was hurt and— *With each time, the same disappointment of a negative answer.*)

MOTHER (*as* CLARA *dials, settles back more comfortably on couch; sighs*): It wasn't much I looked for. Nothing big. Just a house. With a bright kitchen. And—and the kids laughing, playing. And him—smiling. Smiling. That's all. (*Looks at it. Closes eyes. Shakes head.*) At first he thought it was gon' be different up here. No different. Even worse in a way, with them smiling and pattin' him on the back one minute, and the next minute—It made him think of them nodding. Mixed him all up! He couldn't stand it! (*Sighs.*) He'd come from the job and ask for his gun. And if I give it to him, he'd just sit with it; not crying no more, just sittin', thinkin'—In that very same chair. Or—or he'd put it in his pocket and go out! And, Lord, the waitin' and not knowin'! I threw 'way two, three, pistols, one right after another! And he'd jump on me! Then it was the shotguns, like the one in there now. And I'd find the shells and throw 'em out! And he'd jump on me! Jump on— (*Loses control for a moment.*)

CLARA: Emergency receiving? Yes, I'd like to—Al De Leo—De Leo—tonight—we heard he was hurt and—

TIM (*who has been listening, caught between her and* CLARA *at phone*): Mama. You don't have to tell me no more.

MOTHER (*shakes head, gains control, after a moment*): Wasn't much. Wasn't much. Wasn't much at all. But after awhile it just don't much matter. You watch him driving the kids away, shuttin' 'em off, 'cause—'cause, he say: "What can I tell 'em? What can I do for 'em? Ain't up to me what happens to 'em. Up to them damn white folks!"—You know he's wrong somewhere, somehow. But you done got tired. You don't even know what you prayin' for no more. You just doing what you been doing. One day he even ask you, ask you: "Cora? Cora, you still love? After all? You still love, Cora?!" And you look at him and you wonder what that has to do with it. Love is just —just something you remember sometimes; something from way back at the beginning—You don't even know if that was —was what it was—But I guess it must've been— (*Breaks, near tears again.*) Guess it must've been love—

TIM (*as* CLARA *finishes last call*): Please, Mama—! Just—stop! Hear!? Please!

MOTHER (*wiping eyes, breathing deep*): I'm all right—all right. Ain't gon' say no more. No more to say. No more—

(*As* MOTHER *sits* CLARA *slowly rises, phone to ear, listening intently. Hangs up, turns to* TIM.)

CLARA: Thank you. Thank you. Tim—He isn't dead. Al isn't dead. He isn't even on the—critical list. Severe concussion. They're just keeping him for observation—

MOTHER: You mean that boy's gonna be all right, Clara?! He's all right—!

CLARA: Yes, Mother, yes—!! (*Goes to* TIM, *who is standing stunned and dismayed, embraces him.*)

MOTHER: Dear, sweet, Jesus! Forgive my doubts!

CLARA: Tim, don't you understand? He's all right! He's gonna be all right—!

MOTHER: God bless and protect him! May God bless and protect him!

CLARA: Maybe if you go over and talk to him. If he's your friend, Tim, maybe he'll understand, Tim, maybe he won't even tell them who did it.

TIM (*breaking away from her*): Let him tell them! Let 'em come! Let 'em lock me up! Let 'em use their guns! And their sticks! I don't care, hear!? I don't care what he tells 'em! To hell with 'em all!

MOTHER (*pitying tone*): Tim Jr. . . . Tim Jr. . . .

CLARA: Tim, what're you saying? Don't you want a chance? Don't you wanna try?

TIM: Try what, Clara? Mama's Bible says the sentence is three score and ten. We've been wearing stripes and a number since we were born. Didn't you hear her? It's no use, no use.

CLARA: Yes. I heard her! That's where we've been. Not where we have to go! That's yesterday, Tim! Yesterday!

TIM: Yesterday!

MOTHER: Yes, Tim Jr., listen to her. Before you came back, I was laying in there, thinking about what the Reverend said today. You can't lay in ambush, Lord, for yesterday. It ain't ever coming again. Yes, Lord. If I just coulda told that to your father, Tim Jr., if I coulda made him see—

TIM (*for a moment continues intense stare at* CLARA; *then bitterly*): Yesterday is today! Today is still yesterday! Don't you understand!? (*Twists in seat; fists raised. Looking around as though for something to hit.*) Ghosts, huh? Ghosts! I shoulda —shoulda— (*Looks at* CLARA.) Just one. At least one of 'em! If I could make just one of 'em know! Make 'em feel! Make 'em— (*Crumbling in bitter, exasperated rage; pounding arms of chair and his thighs with his fist.*) Hurt 'em. Rip their in-

sides out!—Tear their guts!—Kill 'em! Kill 'em! Kill 'em! Kill 'em! Kill! (*Becoming sobful, mournful chant.*) Kill 'em! Kill 'em! Got to kill 'em—Kill 'em—

CLARA (*goes to him, down on knees; embraces him. He continues kill chant.*)

CLARA: No, Tim, please. Don't. Please don't. Don't do this to us. To yourself. Don't, Tim, please. Tim—Tim—

(*He suddenly looks at her, fist raised as though he is going to strike her; then grabs her in a hug, still shaking his head and swaying from side to side.*)

MOTHER: That's right, Clara, let him lean on you for a minute. You understand it now, baby? Huh, you understand? But you can't hold him long. He's got to rise up pretty soon now. Well, I guess I'll try to sleep a little before we go over and see about that boy. All right Clara, Tim Jr.? I want you to go with me. (CLARA *nods,* TIM *stares stoically.*) Good night, my children.

CLARA: Tim, are you going with us? (TIM *shakes his head.*) Maybe you should go. Try to talk to him. (TIM *shakes his head.*) Maybe you'll feel different tomorrow.

TIM: It's already tomorrow, Clara. Yesterday, today, and tomorrow. It's all the same dirty game.

CLARA: No, Tim. Yesterday it was all different around here, before you came. Nobody looking, nobody seeing. We're looking now, Tim. We're seeing, and if it's there, I'll bet we'll find it. —Night. See you in a little while?

(*She exits.*)

TIM (*moves to center. Looks around*): Nothing's changed. Nothing important. Not a goddamn thing. (*Moves from center to Father's chair.*) But don't you worry, ol' man. Gone be a whole lotta' changes here, soon. Damn soon. Yeh. You jus' keep watchin', ol' man. They gon' know we come from a long line of men—and got a long line comin'. Damn right. Damn right. Damn right. . . .

CURTAIN

145

Charades on East Fourth Street

by LONNE ELDER

Lonne Elder III was born in Georgia and has lived most of his life in New York and New Jersey. Writing of the development of his career, Mr. Elder said, "I started out with the pretension of being a poet and short-story writer—met Douglas Turner Ward in Harlem some years ago—and upon reading a play of Mr. Ward's I made my decision to write exclusively for the theater. I turned to acting, hoping to support my writing, but that didn't work out too cool because of the lack of roles for black actors."

Elder worked as a professional political activist, dock worker, time study and motion man, waiter, numbers runner, and professional gambler. *Ceremonies in Dark Old Men,* originally produced by the Negro Ensemble Company, is his first professionally produced play. Mr. Elder was the coordinator for the Negro Ensemble Company's Directors and Playwrights Unit, is a member of the New Dramatists Committee, and attended the Yale University Drama School film-making division on a Joseph E. Levine fellowship. He has written screen plays and television plays and is currently working on a new play for the fall.

Charades on East Fourth Street was commissioned by Mobilization for Youth, Inc.

CAST OF CHARACTERS (in order of their appearance)

RICHIE
JAKE
ADAM
CLIFF
MANUEL
ANNA
POLICE OFFICER
HORSE

TIME: *Midsummer—somewhere between the hours of nine and twelve* P.M. *this present time.*

PLACE: *The basement of an old movie house somewhere on the Lower East Side of New York City.*

The basement is practically bare with the exception of a few chairs and benches scattered about. A long wide table is against the right wall. There are at least three exits and entrances at the left wall of the room.

At curtain, music can be heard over a loudspeaker system in the far right corner. It is a rhythm and blues composition. Spread out against the walls are five teen-age youths wearing white eye-masks—they are looking at a POLICE OFFICER *in uniform who is chained and handcuffed to an old office-swivel chair on rollers. He is unconscious and his eyes are blind-folded with a black kerchief. His position is at the very center of the floor. The music stops and the voice of a "speaker" is heard trying to get the full attention of the group he is addressing.*

SPEAKER: May I have your attention—may I please have your attention! As soon as we have settled the business of this meeting, there will be more music, and the dance we have planned afterwards. (*The noise and chattering of the crowd continues.*) —Please, people! Please let me have your attention so we can get on with our meeting . . . (*The noise continues as a youthful voice interjects.*)

VOICE: —Let me have that mike— (*The noise and chattering is at a peak.*) —Damnit! You heard what the man said: SHUT UP!

(*The noise and chattering ceases instantly and the five boys down below crack up with laughter.*)

RICHIE: You know who that was snapping his tongue, don't you, Jake?

JAKE: That was ol' rubber-mouth Jim Long . . .

SPEAKER: Thank you, young man . . . My name is Joseph Henderson . . . (*Rah, rah applause.*) —Most of you know me—Well, I'm going to be your chairman for this evening's activities, so I'll make my remarks short. (*Greater rah, rah applause.*) —Well, anyway, we have called this meeting in conjunction with members of our local and city police force along with a large number of our young people in order that we may come to grips with the growing and age-old problem of police-community relations here on the Lower East Side of our city. Our aim here is to uncover the antagonisms that have existed for too long, and thereby—

ADAM: Cut that thing off, Manuel . . .

(MANUEL, *who is standing beneath the speaker, snaps a switch and causes the voice to become silent.*)

148

RICHIE: How long is that police going to stay unconscious, Adam?

ADAM: He will awake soon—You can take your masks off but keep them in your hands.

(*They all take their masks off.*)

JAKE: I hope he hurries up—I want to get this thing over with in time so I can get to that dance upstairs.

ADAM: Why don't you leave now—go on to that meeting, and do your dance.

JAKE: If I wanted to be up there, I wouldn't be down here with you.

ADAM: Then shut up . . . (*Pause.*) Where is that girl, Richie? (RICHIE *does not respond.*) Richie?

RICHIE: You talkin' to me, man, I thought—

ADAM: You thought I was gon call out your real name?

RICHIE: Yeah, why not?

ADAM: Your name is Richie, just as everybody's name is not the name they were born with—You hear me?

RICHIE: Yeah, I hear you . . .

ADAM: You hear what?

RICHIE: I hear that my name is Richie . . .

ADAM: And mine?

RICHIE (*scratches his head as if in doubt*): Adam . . .

ADAM: Everybody got the name I gave them!?

JAKE: Jake!

CLIFF: Cliff!

MANUEL: Manuel!

ADAM (*motions to* RICHIE): Come on, one more time!

RICHIE: Richie . . .

ADAM: Why ain't that girl here?

RICHIE: Late, I guess . . .

ADAM: I know she's late! Why!?

RICHIE: She had to come all the way from the Bronx, that's why!

ADAM (*points to the* POLICE OFFICER): You want to wake him up and tell him where she's from too?

RICHIE: Naw . . .

ADAM: Well, I hope she gets here on time—If not, we'll just have to start without her part of the party.

RICHIE: That's all right by me, but you said that before we did anything, you would have Horse to come down here and identify this cop.

MANUEL: There is no doubt that he is the one—We don't need Horse.

RICHIE: Where is he? He was suppose to be here—didn't you tell us that?

ADAM: He changed his mind and decided he wanted to go to that meeting.

RICHIE: Then somebody go up there and get him!

MANUEL: We don't need Horse—he's the one and I know it! I say, we oughta pluck and peel the skin off his hide like feathers, then everybody can call him a naked-ass chicken!

CLIFF: Bury him with his mama in a pit of snakes!

(*A pretty and shapely teen-age girl enters the room suddenly.*)

ANNA: Snakes!?

(*They freeze momentarily.*)

ADAM: Well, look who's here—about time!

RICHIE (*going to her with his hands out*): Hey, baby!

ADAM: Her name is not baby, it's Anna! You hear me, Anna!

ANNA: Don't you be screaming at Richie!

ADAM: Look, I just want to keep these names straight the way we rehearsed them, now that's Jake, that's Manuel, that's—

ANNA: —And that's Cliff, I know!

ADAM: How you ever got mixed up with a broad all the way up in the Bronx just gets by me, Richie.

ANNA: You think you're so smart, don't you? You know what your trouble is, Adam? Too many people been telling you you got a little brain in your head and you're beginning to believe it!

ADAM: What's wrong with a young boy believing in himself!

JAKE: Why don't you cut out your bullshit, man, and get on with this thing—I want to see my old lady and get to that dance!

ADAM (*has noticed that the* POLICE OFFICER *is awakening*): Shhhhhh! Put your masks on!

CLIFF (*moves to the* OFFICER): Well, the po-lice done come out of their dream—Hey, police, you some kind of drug addict or something? Why do your face look so stupid?

JAKE: He's a police, that's why!

ANNA: You ask dumb questions, you get dumb answers . . .

CLIFF: The big bad "goose man"—So this is whát you look like. I been wanting to meet you for a long time now—done heard so much about you—how you wait in the dark alleys at night, how you don't let too many people get to know you, so you can uphold and keep *law* and *order*. That alley you was fooling around in tonight had a nice little surprise for you, didn't it? (*Turns.*) Say, Jake, you wanta know why they call this bird the "goose-man"?

JAKE: Nawww—

CLIFF: Well, he's got a bad habit of goosing young girls under their arms, like he's playing with them so he can sneak a feel of their "tits." You know the kind . . .

ANNA: Oh yes, I do know the kind.

CLIFF: Course he ain't no real goose. He's a cop! He's a neighborhood cop!

JAKE: And that's the worse kind of cop there is!

(*They all laugh softly.*)

CLIFF (*takes the blindfold from the* OFFICER'*s eyes*): Look, cop, see anybody you know? Take 'em! (*Pushes the chair across the room on a roll. One of the boys catches the chair and pushes it to another with great delight. They roll the chair about frantically, making all sorts of noises and sounds.*)

ADAM (*stepping to the center of the room*): ALL RIGHT! ENOUGH!

(*They stop in their tracks.* ADAM *pushes the chair back to the center of the room.*)

ADAM: Now greet the man in the manner he is accustomed to . . .

ANNA (*moves before the* POLICE OFFICER *and does a curtsy*): Mr. Officer . . . (*Backs away politely.*)

JAKE (*moves before the* OFFICER, *making a slow, draggy "U" turn*): Mr. Police . . .

MANUEL (*steps snappily before the* OFFICER *and comes to a sharp "at attention" pose and salutes*): Policia!

CLIFF (*moves briskly before the* OFFICER, *stops momentarily and continues*): Officer!

RICHIE (*steps politely before the* OFFICER *and stops*): Police-police . . .

ADAM: Now that's better. We don't want this law enforcer here to think that we don't respect him . . .

POLICE OFFICER: All right now—What have you brought me here for?

(*They all laugh.*)

ANNA: Are you a fool, mister!?

RICHIE: We brought you here so you could throw ol' Jake over there in jail—Why don't you go over there and konk him on the head with your big bad stick! Go on! (*Pushes the chair into the arms of* JAKE.)

JAKE (*pushes the chair away with his foot*): Get him away from me. (*Shakes his arms and legs as if to tremble.*) I get nervous 'round the po-lice!

POLICE OFFICER: I'm asking you once again—Why did you bring me down into this cellar!?

ADAM: That's a good question, Officer. We just brought you down here for a little fun. A house party—that's what you can

call it—and we don't want to have this party with nobody else but you because you are our man—we know that. Now, you never heard of the Horse, but the Horse knows all about you, your habits and everything. He told us we would find you in that alley tonight. We waited and there you were—so you have to be the man to have this celebration with us.

POLICE OFFICER: What kind of celebration are you talking about?

ADAM: We answer no questions for you, mister. The game is on and now we play! Manuel!

MANUEL (*moves to the chair directly in front of the* OFFICER *and sits*): You came up to my sister one night while she's with her boyfriend the Horse—You beat Horse and you run him away—Then you tell her you're goin' to run her in because you say she's a whore—You put your hands all over her body and told her if she didn't let you screw her, you was going to take her over to the precinct and book her as a streetwalker.

POLICE OFFICER: I don't know what you're talking about . . .

CLIFF: This is not a trial, so shut up!

MANUEL: Three months later her stomach is sticking out and she gotta tell my mama about it, but my papa don't believe the story and he almost beat her to death. (*Rises.*) My sister is not a whore! This whole neighborhood knows it! But this one man was out to get to my little fifteen-year-old sister! HE PUT HIS HANDS ON HER! This filthy, dirty-minded bastard put his hands on her! (*He backs away, flush against the wall.*)

ADAM: Clifford!

CLIFF (*stands behind the* OFFICER *holding his nightstick in hand*): My brother smokes a lot of cigarettes—That's the only thing he remembers what to do. He used to stay on the street all the time because our house ain't much of a place to live in. And so, he was on the street and he liked to talk a lot and he liked girls a lot, and he met girls on the street and he talked to 'em, but you come along one night and because you wanted to goose up one of them young girls, you tell my brother he's gotta get off the street but he just stands there wondering where the hell he's suppose to go—so you jab him in the gut with this stick—He tries to get out of your way but he don't move too fast, and before he knows it your stick is being crushed up on his neck, arms, his shoulders, and then his head until he can't move no more—He gets himself beat until he forgets how to think. Like I said, he used to talk a lot but now he can't say a damn word! This son of a bitch beat the mind out of him! (*He raises the nightstick to bring down on the* OFFICER's *head.*)

ADAM: CLIFFORD!!!

(CLIFF *holds back the stick.*)

POLICE OFFICER: I have never seen and I know nothing of your brother.

MANUEL: You have nothing to say, Policia!

ADAM: Both of you be quiet! (*Pause.*) It's time we listened in on what's going on upstairs . . . (*Moves to the speaker switch.*)

CLIFF: Here we go again—we've heard enough of that meeting!

ADAM: If you don't want to hear—put your fingers in your ears! (*Cuts the switch on.*)

SPEAKER: My son was killed by a policeman. They say he was attacking this officer with a knife. I do not believe this and I shall take this belief with me to my grave. Now, I have heard some people here tonight say we should wait in dark places and seek revenge on these policemen. To kill them will not bring my son to walk before me tomorrow—to speak to me and smile—not if all the blue devils in this city were blown into hell this very hour. Whether we like it or not, we must be sane and sensible—we must be men, the kind of men they ought to be if—

CLIFF: Cut that damn noise off! I don't want to hear no more speeches!

ADAM: Am I in charge here or not!? (*Cuts the switch off.*)

MANUEL: Cliff is right—Do you think we waited in that stinking alley for three hours to catch this rat, drag him down into this hole just to listen to speeches?

ADAM: And I say we must keep in mind what's going on upstairs. I didn't ask you to let me plan and set up this whole thing—you asked me! Now, we'll do it my way or we don't do it at all!

CLIFF: Why does it have to be your way!?

ADAM: Because I'm smarter than you. And I'm not so sure the kids who went to that rally are not doing the best thing.

MANUEL: Well, if you wanta go to a meeting to hear sad stories about what cops do to us, then you go upstairs and make a speech, Adam.

ADAM: What the hell do you think I'm doing here! I led you into that damn alley!

CLIFF: Then what you so worried about!?

ADAM: I didn't bring this cop down here to kill him, and that's all you and Manuel can think about!

CLIFF: Now who said that? Anybody here hear me and Manuel say anything about killing somebody? If we had, we would've left you home.

153

JAKE: I don't give a damn myself—break his neck!

CLIFF: Now Jake, you know better'n that—Mr. Adam would turn you in to the authorities if you broke this police neck.

ANNA: Well, I'm not for breaking his neck and all that, but we could do something like painting his lips red, polish his nails, put a dress on him, and drop him off at home to his wife and kids.

RICHIE: Send him home to his mama . . .

CLIFF: You got a mama, cop?

MANUEL: Maybe Adam would like to teach him some good manners!

ANNA: I got it! I got it! Why don't we take all of his clothes off, and throw him out on the streets!

ADAM: Very funny, but we have a plan to go through with, and that's what we will do . . .

RICHIE: A little summer sport . . .

ANNA (*struts across the room in front of the* POLICE OFFI-CER): A big lovely house party!

CLIFF: I don't wanta play no games with this snake! Let's do him in and get the hell out of here!

ANNA: You gon be a fool, Cliff? You gon be a fool just like everybody said you would be if we brought this cop here?

CLIFF (*pause*): All right, you can have your sport, but I've seen people break their necks playing games!

MANUEL: And sometimes they even get themselves killed!

ADAM: Nobody gets killed here if I have anything to do about it . . . (*Pause.*) All right, we'll continue . . .

POLICE OFFICER: Damn all of you! Don't you know the trouble you're getting into!?

CLIFF: You're the one that's in trouble!

POLICE OFFICER: You've got to let me out of here sooner or later, and you know it!

MANUEL: Who said so!?

POLICE OFFICER: What are you going to do, kill me? Is that what you're going to do? Now it's my turn to laugh!

ADAM: It is not so funny, mister. That is what's in Manuel's heart. It comes to him in his dreams every night—it was your filthy hands on his sister.

POLICE OFFICER: It was not me, I tell you!

ADAM: You are the one the Horse calls the "goose man"?

POLICE OFFICER: I don't know anything about your damn names!

ADAM: You are to speak to me politely!

JAKE: Even with those chains 'round him, with Cliff and

Manuel a-aching to cut his head off, he's still got a big fat raunchy mouth.

POLICE OFFICER: Whatever you're going to do—do it and get it over with!

ADAM: Don't rush . . . We're going to give you a house party you'll never forget—that's whether you walk out of here on your own two feet—

CLIFF: —Or left lying on this floor bleeding to death. You ain't gon ever hurt nobody in this neighborhood again, not ever! I done been scared of you and I done lived with you all my life! You see how scared I am? I'm so scared I got spit dropping from my mouth like a crazy man!

JAKE: I say forget about the game—give him to Manuel and Cliff, and let's all go to the dance!

ADAM: And suppose he isn't the one we want?

CLIFF: He is, I tell you!

ADAM: How do you know—nobody here has ever seen him . . .

MANUEL: He's pulled Horse in at least three times—he knows him!

RICHIE: What difference do that make whether Horse knows him or not—If we don't fix him up good they'll be hitting us over the head till we get to be shitty old men!

JAKE: If we live that long . . .

ADAM: All right, if it comes to anything serious, we'll send upstairs for Horse. Now ain't that a kick in the head—Horse is the only one that's been near this turkey, and he's upstairs going to a meeting. But I don't think we're going to need him, so we'll begin the game. We'll do it just as we all agreed we would—Nobody is to get tricky and nobody's to get raunchy. (*Stands before the* POLICE OFFICER.) Mister, we have brought you here for nothing more than a little sport—'course the fun is goin' to be all ours. The way we look at it, you owe us a little fun . . . All right, everybody take their positions . . .

(CLIFF *and* MANUEL *move near an open exit and stand . . .* ANNA *and* RICHIE *do likewise at another exit . . .* JAKE *sits on the table next to the wall.*)

ADAM: You see, we all brought little toys to play with— Ain't that something? These big old rusty-ass kids still going around playing with toys . . . Take a look at Anna and Richie over there.

(ANNA *and* RICHIE *giggle as they hold a Polaroid camera up into the air between them. They wink their eyes and click their tongues, pointing into the blankness of the exit.*)

POLICE OFFICER: What are they pointing to?

ADAM: No game is a game without a surprise, policeman
. . . Manuel, Cliff!

(*They roll out a rusty old guillotine halfway in the direction
of the* OFFICER, *then quickly wheel it back near the exit.*)

JAKE: Where did they get that from? That thing couldn't
cut a rotten piece of wood.

CLIFF: His neck ain't no wood . . .

ADAM: Jake!

JAKE (*hops down from the table, brandishing a switchblade
knife. He makes like he is in a sword duel*): And smote him
thus!

ADAM: Shakespeare—I taught him that. That's just like
Jake—old-fashioned—all he could think to bring was that
damn switchblade knife! (*Moves away from the* OFFICER.)

POLICE OFFICER: Just a minute!

ADAM (*stops and turns*): Yes, Cop . . .

POLICE OFFICER: What's your part in this game?

ADAM: You mean you haven't caught on yet?

POLICE OFFICER: No, now stop playing with me and tell me!

JAKE: We don't have to tell you nothing!

ADAM: Now, Jake, the man's got a right to know . . . You
see, Mister Officer, all I've got is my hands— (*Goes into dem-
onstrations of karate motions.*) —feet! body! head! EYES!
(*Ends the karate movements.*) I can break anybody's arm in
this room with one motion . . .

POLICE OFFICER: Karate . . .

ADAM: That's right, screaming and all that stuff, and before
you know it, I'm walking around with your head in my hands.

POLICE OFFICER: You're going to try that on me?

ADAM: No, mister! I'm the only buddy you got here—I'm
going to make sure they don't hurt you, that they don't kill you
with their little games. How do you think I keep this bunch of
young killers in check—with these hands, that's how . . .

POLICE OFFICER: You tell me how you're going to save me
from that contraption over there!

ADAM: That's a good question—I don't know, but I'm thinking on it. Of course you don't have to go through any of this
danger we got set up for you here if you admit your crimes to
us on that stage before all those people upstairs.

POLICE OFFICER: You mean you want me to go up there
and say to those people that I brutalized his brother and that I
raped his sister.

ADAM: That would be the decent thing to do.

POLICE OFFICER: But I would be lying . . .

ADAM: Why don't you make this easier for me and save
yourself, mister!

POLICE OFFICER: But I keep telling you I don't know what you're talking about!

ANNA: Come on, it's getting late, Adam!

ADAM: You're right, he had his chance . . .

CLIFF: I'm first!

JAKE: Naw, I'm first!

RICHIE: I wanta go first!

(*There is a great deal of confusion as each person insists on being "first."*)

ADAM: Stop it! (*Total silence.*) —We'll start with Jake and we'll work our way around the room, and that is how we will do it . . .

JAKE: I'm ready . . .

MANUEL: What if Jake gets him before we do?

ADAM (*points to the* POLICE OFFICER): That is his hard luck, not yours . . .

ANNA: Please let us start, I've got to get home!

ADAM (*snaps his fingers*): Oh, I almost forgot! We got a toy for you too, Policeman—In fact, it's your own toy . . . (*Pulls out the* OFFICER's *revolver and holds it up.*) See your ol' shotgun here; well, I'm giving it back to you, and I'm taking out five of your bullets and I'm putting them into my pocket, but I'm leaving one bullet inside . . . (*Slips the revolver down into the* OFFICER's *holster.*) All right, let's get these chains off him . . .

(*They all join in unchaining him from the chair. After he is freed, they all back away with the exception of* JAKE, *who is now circling the* OFFICER *with his knife drawn in hand.*)

POLICE OFFICER: What do you think I'm going to do now?

ADAM: You're goin' to have to pull that trigger six times to stop Jake from killing you with that knife . . .

POLICE OFFICER (*rises slowly from the chair*): But I don't want to kill this boy!

MANUEL: Remember all them kids with pen knives, attacking big men in blue suits with shotguns—little dangerous, hot-headed punks gettin' their heads blown off!

CLIFF: Get him, Cop! Get him!

(*The* OFFICER *pulls the gun from his holster with his eyes keenly on* JAKE. *The others are cheering* JAKE *with enthusiasm.* JAKE *closes in on the policeman. The* OFFICER, *in defense, pulls the trigger twice. He moves away from* JAKE, *then suddenly turns and runs to a back corner of the room, turns on the boy, pulling the trigger frantically until it reaches the loaded chamber, but the gun does not explode. He continues pulling away on the trigger to no avail. They all burst out in great*

157

laughter. JAKE *charges him with the knife, but Adam blocks his path.*)

ADAM: Give me that knife, Jake . . .

JAKE: You take it from me, Adam—I'm going to get him even if I have to cut a hole in your gut. Now get away from me!

ADAM: I said give me that knife!

(JAKE *tries to lunge by* ADAM *to the* OFFICER *but* ADAM *grabs his arm and wrestles the knife from his grip . . .*

The POLICE OFFICER *runs for the door, but is caught and thrown to the floor by all of the boys. There is a big scuffle as they strip him of his clothes except for his underwear. Meanwhile,* ANNA *and* ADAM *have rolled out a bed and other bedroom paraphernalia into a corner of the room to make it look like a real bedroom setting.* ANNA *strips down to her bra and panties and jumps into the bed. She is on her feet, jumping up and down in the bed as the boys dump the* OFFICER *into the bed at her feet.* RICHIE *moves in quickly with his camera and snaps a picture.*)

RICHIE: How do you like that, Officer? Now I got a picture to send home to your wife, your priest, your precinct, and your mama!

(*They howl in laughter.*)

ANNA (*putting her clothes on*): But we don't have to do a thing like that if you go upstairs and tell them people what you did to Manuel's sister and Cliff's brother.

POLICE OFFICER: I'm going to burn you! I'm going to burn every damn one of you!

ADAM: Put him back in the chair . . .

(*They take him from the bed, chain and handcuff him once again to the chair.*)

CLIFF (*points and moves to the guillotine*): This will get him!

ADAM (*as they are tying him down to the chair*): Tell me something, Officer? Are you a member of the John Birch Society?

(CLIFF *rolls out the guillotine to the center of the floor. It creaks and rattles—*MANUEL *drags out the table to about the same spot, then exits into the back as* CLIFF *arranges the table to the guillotine.*)

JAKE: Say, Adam?

ADAM: Yeah?

JAKE: What's the John Birch Society?

ADAM: A beer company . . .

JAKE: Oh . . .

(MANUEL *returns with an old dirty mannequin and places it on the table.*)

ADAM: You fellows sure take your work serious . . .

POLICE OFFICER: What are you going to do about that guillotine?

ADAM: I'm thinking man, I'm thinking!

CLIFF (*has adjusted the mannequin's head into the guillotine's slot*): Set . . .

MANUEL: All right, let her loose!

(CLIFF *pulls the cord to the guillotine, the blade falls on the neck of the mannequin but does not cut the head—the blade just rests there.*)

ADAM: That thing wouldn't cut butter . . .

CLIFF: We got two more tries—you promised us!

ADAM: Be my guest . . .

(CLIFF *and* MANUEL *set up the guillotine again, raising the blade to the top.*)

ADAM: I think I got it now, Officer—I don't think that thing's goin' to work at all—it's too old for one thing. You see, we gave them three dry runs. Now, if and when they think it's okay, then the next time's gotta be on you. If it doesn't work then, I know I'm gonna have to fight them so you can walk out of here unharmed—but you could make it easier by confessing now—

POLICE OFFICER: I have nothing to confess . . .

ADAM: You are a stubborn man, Officer.

POLICE OFFICER: What if that machine does work?

ADAM: Your head is going to fall on this floor, that's what, and I'm going to be very sorry about that.

CLIFF: We ready . . .

(*The dummy is in place on the table and the blade is up.* CLIFF AND MANUEL *take their positions.*)

MANUEL: Okay, Cliff, let 'er go!

(CLIFF *pulls the cord, the blade falls but sticks in the grooves halfway.*)

ADAM (*laughs*): Didn't I tell you, we got nothing to worry about!

MANUEL: It's got to, I tell you—It's got to work!

CLIFF (*climbs up on the table*): Let me see . . .

MANUEL: You told me it would work! I know I oughtn' listened to you!

CLIFF: Aw, man, shut up and help me with this damn thing! Get the tools!

(MANUEL *rushes to fetch the tools, returning immediately and joining* CLIFF *on the table.*)

ADAM: Screwdrivers, hammers and all that stuff—what are they trying to prove?

POLICE OFFICER: You got time for jokes! They're trying to kill me!

ADAM: I told you not to worry!

(*The two boys are banging away with their tools on the machine.*)

ANNA (*looking up at them*): You fellows having trouble or something?

CLIFF: Richie, will you keep this broad away from us!

ADAM: Now look, fellows, we can't stay here all night waiting for you to get that machine in shape . . . I'm getting impatient myself.

CLIFF: And I'm getting sick and tired of your mouth!

ADAM: That's too bad, either you get that thing to working or we get out of here!

MANUEL: Adam, will you please leave us alone!

ADAM: I will give you ten minutes . . . (*Clicks the speaker on.*) Let me see what's going on upstairs now . . .

(*The sound of music and dancing.*)

JAKE: Uh uh, that's me—the dance is on!

(ADAM *clicks the speaker off.*)

RICHIE: Come on, baby, let's go!

ADAM: You might as well, nothing is happening here.

ANNA: I wanta stay now.

ADAM: For what? Richie, get her out of here.

RICHIE: (*standing at the exit*): Come on, Anna . . .

ANNA (*pause*): All right, I'm coming! (*Moves to the door, stops and turns.*) Adam?

ADAM: Yes, sweetheart?

ANNA: Kiss my foot! (*Rushes out with Richie and Jake.*)

ADAM: Ain't she cute, Mister Police?

POLICE OFFICER: Yeah, cute as a button . . .

ADAM: Look at them—they look like two baggy-ass old women from Brooklyn.

(*As they are banging away on the machine* MANUEL *falls and his head drops into the slot of the guillotine just below the jammed blade.* ADAM *and the* OFFICER *both laugh heartily.*)

CLIFF (*moving down to free him*): Don't worry, I'm coming!

ADAM: That's right, Manuel! Don't you worry, ain't nothing goin' to happen to you! Not in that machine!

CLIFF: Damn you, Adam!

ADAM: Time is running out, fellows! Time is running out!

(*After* MANUEL *is freed, they climb back up on the guillotine to resume their mechanic's work.*)

CLIFF: We'll close our ears and we just won't hear him.

ADAM (*wheeling the* OFFICER *in the chair to a corner of the room*): Why I'm going through all this trouble to save you, I don't know.

POLICE OFFICER: You're just playing a game—you don't want to save me.

ADAM: You're wrong, I do—but for my sake, not yours.

POLICE OFFICER: And still you're going to let them use that thing on me?

ADAM: If it works, I got no choice.

POLICE OFFICER: But I am not the policeman you call the "goose man."

ADAM: You're still a cop, and you're just as much a bastard as a cop can be.

POLICE OFFICER: Look, I'm just a family man that—

ADAM: Manuel and Cliff, they got families too—How do you think Manuel feels about his sister?

POLICE OFFICER: But I have never been near Manuel's sister!

ADAM: You can't prove that.

POLICE OFFICER: But you can! Why don't you go upstairs and get this Horse fellow.

ADAM: Horse wants no part of this—Why do you think he chosed to go to that meeting ?

POLICE OFFICER: The officer you probably want is Murphy —He does those type of things.

ADAM: Then you know about it!

POLICE OFFICER: No, I don't, I just said that——

ADAM: Stop it! Trying to pass your dirty work off on some-body named Murphy. You're the one and you know it—I can see it in your eyes, the way you looked at Anna—You're stupid, you got no soul in you, all you got is your hate and that uniform!

POLICE OFFICER: That is a lie, boy—I have a job to do and I do it well—I am proud of that uniform and I don't go around abusing it by molesting teen-age girls and clubbing innocent people over the head with that nightstick for kicks—and you kinda know that too and that's why you're so damn worried.

ADAM: Me? Worried about you!?

POLICE OFFICER: Yes, because you're not the same as those two over there—You've got a brain on your shoulder, boy, you've got a brain—use it!

ADAM: For what?

POLICE OFFICER: Call this whole thing off and let me out of here before you find yourself sitting in an electric chair.

ADAM: I'm underage—They don't put teen-agers in electric chairs! They rehabilitate us! (*Laughs.*)

POLICE OFFICER: DON'T BE A FOOL, BOY,

CLIFF (*hops down from the table*): We're ready!

MANUEL (*hops down*): All fixed!

(*They start in right away by putting the dummy's head back into the slot of the machine.*)

ADAM: Watch closely, Officer. This is the test that will break their asses.

CLIFF: All set, Manuel!?

MANUEL: Watch the magic!

(*The blade falls on the dummy's head, severing it from the body part. It falls to the floor, rolling about, making awkward, clunking sounds.*)

CLIFF (*jumping up and down in great glee*): We did it, Manuel! We did it!

MANUEL (*jumping up and down*): YIPPEEEEEEEE!

ADAM: Well I'll be damn if they didn't get that thing to working.

POLICE OFFICER: They're crazy!

ADAM: You're right about that.

POLICE OFFICER: You've got to stop them!

ADAM: Speak to them! They set that death trap for you!

(ADAM *shoves the chair on a roll to the boys—it comes to a halt just in front of them.*)

ADAM: Tell them you'll resign from the force and become a social worker.

MANUEL: I don't like social workers either!

ADAM: Tell them you will repent your sins in the middle of that dance upstairs.

POLICE OFFICER: I keep telling you I didn't do anything!

CLIFF: Enough—let's get him on the table.

(*They unchain him from the chair but not without a fierce struggle.*)

POLICE OFFICER: You've got to stop them, Adam! You can't let them do this!

(*They get him adjusted up on the table with his head placed into the slot of the guillotine.*)

MANUEL: I will pull the switch this time, Cliff.

CLIFF: No, I'm gon pull it.

MANUEL: You pulled it three times, now it's my turn!

CLIFF: It's my machine, I found it.

MANUEL: It's my table!

ADAM: Now wait just a minute, fellows!

CLIFF: What is it now?

ADAM: You forgot something.

CLIFF: What's that?

ADAM: The basket . . .

CLIFF: Basket!?

MANUEL: What the hell do we need a basket for?

ADAM: His head—you ain't goin' to let his head roll all over this floor are you—bloodying up everything, and—

CLIFF: I don't understand you, Adam, now stop stalling!

ADAM: You've got to do this thing right . . . Now you bring me a basket and that's all to it.

MANUEL: Where is we going to get a basket this time of night?

ADAM: That's your problem, but I'm not going to let you cut his head off without a basket.

MANUEL: God damn you, Adam—I will go home and steal my mama's clothes basket from the bathroom!

ADAM: Good, you go and get your mama's clothes basket, Manuel.

CLIFF: I'll wait for you here . . .

MANUEL: No, I will not leave unless you go with me.

CLIFF: You don't need me.

MANUEL: I know you—you will try to get him before I come back.

ADAM: He's right—I don't want any trouble from you, Cliff —You go with him.

CLIFFS Okay, but you keep that turkey right where he is.

ADAM: Now get out of here, it's getting late.

(*The two boys rush out.*)

POLICE OFFICER: That was good thinking on your part, getting them out of here.

ADAM: Yeah—I got a good mind . . .

POLICE OFFICER: You better untie me then—you know as well as I—they're going to get that basket.

ADAM: Sure—even if they have to weave one.

POLICE OFFICER: Well, what are you waiting for?

ADAM: I've got to be sure that I'm not turning you loose to go out there and put your filthy hands on somebody else's sister. How do you bring yourself to trust a cop?

POLICE OFFICER: That's your answer for everything; COP! COP! COP! I'm a man! You hear me, a man! Sure, there are some brutes and little Nazis in uniform, and you may think of me as some sort of freak because I am not what you think I am. Being a cop is a nervous and touchy thing—the fear that I know just doesn't happen one morning or two but for a thousand nights and days. What do you think goes on in my heart and mind when a policeman's head has been blown off

for being too damn considerate—shot off by an old crippled man, or gets a knife torn into his gut by thinking it was so easy to handle a harmless-looking fifteen-year-old kid. You've got to be cautious! The only crime I've ever committed in this uniform was being cautious with as much consideration I could possibly give so I could go home every night to my family as any man would want to.

ADAM: How considerate were you the night you raped Manuel's sister!?

POLICE OFFICER: I keep talking about one thing, and you keep blaming me for something I know nothing about!

ADAM: Somebody's to be blamed! That meeting upstairs isn't being held because those people got nothing better to do!

POLICE OFFICER: True! Then why aren't you up there!?

ADAM: I tell you what—There's a way to do this. They do it down at your headquarters. They have all kinds of private and inside ways of making people say things that they are guilty of—they even make people admit to things they're not guilty of.

POLICE OFFICER: What are you going to do?

ADAM: I've got to know! (*He moves to the guillotine and takes the cord in his hand.*) If you don't tell me the truth I'm going to pull this cord myself. I've got to know if I'm going to let you out of here. You've got to say it and I'll let you go! That's the one thing you've got to tell me, you hear! Tell me! Tell me! Tell me!

POLICE OFFICER: Don't pull that cord, Adam! Don't do it!

ADAM: Here it comes, mister!

POLICE OFFICER: All right, God damn it! It was me! It was me! It was me!

ADAM (*pause*): That's all there is to know.

POLICE OFFICER (*pause*): Now, will you please untie me from this table?

ADAM: Sure, sure I'll do that. (*Frees him from the guillotine and handcuffs.*)

POLICE OFFICER: You have my word, I won't mention this to anyone. (*Hops off the table and immediately begins gathering his things together.*)

ADAM: I believe you—God has told me to believe you.

POLICE OFFICER: I just hope that from here on in you don't make a practice of kidnapping policeman. You would have done yourself a better turn at that meeting upstairs.

ADAM (*approaching the officer who is now in the chair tying his shoes*): Yeah, you might be right about that—but tell me something? How does a man come to do what you did to that little girl?

POLICE OFFICER: Don't ask me about it—I told you what you wanted to hear!

ADAM (*standing over him*): But how? *A fifteen-year-old child!*

POLICE OFFICER: How do I tell you that? I don't know—I just don't know how any man could do such a thing!

ADAM (*takes the mask from his eyes and suddenly begins speaking in Spanish*): A girl-child at the mercy of that gun of yours, your old soulless body, your slimy hands. THAT LITTLE GIRL WAS MY SISTER! (*Quickly raises his hand in karate fashion, screams, bringing his hand down on the officer's arm, breaking it.*)

POLICE OFFICER: What! My arm! You bastard! You've broken my arm! (*He backs away from the boy.*)

ADAM (*slowly stalking him*): Yes, that little girl was my sister—Not Manuel's but MINE!!! And now, I'm going to break the veins in your body!

POLICE OFFICER (*still moving away*): You forced me to lie —You tricked me!

ADAM: Yeah—I tricked you and I tricked them. You know what I told them? I told them all we was supposed to do was bring you here and just scare you up so you could go upstairs and make a fool out of yourself. That would have never been enough to cause me to forget what you did to Juliana! (*Catches up to him and breaks the other arm.*)

POLICE OFFICER: NOOOOOOOOO! (*Passes out.*)

(MANUEL, CLIFF, *and* HORSE *enter suddenly.*)

MANUEL: ADAMMMMMMMM!

CLIFF (*rushing to the* OFFICER): What have you done, man!?

ADAM: It worked! Everything I planned worked! He told me everything!

MANUEL: But you promised us you would not hurt him!

ADAM: He admitted it! Don't you hear what I'm saying! He put his hands on Juliana! And I killed him! I killed him!

CLIFF: He's not dead—just fainted—Horse . . . ?

HORSE (*stands over the* OFFICER, *looking down*): He is not the cop that took Juliana away from me that night.

ADAM: But he told me he was . . .

MANUEL: Whether he was or not, you was not suppose to do this!

CLIFF: Are you sure he is not the one, Horse?

HORSE: How could I forget, man—but it's too late for that now. I told you, Cliff—I told you not to trust Adam—He's crazy. He's been talking weird to me about this cop for six

165

months—Called me a faggot because I wouldn't go with y'all into that alley tonight. I told him I didn't have no love for cops either, but I weren't no fool.

CLIFF: You have no honor, man—You should be on the police force your damn self—You had me and Manuel fooling around with that damn machine all night—we did our part because we thought you were together with all of us, but all the time you was laughing at us.

HORSE: And because of him every one of you are gonna be dragged into that precinct tomorrow under those hot lights with every beefy-faced sonofabitch in the precinct blowing spit in your face.

MANUEL: What are we going to do, Cliff? (CLIFF *does not respond and is moving for the exit.*) . . . WHAT ARE WE GOING TO DO, MAN!?

CLIFF (*stops at the speaker and turns*): I don't know, Manuel—I don't know . . .

ADAM: What are you asking him for!? What is he suppose to be? Some kind of answer man? He's just a dumb-ass grammar school dropout who couldn't keep my company if I wasn't so damn generous! I thought this whole thing up, and ran it—not because I'm some kind of genius but because you're so damn stupid! (MANUEL *and* HORSE *join him at the exit.*) . . . You ain't goin' to leave me here with this man, are you? You can't do that—you hear me, you can't do that! (CLIFF *cuts the switch on and the music drowns his voice out.* CLIFF *cuts the switch off.*) . . . WHAT ELSE COULD WE HAVE DONE!?

CLIFF: It's not "we," it's what *you* could have done, and as far as that is concerned; you could've kissed this policeman's ass in Tomkins Square Park for all I care, but *we* should've been upstairs—trying to find out what can be done. As for you, you better call an ambulance before that policeman dies. I may go to jail tomorrow, but for now, I'm going to a dance.

(CLIFF *turns the speaker on—the sound of music. The three boys exit and leave* ADAM *standing in the middle of the floor.*)

CURTAIN

Gabriel

THE STORY OF A SLAVE REBELLION

by CLIFFORD MASON

A member of New Dramatist Committee, Clifford Mason had two productions presented at their theater in 1968. His play *Sister Sadie* was produced at the Eugene O'Neill Memorial Foundation in Waterford, Conn., and again at the Mark Taper Forum in Los Angeles. Mr. Mason has written for *The New York Times* Sunday drama section, *Life* magazine, and the *Amsterdam News*. He is currently teaching at Manhattanville College in New York.

CAST OF CHARACTERS

GABRIEL, Leader of the Revolt
MARTIN, His Older Brother
NANNY, His Wife
CHARLES PROSSER, His Owner
LUCY PROSSER, Charles's Wife
MARY, The Prosser Cook
BILLY, A Young Slave
JACK BOWLER, A Runaway
MOSBY SHEPPARD, Prosser's Neighbor
BIG HENRY STIMPSON, Gabriel's Chief Lieutenant
JAMES MONROE, Governor of Virginia and Judge at the trial
WILLIE, A Specialist in Deception and Death
CAPTAIN, Prosecutor at the Trial
EXTRAS (Plantation Slaves, White Roustabouts, Members of the Rebellion, Court Guards, Court Attendant)

ACT I

Scene 1

Somewhere on the Prosser Plantation, 1880

(*It is mid-afternoon in the fields. As the curtain rises, slaves are picking cotton. There are some men and some women. They are all silent and removed as they go about their work. There is no communication.* MARTIN *comes on from right and surveys the proceedings.*)

MARTIN: All right. Everybody takes five minutes for water. Everybody takes five minutes.

(*They all saunter out right, still without communicating.*)

MARTIN (*picks up stray pieces of cotton and puts them into his cotton bag, which is like the bags the field hands are carrying*): Lazy, no-count. Always leaving scraps around. 'Cause they know I'll pick 'em up. No wonder the foreman is always beatin' 'em. They deserve to be beat—lazy, no-count. You can drag an ass to water, but you sure in hell can't make 'em drink. Lazy, no-count.

(GABRIEL *comes in.*)

GABRIEL: Martin—where've you been?

MARTIN: I been right here, Gabe, all the time. Was you looking for me? Huh? I didn't know you was looking for me, Gabriel.

GABRIEL: Have you seen Nanny?

MARTIN: No. Ain't seen nobody. Somethin' wrong?

GABRIEL: We got any more men?

MARTIN: No. We ain't got no more. If you ask me, we got too much already.

GABRIEL: We can't have too many men when we don't have any guns and we don't even know how to fight like an army.

MARTIN: Yeah, well, you know how niggers is. You tell too many of 'em somethin' and sooner or later it'll get back to massah.

GABRIEL: Yeah. Well, we'll just have to be careful. But we still need men.

MARTIN: How many you figure we got already?

GABRIEL: About 2,000.

MARTIN: Hmph. If two show up that'll be two more'n you should look for.

GABRIEL: Shhh. Somebody's comin'.

MARTIN: Yeah. Or their feet.

(*They both wait.*)

NANNY: Gabe, Jack Bowler ran off.

MARTIN: Oh, no.

GABRIEL: Did they say when?

NANNY: No.

MARTIN: Does it matter?

GABRIEL: If he ran off yesterday he probably went to Richmond or he'd a been here by now. If he ran off today, then he could still be headed this way.

MARTIN: Oh, no!

NANNY: He'll have all a Sheppard's down on us. And they'll end up blaming you for everything.

MARTIN: Let's hope he went south to the sea and got drowned.

NANNY: Let's hope they caught him already and we don't have anything to worry about.

GABRIEL: Let's hope he gets away. If we have to hope for anything.

NANNY and MARTIN: Hmmm.

(*Slaves come back in.*)

NANNY: Well, I have to get back. Oh. I forgot to tell you. Miss Lucy has been asking for you, you lil' ole sweet thing.

GABRIEL: Don't worry about Miss Lucy.

NANNY: Oh, I ain't. She's not worrying about me, I'm sure in hell not worrying about her. I'm just worrying about me. Nobody but me.

GABRIEL: That makes two of us that's worrying about you.

NANNY: Now ain't that sweet. You mean with Jack Bowler, a revolution, and Miss Lucy to worry about, you got time for your wife. Well, ain't that just sweet. (*She exits.*)

GABRIEL: Keep an eye out. Jack's liable to do anything.

MARTIN: Ain't that the truth.

GABRIEL: And you can send 'em in early. With a runaway loose, nobody'll be thinkin' about cotton.

MARTIN: No, they'll be thinkin' about how long it'll take to catch him.

GABRIEL: Or did they shoot him on the spot.

MARTIN: Or did he put up a fight.

GABRIEL: Or how many people saw it.

MARTIN: Or how much a nigger like that worth alive or dead in the first place.

GABRIEL: Dead they ain't worth nothin': black or white.

MARTIN: Ain't that the truth.

GABRIEL: Think I'll go take a look up by the north fence.

MARTIN: You think he may be hidin' up there or somethin'?

GABRIEL: He might.

MARTIN: You want me to wait here for you?

GABRIEL: Yeah. (*He exits.*)

MARTIN: All right, work fast. You're gettin' off early today. (*They begin to leave and he becomes enraged.*) Did I tell you to go, huh? Did I?

THEY: No, but we goin' anyway. (*They leave.*)

MARTIN: Lazy, no-count. (*He mumbles, as he picks up the cotton.*)

(BILLY *enters. He stumbles in from left after the last field hand has left. He falls down on his knees and cries as* MARTIN *turns and frowns at him.*)

MARTIN: Who you?

BILLY: I is Billy, sah. Don't you know poor, stupid, idiot Billy, sah?

MARTIN: Don't call me "sah." Just "mas" that's all, just plain "mas," Mas Martin. I ain't nobody's sah.

BILLY: Yes, sah. I mean mas, sah.

(BILLY *remains agitated and begins to cry.* MARTIN *reluctantly goes to him and rubs him on the head soothingly, with an effect of strong hands.*)

MARTIN: Why you so fretful, boy?

BILLY (*still on his knees and very nervous, almost as if his life depended on it*): 'Cause they been chasin' me and chasin' me an' I ain't done nothin'. Honest I ain't. (*He begins to cry.*) Nothin', I ain't done nothin'.

MARTIN: Hold on now. Who been chasin' you and where? We don't allow them things to go on on Prosser's.

BILLY (*looks up and seems to take courage at* MARTIN'*s words*): I was comin' from town like her told me. (*He speaks quickly and agitatedly.*) When I heard 'em and I begin to sweat and shiver all over. An' I started runnin' for my life. But seems like the more I run, the louder they got an' . . . an' . . .

MARTIN: Hold it, hold it. You done lost me, son. Who is they and who is her?

BILLY (*here he gets up*): Why my missus. Hers the one sent me to town. Her goin' make me free again. Her does it once a year. 'Course I comes right back, 'cause her don't mean it. And when I do, her laughs and says, "See, I knew it. Them darkies don't want to be free. They'd be lost like Jonah in the whale without'n white folks to take care of them." And I says, "Yes, Miss Matty," and goes on roun' to thu kitchen and gets an extra plate a rice for bein' sech a good boy.

MARTIN: Was there any men behind the dogs?

BILLY: Oh, yes, sah. Plenty mens. Some with guns. They

come from Sheppard's. I heard 'em say Jack Bowler is run off.

MARTIN (*becomes startled at this*): You sure?

BILLY: That's what they said. 'Course I wasn't takin' no chances. You know how white folks is. Once they get to huntin' one a we and they can't find the one they want they'll take anyone they can get.

MARTIN: You sure got something there, boy. Come on over here and let me wipe your face. You go around looking like that and nobody'll believe your missus ain't looking for you to whip. (*He sits on stump and wipes* BILLY *with his wet hand-kerchief.*) Does she really make it legal? Settin' you free, I mean.

BILLY: Oh, yes, sah. Her goes through the whole thing, lawyer an' all.

MARTIN: Then why don't you jus' up and take off?

BILLY: Why'd I do a thing like that?

MARTIN: Why? So's you could be your own man, that's why. Come when you like, go when you like, and be what you like.

BILLY (*laughs*): Lawd, Mas Martin, I can do that now. My missus she don't bother me none. I'se free as a bird, 'cep' when there's trouble roun' like now. But most everybody knows idiot Billy. If they gives me some sugar, then I make my face like a monkey. (*He does this.*) And hop aroun' like this. (*He does it.*) And they laugh and walk off.

MARTIN: But don't you know that freedom is a precious thing?

BILLY: But I told you, I ain't in chains. Now they got some blacks at my place what they never let out. (*He becomes furtive here.*) They keep them for special things. (*His eyes widen.*) If you know what I mean.

MARTIN: It's the way it makes you feel. Didn't you ever want to be your own master? Didn't you ever feel that nobody should have the power of life and death over you?

BILLY: Not exactly.

MARTIN: Not exactly! Why you ignorant little fool. Don't you want to be equal?

(BILLY *realizes that he is in disfavor and sulks.*)

MARTIN: Well? (*He shakes* BILLY *by the shoulders and* BILLY *cringes.*) Answer me, boy, 'fore I take a stick to you.

BILLY (*falls on his knees*): Oh, please, Mas Martin, have mu'cy please. I'd be lyin' to you if I said yes, and I know you don't want me to lie to you. I'd rather for them to cut out my tongue than for me to lie to you.

MARTIN: You been lyin' to your missus ever since you can remember, you little black ape. (*He turns from him.*)

BILLY (*pleading*): But that don't count, Mas Martin. We all got to lie to white folks. But lyin' to you, that'd be a sin.

MARTIN (*grabs* BILLY *by the collar and bends down to him*): Boy, havin' you alive is the worst sin I can think of. Havin' you in a black skin and not knowin' that slavery is the sin of the world is the worst sin I know. May God strike you dead, you're an abomination! (*He shakes him violently.*)

(GABRIEL *comes in from left, looking for* MARTIN.)

GABRIEL: Martin, what in the name of heaven are you doing?

(MARTIN *reluctantly pushes* BILLY *from him and moves right.* GABRIEL *comes forward and* MARTIN *turns to address him.* BILLY *is upstage, center.*)

MARTIN: You want to save niggers? Well, let me see you save this one. He's free already, only to him it don't mean nothin' excep' going back to the plantation and gettin' a extra plate of rice for bein' a good boy.

(BILLY *turns to* GABRIEL *and seems to feel immense guilt, although it's clear he doesn't know why.*)

GABRIEL: You don't save niggers by frightening them to death. What's he done?

MARTIN: I just told you.

GABRIEL: All you told me was that he acts the way he's been taught to act. If certain grown men who should know better are afraid of freedom, how can you expect a boy to be any better?

MARTIN: I don't know what you're talkin' about.

GABRIEL: Yeah, I bet you don't. What's your name, son?

BILLY: Billy, sah. Poor, idiot Billy.

MARTIN: Poor, idiot, stupid, black Billy.

GABRIEL: Let the foreman call him names if he wants to, but don't you do it. He'll always act like a slavey in front of white men if the only thing black men ever do for him is call him names.

MARTIN: As dumb as he is, it won't matter what you call him. (*To Billy.*) Show Gabriel your monkey act. Go on.

(BILLY *doesn't know what to do.*)

GABRIEL: You're a monkey act without even trying.

MARTIN: Why you gettin' all excited over this boy for?

GABRIEL: What's he want anyway?

MARTIN: He almost got skinned alive and the flesh hung out to dry 'fore they made walkin' shoes out of him.

GABRIEL: Norfolk toughs or plantation men?

MARTIN: Mosby Sheppard with a whole bunch behind him. Hunting Jack Bowler.

GABRIEL (*to* BILLY): You saw him?

BILLY: No, sah.

GABRIEL (*moves toward* BILLY *as if menacingly*): But you did see the men?

BILLY (*misinterprets* GABRIEL'*s intentions*): Lawd, sah. Have mu'cy, please have mu'cy.

GABRIEL: I'm not going to hurt you, boy. Just tell me what you saw. (*He grabs him.*)

BILLY: Yes, sah, I saw the mens. Plenty mens.

GABRIEL: White men?

BILLY: Yes, sah. White men and dogs. They beatin' the bush all right. He don't stand the chance of a cockroach in a chicken coop.

GABRIEL (*lets him go*): Which way are they headed?

BILLY: Look like they was comin' straight for here.

MARTIN: He'll have all a Sheppard's down on us. And if they catch you with him, that'll be the end of everything.

GABRIEL (*turns away*): You'd better get Billy back to his place and then find Big Henry.

MARTIN: Find Big Henry. What for?

GABRIEL: What do you think for?

MARTIN (*grumbling*): I ain't goin' out there, no, sah, not with the road full of nigger-huntin' whites. If I wanted to kill myself, I'd go. Humph. You young, you go.

GABRIEL: How am I going to hide Jack, and go to Big Henry's at the same time? Huh. Just tell me that.

MARTIN: What do you need Big Henry for? Just hide Jack till in the morning and then let him go for himself. He's young too.

GABRIEL: I might just as well turn him over to Sheppard now. If he is coming here, then we've got to get him on the underground tonight.

MARTIN: Well, if I do have to go out there, I sure ain't takin' him along. A stupid idiot boy who don't even want to be free.

GABRIEL: You might need him as an excuse for being on the road so late. Say he got lost or something and you're taking him home.

MARTIN: You mean I got to go all the way to Hargis and then turn around and go back to Big Henry's. No, sah. You find somebody else. I ain't fixin' to die yet, not for no idiot boy, or no Jack Bowler, no, sah.

GABRIEL: All right, don't go. You stay here and keep Billy with you. And if Jack comes before I get back, hide him in the old water shed. I'll go to Big Henry's.

MARTIN: Hide him. Me! All by myself. Nooo. Supposin' they catch me. You heard what he said. Nooo. I ain't goin' let Sheppard's dogs tear me into little pieces on account of no Jack Bowler who I don't even like anyway. Nooooo.

GABRIEL (*in desperation turns to* BILLY): Billy!

BILLY: Sah.

GABRIEL (*harshly*): Do you want to go back out there now?

BILLY: Sah?

GABRIEL: Come on, boy, answer me. Do you want to go back on the road now with all those men and their dogs out there?

(BILLY *is silent.*)

GABRIEL: If I told you it was important, Billy, not just because you'd be helping to save somebody you don't even know, but because you'd be helping to save a whole lot of other people too; and if I asked you to do it for me, Billy, you would, wouldn't you?

BILLY: You mean I'd be helpin' to make other mens free like me? Is that what I'd be doin', Mas Gabe?

GABRIEL: Something like that, Billy, yes.

BILLY (*grandly*): Oh, yes, sah. Then I'd be glad to do it. (*He puts on his cap, twisting it on his head.*) Yes, sah.

GABRIEL (*to* MARTIN): If you're still afraid, you've got Billy to take you and Big Henry to bring you back.

MARTIN: Did I say I was afraid, huh? Did I say that? I jus' said I didn't want to get killed, that's all. You don't have to try and shame me in front a this idiot boy, jus' because I got sense enough to know that niggers ain't got no business aroun' white folks when they get they blood up.

BILLY: Ain't no shame, Mas Martin. Even my missus don't like to go out by herself at night.

GABRIEL: Shhhhhhh. I hear someone coming. (*He goes left and they stand still and follow him with their eyes. He returns, having seen no one.*) Now what were you saying about not being afraid?

MARTIN: I said it. I said I wasn't afraid. I jus' . . .

GABRIEL (*pushes him right*): Good. With all that courage you should be back before you leave.

MARTIN (*hesitates*): Gabriel, please let me wait till later, then maybe we can both go together.

GABRIEL: Martin, stop it. What do you want me to do, treat you like Charlie's favorite houseboy? What's all the planning for? Why bother with anything? Why risk our lives and Nanny's life and Mary's and everybody else's if you can't even do this?

How are you going to fight, Martin, if you're even afraid to hide?

BILLY: I'se goin' with you, Mas Martin.

MARTIN (*gives* GABRIEL *a last pleading look, then turns to* BILLY): Well, come on then and stop hanging' back, you idiot boy.

(*They exit.*)

(GABRIEL *stands center stage for a half minute. Then* LUCY *comes in from right. She is a woman in her early forties, well preserved, but showing her age in her face. Her hands are thin and she is a little pale. But she has bearing and a wistful way about her. She is not without sexual appeal, although it's beginning to go. These are her last years of desire.*)

LUCY: Good evening, Gabe.

GABRIEL (*looks up and turns away*): Good evening, Miss Lucy.

LUCY: Are you alone?

GABRIEL: Yes, Miss Lucy, I'm alone, all alone.

LUCY: I've been looking for you everywhere. I was afraid you'd gone off somewhere and I wouldn't be able to find you. (*She goes to him and tries to touch him, but he moves off.*)

GABRIEL: Well, you've found me, Miss Lucy, now what do you want?

LUCY: Oh, nothing. I, I brought you a book. It came all the way from England on the Richmond packet. Charles got it for me. I haven't even read it yet. (*She hands it to him. He takes it reluctantly.* LUCY *waits for him to say something; he doesn't and she continues*): I want you to come tonight, Gabe.

GABRIEL: I can't.

LUCY: You've got to.

GABRIEL: I have to help an old woman whose two daughters were sold to 'Sippi.

LUCY: I'll help her. Tell me who she is and I'll fix everything up. And you can see her tomorrow. I'll fix that too, only come tonight.

GABRIEL: Nanny isn't feeling well.

LUCY: She looked fine when I saw her.

GABRIEL: You really want me to come tonight, huh?

LUCY: Oh, yes. I do

GABRIEL: Hmmm. All right.

LUCY: Oh, and come early. When I wait for you for a long time, I get lonely and it makes me sad. And I don't want to be sad when you come, I want to be happy.

GABRIEL (*changing*): And you should be happy. You might be frightened half out of your mind, but you should be happy.

LUCY: Oh, I am, I am. But . . . (*She tries to touch him.*) I hate the waiting. Sometimes you don't come at all and that's when it hurts the most, when you don't even come and I've waited all night for nothing. You've got to come tonight. Please, say you'll really come.

GABRIEL (*moves away*): When I think of the days I've spent pleasing massah and the nights I've spent pleasing you and all the beatings I've taken from the foreman in between, from all the foremen who've ever lived, and all those years, gone, spent, wasted.

LUCY: Sometimes I dream that you did come and when I wake, I'm not sure, because the dream was so real. But then I feel sick inside, and I know it didn't really happen, and I lock my door and I cry. Oh, do I cry.

GABRIEL: When I think of how the white man has made me hate myself and believe that he's everything that's good and wise and noble, then I know what being a slave really means.

LUCY: But you will come tonight, Gabe, won't you? You said you'd come.

GABRIEL (*throws the book away*): I'm tired of reading about all the things white men have done. The white man conquered the New World, the white man discovered the oceans, the white man invented this machine and that medicine and on and on, and all the while, black men did nothing but slave.

LUCY: Tonight, Gabe. You'll remember, won't you?

GABRIEL (*looking at her finally*): How could I not remember.

LUCY: And you'll come early, please.

GABRIEL: Just don't touch me; I'll come early and stay late if you just don't touch me.

LUCY: I won't.

GABRIEL: I'm sick to death of you. I can't even stand the smell of you. So don't touch me. Even when you're getting undressed don't touch me. I don't want to see your face until it's too black out for it to make a difference what you look like.

LUCY: Yes. But I remember when you used to go on and on because you enjoyed it so. I remember when you kissed me until my body was bruised from kisses. I remember when I had to beg you to stop because the pleasure turned to pain. (*She tries to touch him again.*)

GABRIEL: You do, do you? Well, remember this, Miss Lucy. You're old, old, old. I can't even think of anything new that you could do to me to ever get me excited again. It'll be a long night, I can tell you.

LUCY (*using her handkerchief*): I can make you happy again, I know I can.

GABRIEL: As long as I'm a slave nothing will ever make me happy.

LUCY: Then I'll free you. I promise. Just give me a year and I'll let you go.

GABRIEL: A year! Another year of you. (*He makes a hissing sound.*)

LUCY: But I've tried to be good to you.

GABRIEL: And you want to keep on trying, don't you?

LUCY: Yes.

GABRIEL: You don't want me whipped or sold or hanged, do you?

LUCY: No.

GABRIEL: Then listen, listen carefully. Mosby Sheppard is coming here tonight. He'll be looking for one of his slaves. And if he finds him, he'll also probably find that I've tried to help him. Which means he'll want Charles to give me to him to beat. And I want you to make sure that that doesn't happen. Let Charles beat me himself and if he has to, but don't let him give me to Sheppard, no matter what. You understand me, Lucy?

LUCY: Yes, yes, I understand.

GABRIEL: Make sure you do, or I won't be able to come tonight or any other night.

LUCY: Don't say any more, Gabe. I understand. Just give me a kiss before I go, please.

GABRIEL: Tonight, Lucy.

LUCY (*grabbing for him*): Gabe, please.

GABRIEL: I told you, later.

LUCY (*starts grabbing uncontrollably; unsuccessful, she stops, out of breath, and looks at him angrily*): I have to humble myself to Charles for you and you can't even kiss me.

GABRIEL (*agitatedly giving in*): All right, but hurry up.

(LUCY *grabs him and kisses hungrily, while he keeps his arms stiff at his sides.*)

GABRIEL (*forces her away as she resists*): That's enough.

(LUCY *finally relaxes, opens her eyes and runs off right.* GABRIEL *comes back left and sits on stump end, holds his head down and breathes heavily. He seems overwhelmed by his problems. He starts when he hears his name called in a loud whisper. He turns quickly and looks around. The voice calls to him again. It is* JACK BOWLER *who is offstage left.*)

GABRIEL: Jack? Is that you? (*He looks right.*)

JACK (*still offstage*): Over here, Gabe. (*He comes on, look-*

ing weary and hounded. He stumbles and stops. GABRIEL *moves to help him, but he waves him off, being very proud.*) No, I'm all right. Just out of breath. (*He turns to* GABRIEL, *not meaning to be cold.*) Gabe, it's good to see you. (*They embrace manfully, then he turns from him again.*)

GABRIEL: Are you sure you're all right?

JACK: Yeah. I'm tired, but it's more inside, in the soul, than it is in the body.

GABRIEL: I sent Martin to Big Henry Stimpson. We've got to get you out tonight. That boss a yours has everybody and everything beating the bushes looking for you. You're going North on the Underground.

JACK: Why am I going North? All the white men I ever want to see are right here in Virginia, I don't have to go North to find 'em.

GABRIEL: No, they're looking for you, remember? You're not looking for them.

JACK: And you, Gabe, who're you looking for, besides your old white lady?

(GABRIEL *takes a menacing step toward him.*)

JACK: Uh, uh. Not with this. (*He brandishes the knife.*) You can't trick ole Jack, not with this. Now I want to see the great black revolution that a certain head nigger has been preaching about to all the simple folk around here. (*He takes out the knife again.*)

GABRIEL: Give me that.

JACK (*enjoying the idea of holding him at bay*): Why don't you take it?

(GABRIEL *moves toward him.*)

JACK: Ahaaa! (*He goes into a crouch.*)

GABRIEL (*about to do the same, he steps and straightens up*): You fool! Don't you realize that they're after you?

JACK: Then help me to fight them.

GABRIEL: You're not fighting anybody, not tonight anyway.

JACK: The hell I'm not. I'm gonna kill me a whole lot a white men before I die and not you or anybody else is gonna stop me.

GABRIEL: You should've thought of that before. Now is too late to want to fight. I've got too many men depending on me to help you. Even if I didn't have something else planned, helping you fight a few white men with a knife would be like killing the foreman and then running off to hide.

JACK: At least he'd be dead.

GABRIEL: And so will you when they find you. And they're going to find you, if all we do is stand here and talk.

JACK: Then let me join up. Hide me out till you're ready. Anything, but use me, Gabe, don't just let me die for nothing. No more cotton, no more, not for this nigger.

GABRIEL: There won't be any more cotton where you're going.

JACK: But I'm not afraid. Why do I have to be the one to run, when I'm not afraid?

GABRIEL: It's not because you're afraid, it's to help us. It's to keep things quiet.

JACK: And who ever helped ole Jack, who ever cared about him?

GABRIEL: I did, but there are house slaves and field hands and thousands of others who I have to care about too.

JACK (*goes away from* GABRIEL): I don't care nothing about anybody but me. The only thing I know is, you want me to run and I'm not going to. I'm staying, and I'm staying for me, me, not for you or a whole lot a people I don't even know, but for me. I've spent my whole life doing things just to keep the white man from killing me. For once let me stand up to them. I want them to know that Jack Bowler wasn't one of their wide-eyed shaking little houseboys, but a man, you hear me, a man.

GABRIEL: And if we stood and fought together, just the two of us, how many men do you think we'd kill?

JACK: Oh, if we were together we'd slaughter a whole army. We'd go down but we'd die proud.

GABRIEL: Die proud. And what good is that to anybody? The idea is to win, not to die proud.

JACK: You're not talking to the boys in the bush, Gabe, you know you can't win against all of 'em.

GABRIEL: Maybe you think I can't win, but I don't. When I strike I'll be like death in church, unlooked-for but terrible to behold. Come on, it's getting late. I'm going to sneak you out with the evening prayers.

JACK (*holding back*): How are you going to do it, Gabe?

GABRIEL: All the plans have been made. We decided where we'll strike first, how many men we'll need, how we'll do it and where we'll meet. The signals have been arranged and once the rifles get here, we'll move.

JACK: And what about the rest of them? Are you sure they'll fight?

GABRIEL: There's more than just me in this, Jack. There's Big Henry and the boys from Norfolk and field hands from half the plantations in Henrico County.

JACK: And how are you going to teach field hands to act like soldiers?

GABRIEL: They'll be coming for their freedom, and if that doesn't make soldiers out of them, then nothing will.

(NANNY *comes in from right.*)

NANNY: Are you ready?

GABRIEL: Yes, we're ready.

JACK: Hi, Miss Nanny.

NANNY: Don't you say a word to me, you stupid idiot. If it were up to me, I'd let them hang you.

GABRIEL: All right.

NANNY: Are you going with him to Big Henry's?

GABRIEL: Yes.

NANNY: How long will you be gone?

GABRIEL: All night.

NANNY: But you can't. Suppose Charlie asks for you? You know how things get when there's a runaway loose. Besides, if that white captain comes with the guns tonight and you're not here to tell Martin what to do, he'll probably fall apart.

GABRIEL: Martin'll be all right if you show him a little confidence.

NANNY: Well, just be careful. You're all I've got in this stinking world.

GABRIEL: I will, don't worry.

NANNY (*changing*): What about her?

GABRIEL: What about her?

NANNY: You know what I mean. I saw her coming out here. You don't fool me.

GABRIEL: I'm not trying to fool you. I'm just trying to get him out of here before we all get caught and beat half out of our minds.

NANNY: Gabe, I don't want you sleeping with her now. I mean that.

(GABRIEL *doesn't answer.* NANNY *rushes to him and kisses him nervously and exits.* GABRIEL *responds without moving, but accepts the gesture sincerely.*)

JACK: With a sweet gal like that, what do you want with that old sow?

GABRIEL: Nothing, I'm doing it for you, Mas Jack. Just for you.

JACK: But there was a time when you used to do it just for yourself.

GABRIEL: That was a long, long time ago. Come on, let's go. (*The others from opening of scene all file in from right.*) Let's form a circle and pray. When I give the signal, we'll start

singing and move off the fields. Jack, get in there besides Joeby. (*They arrange themselves and* GABRIEL *gets in front of them.*) A great bolt of lightning will flash across the sky and open up the glory of the heavens to the children of sorrow. (*They all answer "Amen."*) Yes, Lord. Answer "Yes, Lord." (*They answer "Yes, Lord."* GABRIEL *starts them singing* "I'm gonna lay down all a my troubles when I get home." *They pick it up and turn to go out right when* MARTIN *and* BILLY *come in anxiously from left.*)

MARTIN: Gabe, they're here!

BILLY: That's right. The mens and the dogs.

(*Four white men come in with dogs on leashes and block both exits. They come from both sides. Then* CHARLES *comes in, followed by* MOSBY SHEPPARD.)

CHARLES: Gabriel, is it true that you have——

MOSBY (*spotting* JACK): That's him, that's the black ape!!

JACK (*takes a step forward*): I wish I was in hell!

END OF SCENE

Scene 2

Gabriel's Shack

(*The room is furnished cheaply and starkly. There is a small bed placed diagonally in the lower right corner. There are some wooden boxes for chairs, a bare table or two and calico curtains.* MARY *is center stage, rocking in an old-style rocker.* MARTIN *and* BILLY *are left, with* BILLY *on the floor at his feet.* NANNY *is right near the bed, standing.*)

MARY: Hmmmmm, Jesus. Hmmm, Jesus. Hmmmmmmmmm, Jeeeesus. Hmmmmmmmm, Jeeesus.

NANNY: Shut up. I've had enough of Jesus for one night.

(MARY *stops and sits quietly.*)

MARTIN (*looks angrily at* NANNY): That ain't no way to talk to your elders.

MARY: Man, shet your mouth. Now ain't the time for you to start any foolishness. My poor baby is frettin' herself to death, and for what, for a no-good worthless man, that's what.

MARTIN: Hmph. Miss Lucy sure don't think he's no good.

NANNY: No, and you don't either, because lying up with Miss Lucy is something big, right . . . pork chop!

MARTIN: Don't call me no pork chop. I'll whup you. I don't care if you is Gabriel's wife. I'd whup you if you was my mammy if you call me a pork chop.

NANNY: Pork chop!

MARTIN (*pretends to be uncontrollable and gets up with much fanfare, but he doesn't cross past* MARY): What! What! Billy, hold me, hold me 'fore I do something I'll be sorry for.

BILLY: Yes, sah, I'm holdin' you. (*He holds him.*)

MARY (*gets up and pushes* MARTIN *back to his box and then pushes him down on it*): I told you to shet your mouth, now shet it, 'fore I shet it for you. Got my poor baby frettin' herself to death. Pork chop. (*She goes back to her rocking chair center. There is a pause as* NANNY *remains removed and* MARTIN *pretends uncontrollable anger on the box.* MARY *starts humming again.*)

NANNY: To hell with Jesus, to hell with you, to hell with all of you.

MARY: Don't be frightened, honey. Mary'll take care a you if that no-count runs off and leaves you. You won't be alone, baby.

NANNY: You'll take care of me. You? How? You going to teach me how to cook so good that I'll always find a massah who'll be kind to me. Ha, ha, ha. He's a pork chop and you're a cotton field.

MARTIN: And what are you?

NANNY: I'm a black gal who wants some of what the white gal's got. I'm too young and too healthy to grow old and die just being Miss Lucy's maid.

MARY: You got them ideas in your head from all the lies he been tellin' you. If he was gonna free anybody, he wouldn't be climbin' into her bed to do it.

NANNY: So what! Let him. If he wants the old bitch that bad, let him. I never knew till now that a good colored gal couldn't satisfy her man more than any dried-up old white bitch. But if he needs it, let him. So long as I don't have to die in this stinking place, let him. Whatever kind of revolution he's planning, so long as it includes me, then let him. And if I have to share a little bit of him in the bargain, that's all right too. Who knows, Nanny may want to do some sharing herself someday.

MARY: And supposin' he don't intend to include you in his so-called revolution?

NANNY: A woman's got to have faith, Mary, honey. Faith in her man or faith in herself, whichever way you want to look at it. At least that's what I keep telling myself.

MARY: Any woman who's fool enough to have faith in a man what's been with a white woman is in for a whole lot of misery. My man ran off and left me with his lyin' self just

because he heard there was white women in Canada what went with nigger men.

NANNY: Your man ran off and left you because you were a cook and you'll always be a cook.

MARY: Ain't no sin in feedin' people.

NANNY: No, ain't no sin. He was just tired a hog maw and greens, that's all.

MARTIN (*starts off loud*): And what's wrong with hog maw? (*He quiets down here.*) I eat 'em all the time.

NANNY: You'll eat anything that comes from a pig . . . pork chop.

MARTIN: You just wait till Gabriel gets here. You just wait.

MARY: You just as bad as she is. All either a you can do is wait for Gabriel. You might just as well wait for Jesus.

NANNY: Well, aren't you always praying to him. You mean you don't really expect an answer one of these days?

MARY: Everybody prays to Jesus, honey, that don't mean nothin'. But only a fool lives in the hope that he'll help you in this life.

NANNY: Mary, I know how much you hate men ever since your man run off and left you, but let's face it, honey, the only chance you and I have is Gabriel.

MARY: Chance for what, to be chained and whipped? I'm too old to start runnin' from dogs and hidin' in the bush.

MARTIN: Well I'm not. I'm gonna be free.

MARY: It ain't never going to be, I tell you. It ain't never going to happen. It's just going to be more misery in the land, more weepin' and moanin' and gnashin' of teeth. Ohhhh.

NANNY: Yeah, well, it's time we had a new way. I don't want any white man crawling over me with his wet clammy hands and his whiskey breath, his nose dilating and his eyes popping out. If there's a place on this earth where I can be the lady, then Gabriel is going to find it for me, or I'm going to find it for myself.

MARY: Ohhh, misery. That's all you gonna get, just plain misery. Ohhh.

MARTIN (*gets up*): Shhhh. He's coming. I can hear his walk. Now I don't want nobody to say nothin' to upset him. You hear me. (*He struts, feeling confident now that* GABRIEL *is here.*) Nobody!

(GABRIEL *comes in from left as they all watch.*)

MARTIN: You all right, Gabriel?

GABRIEL: Yes, I'm all right. (*He looks around.*) I see we have a gathering of the tribe. Is everyone here?

NANNY: Now they are.

GABRIEL: Well, what has the council decided?

MARTIN: Nothin', Gabr'el, they ain't said nothin'.

MARY: Who ain't said nothin'? If you call talkin' about lust and deceit and the sins of the flesh talkin' about nothin' then we ain't said nothin'. If you call preachin' the gospel and then leadin' those who trust you to hell nothin' then we ain't said nothin', no. If you call what happened to Jack Bowler nothin', then you right, nothin', that's what we said, we said nothin'.

GABRIEL: Did they cut him down yet?

MARTIN: No, he's still up there.

GABRIEL: Did they drag it out?

MARY: Don't matter if they dragged it out or if they didn't. He's still dead. And all your speechfyin' can't do nothin' 'bout that.

GABRIEL: Tell it to me, Martin.

MARY: What for, so's you can cry over him now, when it's too late?

GABRIEL: Martin.

MARTIN: Yes, he's still up there. They took him back to Sheppard's and beat him. And he cursed you and spit in their mouths. They kicked him to the ground and he said their mammies were whores. They told him to promise he'd be good and he laughed. He laughed so loud we thought he was laughing because he was in pain. Then they said they'd all share the cost and they put a rope around him. When they told him he had one last chance, he said it was a lie, that his best friend already took his last chance from him. So they jerked the rope up real tight and kept jerking it till the bones snapped and the blood began to pop out and come down his shirt and splatter on the ground. He didn't seem to bleed too long though, but he sure was dead.

GABRIEL: And Big Henry?

MARTIN: He said he'll be here tonight with something for you.

GABRIEL: Tonight!

MARTIN: Yeah.

GABRIEL: He's got them?

MARTIN: Yeah. Says he's bringing one with him.

MARY: Hmmm. Pain and misery.

GABRIEL: Tonight. If Big Henry comes tonight, I can be in Richmond in two days.

NANNY: Ha!

GABRIEL (*looks at her and then turns to* MARY): Mary, you'd better go to bed.

MARY (*starts rocking quickly*): You ain't getting rid a me.

No, suh. I'm not moving from this chair till I'm ready to, no suh.

GABRIEL: It'll be daybreak in a couple of hours. And if you don't want to go to sleep, do it in your own room because I do. I'm tired.

NANNY: You mean Miss Lucy didn't give you any rest at all. Good God, honey. Keep that up and she'll start inviting people over just to see her prize stud in motion. I mean you must be a hell of a sight, sweating over her for all those hours.

GABRIEL: Don't start anything that I'm going to have to finish.

NANNY: Oh, no. You've finished everything you can for one night. It wouldn't be right to ask you to finish anything else.

MARY: They all alike, all of 'em. Once they been with a white woman they're no good, no more. He ain't goin' nowhere. If you believe him, you're a fool. I'm the one what's responsible for you and I say don't you listen to him. I'm telling you before he even opens his mouth not to listen to a word he says. When your mammy died she made me swear I'd take care of you. And I told her—— (GABRIEL *cuts her off*.)

GABRIEL (*bangs on the table*): Shut up. Just shut your mouth. If I have to listen to her, I'm sure as hell not going to let you moan and groan about her dead mammy too. (*There is a pause*.) You got anything else to say to me, Miss Nanny? If we have to have the confessions of a slave before I can get some sleep, then the sooner we get it over with the better.

NANNY: No, Mas Gabe. I got nothing to say to you, nothing at all. You've had your fun and now you've come back to the arms of your ever-loving wife, just like the dutiful husband you are. I'm glad just to see you. For all I know, you might have told Miss Lucy to sell me to Georgia or something, so you wouldn't have to be bothered with my complaining anymore.

GABRIEL: Don't you understand. It all had to do with Jack.

NANNY: That's a lie. He was already dead.

GABRIEL: Right, but I wasn't.

NANNY: Too bad.

GABRIEL: Look, I had to worry about Sheppard, but not anymore. It's all over between me and "Miss" Lucy, for the final and last time.

NANNY: You mean now that Big Henry has the guns it's time to give her up. Well, ain't you the big black prince. How many nigger boys can say their missus was hot for 'em, but it's all over, it's time for bigger and better things.

GABRIEL (*moves to her*): All right. That's enough.

NANNY: Don't you touch me.

(GABRIEL *hesitates.*)

NANNY: Go on, hit me. Hit me, why don't you. I dare you to hit me!

(GABRIEL *withdraws.*)

NANNY: Hit me, you big, no-good thing, hit me! (*She comes at him.*)

(GABRIEL *turns and slaps her against the bed. She falls on it.*)

NANNY: Is that all you can do? Box me around after you've been with her all night, and everybody knowing about it and laughing at me. Is that all you can do? You stay away from me, that's all. Stay far away. I don't want you to touch me, tonight or ever. You've got her smell all over you and if you come near me I'll kill you, so help me, I'll kill you.

GABRIEL (*bending over her and holding her*): What the hell do you want from me? (*He shakes her violently.*) Just tell me that. (*He lets her go and moves away.*)

NANNY: Nothing. There's nothing you can do for me, black boy. The next time I want anything I'll go to a white man for it. He'll do a better job. He's better at everything anyway.

GABRIEL: You can't hurt me, you can only hurt yourself.

NANNY: Because you haven't got any feelings, that's why. I have to lie awake night after night wondering what will happen next. When you'll come back or if you'll come back. You're a whore, a dirty, black whore. I don't know who I hate worse, them or you. Go on, beat me. The bad food and the bad feet that come from standing all day and the bad smell that you can't wash off because you sweat till the sun goes down are no worse than the bad nigger who can't do a thing for his woman but beat her.

GABRIEL: We're all dirty, black whores together. And some of us never even get into the bed because we're too ugly. But I'm going to change all that, Miss Nanny. Little black Gabe is going to change it. I'm going to make black right and white the worst thing a man could be. But I'm not doing it just for me. I'm doing it because the slave boy is going to be proud of his Mary and proud of his Martin and proud of his Nanny. I'm doing it because I can't hold my head up as long as we're the scum of the world, and so I'm doing it for me too, but not just for me.

NANNY: Then do it, for God's sake. Do it and get it over with.

GABRIEL: Martin, you'd better wait for Big Henry down by

the back gate tonight to make sure he gets here without any trouble.

MARTIN: Yeah, sure, Gabe. You want me to go now?

(GABRIEL *nods affectionately at him.*)

MARTIN: Awright, Gabe. Come on, Billy. (*They exit left.*)

NANNY (*to* MARY *first*): Hmph.

GABRIEL: Hmph, what?

NANNY: That trembling old scared-out-of-his-mind fright-ened-half-to-death white man's nigger will turn us all over to Mas Charlie or any other massah, first sign of trouble.

GABRIEL: You're talking about my brother.

NANNY: I'm talking about a slave. I'm talking about a no-good cotton head who'll never be anything else in this life but what he is.

GABRIEL: He's the one who believed in me before anybody else believed: you, her, or Big Henry. He gave me a brother's love, and my faith in him is part of my faith in myself. He's what's left of all that I've come from.

MARY: Which wasn't much to begin with.

GABRIEL: He'll be strong. As long as he doesn't get mixed up, he'll be strong. I know he will. The guns are here and Miss Lucy, old Miss Lucy will keep them off me for one more day at least. I've made certain of that. It's all falling into place, it's all happening. Just as surely as foremen whip field hands, it's happening. Nothing can stop it, nothing will stop it. And he'll be strong, I know he'll be strong.

END OF SCENE

Scene 3

The Prosser Living Room

(*The room is elegantly furnished in the fashion of the period. The only exit needed is from the left. There is a large window rear right, and a table with whiskey on it, also right. As scene opens,* LUCY *is seated right and* CHARLES *is left, standing. He goes to window and looks out, then he returns front stage.*)

CHARLES: All these years I've lived in peace on my land. There've been occasional beatings, but I've never been a part of a slave killing until now. The families have never been broken up, I've never sold the slave children, or permitted the women to be mistreated, and now this, all of this, all at once. First Mosby's runaway gets caught on my place, and who turns out to be aiding him in his escape? Gabriel, my Gabriel, whom I've trusted and thought so well of all these years.

LUCY: When is Mosby coming?

CHARLES: I expect him any minute.

LUCY: What're you going to do?

CHARLES: I don't know. I honestly don't know.

LUCY: Have you talked to Gabriel?

CHARLES: If he has anything to say to me, let him come to me and say it. I've always been as fair with him as I would be with my own son. He's been like a son. But to harbor a renegade Negro on my land. I can't understand how he could've been so ungrateful, after all I've done for him, all these years. Letting him learn to read and write, allowing him to take long trips to Richmond and Norfolk on plantation business, things that no other slave has ever been allowed to do, not in Virginia anyway.

LUCY: Charles, may I have a little bourbon, before anyone comes I mean.

CHARLES: It's not even mid-day, Lucy. You can't be serious.

LUCY: I'm just a little upset, that's all. And that uncouth Mosby will upset me even more.

CHARLES: Then go to your room, my dear. There's no reason why you should listen to his redneck vews on how to treat slaves.

LUCY: But I want to, dear. It isn't fair to leave everything to you all the time.

CHARLES: My brave little girl. (*He goes to her and pats her.*)

LUCY: Just a little with some water.

CHARLES (*goes to table and pours from decanter*): Some ice?

LUCY: Just a little.

CHARLES (*goes left with glass*): Mary. (*He comes forward and hands glass to* LUCY.)

(LUCY *watches him, and as he goes back to call* MARY *again, she gulps drink down and moves quickly to decanter and pours another before he gets far left.*)

CHARLES: Mary. I always have to call twice to get anyone around here.

MARY (*from wings*): Coming, sah. (*She comes in with hands in her apron.*)

(LUCY *is standing right and* CHARLES *comes back, center.*)

CHARLES: Some ice, please, Mary.

MARY: Ice?

CHARLES: Yes, ice.

MARY: What do you want ice for, Mas Charles?

CHARLES: Miss Lucy needs some ice for her drink.

MARY: So early in the morning?

CHARLES: Just get the ice, Mary, that's all.

MARY: Yes, sah. (*She exits.*)

LUCY: Mosby doesn't understand us, Charles, the way we live, how we treat our slaves.

CHARLES: Yes, well he's the newcomer, so it's up to him to change, not us. I'm not going to let him bring his Georgia ways into Virginia, at least not onto Prosser land.

LUCY: But you went along with the hanging.

CHARLES: What else could I do? After all, it was his slave.

LUCY: Then why did you agree to help pay him back for the cost?

CHARLES: Because if we show a common front, then any other slaves who get the same idea will be too frightened to try it.

LUCY: But think of all the money it could cost.

CHARLES: It won't cost me any more money, not again. I wouldn't have done it this time, but that fellow, that Jack was so arrogant. The things he said, the way he laughed at us, and spit at us. The strange thing was that in some twisted way he seemed to blame Gabriel for what happened to him.

LUCY: Are you sure it was Gabe that he was talking about?

CHARLES: What did you say?

LUCY: I said are you sure he was talking about Gabriel?

CHARLES: No, you didn't, you said, "Gabe."

LUCY: Did I?

CHARLES: Yes. You've never called him that before. You aren't getting overly fond of him, are you?

LUCY: What do you mean?

CHARLES: Oh, dear, please. I'm not accusing you of anything, my sweet. It's just that, well, we've never had any children, and you are such a good-natured girl.

LUCY: He's a little old to be thought of as a son, don't you think?

CHARLES: Yes, I suppose so.

MARY (*comes in with ice*): I brought you a tall glass of water, Miss Lucy. Maybe if you drink it, you won't want no hard liquor, leastways not before lunch.

(LUCY *takes the ice from the glass and puts it in her drink and gulps it down in one swallow.*)

MARY (*aghast*): Well, I sure know you don't want nothin' to eat after that.

CHARLES: Just fix lunch the way you always do, Mary. And thank you. (*He ushers her out.*)

MARY (*as she exits*): Humph.

(LUCY *takes another drink from the bottle.*)

CHARLES: Lucy, what's happening to you?

LUCY (*her hands trembling*): I, I don't know, Charles. I feel sick, suddenly.

CHARLES: Don't drink any more of that. (*He tries to take the glass from her, but she holds on.*)

LUCY: I'll be all right. (*She sits and composes herself.*) Well, what are we going to tell Mosby when he comes?

CHARLES (*looks anxiously at her and then returns to his thoughts*): I think I'll send for Gabriel after all, and see what he has to say for himself.

(LUCY *gulps the whiskey down at this and seems to shudder a little.*)

CHARLES (*doesn't know what to make of it; goes left again and calls*): Mary. (*He comes back.*) I'm worried about you, Lucy. This drinking and, I don't know, you haven't been yourself lately. You haven't been yourself for a long time, a long, long time. And I don't know what it means. I think you ought to go to Charleston for a rest. You haven't been home for quite a while.

LUCY: The one place where I couldn't rest is Charleston.

CHARLES: That Mary. (*He goes left again.*) Mary!

MARY (*answers offstage*): Sah?

CHARLES (*angrily*): Come here.

(MARY *comes in, out of breath.*)

CHARLES: Mary, why do I have to call twice before you answer me?

MARY: Because I don't hear you till the second time, sah.

CHARLES: How do you know it's the second time if you didn't hear the first?

MARY: Because you just said it was the second time. You said it, said you called me twice.

CHARLES: Hmmmmm. Well, send Gabriel in here.

MARY (*looks at* LUCY): Lawd, sah. I don't know where he is.

CHARLES: He's supposed to be in his shack.

MARY: But I'm fixin' lunch. I can't leave my cookin' to go looking for nobody.

CHARLES: Then send Nanny or Martin. What's the matter with you anyway?

MARY: Nuthin', sah. I just ain't gettin' mixed up in nuthin', that's all.

CHARLES: What do you mean?

MARY: Nuthin', sah. I don't mean nuthin'.

LUCY: Everyone's afraid that you might let Mosby do to

Gabe, Gabriel what he did to his own slave. And who knows where it would end?

CHARLES: Is that what you think, Mary?

MARY: Sah?

CHARLES: Well, I'll put a stop to that right now. No one is going to get killed. No one. Do you understand me?

MARY: Yes, sah.

LUCY (*quickly*): What about a beating?

CHARLES: No one's going to be beaten either.

(LUCY *and* MARY *exchange meaningful glances.* CHARLES *doesn't see it.*)

CHARLES: Does that satisfy you?

MARY: Oh, yes, sah. Only I don't know if Gabr'el is in his shack. So I'll just go on back to my kitchen and you can send somebody else for him. (*She is about to leave when* CHARLES *speaks. She stops.*)

CHARLES: Mary, you come back here. If Gabriel isn't in his room, then there very well may be a beating and worse than a beating. I gave him very specific orders and he's in enough trouble already.

LUCY: He couldn't have gone anywhere. I'm sure he's around, helping the foreman or something.

CHARLES: He might be around, but he's not helping the foreman, not him. But wherever he is, if you don't find him and quick, there'll be trouble.

MARY (*a little frightened*): I'm goin', sah. I'll find him.

CHARLES: Then hurry up.

(MARY *exits.*)

CHARLES: I'm not going to take any insubordination from him. He's had all the understanding he's going to get from me.

LUCY: Charles, control yourself. Remember you've got Mosby to face.

CHARLES: You seem to think Mosby has an extraordinary influence over me. Well, he doesn't. (*As he's talking, she takes another drink and gulps it down.*)

CHARLES (*so agitated, he just keeps talking*): This is Prosser land and it's been Prosser land for three generations, and no one is going to tell me what to do on it, no one.

(*Just then screams are heard outside.* NANNY *runs in, chased by* MOSBY, *with* MARY *panting as she comes in behind them.*)

CHARLES (*whirls*): What's the meaning of this?

(LUCY *takes another drink and staggers slightly.*)

NANNY (*center stage and breathless*): He tried to hold me down in my own bed when Mary came in and caught him.

MARY: That's right, Mas Charlie. He was in there all right, just like she said.

CHARLES: Well, Mosby?

MOSBY: I just wanted to check up on that buck a yours, Charlie. But looks like that won't be so easy to do, 'cause he ain't there. Fact is, he ain't nowhere at all. I looked high and low for him, and he just ain't here, Charlie, he just ain't here.

LUCY (*holding the bottle in one hand and her glass in the other*): Oh, no. He's gone.

END OF ACT I

ACT II

Scene 1

Brook Swamp

(*It's the dead of the night. There are several lamps that give an eerie glow. They are like smelting pots and are grouped around boxes of powder and stacks of rifles. A young Negro is nodding beside a log at right center. A low whistle is given offstage. He starts, grabs a rifle and looks around seemingly nervous. The whistle is given again. He cocks his rifle and returns the signal cautiously. There is an expectant pause, a rustling sound, and then* GABRIEL *and* BIG HENRY *enter from left. The young man,* WILLIE, *seems relieved and drops the rifle and breathes a sigh of relief. He is about to speak when* GABRIEL *signals him not to, crosses stage and looks right. He seems satisfied and then returns center.*)

GABRIEL: Everything all right, Willie?

WILLIE (*mimickingly*): Everything all right, Willie. I'll be damned if it is. I seen a thousand massahs behind every bush for hours. Everything all right, Willie. I'll never sleep in this life again, unless it's in some place far away from Virginia. When did you say we were gonna take Washington?

GABRIEL: After we take Richmond.

WILLIE: Well, let's get it over with, because everytime I look over here, I think maybe they're over there. And everytime I look over there, I think they done snuk up behind me here.

BIG HENRY: Yeah well, that's why we put you to guard the ammunition, Willie, because we know you're such a good man.

WILLIE: Then you know more'n I know, Big Henry.

BIG HENRY: I don't know why you're always carrying on,

trying to make Gabe think I got the shakingest black boy in the county for the most important job. Who was it poisoned a whole family on Sea Island, Georgia? Huh? Who was it pretended to be a runaway from a slave ship who couldn't speak English when he was caught one time down by the Stono River, and ended up being auctioned off in Norfolk for the third time in one month because he set fire to a schooner he was on when he heard it had changed course and set sail for New Orleans instead a going to South America, and then had to swim for miles before he got picked up by another slaver that put him right back where he started from? Who was it escaped from his massah in broad daylight in a bale of cotton and found himself on a coggle going to Mississippi before he could get the cotton out of his hair, and then drowned the driver the first time he tried to make him cross a stream?

GABRIEL: But how did he get from New Orleans to the ship that brought him back to Norfolk?

BIG HENRY: If I knew that do you think I'd be here now fooling around with you?

WILLIE: Yeah, but that was all in the daytime. I'm a different man when it's light out. But the only thing I know how to do when nature is a nigger is seek eternal rest. My pappy always said, "Son, never fight white folks at night, cause as black as you is, all you got to do is open your eyes and they'll spot you a mile off."

BIG HENRY: Yeah, well go seek some a that rest down by the bridge.

WILLIE: You mean I got to listen to them slimy things slippin' in the water and them bats flying around by myself all over again? You all sure do go through a whole lot a mess just to kill some white eyes. (*He exits with a rifle.*)

(GABRIEL *and* BIG HENRY *chuckle slightly.* GABRIEL *comes forward and* BIG HENRY *picks up a bag of the powder and a rifle and comes forward also. As he kneels on one knee and pours the powder into the rifle and packs it and sets his primer and cocks it,* GABRIEL, *looking away, begins to talk.*)

GABRIEL: We're a fantastic race of people, Big Henry. Look at a boy like that. Only nineteen or twenty and he's already ten times the man all his masters put together will ever be.

BIG HENRY (*on one knee, fixing the gun*): And still slaving.

GABRIEL: That's the hell of it. If there was any justice in this world, he'd have been freed a hundred times over.

BIG HENRY: And then some.

GABRIEL: But there is no justice, except what we make our-

selves. The black man was in his home safe, wishing for no man's country, but his own. And the red man was in his, strong warrior of the north, ruler of the plain.

BIG HENRY: And the white man came and took away both homes.

GABRIEL: And turned one into a home of his own and the other into a storehouse where he went to fill his bags with as much gold as he wanted, for as long as he wanted.

BIG HENRY: Black gold, moaning and dying in the back-waters of the world.

GABRIEL: Black gold that's more precious and more lasting than the gold of the mountains and the hills because it replenishes itself, recreates its own out of its limbs, to be used again in the marketplace so that they can grow fat and sleep well at night and find new ways to break soft young bones.

BIG HENRY: And cook sweet young flesh.

GABRIEL: Where's Martin? I want to get on with the killing, Big Henry, or be sold for a weak little bastard who was willing to live in my own filth rather than die trying to burn the evil out of me.

BIG HENRY: He'll be along soon.

GABRIEL: They'll all be along soon, all 2,000 of them. Men and boys and grandfathers. They'll come like rain to wash away the stink that's in my body, and the smell of unpicked cotton that's in my brain.

BIG HENRY: And their body and their brain.

GABRIEL: When I take care of me, I take care of them. When I strike the white bastard from my life, I strike for all of Africa that never struck for itself.

BIG HENRY: They fought the white man plenty in Africa.

GABRIEL: But they didn't drive him into the sea.

BIG HENRY: You might not drive him into the sea either. You might lose.

GABRIEL: What! Might lose! Me, the son of a used woman who didn't even know what man was doing it at what time, a dumb, toothless sack of flesh who in the end couldn't say anything to me, even when she was dying, except "You ain't gonna last long because you don't know how to shuffle your feet." Might lose. If I have to tear down the walls of every house myself, I'm going to destroy everything that they ever built with my sweat, my hands, my muscle, and my ME. All of me and all of you and all of all of us, all that we haven't stood for and don't know and can't remember and have never seen is all standing there in Richmond waiting for us, for you and for me.

BIG HENRY: Not all of it, Gabe, not all. I gave my little daughter to that wingy bastard, so's he'd let up on me and I'd have more time to get around to the Willies and the Billies. He could a had her anyway, but it was easier for him if she was only half objecting instead of turning completely cold. And there's no redemption for that, nor for your ma.

GABRIEL: You think about the past, the dead leaves of history. I see fires burning and I hear voices singing, "Free at last, oh, Lord I'm free at last." And I close my eyes and everywhere, for as far as I can imagine, the whole world is black, black people dancing and crying with joy, a light in their eyes and a smile on their faces that has never been there before. And if I stay in that dream too long, I swoon, because it's a whole new world, Big Henry, a whole new world that we've never allowed ourselves to even think about. And by tomorrow it will have already happened. To stand on these shores and look out to sea and feel the wet salt on your lips and not have your hands tied and your head hung low, that will be the magnificent moment.

BIG HENRY: All right, we'll talk about it in Richmond over tea.

GABRIEL: Served by little white boys whose fathers will be hanging from the nearest trees.

BIG HENRY: Yeah.

GABRIEL (*slaps his hand on his thigh*): Let's see that rifle.

(BIG HENRY *throws it across the stage. He catches it with his left hand and looks at it. He cocks it back and aims it into the air and brings it down. He turns and looks as if for something to shoot at.* BIG HENRY *becomes apprehensive.*)

GABRIEL: One shot into the cool night air to start the blood burning.

BIG HENRY: Somebody might hear it.

GABRIEL: I'm tired of holding back. There's been too much holding back already. This is the great breaking-out morning, Big Henry. This is the day of the hunt. (*He whirls and fires.*) Aha!

BIG HENRY (*moves quickly from side to side, looking at both exits, but there seems to be no one about*): At least Willie should've heard it.

GABRIEL: Willie knows more about trapping his prey than you think. If he did hear it, he's not going to come charging up here like a fool. He'll just set behind a rock and wait, like the black panther that he is.

BIG HENRY (*a little rattled*): There's just one thing I want to know. You aren't fixing to go crazy on me, are you?

GABRIEL: Just a little crazy, Big Henry, just a little. (*There is a brief flash of lightning. They both look up.*)

BIG HENRY: It's clouding up pretty fast.

GABRIEL: How can you tell, it's as black as your mammy's face up there.

BIG HENRY: I can hear, can't I?

GABRIEL: Yeah. We'd better set up the lines now. The one thing we don't want any of tonight is rain. (*They exit.*)

(MARTIN *and* BILLY *come on from left after a pause.* MARTIN *is tired from the walk. He is leaning heavily on* BILLY'*s shoulder.* BILLY *is walking according to* MARTIN'*s pace.*)

BILLY: Is this the place, Mas Martin?

MARTIN: Of course this is it. Don't it look like it?

BILLY: Oh, yes, say. Except for one thing.

MARTIN: What's that?

BILLY: I ain't never seen it before.

MARTIN (*goes to a box and sits, right, where* WILLIE *had been*): Whew! I'm sure tired.

BILLY: Well, you should be tired, Mas Martin, you done walked almost fifty miles already.

MARTIN: Boy, you sure is one for talkin' foolishness.

BILLY: Foolishness! Why I ain't never worked so hard in my life. I tell you it was fifty if it was a mile. What wid climbalin' over heeills and through all that bush and carryin' you half the time and . . .

MARTIN (*harshly*): Doin' what?

BILLY (*quickly becoming sheepish at the first sign of displeasure*): Nothin', sah, I ain't said nothin'.

MARTIN: Just because I allowed you the privilege of givin' me your shoulder to lean on a few times that don't mean I was really tired.

BILLY: No, suh, but you said you was.

MARTIN: I said I was what?

BILLY: Tired. You said, "Whew! I'm sure tired." And I said . . .

MARTIN: Don't you think I know what I said. You think I'm an idiot, like you?

BILLY: No, sah.

MARTIN: All right then, shut up, just shut up.

BILLY: Yes, sah. (*He slinks back a little.*)

MARTIN (*rubs his legs and wipes his neck with his handkerchief, mumbling to himself as he does so*): I got better things to do than waste my time talking to you. You don't even understand half a what I say anyhow. You better be glad I let you come with me. You hear me?

BILLY: Yes, sah.

MARTIN: You always talkin' about Gabr'el all the time, but he wasn't thinkin' about worryin' with you, was he?

BILLY: No, sah.

MARTIN (*mimickingly*): No, sah, yes, sah. Them lips sure do know how to make the same sounds all the time. (*He gets up and looks left.*) I wonder where he is anyhow. They should a all been here by now. I can't hardly see out there. It'll still be awhile fore it gets light, I reckon.

BILLY (*trying to help*): You want me to look so if I see him for you, Mas Martin?

MARTIN: There you go gettin' uppity again. Didn't your missus teach you how to act round people, once you is let out a your cage? (*He doesn't wait for an answer, but goes back to box and sits. He seems to be thinking.*) Billy, come here. (BILLY *hesitantly comes to him.*)

MARTIN: Come on, I ain't gonna hurt you, come on and sit down here. (BILLY, *more encouraged, sits by him on the ground.*) I wonder what it'll be like, when we're finally free and don't have to massah nobody or bow and grin all the time like some ole ape. 'Course certain types a persons will still have to show respect (*He looks at* BILLY *here.*) to certain other types a persons. You'll still call me "mas," won't you, Billy? When you're free, I mean?

BILLY: I'm free now and I calls you that. I calls everybody almost "mas." My missus her told me to always remember that them what's better than you must be called "mas" and "sah" and all them other titles.

MARTIN: Yeah, well never mind about what your missus said. You ain't going to have no more missus after this.

BILLY: No more missus? What's going to happen to her?

MARTIN: She'll most likely be dead, same as the rest of 'em.

BILLY: Hee, hee, you sure is one for funnin' me, Mas Martin.

MARTIN (*very seriously*): I ain't funnin' you. Gabr'el and Big Henry and them Norfolk niggers they goin' kill everything white in sight, right up to eyeballs and teeth.

BILLY: Oh, no, Mas Martin, you can't mean that. (*He gets up here.*) Oh, no. Kill my missus, what's been good to me all my life. Oh, no. I don't mind you bein' free, Mas Martin, like me, but I ain't gonna let nothin' nor nobody hurt my missus. (*He gets angry.*) Who you think taught me what I know 'bout how to act and talk. Who you think gave me things like my clothes and this hat. (*He takes out a torn and battered old cap and puts it on.*) To wear when it's harvest time and

197

they needs extra hands in the fields? (*He talks to himself.*) Oh, no. Not my missus. My mammy'd never fuhgive me if I let you do that. The last thing she said foh she died, she said, "Billy, we's white folks' niggers. The white folks give us everything we got, everything. If it wasn't for them we'd a died a hunger in the winter a '88. 'Cause we didn't belong to nobody then. We was just like straws in the wind and Miss Matty took us in and claimed us for herself, and that's how come we's alive today. For as long as you live, Billy, if you don't remember anything else in life, remember this: You can't live without white folks." That's what she told me, and she was my mammy, Mas Martin!

MARTIN: I know. Sometimes I get frightened myself when I think on it. Me free like them. Its a powerful thing to think about I tell you. And it 'bout scares me to death. 'Course I don't let Gabriel know. That's why Mary and Nanny treat me the way they do, because they know, but he doesn't. (*Here he gets up.*) Everybody knows but him.

BILLY: How come he don't know?

MARTIN: Because I don't let him know. I pretend soon as I'm around him. The night they were chasin' Jack Bowler and I didn't want to go find Big Henry, he thought it was on account a the dark. But it was them. Them. I been scared a them all my life. They've done some terrible things to me, Billy, terrible, terrible things, way back before he was born, when we didn't belong to Prosser's.

BILLY (*sympathetically*): Don't worry, Mas Martin. Everything's going to be all right. My missus'll take care of us. I know she will.

(GABRIEL *has come quietly back with a rifle in his hand and stands at right entrance, unseen by them.*)

MARTIN (*grabs* BILLY'*s mouth*): Shhhh. Don't talk like that, somebody might hear you. (*He looks left.*) If he ever know. Oh, Lord, deliver me. I don't wanna fight nobody! (*He is wailing at this point.*) I can't fight nobody. I'm too scared. I been scared all my life. Oh, oh, a gun. Billy, go and get me one a them rifles. Maybe if I was to wound myself in the leg, he'd let me stay behind. Billy, you got to help me. Please, Billy, please.

BILLY (*not moving and looking right*): Yes, Mas Martin, 'course I'll help you.

MARTIN: Don't let him find out, Billy. Whatever you do.

(*As he is about to turn to get the rifle,* BILLY *sees* GABRIEL *over* MARTIN'*s shoulder, as* MARTIN *continues to hold tena-*

ciously onto him. His mouth hangs open, as he feels all of
MARTIN'*s fear himself.*)

MARTIN: What's the matter? What you lookin' at? (MARTIN
is afraid to turn around at this point.) Billy, answer me!
(*There is a slight pause.*) Gabe? (*He says it as a question,
still not looking around.*) Is that you, Gabe? Billy, is it him?
(*He is on the verge of terrifying himself by now.*)

GABRIEL (*comes all the way forward*): Yes, sah, it's me,
sah.

MARTIN (*his head bowed down to his knees, reaches out for*
BILLY *as latter backs away to the left;* GABRIEL *stands over
him in thorough disgust.*) Billy, where'd you go, Billy.

(BILLY *is too upset to talk, he just stands there, halfway
between exit and center stage.*)

MARTIN: BILLY! ! !

GABRIEL: Yes, sah, it's me, sah, you son of a raped slave,
you dirty black sambo. It's me! Look at him, Billy, look at
your massah. Your nigger massah, head down in the ground
where it's always been. (*He comes to him and throws him
down and puts his foot on his neck.*) Go on, cry for mercy.
Let me hear you beg for it. (*He presses his foot down and*
MARTIN *gives a gagging sound of pain.*)

BILLY (*rushes forward and goes on his knees*): Please, Mas
Gabe, please don't kill him. Please don't. He don't mean no
wrong. I know he don't. He's good to me and he loves you.
More'n anything in the world, he loves and respects you, Mas
Gabe.

GABRIEL: Not him. The only thing he loves is his stinking
butt, and he'd sell anybody or anything to save it. He'd sell
you and me and the whole damn lot of us.

BILLY (*pulling on* GABRIEL): Please don't, Mas Gabe,
please don't.

GABRIEL (*in throwing* BILLY *off, he accidentally hits him
with the rifle. When he sees* BILLY *fall, apparently hurt, he is
sorry and relents by moving off* MARTIN *and throwing away
the rifle*): All right, then, get up, you sniveling, crawling
scum, you scum of the earth. Why don't you get up?

MARTIN (*gets up, wipes his eyes with his sleeve and goes to
the box again; he still hasn't looked at* GABRIEL): Billy.

GABRIEL (*comes forward quickly*): No, you don't. Don't
touch him, Billy. He's got to deal with me tonight. If it's the
last night on earth for either of us, he's going to have to face
me, me. You hear me, Mas Martin? You hear me, sah, you
dirty, ugly, filthy sah. (*He grabs him and slaps him several
times quickly.* BILLY *rushes over.*)

199

BILLY: Please, Mas Gabe, please don't beat him, please don't. I'm beggin' you, sah.

GABRIEL (*lets* MARTIN *drop*): He's not good enough for you to worry about, Billy. You're an innocent boy who's been robbed of his mind. (*He grabs* BILLY *and holds him at a distance.*) They've turned you into a serving spoon, Billy, but you're still too good for him. You're all of us, all of us in chains. How many hours a day do you sit in one spot chasing flies from your missus?

BILLY: 'Bout six, I reckon.

GABRIEL: For how many days?

BILLY: Eight days a week, 'cep' when I gets a day off.

GABRIEL: For how many years?

BILLY: For as long as I can remember.

GABRIEL: And he's the one who's going to keep you there. Look at him, take a good look. (*He grabs* MARTIN *by the hair and turns his face up.*) At what a slavey's face is like when it's too late to save him.

BILLY: But he said he was goin' kill my missus.

GABRIEL: He said a lot of things for a long time, but he's never meant one of them.

BILLY: You mean he ain't goin' to kill her?

GABRIEL: If your missus has to die, Billy, it will be so we can live.

BILLY: But we's livin' now and she ain't dead.

MARTIN: You got the poor boy confused. He don't understand all them things you said to him. I don't understand half a what you saying myself, nobody does. You just talking to yourself, Gabr'el. All these years you just been talking to yourself. Ain't no niggers goin' fight white men what got cannon and horses and uniforms and we in bare feet, half a us not even knowing how to fire one of them things. (*He turns on him.*) You ain't goin' no place I tell you. I don't care if you do kill me. Go on. Won't make no difference nohow. Inside I've done all the suffering a man can do. I can't do no more, Gabr'el. There just ain't no more feeling left.

GABRIEL: You should have lied just a little while longer. The men are coming, listen. This is the judgment for slave master and pork chops. After I've taken the world, I'll dig you a hole and you can crawl into it and hide forever. Now get away from me before I kill you.

(MARTIN *is about to go when the others come in from both sides.*)

BIG HENRY: It's gettin worse, Gabe, we best to get started.

GABRIEL: We have started. We've started to walk through

hell. (*Thunder and lightning are heard as the men begin now to come in more rapidly. He turns to them.*) Soldiers of the black army, are we ready? (*All the men raise their arms, one arm, and shout:* "YES.") I am Gabriel, the son of a slave, who tonight will fill his hands with death—black death, galloping swift and furious through white Virginia to lay waste all the silk and linen that good brown sweat ever made. Who will we kill?

THE MEN: We'll kill them all.

GABRIEL: When will we stop?

THE MEN: Never, never.

GABRIEL: As long as there is a breath in this black breast, this black hand will crush out every bit of white life that God in an evil moment ever made.

THE MEN: AMEN!

GABRIEL: And again amen.

END OF SCENE

Scene 2

The Road to Richmond

(*The stage is darkened. This is no longer the swamp. Quick and sudden illumination from flashes of lightning and heavy rain come and go. The rain subsides, but the thunder continues.* GABRIEL *comes in, worried, from the right, followed by* BIG HENRY *and some of the others.*)

GABRIEL (*stops left of center and suddenly whirls forward*): This damn rain. What can we do about the rain?

BIG HENRY: Nothing and we've lost a lot of men. Some wouldn't march anymore and some were drowned crossing the bridge at Willow Creek.

WILLIE (*runs in from right*): We can't find Martin. Him and that kid got cut off from the rest by a falling tree and nobody's seen 'em since.

GABRIEL: If he's dead, at least I know he tried. Even if it was just for me, before he died, he tried.

BIG HENRY: We got to do something quick, Gabe. The men are grumbling and the powder's all wet and the rifles are full of water and we still got a lot a miles ahead of us.

GABRIEL: Their powder is no good either and their rifles are full of water too. The same rain that's beating down on us is beating down on them—those dirty, white bastards.

BIG HENRY: But they're warm in bed, rested, and rain don't rust cannon and we ain't got none.

GABRIEL: Men, are we going to let a little rain stop us, just a little rain?

THE MEN (*not enthusiastically*): No.

GABRIEL: That doesn't sound like a rebellion, that sounds like a moan. Men, I say, men, is that the best you can do? Is that all the freedom you want, an idea that made you feel big for a few hours and then went limp from the first water that fell on it. Is that all you can do, hang your heads and give in to that whipped feeling?

BIG HENRY: Take it easy, Gabe. The men are with you. They just figure tonight isn't the right night, that's all.

GABRIEL: Any man who leaves me tonight leaves forever. If you can't face water, then how are you going to face steel? If you can't face whatever the world gives and still give in return, then when are you ever going to get for yourselves? (*He turns from them.*) This is Gabriel, the son of a slave, ready to die this night before he sees another sun with a chain around his heart. And I want to hear from all you sons a bitches . . . WHO'S WITH ME! ! ! !

THE MEN (*turn forward and shout*): ME, ME! !

GABRIEL: Then march on. I want to see the lights of Richmond with a rifle in my hand.

(*They turn to march left, as curtain comes down.*)

END OF SCENE

Scene 3

Sunrise at Highland Springs

(*The same weather as in Scene 2, only more of it. They are all onstage, lying down, except* GABRIEL, BIG HENRY, WILLIE, *and one or two others, who are kneeling. There is a strong wind. They can be seen only when the lightning flashes. Finally the elements subside. There is quiet from all of them, some moaning and sighing.*)

FIRST MAN (*jumps up on his knees*): Oh, Lord, deliver me. This is the judgment day for sure!

(GABRIEL *whirls around and hits him with his rifle butt. He sprawls on his back.*)

GABRIEL: Willie!

(WILLIE *springs on the man and plunges a knife into him. He dies loudly.*)

BIG HENRY (*turning and challenging them*): Who's next?

SECOND MAN: You can't scare me with that young boy. I eat his kind for breakfast. Now I'm with you, but only because I wanna be, not because anybody frightened me. Be-

cause the man who can do that ain't been born yet.

(*They all agree, saying,* "Yeah, that's right, yeah." *The wind picks up a bit.*)

GABRIEL: Willie, take a look.

WILLIE (*goes offstage to left and then comes back*): She's there all right, with the river stretched behind her. But by the time we climbed up about twenty ridges to get away from the flooding and chopped through all them uprooted trees and dodged all that falling rock, it'd be broad daylight.

BIG HENRY: He's right, Gabe. I can almost feel them roosters stirring already.

GABRIEL: Can we stand together now, no matter what? Have we finally proved that we're ready to make a fight of it until we win or lose? Can we go back to the dead life for one more long day and still not change our minds?

BIG HENRY: Yes, Gabe, only you've got to move fast. If we're going to get back to our places before any of us are missed, then we've got to start now.

(*They all get up and he goes among them, grasping their hands and arms. They answer reassuringly.*)

GABRIEL: We'll try again tomorrow. Each one who is here must pass the word to the others. The ones from Prosser's will help Big Henry and me to get the rifles and the powder back to Brook Swamp. Willie, I want you (*He holds him by the shoulders.*) to find Martin for me. No matter how long it takes, find him and bring him to me, or bring his body, to-night when the fires are burning.

WILLIE: You got him. (*He exists right, running.*)

GABRIEL: Tonight, Big Henry.

BIG HENRY: Tonight, Gabriel.

GABRIEL: Men, tonight.

ALL OF THEM: Tonight, Gabe, tonight.

(*They begin to exit methodically, but with an air of resolution that does not need a shout of affirmation. Then the curtain comes down.*)

END OF SCENE

Scene 4

*Somewhere Between Brook Swamp
and the Prosser Plantation*

(MOSBY SHEPPARD, CHARLES, *and five other white men come in. They are all armed, except* CHARLES.)

MOSBY: There's niggers around here somewhere, Charlie. I can smell 'em. Look sharp now, boys. I'm gonna catch me

a coon today. I know it. I got that special feeling. You know how you can tell about some things.

CHARLES: Just don't shoot him down before he has a chance to give himself up.

MOSBY: And miss all the fun of seein' him sweat while we heat the irons right before his eyes. Never in a million years, Charlie boy. But he's a strong one, and he don't frighten easy. We got to be real careful. You hear me, boys. I want you all on your toes now. If everything comes out all right and we get this bull, there's something extra in it for all a you.

(*They nod resolutely, but are obviously apprehensive.*)

CHARLES: You'd think he was one of yours, the way you're so fired up over catching him.

MOSBY: It sticks in my craw to know that one a them slimy things is actually runnin' loose somewhere. Ain't none of 'em supposed to even feel free, for even half an hour, not while I can do anything about it anyway.

CHARLES: Yes, well, you're not going to have much fun today, because I'm going to catch him, take him back and then dispose of him out of the state, and that's going to be that.

MOSBY: You mean you ain't even gonna give him a whippin'?

CHARLES: Why should I? For what reason?

MOSBY: Because he's a nigger, that's why. Since when did a white man ever need a better reason than that?

CHARLES: I need a better reason.

MOSBY: All right. He ran away, didn't he?

CHARLES: It seems that he did, but we can't be sure.

MOSBY: Then why'd you ask me and the boys to come along for, if you didn't . . .

CHARLES: I didn't ask you to do anything of the kind.

MOSBY: You asked, I offered, what's the difference. The point is, Charlie, it ain't right to let us come all the way out here for nothin'.

CHARLES: I told you I'd pay the boys for helping me, and you too, if you want me to.

MOSBY: It ain't the money, Charlie. I'll take care a that. I'm talkin' about seein' the bull bleed a little. You got to make him bleed, just a little, Charlie! (*He gets excited.*)

CHARLES: Absolutely not. If that's what you're after, we can call this whole thing off, right now.

MOSBY: Now take it easy, Charlie, just take it easy. Suppose, just suppose now, that he did try to run out on you. A good talkin', strong, readin' and writin' buck like that, the

pride of your plantation. What's he worth, $1,200 maybe, or even 15, huh?

CHARLES: I know men in South Carolina who'd pay $2,000 for him without a murmur.

MOSBY: Exactly! Now are you gonna tell me that if you find out that a slave worth $2,000 tries to run off, not only robbing you, but breaking the law to boot, the law, mind you, that he don't deserve a whippin'?

CHARLES (*reluctantly*): If he's run away and, as you say, broken the law, then I suppose he does deserve to be punished.

MOSBY: Now you're talkin', Charlie boy.

CHARLES: But no blood, Mosby, there must be no blood.

MOSBY: Believe me, Charlie, he won't bleed. I promise you he won't bleed. Aw right now, let's get ready. Check your guns. (*He takes out a brace of pistols from his belt that had been concealed as were other weapons by his coat, and checks them and puts them back. He takes a saber that is wrapped in oilskin and swishes it about, then puts it back. He takes out his dagger, looks at it, puts it back, checks his rifle and then takes a derringer from his boot.*) Ever seen one a these? Cute, ain't they?

CHARLES: Mosby, what in the name of heaven is all that for?

MOSBY: Jim, you take cover over there. I just wanna be ready, Charlie, that's all. Besides, you know how sneaky they are. Turn your back on 'em for just a wink and they'll slip right through your fingers. Try getting 'em to stand up to you like a man though, and they'll just hang their heads.

CHARLES: I've never seen Gabriel hang his head in all his life.

MOSBY: And that's why he's got to be beat, Charlie, 'cause deep down he ain't no different from all the rest of 'em. This is a hunt, and after we catch the animal we got to skin him.

(CHARLES *is about to protest when* JIM *at left signals them to be quiet.*)

JIM: Shhh. Quiet. I hear somethin'.

(*They all take concealed positions.* MARTIN *and* BILLY *come onstage as in Scene 1 of Act II.*)

MARTIN (*drops down on the stage*): I can't go no further, Billy. I'm 'bout to faint away, I'm so wore out. Look yonder and see if you see anything.

BILLY (*looks slightly to the right*): I don't see a thing, Mas Martin. I think we los'. Which way we headed anyhow, toward the mens or from the mens?

MARTIN: Right now, Billy, I don't care which way we go.

All I wanna do is sleep. I don't wanna do a blessed thing else but sleep. If they'd all only let me alone. Gabr'el and his bunch, the massah with his "do this" and "do that," the women folk with their naggin' 'bout you ain't a man, you're a pork chop. I don't wanna fight nobody.

BILLY: Well, if we can get back to my missus, Mas Martin, maybe you won't have to.

MARTIN: Shhh. Even the rocks have ears. We don't wanna say a thing we don't have to, Billy. You remember that.

BILLY: Yes, sah.

MARTIN (*gets up*): We better keep goin', les' we . . . Ohhhhhhh! (*He slumps back down, holding on to* BILLY's *hand.*) Ohhhh! Billy. Oh, mu'cy, mu'cy. Oh, oh. (*They have all come out with their guns trained on him and* BILLY. BILLY *steps back slightly, confused.*) Billy, don't leave me, Billy, Oh, I can feel the pain already. (*He screams.*) Help me, Billy.

(BILLY *just stands bewildered.*)

MOSBY (*triumphantly goes to* MARTIN *and stands over him laughing*): Ha, ha, ha. If there's one thing I like better than a caught nigger, it's a caught nigger that's already scared half out of his mind, even before I start workin' on him. Ha, ha, ha.

CHARLES: Martin, what are you doing out here? I hope you're not mixed up in this thing with Gabriel, because if you are, you're in trouble.

MOSBY: Of course, he's mixed up in it.

CHARLES: Well, Martin, Are you?

(*He doesn't answer.*)

MOSBY: A little taste of the whip'll loosen his tongue.

CHARLES: Martin, if you don't talk to me, I'll have to turn you over to Mosby. I can't let my personal feelings enter into this. It's a matter of the law. Gabriel has broken the law, and for all I know, you've helped him. Well, Martin?

MOSBY (*cracks his whip*): Don't waste any more of your breath on him, Charlie. (*As he is about to strike,* JIM *calls from his spot again.*)

JIM: Shhh. There's another one coming.

(*One of the men grabs* BILLY, *covering his mouth, and they all hide, leaving* MARTIN *center stage alone, still prone.*)

(WILLIE *comes on warily. He sees* MARTIN *sitting on the ground and goes over to him with quick catlike steps.* MARTIN *looks up at him with widely opened eyes, completely afraid, but says nothing.* WILLIE, *sensing that something is wrong, looks to* MARTIN *for a signal, but when none comes, he relaxes, thinking that* MARTIN *is hurt.*)

WILLIE: You all right, old man? What's the matter? You

can't talk or something? Gabe sent me for you and now that I found you, everything's gonna be all right. (*He tries to help him up, but* MARTIN, *not resisting, just looks up at him, saying nothing but letting his body hang limp in* WILLIE's *hands.* WILLIE *drops him suddenly and jumps back, suspecting something.*) Where's that young boy who was with you? Where's Billy? (*He whirls around just in time to see them come from behind their hiding places with their guns trained on him. He flexes quickly, but stops himself and turns to audience and prepares to meet the situation with a frightened look.*)

MOSBY (*as they all come out*): All right. Just hold it right there, and don't make a move. (*Coming closer.*) Now this is more like it. (*He surveys him.*) This one is full of fight. He's full of plenty fight. Don't let that thinness fool you. You see them shoulders, there's real power in them, I tell you. Oh, it's gonna be fun to watch you sweat, 'cause it'll take a long time, a long, long time. (*He wipes his mouth.*) But you'll sweat. You'll beg for mercy before I'm through with you. You'll . . . (*He gets excited again.*)

CHARLES: Mosby, control yourself. You don't even know who he belongs to.

MOSBY: Yeah, well while you're tryin' to figure it out, I'll just get him warmed up. (*He stretches out his whip.*)

CHARLES: Wait a minute. Can't you see there's something going on here that doesn't quite fit together. You. (*To* WILLIE.) Why were you looking for Martin? And what did you mean when you said, "Everything will be all right now"?

MOSBY: Well, talk up, boy.

(WILLIE *pretends not to comprehend.*)

MOSBY: Come on, talk up! (*He cracks his whip.*)

(WILLIE *mumbles something in Swahili.*)

MOSBY: Oh, you're supposed to be African, eh? Then where're the knife marks on your face? And the beads around your neck, and how come your teeth ain't filed and how come I heard you speakin' English to that one other there? Huh? How come?

CHARLES: Answer the question, son.

(WILLIE *says something else in Swahili.*)

MOSBY (*slaps him.* WILLIE *moves his body forward at* MOSBY *who draws back awkwardly, stumbling over* MARTIN. *Then he comes forward himself*): Why you little ape. Make at me will you?

(CHARLES *comes between them.*)

CHARLES: Hold it, Mosby. Why would he try to make us think he can't speak English when he can?

MOSBY: Because he's scared to death like the other one. That's why.

(*Just then noises are heard offstage right, opposite from where* WILLIE *and* MARTIN *came in.* MARY *and* NANNY *are heard.*)

MARY (*still offstage*): Let's try this way, honey.

(*They come on in a hurry and are out of breath. They are well on before they realize that they are trapped.* MARY *turns and tries to run back, but one of the men blocks her.* NANNY *just freezes. The stage is set thusly:* JIM *and another guard are left wtih their guns on* WILLIE. MARTIN *is on floor far forward and slightly left of center.* MOSBY *and* CHARLES *are on either side of him, turned toward the right. And third guard has* BILLY, *right, upstage. Fourth and fifth guards, who are right, each cover* NANNY *and* MARY, *respectively.*)

MARY: Oh, what misery is this I see here. Martin, you look like the world done turned you over and left you standin' upside down.

(MARTIN *doesn't answer.*)

CHARLES: Mary, Nanny, Martin, Matty Hargis's boy and this strange one, all coming way out here at the same time? Why? What's near here?

MOSBY: Old Brook Swamp is nearby.

CHARLES: And if Gabriel is hiding there, why was Martin coming back in the opposite direction? And why would Mary and Nanny take a chance on meeting him in broad daylight?

MOSBY: You think maybe they were plannin' a raid and somethin' went wrong? That young bull a yours is liable to do almost anything.

CHARLES: Of course, that's it, isn't it, Martin? What was it you said to that boy, "I don't want to fight anybody."

MOSBY (*cracks his whip*): That's right, he sure did.

MARTIN (*facing audience, sitting on the stage*): Oh, no, sah, not the whip. Don't hit me with no whip. I can't take it. Ohhhhh. I knew it wouldn't be no good. I tole Gabr'el that. I tole him, but he wouldn't listen, he jus' wouldn't listen.

MARY: Hesh up, man. Don't you realize what you're sayin'?

MOSBY: If she opens her mouth again, shoot the old bitch. Come over here, Jim, and tie him up nigger style.

(JIM *leaves the other guard with* WILLIE, *gives his rifle to* MOSBY, *and ties* MARTIN'S *hands behind him at the elbows so that he can't relax them.* JIM *moves to right of* MARTIN.)

CHARLES: Whether you get the whip or not is up to you, Martin. Either you tell us what you know or I let Mosby have you. And you know the kind of things he can do. I want

to be fair, but you must see that if you don't tell us what Gabriel is up to, then I'm duty-bound to find out by any means. Well, Martin. I'm waiting.

(*As* MARTIN *is about to speak,* WILLIE *steps slightly forward.*)

MOSBY: Hold that one right there. Jim, tie him up too.

(JIM *goes back to where* WILLIE *is. As he gets between* WILLIE *and the one guarding him, while* MOSBY *and the others have turned back to* MARTIN, WILLIE *springs on* JIM *and knocks him into the other man who had stepped back to give* JIM *room. This knocks the rifle from his hands.* JIM *has left his rifle with* MOSBY. WILLIE *then grabs* JIM *from behind and, with a knife at his throat, holds everyone at bay.*)

WILLIE: Get up, Martin, and let's get out of here. Martin, come on! What the hell are you waiting for? (*They try to box him in and he backs left.*) You. (*To the man nearest him.*) Get over there. Move quick or this one's a dead savage.

MOSBY: Do what he says. He ain't going nowhere.

(*Man comes over to* MOSBY, *leaving* WILLIE *a clear exit.* JIM *does not try to wrestle with him. The knife is still at his throat.*)

WILLIE: Aw right, Martin, you got plenty a runnin' room, now get out a here. (*He waits.*) I'm giving you one last chance to make it.

MARTIN: Nooo. I ain't runnin' nowhere. You see I didn't make a move, didn't you, sah? You seen me, Mas Charlie, you seen I ain't tryin' to run from you, sah. Nooo. Besides, my arms is tied. You young, you run.

WILLIE: I'm gettin' out a here one way or another. If you don't come by yourself, I can't leave you behind, not alive anyhow. You understand me, old man?

MARTIN: I told you I ain't goin' nowhere. Mas Charlie, you'll protect me, won't you, sah?

WILLIE (*tries to move toward* MARTIN, *but man who had crossed over immediately gets somewhat behind him*): Get back, I told you.

MOSBY: Stay where you are. We got him now. All we got to do is move in slow.

(*The man slightly behind* WILLIE *does not have a weapon. When he gets close,* WILLIE *throws* JIM *forward, tripping him as he does so, so that* JIM *falls on* MOSBY *and they both stumble back.* WILLIE *then turns and stabs man behind him in the stomach as he exits left. Man dies loudly, like the other one* WILLIE *killed in Scene 3.* MOSBY *and* JIM *rush to exit.* JIM *goes down on one knee and aims rifle.* MOSBY *stands beside him.*)

MOSBY: Wait, not yet. As soon as he hits the ridge. Now!

(JIM *fires and* WILLIE *is heard falling down a hill with a low groan.*)

MOSBY: Beautiful, Jim boy. You hit him on the wing, dead in the back and he just skipped a step and went plop.

(NANNY *runs to stray rifle and grabs it up to kill* MOSBY. *He wrestles with her, turning it into a sex thing immediately.*)

MOSBY (*grabs her by the waist as he takes away rifle*): This one's a real animal. I knew that the first time I laid eyes on her. And I'd give whole lick a cotton to have her, for just one night.

CHARLES: She happens to belong to me.

MOSBY: How much you want for her? (*He looks at* NANNY *while he speaks.*)

(NANNY *breaks away and tries to run, but they form a ring around her:* MOSBY, CHARLES, JIM, *and the one who was guarding her. One is still guarding* BILLY *and one is guarding* MARY, *who tries to move to her aid, but is blocked out.*)

NANNY (*coming center, breathless*): Dirty, stinking murderers. Filthy animals. Oh, God, how I hate you all. Martin, do something.

MOSBY (*grabs her from behind by the arms*): Now you just stand still, honey. We gonna make that nigger do some talking.

CHARLES: This has gone far enough. We'd better take them all back and send for the authorities.

MOSBY: What's the rush, Charlie? We got a jug a whiskey, a nigger to beat, a black gal to have some fun with, and a young sprig and a mammy to watch it all, so's they won't forget, so's they won't ever forget.

CHARLES: I told you before, Mosby, that I wouldn't stand for any of your disgusting animalism.

MOSBY (*wrestling with* NANNY): You won't stand for it, you. I got one of my best boys, Crayfish, lyin' dead over there. Dead, do you hear me. And all on account a you and that black Gabriel. If I ever get my hands on him.

CHARLES: And I'm telling you for the last time, let her go.

MOSBY: You ain't tellin' nobody nothin', Charlie boy.

JIM: You two better stop wastin' time arguin'. There might be more of 'em around, and there's just six of us left.

MOSBY: You gettin' paid to follow orders, not give 'em. Now, Charlie, that boy o' there what's dead, I figure you owe me for him, and I'll take her as payment.

CHARLES: Payment for what. You haven't lost anything. He's white, and that means he doesn't belong to anyone, so he's not worth anything.

(NANNY *again tries to twist away.*)

MOSBY: If you stay still, sweetie, I won't hurt you. (*He tries to kiss her.*)

NANNY: Get him away from me. Get him away. What's the matter with you anyway? Can't you even fight for what's yours? First you lose your wife, and now your slaves. What's the matter with you, Charlie Prosser, aren't you a man? Don't you have any guts?

MOSBY: I'm gettin' excited just waiting for you. Oh, the things I'm gonna have you do to me, honey!

(NANNY *is still trying to get away.*)

MARY (*goes to* CHARLES *and gets on her knees*): Mas Charlie, I been with you all my life. I raised you from when you was a pup. You sucked my breast before you ever knew your own mammy's. I'm beggin' you, sah, don't give that white devil my baby, please, sah. If'n he wants to whip him (*Looking at* MARTIN.) even unto death, let him. But not my lil' gal. She don't mean what she's saying.

CHARLES: Let her go, Mosby. She's going back with me.

MOSBY: After the way she talked to you.

CHARLES: Yes, even after that. There are traditions, Mosby. A master has a responsibility to his slaves in the same way that they have to obey him.

MOSBY: I don't care about none a that, Charlie. But I want this one. And after all the trouble I've been through today on account of you, I'm takin' her, like it or not.

CHARLES: You've had your fun killing. You don't need any more payment than that.

MOSBY: That ain't nothin' compared to the fun she's going to give me.

(NANNY *begins to kick at* MOSBY's *shins.*)

MARY (*tries to stop her*): No, honey!

(MARTIN *bends his head lower.* BILLY *breaks from his guard and springs at* MOSBY. NANNY *breaks free.* MOSBY *throws* BILLY *away and grabs a rifle from* JIM *and shoots* BILLY *while he is stretched out on the ground.* NANNY, *about to run, stops, turns and comes back.*)

NANNY: You had to kill him, didn't you? If you ever come near me agin', I'll tear that dried-up piece of flesh between your legs off. I'll root it out. Good God, Martin, I didn't think even you could sink to this. Where's Gabriel? He said someone would be waiting at the swamp to take me to him. In the name of heaven where is he?

(MOSBY *moves as if to grab her again,* CHARLES *signals no, and he draws back slightly.*)

NANNY (*coming front*): Wherever he is I hope he kills you

211

all, every last one of you. Tell them, why don't you? (*To* MARTIN.) What can they do about it anyway? By now all of Richmond must be in flames.

(CHARLES, MOSBY, *and the other whites start at this.*)

NANNY: That's right, Richmond! The capital itself. And my Gabe, my man did it. And I'm going to see you hang, every last one of you. I'm going to be the Queen of Virginia, how do you like that, you dirty white bastards?

MARTIN: No you ain't, 'cause they didn't make it. The rain stopped 'em and they had to turn back. Richmond ain't in no flames, no, sah. That's a lie.

MARY: Shut up, you old fool.

MARTIN: It wasn't me what told 'em 'bout Gabr'el. She done it, she was the one.

NANNY: Oh, no. What have I done? Isn't there anything in this world for a black gal like me, besides misery? Oh, Gabe, what have I done?

MOSBY (*grabs* MARTIN *by the hair and yanks his head backward*): You ain't lying now, are you, boy?

MARTIN (*his eyes rolling*): No, sah. If it's one thing I don't do is lie. (*He talks fast now.*) Mas Charlie'll tell you that. Right, Mas Charlie?

CHARLES: How many men?

MARTIN (*grinning*): Close to 2,000, sah.

MARY: You'll burn in hell forever.

CHARLES: Are they going to try again?

MARTIN: Oh, yes, sah.

CHARLES: When?

MARTIN: Tonight.

CHARLES: Where are they going to meet?

MARTIN: Brook Swamp, like you said, sah.

CHARLES: Send a rider to Richmond. We've got to warn the governor. If those blacks surprise the garrison with that many men, there's no telling what can happen. You'd better send two riders.

MOSBY: And what about these?

CHARLES: Martin's the important one now. He must be kept under strict guard. The militia will want to question him. As for the Queen of Virginia, I give her to you along with the old mammy to wash her bruises after you've finished of an evening. I shall go to Norfolk and get an entire new lot as soon as that Gabriel is safe in a cage. Now I must hurry home. I think my wife will find all of this very interesting. Yes, very interesting, indeed.

MOSBY: Imagine, 2,000 niggers together all at the same time. I wonder what that would look like?

ACT III

Scene 1

Trial Room at Richmond

(*The governor's seat is center stage and back on a raised platform. It is set out in the fashion of a judge's bench of the time.* MOSBY *and* CHARLES *are right upstage and at separate ends of a table. There is a uniformed guard between them and the platform. He is downstage. The prosecutor, a captain in the army, is at a small table with chair at right angles with the platform, but on the floor of the stage and to the left, across from* MOSBY *and* CHARLES, *facing the right exit. The* CAPTAIN *is sitting at his table with his back to the left exit, looking at* CHARLES *and* MOSBY, *and also studying his notes. There is another guard at the left exit, also in uniform and armed with a rifle. A young court attendant looks in from left as curtain rises.*)

COURT ATTENDANT: Are you ready, sir?

CAPTAIN: Yes. Has the prisoner been brought up yet?

COURT ATTENDANT: Not yet, sir. I'll send for him right away.

(CAPTAIN *nods and the* ATTENDANT *exits. The* CAPTAIN *stands up and straightens his uniform. The* ATTENDANT *re-enters in a robe and rings a bell once.*)

ATTENDANT: His Excellency, the Governor of Virginia, the Honorable James Monroe.

(MOSBY *and* CHARLES *rise.* MONROE *walks in briskly and with a strong manner. He is carrying his wig in his hand. After he is seated,* CHARLES *and* MOSBY *sit. The* CAPTAIN *remains standing and the* ATTENDANT *goes to the wall at rear and stands, facing the audience.*)

CAPTAIN: Governor, this is Mr. Charles Prosser. (*Indicating which one.*) Owner of the slave Gabriel.

MONROE: He's a lot more than that, Captain. He's the last member of one of Virginia's oldest and proudest families. You're looking well, Charlie. How're things upcountry?

CHARLES: Fine, James.

CAPTAIN: I'm sorry, sir. I didn't know that Mr. Prosser was a friend.

MONROE: He's much more than that. (*He laughs once.*)

The Prossers and the Monroes are all that's left of the finest old Virginia stock. We're the only two families who still have red dirt in our veins instead of blood. Right, Charlie?

CHARLES: Right, James.

MONROE: We've fought Indians, Red Coats, and famine together. Virginia is what it is because of men like us, uh, Charlie?

CHARLES: Right, James.

MONROE: How's the missus?

CHARLES: Fine.

MONROE: As I remember, she's not a Virginia girl, is she?

CHARLES: No.

MONROE: Hmmm. Didn't think so. Well, go on, Captain. (*As if the interruption had been his fault.*)

CAPTAIN: And this is Mr. Mosby Sheppard, a neighbor of Mr. Prosser's, who helped in uncovering the plot.

MONROE (*looking disdainfully at him*): Neighbor! On which side, Charlie?

CHARLES: On the north side, the old Shelby place.

MONROE: Not the old Shelby place, oh no! Charlie, what's happening to us? All the big plantations are breaking up or selling out and people are just sitting back and letting good land go to waste because the tobacco and the rice haven't held up. They're giving in, Charlie, they just don't have the will. Not the way we had it. And it's up to men like us, the ones who care, to stop it.

(MOSBY *gives* CHARLES *a disapproving sneer at this point.*)

MONROE: All these Georgia rednecks and bayou tramps and Frenchies from New Orleans moving in here in droves and buying up all the properties. It's a terrible thing I tell you. It's what's wrong with the country.

(MOSBY *now reacts as if stung by the last remark.*)

CHARLES (*feeling embarrassed for* MOSBY): Some of them are all right.

MONROE (*musing*): Hmmmmmmm.

MOSBY: Are we here to hang a nigger or talk about old times, suh?

MONROE (*ignoring him*): Those Yankees are the real cause of it. Virginians are sensitive people and we're not the main show anymore. Time was when a business failed in Norfolk, somebody got fired in the government. Not anymore. The mistake we made in the first place was letting them put the capital in Washington instead of Fredericksburg.

CHARLES (*tolerating him*): Uh, right, James.

(*There is another pause.*)

MONROE: Well, go on, Captain.

CAPTAIN (*a little startled*): Mr. Prosser has filed for compensation from the state, sir, in the event the prisoner is convicted and hanged.

MONROE: You've got a damned nerve.

CHARLES: I have a right to that money, it's mine.

MONROE: You had a right to it as long as you could keep it.

CHARLES: But you would never have known he was coming if I hadn't told you. The whole city, and God knows what else, would have been destroyed.

MONROE: You don't know what would've been destroyed.

CHARLES: Do you?

MONROE: All right. I'll see that you get the town seal on your coat of arms at the next meeting of the Assizes.

CHARLES: For saving your hide and your garrison and your precious militia.

MONROE: My militia would have run them back into the swamp, warning or no warning.

CHARLES: That's a lie.

MONROE: Now, Charlie, you listen to me. I'll give you $50 for him as confiscated property and not a penny more.

MOSBY: We don't treat our friends like that in Georgia.

MONROE (*to* CAPTAIN): Mr. uh, what's his name?

CAPTAIN: Sheppard.

MONROE: Mr. Sheppard, this is a court of law and unless you are given permission to speak, I expect you to keep quiet, or I'll have you thrown out.

MOSBY (*stands*): I got as much right to talk as he does. I lost a lot a property too. And as Charlie said, if it wasn't for us, you wouldn't a known they were coming.

MONROE: Oh, you did, did you. Well, now, how much land do you own?

MOSBY: What's that got to do with it?

MONROE (*very stern*): Answer me, sir.

MOSBY: Fifteen thousand acres.

MONROE (*nodding*): And how long have you been a resident of this state?

MOSBY: Three years.

MONROE: Well, if you want to keep those 15,000 acres, Mr. what-you-muh-call-it . . .

CAPTAIN: Sheppard.

MONROE (*looks at* CAPTAIN): You'll sit down quietly and wait until I've decided that it's time to talk about how much property you lost. And we'll do that when all the owners are here, Mr. . . . .

CAPTAIN: Sheppard.

MONROE: And not before. There are no privileged persons in my court, sir.

(MOSBY *sits down.*)

MONROE: Now, Charlie, how much was that boy a yours worth?

CHARLES: A great deal. The absolute top price.

MOSBY (*stands again*): I thought you just said we'd talk about that when all the owners are here.

MONROE: Mr. uh (CAPTAIN *is about to give the name again, but* MONROE *waves him off.*) Sheppard, the way I run my court is my business. And what goes on between a Prosser and a Monroe is strictly their own business, in court or out. Do I make myself clear, Mr. . . . Sheppard?

(MOSBY *sits down without answering.*)

MONROE: Answer me, sir. Do I make myself clear? (*He says this last, finally showing the real hardness.*)

MOSBY: Right!

CAPTAIN: Governor, if I may.

MONROE: Yes, Captain, what is it?

CAPTAIN: If the prisoner is acquitted, he would, in due course, be returned to the owner under the law governing slaves tried for capital crimes. In which case, Mr. Prosser will have suffered no loss.

MONROE: With that suggestion, Captain, you have joined the ranks of history's immortal idiots.

CAPTAIN: Begging your pardon, sir, but . . .

MONROE: Begging my pardon, hell! Have you ever heard of a slave being acquitted of any charge as serious as this? Why even if there was no evidence at all, I mean absolutely none, I'd still hang him. But you have enough proof to convict him even if he were white, and you stand there and talk about acquittal. Don't you know that the only reason we're even having a trial in the first place is to satisfy those New England slave lovers? And if I do have to honor a black by letting him into my court, don't make it any harder for me by mentioning acquittal, Captain.

CHARLES: And that's what's really wrong with Virginia, Governor. (*He says it sarcastically.*) It's not the rednecks and the Frenchies who're ruining us, it's the men of power who think they are above the law, who think they can use it as they please because Virginia should only be for the Virginians.

MONROE: What do you want me to do, Charlie, break the law and let him go?

CHARLES: I want you to try him because justice must be served and not because you're embarrassed by Yankees.

MONROE: All right, Charlie boy. I'll tell you what I told

216

your "neighbor." We'll discuss how much you get for him when the rest of the owners are here and not before. Which means you'll get about one tenth of what I might have given you. Now are you satisfied?

CHARLES: I'm not surprised. That's more like the James Monroe I know. And I wouldn't be so contemptuous of Mosby Sheppard if I were you. You're really both very much alike.

MONROE: And what do you mean by that?

CHARLES: Just this. Some men can always profit from the misfortune of others. Some even get rich by selling white children as Negroes. And I know that all of what the owners don't get will not be left in the public funds; just as I know that he (*Pointing to* MOSBY.) would have found a way to do what he did to that poor girl even if there had been no rebellion.

MOSBY: That's a lie!

CHARLES: Is it? I let you have her because of what Gabriel had done, but I didn't think that even you could be that much of an animal.

MOSBY: What happened to her was an accident. I only wanted to have a little fun, that's all.

CHARLES: And you had your fun, didn't you? You had that.

MONROE: That's enough, boys. The court isn't interested in your private differences over slave girls.

CHARLES: It's not a private difference, it's a public crime!

MONROE: Charlie, don't make me treat you like some out-of-state Jew!

CHARLES: Don't treat me any way at all, just do the right thing, for once in your life, do the right thing.

MONROE: I will, Charlie boy, I will. First, I'm going to hang this slave of yours as quick as I can. Then I'm going to instruct the legislature to pass a law making owners responsible for any destruction of property, public or private, by their slaves, so that any talk of compensation will be compensation by the planters, not by the state. I'll have owners sent to school, if necessary, to learn like little boys how to handle their Africans. I'll tighten things up so much around here that if anyone ever slips again, the way you two slipped, I'll confiscate everything he's got and ship him out in his underwear. Now, don't get me mad, Charlie, I'm warning you. (*He sits back.*) Captain, bring in the prisoner.

(CAPTAIN *nods to the* COURT ATTENDANT. COURT ATTENDANT *goes left and says something offstage and then returns to his spot. There is an expectant pause as they all look in that direction.* MONROE *puts on his wig.* GABRIEL *is pushed in. He is blindfolded, and there is some blood on his clothes. He*

217

has chains on his hands and feet, but they are long enough to give him easy movement. Another guard comes in and pushes him forward again, roughly, with the barrel of his rifle. He stumbles center, turns and raises his head, as if he's trying to look up.)

MONROE: Remove the blindfold.

GABRIEL (*blinks and tries to focus. He gets a little dizzy and then manages to see. He looks around at them as if they are strange objects. Then he turns front*): Are they all dead? Big Henry, the boys from Norfolk, Willie, who never came back, Martin and little Billy? I saw some go down, but they died so fast that every hand I touched was turning cold. I tried to hold them up, to tell them not to die. I pleaded with them to live because we had come to get our freedom. "Live," I said, "and be free." I said, "Live . . ." (*He moves as if talking to the imagined dead.*) "Get up, shoot, kill, charge." (*He stops and turns.*) From this spot I will lead my army in one final sweep of sight and sound, one last surge of flesh against cannon and steel. Ten thousand warriors robed in the ancient, tribal way. Their muscles rippling in wave upon wave, their golden spears crouched, glistening in their hands, their painted bodies stretching back beyond the foothills and blocking out the sun. Charge and the echo is heard across the sea by jungle drums that tell the kings of Africa we have destroyed our dishonor with black death. Men, don't die. Touch the ground that we made holy with our blood, fall on it, reach in and kiss the lips of an unknown child: mother and daughter and queen. (*He falls down on his knees here.*) Caress the sad, still face that never knew a day of rest in all its life, but don't die! (*He falls all the way down here.*) Don't die!!

MONROE (*motions to the guard to take him to the bar, left. The guard goes and helps him up and leads him there while* GABRIEL's *head remains bowed*): Proceed, Captain.

CAPTAIN: Are you Gabriel, slave of Charles Prosser?

GABRIEL (*his head down*): Yes.

CAPTAIN: How old are you?

GABRIEL: Thirty-one.

CAPTAIN: Born in Southampton County, State of Virginia?

GABRIEL: Yes.

CAPTAIN: And do you, to the best of your knowledge, have any slave children?

GABRIEL: No.

CAPTAIN: Any slave brothers or sisters?

GABRIEL: Two brothers.

CAPTAIN: What are their names?

GABRIEL: Solomon and Martin.

CAPTAIN: And where are they now, to the best of your knowledge?

GABRIEL: Dead, all dead. Nanny's dead too.

MONROE: Just answer the question.

GABRIEL (*looks up and sees* CHARLES): Charlie, Mas Charlie, is that you? Tell me, please tell ole Gabe where his sweet Nanny is. All I ever did for her in my whole life was to cause her pain . . . Charlie Prosser (*Angrily.*), what did you do with her? (*Shouting.*) Answer me, Charlie, or I'll kill you! (*He comes out from the bar. The* CAPTAIN *tries to gently stop him, but he pulls away and takes a step toward* CHARLES, *who stands up and backs away as does* MOSBY. MONROE *is amused by this.*) No, not anymore, not like that anymore. (*He sinks back, then he falls on his knees again. He looks up at* CHARLES *and pleads with him.*) Mas Charlie, I'm begging you to forgive me. I'm begging you to be kind, like you used to be. Have mercy on me, Mas Charlie, and tell me that you didn't let them hurt her. Go on, say it. (*Coaxingly.*) Say she's back doing for the missus the way she always did. (*He half laughs and half sobs as he tries to get an answer.*) Say she is, please say it.

CHARLES (*taking courage and leaning forward on the table and looking down at him*): No, Mas Gabe, that's not the way it is, because you didn't want it that way. You wanted bloodshed and killing. You wanted to destroy those who'd been kind to you all your life, but you destroyed yourself instead. You and all your people will suffer torture and worse than torture many a long night because Gabriel wanted to rob and steal and take what belonged to others. What others had worked for and built, he wanted to have for himself. Nanny is dead because she believed in a man who loved himself too much to care about anyone else.

GABRIEL: Dead? How? Why?

CHARLES: She was killed by someone whose greed was not unlike your greed, and whose death, if this were a just world, should not be unlike your death. But she was killed most of all by you.

(GABRIEL *bends his head forward and heaves.*)

MONROE: Very touching, Charlie, but a little out of place. Captain, set the prisoner back at the bar and continue. (*The* ATTENDANT *and the* CAPTAIN *help* GABRIEL *up and back to the bar. His hands are folded and head is still bowed. The* CAPTAIN *goes back to his table.*)

CAPTAIN: Do you have any other slave family alive that you know of?

GABRIEL: No.

CAPTAIN: Were you the leader in the plot to attack this city and take it over by force?

(*There is a pause.*)

GABRIEL (*heaving*): Yes. (*Then he holds up his head.*) Yes, I am the leader.

MONROE (*noticing a change*): Once is enough.

CAPTAIN: How many slaves were with you?

GABRIEL: Slaves? There were no slaves, there were only men, men who would have matched your army two to one in hand-to-hand combat and driven you into the sea.

MONROE (*nods to* CAPTAIN): That'll be enough of that, Captain. And if the prisoner has another outburst, you know what to do.

CAPTAIN: Yes, sir. And arms, what arms did you have?

GABRIEL: We had fifty rifles and ten pounds of powder for each.

MONROE: Hardly enough to fight a man's war.

CAPTAIN: Where did you get the weapons and the powder from?

GABRIEL: From a white man who believed all men were born to be free, and that any man who could enslave another man shouldn't be allowed to walk the earth.

MONROE: You'll get your chance to make your speech, slave Gabriel. But you must wait until we tell you to. Do you understand me, boy?

GABRIEL: If I had won, it would have been a black man's court this day in Richmond.

MONROE: If you had won, but you didn't.

GABRIEL: If I had won, we would have shown you what real justice was like. You would have been in the dock, Governor, and I would have made you sweat. Every slave law that you ever passed would have been used against you and I would have made you sweat before I hanged you from a cottonwood tree, believe me.

MONROE: The law is clear on the crime you have committed, slave Gabriel.

GABRIEL: The law. What law? Don't talk to me about law. White man's law has made the black man an ox with a ring in his nose. Is that the law you're talking about? The only law that means anything is a law that's made to save men from oppression, not destroy them. Show me a law that's of the spirit and not the gun, and then you'll be talking about a law that I can respect. I did what any man would do to free his own from bondage. I did what all the men of every generation have done when they were faced with the choice of trading

their honor for their lives. And if it hadn't rained, it would have been a black man's court this day in Richmond!

MONROE: We're not interested in your rantings about what might have been, slave Gabriel, nor what you think about the law. I allowed you to ramble on at first because you amused me, but you don't anymore. And you'll be quiet from now on if you want to save your hide from any more beatings. Captain, I want the prisoner made to bend if he refuses to obey.

GABRIEL: And how's he going to do that?

MONROE: You dirty black! You dare challenge my court.

GABRIEL: Damn your court and damn you, and all your women and all your sons. May they all be born dead.

MONROE: Before I let you carry on like this anymore, I'll run you through myself! Do you hear me?

GABRIEL (*laughs*): Ha, ha, ha. Come down, Monroe, come down and do it. Ha, ha, ha. Come down and do it. Come down, if you're man enough to die, and do it!

MONROE (*sits back*): Is this your doing, Charlie? Did you teach this African to talk to white men this way, huh?

(CHARLES *doesn't answer.*)

MOSBY: I think the governor's having a little trouble, Charlie. Why don't you help him out? After all, you two are all that's left of the old Virginia.

CHARLES: Gabriel, you know you're going to die. No matter what happens, you're going to die. That was decided before you even came in here.

GABRIEL: That was decided before I was born.

CHARLES: Yes, Gabe, but don't make it harder for yourself or the others. Answer the questions and just let them hang you quietly and without any more violence. That's all they want from you now.

GABRIEL: How do you hang a man without violence? (*He comes forward.*) Oh, God! What a terrible thing my hope for becoming a man has turned out to be. Did God put us here to suffer like this? Won't we ever be free? (*He turns on them.*) Are you going to keep us all in chains for always? Even the unborn babies and the innocent children? Don't you have any pity, any of you? (*There is a moment of quiet.*)

MONROE: This is a court of law. And the only thing that we are here to decide is your guilt or innocence to the charge that on the night of April 26, in the year of Our Lord 1800 you did incite and lead a rebellious band of slaves against the city of Richmond.

GABRIEL: And you think that when you hang me you'll end it?

MONROE: When I hang you, I'll let the body dry out in the

221

hot sun, for days and weeks, until there's nothing left but bones. And I'll turn your face out toward the harbor so the wind will blow the odor away. And the blood of every rebellious dog that we track down and hound out will flow past the dead eyes and empty skull, down the river and out into the sea.

GABRIEL: And when the bones fall and tree withers, there will be other Gabriels, not yet born, to try again. You'll never be safe in your beds until you give us our freedom.

MONROE: Give you your freedom. Does a master give a dog its freedom? No, because the dog wouldn't know what to do with it even if it had it. And that's what you are, that's what all of you are. That's what you were when the white man found you, savage dogs who roamed the jungle naked, with cow dung in your hair and snake blood on your face, killing each other, eating each other and selling each other.

GABRIEL: You've bought the victim from the victor and pretended you conquered the best of the race. All the ones who were ever sold into bondage were beaten men. And those who won the battles still stand proud, master in their own country, ready to kill anyone who tries to take from them what is theirs.

MONROE: Is that how you came to be here, victim, because you were beaten?

GABRIEL: No, I was born of woman in a land of pain, chained at the breast and beaten to the grave.

MONROE: You and all your brothers, the whole rotten lot. Gabriel, slave of Charles Prosser, you shall be taken from this place to another place, and from there to a place of execution, where you shall be hanged by the neck at the first sunrise, until dead. And may the Lord send your black soul to hell with all the other black devils.

GABRIEL: Then lead a good life, Monroe, because if he ever sends you down there too, I'll kill you forever. (*He turns and is about to go.*)

MONROE: I'm not finished with you. Send in the other one.

(*They all wait while the* ATTENDANT *goes left. He returns and stands by the exit as* MARTIN *is pushed in.*)

MARTIN (*is holding his head and doesn't see* GABRIEL): Oh, please, sah, have mu'cy. It warn't me what done it. I swear it warn't. (*He looks up when no one hits him and then sees* GABRIEL.)

(GABRIEL *turns to* MARTIN *and* MARTIN *comes to him and falls on his knees in front of him.*)

MARTIN: Don't shame me, Gabe, please, don't shame me. I tried, God knows I tried.

(GABRIEL *bends to him and cups* MARTIN'S *head in his hands.* MONROE *rears back and laughs loudly.*)

END OF SCENE

Scene 2

Gabriel's Cell

(GABRIEL *is sitting on a small bed with his head in his hands. He is chained by one leg to a giant ring in the wall. There is a small window above the bed and to the left of it, with iron bars in it. He gets up and moves about nervously. Then he sits down again and holds his head in his hands. There are shouts from the street which can be heard through the window.* "Get that nigger over there. Quick, grab him before he gets away . . . Hang him, lynch him. It's open season on all niggers!" *Crowd responds with a roar.* GABRIEL *goes quickly to the window and peers out. He has to strain to see what's going on, but he manages. He breathes deeply as he does so. The victim's voice is then heard.* "Lawd, Lawd, have mercy. AAAAAAAA-AAhhhhhhhhhhhhhhhggggg." *Sounds of the man being tortured are heard as he dies. The crowd send up another cheer.* GABRIEL *slowly releases the bars and comes back, center stage. He wrenches at his leg iron, then he goes to wall and tries to tear out the iron ring. Then crowd is heard at his window.* "Now let's get the one in there. Let's burn him. NIGGUH, you in there?" GABRIEL *sinks to the floor still holding onto the chain, but recoiling from the sounds.*)

(CAPTAIN *comes in as a guard, who unlocks the door, stands there with a rifle. He goes over to* GABRIEL *and looks apprehensively at him.* GABRIEL *is curled up beside the wall, holding the chain. He looks up at the* CAPTAIN *with eyes of desperation, hate, incapacity, and defeat.*)

CAPTAIN: What's the matter, are you sick? (*He then hears the shouts outside and seems to comprehend. He goes left.*) Guard, disperse that crowd.

(GUARD *leaves and crowd is heard being ordered away by the time the* CAPTAIN *gets back to* GABRIEL. GABRIEL *gets up and slowly comes forward.*)

CAPTAIN: I've come to tell you that you've been granted a last wish. You can have anything that a white man can have who's going to die.

GABRIEL: What's happened to Martin?

CAPTAIN: The governor returned him to Mr. Prosser and he sold him to Mr. Sheppard.

GABRIEL: And the others, what about them?

223

CAPTAIN: We caught the one they call Big Henry. He was wounded but alive. I think all those who weren't hanged or shot outright will be put on a coffle and sold out of the state.

GABRIEL: But before you kill me, I can have a chicken dinner.

CAPTAIN: If that's what you want.

GABRIEL: Of course. That's what all of us want. Give a nigger a chicken dinner and he'll do anything for you, even die happy.

(*Noises are heard from the street again. They both turn.*)

GABRIEL (*moving away from the* CAPTAIN): Facing them would be the best death. Let the howling mob that I wanted to destroy, destroy me. Let me look into their eyes while they burn the flesh and tear off the limbs. Let me see their hate full force. Let the grinning faces and the screaming voices of the real world, the world of power and of the future devour me. Let me be consumed by my defeat. Let me die the way all black men die in this country. Let me feel the struggle and give into the pain. Let me know in the end that I was weak.

CAPTAIN: I'm afraid the governor would never allow it. Your death will be a model of military efficiency. The ceremony might be cold, but it will be well ordered. And you'll hang. You won't be tortured or burned or any of those things. (*There is a pause.*) You have a visitor. And I'll come back in case you change your mind. (*He goes to the door and* LUCY *comes in.*) The door will be open and the guard will be right outside. He's chained and can't come beyond this point. (*He indicates with his hand. She nods and he leaves.*)

LUCY (*feels her way and watches where she walks*): So this is what you were planning? This is why you wanted me to keep Mosby and Charles away, so you could start your little revolution. But it didn't work, did it, Gabe? Do I still look old to you? Tell me that, do you still think I'm old and ugly? I bet you'd give half the blacks in Africa just to be able to touch me now. Ha, ha, ha, ha. Poor, poor Gabriel. Poor, poor slave. Poor, poor, dead nigger. Your missus won't ever be good to you again in life, boy, because you did a bad thing, didn't you? (*She laughs again.* GABRIEL *doesn't answer.*) Now that must be the first time in your life that you didn't have an answer for somebody, the first time that you didn't rise up in righteous hatred and scream and shout. Anyway, I came to thank you for what you taught me. You taught me that it's not love that counts in this world, it's getting something you can kick around until you feel good. There's nothing like playing massah, is there, Mas Gabe? The way you played it with me. That's really the greatest game of all, isn't it? (*She goes left*

and calls.) Boy, come here. (*A Negro youth comes in.*) Boy, kiss your missus' feet.

BOY: Yes'm. (*He does so, remaining in that position.*)

LUCY: Get up, boy.

BOY: Yes'm. (*He gets up.*)

LUCY: Come here. (*He goes very close to her. She feels him lustfully.*) Nice, firm young boy. Do you like it when I touch you, boy?

BOY: Oh, yes'm, yes'm.

LUCY: You see him, boy? (*He nods.*) He tried to hurt your missus. What do you think of that?

BOY: I think that's just awful, just awful.

LUCY: Right, now you show him what you think of him for doing that.

BOY: Yes'm. (*He goes to* GABRIEL *and spits in his face. Then he comes back to her.*)

LUCY: Good, boy. I'm going to kiss you for that, boy. (*She grabs him in her arms and devours him with a rapacious kiss.*) Does that make you feel hot down below, boy?

BOY: Oh, yes'm. It sure do.

(LUCY *looks triumphantly at* GABRIEL *and then laughs. She leads the boy out. Sounds come from the window again.* "There's another coon. Don't let him get away." *Crowd is heard running down the street away from jail.* GABRIEL *goes back to the bed and sinks down and holds his head in his arms.*)

CAPTAIN (*reenters*): Well, this is your last chance. Are you sure you don't want anything? It's going to be a long and lonely night.

(*The crowd is heard charging back past the window. A Negro is heard screaming in terror. They both look at the window.* GABRIEL *gets up.*)

CAPTAIN: And that won't make it any easier.

GABRIEL (*reminiscing*): Ten thousand warriors robed in the ancient, tribal way . . . If only the rain hadn't come. One night, that's all I needed, just one night. I set myself against them, against all of them. But I failed and all of my people died because of it. If I had left Nanny and Martin and the rest of them the way they were, if I had left the world the way I found it, I would have died even unhappier than I'm dying now. And that's all I can say for myself.

CAPTAIN: Then let me say that what you did today, the way you stood up to the most powerful man in the state, was a great thing, the greatest thing that a black man has ever done in this country. It will go down in history and one day

225

you will be remembered and your name will be honored by
your people. I'm sure of it.

GABRIEL: I'll kill you! (*He moves, but not all the way.*)
You stand there looking at a chained, beaten dog and tell him
that he'll be remembered. That's the one thing I don't ever
want to be, remembered. Remembered because I couldn't win,
remembered because I let them tie me down and kick me and
rape my wife and turn my brother into a frightened ape.
Remember me! I'll kill you. I'll kill you all. Oh, it's the only
way. It's all that's left. It's got to happen someday. (*He bends
into himself, then he falls on his knees.*) Any black man anywhere who ever kills a white man, woman, cripple or child
will be killing for me who didn't kill for himself, and when he
does, I'll praise his name in heaven or in hell.

(CAPTAIN *looks at him coldly and then leaves. The gate is
closed loudly by the guard and then locked. The crowd is
heard again.* GABRIEL *falls forward and gives a loud anguished
cry.*)

END OF SCENE

Scene 3

The Road to Georgia

(*Moaning is heard offstage. Slaves come on tied to a coffle.*
JIM *comes in with them.*)

JIM (*goes right and then returns*): Awright, we res' here.

(*They all fall down on the ground.* MARY, MARTIN, *and* BIG
HENRY *are in the middle and center stage.* JIM *wipes his face.*
MOSBY *comes in smoking a cigar.*)

MOSBY: Jim, what're you doin', tryin' to spoil 'em. They
don't pay top price for spoiled niggers in Atlanta.

JIM: I told 'em to rest because we got that river to cross
and I know you don't want to lose none of 'em on the way,
leastwise not if you can help it.

MOSBY: Hmmm. Well, don't any a you coons get any ideas.
If one a you gets sick or injured and cost me any money, so
help me, I'll kill you where you stand.

(*They moan in response.*)

MOSBY: All right. Let's see that river.

(*They exit right.*)

MARTIN: Oh, why didn't they jus' kill me along with Gabe
and get it over with?

MARY (*between* MARTIN *and* BIG HENRY): 'Cause your
black ass is worth more alive than dead.

BIG HENRY: Not to me it ain't. (*He makes at* MARTIN *but*
MARY *gets in between.*)

MARY: What you tryin' to do, make it worse? You want him to come back in here and beat us all? Ain't you men caused enough trouble already with your wuthless selves? I ain't never met a black man yet who had any sense.

(*They all sit down.*)

WOMAN ON THE COFFLE: I wonder if they cut him down yet?

MARY: They ain't never goin' cut him down.

WOMAN: The wind kept blowin' all day and his body was jus' blowin' back and forth with it.

(*Everyone answers with a moan.*)

MARY: With his soul already in hell.

MARTIN: His soul will never leave him.

MARY: 'Cause he never had one in the first place.

BIG HENRY: Woman, shut your mouth.

MARY: Why? He ain't the only one swinging from a tree. We all swinging now. And they ain't never goin' cut us down. They jus' goin' let us swing and swing, back and forth and back and forth, till the neck rots and splits. And then the body'll fall off and dogs'll rip it to pieces. Only it'll be so tough that they'll have to drag it for miles before it'll tear. And then they'll eat it. You goin' feel them eatin' you. Your back bones goin' pop in they teeth, your knee joint goin' crackle in they jaws and your blood goin' spill all over they lips. You'll see the judgment, but you ain't goin' get no salvation.

(*They all answer again with a moan.*)

MARTIN (*falls forward with a moan*): I'se jus' a poor, dumb nigger, sah, that don't mean no harm. Please sah, ah beggin' you, foh Gawd, don't hit me with that stick again.

BIG HENRY: Who you talking to? You lost your mind or something?

MARTIN: Nooo. I'm just practicin'.

MARY: You ain't never needed no practice being a sambo, you was born that way.

(MOSBY *and* JIM *reenter.*)

MOSBY: All right, get up off your black butts. (*He kicks at them as he passes. Some jump up quickly to avoid the boot, others take it and get up slowly, like* BIG HENRY.) Come on, Jim boy, let me see you use that whip. I'm goin' home to Georgia with twice the money I had when I lef'. Yes, sah.

JIM (*reluctantly*): Awright, let's go. (*He cracks the whip and they move out slowly, moaning.*)

MOSBY (*stands triumphantly, puffing his cigar*): Ha, ha, ha. Ain't that a lovely sight.

END OF PLAY

Brotherhood

A SHORT ONE-ACT PLAY

by DOUGLAS TURNER WARD

Douglas Turner Ward's first produced plays, *Happy Ending* and *Day of Absence,* were presented by Robert Hooks at the St. Marks Playhouse, with Ward and Hooks also acting major roles in them. The satiric double-bill were the winners of the Vernon Rice-Drama Desk and Obie Awards, and had a run of well over a year. In August of 1966 Mr. Ward wrote an article for *The New York Times* in which he called for the establishment of a Negro-oriented theater in New York. He envisioned it as combining professional performances by a resident company and an extensive training program for promising actors, playwrights, directors, managerial and technical personnel. It is that vision which has been realized in the establishment of the Negro Ensemble Company, which under Mr. Ward's guidance as artistic director launched its first highly successful season in January of 1968.

CAST OF CHARACTERS (in order of appearance)

TOM JASON
RUTH JASON
JAMES JOHNSON
LUANN JOHNSON

TIME *is the present.*

SETTING: *The living room of the* JASONS' *typical suburban home.* TOM *and* RUTH JASON *are exemplars of this attractive, sophisticated, middle-class, Caucasian environment.* TOM, *a big, open-faced, temple-grayed man with the beginnings of a slight pot-bulge around the waist, dressed casually—shirt open at the collar and wrinkled slacks.* RUTH, *tanned and pretty,*

also wears slacks, topped by a man's checked shirt tied in a bow around her rib cage, leaving midriff bare.

Curtain rises on the couple frantically rushing to prepare for expected visitors, snarling and shouting at each other as they strip the room of furniture and other articles. Little by little, the room is taking on an empty appearance.

NOTE ON PRODUCTION: *Every item removed in this opening scene must be cleverly cloaked to prevent the audience from guessing identities. At no time should the audience recognize objects being removed. An alternative suggestion is to pantomime this first section so as not to impede the flow of continuous movement.*

TOM (*standing on back rim of sofa, draping cloth over a painting*): I told you to take care of this while I was at the office!

RUTH: How could I with all the—Oh, my God! (*Rushing to grab item.*) Didn't you put this with the others?!

TOM (*turning to see*): I thought I had. Must have missed it.

RUTH (*rushing out, lugging weighty object. Sternly on exit*): We can't afford to miss anything!

TOM (*shouting to her offstage*): Why didn't you check! If you'da made a list, we'd be operating with an itemized inventory. Can't you do anything organizedly! (*Leaping from couch on spying another object.*) Another one! (*Grabs it as she rushes back in.*)

RUTH: Where?

TOM: Right here! (*Rushing out.*) This one could be real disaster. I told you to give it priority!

RUTH: The others were just as crucial! Don't underestimate them!

TOM (*reentering*): I'm not underestimating anything! They're all dangerous!

RUTH (*interrupting*): Look, there! Another one!

TOM: Where?!

RUTH: THERE!

TOM: Oh, my aching fanny!

RUTH: Let's move it.

TOM: Not enough time. Cover it up! (*She snatches for a large cloth.*) Not that! It's being used! . . . Take that one!

RUTH: It's being used too!

TOM: Get a sheet from the closet!

RUTH: Used 'em up already!

TOM: The spread off the bed!

RUTH: In use too!

TOM: The blanket on the kids' bed!?

RUTH: It's free!

TOM: Snatch it! (*She rushes out. He climbs back up on the couch to finish draping. She dashes back with blanket. He jumps down to help her.*) What time is it?

RUTH: Almost eight!

TOM: We're late!

RUTH (*suddenly cracking under the strain*): I can't do it! (*Verging on tears.*)

TOM: Don't panic! We're almost through. Just keep your equilibrium. We can do it if we attack this thing systematically . . . Now, you start from that end, I'll start from this corner. We'll scout thoroughly until we connect. Okay . . . ?

RUTH: I'll try.

(*They take positions on opposite sides of the room.*)

TOM: Ready . . . ??? . . . Let's go!

(*They scurry around in a tight-lipped, stylized ballet of search and seizure, removal, departure and return—all done with underlying hysteria. As they converge on the center of the room, the doorbell rings. They stiffen. Panic startles their faces.* RUTH *breaks for the door.*)

TOM (*in passionate whisper*): Wait!!!

(*Through sign language, he indicates they must complete the survey. Resuming, they hurriedly pace back and forth until they bump shoulders in the center of floor. Siamese-bound like toy soldiers in a mechanical drill, they march shoulder to shoulder over final space.*)

RUTH: Now . . . ?

TOM: Yes—NO! Wait! . . . Let me check the closet again. (*He exits as she freezes, eyes fixed on door from whence insistent bell is ringing.*)

TOM (*reentering*): It's all right. Just had to cram a little tighter.

(RUTH *primps, brushing hair and smoothing slacks.* TOM *repairs own disarray.* RUTH *starts toward door, destiffening her face en route. Reaching the door, her face blossoms into a radiant smile.* TOM's, *likewise. With great flourish, she swings door open.*)

RUTH: Helllooooooo!

(*Standing there are* JAMES *and* LUANN JOHNSON, *a Negro couple of the Jasons' age-group.* JAMES *is so sharply dressed that the crease in his pants legs gleams threateningly like a brand-new razor blade.* LUANN *equally dazzles in a stylish ensemble that would make a Dior model look like a frump. They enter.*)

231

JAMES: How are you?

TOM: Hi.

LUANN: Hello.

TOM (*introducing*): James, my wife, Ruth.

JAMES: My wife, LuAnn.

LUANN: Hello.

RUTH: Hi.

JAMES: Glad to meet you.

TOM: Delighted you made it. Have any trouble finding the place?

JAMES: No, but for a moment we didn't think we had the right house. Nobody seemed to be home.

RUTH: Oh, that! . . . Our bell is rather erratic—temperamental, you know. Sometimes it beeps and other times it blares, ha, ha, ha . . . Almost didn't hear it. Wouldn't it have been terrible, I mean if we hadn't heard it at all, ha, ha, ha.

TOM: Enter our little domain . . . Not lavish, but livable. (*Intercepts* JAMES *from sitting in chair flanked by one of the covered objects.*) Wait a minute! Not there, more comfortable over here. (*Leads* LUANN *away from another draped item.*) And you . . . here . . . That's just fine. (*As* LUANN *is about to sit,* RUTH *whisks something from seat of chair and backs out sheepishly.*)

JAMES: We aren't late, are we?

TOM: Of course not.

JAMES: We dreaded being tardy birds for our first get-together.

TOM: Right on the dot . . . Ruth, scrape up some refreshments. What's your pleasure?

JAMES: Both Scotch, if you don't mind.

RUTH: Splendid. We share similar tastes. Scotches coming up.

LUANN: Can I help you?

RUTH: No! . . . I don't permit guests to even lift a pinky. (*Exits.*)

JAMES (*taking out a cigarette*): Might I smoke?

TOM: Certainly, by all means, go right ahead.

JAMES (*looking around on discovering no ashtrays*): Er . . . do you have an ashtray handy?

TOM (*face reddens*): Oh . . . don't bother. Just flick 'em on the floor. Ruth and I don't use them . . . Out of nostalgia for the days of coldwater flats, bohemian disorder and dangerous contretemps. Wonderful period. We elected to keep ashtrays in eternal banishment to remind us that a house should never become a museum.

JAMES: Very original. Never thought of it that way.

TOM: Scatter them freely. The house will survive.

LUANN (*who has lit her own cigarette, letting the ashes fly*): It's exquisite . . . such an interesting room.

TOM (*who has been smiling sickly at the flying ashes, recovers quickly*): Yes, yes! . . . Er . . . the latest in decor, you know! . . . The modern trend is to dispense with as much bric-a-brac as possible . . . Leaves more room for the expansion of the people within.

JAMES: An interesting concept, er, er . . . ?

TOM: Tom, James. Tom. No need for formality with us. We're going to be old buddies—(*Sees* RUTH *approaching with a tray of drinks.*) RUTH!

(*Startled by his shout,* RUTH *glances at label on bottle, then hastily hides it behind her back, backing out with an embarrassed grin on her face.*)

JAMES: Is something the matter?

TOM: Er . . . ha, ha . . . It's nothing . . . It's just . . . It's just a thing between us. Ruth is so absent-minded, ha, ha, ha. She always gets the drinks ready and forgets to bring the DRINK! Ha, ha, ha. You ever heard of anything so absurd! Ha, ha, ha! (RUTH *reenters, smiling sheepishly, carrying a bottle of Black and White.*) You are so ridiculous, my dear, ha, ha, ha!

RUTH (*to* JAMES *and* LUANN *as she sets tray down.*) Mixed or straight? On the rocks or off?

JAMES: Straight, on.

LUANN: Same for me.

RUTH: Should I pour?

JAMES: Good enough for me.

LUANN: Me, too.

RUTH (*pouring*): Say when?

JAMES: . . . When.

LUANN: . . . Fine.

RUTH: I forgot stirrers.

TOM: What'd I tell you, a regular sieve in her memory, ha, ha.

JAMES: Use your finger, probably make it sweeter, ha, ha.

RUTH: What a nice thing to say.

LUANN: Oh, James is always loaded with nice sayings.

RUTH: What an absolutely gorgeous dress, er, er . . . ?

LUANN: LuAnn, LuAnn.

TOM: I was just advising that we drop the formality, Ruth. Among friends there's no need to trade in last names.

RUTH: It is a gorgeous dress, LuAnn.

233

LUANN: Thank you, Ruth. James selected it.

RUTH: Oh, how nice! Tom should only have such refinement.

TOM: Feminine apparel is not up my alley, James.

RUTH: You must help him sharpen his appreciation.

JAMES: Be glad to give a few pointers.

RUTH (*sits at* JAMES' *feet*): How nice. Isn't that nice, Tom?

TOM: I'm afraid you have a bad pupil here, James. New tricks for an old mongoose is quite a feat.

JAMES: Really nothing to it, Tom. Developing an eye for the female anatomy can be acquired even if you aren't gifted with natural instincts. With a little concentrated observation, skill becomes embedded in your sensory equipment. Your retinal fibers become so honed until you can tell at a glance whether a woman needs more draping to highlight a virtue or more ballooning to suppress a defect. It's like art: the more you look, the more you see . . . Like that draped painting over there—

TOM (*blanches as* JAMES *focuses on wall spot*): Oh . . . It's not draped—James. The way it is . . . Yes . . . the painting itself. It's the latest thing . . . Called "Fabric Over Frame" . . . A radical departure . . . Creating quite a stir in the art world. Indeed it is!

LUANN: That's fabulous. You must recommend us to your dealer so we can appraise one for possible purchase. It's fascinating! . . . Oh, James! We have so much to learn! (*Turns to* TOM *and* RUTH.) You have no idea how limiting our old environment was!

RUTH: Not if your taste in clothes is any barometer . . . Why, Tom and I, even with the most determined effort, could never aspire to your chic and elegance!

LUANN: Oh, that's different! So easy. Insignificant! . . . As James says, all you have to do is alert your eyes. Clothes are paraded around you. People wear them, shops exhibit them, publications hawk them. Why, even a Hottentot would find it difficult to avoid the preeminence of fashion and modiste. But acquiring taste and appreciation of such subtleties as the fine arts completely eludes the reach of one not correctly exposed. We've been seeking this atmosphere for so long. We're going to love it. I just know it!

TOM: Benefits will work both ways. I sensed that immediately, didn't I, dear?

RUTH: We both did.

LUANN: Oh, but we have so much more to gain . . . discover . . . explore! Don't we, James?

JAMES: Absolutely!

TOM: Come now! You're underestimating yourselves. Aren't they, Ruth?

LUANN: But we do!

TOM, RUTH: Oh, no!

JAMES: Yes, it's true!

RUTH: Now, we aren't going to permit you to be overmodest. *You're* the catalyst which will metamorphize *our* existence. Any other attitude is completely retrogressive.

JAMES: But consider the ignorance we've already displayed. (*Points to a draped object.*) Ordinarily, I would have taken this for just another covered piece of furniture or decoration. However, noticing how it matches so perfectly with the Ahvant painting, I now suspect it is a companion piece—probably sculpturally—of the same artistic style.

TOM: (*flushing*): Right!

RUTH: Yes!

TOM: What perception. It would have taken eons for someone else to have grasped that so quick. Wouldn't it, Ruth?

RUTH: Uncanny!

JAMES: Never would have occurred to me without your generous guidance. (*Rises and walks over to object in question.* TOM *and* RUTH *are paralyzed in fearful anticipation.*) Now I'm stimulated further. My curiosity is whetted as to how the result was achieved—the technique behind the underlying conception creating this hanging effect of draped folds— (*Reaches toward object.* TOM *and* RUTH *are apoplectic.*)

TOM, RUTH: NO!

TOM: Don't touch it! You'll ruin it! . . . It's . . . it's integral! . . . If disturbed, the form will be unalterably destroyed!

LUANN: Stop, James!

JAMES (*quickly backing away*): I'm sorry . . . What a boob I am. Forgive me . . . I have so much to learn . . . Please have patience; with your assistance, in time I will though. (*Sits down disconsolate.*)

TOM (*attempting to cheer him up*): It's really nothing, James. No harm done. We were just a trifle excited. We owe you an apology.

JAMES: No, it's all my fault.

RUTH: That's not so. Don't ever feel that way!

TOM: DEFINITELY NOT! . . . Now don't be gloomy. A little music. Just what we need. (*Rushes to record stand and twists knob on player. Record drops. He starts to walk away as tune is about to begin.*)

RUTH (*shouting*): TOM!

TOM (*jumping back to machine*): I always forget! (*Quickly turns another knob. Music blares out in a frenzied discord of Donald Duck gibberish.*)

JAMES (*listening puzzledly*): Right speed?

TOM: Oh, yes, definitely. The latest sound. If you don't adjust it to this speed, the record is ruined. Quite delicate these days.

JAMES: Another example of our deprivation. If I had stumbled upon this music alone, I would have sworn the record was at the wrong speed. Something new absorbed again.

LUANN: In one sitting, we're ingesting more than the rest of our life.

TOM: Consuming from each other! Mutual give and take . . . Like this Scotch, wouldn't you say, James? Rather symbolic, don't you think? (*Displaying Black and White prominently.*)

JAMES: Good Scotch.

TOM (*waxing rhapsodic*): You don't know what pleasure it gives us to have you. Before your arrival, I told Ruth what a relief it would be escaping the treadmill of our regular social monotony—staring into the same old faces, suffocating in stale chatter, bogged down in ridiculous routines. Stagnating! Utter stagnation! . . . Ruth, I said, it's our privilege to receive James and his wife. They honor us by sharing our company this evening. Many evenings more, Ruth, I said—

LUANN (*rising, fidgety*): Pardon me, but could I use your bathroom?

TOM: Why of course. By all means. Go through that door—

RUTH: NO, TOM!

TOM: (*intercepting* LUANN): NO, WAIT! . . . I forgot . . . We've been doing a lot of renovation and the bathroom's an absolute mess.

LUANN: . . . Oh? . . . That's all right, I'll manage. I just need enough room to squeeze in, ha, ha, ha . . .

TOM: No, that's what I mean . . . It's out of whack . . . out of order, you see . . . (*Greatly embarrassed.*) I'm afraid the only thing we have to offer you is the . . . is the . . . kids' . . . the kids' . . . potty?

LUANN: ??? . . . I . . . I . . . think I'll have to use that . . .

TOM: Come, I'll get it for you. (*Starts to lead her to another exit.*)

RUTH: She can't get through there, either, Tom! The other things are in the way!

TOM: That's right! I'm sorry . . .

LUANN: ??? . . . Well, I'll just go outside, if it's all right?

TOM: Of course; I'll show you.

RUTH: *I'll* show her, Tom. Come, LuAnn, I know just the spot.

(*They exit.*)

TOM: Awfully sorry about the inconvenience, James.

JAMES: Don't give it a thought, Tom. I understand perfectly. Things like this happen. Can't be avoided.

TOM: Glad you understand.

JAMES: Would be idiotic not to, Tom. I've always considered a true mark of friendship the ability to accept minor inconveniences. Aware of how imperfect we all can be in striving to provide utmost comfort for the other.

TOM: Very generous, James.

JAMES: We should never allow our own impatience to communicate itself.

TOM: Shrewd observation.

JAMES: —not expect ideal circumstances as a gauge of our friends' feelings toward us—

TOM: So true!

JAMES: —not place too much value on inconvenience—

TOM: Certainly!

JAMES: —because, after all, an inconvenience to us is also an inconvenience to our friends—

TOM: Right!

JAMES: —and nobody likes to be inconvenienced—

TOM: How true!

JAMES: Therefore, an inconvenience which perturbs a friend and causes inconvenience for one's self cannot be calculated because no one knowingly inconveniences themselves.

TOM: Perfect!

JAMES: So if it's not done on purpose, there's no reason why it should figure in judgment!

TOM: Admirable thinking! (RUTH *and* LUANN *reenter.*) That was quick. Everything flow smoothly?

RUTH: Without a hitch.

LUANN: No trouble at all. Quite prophetic. I don't think it's possible that anything—absolutely nothing—could happen which would ruffle the tranquility of this evening's encounter. When we—

RUTH: TOM!!!

TOM (*startled*): What!!!?

RUTH: The . . . check! . . . The children!

TOM: ??? Check . . . children?—Jesus Christ, yes! (*He dashes out.*)

JAMES: Can we be of any help?

237

RUTH: No, no! Sit right there, where you are. It's nothing. Just . . . Just . . . a check—for the children . . . the children . . . YOUR CHILDREN! . . . Yes! . . . Your children! I was telling Tom how nice it would be if—(*Raising voice loudly.*) Tom, Tom! I said, if you don't remember it right away, you're going to forget the check for the children. Tom! Don't forget the check we promised for James and his wife's children. Don't forget the check now, Tom!

TOM (*offstage*): Thanks for reminding me, dear.

JAMES: I don't understand?

RUTH: You see, Tom and I felt that since we were embarking on a beautiful friendship with extraordinary people, wouldn't it be nice to inaugurate the occasion with a memento of a gift to the kiddies. An expressive token of our affection—a tangible gesture which would embrace them even in their absence . . . Don't you think it would please them?

LUANN: It's a beautiful thought, but we couldn't accept it.

JAMES: Wouldn't think of it. The sentiment's more than adequate.

RUTH (*addressing* TOM *as he reenters*): All right?

TOM: Just in time. Loosened a bit, but fixed.

RUTH: I was just explaining to James and LuAnn about their children's involvement through the check.

TOM: Here it is. Take it.

LUANN: Wouldn't think of it.

TOM: We want you to.

LUANN: The kids will be overjoyed to merely know that Mommy and Daddy were among friends.

JAMES: That's right.

TOM: No, please take it. It would mean so much to us.

JAMES (*pauses as* TOM *stands before him offering check forlornly*): All right! We accept.

TOM (*greatly relieved*): Thank you. (*Hands* JAMES *check.*)

JAMES: *We* thank *you* . . . And since the gesture is too immaculate to be incarnated in materiality, we enshrine the sentiment in our memory by—(*With deliberate, dramatic flourish, he tears check into quarters.*) All right?

TOM (*extremely moved*): Fair enough!

RUTH (*awe-stricken*): What an absolutely beautiful poetic gesture.

LUANN: It hardly measures the beauty of your thought. We will convey your sentiments to our little ones . . . I'm ashamed we didn't think of some comparable gesture toward yours . . . Are they here?

RUTH: They—

TOM: —went to their grandparents. We didn't want anything to distract from this first evening with you. You know what a nuisance kids can be in strange company.

LUANN: They wouldn't have bothered us . . . Give them our love.

RUTH: We certainly will.

JAMES: Our pair and your duo must also get together for comradely introductions. If yours can be as enlightening with ours as you have already been with us, then ours are sure to be rewarded as beneficiaries of a rich experience and a wealth of insight.

RUTH: And yours on ours.

TOM: Let's drink to that!

JAMES: Right!

(*Glasses are lifted.*)

TOM: Nothing stimulates greater bonhommie than consorting with harmonious companions—

JAMES: Sipping good Scotch—

LUANN: In ideal surroundings—

RUTH: Exchanging climactic experiences!

TOM: Forever and all evenings to come!

ALL: SKOAL!!!

(*Scene freezes into a still-life frame with the seated foursome remaining statically positioned, glasses aloft. They remain motionless long enough to create a passage-of-time effect. The frieze is broken finally and the quartet abruptly resume activity.* JAMES *and* LUANN *are rising to depart.*)

LUANN: Marvelous evening!

RUTH: Glorious gathering!

TOM: Must do a repeat soon, huh, James?

JAMES: You bet.

TOM: Haven't had such a time in eras.

JAMES: Neither have I.

LUANN: Our turn next time.

RUTH: Looking forward to it.

JAMES: We're anxious for more enlightenment.

RUTH: You've got to teach *us!*

TOM: Exchange instructions, huh?

JAMES: Great!

LUANN (*moving toward door*): Lovely time. Couldn't have been lovelier.

RUTH: We're so glad.

TOM: Keep in touch.

RUTH: Wouldn't forgive you if you didn't!

JAMES: Don't worry.

LUANN: 'Bye now.

JAMES: 'Night.

(*He and* LUANN *exit through door.*)

TOM: Be careful on the way home.

RUTH: Please do . . . And keep James spouting those deliciously quaint compliments, LuAnn.

LUANN (*offstage*): I couldn't stop him . . . Our affection to the kids.

RUTH: Yes. Same to yours. 'Night.

JAMES, LUANN (*offstage*): 'Night.

(TOM *and* RUTH *remain in door watching them disappear. They shut door, moving to window to watch some more. Finally, they turn, wordless, gazing into each other's eyes. The dam breaks, hysteria erupts. They clutch. Locked in embrace, they bound around the room, laughing and crying deliriously.* TOM *elevates* RUTH *in his arms and whirls her around. Suddenly stopping, their faces light up in maniacal glee. Hands are rubbed vigorously, eyes dart madly around the room. On the verge of proceeding,* TOM *stops* RUTH. "WAIT!" . . . *He tiptoes back to window, looks out carefully. Satisfied, he bellows:* "NOW!"*

Opening scene procedure is reversed. Now, the couple scurry around returning objects to original positions. Husband and spouse seem possessed of superhuman strength. Statues beyond weight are carried with ridiculous ease. Each item is caressed and drooled over. Each elicits mad pleasure on unveilment.

The scene is one of controlled frenzy—a gargoyle ballet. In time, the room spills over with a grotesque menagerie of Negro plantation statuettes: crimson-lipped, white eye-rimmed jockeys; bandanaed mammies; bare-assed ashtray blacks; ebony pissing-stanced lamps, and a staggering profusion of diverse artifacts of "Niggerphalia."

The "Fabric Over Frame" painting is undraped and deliciously sadistic scenes of Negroes being brutalized dominate the motif.

The record box is clicked to its right speed and "Old Black Joe" blares out.

The unveiling is accomplished with swift impact. When finished, the fiendishly contented couple sit, limp, relishing the scene, panting in joy and relief, yet weary.)

RUTH: I'll fix us a drink.

TOM: Good.

(RUTH *exits as* TOM *lights a "Nigger-pipe" and cushions feet on a "Niggercomfort-Footrest."* RUTH *soon returns with*

two gleaming mint juleps. Sets hers down after handing one to TOM, *picks up the Black and White bottle and smashes it, ship-christening fashion, against one of the statuettes. She plops down on couch, suddenly jumping up abruptly.*)

RUTH: The children! We forgot! They might have gagged to death in the closet!

TOM (*too weary for concern*): You see 'bout 'em, I'm too pooped.

(RUTH *hurries offstage. Briefly, a shout is heard.*)

RUTH (*offstage*): THANK GOD, THEY'RE ALL RIGHT . . . Yes, darlings, it's all right now . . . Daddy and Mommy had to do it . . . Yes, we love you . . . Yes, dears, you can sing to your heart's content now.

(*As she returns onstage, we hear two high-pitched adolescent voices singsonging the mixed strains of "Eeny Meeny" and "Little Black Sambo," which drifts in and mingles with "Swanee River," now issuing from the record player.*)

RUTH (*retrieving her drink and sitting*): . . . What about next time?

TOM: . . . Just hafta get started sooner, that's all.

(*Lights dim.*)

END OF SCENE

Dramatic Epilogue

(*Lights rise on two figures emerging out of darkness, making strange motions on approach.* JAMES *and* LUANN *are recognized.* JAMES *is gnashing his teeth viciously, crooking one arm about an invisible throat and with the other hand, slashing it brutally with a gigantic knife.* LUANN *trails behind, raptly concentrated on repeatedly sticking a long hatpin into a voodoo-doll likeness of* RUTH.)

LUANN (*without pausing in her attention*): What about the check?

JAMES: I'll paste it together when we git home.

(*They continue their ministrations as they head offstage. Lights dim to blackout.*)

THE END . . . . ?

The One

A PLAY

by OLIVER PITCHER

Oliver Pitcher has taught at Bard College, the New School, and the American Negro Theater. He is currently teaching black drama at Vassar College. Several of his plays have been optioned for Off-Broadway and Off-Off-Broadway. His poetry is represented in numerous anthologies of black poets.

CAST

BOOBOO, a young Negro

(*A small gray box of a room. Three walls. Left, right, and upstage. No doors, no windows. In blackout. Sound of frantic pounding on a door . . . Silence . . . Light.*)

BOOBOO (*in a fit of agony*): You turn me on yeh yeh yeh where the machine gun was on top of the truck cabin yeh yeh yeh WHERE'S A BRICK? yeh yeh yeh you turn me on yeh yeh yeh YOU OLD BAG yeh yeh yeh you turn me on yeh yeh yeh. SOMEBODY STOP HIM.

(*Lies out motionless on a heap of rags. More light. A low stool. One yellow sock hangs high on right wall. BOOBOO, a young Negro, wears a sweater, pants, one yellow sock, one green sock, no shoes.*)

No; it doesn't seem . . . no, not that way, not at all . . . Yet I do remember it being . . . well . . . sort of . . . (*Elated.*) Yes! it was that way. (*Downcast.*) Exactly as I knew it was going to be, even before it unfortunately happened. Unfortunately. (*Enumerates. Gibberish. Then, highly satisfied.*) Yeh-be-it! EXACTLY. Punctiliously to the letter! "HAAA-OOO!" comes the joy-cry from Genitalia! Not even an echo? In the not too distant midlands? . . . Midlands? Fair-to-middlin'?

(*Shrugs. Contagion. Head, shoulders, toes, twitch. He discovers an imaginary audience, bows deeply, smiles charmingly.*)

Hi. No matter what anybody will tell you, I really get my kicks from instant dancing. An eye screens, a shoulder shudders, the chin betrays; thechinbetraysashouldershuddersaneye screens. I both lead and follow. And toes—

(*Discovers his yellow and green feet, stares, searches among the floor debris, speaking offhandedly.*)

Music, of course; I'm not that far gone. And I've been doing it, instant dancing, ever since I was a child. (*Trips over*

a garment.) Ooops, my one-and-only Mommy. Excuse me, Ma. (*To audience.*) As you can see, I live in a collage . . . My mother used to say I never was. A child. BRAGGED ABOUT IT. Well, you saw to that, you old bag.

(*Hangs a dilapidated dress by the shoulder seams on left wall. Distracted by indistinguishable sounds,* BOOBOO *goes to a far wall, listens . . .*)

Whew. I thought they'd come. The invasion, the Marching Multitude. Mice. Did you ever notice how sometimes people's voices a long way off sound like mice chewing wood? (*Listens. Laughs.*) You should've heard what he said AFTER he got out of bed! But she had the last laugh. It wasn't until he was outside the building, and locked out, that he realized he was wearing HER shoes! Ohhh, I'm sorry to say one thing but mean . . . another. It's cruel, and isn't that what confusion is, cruelty? Confusion is a common dominion but, thank God, we can come to conclusions in the sacred privacy of our nodding skulls. (*Listens at wall . . . Irritated almost beyond control.*) IF ONLY PAUL KLEE DIDN'T SOUND THE WAY ARNOLD SCHOENBERG LOOKS. Ooops, dropped another name. (*Returns to searching, speaking offhandedly.*) What the hell drop away nothing shatters easily these days everything is made of gray dough except the days themselves and they droppeth like the gently rain from heaven SHATTERING. (*Discovers garter belt with nylon hose attached.*) Ah luv luv luv luv luv luv luv luv etceterahh.

(*Embraces, caresses belt; capers, hum-mumbles. Eventually, he gets stocking from belt, hangs belt on upstage wall, lays stockings out on debris heap. He throws kisses at them as he removes sweater. He lies down beside* LUV *to make tender love . . .*)

Each time I'm with you, One-and-only, I AM A KING . . . I know as a king knows: every appearance invites assassination. But, then, haven't I been knitting and purling my own shroud? . . . So wha wha wha to do? Why, come we all to everyone else's nothing. Mouse turd. Nobody but nobody comes to looksee for nada. Expectation is why we inhale and exhale . . . albeit only occasionally. (*Starts to kiss* LUV, *recoils.*) GodDAMN. (*Scrambles about, finds sweater, rises, puts on sweater.*) Wherever I press my mouth to you damn if I don't taste somebody else! Disconcerting, baby! I have never been that fond of smorgasbord.

"Just one minute, baby! You turn me on, yes, we turn each other on, but I see where I'm gonna have to turn you loose, find me a man what comes on strong. You don't come

on NO kinda way, draggin' me 'roun' to them ole coffee houses an' art films and things. Don't you be poppin' you eyes at me, I know what's wrong wiff you. You evil cause you ain't white!" (*Stunned, a dull voice.*)

I never wanted to be a white man, One-and-only. I've always wanted white man's rights. I accept my color. I can't accept my role.

"That's what you *say* . . . I kinda think I would go real fine wiff the decor at the Persian Room, don't you think?" (*A sudden, fierce retaliation.*) "WHEN YA GOT BREAD, FOOL, YA CAN COME ON STRONG. That's it, that did it, I'm just gonna have to find me a white man! Get up off my eyelashes!"

I just stood there and looked at the bitch . . . I had trouble all right. So I went to the UN.

(*Stares at audience, suddenly whirls about, touches left wall. Panic is mounting as he rushes to upstage wall.*)

ISN'T THIS THE UN?? . . . TESTING! TESTING! 0 9 8 7 6 5 4 3 2 1! . . . 1?? . . . WHAT COMES AFTER 1???

(*Mauls walls, reaching, jumping up and down, trying to climb over . . . He stands panting for a moment . . . Defeated.*)

Okay . . . So? So this is not the UN.

(*Blackout except for small spotlight on stool area. This area is bare, no rags, just the stool. In lighted area,* BOOBOO's *expressions, eyes, roving fingers indicate he is carefully making a selection . . .*)

According to the critics on the dust jacket, this is a . . . "Profound," "Penetrating," "Persuasive," "Purging" . . . work of literary art . . . Hmm. "Two for a quarter."

(*Blows dust from imaginary book, coughs, clears the air, opens book, "reads."*)

"Entering upon a sheet of snow a slow convoy of army trucks and Negro soldiers but this was another war, World War Two, and this unit which was attached to front-line tank units although somehow possibly by the slip of some red tape they were never classified as invasion forces or given the dubious credit.

Entering Germany, there had been and still was much fighting . . . snipers . . . plucked out of rock gardens, bodies . . . nerves . . . and German soldiers surrendering. The surrendering had become so common . . . we men had become so bored . . . giddy . . . distrustful of war . . . none of us could arouse . . . surprise . . . elation . . . or even wry amusement. Delicate instincts . . . even sensibilities . . . cached away in hollowed-out vacuous 50 mm. shells somewhere

245

passed . . . waiting to be taken up . . . nourished another time if such was the possibility. We men rode along slowly in the convoy . . . watched the voluntary Nazi prisoners pass by . . . hands clasped behind their heads in surrender . . . dimly aware but hardly seeing. (BOOBOO's *interest begins to mount.*)

There was one fellow, Private A., riding on our truck. Everyone knew this colored Arkansas boy was intensely anti-white, but too many of us soldiers shared the same animosity, in lesser degrees, to give a damn about his feelings or lack of feelings. Familiarity had bred unconcern. Private A. would never even look our white officers in their faces; such was his contempt. He would always look just past them; his cheek muscles would flex spasmodically. (BOOBOO *is no longer reading—he discards the book—yet, reliving, he continues the story.*)

How did he keep his sense of humor? He would say, "I salutes um. Then I shoots um. POW POW POW POW POW. Click. Click. Click." He had lived with the color of his skin all of his life, he accepted that. But he had never accepted his role. The convoy stopped. Five-minute break. Short puffs of steam . . . from mouths . . . nostrils. Conversation hushed . . . Ahead . . . more surrendering Nazis . . . half-stumbling . . . snow packed . . . polished to ice on the soles of their shoes. Some . . . obscure compulsion lifted him from his seat . . . propelled him stealthily to the front of the truck where the machine gun was on top of the truck cabin . . . SOMEBODY STOP HIM. (*Loud blasts of machine-gun fire.*) "You WHITE bastards. You WHITE dogs. You WHITE sons of a bitch." . . . Not once did he say NAZI . . .

For a detached moment, Private A. experienced pure awe. He never dreamed in his confusion of sleep out of tune with compassion that men so pale could gush forth so much blood glaringly red! from their skulls . . . from their groins . . . Our white officers mistook the shooting for snipers being plucked from trees . . . Not one of us spoke up.

The break's up. The signal given. Gears went into place. The convoy . . . some many-legged, long, carnivorous creature . . . slowly moved on. Fifteen soldiers lie off to the side of the road. Fourteen soldiers dead. The fifteenth one . . . he moves a leg in slow spasms. Snow and silence curtains the scene.

(*Silent pause.* BOOBOO *"retrieves" the book from floor, brushes off cover, scans some pages, throws it on floor.*)

That sure is a piece of bad-ass writing!

(*But his mood is heavy; he attempts to toss it off, singing to the tune of "Carolina Moon."* "Sauerbraten moon, stop shin-

ing, Shining on . . . the one? . . . the one . . . the one!" *Horrible memory-images stop him, his body contracts in slow spasms, tears come to his eyes. Suddenly he is screaming and screaming, clawing the air, until he topples over, and into the debris, exhausted. He lies panting for a moment. Across the room he sees the hanging dress. He quickly rises up on his knees.*)

Ma? . . . Ma! (*A rare moment of complete lucidity.*) I watched you grow inward and inward until you were nothing more than a fly speck. You had too little to begin with. Naturally, the next step? You went to work on Pa, belittle him for not being a young prince come riding up in a white Cadillac. You belittled him into brittle hostility and you held out and won. You hammered away until he was bite-size . . . good, crunchy eatin'. What were your words, Ma? "Anything ANY white woman can do, I can do better!" How right you were. Yes, you did the job better. The job of emasculating, *castrating,* my father. And when the job was finished? What were your words, Ma? "He shouldn't've been so *weak.*" (*Chuckles to himself.*)

When I was fifteen, I called you a transvestite. You asked me what the word meant. I said it meant Chairman of the Board. In capital letters! You liked that. You loved that! . . . After that, how could I call you an old bag? Even though you are an old bag. I was always your Little Man—caps again!— because you wanted to save me from everything you were afraid of. You tried. It didn't quite work. It never does. Amen. (*Still on his knees, he walks to dress.*) Maybe we've hung each other up, Fatso. I'll say I'm sorry . . . Will you? . . . Please??

(*Rises, climbs up into dress until he is half covered. Small spot picks out yellow sock hanging high on opposite wall. Turning around inside dress, one of* BOOBOO's *eyes is visible through a rip in dress. Pointing, he spots the sock and comes out of dress. Elation. He opens his arms wide but with each step toward the sock his arms mechanically close about his chest until, right at the sock, he is clutching his chest tightly as though in a straitjacket. Confusion, alarm, struggle, panic. No success. Panting . . . Idea. He faces the wall, then methodically retraces his steps, walking backward to opposite wall. In doing so, arms unfold until he is in his former position.*)

Anybody'd think I was out of my mind: talking to myself like this. SILENCE. (*Sits, gets comfortable on debris. Pause.*) That's more like it. I DEMAND SILENCE . . . ME . . . "Who?" . . . I! . . . "Oh. 'I' who? Sorry, 'I' WHOM?" . . . That's better. The many Me's of the one and only "I" demand silence from the . . . one and only . . . "I" . . . which is only

247

. . . One. (*Staring. Appalled.*) Yeh, yeh, yeh, yeh, yeh, yeh. (*Frightened.*) Oh God! NO ONE ELSE TO FACE? . . . NO ONE . . . (*Snaps out of it; confidential, to audience.*) You see, I am not Christ. In the script it says I am to SCREAM, scream, mind you!—I, AND I ALONE, AM TO BLAME FOR IT ALL . . . BLAME?? No thank you. I turn down the part, I am not Christ. Mankind—as I know it—is the very sick playwright. (*Spotlight on sock goes on and off, playfully winking . . . Chortling.*) Wink on, wink on, Sneaky . . . Like hell you do, Sneaky, and you know it! Nah, you're just saying that, and you know—! (*Spotlight has gone off . . .*) How'd I ever confuse THIS place with the UN? The UN is glass . . . vulnerable . . . and real! Real as anything! (*His eyes light up diabolically.*) Oh yes, look at all that glass! (*Pantomime: search and discovery of a brick. He "throws" brick, looks to ground mock-dolefully.*) Tch tch tch. Look at all that glass! "Whatever got into that boy to do a thing like that!" . . . Well, now, Mr. U Thant.* I'll tell you, it's like this—(*Sound of pounding . . . A fit of agony.*)

You turn me on yeh yeh yeh where the machine gun was on top of the truck cabin yeh yeh yeh WHERE'S A BRICK? yeh yeh yeh YOU OLD BAG yeh yeh yeh you turn me on yeh yeh yeh. RUNNING! RUNNING!—SCREAMING IN THE NIGHT—FROM A SLIPPERY SPOOK NAMED AMBIGUITY, I CAME TO A DOOR, I POUNDED AND I POUNDED. A VOICE CALLING ITSELF PARADOX ANSWERED. HE DID NOT LET ME IN . . . And all I wanted to ask was a question, just one simple question, as a beggar might ask for a dime. WHY AM I ALWAYS FIGHTING MY OWN WAR? And this is a war I have less choice to fight than any war I'm forced to fight . . . Why have I not learned to love that which I do not know? Stupid stupid stupid of me! Simple questions always have complex answers. Anyone will tell you that . . . who cannot or prefers not to answer . . . So, you see, Mr. U Thant, I was a long time making it here to Sanctuary. I just barely managed to get enough plaid stamps.

(*Blackout. And immediately the tiny spot comes on downstage, on floor, shining brightly.*)

Where does that speck of light keep coming from? The Marching Multitude? Damn, I must be losing my mind! (*Gets down on all fours with his head in spotlight close to floor.*) A peephole? . . . Crack? In the wall? At the bottom of the wall, a crack! Well, dearie me! And . . . people OUTside???

* Or whoever is currently Secretary General.

Shucks. Maybe just maybe?? TESTING. TESTING. (*Clears his throat, makes all the pompous gestures of one about to make a history-making speech, then shouts through the "hole."*) WHY DO MICE HAVE SMALL BALLS? (*Waits for an answer, then.*) BECAUSE THEY REALLY DON'T LIKE TO DANCE. (*Sotto voce.*) Anybody'd laugh at that I wouldn't want to address anyway, my audience is . . . (*His eyes light up.*) My audience is . . . ALL THE UNBORN BABIES.

(*Aloud, resounding WHACK like a smack across the face. The impact of it makes* BOOBOO *topple over. Another whack— which, groveling about—he almost misses. His head is thrown back suddenly, skyward. There is a two-way dialogue going on; however, the other party is not heard . . .*)

Yezzuh . . . Yep . . . B—but . . . YezZUH . . . Aw, c'mon, man . . . Blasphemy??? . . . What do you mean: BLASPHEMY?! . . . B—but . . . I only want to address . . . my audience . . . which just so happens to be . . . SO??? . . . They've got to start somewhere! Sooner the—!

(*More WHACKS.* BOOBOO *topples over backward in the debris like somersaults . . . Finally, a sudden logomanticity like an open deluge of words held back for centuries.*)

PAROLE TIME! HALLELUJAH, IT'S STAR-TURN TIME FOR THE PAROLEES! I AM MAN AND I'M GIVING YOU ANOTHER CHANCE! YOU!! LETTING YOU OUT ON PAROLE BECAUSE, IN YOUR SELF-IMPOSED EXILE, IT WAS HARD TO FIND A JOB FOR YOU. NOT BECAUSE YOU WEREN'T AN A-OK CARPENTER, IT'S JUST THAT THERE'S AUTOMATION NOW. BUT, JUST THINK, ANOTHER CHANCE! AND MAN! REMEMBER! WHICH YOU CREATED IN YOUR IMAGE IS GOING TO GIVE YOU ANOTHER—! (*Covers his nose. Silence . . .*) Okay, Okay, you made your point . . . I've got a bloody nose . . . BLOOD! . . .

YOUR point, yeh, you've MADE IT! . . . Damn, you sure pack a mean right! (*Searches in the pockets of his Eisenhower jacket, finds a Band-Aid, tapes one nostril, holds his head back.*) Why do I all the time have to keep looking up at them cotton-candy clouds . . . just like I could, should, would, just might, see You? . . . There, now. Did you create me in Your image?

(*One loud blast on a whistle—like a police whistle—and immediately the sound of marching feet.* BOOBOO *keeps one eye cocked to the heavens. He is itching to blast out his message to the world but after this last clobbering he is very hesi-*

tant. Careful, actor. Do not make him cute; he is quite the opposite: wretchedly conniving, almost sinister.)

Uh-oh . . . The Marching Multitude. They're coming! . . . (*Blasts out rapidly as possible.*) UNBORN BABIES, listen to me, put away your knitting needles, knitting and purling your own shrouds, I beg you, listen to me, listen to me, LIVE A LITTLE. (*The sound of marching feet is pressing in on him; he is fearful of being trampled.*) I have five Words! (*But he is forced into the marching line which is marching in a circular pattern. He breaks out, lies flat, shouts through the "hole."*) Number One is: COMB THE BERRIES FROM YOUR WILD HAIR and Number Two is—(*Same procedure as before but with variations each time. Shouting through "hole."*) Number Two is: No matter what they tell you at the Art Students League the road we walk does not diminish into nothingness at the horizon only if you walk backward, and who in their right mind would do THAT? Number Three is— (*Same procedure.*) Number Three is: City birds don't sing canaries of course but they've been brainwashed: "SING, ya little bastard, whatta ya wanna do, ruin my business?!" Number four is—(*The sound of marching feet has passed by.* BOO-BOO *is surprised, then pleased.*) And Number Four is: (*Sings to tune of "Rockabye Baby":*

"Give your straitjacket
The Nehru Look
Formed but not fitted—."

(*Has been moving in a drifting, circular movement of total isolation, then . . .*) Number Five . . . is . . . forthcoming . . .

(*His frustration turns to rage . . . Grunting, growling, he claws at the toes of his socks until the toes of both socks are, identically, ripped away. He becomes popeyed; glow of revelation fills his face and entire being.*)

THEY MATCH.

(*Bright yellow light.* Music. *Triumphal March of the Devil from Stravinsky's "L'Histoire du Soldat."* BOOBOO *snatches his wrinkled, moth-eaten Eisenhower jacket from debris, puts it on backward, does a grotesque Dance of Victory over Trivia . . . When* Music *and dance are completed, he topples over on debris laughing hilariously . . . mimicking a metallic-voiced authority—like the Recorded Announcement voice on the telephone.*)

"Oohh, MISter Booboo, if you ONly knew! The psychiatrists have JUST had their last consultation on YOU. If you but knew how proud WE are! The progress of science should make you proud to be alive! Just think! In two weeks you will be

free to face the world and find your rightful place in Society!" This is a recorded announcement. (*A sober silence . . .*) Ah sweet mystery of life.

(*Casually folds Eisenhower jacket, removes dress and garter belt from walls, folds, drops them in a heap. Facing each of the walls.*)

Wall number one. Ah sweet mystery of life at last I've found thee. Wall number two. Love does not make my world go round. Wall number three. It's Paradox and Ambiguity playing hotsy-totsy hanky-panky flim-flam. Wall number four. (*Quietly, without mimicry; immersed in another, deeper involvement.*) "Do you hear what I'm saying, Mr. Booboo? Doesn't looking forward just THRILL you to the bone? You are going to be a FREE man. Free to find your rightful place in Society." (*The drifting, circular movement of total isolation.*) One. Two. Three. Four.

(*At center, he shudders almost uncontrollably but stifles an outburst of sound . . . The whistle blows loudly, then the sound of marching feet . . . Dead sober . . .*)

And Number Five is: are they kidding??? (*He neatly folds several of memory pieces. sits on them, looks out to audience, unalterably.*) I've got it made. (*Remains standing at center, looking out soberly to audience, motionless, unalterable.*)

The Marriage

A PLAY IN TWO ACTS

by DONALD GREAVES

Donald Greaves, who was born in Harlem in 1943, is the author of two screenplays, *Somewhere in the City* and *666*, and co-author of a third, *The Sweet Flypaper of Life*, which is an adaptation from a book by Langston Hughes and Roy DeCarava. Also a poet, he plans to introduce his poetry in the context of an experimental verse drama to be called *Kitsu Meusi*. *The Marriage*, for the most part, was written while he was still in high school.

The scene is the living room of a three-room apartment of a tenement. Only the doorways of the other rooms—bedroom, kitchen, bathroom—are visible although action takes place within; the doorway of the bedroom is in downstage left corner; the doorway of the kitchen and bathroom are somewhere in left wall. In upstage center wall is the only visible window of the apartment and it is dust-covered as are the curtains that hang before it. But through this window tenement rooftops can be seen, near and far. In downstage right corner is the door to the apartment. Now, because this living room doubles as a bedroom, there is a clothes closet and a bureau (mirrorless) against right wall; the sofa in upstage right corner is convertible into bed; the coffee table that stands before sofa bears a bedside lamp, etc. There is an armchair and a television in upstage left corner. The television is not working; it only supports a phonograph; on floor on side of television that is visible to audience is a stack of records.

It is late afternoon of a May day and the fading sun casts fading rays through dust-covered window and curtains.

PHILIP KITCHENER *lives in this apartment with his wife, his mother, and her lover. The curtain rises on* PHILIP KITCHENER *sprawled on sofa, enjoying one of many comic books stacked high on floor beside sofa. He reads, chuckling now and then.* PHILIP *is a tense boy of eighteen, tall and thin. He is possessed of much nervous energy which he spends not in movement—for he moves about with a rebellious, self-centered slowness—but in sudden changes of expression and in his intense expressiveness. For all at once his joy can become sadness, his smile a frown; he gesticulates urgently, saying much with his hands.*

There is a broodiness about PHILIP *that is noticeable even under his laughter.* PHILIP *reads and chuckles some moments before a girl,* ELAINE, *enters apartment. She is* PHILIP's *wife. Of medium height, attractive build, she is very attractive. She*

253

*is a very intelligent girl, very sensitive, with a very passionate
soul that is shielded by a calm and modest exterior. As she
opens the door her movements are furtive.* PHILIP *is at first
unaware of her, but notices her as she quietly closes the door.*

PHILIP (*returning to comic*): Oh. Hi.

ELAINE: Hi! I—I thought you were sleeping still. It's only
about quarter to five—you never wake that early on a Friday.

PHILIP (*not looking up from comic*): Umm!

(ELAINE *briefly stands watching him, then she starts to
move past him toward window.*)

PHILIP (*still reading*): Where was you?

ELAINE (*stopping abruptly, nervously playing with light
sweater which she has removed*): Walking . . . (*She continues
on to window where she sits on sill, looking out.*) It was so
nice out, I just walked and walked and walked . . . the streets
were so clean . . . the men in the big white water truck came
around and washed them early this morning . . . Funny how
they only wash the streets in summer, Phil. (*Pauses.*) Oh, but
you should have seen the dogs, all the dogs in the neighborhood, it seemed like . . . running with the truck and barking
at the man inside. It was so funny, I laughed all the way down
the block. I think they should wash the streets in winter too.
The dogs have so much fun. (*Pause.*) Phil, you're not listening
to me. (PHILIP *chuckles at something humorous in the comic
book and goes on reading.*) Ph-i-i-i-l!

PHILIP (*not looking up*): Umn!

(*Pause.*)

ELAINE: There aren't any jobs listed in those comic books,
Phil. (PHILIP *bursts into uproarious laughter again at something humorous in the comic book.*) Okay, Phil! You go on
and have fun reading those books, you hear? (*She comes away
from window, and crosses to bureau, right, from which she
takes pair of pants and a sweater belonging to* PHILIP.) Just
have some story ready to explain to your mother why you
haven't got a job yet. (*She crosses from bureau to bathroom,
left, where she will change. She leaves the bathroom door
ajar. Still in response to the comic book,* PHILIP *chuckles
throughout.*) Not that she'll be wanting to hear another story,
hard as she works. It's really a wonder that she puts up with
us! My goodness! I sure do hope our kids won't grow up so
dependent on us as we are on her. (*Pause.*) Umn, umn, umnh!
Have you ever seen such weather, Phil? I'd say it was at least
ninety degrees outside. (*Pause, poking head out of door.*) So
what're you going to tell your dear mother today when she
comes in, Phil—about your not looking for a job and all?

(*She goes back inside, appearing a moment later as she walks out into living room. Exasperatedly.*) Ph-i-i-i-l!

PHILIP (*raising up on one elbow in acute annoyance*): What, Elaine? What?!

ELAINE: Well, Phil, don't get all annoyed!

PHILIP: Um not annoyed, Elaine! But don't you see um reading? Gosh, the way you call my name: Ph-i-i-i-l! Why you gotta say it like that? Um not deaf!

ELAINE: Hummph, who says you're not? Who have I been talking to but myself all this time?

PHILIP: Okay, Elaine, let's don't start nothin'! Can all that stuff an' get to the point! What's the point you're makin'? What're you tryin' to say?

ELAINE: Oh, Phil . . . Phil, you must try and talk that way all of the time—I mean, the way you said "What's the point you're making, what're you trying to say"—it's so thrilling! (*She laughs; he has to laugh too.* PHILIP *rises from sofa and moves to* ELAINE.)

PHILIP (*putting his arms about her waist, his face in her hair*): How you feel, hah, baby? How you feel today?

ELAINE (*grasping both his hands in hers behind her back*): Okay, Phil . . . I guess . . .

PHILIP: You guess! Damn it, I say you look great!

(*They chuckle briefly.*)

ELAINE: Phil . . .

PHILIP (*going away, sniffing her hair*): Umn, an' your hair smells so good! Hey Elaine, what'd you put in it?

ELAINE (*turning her head, showing it off*): You like it?

PHILIP: Doggone right I do!

ELAINE: I washed and shampooed it this morning while you were sleeping.

PHILIP: For me?

ELAINE: If not for you, then for who?

PHILIP: My woman!

ELAINE: . . . so crude! But you know something? I like it. (*Pause.*) But, Phil . . .

PHILIP: Aw, Elaine! You know somethin', you really wanna know somethin'? (*Standing away a little, gesticulating passionately.*) I wanna dress you up like you oughta be dressed up. I wanna someday take you 'round to all them high sedidy dress places down around Fifth Avenue an' stuff! An' wouldn' that be real boss? 'Cause if I had that kinda dough, I maybe could afford to get us a little apartment, know what I mean, sweetie? Someplace that'd be ours: with nobody, I mean nobody feelin' like we parasitin' off them . . . You know . . . the kinda way my mother's been actin' lately . . .

255

ELAINE: Phil, that's not really fair! I don't think it's fair at all, you speaking about your mother as though . . .

PHILIP (*walking away toward window*): Go on, side with *her,* side with *her!*

ELAINE (*following*): Oh, Phil . . . it's not that I'm siding with anyone . . . well, I'm just trying to say that . . .

PHILIP (*turning around, turning on her*): I'll bet you ain't! Think I didn' hear you yukkin' away while I was readin'? Think I din' hear you mumblin' and grumblin' about how lazy I am an' all that type o' . . .

ELAINE: If you hear that much, you know darn well that I never said you were lazy, and I wasn't mumbling and grumbling, as you say . . . nor was I "yukkin'." I was only . . .

PHILIP: Don't ape my speech, Elaine.

ELAINE: Oh, don't be imposs—

PHILIP: Okay, so you didn' say it right out—no doubt that'll come with time—but you sure implied it with all that stuff about you "hope you never have kids as dependent on you as we are on my mother"—In other words, me. Why don't you come right out and say it, 'stead o' makin' sly remarks about it. And that's another thing—I can't stand little sneaky remarks about my character. Not from my mother, not from that bastard, Jake, not from you . . .

ELAINE: Please don't associate me with that slippery . . .

PHILIP: . . . Yet it was only yesterday that you wouldn' hear nothing I had to say to you about . . .

ELAINE: Because he's your mother's friend, that why.

(PHILIP *goes to sofa, sits, and starts gathering comics.*)

PHILIP (*brooding heavily*): An' um her son—yet he's inside while um in the doghouse; the way she acts to me sometime. (*Pause. Cruelly*). What'd he do, try to rape you while I was out las' night 'r somethin'?

ELAINE: Stop it right now, Phil!

PHILIP: Aw, um sorry, baby! I—I didn' really mean that. Um sorry—but the way he looks at you; sometimes I think you ain' got a stitch on, the way he looks at you . . .

(ELAINE *moves to sofa and begins gathering comics with* PHILIP.)

ELAINE: I know. I always feel that too . . . it makes me warm all over . . .

PHILIP: Filthy bastard!

ELAINE: . . . I mean . . . it's so annoying . . . and embarrassing . . .

(*Pause.*)

PHILIP: But you should watch how you go around, too, sweetie. (*He rises with comic books and takes them over to*

bureau, inside of which he deposits them.) 'Cause you do dress kinda careless sometimes . . .

ELAINE: Phil, I'm home! I'm in my home, Phil! Where else can I relax if not at home?

PHILIP (*hurriedly, guiltily*): Yeah—yeah, well, we should have our own place—you got a point there, I mean it, I really do mean it!

ELAINE: When one is in one's home, one ought to at least be able to wear one's bathrobe and feel at ease.

PHILIP: 'Cause we ain' gonna be here forever, you know what I mean? We ain' gonna be here forever. (*Pause.*) You know?

ELAINE (*dutifully*): Yes.

PHILIP: No, I mean, do you?

ELAINE (*straightening sofa cover, just busying herself*): Yes, Phil. Yes! You just told me we wouldn't, didn't you?

PHILIP: Well, yeah—but I mean . . . (*Short, uncomfortable laugh.*) . . . Well, the way you answered . . . as if you doubted what I said 'r somethin' . . . (*Pause.*) You doubt me, don't you? (*No answer.*) Well?

ELAINE (*stopping activity*): I'm your wife, Phil.

PHILIP (*voice perceptibly raised*): But do you doubt me, I said!

ELAINE: No . . . but you'll have to admit that you haven't given anyone much justification for faith—I mean, for my part the faith is there, it's there . . . you haven't done very much to justify it, though. (*Pause.*) Phil?

(*Silence. Eventually* PHILIP *strolls to window. He pulls back the dusty curtain and looks down on street for some time. Finally.*)

ELAINE: Phil, I don't . . .

PHILIP (*his voice hoarse and subdued*): Street's empty . . .

ELAINE (*disconcertedly*): I know—it's so hot. (*Presently,* PHILIP *goes to coffee table on which rests a half-filled ashtray, from which he selects a half-smoked cigarette—a butt—which he lights. His jaws slam tightly on cigarette, his head goes back a little: he is defiant. As* PHILIP *moves to exit, down right.*) Phil.

PHILIP (*stopping and turning*): Yeah?

ELAINE (*rising slowly from sofa*): Where are you going?

PHILIP: Difference does it make?—(*Resuming his march.*) To the street.

(*Pause.*)

ELAINE: You'll accuse me of nagging you, but your mother did ask me to tell you about the windows today—she says you've been promising to wash them.

PHILIP: Thanks. You can tell her that you tol' me.

Donald Greaves

ELAINE: You'll wash them today?

PHILIP: Probably today.

ELAINE: Because she may be very angry if they're still not washed today—she's expecting they'll be done today, Phil.

PHILIP: Yeah?

ELAINE: Well, yes!

PHILIP *laughs genuinely as he goes out. Disturbed,* ELAINE *watches him go. She stands a moment longer, then slowly seats herself upon arm of sofa, worrying. She sighs and rises abruptly, having made a decision: she will straighten up in general and wash the windows herself. With this purpose she enters bathroom, left. We hear: pail being banged around, filled with water. There is a knock at the outside door, down right.* ELAINE *comes out of bathroom, pail of water, rags, and soap powder in one hand, with other brushing back hair from forehead which now shows beads of perspiration. She sets all items down on floor.*

ELAINE: Who is it? (*A muffled voice sounds through.* ELAINE *becomes aware of her appearance and looks briefly upon herself.*) Philip isn't here, Theodore. (*More muffled tones and* ELAINE *goes to door, down right, and opens it.*) Hi.

(*Enter* THEODORE *carrying school books. He is eighteen years of age, a little taller than average, fairly good-looking. He is very ambitious, envisioning high-minded stuff about "someday achievements." But he works hard too; the epitome of all that is determined. And he is aggressive, a "taker." There is a "point" to* THEODORE—*his very movements seem to manifest purpose, themselves being purposive and precise.* THEODORE *is an egotist but it seems he tries to obfuscate this truth —because people do not like egotists—with behavior patterns that point to modesty. But he is a liar in this; he is ostensibly outgoing but truly he is deeply involved with himself. He very often unconsciously cleans his fingernails when being spoken to. We do not especially "like"* THEODORE *but we cannot help but admire, indeed, if not envy him. Generally his spirits remain on a considerably even keel, but today they are especially high and his eyes are accordingly bright.*)

THEODORE: Hi, Elaine. Where's Phil?

ELAINE: Out. You didn't see him downstairs?

THEODORE (*on his way inside*): No. He say where he was going? (*He puts down his books on coffee table.*)

ELAINE (*closing door*): No, he just stalked out. Wait for him if you like.

THEODORE: Thanks. Stalked out—mad, hah?

ELAINE (*wanting to air it all, feeling it's not* THEODORE'*s business*): Oh, skip it, Theodore.

258

THEODORE (*massaging left wrist and arm*): He'll get a job, don't worry . . . I'm convinced that the most difficult aspect of education is the book-carrying. (*Pointing to books on table.*) I tell you, these things nearly took my arm off on the train.

ELAINE: Heavy, ha?

THEODORE: Grossly understated, Elaine.

(*She smiles.*)

ELAINE (*moving to pail of water, etc.*): Excuse me while I get some of this work done, Theodore?

THEODORE (*sitting down on sofa*): What, can I help?

ELAINE (*taking equipment to window, she smiles briefly in appreciation*): No. No, that's all right. Thanks. (*She begins taking curtains down from window.*)

THEODORE: Say, you know your hair suits you very well that way?

ELAINE: Oh. Does it?

THEODORE: Very well—fact it's the best I've ever seen you with it.

ELAINE: Thank you. Just a new hair style I thought I'd try. So, how are you, Theodore?

THEODORE: You ought to wear it that way all the time—oh, you know, making it, I guess.

ELAINE (*laughing*): You'd say that if you were gaining the world, wouldn't you? (ELAINE *takes curtains into bathroom where she is heard running water over them.*)

THEODORE (*rising; this talk that is gravitating to himself fascinates him. Laughs briefly*): No, what do you mean? (*Ambling to bathroom door.*) Why do you say that?

ELAINE (*coming out, returning to window*): Oh, you're so conservative in your evaluation of yourself and all.

THEODORE (*brief laugh*): Okay, well, I'm doing good, okay? I'm doing very good, actually!

ELAINE (*attacking windows with vigor, she laughs*): There, you see?

(*He laughs again briefly and picks up paperback from bureau.*)

THEODORE (*reading title*): . . . Tropic of Cancer . . .

ELAINE: You read it?

THEODORE: Ah hah—made a couple of interesting points. But you know, I've fallen behind in my reading? I mean, I haven't picked up a book in nearly two weeks. I'm always doing reading for school, of course, but my own's been suffering. School's finished for the week, though. Figure I'll get some reading done over the weekend.

ELAINE: You'll catch up. (*Pause.*) But how *is* school?

THEODORE: Good. Good. Pulled a ninety-four on a math

259

exam I took last week. Gave us back our papers today.

ELAINE: Really? Ninety-four? Oh, well, you're very smart, anyway.

THEODORE (*smiling as he stands somewhat behind her, watching her activity*): Well, I studied. You know. But I'm really going to catch hell now that I'm working full-time.

ELAINE (*stopping what she is doing*): Oh, you must be kidding!—Not and go to school too.

THEODORE: Got to! Got to raise my full term money. You know, books, tuition—and I've been thinking about a car. Since I can use one. I can do it!

(ELAINE *stares at* THEODORE *in wonder and stronger admiration.*)

THEODORE (*continuing, reveling in it*): Think I'm crazy? I'm not.

ELAINE: How is it done, Theodore? How do you do it? (*He laughs.*) No, really, how?

THEODORE: Tell myself that I can do it.

ELAINE: That's all . . .

THEODORE: And that I want to.

(*Pause.*)

ELAINE: I'm going to read about you someday!

THEODORE: Well, that's to be seen . . . but I do try.

(ELAINE *resumes window-washing. The sun is almost completely down and only the last red tip can be seen above the tenement rooftops in the distance. Shadows in the living room are plentiful.*)

THEODORE (*continuing, seated on couch again*): Why don't you come to college, Elaine?

ELAINE: I wanted to very much when I was in high school but . . . oh, no—anyway, I'd have so much to make up before I were accepted.

THEODORE: You're intelligent—it wouldn't take you long. You should, you know.

ELAINE: Oh, Theodore, I'm married now.

THEODORE: And?

ELAINE (*stopping work*): And—well, I'm married.

THEODORE: So what? Because you're married's no reason why you should stop developing, is it? As a matter of fact, that's more reason why you should be concerned about development—having something to offer your kids besides love— which I'm sure is charming—but, I mean, something they can touch, something . . .

(*Afraid of the desire* THEODORE *threatens to revive,* ELAINE *has perceptibly accelerated her pace of work.*)

ELAINE (*laughing briefly, insincerely*): Theodore, will you

shut up before you have me breaking up housekeeping in order to contemplate it?

THEODORE (*smiling vaguely*): Why should you have to break up housekeeping? (*Silence while she seeks the answer. Finally she makes futile movements with her head and hand.*) Phil wouldn't mind, would he?

ELAINE: Oh, no . . . he wouldn't mind . . . !

THEODORE: I hardly thought he would.

ELAINE: It's just that—well, I guess I'm just more interested in my Mrs. than my Ph.D.

THEODORE (*chiding gently*): Humn!

ELAINE: No, really . . . !

THEODORE: Oh, I don't mean to say that you aren't sincere. I—oh, let's forget it, Elaine.

ELAINE (*smiling, relieved*): Okay, let's!

(*Brief pause.*)

THEODORE: I'm thirsty. You?

ELAINE: As a matter of fact, I am.

THEODORE (*rising*): I'll get us both some water.

ELAINE: Oh, Theodore, I forgot—there's some grape Cool-Aid in the refrigerator.

THEODORE: Good.

ELAINE: Excuse me for not offering.

(THEODORE *goes out upper left to kitchen, whistling. Pause.*)

THEODORE (*from kitchen*): S'getting pretty dark in here, isn't it?

ELAINE: My eyes are so accustomed I hadn't noticed it.

(*She crosses to light switch somewhere in upper left, as* THEODORE *enters from kitchen with drinks.*)

THEODORE: "And there was light." (*Squinting.*) My eyes feel as though I've just emerged from the Bottomless Pit. (*He gives one drink to* ELAINE.)

ELAINE: So do mine. (*She takes drink and sips.*) Umn! I needed that. It's good.

THEODORE: I'm a hell of a cook when I put my mind to it. (*They laugh a little.*)

ELAINE (*surveying her work*): Hey, I think that window will pass, don't you?

THEODORE: If you polish it anymore the glass'll fall out—leave it!

ELAINE (*setting drink down on table*): Exactly what I'm going to do. I should really have gotten much more done; I planned to clean the house in general. But I so enjoy talking to you, Theodore! (*She goes about the business of putting away things she has used. From bathroom.*) These curtains can soak

at least another two hours—they're filthy. (*Appearing in bathroom doorway.*) Play some records, Theodore.

THEODORE: Get any new ones?

ELAINE: There may be one or two new ones there.

(*As he moves to phonograph,* THEODORE *snaps fingers in time to some tune he hums or whistles.*)

THEODORE: You know, I hardly get to listen to records anymore?

ELAINE (*from bathroom*): Busy man. With me it's not that I don't have the time; I have the time all right but not the mood. I just don't . . .

THEODORE (*has put on a record of the day and younger set; it plays on low volume but will rise*): With me too. I'm usually not in the mood myself.

ELAINE (*entering, jokingly*): Think we're getting old, Theodore? (*She starts snapping her fingers.*)

THEODORE (*very serious*): Could be. (*He keeps time with a pencil, tapping it on ashtray. They are both moved by the music, yet they seem consciously to avoid physical contact— they will not dance: wherefore the fact is salient, the situation awkward. Pause. They sit on sofa. A voice from the street suddenly rises above the music, entering apartment via open window.*)

VOICE: A-a-a-ye, Phil . . . !

ELAINE (*starting*): That big-mouthed Harry!

(THEODORE *laughs, goes to window. When* THEODORE *relates to "the boys" from the neighborhood, he adopts certain new modes of behavior: he becomes callous, cursing more than usual and being generally vulgar. He assumes a sort of "I-don't-give-a-damn" attitude. And the curious thing about this transformation is that it is, as it seems, automatic, unconscious, for the most part. But* THEODORE *takes some pride in his ability to mingle with the gang, to be an integral part of it, while yet retaining an identity, striving contrarily.*)

THEODORE (*leaning out of window, yelling down to street*): Yo! Wha's happenin', Harry?

VOICE OF HARRY: Ain' nothin' goin' on yet. Where's Phil?

THEODORE: Don' know. Um waitin' for 'im.

VOICE OF HARRY: Well, tell 'im I was looking for 'im when you see 'im.

THEODORE (*he stays a moment longer, then comes in, a pleased expression on his face*): Harry. He's looking for Phil.

ELAINE (*putting down* THEODORE's *book*): What's he do for a living, anyway?

THEODORE (*laughs*): Anything . . .

ELAINE (*becoming alarmed*): Really?—you mean he . . . ?

THEODORE: No, he's working—I think.

ELAINE: And why does Phil associate so closely with him?

THEODORE (*nearly a boast*): Aw, we all grew up together, Elaine.

ELAINE: Oh, yes, that's right—you associate with him too, don't you?

THEODORE: You've got to know how to hang out.

ELAINE: And why must one know how to "hang out," as you say?

THEODORE (*shrugs shoulders, pauses*): Well actually, it's pretty much like the textbooks say, I guess—acceptance, needing to be one of "the boys." Of course, it's much more than just that with me, though; I kind of think it marvelous that a guy like me—I mean, wanting the things that I want—knows how to sit down on some stoop Saturday night and drink a pint of wine, or make it with the girls, or just sit around shooting the bull . . . and yet keep on wanting the same things he started out wanting. None of this . . . (*gestures*) . . . this snobbery just because you happen to want particular things, know what I mean?

ELAINE (*protesting*): Yes, but with you it's different, Theodore. I mean . . . well, you've got a certain strength, a strength few people have—you can do it, but, Theodore, not everyone can. You must realize that. (THEODORE *smiles as though to concede, as though to say, "Yes, you are right!" Softly.*) Oh, I wish Phil would concern himself more with making our marriage work and less with that sort of thing—if that has anything to do with his attitude. (*Pause.*) You're the only one I can talk to, Theodore! I mean, well . . . I'm so alone with my thoughts, my feelings . . . I don't go anywhere, don't meet anyone . . . and Philip . . . Philip's so hostile lately . . . the slightest thing sends him into rage. The slight . . .

THEODORE: Oh, he'll probably change . . .

ELAINE (*rising and facing, wringing hands*): But he's got to change. He's got to because I need him to . . . and yet he's got to change . . . well, because it's in him to change, because he wants to . . . and not because of any pressure from his mother or from me. Oh, I know he . . .

(*A key in the apartment-door lock, down right.* ELAINE *starts, then goes to record player and tinkers. Enter* PHILIP *carrying a broom handle, used by city boys to make what are called "stick-ball bats"; the balls used being made of rubber and close in size to those used in tennis. "Stick-ball" is the game.* PHILIP *carries bat in one hand, a cigarette dangles precariously from mouth; he wears sneakers—something is incongruous about it all.*)

THEODORE: Aye, man! Where you been?

PHILIP (*seeing* THEODORE): Say, Teddy! Wha's goin' on?

THEODORE: Been waitin' for you coupla hours, hah, Elaine?

ELAINE: About that, I guess.

PHILIP: So what's happenin'? I mean, wha's new?

THEODORE: Same ol' thing, I guess. You know, tryin' to make it. How's things with you?

PHILIP: I's a drag, Ted . . . I's a drag.

(PHILIP *leans bat against wall. Unnoticed by* PHILIP, ELAINE *removes bat and puts it behind bureau.*)

THEODORE: Oh, what's-his-name was lookin' for you. Harry.

PHILIP (*fanning the air with hand*): Damn, I wish 'e'd get off my back. (*He has noticed record spinning on phonograph and he turns up volume. He executes some good quick steps very, very skillfully. The music is Latin.*)

THEODORE: Umn humn! Yeah! Get um, Phil!

(PHILIP *laughs and "Gets 'um."*)

THEODORE (*to* ELAINE *who has not been watching*): Can't beat this man when it comes to dancing. (ELAINE *only looks away.*) Go 'head, Phil! Get mean!

(PHILIP *goes through a couple of steps more, then stops abruptly.*)

PHILIP: How long ago was it?—I mean, that Harry was here? He come up here?

THEODORE: Uh uh! Just yelled up from downstairs about fifteen minutes ago, said 'e'd be back. You know Harry an' his mouth. (*Laughs.*) Rubbed Elaine's fur—the yellin'.

PHILIP: Yeah—he say when?

THEODORE: Ah ah! (PHILIP *kisses teeth.*) What's he want?

PHILIP: I'll tell you afterwards. (*Nods in* ELAINE'S *direction, perfunctorily.*) So you doin' good in college, Teddy?

THEODORE (*starting to stroll*): Yeah, Phil, um doin' okay. Doin' real boss . . . (*Smiling.*) Been thinkin' about a car, Phil.

(*Simultaneously with the mention of a car,* PHILIP'S *whole countenance is aglow.*)

PHILIP: Yeah? (THEODORE *nods affirmatively, smiling. Pause.*) You jivin' me . . .

THEODORE: No, I was just tellin' Elaine—right, Elaine?

ELAINE (*who has dissolved into the background*): Yes.

PHILIP (*staring at* THEODORE): Oh, man! Oh, man, Teddy! (*Pause.* PHILIP *dreams.*)

THEODORE: Probably be somethin' like a '59, you know? Can't take nothin' too expensive right now—college and all . . .

PHILIP (*who has been dreaming*): . . . aw, man . . . but how you gonna, I mean, where you gonna get the . . .

THEODORE: Got a job—full-time, pays all right too.

(PHILIP *sits down slowly upon arm of sofa, chin in both hands, both elbows on both knees, dreaming and lamenting.*)

PHILIP: . . . Aw, man . . . If I could . . . I wish I could . . . (*Looking up at* THEODORE.) Think they'd hire me too, Teddy?

THEODORE: Well, see, I got the job from school, Phil—las' spring I took a test . . .

PHILIP (*kisses teeth, annoyed*): Well, what you gotta do, hah, man? I mean, i's hard?

THEODORE: Aw, it's light action if you know (*reaches in suit jacket pocket and removes very choice cigarette case and lighter*) how to work your logarithms, functions, variables . . . (*lights cigarette for self and extends case to* PHILIP *who also takes cigarette which the former lights as he talks*) . . . that kinda jive. See, because what you gotta do is feed info' to computers and you can't afford to make mistakes, see. 'Cause you figure, you feed the machine certain information that's, say, one integer off and the whole project gets goofed, know what I mean? 'Cause the machine ain' never wrong; it works accurately with respect to whatever you give it.

(PHILIP *listens, fascinated at first; then his expression changes to one of envy and annoyance. He rises, goes to window and looks out briefly.*)

PHILIP (*coming inside*): Tha's really somethin', Teddy. (*To* ELAINE.): Wha's for dinner?

ELAINE: Your mother hasn't come in yet, Phil.

PHILIP (*laughing sardonically*): How you like that, Teddy? Gotta wait till my mother gets home before my wife can give us somethin' to eat.

(THEODORE *smiles awkwardly.*)

ELAINE: Well, Phil . . .

PHILIP (*harshly*): Yeah, yeah, I know—don' say nothin', will you? Gonna probably hear enough when my mother gets home. (*Pause.*) Play some records 'r somethin', Teddy. S'like a morgue in here.

(THEODORE *goes to phonograph, selects and plays record. A key in the door lock, down right, followed by the entrance of* JAKE. JAKE *is fifty-four years of age, but there is an astonishing youthfulness about him. Instead of walking, he nearly prances. He is of medium height, but muscular and virile, and these things strike us about him. He has been subject to some of life's more intensive floggings and although he has not "bent his head" he "cries aloud." For his is that bitter sort of pride of one pitted, circumstantially, against insuperable odds, who has emerged, very scarred, but who nevertheless has emerged: that fact in itself being something of a wonder. His*

265

face is hard to the point of ugliness. His hands are rough and heavily calloused, broken fingernails. His eyes are narrow and wary, his teeth strong; and it is not uncommon to see him bite enthusiastically into a raw onion, gulp down a raw egg, or swallow a handful of red-hot peppers without even a sigh. JAKE *is tougher than life.*)

JAKE (*to no one in particular*): Where's Mom?

THEODORE: Hello, Jake.

JAKE: Hi, kid. (*Ripping back the curtain that shuts off the one bedroom, down left.*) Hah? Mom come home yet?

PHILIP: No.

JAKE (*over the noise from the phonograph, knitting his face*): Hah?

PHILIP: I said, no!

JAKE: . . . The hell is she, then?—Chris', been to 'er job an' everything!

PHILIP: How the hell um supposed to know?

JAKE: Watch yer mouth, Phil! Um just askin'!

PHILIP: Well, you act like . . .

JAKE: Just watch yer mouth—damned kids got no respect nowadays. (PHILIP *kisses teeth. Slight pause.*) Gotchore self a job yet? (PHILIP *kisses teeth again. Marching off to kitchen, up left, triumphantly.*) Didn' think you did—lazy son of a gun, you . . .

PHILIP (*approaching still-dark kitchen in anger*): Um lazy? Um lazy? Well, mister, where's your job? (*Loud.*) I said, where the hell's your job?

JAKE (*appearing now in doorway, a bottle of red-hot peppers in one hand, a handful of the peppers in the other*): Listen, kid. (*He pitches some of the peppers down throat.*) You got no right askin' me where's my job.

PHILIP: But you can ask . . .

JAKE: Makes no difference, I'm oldern' you. I was workin' almost from the time I was walkin'. You got no right asking me that—where's my job.

PHILIP: Aw, Jake . . .

JAKE: I—I say you got no right . . . an' don' do it again because I'll make you sorry. I don't need a job, see? (*Vainly attempting to offset the intimidation,* PHILIP *kisses teeth, walking past* PHILIP, *peppers in bottle and in hand.*) Just forget it! (PHILIP *fans hand at* JAKE *as the latter moves out into living room toward phonograph, knitting face as he does so.* JAKE *turns down volume on phono and addresses all after a swallow of more peppers.*) See, when I was a kid you-all's age—and I say "kid," knowin' some o' you're married, because you're still kids to me—(*Pause.*) When I was a kid, I didn' have

nobody worryin' about me all the time. Nobody was concerned about where I slept or what I was gonna eat . . . there wasn' nobody there to see if I had a bathroom to go to—now I ain' tellin' you this to make you feel sorry . . . after all, what the hell do you care . . . but I want you to have a idea o' why it is I don' like to see you kids havin' life so easy as you do nowadays. I's jus' a . . . (*The voice of* ANNIE, PHILIP'*s mother rising up from street, calling:* PHILIP *and* JAKE *sticking head out of window.* JAKE, *harshly.*) Where you been? (*Again* PHILIP *fans hand at* JAKE'*s back.* JAKE *comes inside. To* PHILIP.) Go on downstairs an' get them packages your mother's got, Phil. She can't carry 'em. (*After a rebellious delay,* PHILIP *ambles off toward outside door.*) Take the lead out, will you, Phil? (PHILIP *goes out.*) Jesus, that kid! (*Pause.*) So how you doin'—wha's your name?

THEODORE: Theodore!

JAKE: Tha's it—(*Laughing half-jokingly.*) But it was so many o' you damned kids in an' outta here all hours o' day an' night when you was younger, I forget—you gotta excuse me.

THEODORE: That's quite all right.

JAKE: 'Cause see, I'll tell you (*articulating each word*) I Don't-Like-Teen-agers. They get on my nerves . . . bein' perfectly frank with you. An' see (*points to head*) I got a condition—nervous, um very nervous. Tha's what your Uncle Sam did for me durin' your las' war . . . you remember hearin' about Guadalcanal . . . they teach you in school . . .

THEODORE: Umn humn!

JAKE: Yeah, 'cause you was nothin' but a kid then—Guadalcanal, Guam. Guam's where I got my condition at—goin' over the hill, went over twice. I was with the 41st division, bombadeer specials we was called. Well, I went over the hill, an' I got it—enemy shell grazed me. (*Leaning toward* THEODORE, *displaying scalp.*) Right here. Believe you can still see the scar, right there. (*Pointing.*) Here, see it?

THEODORE (*leaning over, looking*): Oh, yes. I see it.

JAKE (*triumphantly*): Sure! I ain' gotta lie to you about it, 'cause it's right there where you can see it yourself. Doctors, they said a fraction deeper an' it'd o' been all over for me—no more drinkin', no more dancin', no more women . . . not nothin'! But um here, ain' I? An' um still kickin', though they had to put a plate in my head. Not suppose to drink whiskey, but I drink a little now an' then, 'cause what the hell, am I suppose to stop livin'? Private stock's what I really drink, though. (*Laughs.*) You know what I mean, don't you?

THEODORE: Sure, you and I got together on some coupla times, remember?

JAKE: Yeah, yeah, tha's right, me an' you, wine. See that? But you know somethin', kid . . . 'scuse me for callin' you kid, you don't mind, do you?

THEODORE: If you feel like calling me that, go ahead.

JAKE: No, 'cause see, um so accustomed to sayin' that; all the teen-agers, most of 'em, I should say—why, they're kids to me. But, now tha's what I was gettin' ready to say, i's a funny thing but I don' consider you a kid.

(ELAINE, *exasperated, rises and crosses to kitchen, up left.*)

THEODORE: I don't profess to be so old—but thank you.

JAKE: No-o-o-o, I mean, but you know how to carry yourself with oldsters like myself—see, 'cause um fifty-four years of age—would you believe it?

THEODORE (*removing nail file from inner pocket*): Not if you hadn't told me before, and Phil verified it. (*He begins filing nails.*) Every time you tell me, though, I'm almost astonished as the last time—it's really hard to believe, Jake.

JAKE: Yet it's so right on; fifty-four years of age, nearly sixty, but um just as spry as any o' the teen-agers out here in the street, ain' I?

(ELAINE *rises and goes into kitchen.*)

THEODORE: It's amazing!

JAKE: Well, tha's what um sayin'—but I demand respect, not for who I am necessarily, 'cause, after all, who am I?—but for my age, if nothin' else. Respect. Without that—'scuse me for puttin' it this way, but you're no kid—without that, the world ain' shit. I mean that! Now you take your friend Phil: what kinda respect's he got? None. Not for me, not for his mother, not for school; 'course not—he quit. (*In subdued tones after glancing around.*) Not for his marriage to this girl, here, not for 'nothin'. An' when that happens—this I truly believe—you get your vandalisms, your so-called delinquents, your dope addicts an' your pushers, you get your unwed mothers. (*Lowers voice yet.*) They may not've tol' you, but tha's what they was afraid she was (*nods head toward kitchen*) til your friend here married 'er. Now if this don't make you get my point, nothin' will. (*Beginning nearly as a whisper, but rising.*) Him an' her in his mother's room. Yeah! I know. I didn' say nothin'. Tha's they business—now ain't it? But what I'm meanin' to show you is what um sayin' about respect. I come in here coupla times an' what I see but them two—him an' her—emergin' sheepishly, tail between legs, know what I mean? Know what um tryin' to say? All right then, so you gotta have respect, first of all. Oh, don't get me wrong. I ain' settin' myself up as no angel, for I was a kid myself once, an' I'll tell you about that some time, but (*articulating each*

word) I-had-respect! An' I say without it, the world ain' shit. Without it, you got nation warrin' agains' nation. You got one nation not respectin' the other, maybe 'cause the other's smaller, maybe anything—but war's the bitter result. (*Pointing to scar on head.*) I know! (*In fatherly manner, he pats* THEO-DORE *on shoulder, the latter now being seated on sofa.*) But I wanna sit down some time an' talk to you about some o' this, kid. 'Cause, see, I have *touched* what I know an' talk about! My knowledge ain' from none o' your textbooks—I have lived! My mother threw me out when I wasn' but a kid seven years old. Been shifin' for myself ever since. (*He goes to window and hollers out.*) Hey, Mom! Hey, Annie!

(*He comes in from window, shaking his head as if to say "You ever see anything like this?" He goes out. Pause.* THEO-DORE *rises, strolls about, stopping in front of mirror. There he appraises himself. His manner is that of one wanting to admire himself at length but feeling somehow guilty about doing so. He leaves mirror, strolls, returns, strolls again.*

Enter PHILIP, JAKE, ANNIE, *who carries one small package. Now,* ANNIE *is about forty years of age: a working woman, hard-working. But there can yet be seen about her something of the glamorousness that was hers in youth. In her hey-day she was doubtless pursued by all of the young men of her set; but now she must look to her future and more concrete things and she finds herself caught in that groove, the hard work-a-day world where one scuffles solely in terms of the present, having access only to a kind of moment-to-moment reality.*)

ANNIE (*entering behind* JAKE *and* PHILIP, *who carry large packages*): Whewww! Oh, I'm so tired. An' those stairs, my goodness! Jake, you an' Phil put some o' those things away for me please? I'm so tired.

JAKE (*going toward kitchen,* PHILIP *following*): Sure, Mom! Come on, Phil!

ANNIE (*sitting on sofa*): Whew!

THEODORE (*sitting in armchair in upstage left corner*): Hello, Mrs. Kitchener. How are you feeling?

(ELAINE *enters from the kitchen.*)

ANNIE (*noticing him for the first time*): Oh, hello, Theodore —um dead on my feet.

ELAINE: Hello, Annie.

ANNIE: Put something decent on, Elaine! Don't you know you've got company?

ELAINE: Oh, Annie, I know. But it's all I've—I've got . . . And there's nothing wrong with . . .

ANNIE: Don't say it's all you've got—an' there is something wrong with . . .

ELAINE: But it is all I have . . .

ANNIE: I told you, don't say that. Hush up an' listen to me. (*In subdued tones which emerge from the side of her now slightly twisted mouth.*) What you've got on is not decent! You can see everything through what you've got on—that's no way to carry yourself in front of your husband's friends; after all, show your husband a little *respect*. Now go 'head. Go 'head an' make yourself presentable, Elaine.

ELAINE: Honestly, Annie!—Everyone makes me feel so . . . so like (*Pause.*) Well a—a harlot or something—a lewd woman. First . . . well, first Phil . . . and now you. You make me so conscious of myself . . .

ANNIE: Conscious! How do you mean we make you concious?

ELAINE (*flustered*): Conscious, that's all. You just make me conscious! (*Pause.*) I—I'll try to find something else, Annie.

ANNIE: You can, Elaine.

(ELAINE *goes to bureau and rummages through contents.*)

JAKE (*from kitchen*): Where you want to put these chops, top or bottom?

ANNIE: Oh, leave 'em out, Jake. Just as well have 'em for dinner. (*Pause.*) An', Elaine . . . a woman's got no choice but to be, first of all, conscious of herself. (ELAINE *continues to search through contents of bureau, casting nod in direction of kitchen.*) He do what I ask 'im to do?

ELAINE (*brief pause*): Uh—yes . . . uh—he didn't get to your window and the kitchen, Annie . . . but he did this one; that's some—oh, and he even put the curtains to soak. (*Smiling.*) See? (ELAINE *points to window, smiling, then casts glance at* THEODORE.)

ANNIE (*rising and going to window, inspecting it*): Elaine! Elaine . . . do you suppose something's come over that boy? Think he's changin'?

ELAINE: Oh, I know he will, Annie, I just know he will— if we give him a little time, if we just don't pressure him too much . . .

ANNIE: Well, I never! An' curtains too, no less . . . !

ELAINE: But please, Annie, don't say anything to him about it this time. Just sort of take it for granted, you know. Don't make him self-conscious. It may spoil everything . . .

ANNIE: Okay, Elaine . . . don't get panicky. I'll just go on in my room. (*She bypasses kitchen and enters bedroom; whereupon,* ELAINE *sighs, relieved, again glancing at* THEODORE *who stands, back to window, smoking cigarette. She takes out some sort of evening-out attire, probably an evening*

gown—a remnant of her middle class heritage. She looks at the gown which is somewhat wrinkled and losing its form, hopelessly shaking her head. She enters bathroom where she will change. Now JAKE *enters living room from kitchen.*)

JAKE (*looking around*): Mom! (*To* THEODORE.) Where'd his mother go?

THEODORE (*pointing to bedroom, downstage left*): Inside, I believe.

(JAKE *moves down to bedroom.*)

JAKE (*ripping back curtain and entering*): Lemme have ten dollars, Mom! (*He draws the curtain and continues talking to* ANNIE *in progressively indistinguishable tones.* PHILIP *now comes out into living room also.*)

PHILIP (*to* THEODORE): Where'd he go? (THEODORE *indicates bedroom with nod of head.* PHILIP *waves hand in that direction.*) Bastard, isn' 'e?!

THEODORE: Well . . .

PHILIP (*interrupting*): Got a cigarette, Ted? (THEODORE *reaches in pocket, takes out cigarette case, which he extends to* PHILIP. *He lights cigarette that* PHILIP *takes.* PHILIP *blows out smoke, puts hand on* THEODORE'S *shoulder.*) Say, listen, man, um sorry. You know, for goin' back an' forth an' all while you were waitin' for me. But you see how it is, Teddy. (*As he talks,* PHILIP *guides* THEODORE *to sofa where they sit.*)

THEODORE (*blowing out smoke*): Aw, Phil, what're you talkin' about? That ain' nothin! Lots of times you used to wait for me, right?

PHILIP: Well, sure, Ted, but . . .

THEODORE: Aw, shuddup . . . just shuddup . . .

(*They laugh a little, healthily. A good pause.*)

PHILIP: You know, I still remember them days, Ted?

THEODORE (*laughing*): You make it sound like it's history already—them days!

PHILIP: Oh, well. I mean—a lot of things've happened since.

THEODORE: Tha's true.

PHILIP: You goin' to college, workin', Uncle Sam's got Johnny up right. Richard's in jail, Harry wit' all the money (*pause*) an' um married!

THEODORE: Well, don' say it like *that,* man!

PHILIP (*rising, very agitated*): But I mean, Teddy . . . I—I live those days . . . (*Pacing now.*) . . . I live those days all the time! Talkin' an' schemin' on all the girls, drinkin', stayin' out, partyin' late an' not comin' home till all hours o' the mornin'! Dances, parties—fun, Ted, a lotta fun!

THEODORE: It was. It was fun. (*Pause. He notices stick-ball bat behind bureau.*) You was playin' stick-ball today, hah?

271

PHILIP (*going to window*): Aw, just for a little while with the kids. (*Staring out of window, down to street.*) There's nobody else out there to play with. I mean, they're fourteen and fifteen, on up like that . . . but they're kids to me, you know?—hard to get 'em to play a serious game.

THEODORE (*rising, cigarette in mouth*): Hummm! (*He walks down to bureau and takes bat from behind it. He stands as though "at the plate," wide stance, testing the weight of the bat in his hands. He glances about himself quickly, then abruptly swings.*) Swoosh! (*He swings again.*) Swoosh! Damn, you know I can't remember the last time I even held one o' these?

PHILIP (*has turned from window to watch* THEODORE): Long time . . .

THEODORE: Damned long time! Think maybe I'd like to go a coupla innings one day, Phil.

PHILIP (*moving to* THEODORE, *profoundly happy*): Yeah? Okay, swingin'! Swingin'! Here, Ted, lemme show you a kinda wris' action I been developin'! (*Takes bat, flexes wrists in particular way and swings.*) See? (*Swings again and again. Breathing with excitement and exertion.*) See what I mean? That way you got more pull, more action, but less effort, know what I mean?

THEODORE (*nodding affirmatively*): Uh hah! Yeah, well I'd like to get out there sometime . . . try some o' that stuff again . . .

PHILIP (*smiling, truly happy*): Crazy, Ted! Swingin'!

THEODORE: We'll teach them boys out there somethin' from the old school, from the masters . . .

PHILIP (*replacing bat*): Masters, hah?

THEODORE: Dig it!

PHILIP (*moving toward* THEODORE) I like that. I really like that!

(*They laugh a little, until* ELAINE *enters, at which time* PHILIP's *laughter tapers off conspicuously into a sullen expression.* ELAINE *is dressed in the evening gown but she still wears low-cut sneakers, the backs of which are mashed down. She is attractive.*)

THEODORE: Well! (*She smiles.*) Look at your wife, Phil.

PHILIP: Where're you going?

ELAINE (*moving in*): Nowhere.

PHILIP: Oh.

ELAINE: Your mother told me I should put something else on.

PHILIP: Oh. (*Pauses.*) So ah . . .

ELAINE: Thank you, Theodore. (*She moves downstage left*

to bedroom where JAKE *and* ANNIE *carry on muffled conversation. Standing in front of drawn curtains.*) Annie, is it all right if I fix something for dinner?

ANNIE (*from within*): Oh—yeah, yeah, go on. But use the chops!

ELAINE (*moving back upstage. She pauses briefly, her tone apologetic*): Chops again, Phil. (*No response.*) Do you feel like eating chops?

PHILIP: I feel like eatin' steak.

(THEODORE *laughs raucously, quickly becomes aware that no one else is laughing, and quickly becomes silent again.*)

ELAINE: Phil, I . . .

PHILIP: I know—you was just askin' . . .

ELAINE (*turning around as she reaches kitchen doorway*): I'm sorry I can't offer you anything, Theodore, but . . .

THEODORE: Aw, that's all right, Elaine—I'm not hungry. Had a big lunch in the cafeteria before I left school.

(ELAINE *enters kitchen; we hear pots and pans rattling. Pause.*)

PHILIP: What was we talkin' about?

THEODORE: Hah?—Oh, stick-ball and what not.

PHILIP: Yeah—so you gonna play sometime, hah?

THEODORE: Yeah . . . um gonna play—think I'd like to . . .

PHILIP: Boss!

THEODORE: . . . when I get some time. (*Silence.*) What coulda happened to Harry, I wonder? I told you he said 'e'd be back in a little while—that was at least an hour ago.

PHILIP: Ah, what the hell! (*Lowers voice.*) Wants me to mess around with the digits.

THEODORE: Digits?

PHILIP: The numbers.

THEODORE: Ah hah! Ah hah! Tha's whatchoo said you'd tell me?

PHILIP (*starting to pace*): Ah hah! Hell, man, I don' wanna mess with that jive, know what I mean?

THEODORE: I know exactly what you mean. What's it he wants you to do exactly—say you mind me askin'?

PHILIP: Come off it, Teddy!

THEODORE: No, 'cause I mean . . .

PHILIP: You know I'd tell you anything.

THEODORE: But that don' necessarily mean . . .

PHILIP: Yeah, but still!—wants me to take 'em.

THEODORE: Aw, you don' wanna do that, man.

PHILIP: I know. (*Pause.*) Although it is a lotta dough I could make, and fast.

THEODORE: Well . . .

273

PHILIP: Fast dough . . . !

(*Pause.* THEODORE *gets up and goes to window. Pause.*)

THEODORE (*looking down on street*): Well, think about it hard, Phil! You know. (PHILIP *ponders the matter, nods his head several times. Pause. Turning from window, toward* PHILIP.) How much you figure you could make, and in what time?

PHILIP: Well, see, I never even really discussed the matter wit' 'im, but I figure it'd be somewhere around five hundred in a month. (THEODORE *whistles.*) Maybe even more, who knows?

THEODORE: S'lotta dough! S'*whole* lotta dough, as a matter o' fact! But why's 'e want you? I mean, why's 'e keep botherin' you with the proposition?

PHILIP: Yeah—well, see, this is more or less my neighborhood, see? Um sorta on to all the people that play the numbers around here.

THEODORE (*moving to* PHILIP): Ah hah! Ah hah! (*Pause.*) Well, I wouldn't think too seriously in favor of it myself, you know what I mean, Phil?

PHILIP: Ah hah! I think I know whatchoo mean . . .

(*Pause.*)

THEODORE (*cocking head*): Say, listen!

PHILIP (*doing same*): What? Wha' wrong?

THEODORE (*moving to phono*): The record player, humming sorta—it's been on all the . . .

PHILIP (*finger to lips*): Sssssh! (*Points to bedroom.*) He'll wanna pitch a bitch if he finds out.

THEODORE: But he's the one who turned it down; tha's why we couldn' hear it . . .

PHILIP (*going to phonograph*): Still (*lowered voice*), you don' know 'im like I do . . . He's a bastard—always stirrin' up trouble between me an' my mother.

THEODORE: Oh. Say, Phil, put on that record you was dancin' to.

PHILIP (*perceptibly annoyed at* THEODORE'S *sluffing off his grievance*): What, man?

THEODORE (*missing* PHILIP'S *annoyance*): You know, the Latin one.

PHILIP: *Siempre me gusta por la noche.*

THEODORE: The one you was dancin' to—I guess tha's it. (PHILIP *puts on record at considerably high volume.*) Yeah, tha's it.

(PHILIP *has taken up ashtray and* THEODORE'S *pencil; he now rhythmically taps ashtray with pencil, singing along with record.*)

PHILIP:

> *Eh, muchacha mia*
> *No me besas por el dia*
> *Por-que cuando tu me besas*
> *Me gusta mas por la noche*

THEODORE: Tha's boss! Tha's really boss . . . an' those was some real nice steps you was doin' before, real nice.

PHILIP: Thanks.

THEODORE (*demonstrating*): I think you did somethin' like . . .

PHILIP: No, Teddy, it was . . . (*He demonstrates.*)

THEODORE: Tha's nice, tha's very nice, Phil!

(PHILIP *is caught up with the music and hardly hears* THEODORE. PHILIP *is dancing.*)

JAKE (*from within*): Turn that goddamned record player down!

(PHILIP *stops abruptly, frozen, an intensely angry expression on his whole being. Presently, he moves to phono and turns it off.* JAKE *continues to mumble angrily within.*)

PHILIP (*softly*): I may kill him one day.

THEODORE: Be cool, Phil!

PHILIP: I may kill that son of a—

THEODORE (*moving toward* PHILIP): Look, you feel like makin' a dance tonight?

(*At the mention of a dance,* PHILIP'*s anger vanishes.*)

PHILIP: No jive.

THEODORE: Um serious.

PHILIP: You mean, you goin' too?

THEODORE: Yeah. I mean, what the hell, um sorta outta the groove now, but . . .

PHILIP: Crazy! Aw, but I ain' got no dough.

THEODORE: Tha's arright, I'll pay your way . . . this time, an' get us somethin' for the head—cool?

PHILIP: I could go for that; tha's boss . . .

THEODORE: 'Cause I gotta' keep in touch, you know?

PHILIP: Tha's it, Ted, tha's it! You know, you had me worried aboutchoo for a while, man! I mean, nobody don' never see you—or nothin' cause you studyin' so much an' what not. I mean, maybe you wouldn' go crazy or nothin' . . . but man, you could! All that studyin's bad for you!

THEODORE (*smiling*): Well . . .

PHILIP: I mean it, Teddy!

THEODORE: Ah hah! . . . so you wanna?

(ELAINE *appears in kitchen doorway.*)

ELAINE: It's ready, Phil.

PHILIP: Ah—Elaine . . . just put it on the stove for me . . .

I got to go somewhere . . . um goin' to a dance. (*Hurt is readable in her expression. She turns and reenters kitchen.*) Ah-um gonna get ready—now, Ted.

THEODORE: Arright. Listen, umma go get that taste, okay?

PHILIP: Okay, Teddy. Pull the door in, will you?

(THEODORE *starts for door, downstage right;* PHILIP *goes to bureau and removes towel, shirt and underwear as* JAKE *parts curtains of bedroom and strides to bathroom, left, wearing bathrobe, towel in hand.*)

JAKE: You know better'n to play that record player so damned loud!—think you the only one livin' here or somethin' . . . ?

(*He enters bathroom, excitement can be seen to well up in* PHILIP.)

THEODORE (*touching his arm*): Don't panic, man. Ignore him!

(PHILIP *ignores* JAKE *and, putting the towel down, proceeds to take a pair of shoes from under bureau.* THEODORE *goes out. Suddenly* ELAINE *enters from kitchen and darts left to bathroom. At the sound of* JAKE'S *voice, she stops abruptly.*)

JAKE (*booming agitatedly from within*): Phil! Get these rags outta the tub!

ANNIE (*yelling from bedroom*): It's all right, Jake!

JAKE (*storming out of bathroom*): No, it ain' all right, Mom!—um tryin' to take a bath so we can get the hell outta here!

ELAINE (*urgently*): I'll take them out, Jake! (*She enters bathroom: the sound of water splashing within.*)

PHILIP (*forcefully throwing shoes to ground*): Let 'im take them out 'imself!

JAKE: Shet up, Phil! Chris', don't you ever know when you wrong? You put them in there—which was good—but that don' mean you got to give us all a pain in the behin' cause you done somethin' for a change.

(ELAINE *appears in bathroom doorway, holding curtains, which she has wrung out, on scrub-board. She leans against door post in a kind of "come wind, blow wrack" attitude; she is prepared for the onslaught.*

PHILIP: See, now, you wrong! You wrong!—I ain' put nothin' in that tub, not nothin'! You wrong, Jake!

JAKE (*pointing to curtains* ELAINE *holds*): You didn' put them in the tub when you washed the windows?

ANNIE (*entering living room, wearing housecoat*): Phil, you didn' wash the windows?

(PHILIP *kisses his teeth.*)

JAKE (*entering bathroom*): 'Scuse me for accusin' you, Phil.

PHILIP (*as* ELAINE *passes him on way to kitchen*): You shouldn't've done that—said I did them windows. (*She says nothing; he follows her.*) You said I washed them windows, didn't you?

ELAINE (*entering kitchen*): Yes.

PHILIP (*following to threshold of kitchen*): You shouldn't've done that, Elaine.

ANNIE (*reentering bedroom*): Hang 'em up where they'll dry, Elaine.

(*Pause.* PHILIP *starts on a pitch almost devoid of emotion, but, although he never really raises his voice, the emotion in it is progressively intensified, until at last it is cold rage.*)

PHILIP: You think you're smart, don't you? (*Silence.*) Well, um just tellin' you, don' pull nothin' like that again. See, 'cause um not the kid you seem to think I am. See, I just ain' no kid. You may think I am maybe, you may talk about me and to me as if um one, but I ain'. An' when I don' do somethin', s'not 'cause I don' know how or can't or nothin' like that—it's 'cause I got reasons, it's 'cause I probably got my reasons when I don' do somethin'. An' . . . (*in reference to curtain-hanging*) don' do that when um talkin' to you, sweetie.

ELAINE: The curtains are wet, Phil. You heard what your mother . . .

PHILIP: Yeah, I heard what she said an' I don' give a damn what she said, I don' give a damn. Um talkin' to you now. (*Pause.*) An' so I probably got my reasons . . . I don' need you to front for me. I don' need you takin' me by the hand like I was a little boy . . .

ELAINE: Nobody's taking you . . .

PHILIP: *You're* taking me by the hand, *you're* actin' like I was a kid!

(*Silence.*)

PHILIP: You didn't think I was any kind of a goddamned kid when I married you, though, did you?

ELAINE: No—I didn't.

(*Pause.* ELAINE *comes out into living room, takes ashtray from coffee table and goes back into kitchen where she empties it. She returns with ashtray. While this action occurs,* PHILIP *talks.*)

PHILIP: You know, sweetie, you got yourself an attitude lately. You gotchore self a stinkin' attitude that I hate! (*Gesticulates.*) You're up here! All of a sudden you're up here, lookin' down on me, talking down to me. Why I wonder.

Don'tchoo know you ain' livin' out there in them suburbs no
more?

ELAINE: Please, Phil! I've never acted that way toward you
and you know it!

PHILIP: . . . All of a sudden, high falutin', hinkty—well,
where the hell's it comin' from, that attitude? (*Laughs shortly.*)
Baby, you better come back down to earth, otherwise you
liable to fall on your face.

ELAINE: What does that mean?

PHILIP: It means whatever you think it means, tha's what
it means.

(*Pause.*)

ELAINE: Phil . . . when I first came here, when we thought
I was pregnant and I came here to live, Phil . . . you told me
things weren't perfect here, that I shouldn't expect much at
first, the way you said things were and all, and you told me
that I'd be better off going back to my mother's . . . and what
did I say, Phil? (*No response. Pause.*) I told you I loved you,
Phil . . . and that I didn't want to go back to my mother's
although she'd wrote and said I could. I told you I loved you
and that I didn't care how hard it was for us at first; that I still
wanted to live with you, even though we'd discovered that I
wasn't pregnant after all . . .

PHILIP: And then we got married . . . and then your mother
slammed the castle door shut . . . and then you started gettin'
that attitude, lookin' down your nose, findin' fault with all that
I do . . . an' don' do . . . just like them two . . .

ELAINE: Oh, Phil . . . I've tried so hard to be patient! I
have, Phil. I have tried! But don't you see that there's got to
be an end to this, whether I like it or not, things've got to start
happening? Because . . . (PHILIP *is unaware of the slight
movement of her hand to upper abdomen.*) . . . Oh, Phil . . .
because . . .

(ANNIE *enters living room on way to kitchen.*)

ANNIE (*over her shoulder*): Boy, are you still harping on
them curtains?

ELAINE: Philip isn't talking about any curtains, Annie!

ANNIE (*coming to kitchen threshold, surprised at* ELAINE's
assertion of the fact and of herself): What did you say?

(*Slight pause.*)

ELAINE (*less certain of herself*): I said, Philip isn't talking
about the curtains.

(*Pause.*)

ANNIE: And he needed you to say that for him.

ELAINE: Annie, he . . .

PHILIP: I don't need her to say nothin' for me. (*To* ELAINE.)

An' don' say nothin', don' say nothin' for me no more. (*To* ANNIE.) And I don' have to say nothin' to you, either. Wait a minute, Ma . . . Ma, you think 'cause you doin' me a favor, 'cause you lettin' me stay in your house for awhile, you think I gotta answer to you or somethin', hah? You think that, don't you?

ANNIE (*starting to turn*): Oh, Philip, stop!

PHILIP (*going to her and grasping her by arm*): You think you can tell me what to do an' all, don't you, scoldin' about this, scoldin' about that . . . you really think you can treat me like a kid, don'tchoo?

ANNIE: I just want you to learn to stand on your own two feet and be a man, tha's all . . . !

PHILIP (*dropping his hold, turning from her*): I *am* a man! Hell! I *am* a man!

(*Enter* JAKE *from bathroom, laughing, briskly rubbing witch hazel into clean-shaven face. He says nothing, just moves to bedroom, the laughter tapering to a cruel chuckle,* PHILIP *just stares after* JAKE; *he is paralyzed with hatred. At once* PHILIP *starts laughing, an inappropriate kind of laughter.*)

JAKE (*yelling from bedroom, interrupting* PHILIP's *laughter*): You all ready there, Mom?

ANNIE (*entering kitchen*): Yeah, Jake. Um just gettin' a little bite or so. (*Still laughing,* PHILIP *enters bathroom and slams door in absolute frustration. To threshold*): Hey!

(*We continue to hear his laughter until at last it is drowned out by the water running full force in there.* ANNIE *reenters kitchen.* ELAINE *stands in middle of living room, "shut out," tears streaming from her eyes. Presently, compelled to movement,* ELAINE *goes to sofa, sits and picks up one of* THEODORE's *textbooks; she tries to interest herself in it. She puts it down, rises and goes to window. She sits on sill.*

Presently there is a knock at the outside door, down right, directly followed by the entrance of THEODORE *and* HARRY, *the local boy.*)

THEODORE (*entering, carrying quart bottle of liquor in bag so shaped*): Me! (ELAINE *rises, hastily wiping eyes with back of hand. We recognize* HARRY: *he is "the city slicker." He wears "long" shoes, long collars, shirt with flashy cuff links, tie clip, etc., fairly narrow tie, dark-colored silk suit, wide-brimmed hat that is deep-rolled. Moving with* HARRY *toward* ELAINE.) You've met Harry, haven't you?

ELAINE: Ah . . .

THEODORE: Well, just in case, this is Harry. Harry, Elaine, Phil's wife.

ELAINE: Hello.

HARRY (*appraising her, looking at her steadily*): How you feel, sweetheart?

ELAINE (*ill-at-ease*): Fine, thank you.

THEODORE: Say, you been crying?

ELAINE: No.

THEODORE: Oh. Your eyes are sort of red . . . Phil ready yet?

ELAINE (*returning to window sill*): He's in there. (*She points to bathroom.*)

ANNIE (*coming to threshold of kitchen*): Who is it, Elaine?

ELAINE: Some friends for Philip. (*To* THEODORE *and* HARRY, *starting to rise.*) Won't you have a seat?

(ANNIE *reenters kitchen.*)

THEODORE: No, thanks, Elaine—we're not staying long. (*Walking toward bathroom.*) Say, Phil, come on!

(*The sound of running water ceases.*)

PHILIP (*from within*): Teddy?

THEODORE: Yeah, man. S'gettin' late.

PHILIP (*from within*): Be out in a few minutes.

THEODORE: Hurry up! (*Walking back to* HARRY, *who is now in the process of lighting a cigarette.*) What's this remin' you of, Harry?

HARRY (*blowing out smoke, laughing briefly, a throaty laugh*): Ol' times . . . when we all was hangin' out together, makin' all the sets, all the happenin's—some swingin' times! (*Pause.*) Guess who's out.

THEODORE (*lighting cigarette*): Out o' what?

HARRY (*glances first in* ELAINE'*s direction, then lowers voice*): The Slams.

THEODORE (*after a brief pause*): Not Richard! (HARRY *nods to say, yes, Richard.*) No jive!

HARRY: I ain' jivin'. Lotta people don' know yet. His mom's livin' cross town now. He's stayin' wit 'er.

THEODORE: Well, when, man? When'd 'e get out? Think I'd like to maybe see the cat sometime.

HARRY: Yeah, well . . . (*Enter* PHILIP *from bathroom, dressed, brushing hair.*) Wha's happenin', my man? Lookin' sharp there!

THEODORE (*quickly*): Harry's makin' it with us, arright?

PHILIP (*perceptibly disappointed and annoyed, he nods after a slight pause*): Arright.

THEODORE: So are we ready?

PHILIP: Yeah. Le's go! (*He and they move toward outside door. Turning around, to* ELAINE.) Ah— you feel like goin'?

(*No answer.*) Elaine. (*She looks at him.*) I said, do you feel like goin'?

ELAINE: No. No, I don't feel like going, Phil.

PHILIP: Well—ah . . . I'll be back about three. (*To* THEODORE *and* HARRY.) Come on.

THEODORE (*to* ELAINE): See you, Elaine.

(*No answer. He shrugs shoulders and starts out of door.*)

HARRY (*as he goes out behind* THEODORE): But, you know, Teddy, Richard didn' have to get busted in the first place—I mean, if 'e'd used his head . . .

(PHILIP *closes door behind them and they are heard descending stairs.* ELAINE *leans head on window post, crying, and . . . the light dims out and comes up some hours later on the same scene.*

But now the sofa is pulled out into its bed form. ELAINE, *clad in nightgown, slowly and disconsolately goes about the business of tucking sheet ends under edges of sofa. Lights are relatively dim and there is a loneliness about the place and about* ELAINE. *A street lamp outside rudely throws some of its light inside the apartment via the open window whose curtains are now pulled to one side and hitched to a nail.* ELAINE *tucks a second sheet in on top of the first, then sits on bed. Presently, she rises, restlessly, goes to phonograph and turns it on. Now she selects record from stack and places it on machine. A very cheerful tune is what we hear. Because the record is badly scratched and unclear, we surmise that the record is old. Leaning against the wall,* ELAINE *listens reminiscently. Before the piece finishes, she abruptly removes needle of phonograph from record, interrupting the piece. She snaps phono off, returns to sofa, and switches off lamp that is on coffee table, which now is situated alongside sofa.*

Now the living room receives its little illumination solely from the glare of the street lamp outside; and ELAINE *is little more than a silhouette; she sits on bed once again and kicks the low-cut sneakers from her feet. Now she slides under the end of upper sheet that is turned down. A stumbling ascent of the outside stairs is heard.* ELAINE *rises a little with a start. More stumbling accompanied by loud talking and finally the sound of a key in door lock;* ELAINE *falls back to former position. Enter* PHILIP *intoxicated, assisted by* THEODORE *who is also under the influence, though to a lesser degree.*)

PHILIP (*fiercely struggling against* THEODORE'S *firm hold*): Will you quit hangin' on me, Teddy?

ELAINE (*rising to sitting-up position, switching on light*): What's happened, what's the matter? (*She pulls sheet from*

herself altogether, gets out of bed and hurries over to PHILIP.)
What's happened, Teddy?

THEODORE (*swaying slightly*): Ah, he's drunk! Had to bring
'im home!

ELAINE: Thanks an awfully lot, Ted!

PHILIP (*struggling harder*): Quit lyin'! You didn' have to
bring me home, nothin'! Get off me!

THEODORE (*tugging at* PHILIP): Will you stop acting like
an idiot an' let somebody help you out? Now, you're drunk,
Phil! Drunk as hell!

(ELAINE *goes to open door and closes it. She returns to*
PHILIP *and* THEODORE.)

ELAINE (*hand on* PHILIP's *arm, moving toward bed*): Bring
him over here.

(*With a final, violent jerk,* PHILIP *frees himself.*)

PHILIP: Damn it, get off me, I said! I don't need y'all pawin'
all over me!

(*Pause.*)

THEODORE (*abruptly, starting toward sofa*): You're a sim-
pleton, Phil. Let me get the hell out of here—where're my
books, Elaine?

ELAINE: I'll get them. (*She goes to table beside sofa-bed.*)
I put them . . . (PHILIP *is staring at* THEODORE, *deeply angered.
Returning with books.*) Here they are.

THEODORE (*taking books and starting for door*): Thank
you, Elaine. Good night.

PHILIP (*stepping into* THEODORE's *path*): Wait a secon',
my man!

THEODORE (*stopping short before* PHILIP, *surprised*):
What?!

ELAINE (*moving toward* PHILIP): Oh, Philip, stop . . . !

PHILIP (*snapping, his drunkenness falling away before his
anger*): Shaddup! You stay the hell outta this for a change!

(THEODORE *slowly puts books down on floor next to him.*)

PHILIP (*noting this action*): Yeah, tha's right, tha's arright
too—put 'em down, Teddy. Le's see how good you handle
yourself withoutchore books.

ELAINE (*moving to* PHILIP *once again*): Phil, I'm not going
to let . . . (*He shoves her away from him. Shocked.*) Phil . . . !

PHILIP: Well, I said keep out, didn' I?

THEODORE (*yelling*): What the hell's wrong with you, pushing her that way, hah, Phil?

PHILIP (*looking at* THEODORE *steadily. In low voice*): You
defendin' her 'r somethin', Ted?

THEODORE: You're damned right I'm defending her! You
must be insane!

PHILIP: No, um not insane. In fact, um more sane than you think I am! So watch yourself . . .

THEODORE: What're you talking about now?

PHILIP: There you go—how come you always talk so proper when she's around?

THEODORE: What do you mean, what are you talking about?

PHILIP: You know what I mean. You think you're slick . . . but um on to you, Ted. Um on to you!

THEODORE: You're crazy!

PHILIP: An' like tonight—that Daddy act you was pullin'! (*Brief pause.*) Don' try that kinda jive no more!

(THEODORE *stands there a moment longer, staring at* PHILIP.)

THEODORE (*abruptly stooping and picking up books*): You're nuts, that's whatchoo are!

PHILIP: Just you don' try that no more, tha's all!

THEODORE (*starting to brush past* PHILIP): You're nuts . . . let me get—

(PHILIP *shoves* THEODORE.)

ELAINE: Phil . . . !

THEODORE: Now, watch yourself, Phil!

PHILIP: You watch yourself—from now on, chump! Don't think you're the only one who's got any brains.

(PHILIP *walks away toward sofa, ripping off already loosened tie as he goes. He throws himself down upon bed.* THEODORE *stares after* PHILIP. ELAINE *watches* THEODORE.)

THEODORE (*abruptly, moving for door*): Good night, Elaine. I may see you around. (*He exits. Pause.*)

ELAINE: I think you've lost a friend.

PHILIP: What d'you care? You've gained one.

(*Pause.*)

ELAINE: Why are you so angry with me?

PHILIP: I say I was angry with you?

ELAINE: A person doesn't have to be told all of the time . . . sometimes when it's there . . . you just feel it . . .

PHILIP: Um sorry I pushed you. But you forced me.

ELAINE: No, no . . . the shoving doesn't hurt me half as much as the anger behind it . . . it's the anger behind it that hurts me, Phil . . . deep down behind the words. It hurts, Phil. It hurts so much! (PHILIP *rises from bed and goes to window. Taking a step closer to* PHILIP.) You're angry with everyone . . . with everyone . . . with the whole world . . . !

PHILIP: I got reason to be! I got troubles . . . I go around with headaches most o' the time!

ELAINE: But being angry with everyone's not going to . . .

Donald Greaves

PHILIP: I don' care! I don' care . . . an' why can't I show um mad when I *am* mad?

ELAINE: Because you often lose friends and . . . people who mean a lot to you—you shut yourself off from the world. You just can't be angry with the world you live in . . .

PHILIP: You're preachin'!

ELAINE (*slowly moving closer*): I don't mean to.

PHILIP: But you're preachin'!

ELAINE: Oh, Phil . . . I just mean to say . . . you can't shut out the whole world . . . because I'm in it . . . and I need you very much . . . you can't shut out the world! I'm not preaching. I just want to make things right with us. I want to stop feeling like something under your feet that's keeping you from better things. I want you to want me around you . . . to need me around you . . . (*She is standing directly in front of him now; and her plea and her closeness are visibly disconcerting to him.*)

PHILIP: Aw, Chris', Elaine . . . I told you all that long long ago . . .

ELAINE: But now, Phil. I need you to tell me now! (*Pause.*) Phil . . . ?

PHILIP: I hear you.

(*Pause.*)

ELAINE: . . . it was the clinic I went to while you were sleeping this morning. I'm going to have a baby . . . Phil . . . (*Pause.*) I was afraid to tell you—I thought you'd be sorry.

(*Silence.* PHILIP *slowly sits upon window sill. He starts making a loudly rasping sound with some object he finds out there, perhaps a can opener. He is looking down on street.*)

ELAINE: Please don't be sorry, Phil. (*Pause, moving closer to him yet, gently resting hand on his neck.*) Please don't be sorry.

PHILIP: I ain' sorry. No, I ain' sorry, baby. (*He puts down the object. Pause. Suddenly he puts his arms about her, pulling her close to him, repeating almost reassuringly to himself.*) I ain' sorry, I ain' sorry . . . !

CURTAIN

ACT II

Scene 1

(*It is evening of fall and the lights rise to dimly illumine the living room of* THEODORE. *Soft music of strings is vaguely heard; it emanates from the phonograph situated in a corner;*
284

it is the orchestra of Mantovani playing "Music to a Dead Princess." A bottle of liquor, glasses, etc., are barely discernible atop the phonograph, in front of which stands THEODORE, *fixing drinks. The odd intensity of his activity expresses the anxiety of his mood.* ELAINE *is easily visible to us as she lies on a sofa, not disarranged, though her high-heel shoes are on the floor at one end of sofa.*)

ELAINE: . . . Because he seemed so unconcerned about everything. I guess . . . so able not to care . . . about anybody, about *anything*—the way he moved—so slowly . . . as if to say "Everyone, everything must wait for me." I used to think of him as being so frightfully strong in that way, so very much stronger than I could ever have been with my parents, with people I knew and had to deal with. I guess I thought I'd found strength in Philip—I was pregnant, young, and afraid. It cost us a lot to find out how wrong I was.

(THEODORE *moves to sofa with tray of drinks.*)

THEODORE: I've wished a hundred times that I'd met you before Philip did. (THEODORE *sits on sofa. He gives one of the drinks to* ELAINE, *takes the other himself and sets tray down on floor beside sofa.*)

ELAINE (*raising up, now making herself visible*): Teddy . . . ?

THEODORE (*a hand to her cheek*): Humnh?

ELAINE: . . . Teddy, would you have married me—I mean, in the same circumstances that Philip did?

(*Awkward pause.*)

THEODORE (*dropping hand*): Aw, you can't compare me and Philip—I mean, we're so different. We're different people altogether . . .

ELAINE (*with increasing urgency*): But would you have married me?!

THEODORE (*raising his glass to hers*): To success! (ELAINE *sips. Consuming drink in a swallow.*) I'd probably have married you, sure! It'd've depended though . . .

ELAINE: On what, Teddy? Why must it have depended on anything?!

THEODORE (*rising restlessly*): Because everything must depend on something, Elaine. Because there's a rational way of doing things . . . and there's an irrational way. (*Starting to pace.*) I'm the rational type. I don't take train rides to nowhere. When I board a train, any train, I ask to know where that train is headed. I've got to know where I'm going and why. (*Pause.*) Plato says, "Don't be a fool and learn by experience"—I'm in touch with that. For me to have married you, our attitudes, our aims, yours and mine, must at least

285

have approximated each other . . . if they weren't the same. (*Pause.*) I read you as wanting particular things in life, sweetie. And I'm in touch with those things. I read you . . .

ELAINE: But me, Teddy . . . are you in touch with me?

THEODORE (*moving around back of sofa, taking her face in his hands*): Aw, yeah, baby . . . with you, yeah! You know I am; I know you so well . . . !

ELAINE: And that's the bridge between us.

(*Brief pause.*)

THEODORE (*walking away a little*): Well, yeah! What other bridge could there be between two people . . . but their knowing each other? (*Turning to* ELAINE.) Well, isn't that right? I've got to have a knowledge of you before I can be in touch with you . . . and I know you . . .

ELAINE: What about love . . . do you love me?

THEODORE (*agitated*): These sprawling terms! (*Pause. Trying to reason with her.*) Elaine . . . Love is simply a misnomer of the result of basic drives. Wouldn't be a bad word in itself —after all, what is a word but intelligently arranged letters; it's what people expect of it that makes the careless use of it dangerous. They use it like a magic wand or something, a kind of abracadabra to unite incompatible characters.

ELAINE (*rising and walking to window*): You can make everything sound so worthless, so stupid.

THEODORE: I don't mean to, Elaine. It's just that . . . well, some notions are worthless . . . and stupid . . . and I think we'd better recognize which ones they are. (*Pause. Growing apprehensive over her mood.*) Look, Elaine . . . didn't Phil ever say he loved you?

ELAINE: Many times.

THEODORE: And haven't you told him the same?

ELAINE: So many times . . .

THEODORE (*moving to her*): You see? And so what? (*She looks at him.*) I mean, you're standing in *my* living room with your shoes off . . . beautiful! A minute ago you lay in my couch—see . . . it ain' in what you say, baby, it's in what you do. (*He is standing close behind her now and he puts his arms about her waist; he starts kissing her passionately on neck.* ELAINE *at first yields to this, then abruptly disengages herself. She moves away, toward sofa.*) What's the matter . . . ? (*No answer.*) Hah? What'd I do? I say something?

(*Pause.*)

ELAINE (*slowly and deliberately*): If—Philip—would give me—a divorce—Teddy, would you marry me . . . ? (*Silence.* THEODORE *turns from her slightly. He reaches in a pocket, takes out cigarette and lights it.* ELAINE *awaits him in silence.*

Slowly moving to him.) Teddy? Would you . . . ? (*His back is slightly turned to her; when she reaches him, she puts her arms about him and leans head on back of his shoulder.*) Teddy?!

(*Pause.*)

THEODORE: Sweetie, I—I can't. (*Pause.*) I can't.

(*Silence.* ELAINE *drops her arms to her sides and stands looking at* THEODORE *a moment, then she slowly goes to side of sofa and puts on shoes.* THEODORE *slowly follows to sofa, and walks slowly around it, stopping at back of it, downstage center.*)

THEODORE: You understand, don't you? (ELAINE *looks at him intently.*) S'not that I don't want to. (*Pause. He laughs shortly, a peculiar, self-involved laugh.*) See . . . so many places I want to go . . . so many things I want to see—so many things—I've got to be . . . !

(ELAINE *dons coat and the lights dim out.*)

Scene 2

(*Bright lights rise on the* KITCHENER *household a little later the same evening. Changes have been made in the apartment; the old sofa has been replaced by a new one. Where once stood the broken-down television which supported the old-fashioned phonograph, a brand-new TV–Stereo combination now stands, stacked high with record albums and forty-five-speed discs alone. A brand-new floor covering. Full drapes at the window. An easy chair, etc. The place looks good.* ELAINE, *in outdoor dress, changes her baby's diapers; she sits on sofa as she does this. The baby, her clothing and blankets on side to which she is now turned; her books on the other.* PHILIP *stands with back to window, a quart bottle of whiskey in one hand, a half-filled glass of the whiskey in the other. He is watching* ELAINE *intently. His dress is very like that of* HARRY. PHILIP *is dressed in the tradition of the "city slicker," the "hustler." His shoes are "long" and very shiny. He wears highly tailored pants, a rust-colored suede jacket, the belt of which hangs in casual support of the "cool" air which he sporadically tries desperately to maintain whenever he remembers his "image"; that is, often. He also wears a black, long-collared shirt, open at top, a "Big Apple" cap worn on an exaggerated slant; more than one flashy ring is worn on his fingers. At rise of curtain there is intense silence which lasts for quite some moments.*)

PHILIP (*his voice husky with emotion*): Friday night . . . I get a chance to be with you . . . but you're goin' someplace as usual . . . (*Without responding to* PHILIP, *seeming not to hear*

287

him at all, ELAINE *continues with her activity. After a brief pause,* PHILIP *raises glass to mouth and empties it completely of contents. He goes to the new coffee table and sets both bottle and glass down upon it. Moving* ELAINE'S *books to coffee table,* PHILIP *seats himself at her back; for she is turned away from him, toward baby.* PHILIP *reaches out uncertainly to touch* ELAINE'S *back, but he retracts his arm and plays with her hair instead.*) Baby, can't you just stay home tonight? I mean, I—I don' never get a chance to see you no more. (*Pause.*) Please?

ELAINE (*unceasing in activity*): You know that I have to go to school.

PHILIP (*still playing in her hair*): But every night, sweetie, not every night! An' then all that homework!

ELAINE (*turning head in order to disengage his hand*): Stop! You'd just as well get used to it because I have a year to go.

PHILIP (*rising, anxiety-ridden*): Then what? (*Walking around frustratedly.*) Aw, Elaine, you just can't keep this up forever—'cause . . . well, what about me?

(ELAINE *rises, diapers and other items of the baby in hand, crosses to bathroom. Her steps are brisk, directed.*)

ELAINE: Right now, all I'm concerned about is this baby's future . . . and mine . . .

PHILIP (*following her*): Please don' say that. I mean, don' make it seem like you're the only one that cares about the kid, 'cause I care too! I care about the both o' you-all!

ELAINE (*turning in doorway of bathroom*): Let's face it, Philip—you don't really care about anyone . . .

PHILIP: Aw, but I do . . .

ELAINE: No, you don't; not really. All you ever care about is yourself—how you feel and how you don't feel. You have a notion that everything and everyone's to revolve about you—it's disgusting! (*She enters bathroom.* PHILIP *follows to doorway as she runs water over diapers in tub. Pause.*)

PHILIP: Is that why I run all over this neighborhood the whole week? Riskin' jail an' everything, maybe even gettin' held up? (ELAINE *does not answer but turns water off, puts out light, and strides past him on way to kitchen, to which* PHILIP *follows.*) Answer me, Elaine! Is that why I risk goin' to jail every day—if I didn't care about nobody or nothin' like you say—tell me, do you think I'd do that?

(ELAINE *puts out light in kitchen and comes out into living room, testing warmth of baby's two bottles.*)

ELAINE: Philip, I don't feel like going back over all of this with you; honestly, I don't. I mean, you've set yourself on what you want to do and you're doing it. (*She sits down on*

sofa next to baby and begins feeding her one of the two bottles.) And you needn't try to sound like a martyr either, because as far as I'm concerned you're not. There were jobs you could have found if you'd had a mind to find them, but you didn't and that's that.

(*Silence.*)

PHILIP: Takin' number's the only thing I know how to do . . .

ELAINE: Oh, Philip, please . . .

PHILIP: It is. I don't know nothin' about computers an' stuff.

ELAINE: I know there were jobs! Of course, not white collar but . . .

PHILIP (*vigorously shaking head*): Umnh! Umnh! None! Only messenger.

ELAINE: Yes, you're too much above that.

(*Pause.*)

PHILIP: I wannid to get a nice apartment, fixed up an' everything, cross town, for the four of us—my mother, you, me, and the kid. Couldn' do it runnin' errands.

ELAINE: I've told you so many times already, I'm not impressed, Philip. You chose to take numbers because the big money you made let you feel important; all that big talk I've heard you and Harry with about big cars—Cadillacs and Chryslers, boasting about your thirty-dollar shoes, your expensive clothes.

PHILIP: An' can you blame me 'cause I wanna feel important?

ELAINE: No, I couldn't. But . . .

PHILIP: Everybody's gotta feel important in some way. (*Pause.*) And I don't want those things only for myself.

ELAINE: And I don't want them for myself, nor for my child . . . not that way, at least. (*With note of cruelty.*) And your mother doesn't seem to want them especially either.

(*Pause.*)

PHILIP: Seems like my mother don't want *nothin'* from me! (*Pause.*) But, Elaine . . .

ELAINE: Philip, I don't have time to talk to you anymore— Ted will be blowing his horn any minute.

PHILIP: If I had a car . . . would you mind if I drove you to school?

ELAINE (*stopping and turning to him in amazement*): You would buy a car so you could drive me to school!

(*Misreading* ELAINE'S *amazement as enthusiasm,* PHILIP *smiles and nods head affirmatively, deeply pleased. As* ELAINE *continues to look at* PHILIP, *the latter's face reveals fast-growing expectation. Pause.* ELAINE *turns away from him to pick*

up coat from sofa. PHILIP *moves to her and assists, striving to please her.*)

PHILIP (*holding her coat as she slips into it, overjoyed*): I got nearly three thousand dollars saved up . . . An' I won't get a big car.

ELAINE (*buttoning coat*): Thank you.

PHILIP: So you know what I mean? Somethin' nice, but not too big. (*Smiling.*) I'll take you to school.

ELAINE: Oh, do something else with your money, Phil. (*There is a tone in her voice of some feeling for him now. But it smacks of pity.*)

PHILIP (*deeply frustrated*): Like what, Elaine?

ELAINE (*gesticulating vaguely*): I don't know . . .

PHILIP (*angering*): Like what!

ELAINE: I don't know, I said. (*Pause.*) But something practical, anyway.

(*Silence.* ELAINE *goes into kitchen with one bottle. After a brief pause,* PHILIP *goes over to sofa and picks up baby.*)

PHILIP (*holding baby in arms*): What um gonna do? Hah? What um gonna do? Everything I got, nobody don' want. (*Putting face close to baby's.*) Gimme some sugar! (*Baby begins to wail.*) Aw, don' cry, baby! Ssh! Ssh! Baby, please don' cry!

(*Baby continues to wail.*)

ELAINE (*hurrying into living room*): Oh, what'd you do? She was so quiet . . . (*She takes baby from* PHILIP. *Talking baby language.*) Mommy's heah. Yeah, baby, ssh! . . . she's heah, don't cry. Umn! Tha's a good girl.

(*Baby smiles then begins to laugh. Pause.*)

PHILIP (*his hands jammed tightly in pockets*): Kid ain' suppose to just start cryin' like that—for no reason, start cryin' when all somebody does is pick her up. It ain' normal.

ELAINE: Well, the amount of liquor you've got on your breath would make anyone cry.

PHILIP: She almos' never gets a chance to see me—tha's the trouble. You'd almos' think she didn' know me, the way she acts.

ELAINE: She knows you.

PHILIP: How can she in the little time she's here every day?

ELAINE: What are you saying?

(*Pause.*)

PHILIP (*pacing*): Every time I come home you're gone— work and school, you say, or somethin'. Kid's stayin' wit' a lotta strange people. For instance, I don' know this Miss Wilson that keeps her—for all I know, she could be anybody. (*Pause.*) Riff-raff, even. (ELAINE *does not look at him. Pause.*

PHILIP *himself looks away.*) Kid needs her mother around . . . 'specially now when she's young. (*Pause. Turning to* ELAINE, *moving to her.*) An' what if somethin' happened to her while she was over there—God forbid!—but just what if; where's her mother? Gone. Makin' a dollar that she don't have to make! School! Ambition, hell!—that kid ain' gonna care nothin' about your ambition then . . . think she's gonna care?

ELAINE: Well, I . . .

PHILIP (*leaning into her face*): She won't! She ain' gonna care!

ELAINE (*looking down at baby*): She'll understand . . .

PHILIP: No! No, don' believe that! All she's gonna understand is that you wasn't there when she needed you! (*Pause.*) Kid needs her mother around . . .

(*The horn of a car in the street honks three times.*)

ELAINE: Ted—I've got to go.

PHILIP: I think you should give up school.

ELAINE (*packing baby's items into shoulder bag*): I can't. I can't and I'm not going to.

PHILIP: What if I say you gotta?

ELAINE: No. (*Determinedly putting books into fairly large handbag.*) No, that's the last thing you can tell me.

(*Pause.*)

PHILIP: Aw, baby, le's forget about all I've done and didn't do . . . can't you see we're caught up in the present now . . . you and me? (*Pause.*) You're so far away from me, Elaine . . . baby, everybody's so far away nowadays. You know? Hah, sweetie? You know what I mean? You're so far away—I—I can't reach you no more . . . all of a sudden you're driftin' away . . . driftin' away from our dream; baby, you used to hold the world together . . . but not now . . . not no more. Now all you say . . .

ELAINE: I've got to go, Philip! I've got to go . . .

(*A knock at the door is immediately followed by the appearance of* HARRY *who enters with exceeding familiarity, practically as though he owned the place.*)

HARRY (*to* ELAINE *who is close to exit now*): How you feelin', Elaine? (*She ignores him. To* PHILIP.) Say, Spody Ody!

PHILIP (*moving past him toward* ELAINE *who is about to exit*): Elaine . . . (*She pauses without answering.*) Call me Phil, like you used to. When you call me Philip . . . I know I'm a stranger.

ELAINE: I must go, Phil! (ELAINE *goes out carrying baby and books. Pause.*)

HARRY: Looks like you got a case of woman trouble on your hands.

(*Without reply,* PHILIP *moves to coffee table. He stands there, unmoving for some moments. Finally he takes up bottle of liquor and raises it to mouth, drinking deeply. In an abrupt upsurge of emotion he flings the bottle into television screen, causing a minor explosion.*)

HARRY (*startled*): What was that for?

PHILIP (*looking at* HARRY *askance*): Felt like it! (*Turning.*) Wha's happenin'!

HARRY: You know. Same ol' thing . . . so you gonna leave the bottle in there? I's a shame to goof a boss set like that. (*Going over to it, examining.*) Liquor's running all out the front; the wires must be in some kinda trouble, my man!

PHILIP (*walking to window*): So what?

(HARRY *lights a a cigarette. Pause.*)

HARRY (*talking around cigarette*): Cigarette, Phil? (PHILIP *shakes head to say "no."* HARRY *blows out smoke. Pause.*) Your kid's gettin' big, Phil. Growin' as fast as she's growin', she'll be on 'er own in no time at all.

(PHILIP *moves to sofa, reaches down behind it and takes out a pint of liquor; a reserve. He unscrews cap and drinks. Wiping mouth with handkerchief, he extends bottle to* HARRY *who also drinks.* HARRY *returns bottle.* PHILIP *returns it to place of concealment; taking pack of cigarettes out again, extending it toward back of* PHILIP, *who once again stands looking out of window.*)

HARRY: Sure you don' wan' a cigarette, Phil? (PHILIP *shakes head negatively again. Abruptly walks toward sofa.*) I know it ain' really none o' my business, Phil . . . but I just wanna know: How you let Teddy drive your wife aroun' and what not? I mean, Teddy's arright wit' me, don' misunderstan' me—cat's got a lot on the ball . . . but he is gettin' pretty familiar from what I see . . . an' hear. (*Quickly.*) Aw, I ain' sayin' the cat's tryin' to pull her from you or nothin' like that, man . . . but . . . well damn! You know what I mean? An' another thing—they seem to have the same kinda ideas about things—jus' lissen to 'em talk some time—sorta like watchoo might call a philosophy they seem to have . . . about . . . well, jus' Life, you know? Jus' Life! They ain' nothin' like you an' me, they don' think like you an' me think; they want different things outa life. If you jus' notice em a little bit, you dig what I mean. (*Pause.*) Better watch 'im, Phil! He's got a lot on the ball. He . . .

PHILIP: Sheddup, Harry!

HARRY: Well, um jus' tryin' to pull your coat, Phil—show you wha's goin' down 'cause . . .

PHILIP: When 'e gets as familiar as you think he's tryin' to get, I'll kill him!

HARRY: Now, wait, Phil . . . I didn' say nothin' about killin' nobody; all um sayin' is . . .

PHILIP: I'll kill him!

HARRY: Still ain' gonna change nothin', man! So he's dead, so what? That ain' gonna help you reach *her* . . . !

PHILIP: Harry, sheddup . . . !

HARRY: . . . which is whatchoo want after all, ain' it?

PHILIP (*turning and yelling, enraged*): Sheddup, Harry! Sheddup!

HARRY: Okay. Don't panic. I'll sheddup.

(*Pause.* HARRY *calmly sits on sofa, lights another cigarette.* PHILIP *glances at him apprehensively.*)

PHILIP (*looking out of window*): Lissen, Harry, don' take me serious . . . I mean, um serious, but I mean . . . (*Pause. turning to* HARRY.) Aw, hell . . . you understan' what I mean?

PHILIP: What're you doin', Harry? (*Takes a step closer.*) Wha's wrong, Harry? (HARRY *just smiles. Pause. Calmly.*) Okay, shoot. Go 'head 'n' shoot me! (*Laughs.*) I don' care.

HARRY: Don't you want it?

PHILIP: What?

HARRY: The gun—um givin' it to you. Here, take it!

PHILIP (*moving to coffee table*): Y-You were just kiddin'? (*He puts drinking "equipment" down on table and takes gun from* HARRY, *who laughs.*)

HARRY: Now, why would I wanna shoot you?

PHILIP (*examining gun awkwardly*): Why not?

HARRY: Go 'head, man! I's yours. It ain' loaded.

PHILIP: But what am I gonna do with it?

HARRY: Night track—in a couple o' days we gonna be workin' the night track.

PHILIP: What happened to Slim? I thought that was his show.

HARRY: Got busted a little while ago—cops walked right up on 'im in one o' them hallways on the avenue, caught 'im wit' some digits.

(*Pause.*)

PHILIP: An' the gun?

HARRY: Protection.

(*Pause. Despite* PHILIP's *show of antipathy for the gun, we sense his inner fascination with it; for he fingers it, even as he verbally rejects it.*)

PHILIP: I—I . . . Damn, Harry , . . . I—I don' know—not no gun!

HARRY: You sound like you already forgot what happened to Slim las' month.

PHILIP: No. Ah, ah! I didn' forget!

HARRY: Okay, then. Unless you wanna get your head whipped an' your money taken, carry the gun, an' *let* people know you carryin' it; people get a whole lotta heart at night, you know.

PHILIP: Sure is pretty, though. Boss!

HARRY: Ain' it? And dig the safety. (PHILIP *examines the safety catch.*) See there? Fits right into the side o' the gun itself . . .

PHILIP: Sure is pretty. (*Pause.*) How much?

HARRY: How much what? The gun? You own it.

PHILIP: Yeah? Aw, you jivin' me!

HARRY (*laughing*): No, I ain' kiddin' you, Phil. (PHILIP *is fascinated with the gun. He turns it in his hands fondly, staring at it. Reaching into pocket.*) Bought you some shells too. Maybe you can take a couple o' shots on the roof, you know?

PHILIP: Nobody don' ever go up there.

HARRY: Yeah, well you can take a couple o' shots, develop your eye. Know how to load it? (PHILIP *shakes head negatively.* HARRY *takes gun from* PHILIP.) Here's your clip, see? Slides out like this. Put your shells in, this way. Now, you got six shots. Slide it back in—catches by itself, you don' hafta do nothin'—slide it back in . . . an' you're all set. (*He returns gun to* PHILIP.) Try it. (PHILIP *fumbles with gun.*) Ain' nothin' to it—you'll get the hang of it! (*Pause.*) Say, can we get that taste now? (PHILIP *continues to fumble with gun.*) Phil?

PHILIP (*hearing him for the first time*): Hah?

HARRY: Can we get that drink?

PHILIP: Oh. Yeah! Yeah, we can get it.

HARRY: Better let me take them shells out till you get more familiar with it, otherwise . . .

PHILIP: Yeah, I know. (*Hands gun to* HARRY.) Um gonna put it away now. (HARRY *returns it along with removed shells.*) I'll keep it down in that armchair—nobody sits in it much. (PHILIP *wraps shells in handkerchief and puts handkerchief and gun down in armchair, upstage left corner, while* HARRY *pours drinks.*)

HARRY: Man, you got fancy!—tongs, icebucket. (*Pause.* PHILIP *joins him.*) Hey, le's make a toas', Phil!

(*They lift glasses.*)

HARRY (*touching his glass to that of* PHILIP): To all the money that you an' me 're gonna make.

(PHILIP *smiles weakly.*)

PHILIP: Thanks for the gun, Harry.

HARRY: Forget it! I'd like us to be frien's! You know, hang out together again. (*Pause.*) You wanna?

PHILIP: Sure, Harry.

(*Lights dim out.*)

Scene 3

(*It is the same scene in the afternoon of the following day.* ELAINE *is removing her belongings from a new bureau against the wall upstage somewhere which replaces the old one. As she stacks some of the contents on top,* ANNIE *watches her resolute activity with anxiety, saying nothing.*)

ANNIE: He know you're leaving?

ELAINE (*not looking up*): No.

(*Pause.*)

ANNIE: What's he gonna say when he finds out, honey? (*Pause.*) Humnh? What's he gonna say?

ELAINE: I don't know, Annie.

(*Pause.*)

ANNIE: He's been so upset lately—you'll kill 'im by leaving 'im, honey, I swear you'll kill 'im by leaving 'im now.

ELAINE: And I'll kill him by staying. I'm just telling a great big lie staying here—I don't love him . . .

ANNIE: Oh, but he needs you, Elaine . . . he needs you more than ever now! I know he does!

ELAINE: Annie . . . Philip only needs and wants.

ANNIE: I know it. (*Pause.*) Most of us do. I know it.

(*A key in the door lock. Enter* PHILIP, *flashing a huge bankroll, counting, much ado about it. He affects air of great importance and deep involvement with his work as he pauses to calculate mentally and make a note.*)

PHILIP (*announcing proudly, hoping to tempt*): Well, I made close to another five hundred this week and if business goes like we plan, it'll probably be around a grand working day and night . . . not bad for a cat who's not supposed to have nothin' on the ball. (*He forces a laugh. Unimpressed,* ELAINE *puts on her coat and heads for exit.*) Where's she going?

ANNIE: I think you should ask her.

PHILIP: What for? It ain' nothin' to me what she does no more.

ANNIE: Well, it should be.

(ELAINE *exits.*)

PHILIP: Ain' no woman gonna blow my mind—I ain' no chump!

ANNIE: I think you'd better think . . .

PHILIP (*impatiently*): Listen, Ma, I got other things to think about—I wanna talk to you about somethin'.

(ANNIE *starts dusting.*)

ANNIE: Go ahead, I'm listening. But I still say . . .

PHILIP: Ma, will you forget that for a minute and hear what um gettin' ready to say? This is important!

ANNIE (*stopping the dusting momentarily*): I hear you, Phil! I hear you, for goodness sake!

PHILIP: Arright, then. Now listen. (*Muffling his voice.*) Remember a while ago I mentioned to you about a house?

ANNIE: Go on. (*She resumes the dusting,* PHILIP *consequently follows her around in order to address her.*)

PHILIP: Well, I got nearly three thousand dollars saved up —Um gonna buy us a house. You want a house, don'tchoo?

ANNIE: Son, how will I ever make you see?! Sure I want a house, who don't want one? But what good's a house without nobody livin' in it? I'd stay in it, sure, and you'd stay in it, so you say. But when you get a little older, when you . . .

PHILIP (*trying to lean around in front of her, fervently*): No, I swear, Ma! I swear I wouldn't ever leave!

ANNIE: You would! I know you would. You'll get older and when you do, you'll begin to see things all differently. You'll want a life of your own, and rightfully . . .

PHILIP: But I'd never leave, never . . . !

ANNIE: Maybe you wouldn't, maybe you are like that at heart—faithful. But it'd destroy you *inside*. It'd destroy *me* to know I was such a burden to you. I'm getting old, whether it pleases you to hear it or not. You, you've got a lifetime yet . . . live it, Philip! Learn to live it on your own!

PHILIP (*flopping down into sofa, despairingly*): What am I gonna do, hah, Ma? Ma, what am I gonna do?

ANNIE: That's your decision. Nobody can make it for you —what you're gonna do, how you're gonna live. But all I wanna say is, however you live, whatever you do, be a man! Be a man and life won't come so hard to you. Sometimes I feel you think I'm cold. I'm not. Um your mother. But when I seem so, when I seem like I don't care, it ain' that—it's just because I'm determined that you'll be a man, not dependin' on me or nobody for the strength to live. 'Cause nobody can ever really give you that. Even I can't give it to you, though you seem to think I can, but I sure can take it away from you, whatever of it is in you. I can take it away, kill it, never give it a chance to grow by pushin' against the doors that you oughta open for yourself, by pickin' up the weights you oughta pick up . . . by livin' your life, Philip, like you want me to . . . I'd

become your life . . . and that's when you'd die—in spirit. Nobody'd live in that house you speak of buyin' for us. We'd only *be* in it. Buy it for your wife and child, Philip! Make a life with them!

PHILIP: I ain' got a wife no more.

ANNIE: Don't *say that,* Philip!

PHILIP: I ain' got a wife, I ain' got a wife!

ANNIE: Now, Philip, she . . .

PHILIP (*nearly screaming*): Don't talk to me about her! I—I'm talkin' about me and you. Us! Nobody else!

ANNIE (*startled*): Philip! Philip, what's the matter with you? There's more than me an' you in this world . . . in this house—there's your child, your wife . . . Jake . . .

PHILIP (*nearly screaming again*): To hell with Jake! He ain' got nothin' to do with my life, with nothin' . . . with me buyin' us a house . . .

ANNIE: You're wrong, son . . . you're so wrong. Jake's got more to do with your life than you'll ever imagine, much more . . . so don't you ever knock him. When you do that, you knock me too—the both of us.

PHILIP: W-what're you tryin' to say, Ma? Hah? What're you tryin' to say? (*Silence.*) H-He ain' my father . . .

ANNIE: Might as well be . . . I think sometime . . .

(*Brief pause.*)

PHILIP: Talk to me, Ma. What're you tryin' to say? He ain' my father. He ain' got nothin' to do with my life. He's just a idle bum hangin' on for a handout—ain't that right—an' now he'd like it if he could crawl in somewhere new.

ANNIE: That's not so.

PHILIP (*snapping, loud*): Then why the hell's it I can't buy you a house, why's it you won' never take nothin' from me. You know I couldn' stand for him to share a house witchoo, don't choo? (*Pause.*) Why's 'e gotta figure in to everything? (*Pause.*) Why does 'e live here . . . ?

ANNIE: Jake's the only *man* I ever knew.

(*Pause.*)

PHILIP: Make 'im go, Ma. Please make 'im go!

(*She does not answer. Silence.* JAKE *appears in doorway of bedroom, wiping sleep out of his eyes, a comb in one hand. He is unnoticed by* PHILIP *and* ANNIE. *He is combing his hair, his appearance indicative of his having not long awakened. The expression on his face is of profound anger, though he calmly stands there, combing his hair.*)

PHILIP: Ma, will you make 'im go . . . lemme buy us a house?

JAKE: Lissen, kid!

(PHILIP *turns, startled.* ELAINE *reenters carrying two suitcases, wrapped. Amidst their dialogue she continues preparations to leave, virtually unregarded by them.*)

JAKE: I took you in when that spineless . . .

ANNIE (*quickly moving to* JAKE): Hush up that talk, Jake! Hush!

JAKE: Damn it, Annie—tell 'im the truth! (*To* PHILIP.) When that spineless father o' yours run out on you, you wasn' but a small kid three years old then, so you couldn' remember. But before you start talkin' about puttin' me outta *my own house, mine,* about me bein' some kinda bum an' all, lookin' for a handout from a punk kid that thinks he's a big shit 'cause 'e's got a little chump change in 'is pocket—which 'e hustled off some por black people, on welfare some of 'em— before you start sayin' them things, before you actually start believin' that shit, I just wantchoo to know what I told you, son.

PHILIP (*dumbfounded, shocked, angry, standing very still, softly, half to himself*): You a goddamn liar, Jake! You a goddamn liar!

JAKE: Oh, so now I got to be everything you want me to be and "a goddamn liar" too, huh? Annie, tell 'im how . . .

PHILIP: Liar, sheddup! You better sheddup, um warnin' you!

(ELAINE *cringes as he rears back and kicks out one of the legs on coffee table so that objects come crashing to floor.*)

ANNIE (*moving between them*): Jake! Philip! Both of you stop all of this quarreling this minute!

(ELAINE *has frozen in her activity, feeling* PHILIP'S *pain.*)

JAKE (*moving toward* PHILIP, *pointing "finger of truth" at him, restrained by* ANNIE *who stands between them, shielding* PHILIP): I'll stop it when this foolish kid gets the truth and not before. You better tell 'im, Annie, if you don't want me to, because he's gonna get the truth about things for once in 'is dad-blamed life, he's gonna get the truth, about me an' you, an' him, an' all of it—you hear me?! Um not going to have no more of his damned disrespect, an' no more of this babyin' him; so just you go on an' tell 'im all of it . . . tell him how 'is father run out on you in the depression.

ANNIE (*putting hand in his face*): Doggone it, Jake, I said . . . !

PHILIP (*screaming, darts for armchair*): Okay, nigga, I got somethin' to make you sheddup . . . !

ANNIE: Philip! (*As* PHILIP *produces gun, gasping.*) Philip!!!

ELAINE: Philip! Don't!

PHILIP (*trembling, his gun-hand shaking violently*): So help me God, I'll kill you if you say another word, nigga!

JAKE (*hardboiled, unfazed*): Um for real, son. That gun ain' nothin' to the truth, reality. Everything is real, ain' it, Mom?! Tell 'im how you had 'im with no place to live, nothin' to eat, how they wasn' no jobs or nothin'. (ANNIE'*s face is turned away. Tears pour down* PHILIP'*s face as the gun shakes uselessly in his hands.*) Tell 'im how I took you an' him in, Annie, sure . . . an' volunteered for the service when the war broke out, had them send you my paycheck every month to take care o' you an' him, keep house for me—I had nobody. But you see this? See how he hates me? (*Turning to include* ELAINE.) I mean, he honest-to-God hates me! (*To* ANNIE.) How the hell you think I feel to come to find out the kid's been hatin' me all these years? After I done put my life on the line for you and him, supported you all them years, a better father to 'im than 'is own father. You got this kid all et up with hate, Mom!

PHILIP (*tearfully*): I got to kill you, Jake. I got to kill . . .

(*Instantaneously* JAKE *kicks* ELAINE'*s luggage into* PHILIP'*s face, screaming insanely as he does so, and flies at* PHILIP *in the spirit and technique of karate. He is upon him before the latter has time to rally. The gun goes flying.*)

ANNIE and ELAINE (*as* PHILIP *for the briefest moment struggles against* JAKE): No, Jake! Oh, no, Philip!

(ANNIE *runs and picks up gun.*)

JAKE (*pinioning* PHILIP *helplessly, hand raised edgewise instinctively in anticipation of bringing death, breathing with excitement to kill*): I could kill you. Son, did you know that I can kill you?!

ANNIE (*crying, gun trembling*): Jake, so help me God!

ELAINE: Annie! Jake!! No, please. No!

JAKE: That I can sen' your nose-bone rippin' through your brain . . . ?!

ANNIE and ELAINE (*screaming*): Let him go, Jake.

ANNIE: For heaven's sake, let him go!

(*Pause.* JAKE *releases hold.*)

ANNIE: Now, just rise on up, Jake, just get right on up—you done enough damage already.

JAKE (*rising*): No it's you done the damage, keepin' everything covered up with lies and silence, instead o' tellin' 'im like it really is. I just tol' im all the things you shoulda tol' im long ago. Whatchoo think you was doin' when I tried to, tellin' me "hush" but robbin' him of one of the few chances for 'e can

299

show 'is manhood in a way that can really count for somethin'. Year in and year out, you're naggin' 'im "Be a man! Be a man." How can he, by shuttin' his eyes the way you shut yours—to truth, to reality, to manhood? There's no spine in that old ostrich trick. Why would you take his spine that way, why would you do that to him, huh? (*Addressing both* ANNIE *and* ELAINE.) Your needs alone ain' the las' word on what a man is, think they are? Why would you do that to us? An' a man ain' never a man if 'e's got to keep on havin' what a man is defined for 'im!—by two women?! (*He walks over to* ANNIE *and rips gun out of her hand after slapping her.*) Gimme dat thing, woman! You ain' ready for me!

ANNIE (*sniffling, deeply ashamed*): Oh, Jake . . . !

JAKE: Tried to bring a little light into you-all's life, a little happiness. Butchoo wasn' ready for me. 'Cause you never really *loved* me—you *used* me, from the jump . . .

ANNIE: No, Jake . . .

JAKE: Yes you did, from the jump you used me—else the truth an' tellin' it to him never woulda been so hard to you. (*He puts the gun in his pocket and walks out, grabbing coat off the doorknob on way out.* PHILIP *is crying on floor.*)

ANNIE: Forgive me, Jake, I . . . don't go . . . where you goin', Jake . . . ?

(*Door slams in her face.*)

ANNIE (*crushed*): He's right. Oh, God—the man is right . . . the only man I . . . (*To* ELAINE.) Oh, honey, dontchoo go doin' like me—see what I've done to three men?! To Jake, my son, to his father, the man I left like you are leaving, when times were rough and he needed me most, dying for my love. (*En route to door.*) You can't leave Phil, I know you can't, Elaine, now that you see. Because I did leave his father—he didn't leave me, though Jake and Phil never knew. How could I explain such pride that wouldn' let me return after I had left? (*Fetching coat from bedroom, she prepares to leave.*) I must catch Jake or I'll lose him too for sure! (ANNIE *exits.*)

ELAINE (*as she stands looking down at* PHIL, *crying on floor*): We were so young . . . and full of dreams . . . about everything . . . about each other . . . and now . . oh, Phil . . . !

CURTAIN

The Owl Killer

A SHORT PLAY

by PHILIP HAYES DEAN

Philip Hayes Dean was born in Chicago. He moved to Pontiac, Michigan, where he attended high school. He then came to New York where he became an actor. He appeared on Broadway in *Waiting for Godot* and *Wisteria Trees*. He wrote *Johnny Ghost* for the television series *On Being Black*. His plays have been presented at the American Place Theater and the Chelsea Theater Center.

The interior of the HAMILTON *home, located in a small city in the Midwest called Moloch. The house is no different than the other small, two-story frame houses owned by blue-collar workers across America. It has a kitchen, a living room, and a dining room. It is clean and comfortable for habitation.*

EMMA HAMILTON *is seated in the kitchen snapping string beans and putting them in a large white pot. She is a good-looking woman about sixty years old with a quiet kind of grace.*

NOAH HAMILTON *enters the porch and into the house. He is about the same age as* EMMA. *He is a little man with a cast-iron face, dressed in a faded brown jacket and matching hat.*

The time of the play is anytime during what is called the Black Revolution. It is evening in the autumn of the year and there is a threat of rain.

EMMA: What you doin' home . . . thought you'd be at work by this time?

NOAH (*moving into kitchen*): I didn't feel like goin' in tonight. Got as far as the gate. Here. (*Hands her a brown paper bag containing his lunch.*)

EMMA (*takes bag*): I'll put it in the refrigerator an' use it for your lunch tomorrow night.

NOAH: Throw it away.

EMMA: I can save it and use it for your lunch tomorrow night.

NOAH: Throw it away! (*He takes bag and drops it into garbage can.*)

EMMA: You ain't sick, are you, Noah?

NOAH: Naw, I ain't sick.

EMMA: Your stomach trouble ain't botherin' you, is it?

NOAH: Naw.

EMMA: I was just gettin' ready to put on supper. I was gonna have a nice hot supper when you came in tonight. I was

301

gonna have string beans and white potatoes. And I was gonna bake some corn bread . . . bake some sweet potatoes . . . (*She breaks down and starts to cry.*)

NOAH: Ain't no use cryin' now.

EMMA: I wasn't cryin' . . . just kinda . . . I don't feel too well, I reckon.

NOAH: What's wrong with you?

EMMA: I dunno.

NOAH: You got a complaint, you oughta see th' doctor.

EMMA: I don't have no special complaint . . . just old and tired. Wore out. (*There is a long silence. She sits down and returns to her potatoes. He moves to sink and gets a glass of water.*)

NOAH: Looks like it's gonna rain tonight. If it does it'll turn cold tomorrow. Yes sir, if it rains tonight it'll turn cold tomorrow . . . just watch what I tell you.

EMMA (*trying to hide tears in her voice*): We've sure, Lord, have had good weather this year. Here it is almost November and it's still warm.

NOAH: I reckon I'd better get in a ton of coal tomorrow.

EMMA: I'll call Mr. Anderson and tell him to bring us over a ton.

NOAH: Tell him to bring over blue coal. Tell him I don't want no slag in it. Tell him if there's slag in it he's gonna take it right back.

EMMA: Mr. Anderson wouldn't cheat us, Noah.

NOAH: They slip in that slag on him in the coal yard. They got what they call the nigger coal pile over there in the coal yard and they throw all the slag into it. Coal can't breath with all that slag in it. If they put in any slag in it he's gonna take it right back. Better tell you that so he can check it before he bring it over here. Cost me too much money to heat this house last year.

EMMA: I'll tell him.

NOAH: Ed Anderson oughta have sense enough not to let them slip that slag in on him. He ain't got that much sense.

EMMA: I reckon he does the best he can.

NOAH: Scared of white folks.

EMMA: He's a nice man . . .

NOAH: He ain't nothin'.

EMMA (*repeating*): He ain't nothin'.

NOAH (*after a pause*): Would you call the plaint for me? Tell 'em I won't be in tonight.

EMMA: All right, Noah, (*She crosses into dining room to a small table by the window where the telephone is placed.*)

What's the number?

NOAH: You don't know th' number out at that plaint?

EMMA: I'll look it up.

NOAH: S-T . . . 4-6772. Ask for plaint nine . . . time-keeper's office.

EMMA (*dialing the telephone*): Anybody special I should ask for in th' time-keeper's office?

NOAH: Just ask for the time-keeper's office.

EMMA: Hello . . . is this Moloch Motors? May I have plaint nine, please? Hello . . . is this plaint nine? Time-keeper's office? Well, I'm callin' for Noah Hamilton. Badge?

NOAH: Badge 917-218.

EMMA: Badge 917-218. He won't be in tonight. (*Looks at* NOAH.) Well, he's not feelin' too well. Tomorrow night? Yes . . . if he feels better. All right, I'll tell him. (*Hangs up phone.*) Said if you're out for three days you'll hafta have a note from the doctor.

NOAH: He oughta have sense enough to know that I know that. I should after almost thirty years.

EMMA: I reckon they tell that to everybody.

NOAH: I bound you ole Whitehead was waitin' for me to come in this evenin'. I bound you he just couldn't wait for me to come in tonight.

EMMA: You an' Whitehead.

NOAH: That cracker foreman scared I ain't gonna work myself to death.

EMMA: I reckon that man ain't even studyin' 'bout you.

NOAH: By rights I shoulda been a foreman by now . . .

EMMA: You didn't have the education, Noah.

NOAH: I got 'bout as much as that cracker foreman Whitehead.

EMMA: Maybe you should've gone on in tonight, Noah . . . coulda kept your mind occupied.

NOAH: Wouldn't been occupied with Whitehead. Bet he done read the papers. They had to put our names and address in th' papers. Su'prise that phone ain't been ringin' all day . . .

EMMA: I wish somebody would come callin' here an' sayin' one thing to me about it. I'd tell them to kiss my foot.

NOAH: What good would that do?

EMMA: Nobody better come askin' me one word about Lamar.

NOAH: Well, they sure gonna ask you. And ain't no need gettin' mad at folks.

EMMA: They better not asking me about it if they don't want to get set out!

NOAH: You must be a fool. Gonna set folks out because you're mad at them for askin' why somebody would pull a dirty trick like what Lamar did. Now that shows you're a fool!

EMMA: All right, I'm a fool.

NOAH: I ain't covering up for nobody's wrongdoin's.

EMMA: I ain't tryin' to cover up.

NOAH: I hope they catch that thing an' put his behind under th' jail.

EMMA: He's still our son.

NOAH: I wouldn't care if he was my Siamese twin . . . They would just have to cut him loose from me and take his behind onto jail.

EMMA: Don't carry on so.

NOAH: Police been back here?

EMMA: Not since you talk to them this mornin'.

NOAH: That thing better not show his behind here, 'cause I'm sure gonna run him on away from around here.

EMMA: Noah . . . ?

NOAH: Wasn't enough to go out there on Telegraph Road and rob that supermarket and kill that man—he had to go and cut th' man's waterspout off . . .

EMMA: Please, no . . .

NOAH: Mutilate that man like that.

EMMA: I don't want to hear about it, Noah.

NOAH: I know you don't want to hear about it.

EMMA: It's done now . . . ain't no use of keep talkin' about it.

NOAH: I'd just like to know what was in that thing's head to make him pull a trick like that.

EMMA: Lamar must have somethin' th' matter with him.

NOAH: Must have? You tellin' me he must have.

EMMA: Lamar always was a little perculiar.

NOAH: That thing just ain't no good.

EMMA: Stop callin' him a thing.

NOAH: I can't think of anything low enough to call him. That is the low-downest trick I have heard of in all my born days.

EMMA: Oh, Jesus . . . I'm so tired of hearin' about all this mess.

NOAH: You know it's your fault, don't y'?

EMMA: My fault? How is it my fault? I didn't know how you'd do it but I knew I'd get blame for this just like I get blame for everything.

NOAH: I told you there was somethin' wrong with Lamar. I looked at th' thing th' day he was born an' knew he wasn't

right. No sir . . . I knew that thing was not right. Shootin' owls! First time I caught that thing shootin' owls I shoulda . . .

EMMA: Lot of boys hunt.

NOAH: That thing's whole room full of stuffed owls. I bound I'm goin' throw them things out. Every last one of 'em.

EMMA: I tried to get him to get rid of 'em.

NOAH: I want you to throw 'em out.

EMMA: I don't wanna touch them things . . . makes my skin crawl.

NOAH: I don't want 'em in my house.

EMMA: Well you throw 'em out then.

NOAH: Stuff 'em in the furnace and burn 'em.

EMMA: Maybe we oughta see if Stella Mae'll take 'em. He might still want 'em.

NOAH: Let her take 'em, then . . . but I want 'em out of here.

EMMA: I'll call Stella Mae and tell her to come get 'em.

NOAH: I don't want her behind parts around here . . . I've told you that.

EMMA: Then how I gonna give her the stuffed owls?

NOAH: I don't want her behind here.

EMMA: Then I'm gonna hafta lug them all th' way over to th' south side.

NOAH: Think you'd be rarin' t' get over there to smell her up.

EMMA: I ain't smellin' nobody up.

NOAH: Ain't you got sense enough t' know that I know you sneak over there behind my back when I'm gone to work.

EMMA: Sneak! I don't haffta sneak off to see my own child.

NOAH: I told you to stay away from that thing.

EMMA: You can't tell me not to have anythin' to do with th' child I brought into this world.

NOAH: Then you oughta carry your behind on over there and stay with her. Let her make your livin' for you.

EMMA: She's my child, Noah . . .

NOAH: I have washed my hands of her and Lamar. I fought the good fight with both of 'em but I give them up into more powerful hands than mine.

(*The telephone rings and* EMMA *crosses into dining room.*)

EMMA: Hello . . . Yes, he's here. Who is this?

NOAH: Who is it?

EMMA: Whitehead.

NOAH: What's he doin' callin' me?

EMMA: You wanna speak to him?

NOAH: He ain't suppose t' be callin' me at home.

EMMA: What shall I tell him?

305

NOAH: Cracker callin' me . . . !

EMMA: Shall I tell him that you can't come to th' phone.

NOAH (*taking phone but covering up receiver*): I don't haff'ta lie to no cracker. Hello . . . Mr. Whitehead. Yes, sir. Yes, sir. Well, I'll be in tomorrow, Mr. Whitehead. Yes, sir, you can count on me . . . I'll be in tomorrow night, all right. No, sir, I ain't heard nothin' yet about it. Er . . . well . . . th' police was here this mornin' . . . Yes, sir . . . I don't rightly know. Good-bye, sir. (*Hangs up.*) That damn cracker got a whole lotta nerve.

EMMA: What'cha talk to him for?

NOAH: I ain't scared to talk to him.

EMMA: You shoulda hung up on him.

NOAH: I don't need you to tell me who I shoulda hung up on.

EMMA: Did he ask you about Lamar?

NOAH: None of your business what he ask me about. You're always listenin' to all folks' conversations an' dippin' in.

EMMA: That man's gonna drive you crazy.

NOAH: I got my time set to tell that cracker off.

EMMA: You been goin' t' tell him off for thirty years.

NOAH: He's gonna fool with me one time too many.

EMMA: An' you're gonna lay him in the sweet peas.

NOAH: He fool with me once more an' I'll knock him cold as a milkshake.

EMMA: Unhuh.

NOAH: What do you mean, unhuh?

EMMA: Nothin'

NOAH: If you mean nothin' what'd you sayin' unhuh for?

EMMA: Can't I say unhuh if I want to?

NOAH: Fool talk. That's why I hate to be around ignorant folks.

EMMA: Everybody knows you got all the sense.

NOAH: Some more of your old fool talk. That's why I like intelligent folks. Because you don't haff'ta listen to no fool talk.

EMMA: Noah, why don't you go on somewhere and lie down. I'm upset enough without havin' to listen to your mouth.

NOAH: Go upstairs and get them stuffed owls and burn 'em.

EMMA: Thought you was gonna let Stella Mae keep 'em for Lamar.

NOAH: She don't need them things.

EMMA: Shouldn't burn up his things.

NOAH: By th' time that thing gets outta jail he won't need no stuffed owls.

EMMA: Let me take 'em over to Stella Mae's.

NOAH: I'm gonna burn 'em up.

EMMA (*resigned*): All right . . . go ahead . . . burn them.

NOAH: Put 'em in the furnace and burn 'em up.

(NOAH *moves to the staircase and exits up to the bedroom.* EMMA *is placing the food she has prepared into the oven. Outside of the window the light of lightning is reflected through the window. A knock is heard at the door. She crosses through the living room and moves to the door.* STELLA MAE *enters. She is a young woman of about twenty-five, dressed in beige housecoat with a scarf tied around her head.*)

EMMA: Stella Mae . . . ?

STELLA MAE (*moving into house*): Hello, Mama . . .

EMMA: What you doin' here?

STELLA MAE: Lamar call?

EMMA: I ain't heard from Lamar.

STELLA MAE: Have you been at the phone?

EMMA: Except for the time I was doin' the washing.

STELLA MAE: Mama, I told you to stay by that phone.

EMMA: I had my washing to do.

STELLA MAE: He could have called here . . .

EMMA: I listen for th' telephone.

STELLA MAE: Down in th' cellar with that washin' machine goin' he could've called here and you never heard the phone ringing.

EMMA: I had to do my washing.

STELLA MAE: Your washing!

EMMA: Shhh! Don't talk so loud. Your daddy's home.

STELLA MAE: I thought he was suppose to be at work.

EMMA: He didn't feel like goin' in tonight.

STELLA MAE: Suppose Lamar came home?

EMMA: Noah's not gonna let him hide out here.

STELLA MAE: Here and my house is the only place he could come.

EMMA: Ain't no place for him to hide here. Police done been here twice already.

STELLA MAE: He's gotta go someplace.

EMMA: Ain't no need for him to come here, because Noah sure ain't gonna help him evade the law.

STELLA MAE: The law!

EMMA: What he should do is just go right on downtown and give himself up.

STELLA MAE: He's got to get out of this town before they catch up with him.

EMMA (*looking out of the window*): Probably watchin' th' house.

307

STELLA MAE: I didn't see anybody when I came in.

EMMA: Just 'cause you didn't see them don't mean that they ain't out there.

STELLA MAE: Mama, ain't nobody watchin' th' house.

EMMA (*moves to the kitchen window and looks out*): They could be lurkin' around out in back . . . (*She pauses.*)

STELLA MAE (*looking out back window*): Mama, there's nobody out there.

EMMA: There's a hoot owl sittin' out there on the apple tree.

STELLA MAE: A hoot owl?

EMMA: I reckon if Lamar was home . . . he'd sneak out there an' try to kill it. Have it stuffed . . . stick it up there in his room.

STELLA MAE: Maybe he doesn't like hoot owls?

EMMA: Do you want 'em?

STELLA MAE: What?

EMMA: Lamar's hoot owls.

STELLA MAE: What would I do with them?

EMMA: Noah is goin' to throw them in th' furnace.

STELLA MAE: Why can't he leave 'em up there in Lamar's room?

EMMA: Have to ask him that.

STELLA MAE: They belong to Lamar.

EMMA: It's Noah's house.

STELLA MAE: Why doesn't he burn up all his clothes?

EMMA: Noah never did like them things.

STELLA MAE: And you're going to let him do it?

EMMA: I can't stop Noah from doin' anythin' he wants to do.

STELLA MAE (*after a pause*): Did you ask him what I told you to ask him?

EMMA: No.

STELLA MAE: Why not?

EMMA: Because I know what he's gonna say.

STELLA MAE: Mama, will you please ask him?

EMMA: Now there ain't no need of me askin' him for no money for Lamar, 'cause it ain't gonna do nothin' but start a whole lotta trouble. I don't feel like hearin' his mouth this night. Now . . . you better go on before he comes downstairs and catches you here.

STELLA MAE: Let him catch me.

EMMA: I don't feel like no excitement. My heart's too weak. This whole mess done took too much out of me. You go on before he comes down and you two start up. You know he don't want you here.

STELLA MAE: I don't give a damn what he wants.

EMMA: Look like you'd do it for me. Look like you would say, . . . I don't want to worry Mother . . .

STELLA MAE: What about Lamar?

EMMA: Jesus, I'm so tired! Lord Jesus, I'm tired. You two have almost worried me to death. If it ain't you, it's Lamar. Sometimes, Jesus, I wish that I was dead an' sleepin' in my grave.

STELLA MAE: Mama, don't start dying. You have been dying since I was seven years old.

EMMA: I'm so sick of you two I don't know what to do. You two have almost driven me into bad health. My heart just won't take no more. No more, Jesus. Just wearing me out. Lamar done gone out here and killed a man . . . then muti-lated him like that. I have not heard of a trick like that since in this world I've been. He's gonna have to give an account for doin' a thing like that. I never knew he had that kind of dirt inside of him. He must be crazy. He couldn't have all that belongs to him and go out and pull a trick like that.

STELLA MAE: Mama, you gotta talk to Papa.

EMMA: What could make somebody wanna do a thing like that?

STELLA MAE: Mama, I got somebody to drive him out of town . . . out of the state, up to Ohio, but he's got to have some money. That is, if I can find him before the police.

EMMA: Noah ain't gonna help him escape.

STELLA MAE: You didn't even ask him.

EMMA: Can't you give him somethin'?

STELLA MAE: I haven't got any money.

EMMA: Can't you borrow some from somebody?

STELLA MAE: You've got to get Papa to help.

EMMA: Maybe if you could get somebody to get him out of town . . . later on you an' me could send him a little somethin'.

STELLA MAE: We have to pay someone to drive him out of here.

EMMA: You gotta pay 'em?

STELLA MAE: Can't ask people to risk going to jail for nothing.

EMMA: You're suppose to have so many friends.

STELLA MAE: Mama . . .

EMMA: Always talkin' about what good friends you got.

STELLA MAE: You're his mother and you don't wanna . . .

EMMA: Please go, Stella Mae.

STELLA MAE: You're just going to sit here and do nothing.

EMMA: There ain't nothin' I can do.

STELLA MAE: Just so scared of Papa . . .

EMMA: I ain't scared of your daddy. Because I don't want to help Lamar, that makes me scared of Noah?

STELLA MAE: You're just going to hide.

EMMA: I ain't hiding.

STELLA MAE: Just the way you hide that night when Papa put me out. He threw my clothes out into the street and you ran down in the cellar and hid away.

EMMA: I tried to talk to Noah, but you know how he is.

STELLA MAE: I know how you are.

EMMA: That's right, go on an' blame me. I tried my best to keep you off that Square . . . but you went right ahead with your fast tail. You just weren't satisfied until you had took another woman's husband.

STELLA MAE: Let's not start on that.

EMMA: Every time I see poor Mrs. Watkins I just want to crawl under the seats in church.

STELLA MAE: I'm Mrs. Watkins now, Mama.

EMMA: Common law. Carried your behind out an' got yourself a baby and took that woman's husband.

STELLA MAE: What did you expect me to do? I survive, Mama . . . that's all I know. And if you have to take something that belongs to somebody else . . . well, so what. Think I was just gonna sit up in this house day in and day out. Then go sit up in that church all day Sunday.

EMMA: Church didn't do you much good.

STELLA MAE: You oughta get out of this house once in awhile and find out what's going on.

EMMA: You married to a hustler.

STELLA MAE: It was all right when Mrs. Watkins was with him.

EMMA: She ain't my child.

STELLA MAE: We live . . . Mama . . . we have a ball. Stan is good to me.

EMMA: Gettin' drunk an' foolin' 'round with dope.

STELLA MAE: The only thing in life is kicks. I'm going to get my kicks while I'm alive.

EMMA: Why don't you ask Stan to get you the money?

STELLA MAE: It's your responsibility.

EMMA: It was your responsibility not to take that woman's husband.

STELLA MAE: I took what I wanted. I saw him . . . I wanted him, and I took him!

EMMA: He's old enough to be your father.

STELLA MAE (*pauses*): You sure know how to change the subject, don't you?

EMMA: Huh?

STELLA MAE: You're an expert on that.

EMMA: I wish that I could just go on away from all of y'all. Just go somewhere and be by myself.

STELLA MAE (*moves to the stairs*): Papa!

EMMA: Stella Mae!

STELLA MAE: Papa!!

EMMA: What'd you wanna start him up for?

STELLA MAE: Papa!!!

EMMA: You wanna kill me, don't you?

(NOAH *enters on the staircase. There is a cold dead silence as the three of them face each other.* EMMA *knows that there is nothing she can do to stop the clash that is coming.*)

NOAH: What you doin' all that hollerin' for? An' I thought I told you to keep your behind parts away from my house.

STELLA MAE (*a little frightened*): I want to talk to you, Papa . . . about Lamar.

NOAH: You got nothin' to talk to me about . . . Lamar or anythin' else.

EMMA: Stella Mae, will you please go.

NOAH: Didn't I tell you that I didn't want this thing in my house. I done run her butt away from around here once.

EMMA: Noah, don't start. (*To* STELLA MAE.) You see, you're makin' it hard on me.

STELLA MAE: I want you to listen to me, Papa.

NOAH: You'd better get on away from around me before I get mad.

STELLA MAE: Nobody can talk to you, can they. But you can say anything you want to.

NOAH: You're gonna fool around and make me hurt you.

EMMA (*sensing danger, moves to oven*): Lord, my supper'll be done burned.

STELLA MAE: Mama, stop cookin' that food.

NOAH: Who you talkin' to? You tryin' to run my house?

STELLA MAE: No, I'm not tryin' to run your house.

NOAH: Then let me know it!

STELLA MAE: It's your house!

NOAH: If you don't know who you're foolin' with you better ask somebody. Now, you get your behind parts out of here.

STELLA MAE: Not until you hear what I've got to say.

NOAH: You better talk to this fool, Emma.

EMMA: Why do you act so ugly to each other?

STELLA MAE: I want you to help Lamar.

NOAH: I didn't help him rob that store, did I?

STELLA MAE: No, you didn't.

NOAH: I didn't help him murder that man.

STELLA MAE: No.

NOAH: And I didn't help him . . .

STELLA MAE: No.

NOAH: And I ain't gonna help his butt now.

STELLA MAE: Just turn your back on him.

NOAH: He oughta be in hell with his neck broke.

EMMA: Don't say things like that.

NOAH: Ain't worth the salt that goes in your bread . . . either one of you.

STELLA MAE: You're so self-righteous, aren't you?

NOAH: You wanna try me?

STELLA MAE: No, Papa, I don't wanna try you.

NOAH: You must.

EMMA: Noah!

NOAH (*stopping himself*): Don't come messin' around me 'cause I'll walk you like Christ walk th' water.

STELLA MAE: Papa . . .

NOAH: And don't be givin' me no two for one. Every word I say, you got two to come back with.

STELLA MAE: I'm not giving you two for one.

EMMA: Y'all gonna keep on until you get into it.

NOAH: You told her to come over here.

EMMA: I didn't tell her nothing. Did I tell you to come over here, Stella Mae?

NOAH: I ain't gonna raise one finger to help that thing.

STELLA MAE: You ignorant old fool!

NOAH (*moving toward her*): You done gone crazy!

STELLA MAE: Go on hit me . . . knock me down.

NOAH: I reckon I'd just better go on an' kill you and go serve my time.

EMMA: Stop it! (*Trying to get in between them.*)

STELLA MAE: Let him c'mon.

NOAH (*grabbing her by the neck*): I'm gonna kill you . . . You oughta been born dead. I wish you both had been born dead!

EMMA: You gonna kill me! (*She runs to cellar door and exits.*)

STELLA MAE (*gagging*): Mama!

(NOAH *stops himself, letting her fall to the floor.*)

NOAH: You'd better go on . . . I'm tellin' you.

STELLA MAE (*trying to get up*): You almost cut off my wind.

NOAH: Should have cut off your wind. You should be in hell right now.

STELLA MAE (*getting to her feet*): That's all you know, isn't it? How to knock somebody down.

NOAH: Didn't knock your butt down enough. If I had, you'd be straight now. I'd rather see you dead and in your grave than the way you are.

STELLA MAE: Beat! And beat! And beat! Every time I think of the beatin's I took from you I hate you.

NOAH: Don't you stand up in my face and tell me you hate me.

STELLA MAE: What'd you expect?

NOAH: Work for chaps like a dog and they stand up an' tell you to your face they hate you.

STELLA MAE: And you never let anybody forget that you were feedin' 'em.

NOAH: I tried my best to make something out of you. Just didn't have right in you.

STELLA MAE: What you thought was right.

NOAH: I woulda sent you to school . . .

STELLA MAE: Maybe I didn't want to go.

NOAH: You didn't have that much sense.

STELLA MAE: I got tired of marching up to Moloch High every day wearing the same clothes.

NOAH: You had fine clothes.

STELLA MAE: The cheapest you could find.

NOAH: You had better than I ever had.

STELLA MAE: And you had the money. You worked every day . . . you were too cheap and mean to buy us anything more than what we needed to get by.

NOAH: You chaps were blessed and you didn't know it. I didn't go to school much. And when I did go, you know what I carried for my lunch? Syrup and bread. Had to walk two miles to the schoolhouse.

STELLA MAE: Going to that school every day was like going to prison. Sent us there to get rid of us so we wouldn't be around.

NOAH: Now, I know you ain't got all that belongs to you.

STELLA MAE: I use to come home and find empty ice cream boxes in the garbage can. You and Mama use to buy ice cream while we were in school and eat it up before we got home.

NOAH: Don't watch chaps they'll eat up everything in sight.

STELLA MAE: Keeping the pies and cakes under lock and key in your room. You and Mama eating them when you came in at night from work. Me and Lamar use to sneak down the stairs early in the morning—before daybreak—to see if you or Mama had forgotten to take the pies and cakes with you.

NOAH: You two always had aplenty to eat.

STELLA MAE: Except for dessert. I use to save up my money and buy a cake from the bakery and eat it in the bathroom at school.

NOAH: Chaps don't need a whole lotta sweets.

STELLA MAE: That's why I try to give my children . . .

NOAH: I don't want to hear nothin' 'bout that litter. Four or five chaps an' all with different fathers.

STELLA MAE: That's my business.

NOAH: And got the nerve to come struttin' into church every Sunday mornin'. If you had any sense you would be hidin' them.

STELLA MAE: I don't care what people think.

NOAH: You must not. Otherwise you wouldn't gone out here an' got a whole bunch of bastard children.

STELLA MAE: Don't call my children bastards.

NOAH: That's what they are. Started out takin' one woman's house . . . Now numbers! Somebody always comin' up to me in th' plaint askin' me if I would turn in their number to you for them.

STELLA MAE: I have to make a living.

NOAH: Go out and get yourself a respectable job is too much like right.

STELLA MAE: What should I do? Go out to LaBlanch Hill and scrub floors?

NOAH: Lily Lightfoot ain't scrubbin' floors. Sittin' out there at the union hall poundin' that typewriter.

STELLA MAE: Papa, I don't want to hear about Lily Lightfoot.

NOAH: I know you don't.

STELLA MAE: Still throwing her up in my face!

NOAH: Th' truth is th' light.

STELLA MAE: And Lily Lightfoot is the light.

NOAH: I give that girl her due. She was determined to be somebody. You should have used her as an example.

STELLA MAE: She married and had a baby awful quick.

NOAH: You ain't nothin'. Always tryin' to bring folks down to your level. You're low class . . . just low class. That's why you lay 'round on that Square . . . feel comfortable with them low-class folks.

STELLA MAE: At least they ain't tryin' to be something they are not, like Lily Lightfoot.

NOAH: I give her credit . . . she ain't tryin' to be a slut.

STELLA MAE: Don't call me a slut!

NOAH: What'd you call them things that hustle up on the Square?

STELLA MAE: I see Lily Lightfoot sneakin' around there.

NOAH: You're a lie!

STELLA MAE: She sneak up there every chance she gets.

NOAH: What makes you stand up an' tell a bare-face lie like that?

STELLA MAE: You can find her right down in the hole now with Pretty Eddy.

NOAH: What would she be doin' with that nut?

STELLA MAE: You'd have to ask her that.

NOAH: If she fools with that thing she ain't no-count either.

STELLA MAE: But she's the great Lily Lightfoot.

NOAH: Anything that hangs up on that Square ain't nothin'. Just ain't nothin'. I would care if it was my mother.

STELLA MAE: If she lived in this town . . . she would.

NOAH: That's what I think is wrong with Lamar.

STELLA MAE: The Square is not what's wrong with Lamar.

NOAH: Tried my best to keep his behind from down there.

STELLA MAE: He wasn't around the Square that much.

NOAH: If you had anything in you, you would have run his behind away from down there.

STELLA MAE: I have seen Lamar up on the Square exactly twice.

NOAH: If you hadn't set such a bad example for him he might not be in this trouble he's in now.

STELLA MAE: You're the cause he's in the trouble he's in.

NOAH: Sounds like some more of your fool talk.

STELLA MAE: He's scared of you, Papa.

NOAH: Scared of me?

STELLA MAE: He's so scared of you . . .

NOAH: He wasn't too scared to go out and kill a man.

STELLA MAE: I use to be scared of you. I got so I was scared to even open my mouth when you were around. That's why Lamar stutters when he speaks.

NOAH: That thing is too lazy to open his mouth and talk.

STELLA MAE: He stutters because he is afraid of you. The way you beat him . . . like he was a dog.

NOAH: Didn't beat his behind enough.

STELLA MAE: I use to hide when I saw you coming.

NOAH: Probably was wrongdoing.

STELLA MAE: I was scared.

NOAH: You weren't too scared to eat up my food and sleep out my bedclothes.

STELLA MAE: I use to wish that you would go away and never come back. I use to pray to God that there would be an accident out at Moloch Motors and you'd die so I'd never have to look into your face again.

NOAH: You work for 'em . . . to give 'em something more than you ever got and that the way they talk to you. I've worn cardboard in my shoes to put shoes on your feet.

STELLA MAE: That was your job.

NOAH: Get any thanks for it?

STELLA MAE: Nobody owe you a lifetime of gratitude.

NOAH: Your mother never had to stand out there and wait for me on Friday at the gate at Moloch Motors. You see 'em every Friday evenin' . . . women waitin' for their husband to try and beg for a little money, to feed their children and put clothes on their backs. Your mama never had to do that. I never threw my money away gamblin' and runnin' around on that Square foolin' 'round with women. No, sir, I never even cashed my check until I got home. I took care of my family. Your mama never had to go out to no welfare and beg to get y'all somethin' to eat. I can prove that by your mama. Emma! Emma! (*He crosses to the cellar door.*) Come up here.

EMMA (*offstage*): Y'all done stopped?

NOAH: Come up here.

EMMA (*appearing at the cellar door*): What'd you want?

NOAH: Did you ever have to come out to that plaint on Friday evening like other women?

EMMA: No, Noah.

NOAH: Did I ever once cash my check before I got home from work?

EMMA: No, Noah, you never did.

NOAH: Did you and the children ever miss a meal?

EMMA: You were always a good provider.

STELLA MAE (*to* EMMA): You're going to stand there and just say everything he tells you to say.

NOAH (*moving to basket of stuffed owls*): I have done my part.

EMMA: Noah . . . don't burn them. Let Stella Mae take them.

NOAH: She don't need these things.

STELLA MAE: Just put 'em somewhere and I come and get them.

NOAH: What do you want with them?

EMMA: Save 'em for Lamar.

NOAH: He won't need them where he's going.

STELLA MAE: He might want them.

NOAH: Ain't gonna do him no good.

EMMA: Don't be so hateful.

NOAH (*putting the box down*): You want these things, take 'em now.

STELLA MAE: I couldn't carry that box all the way to my house. Besides I still have to see if I can find Lamar.

NOAH: I bound the police got his butt by now.

EMMA: Don't say that.

NOAH: You want him to get away, don't y'?

EMMA: He's my son.

NOAH: That man was somebody's son, too.

EMMA: What about when he gets out? He might want them when he gets out.

NOAH: He ain't never gonna get out.

EMMA: You don't know that. They don't have capital punishment in this state.

NOAH: Even if I'm still living I'd never let that thing back into my house anymore.

EMMA: This is my house too, Noah.

NOAH: I pay the rent for this roof.

EMMA: I'm not a child, Noah, don't talk to me like that.

NOAH: Then stop talkin' crazy.

EMMA: You're the one that talks crazy.

NOAH: I know you done lost your mind.

STELLA MAE (*moves to box*): I'll try and carry them.

NOAH: Don't touch 'em.

STELLA MAE: I'll take them now. I'll take them out of your house!

NOAH: You ain't takin' them nowhere.

EMMA: You wanna burn them up, don't you?

NOAH: You goddamn right I do.

EMMA: Don't swear at me.

NOAH: Then keep your old silly mouth shut.

EMMA (*moves to box and picks it up*): Here, Stella Mae . . . take it home.

STELLA MAE (*taking the box*): I'll keep it from him.

NOAH: Just gonna run over me!

EMMA: Ain't gonna run over you, Mr. Fool!

NOAH: Put that box down, Stella Mae!

STELLA MAE: Papa!

EMMA: Leave her alone.

NOAH: Put the goddamn box down.

EMMA (*ushering* STELLA MAE *to door*): Go on home, Stella Mae.

NOAH (*hollering*): Don't take the goddamn box outta here!

EMMA: Will you stop that hollerin', crazy man.

NOAH (*whistling to them*): Give me the box!

EMMA: Stop whistling at me.

NOAH (*crosses and takes box from* STELLA MAE): I'll let you pay the rent if you're gonna run my roof.

EMMA: Mr. Crazy man!

NOAH (*crosses to cellar*): I ain't nothin' . . . just somethin' to run over.

EMMA: Don't burn Lamar's hoot owls.

NOAH: Right into the furnace.

EMMA: You got a whole dirt in you, Noah. Do you know that?

NOAH: I been eatin' it for thirty years. I should have.

EMMA: Mr. Nut . . . don't you burn Lamar's things.

NOAH (*exiting through cellar door*): Know what you can do . . . get out!

EMMA (*at cellar door*): Noah . . . Noah . . . (*She closes the cellar door. Something inside of her has collapsed. She crosses to kitchen table and sits down in the chair.*)

STELLA MAE (*watching her*): Mama . . . (*She crosses to her slowly.*)

EMMA: Lord, I'm tired . . . Jesus, I'm so tired.

STELLA MAE: I guess I better . . . Maybe he's called over at my house. I should be checking in.

EMMA: If I had some money I'd give it to you for Lamar.

STELLA MAE: Never mind. If I can find him, I'll find some way to help him.

EMMA: I reckon I should do somethin'. I just don't know what to do.

STELLA MAE: Don't worry yourself about it.

EMMA: Can't do anything with Noah.

STELLA MAE: No, I guess you can't.

EMMA: I tried. Didn't I try?

STELLA MAE (*softly*): Yes, you tried.

EMMA: Can't do anythin' with Noah. Tired of tryin'.

STELLA MAE (*after a pause*): Do you know how I had to live when I left home . . .

EMMA: Stella Mae, please . . . I can't take anymore this night.

STELLA MAE: After Papa threw my things out . . . I walked up to the Square . . .

EMMA: I don't want to hear anythin' bout that Square. Somebody oughta burn it down.

STELLA MAE: I was three months pregnant with Bobby and didn't have no place to go.

EMMA: I begged Noah not to do it.

STELLA MAE: You hid in the cellar.

EMMA: I talked to Noah . . .

STELLA MAE: I was sixteen years old. So I went down on the Square and I had to learn how to survive.

EMMA: You didn't stand on the street, did you?

STELLA MAE: I did what I had to do.

EMMA: You sold yourself down on that Square.

STELLA MAE: What did you want me to do . . . stand on the streets and starve to death?

EMMA (*exhausted*): Jesus, have mercy.

STELLA MAE: That's what I use to say every time I had to flag down a car with one of them honkies in 'em. But that didn't do much good. All the prayin' an' callin' on th' Lord don't put no pork chops in your pot. That's what's important . . . gettin' some pork chops in your pot an' keepin' th' wind off your tail.

EMMA: I would have picked manure with the chicken first.

STELLA MAE: That's easy for you to say. You sit in this house year on end, never put your foot out of that door.

EMMA: I always get the blame.

STELLA MAE: I blame you, Mama . . . think I blame you more than Papa.

EMMA: Go home, Stella Mae.

STELLA MAE: Just go home and forget about it, huh?

EMMA: Will you please go home before Noah comes back up here.

STELLA MAE (*crossing to door*): If Lamar calls here, tell him to call me.

EMMA: If he calls here . . . I'll tell him.

STELLA MAE: Good-bye, Mama. (*She exits.*)

(NOAH *emerges out of the cellar and stands silently on the threshold of the cellar door looking at* EMMA *who sits motionless at the kitchen table. He moves to the sink to wash his hands.*)

EMMA: I was gonna have such a good supper tonight . . . string beans and sweet potatoes . . .

NOAH: Couldn't eat anythin' tonight anyhow.

EMMA: Stomach troublin' you?

NOAH: Yes.

EMMA: Told you not to upset yourself. Now you gonna keep me up half the night. You want me to fix you some hot milk?

NOAH: Might make me rest better. (*He moves to the table.*) I reckon I oughta transfer to the day shift.

EMMA: Night rest is your best rest. An' we don't need the extra money anymore.

NOAH: Have to get Whitehead to okay it.

EMMA (*rises, gets pan and milk from refrigerator*): Why wouldn't he?

NOAH: I reckon maybe I will put in for a transfer.

EMMA (*at stove*): I think you should.

NOAH: Gettin' too old to work th' night shift.

EMMA: Just explain it to Whitehead.

NOAH: Haffta bump somebody off the day shift. Could bump a whole lotta of 'em with my seniority.

EMMA (*stirring milk in pan*): Lord, it's really rainin' . . . it's really comin' down! Lamar is out there somewhere in all that rain.

NOAH: I ain't helpin' nobody beat th' law.

EMMA: If he don't get away he's gonna haffta have a lawyer.

NOAH: I ain't got no money to throw away tryin' to help nobody beat the consequence of their wrongdoings.

EMMA: I think we should find some way to help Lamar.

NOAH: Then you better go on out and get yourself a job.

EMMA: Ain't I got nothin' to say?

NOAH: Not to me . . . about this . . . you haven't.

EMMA: You'd like to see Lamar in jail, wouldn't you?

NOAH: Woman, what are you talkin' about?

EMMA: Nothin'.

NOAH: That's right, you're talkin' 'bout nothin'. I've done my part an' I ain't doin' no more.

EMMA: You're so hateful, Noah. That's why your stomach is always botherin' you.

NOAH: Now you're a doctor.

EMMA: I don't have to be no doctor to know you're hateful.

NOAH: 'Cause I'm sick of folks tellin' me I'm hateful. Even iron wears out.

EMMA: People wear out too, Noah.

NOAH: That's right and they have worn me out.

EMMA: You wore out Lamar . . . and Stella Mae. Had that boy tremblin' at the sight of you.

NOAH: Worked my fingers to the bone for 'em.

EMMA: And you hate them for it.

NOAH: It was for their behinds I was doin' it.

EMMA: And you made them pay for it. Comin' in here on Friday rollin' your eyes . . . hollerin' at everybody. Make 'em scared to breathe. Scared to talk. Tell 'em to shut up.

NOAH: I know you ain't got good sense.

EMMA: I watch you come through that door every Friday for thirty years with your mouth poked out and your fist doubled up. Just waitin' for one of 'em to crook so you could beat 'em.

NOAH: Try to make 'em straight.

EMMA: You took it out on them.

NOAH: Took out what?

EMMA: All your anger! I use to wish that you would just go out one week and throw your money away. Then I wouldn't have to hear you talkin' 'bout that check.

NOAH: You spent it, though. You sat up here on your butt and spent it.

EMMA: You ruled this house like a crazy man!

NOAH: Suppose to rule my house.

EMMA: Then when you went downtown . . .

NOAH: Downtown what?

EMMA: Lettin' the children see you . . .

NOAH: Lettin' the children see me . . .

EMMA: Bowin' and scrapin' in front of white folks.

NOAH: I ain't never bowed and scaped to no cracker!

EMMA: You bowed and scraped all your life. Then came home and took it out on me and the children.

NOAH: You don't know what you're talkin' about.

EMMA: I use to watch Lamar and Stella Mae scringe when we went downtown. They saw all your loud talk and bluff just evaporate in front of white folks.

NOAH: Didn't I tell you I ain't never . . .

EMMA: You been bowin' an' scrapin' to Whitehead for thirty years. Sometimes I use to think I was sleepin' with Whitehead.

NOAH: You better stop talkin' to me.

EMMA: Use to talk in your sleep about that man.

NOAH: I got my time set for Whitehead.

EMMA: I been hearin' that for thirty years.

NOAH: I get no thanks whatsoever, do I? I've eaten that dust for thirty years without any thanks for it. Don't come talkin' no foolishness like this to me because I've done my part. Every day the Lord sent I got up and went out there to that plaint . . . sometimes half sick. But I went every day the Lord sent. I've spent near 'bout half my life in that place. Standin' in front of a red-hot oven snatchin' plates full of white steel.

Eatin' blue dust and sweatin' like a pig. How much dirt you reckon I've eaten in that plaint in thirty years? You ain't never tasted no dirt like that foundry dirt. It ain't real dirt . . . like earth, I mean. It's somethin' they make over there in plaint six. They make it outta sand. Then they dye and mix it with some kind of chemical. The taste of it gets on your tongue an' you get so you taste it no matter where you are. Can't wash it off, strongest soap in the world won't wash the smell of it off. I can smell it in my pores right this minute. Gets down below the surface of your skin . . . changes the color of your skin. And it ain't even much real dirt . . . like earth. (*Pause.*) You know I read somewhere once . . . sweat is like blood. It's the air that turns it red. For thirty years that hot oven has been suckin' th' sweat outta me. And y'all layin' up on your behind parts . . . ridin' me. Eatin' up my grub an' sleepin' out my bed-clothes. Yes, I hated all y'all sittin' around while I had to go an' meet that man every day. How'd you think I felt . . . knowin' y'all hated to see me comin'. All y'all ever wanted from me was what I was slavin' to get ahold of. That's all you ever wanted from me was a place to lay your head an' some-thin' to put in your stomach. Use to wish th' house would burn down with all y'all in it so I wouldn't have to feed your behinds. Yes, I took that cracker's shit . . . I had to. Couldn't do no better. 'Cause if I had knock him on his butt you wouldn't have nothin' to eat an' neither would them chaps. Why weren't they born dead . . . why weren't they just born dead . . .

EMMA: Listen to yourself. Listen to what you're sayin'?

NOAH: What have I gotten for it?

EMMA: What does anybody get?

NOAH: More than I ever got.

EMMA: You wanted pay.

NOAH: Somethin' to make it worthwhile.

EMMA: I never really knew how much you hated us.

NOAH: You know it now.

EMMA: That's the Lord's truth.

NOAH: Many a night I thought I just get on that bus down-town and ask th' driver to take me to parts unknown. Run away and leave your behinds for somebody else to take care of. 'Cause I never got no thanks!

EMMA: Then why didn't you just walk on away from us?

NOAH: 'Cause I had my part to do.

EMMA: I wished you had walked away and never looked back. I'd rather you had just gone on down the road than had to put up with you.

NOAH (*shaking his head, rises, crosses to stairs*): No thanks!

EMMA: Where you goin'?

NOAH: I'm going upstairs to lie down.

EMMA: Don't you feel well?

NOAH: I just want to lie down.

EMMA: What about your hot milk?

NOAH: I feel like I've got to lie down.

EMMA: You want me to bring it up to you?

NOAH: You can if you want to.

EMMA: I'll bring it up in a minute.

NOAH: Thank you. (*He exits upstairs.*)

(EMMA *pours the milk into a cup which she places on a tray. She crosses to the staircase.*)

LAMAR'S VOICE (*offstage, knocking on door*): Mama!

EMMA: Lamar!

LAMAR'S VOICE: Mama! (*Knocks on door again.*)

NOAH'S VOICE (*offstage*): Who is it?

EMMA: Noah . . . ?

LAMAR'S VOICE: Mama . . . open the door?

EMMA: It's Lamar!

NOAH (*offstage*): Don't you open that door!

EMMA: Please, Noah!

NOAH (*offstage*): You can go out there with him if you want to.

EMMA: Noah!

NOAH (*enters*): You ain't opening that door!

EMMA (*at door*): Lamar . . . Lamar!

NOAH: Go on with him!

EMMA (*bends down to floor*): It's blood!

NOAH: Blood?

EMMA (*opening the door and screaming as she finds an owl hanging in the doorway from a rope*): Lamar!

NOAH (*calling out*): Lamar!! (*He gets a knife and cuts it down.*)

EMMA (*going out onto the kitchen porch*): Lamar?

NOAH: Is he out there?

EMMA (*closing door behind her*): I don't see anybody.

NOAH: Why did he do that?

EMMA: Throw that thing away!

NOAH: What's in that thing's mind?

EMMA: Get rid of that thing.

NOAH: I'll throw it into the furnace. (*He crosses to cellar and exits.*)

(EMMA *crosses into living room and looks out, trying to find some sight of* LAMAR. NOAH, *offstage, screams.*)

EMMA: Noah! (*Moves to cellar door.*) Noah, what's the matter? (*He screams again and again.*) Noah . . . ? (*She descends the staircase.*) Noah—(*She screams. She comes up out of the cellar followed by the groans of* NOAH *coming from the cellar below. She moves to the telephone and dials.*) Stella Mae! Stella Mae! Come over here quick. Your daddy! Your daddy, your daddy! He stuck his head in the furnace. Call a doctor! Quick—(*She hangs up phone and crosses to cellar and exits.*)

FADE OUT

Requiem for Brother X
by WILLIAM WELLINGTON MACKEY

William Wellington Mackey is a native of Miami, Florida. He attended Southern University in Baton Rouge, Louisiana, and the University of Minnesota. He is the author of the book for *Billy Noname,* the critically acclaimed musical presented Off-Broadway in New York during the 1969–70 season. *Requiem for Brother X* has been presented at various experimental theaters and university groups around the country, including a summer's run at Chicago's Hull House Parkway Theater. His full-length play, *Behold! Cometh the Vanderkellans,* is scheduled for an Off-Broadway opening during the 1970–71 season. Presently living in New York City, and the recipient of a Rockefeller Foundation playwright's grant, he is at work on a new full-length play as well as the book for a new musical.

Introduction

Requiem for Brother X is a dramatic dialogue about black people trapped in the ghetto. It is an expression of repressed feelings of anxiety and deep inner frustrations. It is a shout, a cry of mercy, a lamentation for understanding. It is a spit at the black middle class for turning their backs on the black masses still in bondage. It is triggered anger and hostility toward the white masses. It is the trillion hallelujahs and amens of a dirge—a black mass. It is a requiem for the dead black people buried in the stone jungles of this country.

The play is about the impact of a man called Malcom. It is about people who cannot talk . . . who just exist from day to day. They cannot talk because they have never been allowed to talk. *Requiem* is about Harlem, Chicago's South Side, and a sickening memory from my childhood of a place called Goodbread Alley. *Requiem* is about a place called Watts—a recent example of the tragedy of people who have been unable to find expression. It is about other places that have yet to define themselves; other places ever sweltering and abounding with anxieties and frustrations of people overcome by impotence and helplessness . . . people on the verge of the breaking point. Whatever that breaking point is, only God knows. Only time will tell.

Denver, Colorado
May 28, 1966

—where can you go in a circle?

Inquiries concerning performance and translation rights should be addressed to Jack Rich, Esq., 349 East 149 Street, Bronx, New York 10451.

William Wellington Mackey

Author's Notes on Staging of the Play

1. The mood of the play is *black;* very *black.* If this is not accomplished the play fails in its intention.

2. The actors should be completely separated from the audience. Cage them in. Erect a non-shield of metal poles between the audience and the stage. The play works extremely well if presented in an arena-type theater.

3. The set should be separated into six major playing areas.

    AREA I: Center stage right. A raised platform on which Nate performs. Nate is the only character allowed movement throughout the production.

    AREA II: The same platform on which Nate performs but extended; and that part which is located at center stage. Matt, dressed in a post office worker's uniform, is seated here on a stool. He never rises from the stool.

    AREA III: Downstage left. Martha, seated on a chair at floor level. She remains seated throughout the performance.

    AREA IV: Floor level, primarily in the center of the space between areas III and IV. The main playing area for Bonita. Movement is optional.

    AREA V: A raised platform upstage left. For the little white girl in labor with child, lying on a bed draped with white sheets.

    AREA VI: Downstage right. Jude, in a wheelchair. During the course of the play, he maneuvers himself about in the floor space between areas III and IV. A lightbulb hangs from the flies just above Jude's primary location. At the end of Part One of the play (just prior to Nate's entrance), Jude reaches up and turns the light off. *Note:* Jude is arthritic: he is paralyzed from the waist down.

4. The lighting plot allows for either a single room or a whole house.

5. In the background, somewhere around upstage left, a coffin hangs from the flies. Five lilies are placed at the head of the coffin. Dim lighting is on the coffin throughout the play.

6. Sound effects overlapping and interchangeable as specified at various points during the course of the play.

    a. The RAW quality of the pulsating sound of a living heart pumping blood throughout a living body.

    b. The beautiful, terrifying cries of a woman in labor, about to give birth to a new living being. The cries encompass joy, sorrow, fear, and (most important) pain. These outbursts should be so employed throughout the play that

326

they profoundly establish the mood and tempo of the production. They should provide a unique continuity that will, as a lament, musically accent the dialogue—which is, in fact, what the play really is: a dialogue of confrontation.

c. The ringing of chimes, with a gong quality (at specified points in the play).

d. A baby crying (at specified points in the play).

7. The time of the play: The eve of an American tragedy. (This should be inscribed in the program.)

8. The place: America: sweet, sweet land of Liberty . . . of thee I sing this lament. (This should also be inscribed in the program.)

9. Music: Just prior to the start of the play, as the house-lights dim, enter music embellished with a very "distant" spirit—with an African quality and a suggestion of spirituality: perhaps the "Kyrie" and others from the "Misa Luba," the Catholic Mass as sung in Congolese on a recent popular recording. Whatever music is used for the desired effect should be repeated as the lights are dimmed at the end of the play.

New York City
January 1, 1969

THE CHARACTERS

JUDE   Old, graying man, on the verge of senility. He is crippled and sits in a wheelchair.

BONITA   Teen-ager, but older in mind and spirit because of her "ghetto" experience. A bundle of fire; dynamite; always near the point of ignition.

NATE   Tall and lanky; around twenty-two years old. The key to his character: too much insight about too many things . . . too soon.

MATT   The oldest of three children. Accepts this role seriously; very seriously. Believes that there is a better day ahead.

MARTHA   Matt's wife. Charming and pleasant. Around thirty years old. Has a quaint but "hopeful" sad expression almost constantly on her face.

(*Darkness, The sound of a heartbeat. Lights open on* MARTHA *and* MATT.)

MARTHA (*calling*): Any sign of Nate, honey? Matt . . . Matt . . .

JUDE (*in darkness*): Ha, ha, ha, ha . . .

MATT (*overlapping*): No, Martha. Don't see him. Guess he went downtown.

JUDE (*still in darkness*): Hah!

MATT (*snappingly*): And you needn't start either.

(*Lights open on* JUDE.)

JUDE (*growling*): Boy! You listen to me. I'm gettin' tired o' this being pushed around all the time. This is still my house. Best you remember that.

MATT: Yeah, yeah, Daddy. Okay. Okay. I remember.

JUDE: How many times I have to remind all of you! This is still my house. And I'll speak and do what I damn well please. Don't care if you are . . .

MATT: All right, Daddy. All right!

MARTHA: You two . . . Just listen to you. I have never before seen a daddy and son argue the way you two do. Now behave, both of you.

JUDE: Martha, didn't nobody ask you a damn thing. Can't even open your mouth in this place nomore.

MARTHA: Oh, hush, hush now, Daddy. Here. Come on now. Time to eat. Time to get something into that empty stomach.

JUDE (*antagonized*): I ain't no baby, woman. Uhm in a wheelchair. But I ain't no damn baby. Lemme go now. Damnit! Lemme go!

MARTHA: Okay. Okay. If you have to be so mean about it. But please . . . let's have some peace, Daddy, huh? Okay?

(*A slight pause.*)

MARTHA (*continuing*): My! What a gloriously beautiful day!

JUDE: Some wife you got, boy. Here it's raining like hell outside, and what does this fool say? (*Mockingly.*) "It's a gloooooriously buuuuueeetiful day." Hmph! Dumb fool!

MARTHA: Oh, Daddy, you know what I mean. Mary . . . the little girl; the baby and all. Ain't every day a woman can be blessed with a brand-new little baby. Ain't it just wonderful? I mean it really is! All clean and decent and pure. Sweet as an angel!

JUDE: Hmph! Yeah! Sweet all right! Just one more to add to the flock. An angel with no mercy! Another bastard to be blessed with the holy waters of Mr. President's Anti-Poverty Program. Hmph! Another mouth to feed. Crazy fool! Messin' 'round all the time.

MATT: For God's sake, Daddy. Do you have to? Do you have to all the time?

JUDE: Well, it's the truth. It's the God's truth, and you know it. He's just plain no good. A bum! A goddamn bum!

And that ain't all, either. He's sick. He's sick too! Something terrible gonna happen to that boy. Mark my word. Something terrible gonna happen to him.

MARTHA: Oh, Daddy, Nate'll find himself eventually. Sometimes it takes some people longer than others to find themselves. He'll be all right. When we move, maybe then Nate'll . . .

JUDE (*snapping*): Moving ain't gonna do one damn thing for that boy. Nothing! He's a bum. Hmph! I knew something was coming. Knew something was gonna happen sooner or later. Told you so, too. But you wouldn't listen. (*Mockingly.*) I'm an old, stupid, foolish man! Hmph! I know a bum when I see one. Son or no son, he's a bum. Screwing every white bitch he can get his hands on.

MATT: Goddamnit! Will you shut up and eat your food. Do you have to talk that way in front of Martha? Jesus! It'll be good to get out of this dump!

(*Enter the sound of the cries. The cries continue throughout the dialogue.*)

MARTHA: Matt, please . . .

JUDE (*overlapping*): Ayeeee . . . So it's a dump now, is it? It's a dump! You done got so high and mighty, it's a dump now. Well you were born right in that room, fool! Right in there, and with a name. And now you can sit there and tell me, your father . . . Hmph! A dump! Ungrateful as hell! All of you! At least you got rightful claims to being born, fool! You ain't like that whore in there. YOU GOT RIGHTFUL CLAIMS TO BEING BORN.

MATT: Being born—big deal. If only people could do something about being born and not being born. What's worth anything when you come to the point of knowing what you are, and who you are, and who's responsible for what never should have been?

JUDE: What's that? What do you mean? Don't talk that double-talk to me. Think you talking over my head, don't you? Think you making a fool of me? Well you ain't, you know.

MARTHA: Matt, honey, that's enough now. It don't really matter. Don't argue with him. Just leave him be. Leave him be. He's still your daddy.

MATT: Daddy! Sometimes I wonder if he ever knew the meaning of the word.

JUDE: Don't you sass me, boy. Don't sass me. Don't you ever think you're too big for me not to knock off your feet.

MARTHA: Oh, hush, Daddy. Everything's all right. Daddy, you're going to be a grandpapa. That lil' girl in there's having

329

your grandchild. Daddy, this is your first grandchild.

JUDE: First grandchild! Hah! If I could count the times the gals have been to that door trying to get me to make these boys marry them. (*Teasingly.*) That's right. You too, Mr. Postalman. You ain't always been so high and mighty. Hmph! I probably been a grandpapa least a dozen times for the both of them. Girl, this is Harlem, U.S.A. Ain't nothing for um to do but lay um and blow um up from the time they're knee high to a car in this place. (*Again teasingly.*) Ain't that right, Matt? Ain't that right, Mr. Postalman? Hmph! (*Slight pause.*) Course I don't know . . . This one's white. Lord knows that kind can be something else when they get their nose open for a spook.

MATT: My God! This man's mind stays in the gutter.

JUDE: Gutter! Yeah, gutter it is. There ain't much but the gutter, boy. I ain't that old or foolish not to know there ain't much but the gutter. Been in and outta gutters all my life. EVERYTHING'S GUTTER! There ain't nothing much that THEY can do to change it, either. THEY'RE ROT-BUCKET GUTTER THEMSELVES! ALL OF THEM! GUTTER EVERYWHERE! THE WHOLE GODDAMN COUNTRY! YOU BORN IN IT AND YOU DIE IN IT. Ain't ever possible to forget that. YOU THINK GUTTER AND YOU LIVE GUTTER AND YOU DIE GUTTER! (*Nervously.*) Them . . . them crooks in Washington, D.C., and . . . and . . . downtown: the mayor and . . . and Peace Corps; goddamn poverty-assed programs, and all that shit! EVERYTHING'S GUTTER! Remember that, boy! EVERYTHING'S GUTTER! You wind up in the crazy house or the 'lectric chair the minute you're stupid enough to think you're better'n the gutter.

MATT: Okay, Daddy. Okay, Okay, you win. I can't fight you. (*Slight pause.*) Martha . . . honey . . . Oh now, honey, what you crying for? Don't pay any attention to him. He . . . he's just an old man . . . an old, bitter, angry man that just don't understand nothing no more.

JUDE: I heard that! I heard that! An old man . . . an old man. Hmph! You'll see. You'll see. I know what I'm talking 'bout. I been 'round a long time, boy. DON'T TRUST UM! DON'T YOU TRUST UM! They'll kick you in the ass the minute you turn your back. Boy, you ain't been the same since that damn post office. The Man got you fooled like he done fooled all of us for as long as I can remember. I'm telling you, boy. DON'T YOU EVER TRUST UM! They ain't never fooled me once. NEVER!

MATT: Tell you what, Daddy. Tell you what. You go right

ahead not trusting them. It's okay with me. Damn okay with me.

JUDE: Weak! You're weak! A spineless Uncle-Tom weakling. Least Nate does have fire. Got fire in his blood! Least Nate knows them for what they are.

MATT: Daddy, Nate is somewhere lost in the middle. Thank God I've passed that stage. I've had that experience. And . . . and WE ARE WHERE WE ARE, AREN'T WE? EVEN YOU HAVE TO ADMIT THAT. No. No, you just go right on hating them, Daddy. Go right on hating them. Just keep in mind where the check comes from every month. That's all I got to say.

(*For a second or so only the cries are heard. And then a piercing scream. The three lights dim a bit as a fourth light opens on* BONITA.)

BONITA (*sprightly*): What did I do to deserve this? What a drag! You people have a lot of nerve. This ain't fair. This ain't fair at all.

MARTHA: I know, honey. I know. Soon all this will be far behind us. We'll be able to breathe again.

MATT: Have we ever, Martha?

JUDE: Hah!

BONITA: Hang it up, Matt! Hmph! This ain't fair. I wake up this morning; clean up; cook breakfast; wash the dishes; go to school and labor in classes trying to better my lot like the good white father tells us to . . . and for what? To go to my nice lil' job and flunky for Mr. Fineburg? And then when I get back to this place, what do I find? Some dizzy chick having a baby in my room.

MARTHA: Honey, honey, please . . .

BONITA: But wait! Wait! That's not the half of it. Oh no! I wind up having to help deliver this broad's baby; the enemy's little bastard; the white chick who'll spit on me uptown; the clean and decent ofay baby who scrutinizes me up and down every day in gym class to see if I have sores and scales over my body.

JUDE: Mind your mouth, Bonita! Remember who you're talking to. Fuss with these two. Don't get mad with me. I'm old, too old to know anything anymore.

MARTHA: How's the little girl coming, Bonita?

BONITA: What do you mean, Martha, "How's the little girl coming?" THE LITTLE WHITE GIRL? She came nine months ago, and now she's having a baby! That's how she's coming! Lord! That brother of mine. I knew something was going to happen. I told him to quit running behind everything in a skirt just because it was white. Every last one of them

gets special pleasure outta wrapping colored boys around their fingers. You should see them at school. Our boys so damn hot after them just because they're white. You think that's all they lived for—screwing some white girl.

MATT (*angrily*): Bonita!

JUDE (*overlapping*): Ha, ha, ha . . . tell him, daughter! Tell him the facts of life. Ha, ha, ha . . .

MARTHA: Daddy! You should be ashamed of yourself!

JUDE: Of what. The facts of life? Ha, ha, ha, ha . . .

BONITA: Why is she here? She doesn't have to be here. What's she trying to prove? Hmph! I'll tell you what she's doing. Everything's recorded these days, you know. Everything! That baby of hers is going to show up on Mr. White Man's statistics and warp-sided studies. That's just what's going to happen. And the fact that that broad is white just ain't gonna show. Like it always is. Those statistics will be made up of BLACK FIGURES: BLACK NUMBERS! Hmph! BLACK SOCIAL DISORGANIZATION! This is the kind of mess they throw in our faces in school. Every time the counselor calls us in, he never once forgets to remind us that WE . . . that WE ARE THE DEPRIVED: THE SOCIAL DISOR-GANIZED: THE HELPLESS. NOT THEM! NOT HER! Why should we always be so doggone helpful to them all the time?

MARTHA: The point is, she's here, Bonita. There's nothing we can do but be kind to the girl and help her as best we can. Least until she's able to leave.

BONITA: Well, LEAVE is right! You people don't have to listen and take all that crap every day like I do in school. Look. I'm the one that's suppose to be dirty. My kind is suppose to be no good. NOT HER! NOT THEM! BLACK IS DIRTY! NOT WHITE! I'm suppose to be in there screaming and carry-ing on with a baby in my belly. WE'RE SUPPOSE TO BE THE ONES WHO MAKE MISTAKES! NOT THEM! Their daddy's got the bread to slip under the table to some doctor; the money to pay the Man to keep them off the state's records. So when one of them messes up and gets caught in the trick, I say hallelujah!

JUDE: Amen!

BONITA: And don't any of you pull that age crap on me either. The facts are, I'm sixteen and unfortunately a NIG-GER! A NIGGER! I'm bucking this rotten city like all of you. I know the facts of life the way all NIGGERS do by the time they're sixteen in this place. I SAY SHE HAS TO GO! It's rough for everybody.

MATT: Oh, girl, go on in and help Dr. Hanley. For Christ's sake!

BONITA: Drop dead, Matt! Don't be giving me any orders. I'm not your slave. And since when did you get on this Dr. Hanley kick? He's a phony—a quack! He ain't been able to practice for years. I know right from wrong. Do you think I'm stupid or something.

MATT: All right, all right! I'm sorry. I shouldn't have yelled. But Bonita, we've gone this far. Please help us, will you? I'm sorry I let things go this far.

BONITA: Just don't bark at me as if I was some child. Ain't nobody ever a child in this place . . . don't ever have the time.

(*A slight pause as the lights on* BONITA *dim.*)

MATT: Nate oughta be here. Maybe I should go and try to find him.

JUDE: For what? Nate couldn't care less 'bout no broad having no baby. Hah! He's done it! He's done it! Didn't know what it was gonna be; but when he came back from school, I knew he had something on his mind.

MATT: Yeah. I should have known . . . and . . . and joining up with those crazy people. And following that man around as if he were Jesus on the cross. And this hate—all this hate! God! I should have been able to do something.

BONITA: Yes siree, Daddy. That's just what they call us, those teachers and social workers. "Nita," they say, "Honey, we're not prejudiced. Why do you think that about us? Dear little girl, we loves your people. We really do! That's why we're here, honey. Why just last year we spent our whole year on the South Side of Chicago with the Special Project for Deprived and Underprivileged Children. Poor little colored girl, please let us in. Please. We really love you all. We do. Why are you so paranoid? You lil' nigra children just carry this chip on your shoulders. (*Elated.*) Oh, I know! I know! We're just gonna make this our thesis project when we're in graduate school next summer. That's just what we're gonna do. There just has to be a reason for this nigra paranoia. There just has to be a reason." Yeah, Daddy. They think we're all crazy. (*The lights on* BONITA *begin to fade.*) We're no more crazy than they are, or that white girl in there. And you should see her . . . those big blue eyes staring at the dirty walls; and that whatever-it-is inside her, kicking and tearing away at her guts. She just lies there, staring, scared as hell, staring and . . . and . . . (*A scream from offstage.*) Damn! Screams like a damn coyote! (*Slight pause.*) Well, here goes old black mammy again. Lord . . . Ain't this role ever gonna change? (*Lights on Bonita fade off.*)

JUDE: Ha, ha, ha, ha . . . That's my girl! That's my daughter! Strong she is! Guts! Ain't afraid of nothing. She knows the score. She knows THEM! Take note from that girl, Martha. Take note! Might learn something. You might learn a few things.

MARTHA (*wounded*): I . . . learn something, Daddy . . . from little Bonita?

MATT: Don't pay any attention to him, Martha. Here. Want a cigarette?

MARTHA: No. No, Matt. No, honey. I, I think I'll just go in and see if there's anything I can do. I, I, and well . . . learn something. (*The light on* MARTHA *fades off.*)

MATT (*after a slight pause*): You want to watch television, Daddy? Its almost time for the news.

JUDE: Nawh. There ain't too much that we don't know about.

MATT: Yeah, I guess so.

JUDE: Gets so it's like dying a little every time you listen to that damn thing.

MATT: You tired? Want to go in awhile?

JUDE (*jokingly*): Ha, ha, ha, ha . . . "Tired of living and scared of dying," so the man says.

MATT (*amused*): Daddy, you're too much. You're just too much.

JUDE (*teasingly*): And old and foolish. Tell you one thing. You gonna see more than "too much" if I don't hurry and pay my respects to the john.

MATT: Ha, ha, ha, ha . . . Here, let me help you.

JUDE: No. no. No. I can wheel myself in. I ain't that help-less.

(*The lights on* JUDE *and* MATT *begin to fade.*)

MATT (*overlapping*): Oh, come on, Daddy. Come on. Quit being such a . . . Daddy, you know one thing? You, you ain't old at all. You're still just a big baby. That's what you are—a big baby.

JUDE (*overlapping*): Lemme go. Damnit all. Lemme go. Will you lemme . . .

(*Darkness. The cries stop. The sound of the heartbeat continues. After a second or so, the lights open on* NATE *and* MATT.)

NATE: 'Lo.

MATT: Where you been?

NATE (*matter-of-factly*): None of your damn business.

MATT: Yeah. Well, how did it go?

NATE: Meeting.

MATT (*concerned*): Again? I thought you people met last night.

NATE: Things getting worse. Gotta meet. Won't be long now though. Few more days, I figure.

MATT: Well, did they catch them? Have they gotten them yet?

NATE: Nawh. But we'll find them. They can't get too far that we can't find them. Like we've got our own force now, you know; a dragnet, right now; clear around Harlem.

MATT: Nate, you people don't plan to take the law into your own hands . . .

NATE: What law?

MATT: Nate, you're not going to get into trouble? You promised . . .

NATE: What law?

MATT: Oh, for God's sake. Quit playing games. The law! The police! Let them handle this thing. You people don't have any right to take the law . . .

NATE: What you mean is Mr. White Man's Law, right? Like on the Man's Law is right. MR. WHITE MAN! Like hell it is, boy. Like hell it is! Ain't nothing he can do for us. He could care less about what happened. So screw him! But like those bastards who shot my Brother will pay. We'll get them—and when we do . . . boy, when we do.

MATT: Nate, why don't you wake up before it's too late. You and that hate mob of cutthroats are so sick and pitiful, you make everything that those people in Mississippi are doing meaningless. Wake up and open your eyes to the facts of life, boy!

NATE (*cutting*): The facts of life are "X's" boy. "X"! Dig? Don't hand me none of that nonviolent crap. Wars ain't never been won by bending over and getting kicked in the ass. AND THIS IS WAR! And there ain't but one way to fight this kind of war. AND THAT'S THE WAY! WE GOTTA ORGANIZE! ALL BLACK PEOPLE! GOTTA BAND TOGETHER AND MARCH, MATT. MARCH ALL OVER THE GODDAMN COUNTRY. Following the word of the Brother. Just can't let him die for nothing. He knew what he was talking about. God knows he knew how to deal with Mister Charlie. I'd bet anything that at the bottom of that man's assassination, I'd bet anybody that Mister Charlie planned the whole rotten dirty business.

MATT: I wish you'd listen. GROW UP, NATE. GROW UP! Hanging around that corner every night and listening to all those speeches of hate will get you nowhere.

NATE: As if you're somewhere. Like you're living on Park Avenue. Like sorting Mister Charlie's mail and licking his ass from sunrise to sunset gonna get you that fine white house and beautifully landscaped yard in Westchester. Like hell it is. Like hell, fool! That promotion of yours don't mean from shit. You're gonna rot right here with the rest of your black brothers.

MATT: My God, you're hopeless. Nate, everything's just laid out for you to take advantage of. Boy, if you had to go through . . .

NATE: Don't start that crap again. Hell! Everything is nothing! Bullshit and promises! Promises from the Man. Promises which don't mean nothing. And I say the hell with him. Who needs him? A piece of paper ain't gonna change that damn white man. Just the latest hypocritical move he's made to keep black people off guard. Civil rights bill or no civil rights bill, the white man don't care from nothing about black people. Shit! He's scared, Matt. That's all. He's scared as hell. Too many people all over this world beginning to look at that Man at last; finally beginning to call him down for what he really is. And that shit; pure shit. He ain't the big daddy he's fooled everybody into believing he is, no more. HE AIN'T NO MORE THE WHITE FATHER OF MANKIND! POWER! THAT'S THE KEY, MATT. POWER IN THE HANDS OF MILLIONS OF BLACK PEOPLE ALL OVER THE WORLD. AND POWER IN THE HANDS OF BLACK PEOPLE. YES SIREE, MATT. POWER IN THE HANDS OF BLACK PEOPLE. HAH HAHH! AFRICA HAS RISEN AT LAST. THE GREAT WHITE DADDY OF THE GOOD OLD U.S.A. AIN'T BIG DADDY NO MORE.

MATT: Jesus Christ! That corner . . . Damn that corner!

NATE (*snidely*): Freedom of speech, Matt. ha, ha, ha . . . Freedom of speech.

MATT: Stay away from that corner, Nate. And, and . . . that man. And, and those, those, stupid, ignorant fools.

NATE: What's the matter, brother? What's the matter? Us poor colored folks turn your stomach, brother? Hmph! That's funny. Once a white boy told me exactly the same thing. Instead of "turn," he said, "You churns my stomach, nigger! You churns my guts!" What's the matter, Matt? Make you sick on the stomach to see people your color PROUD OF BEING YOUR COLOR? That's the key, you know: BLACK PEOPLE PROUD OF BEING BLACK!

MATT: Yeah, yeah, yeah, I know. I saw. I heard.

NATE: Then what the hell's bugging you? Get off my back.

MATT (*almost pleading*): Nate, do you know what it is about your corner that turns my stomach, boy? Yeah, and that, that CHURNS my guts? Do you know what I see every time I stop to listen on your corner? Do you know what they call those tactics that, that your Brother used? DO YOU KNOW WHAT IT IS, NATE? BRAINWASHING! BRAIN-WASHING, NATE. TAKING ADVANTAGE OF POOR, STUPID, IGNORANT PEOPLE.

NATE: BRAINWASHING? Hah! What the hell's Radio Free whatever-they-call-it? What the hell's election time in this crazy country? What the hell's any goddamn thing? And what the hell do you mean, POOR PEOPLE, IGNORANT PEOPLE? Who the hell you think you are—BLACK JESUS OR SOMETHING? Matt, your kind really stinks! For every one of your kind, there are hundreds of black people all over this mother-fucking country still in bondage to the goddamn white man. That government badge you wear to work don't mean one damn thing to them. Ain't no hope for them as long as black people like you make off the black scene and forget about your black brothers.

MATT: Oh, drop it! Drop it! Talking to you is a waste of time. I'd rather follow the good preacher in Mississippi any day before being suckered into that crap.

NATE: Matt, you're my brother, but I swear I'll never understand you. Man, you're a hypocrite. Following the good preacher in Mississippi . . . Why aren't you down there? At least I'm on the corner every night. At least I go to the meetings.

MATT: Yeah. And spread the word of hate.

NATE: But I'm in, man. I identify. I'm somebody. A PROUD BLACK SOMEBODY! I'M PART OF WHAT'S HAPPENING IN THE WORLD TODAY, MAN. WHERE ARE YOU? YOU AIN'T NOWHERE. Preacher man's in Mississippi or Alabama or Chicago or someplace right now. Where are you? Those three boys from up here went down there to Mississippi and got themselves killed for you, man. Where are you? YOU AIN'T PART OF NOTHING! YOU AIN'T GOT NOTHING TO LIVE OR DIE FOR. YOU AIN'T BLACK OR WHITE. YOU ONE OF THEM HALF-ASSED NIGGERS. YOU SO SCARED TO LOSE A DIME YOU CAN'T EVEN TAKE A DECENT SHIT ON YOUR FUCKING JOB. (*Shouting.*) HALF-ASSED NIGGER! THAT'S WHAT YOU ARE! All you do is talk and play post office for Mister Charlie all day. You don't do a damn thing but punch Charlie government's clock and sucker him outta

that GI loan to get you that white house in Westchester.

MATT: You'll be part of that house, Nate. It'll be yours too.

NATE: Like hell I will! That's your problem; not mine. If you're stupid enough to believe that a white house and picket fence will change this boy's color, you do have problems. Those white people don't want you, boy. They don't want no part of you being near them. That's when you really find out you're a nigger and that your color ain't going to ever change.

MATT: I still say this hate is no good, Nate. No good at all. This hate for everything.

NATE: EVERYTHING THAT'S WHITE! CLARIFY! BE SPECIFIC!

MATT: It just don't make any sense. You haven't had it so bad. You've had every chance to . . . we've all worked hard to give you every chance to . . . to . . . But you're still so bitter. What are you doing on that corner? Make me understand, boy. Nate, you've been to college. You can count on one hand the kids on this block who've had that chance. But what do you do? You quit school outta the clear blue sky and join in cahoots with that . . . Why in hell didn't you join CORE or SNICK or some of the others if you just had to get involved in the movement? We'd understand that. Sure . . . sure, these are the times for COREs and SNICKs and movements. But why this?

NATE: You really want to know, Matt?

MATT: I only want to understand.

NATE: Matt, I learned one thing at that righteous, phony, liberal-assed school. Like the old saying goes . . .

MATT: What are you talking about?

NATE (*snappingly*): The goddamn white man is governed; he believes—oh the hell, you know what I'm trying to say. "IF YOU'RE WHITE, YOU'RE ALL RIGHT! BUT IF YOU'RE BLACK, STEP BACK, NIGGER . . . STEP BACK!" They only go so far, white people, when it comes to giving of themselves, Matt. Hell! You can forget it! You can fart on it! I know what I'm talking about. I tried. I tried. And that . . . that sonuvabitch!

MATT: The kid? The boy you brought home with you Christmas?

NATE: Yeah. The white father's clean-cut, blue-eyed American boy. Sonuvabitch! First damn true-blue white bastard I ever got to know. Ain't worth it, Matt. Damn sure ain't. Take it from me: if you have to know white people, stick to Jews or Italians. ANYTHING but the true-blue pure American.

They ain't from nothing. At least Jews and Dagos got peculiar problems too. But Mr. America? Matt, this is his goddamn country. And he don't care from shit about nobody but himself.

MATT: What happened? What happened, Nate? I thought that . . . I liked that boy. He seemed like a nice kid. I thought you two were . . .

NATE: Yeah . . . very nice. He was very nice. That's what they all are in that part of the country. Made a first-class ass outta me.

MATT: You loved him! Nate, you . . . loved him.

NATE: Loved him? Are you outta your fuckin' mind? A white boy?

MATT: Nate, I'm your brother. I know you.

NATE: All right! All right! Yeah. I guess so. Yeah. I loved that one white boy. Like a typical nigger, I loved. (*Nervous exasperation.*) We were brothers. Least I thought we were. Hmph! I never thought it was possible to have a special feeling for a white person. But . . . but, I loved. Yes, I loved. Things happened so quickly. We were doing so many things together; things I never dreamed were possible. As if he were just another person . . . a friend. God, I forgot that he was even white. Ain't that a bitch, Matt? (*Slight pause.*) That boy even took me home with him—there, in that part of the country. Out there it's something else when an ofay cat takes you home with him. Those hicks in those little towns are too much. Most of them don't even know what a Negro looks like. He was so goddamn straight . . . swinging. Like yes. I guess I did love him . . . that one white boy. I guess I really did. He proved to me—least I thought so at the time—that it was possible; that there were some white people who were like . . . decent . . . like . . . swinging.

MATT: Nate, you needn't. I . . . think I understand.

NATT (*snappingly*): YOU ASKED! SO LISTEN! (*A slight pause.*) Yeah. I loved that white boy, damn him. (*In pain.*) Dear God! I loved. (*Nervous exasperation.*) Something happened. It had to, I guess. Love is a funny thing. It demands. If it's there, people communicate for the first time in their lives. There . . . there can be no breakdown in that communication or the results will be tragic and . . . and . . . unforgiveable. He, he castrated me, Matt. Like all the white beasts have done to all the centuries of black grandfathers before us. And I, I taught him the facts of life. Like a fetus in a womb, I nurtured him. We walked a dark, lonely road together. His manhood in the palm of my hand. And the

strangest revelation was the satisfaction, Matt. I was proud. I felt good. I had won the heart, the sincerity, the love of a white boy. His heart, my heart. His soul, my soul. No black, no white. Just love. (*Slight pause.*) Dear God! What is love? (*Slight pause.*) That white boy used the hell outta me, Matt. He used me. He was a first-class nobody when I met him. I made him. The classic story all over again. Negroes like me have been saving the souls of white people since the country started. White people have been feeding off the breast of mammies and sucking away at the hearts of Toms and Sams and Rufuses for SO LONG . . . TOO LONG. And, and it'll always be that way unless we do something about it . . . and NOW. NOW! BEFORE IT'S TOO LATE.

MATT: Nate, don't judge them all, everything about them, because of this one experience.

NATE (*almost pleading*): Oh, Matt. Don't you know what I'm trying to say? Ain't you a Negro no more? Don't you know what it means to be a Negro in this goddamn country? It don't matter how far you go or how high you get or how good things may seem to be. Something always happens. SOME GODDAMN THING ALWAYS HAPPENS WHEN YOU LEAST EXPECT IT! AND IT HURTS, MATT! GOD, IT HURTS! AND I JUST CAN'T TAKE THAT KIND OF HURT NO MORE. IT'S MORE THAN A COLOR OF A WHITE MAN'S SKIN. IT'S THOSE MILLIONS OF MONSTERS INSIDE THAT MAN . . . THOSE WHITE DEVILS INSIDE THAT MAN'S SOUL THAT I'M SCARED OF, MATT. THOSE DEVILS . . . ALWAYS WAITING FOR THE CHANCE TO DESTROY ME. EVERY TIME I SEE A WHITE FACE, I KNOW THEY'RE THERE. YOU DON'T SEE THEM. BUT YOU KNOW THEY'RE THERE . . . HIDDEN BEHIND THAT WHITE MASK. (*Slight pause.*) AND MATT . . . THAT'S AMERICA: ONE HUGE MONSTROUS WHITE MASK. (*Long pause.*) No, never again, brother. Never again. Negroes should always be on guard and aware of what that man is capable of doing. We shouldn't ever give completely of ourselves to them again. If we do, we're left with nothing. I hate and I love. Finality! The end! The essence of the complete castration. Omega. The beasts neither hate nor love. Alpha. They're somewhere in the middle . . . somewhere in the middle.

MATT: Maybe he never got to understand you, Nate. Maybe there wasn't enough time for understanding.

NATE: He understood. He understood. But like most of them, he's afraid . . . afraid of life . . . afraid to live—to

touch, to feel, to be. They're animals, Matt. Beasts! Their very existence is one of chaotic nothingness. When forced to touch, they devour. When made to feel, they castrate. And . . . and when given the chance to re . . . to LIVE, THEY . . . THEY DESTROY. (*Pause.*) Funny, I know that boy don't really want that, Matt. He don't want that at all. He found out from me what living's about. And, and he'll miss living. That's his tragedy. He'll want to live.

MATT: And you in the meantime will continue feeling sorry for yourself.

NATE: Oh no, brother. Oh no. Like hell I will. Like Nate's gonna swing, baby. Nate's gonna swing with the man! DOWN WITH THE GREAT WHITE FATHERS! DOWN WITH THE WHITE BEAST! SWING WITH ME, MATT! SWING WITH THE BROTHER. TAKES GUTS TO SWING, BABY! GOOD . . . STRONG . . . BLACK GUTS!

MATT: Oh, Nate! What are you living for?

NATE: Me, baby! ME! I relate to everything and at the same time to NOTHING! Like the beast when he's doing the Twist . . . the Jerk . . . the Monkey . . . the Fly, and all that other crap. Relate to NOTHING! DON'T TOUCH! DON'T FEEL! JUST DO! NO MEANING! JUST DO! (*With exhilaration.*) PRETEND! MAKE LIKE REAL! BUT DON'T BE! DON'T BE!

MATT (*angered*): Yeah, and just where will that get you?

NATE: To hell if I don't pray. But like most niggers, I pray. I pray in spite of it all. Like that spook chick I was with the other night. Man, colored gals are too much lately; really getting carried away with themselves. Like most Negroes— always praying and hoping for something different. You know what I mean?

MATT: Yeah . . . always hoping.

NATE: Man, we were getting ready to go to lil' Joe's party. Rose had dolled herself up with Miss White Woman's cosmetics and all. She was primping away like Miss Ann. She was saying "Mirror, mirror on the wall, who's the fairest of them all?" (*Breaking up.*) Man, I screamed! Ha, ha, ha, ha . . . I cracked up! I told her "SNOW WHITE, YOU BLACK BITCH. AND DON'T YOU EVER FORGET IT."

MATT: My God! You're hopeless, Nate. There's no hope for you.

NATE: And up yours, too, Uncle Tom! UP YOURS!

MATT (*snapping back*): Now just a goddamn minute. Who the hell you think you're talking to? There's just so much,

341

Nate—just so much, boy. Not for one goddamn minute do I have to listen to this.

NATE: THE HELL YOU DON'T! THE HELL YOU DON'T. I'm trying to save you, BOY! TRYING TO SAVE YOU BEFORE IT'S TOO LATE. TRYING TO PUT SOME STRONG BLACK GUTS INTO YOUR CHICKEN-SHIT BAG OF BONES.

MATT (*nervous exasperation*): JUST SO MUCH, NATE. JUST SO MUCH, BOY. LEMME TELL YOU ONE DAMN THING, BOY. SO HELP ME GOD AS I'M STANDING HERE . . . I WILL KNOCK THE LIVING . . .

NATE (*overlapping*): Ha, ha, ha, ha . . . What's the matter, BOY? (*Teasingly.*) What's the matter, UNCLE TOM? (*Resoundingly.*) WHAT'S THE MATTER? YOU DON'T LIKE TO HEAR THE TRUTH, DO YOU? THAT JUST WHAT THE BROTHER SAID ABOUT YOU NIGGERS! YOU DON'T LIKE TO HEAR THE WAY IT IS! HE WAS RIGHT, MY BROTHER! LORD KNOWS HE WAS RIGHT. THAT'S THE TROUBLE, BOY. TOO MANY DAMN UNCLE TOM NIGGERS LIKE YOU ALL OVER THIS GODDAMN COUNTRY. THE WHITE DEVIL GOT YOU ALL "BRAINWASHED." All this patriotism crap since the march on Washington. (*Mockingly.*) EVERYBODY LOVES EVERYBODY ALL OF A SUDDEN. Jesus Christ! When will you stupid niggers ever learn? Damnit, Matt. We're just a stone's throw from the cotton fields! Yesterday is but a fart's smell away! That's what was so beautiful about the Brother. He knew. "Don't be fooled," he told us. "They need you. They need your blood again! They need your sweat; your guts; those STINKING SMELLY BLACK GUTS THAT BUILT THIS COUNTRY!" And man, was he right! Look at what's happening. THE WHOLE GODDAMN WORLD IS FUCKED UP! AND MIGHTY, MIGHTY US! WE! IT! THE BEAST IS JERKING OFF AGAIN. PISS-ASSING AROUND WITH EVERY GODDAMN BODY . . . TRYING TO PLAY JESUS! WE'RE SITTING ON A TIME BOMB, BABY. THERE'S GONNA BE A BIG EXPLOSION LIKE NOBODY'S EVER SEEN BEFORE, MATT. AND WHITEY . . . WHITEY AIN'T PREPARED FOR THAT KIND OF BATTLE. STRONG BLACK GUTS WILL BE NEEDED AGAIN! THOSE STRONG BLACK GUTS THAT PICKED ALL THAT COTTON AND SWEATED IN THOSE FIELDS WILL HAVE TO BLEED AGAIN. Yes siree! Whitey's gonna keep pushing people around until we wake up to the sound of hundreds of bombs dropping on us. And Whitey ain't used

to that, boy. Suffering, he ain't used to. Ain't no way in the world he could adjust to that, boy. But black people? Niggers? Man . . . BLACK . . . NIGGER . . . SPOOK . . . COON. They all mean the same thing. SUFFERING! We'll make it through whatever happens. Whitey knows that. He knows that all too well . . . all too well.

MATT: My God! If you're not a sickening sight! (*With disgust.*) Just look at you. Yeah. You're right about one thing. War is coming. And thank God you'll probably be in it. War'd be the best thing that could happen to somebody like you. You might grow up and get this damn black-ass chip off your shoulders.

NATE: BULLSHIT! Like the war won't just be starting. Like we're already at war . . . BOY! Niggers are already at war. Like Alabama ain't a battlefield? Like that minister wasn't on the firing line? Like those white bastards that killed that lady won't be acquitted in the name of white sovereignty? THAT'S MY WAR, BOY! THAT'S MY BAT-TLEFIELD! Ain't got no time to waste fucking around with people who don't give a damn about me. Those Vietnamese could care less about my troubles. But those bastards in Mississippi do. Yes siree, boy! That's my battle. Ha, ha, ha, ha.

(*Enter the sound of* JUDE's *laughter. In darkness.*)

MATT (*overlapping, as* NATE *enters into the laughter*): Goddamnit boy . . . what the hell's the matter with you. You crazy or something?

NATE: Crazy? (*Sarcastically.*) Yeah. NIGGER CRAZY! Ha, ha, ha, ha . . . (*Sinking deeply; intensely hysterical to a point; almost drifting senselessly.*) Ha, ha, ha, ha . . . it hurts. It's killing me! Ha, ha, ha, ha . . . ME! THE GREATEST MAN ALIVE! Ha, ha, ha, ha . . . IT'S SO FUNNY. NIGGER CRAZY! Ha, ha, ha, ha . . . THE BLACK MAN; THE WORLD AT MY FEET: LOVING ME AND HATING ME. I AM THE POPE . . . THE SAINT . . . THE HOOOOLY MAN. Ha, ha, ha, ha . . . Why do they love me and hate me? I CANNOT DIE. I REFUSE TO DIE. FOR I AM THE BOMB . . . THE CONGREEEEGATION! (*Joyfully.*) SING, BROTHERS, SING! SING ON, YOU FUNKY NIGGERS! ONLY YOU CAN SAVE THEM! Ha, ha, ha, ha . . . (*Sings.*) "Oh, when the Saints go marching in. Oh, when the Spooks go marching in. Oh, Lord, I want to be in that number, when those NIGGERS go marching in. Ha, ha, ha, ha . . .

(*He repeats the singing and then overlaps into laughing again. Enter the sound of chimes; the gong quality of death chimes.*)

MATT (*screaming, overlapping the singing*): Boy! What the hell's the matter with you? Nate! Nate! What the hell you doing? Nate, for God's sake, stop it. Shut up! Stop it! You hear me? I said STOP IT! (*Bitterly.*) You sorry sonuvabitch! Bum! No good bum! You're no brother of mine. You're a goddamn animal. An ANIMAL! ANIMALLLLLL . . . Who the hell you think you are? What gives you the right to condemn any goddamn body? Sonuvabitch!

NATE (*overlapping*): Ha, ha, ha, ha, ha . . . Yeah! Gotta go, baby! Gotta die! Gotta be freeee . . . Ha, ha, ha, ha . . . Like that's the way, baby. That's the only way.

JUDE (*still in darkness*): Ha, ha, ha, ha . . . Tell him, son. Tell him the way it is.

NATE: Like man, I got it all figured out.

(*The lights open on* JUDE.)

JUDE: My boy! I hear my son. Tell him, son. Speak the truth, son. Ha, ha, ha, ha . . .

MATT: My boy! I hear my son. Tell him, son. Speak the truth, son. Ha, ha, ha, ha . . . (*Overlapping* JUDE.) Oh, my God! Daddy, will you get out of here.

NATE (*in a preaching manner—in the old Southern Baptist tradition*): Like, man, if they call me for some fucking examination, I'll show them. I'll be ready. I'm gonna spend two weeks just letting this kinky hair of mine grow like it's never grown before.

JUDE: Ha, ha, ha, ha . . . Speak, son. Tell him, son. Glory hallelujah!

NATE: And I'm not going to get a haircut for damn near two months before that white man's examination. TWO MONTHS! YOU HEAR ME? And I ain't crazy. I ain't nobody's fool. (*The sound of the woman's cries enter again. The sound of the heartbeat and chimes intensify.*) They say all niggers are wild animals anyway. And, boy, I'm not going to take a bath for two weeks. Boy, am I gonna stink. Am I gonna stink!

JUDE: Ha, ha, ha, ha . . . You shore is, son. Amen! Hallelujah!

MATT: Daddy, will you shut up?

NATE (*overlapping*): Then . . . I ain't gonna shave for a week and a whole half.

JUDE: Aaaaamen! Preach the word! He's lost, son. Preach the word. Save your brother. They're after him. Save your brother before it's too late.

NATE: And when I go for that white man's examination,

344

I'm gonna wear clothes I'd have left in the alley for another week.

JUDE (*bursting hysterically*): Ha, ha, ha, ha, ha, ha, ha . . .

MATT (*overlapping*): Oh, my God! My God! My God!

NATE: And the rats and roaches will have laid at least a million baby rats and roach eggs. And them eggs will just be a-sticking to them clothes. Ha, ha, ha, ha . . .

JUDE (*chanting*):

> I've been buked and I've been scorned.
> I've been buked and I've been scorned.
> I've been talked about sho' as you born.

(*Repeats a second time.*)

NATE (*overlapping, still in the preaching manner*): But first . . . I'll take them clothes and throw them back into the smutch pot and START THAT FIRE . . . START THAT FIRE!

JUDE (*bursting gloriously; with revelation*): START THAT FIRE, SON! START THAT FIRE! Ha, ha, ha, ha, ha . . .

MATT (*overlapping*): Nate, don't . . . please, don't . . .

NATE: And I'll just let them clothes soak all the goddamn day!

JUDE (*chanting*):

> There is trouble all over this world.
> There is trouble all over this world.
> There is trouble all over this world.

(*Repeats a second time.*)

NATE (*overlapping*): And those rats and roaches will just dissolve all PRETTY-LIKE into a beautiful RED . . . GREEN . . . BLUE . . . BLACK! And when them clothes are dry, I'll just throw them back into the alley so that the rat and roach community can sing praises to their dearly beloved ones who are now singing praises in the rat and roach heaven ABOVE! Ha, ha, ha, ha, ha . . .

JUDE (*joyfully*): Ha, ha, ha, ha, ha . . . Tell him, son! Tell him the word! The God's truth! (*Chanting again.*)

> There is trouble all over this world.
> There is trouble all over this world.
> There is trouble all over this world.

(JUDE *will chant the lyrics to the spiritual throughout the remainder of* NATE's *monologue. The chanting is broken by occasional outbursts of spirited laughter.*)

NATE (*overlapping* JUDE, *still in the preaching manner*): And, Daddy . . . just before the actual examination . . . I'm gonna sneak around to the toilet. Ha, ha, ha, ha, ha . . . And

345

I'm gonna have milk and crackers and crumble them and mix them up all together in a real pretty slimy mess and put um in the commode, Daddy. Oh, yes, I am . . . straight into the commode.

JUDE: That's right, son. Tell him, son. Tell him the word, son.

NATE (*almost in desperate response to* JUDE's *sickening enlightenment*): And, DADDYYYYEEEE . . .

JUDE (*quickly, spasmodically*): Yeah, son? Yeah, son? What is it, boy? What is it, son?

NATE (*resoundingly, pitifully*): DADDYYYYYEEEEE . . .

JUDE (*frightfully*): Easy, son. Easy now. Your daddy's here, boy. I'm here. Easy, son.

NATE (*bitterly, yet with passion*): And, Daddy . . . Oh, Daddy (*Near tears.*), if they tell me that (*Struggling for words.*) that I passed that examination . . .

JUDE (*expectantly*): That's right, son! That's right! Tell him, son! Precious Lord! Ha, ha, ha . . .

NATE (*abruptly—and breaking from the preaching mood to a dead serious manner*): Like why should I let myself be taken by a bunch of white brass to fight for something that ain't really mine? With all my troubles just staying alive in this fucking place . . . I, I, don't give a damn if these Vietnamese or any of them wanna play cowboys and Indians with these bastards. (*Now bursting again.*) LIKE I'M GONNA RUN; SCREAMING AND CARRYING ON; STRAIGHT INTO THE TOILET. I'M GONNA FLY INTO THAT TOILET AND GET ON MY KNEES AND START A-PRAYING AND CARRYING ON LIKE I NEVER DONE BEFORE.

JUDE (*fearfully*): No, son. No. No. No, son. No. No, son. No. No. No.

MATT (*at the breaking point, bursting*): GOOD LORD! MY GOD! MY GOD! HELP US ALL. (*Bitterly, very bitterly.*) ANIMALLL! (*To* NATE.) YOU ANIMALLLLL! OH, DEAR GOD! STRIKE THIS, THIS, THIS THING DEAD! DEAD! LET HIS SOUL ROT IN HELL FROM WHENCE HE HAS COME! (*To* NATE.) HELL'S DAMNATIONS TO YOUUUUU. YOU THING! HELL'S DAMNATIONS TO YOU! ANIMALLLLLL! HELL'S DAMNATIONS TO YOU!

(*All sounds stop—heartbeat, chimes, cries; all stop abruptly. There is a second of absolute silence over which* JUDE's *chanting overlaps.*)

JUDE (*as if searching; prying deeply into the inner depths of something about* NATE *which is over and beyond his grasp*):

I've been buked and I've been scorned.
I've been buked and I've been scorned.
I've been buked and I've been scorned.
(*Repeats a second time.*)

NATE (*with passion, pathetically, overlapping* JUDE *as he chants the second time*): My soul will rot in hell. HELL . . . HELLLL . . . HELL! I must be looking for hell—hell or someplace. If I had to choose between heaven and hell, I think I'd choose hell. Heaven . . . Heaven would probably be this rotten, stinking world all over again. Don't think I could buck it a second time. Don't think I could take it. Couldn't take it.

(*From offstage: a loud piercing scream—and then a dirgeful moaning sound; a lament of relief, freedom. And then a second of quiet.*)

NATE (*puzzled*): What . . . what the hell's going on?

(*Offstage: the sound of a baby crying; beautiful, tender. The lights open on* MARTHA *and* BONITA.)

MARTHA (*excitedly*): Oh, Matt, Matt . . . A boy! A boy! A little boy!

BONITA (*weary, exhausted, but reveling*): Well, I'll be darn. I never want to go through that again. Nate . . . How about that? A fiery little devil and cute too. Congratulations!

(*The baby's cries continue to curtain.*)

NATE (*matter-of-factly*): Congratulations . . . for what?

MARTHA: Matt . . . you mean you haven't told him? Oh, my God, no! Nate, honey . . . the little girl . . . the little white girl . . . what's her name? You're a father, boy. You're a father.

(JUDE *begins laughing in a rather teasing manner. The laughter will build up and reach a resounding crescendo at darkness.*)

NATE: Father! She's here. (*Slight pause.*) A father! Hmph! Ain't that a bitch! That's tough! Hmph! Tough shit! Tough shit!

JUDE (*screamingly*): Ha, ha, ha, ha, ha, ha, ha . . . Hallelujah! Ha, ha, ha, ha, ha, ha, ha . . .

(*The sound of the baby's crying intensifies. Lights slowly fade out. Darkness.*)

CURTAIN

Ododo

A MUSICAL EPIC IN TWO ACTS
Book and Lyrics by JOSEPH A. WALKER

Joseph A. Walker received his B.A. in philosophy at Howard University and his M.F.A. in drama at Catholic University in Washington, D.C., where he acted the leading roles in a number of productions, including *Prometheus Bound* and *Othello*. After arriving in New York in 1965 he became a member of Voices, Inc. There he co-authored, designed the set, and played the leading role in the Off-Broadway production of *The Believers* in 1968. In December of 1969 the Negro Ensemble Company opened its season with a production of his play *The Harangues*.

ACT I

(*The setting is abstract, consisting of a bare stage. Gigantic African symbols dangle up right and up left—dominated by the love symbol. A scrim stretched across the upstage wall separates the musicians from the playing area. The musicians have individual spots directed upon them so that they may be seen when deemed necessary. The scrim is also lighted from the front. There are times, therefore, when the musicians are not seen. There is a platform in front of the scrim. The* MUSICIANS: *a bassist, a trap drummer, a conga drummer, an electric guitarist, and a pianist.*

The PERFORMERS *will be designated arbitrarily by letters of the alphabet. All the* MEN *are costumed in a rich reddish brown, gold-streaked daishikis and colorful contrasting African print, bell-bottom pants. They wear medallions and beads.* ACTOR L, *who is also the lead singer and conjuror, wears a purple, green-streaked daishiki and contrasting African print, bell-bottom pants. Around his neck he wears a set of bells.*

The WOMEN *wear colorful red and blue African blouses* [bubas] *with matching orange-red, floor-length culottes. The* WOMEN *also wear beads and medallions. All the actors wear bells on their legs. The men's bells are heavier in pitch.*

The time is before the beginning of time.

At rise the stage is vacant and completely dark. ACTOR L *enters. He circumnavigates the entire stage. He improvises an eerie melody as he walks. From time to time he stops and plays runs on a flute. The singer is invoking the spirits of life's beginnings. He calls them to return and show again the start of creation. The* SINGER *ends up stage center. He makes a weird sound—an invoking sound—and immediately an electric guitar and bass are heard in answer. Blue lights fade up. The* SINGER *makes another sound and the piano answers; another call and the flute answers; another, and African drums answer.*

Joseph A. Walker

The music fades as the SINGER *raises his hands in a final gesture and a final call—more distinctive than the others.*

At this cue, the ACTORS *file onstage, passing between each other. The* ACTORS *are the spirits of the beginnings of man, and they move as if not quite awake from a million years of slumber. They take weird but restful positions onstage. There is a pause, after which the actor down left—*ACTOR M*—begins making cosmic sound of reawakening.)*

ACTOR M: Sh-sh, sh-sh . . . sh-sh, sh-sh . . .

ACTOR G (*stuttering*): Uh uh uh uh uh uh uh uh—

(ACTOR G *rises from floor and begins to move, slowly at first, then faster. He completely circles the stage and as he reaches* ACTORS *they fall in behind him with their own sounds. Soon the entire group becomes a moving circle, and the cosmic sounds build to a high pitch. All sound ceases and* ACTORS *freeze for a beat before they chant the following lines and move into a half-circle position around the stage.)*

ALL: Africa is the cradle of all creation. (*Everyone again freezes, then raise hands to the sky as they sing the following.*) E-E-E-E—AH-AH-AH-AH!

(*All bodies drop to a limp position; music accompaniment cues* ACTORS *to African theme, which* ACTORS *come up to a standing position singing on an AH syllable. The* WOMEN *immediately go into a musical round to give an echo-effect to the following lines.)*

ACTRESS J (*as was said, each of her lines is repeated by each* WOMAN *in company.* ACTRESS J *begins each phrase on pitch*):

In the beginning	(WOMEN *repeat in round.*)
God created the heavens	(WOMEN *repeat.*)
And the earth	(WOMEN *repeat.*)
And the earth was without form	(WOMEN *repeat.*)
And void	(WOMEN *repeat.*)
And darkness was upon the face of the deep.	(WOMEN *repeat.*)

ACTOR J: And God stepped out on space . . .

WOMEN (*singing*): Space . . .

ACTOR W: And he looked around and he said, "I'm lonely . . ."

WOMEN (*singing*): Lonely . . .

ACTOR W: I'll make me a world!

ACTRESS M (*in African accent*): In the beginning, Kabezya Mpungu had four children: Sun, Moon, Darkness, and Rain.

ACTOR A: In the beginning, Kabezya Mpungu, the King of Gods, created the sky, the earth, man and woman. To man

350

and woman He gave the gift of reason. He did not however
give them a heart. In the beginning, Kabezya Mpungu, the
God of Gods, had four children: Sun— (*points to* ACTOR J.)
Moon— (*Points to* ACTRESS L.) Darkness— (*To* ACTOR W.)
and Rain—. (*To* ACTRESS M.) He gathered them all together
and said to them, "I must go now to my home in the sky, but
first I would like to know how you plan to treat my creatures.
You, Sun, tell me what you plan to do!"

ACTOR J (*proudly*): I intend to shine hotly, and burn everything beneath me.

ACTOR A: "And what about you, Rain?"

ACTRESS M (*sinisterly*): I will fall forever and make the
earth one great ocean.

ACTOR A: "And what about you, Moon and Darkness?"

ACTRESS L *and* ACTOR W: We intend to rule together—continually.

ACTOR A: "Ah, my children," said Kabezya Mpungu, "how
do you expect my creatures to live if you act so foolishly?
First, Sun, you must shine a little and dry the earth. Then you
must give Rain a chance to cool and water the earth. And you,
Moon and Darkness, you must take turns with Sun so that my
creatures may have time to sleep. Now I must go . . . (*Company motions toward him, and sighs disappointedly.*) But I
will send down Heart in My place." And so Kabezya Mpungu
left the earth in care of his children. Soon after, Heart came
down to earth in a small container and Heart cried without
ceasing:

VILLAGERS (*singing*): Where is our father, Kabezya
Mpungu?

ACTOR A: Sun, Moon, Darkness, and Rain cried also.

HIS CHILDREN (*singing*): Where is our father, Kabezya
Mpungu?

ACTOR A: Finally Heart said, "Since man has no heart, and
since he is the greatest of my father's creatures, I will enter
into man and wait the return of my father." And so he did.
From that time, all children born of man possess a heart which
is in reality—a longing for the return of God.

(*Company applauds and congratulates the storyteller.*)

ACTRESS M: Look! The moon is full. Time to put the children to bed.

(*A* WOMAN *starts clapping a definite rhythm. The* MEN *pantomime holding a baby as the* WOMEN *begin singing the following African lullaby.*)

WOMEN (*singing as they move*):
    Yeke omo mi, omo mi yeke.   (Oh, do not cry,
       my little treasure)

(MEN *begin swaying to music as they gradually go to the floor, place imaginary baby on floor and scold it—all in tempo as* WOMEN *continue to sing.*)

Yeke omo mi, omo yeke.   Emi mi ni iyare.
(For here is your mother)

(MEN *take babies to* WOMEN *as* WOMEN *continue to sing.* WOMEN *take babies to positions around stage and pantomime putting them to sleep as they sing.* MEN *gather center stage and converse with each other in Swahili:* Hujambo! Sijambo! Kazuri, Kazuri, *and other ad-libs.*)

Yeke omo mi, omo mi yeke. Emi ni iyare.
Yeke omo mi, omo yeke.

Oto omo mi, omo mi oto   (Oh, hushabye,
   my little treasure)
Oto omo mi, omo mi oto. Emi ni babare
(For here is your father)

Oto omo mi, omo mi oto.   Emi ni babare.
Yeke omo mi, omo mi oto . . .

ACTRESS M: Beautiful! They are all asleep!

MEN (*softly nodding*): Kazuri! Kazuri!

NARRATOR: Let us pour a libation to Ogun, God of contracts and covenants. Let us pour this libation to Ogun in honor of Olugbala and Ifetayo! Let us call their names to the fields.

COMPANY (*chants*): Olugbala! Ifetayo!

NARRATOR: Let us whisper their names through the tall elephant grass.

COMPANY: Olugbala! Ifetayo!

NARRATOR: And through the waterfalls and to the top of the Rima tree. Let us cup our hands and blow their names through the mouth of the calabash and carry the calabash on the heads of our women and dance to the drum and sing to the kora with their names on our heads. And the dundun, the drum that talks, let it shout their names to the mountains and the sun and the stars and the sky itself. Let us dance a poem and sing a vision with their names swaying and bouncing in the calabash on the heads of our beautiful, budding black maidens. Let our children draw their names through the nipples of their contented mothers.

COMPANY: Olugbala! Ifetayo!

NARRATOR: Everything in life is foretold! Only it takes a person with special eyes to read the telling. Thus it was foretold that Olugbala would be born with a veil over the length

of his body and that he would be endowed with such special eyes.

COMPANY (*raises imaginary baby*): Olugbala!

NARRATOR (WOMAN): Thus it was foretold in dreams and ancestral bones and the dry rattles of the sacred gourds, two generations before, that Oba our king would have seven sons and nine daughters and that the ninth daughter would be called Ifetayo, which means love excels all. It was foretold that she would be so lovely that when she walked all the women of the village would try to imitate her walk and when she paused they too would pause . . . (*The* NARRATOR *walks.* WOMEN *imitate her. She pauses.* WOMEN *pause in like manner.*) But when she smiled the women would cover their faces in envy.

COMPANY: Ifetayo! Ifetayo!

NARRATOR (MAN): It was foretold that Olugbala . . .

COMPANY: Olugbala!

NARRATOR (MAN): Would not know the love of a woman until he was two and seventy years.

NARRATOR (WOMAN): And that Ifetayo, who would then be ten and five, would be his first and only love.

NARRATOR (MAN): And on that day, the mountains would shudder . . .

NARRATOR (WOMAN): And dissolve into soft billowing clouds, that the sea would sing a song . . . (COMPANY *chants in rising crescendo the word* Yemaya *which means goddess of the sea and mother of the other gods.*) I say the sea would sing a song as it rises to replace the sky. (*Chanting fades.*)

NARRATOR (MAN): And that the drums would tell Obantala —the creator—that his world had been turned upside-down. (*Chanting rises, fades down and under.*) And Olugbala became a great priest and men listened to the young Olugbala, for they knew that nothing lingered with his words but the truth. And men praised the old Olugbala for it had been said that he was so loved by the Obantala that even the treacherous leopards purred when he walked among them. Olugbala grew so great that Oba, the king, came to look upon him as his second father and would not attend a ceremony unless Olugbala was there to conduct the drummers and announce the arrival of the gods.

COMPANY: Olugbala! Dance a poem and sing a vision to Olugbala. (COMPANY *does short, stylized dance.*)

NARRATOR (WOMAN): But the king's daughter, Ifetayo, it had been prophesied, would marry Olugbala when she was ten and five and he two and seventy. Oba spoke of his fear to Olugbala, whom he loved as a father, but Olugbala said nothing. Oba, therefore, decreed that none of the prophecy would

353

ever reach the ears of his ninth daughter, Ifetayo. And as she approached her fifteenth year she was to be guarded night and day. She was not even to converse with her own sisters and brothers. For she was not to marry Olugbala. She was to marry Akin. It had been agreed upon before Ifetayo was born.

COMPANY: Ifetayo! Dance a poem and sing a vision to Ifetayo. (COMPANY *dances short, stylized dance.*)

NARRATOR (MAN): When Olugbala reached two and seventy, he had all of his belongings taken to the mountains— to a beautiful silver-streaked cavern in the mountains, and there it was said he sang and played the kora and spoke with his ancestors. And there it is said he waited for Ifetayo.

NARRATOR (WOMAN): Three days before Ifetayo reached her fifteenth year, Oba's lovely daughter fell into a sleep— deep as the core of the earth itself—and she slept for three days and nights. And the king brought in his men of medicine, his seers and prophets. They all knew the answer; it had been foretold. But they were afraid to tell Oba. These wise men knew that Ifetayo was dreaming. That in her dreams Olugbala sat crosslegged in a silver-streaked cavern and spoke to her. These wise men knew that she would awaken on the fourth day, which marked her fifteenth year, that she would bathe under the waterfall, spread the scent of flowers over her body, adorn the wedding garments, and go not to her wedding with Akin, but to the mountains where her beloved who was two and seventy awaited her.

NARRATOR (MAN): The people lined the village. People from other villages came and squatted on the great ridge before the mountain.

COMPANY: Do not go, Ifetayo. Please do not go. We will miss the mystery of your eyes and the glow of your spirit. Do not go. He is much too old.

NARRATOR (WOMAN): The queen poured libations mingled with tears.

NARRATOR (MAN): Oba, the king, told them not to interfere. It was impossible to make bargains with fate. His eyes retreated into his soul, and he said no more.

NARRATOR (WOMAN): Ifetayo passed the ridge without seeing anyone or anything but Olugbala, squatting, his great shoulders erect, his eyes closed, waiting for her. The people did not obey their king. Their hearts were too full.

COMPANY (*running to another position*): Do not go, Ifetayo. We will miss your smile, your burnished copper skin, your dancing hands. He is much too old.

NARRATOR (MAN): Ifetayo did not hear them. Her long brown legs caressed the earth as she walked. She stood before

the mountain. Her black eyes wide, housing all the suns of the universe, on her round lips a chant of love and sighs. (COMPANY *begins* Yemaya *chant underneath.*) A stinging strangeness in her heart, a wild ache in her breasts. For Olugbala had waited for two and seventy.

COMPANY (*one last effort*): Do not go! Ifetayo. We love you! You will never come back if you go. It has been foretold. He is much too old.

NARRATOR (WOMAN): Olugbala frowned from inside the cavern, and the mountain opened up to receive his young wife.

NARRATOR (MAN): The mountains shuddered, dissolved into soft billowy clouds, and Ifetayo walked in while the sea sang a song as it replaced the blue of the sky, and the drums told Obantala—the creator—that his world stood on its head. Then the mountain closed.

NARRATOR (WOMAN): It was foretold that no one would ever see Olugbala or Ifetayo after that.

COMPANY: Let us dance a poem and sing a vision to the fierce determination of love. (*Sings.*)

> Love is a magic you can't deny
> It's in the ocean
> It's in the sky
>
> We are the children of Mother Earth
> She set in motion
> The act of birth
>
> Love's been around a long long time
> Before the mountains
> Began their climb
>
> Never, never say no to love
> Never try to stop the flow of love
> Never think you know the might of love
> Never try to win a fight with love.
>
> Love is a magic you can't deny
> It's in the ocean
> It's in the sky.

(COMPANY *executes a stylized dance of love.*)

NARRATORS: Nyeusi! (*Swahili word for "black."*)

COMPANY (*shouts*): Nyeusi! (*Music with Nyeusi—Swahili word for blackness—theme comes in under as* COMPANY *moves toward audience with great pride and forms two broken lines at foot of stage—*MEN *in the rear.* COMPANY *pauses and stares at the audience, then speaks in unison the following.*) Why do we revel in these things? Surely blacks have no

tales to tell. Surely blacks are without roots, without culture, without . . . wisdom.

ACTRESSES Y *and* J (*imitating Southern belles, giggling*): Africans do like to talk, however.

COMPANY: Even if what they say is nonsense.

ACTRESS L: The ruin of a nation begins in the homes of its people.

ACTRESS D: The friends of our friends are our friends.

ACTRESS Y: A cow gave birth to a fire. She tried to lick it, but it burned. She wanted to leave it, but she could not because it was her own child.

ACTRESS J: By the time the fool has learned the game, the players have gone away.

ACTRESS E: When a man is coming toward you, you need not say come here.

ACTRESS M: Love is like a baby. It needs to be treated tenderly.

WOMEN (*shouting*): NYEUSI! (*They turn upstage and kneel.*)

MEN (*shouting*): NYEUSI!

ACTOR W: A log may remain ten years in water, but it will never become a crocodile.

ACTOR H: He who dances badly will say that the drum is bad.

ACTOR M: What is said over the dead lion's body could not have been said if he were alive.

ACTOR A: Two birds argued over a grain of corn, when a third bird swooped down and carried it off.

ACTOR J: When you are rich, you are hated, when you are poor you are despised.

ACTOR L: Those who are absent are always wrong.

ACTOR G: When spider webs unite, they can tie up a lion.

COMPANY: Surely blacks have no tales to tell. Surely blacks are without roots, without culture, without . . . wisdom.

WOMEN (*Nyeusi theme fades as women rise and sing*): NYEUSI! (WOMEN *move through* MEN *and form dance positions as* MEN *move stage right and left and remove their daishikis which they hang on hooks provided on stage left and right flats.*) NYEUSI!

(WOMEN *dance to Nyeusi music. At the end of the dance the* WOMEN *go to kneeling positions on the floor. They yell in rhythm:* N—YE—U—SI *as they place hands on the floor. This is the cue for the* MEN *to come out in rhythm and dance. At the end of the dance* ACTOR M *does a solo dance which increases in tempo until he ends it with a leap. The rhythm slows down to a speech tempo as* ACTOR M, *who has not stopped*

moving, yells: N—YE—U—SI, *at which point the* WOMEN *form a circle around him. The following is chanted in strict tempo.*)

ACTOR M (*shouting*): AFRICA, THE OLD . . .

COMPANY: ANCIENT!

ACTOR M: THE NILE IS OLD . . .

COMPANY: ANCIENT!

ACTOR M: THE NIGER IS OLD . . .

COMPANY: MALI, SONGHAY, TIMBUKTU, GHANA

ACTOR M: TEN THOUSAND YEARS OLDER . . .

COMPANY: TEN THOUSAND

ACTOR M: THAN EUROPE'S OLDEST . . .

COMPANY: THAN EUROPE'S (*Pause.*) CIVILIZATION.

ACTOR M: VALUES . . .

COMPANY: OF THE SPIRIT . . . OF THE SOUL

ACTOR M: BECAME . . .

COMPANY: THE SUPREME VALUES

ACTOR M: WHILE EUROPE CULTIVATED . . .

COMPANY: AH, HER CATHEDRALS
AH, HER MACHINES
AH, HER SCIENCE . . .

ACTOR M: WE . . .

COMPANY: WE CULTIVATED THE SOUL, SOUL, SOUL . . .

(Soul *is repeated softly in rhythm while the* WOMEN *take up* Yeke Omo Mi *under.* MEN *take their* WOMEN, *wave goodbye and go to their positions on the floor. They settle down to sleep.*)

ACTOR A (*walking toward the audience*): We lay down to rest; strangers come amongst us . . . (*actors sit upright, startled. The* MEN *move up left as if to protect their* WOMEN. *The* MEN *then move center stage as if to confer*) seeking food and shelter for the night. And since our hearts—in our lack of culture—have always been open; and since our homes, in our lack of culture—have always been open—we took them into our hearts and our homes. The wise old mothers of the village said:

WOMEN: How can there be men who are not the color of earth, for surely all men sprang from the earth.

ACTRESS Y: It must be an illness, a disease.

WOMEN: Let us take them in and nourish them that they may again return to the rich brown of Mother Earth, of whom surely they are children.

ACTOR A: The wise old fathers of the village said simply:

MEN: They are men. We will take them in.

ACTRESS Y: So we gave them our fire . . . (COMPANY *ges-*

357

tures in unison to indicate fire.*) And our cassava . . . (COM-
PANY *gestures.*) And the meat of the waterbuck . . . (MEN
throw imaginary spears.) And our kola nuts . . . (COMPANY
gestures.) And our village returned to its slumbers. When we
awoke to see the sun, we found that we could not stretch our
limbs because our hands were tied. Our whole village was
tied. (COMPANY *pantomimes trying to free hands.* COMPANY
*then rises to knees, looks around in stark terror. All through
this sequence, the* COMPANY *makes sounds of horror.*) Our
hearts were tied.

COMPANY (*angrily to audience*): So first they took our hospitality and then they took us. (COMPANY *falls back to floor
in dejected exhaustion, but musical sounds of severe whipping
come in immediately. In agony, the* COMPANY *scrambles to
feet. The* WOMEN *are forcibly separated from their* MEN. *The*
WOMEN *end stage right, hands crossed as if in chains. The*
MEN *end stage left in the same manner. The* COMPANY *sways
and sings* Yea, yea, yea, yea. *The* MEN *raise their torsos to an
upright position and begin speaking. The* Yea's *provide the
background.*)

MEN: We are separated from our women.

ACTOR W: We are forced to lie naked on the floor, on the
damp floor, a floor which reeks of human waste.

MEN: We cannot move.

ACTOR A: We are chained to the floor.

(MEN *open arms and lock them across their waists as if
they are chained to each other.*)

MEN: We cannot move.

ACTOR A: Our brothers are so close that our sweat inter-
mingles. We are forced to do everything . . .

MEN: Eat, sleep, relieve ourselves—all in this one spot.

ACTOR A: The stench is human, and so inhuman.

ACTOR W: At night there are rats, the size of which we
have never seen before. They are wise. They must have learned
that human flesh is nourishing and that our feet are the most
defenseless part of us.

ACTOR A: At night there are rats and above the screams of
those being eaten by the rats, we hear yet other screams.
(WOMEN *give a musical scream.*) They come from our women.

MEN: We are separated from our women. (MEN *bend and
take up the swaying as they start the* Yea's *as the* WOMEN *rise
to speak.*)

WOMEN: We are separated from our husbands, our lovers,
our sons. We are chained also to the floor underneath the
place where the crew lives. This morning Nelaja had her baby.
They took her baby and threw him overboard. They did not

wish to take care of a baby. Nelaja has not stopped crying. At night there are rats, but they are human. Or so we think. They take the youngest for their pleasure. They took Folami for their captain. What is a captain? She is a princess. She is proud. She would not eat. The Captain used a very sharp knife to force her lips apart so that she would eat. The girls are screaming. Folami can be heard above the others. Now she returns. Her lips are bleeding, so is her back, but what bleeds most is her heart—pledged to Adejola, who is the son of our king. At night there are rats, but they are human, or so we think.

(*Music for "How Far Can a Ship Sail" swells.* ACTOR L *moves center stage.*)

ACTOR L (*sings*):
> How far can a ship sail
> Underneath a moon that is too pale,
> On a dead sea of tears and blood?
>
> How far can a ship sail
> Underneath a sky where the winds fail,
> On a dead sea of tears and blood?
>
> Propelled only by the breeze of a labored breath,
> Crying, sighing, moaning, dying . . .
> In the stillness of a sea which is red.

MEN: The crew, having finished with our mothers, our sisters, our wives, and our lovers . . .

ACTOR A: The crew dreams of Virginia and Georgia and Mississippi, drugged with West Indian rum, not knowing that a valuable piece of black merchandise named Adejola has pulled himself free and is now freeing his brothers. We pull . . . one . . . then two . . . then three . . . then four . . . then many, many more.

(*Actors move across the stage to the* WOMEN. *They move stealthily and silently. They pantomime freeing their* WOMEN, *at which point the* MEN *break away in anger—attention now focused on the mutiny.* ADEJOLA—ACTOR J—*gives the signal and moves in a circle. The* COMPANY *also moves in a circle, signifying coming on the deck of a ship. The* MEN *spread out and take positions of battle. The* WOMEN *take positions next to them. All this time eerie music in the foreground has set the mood. At this point the music swells.*)

ACTRESS Y: Silently our strongest warriors strangle the members of the crew who sleep on deck. (MEN *pantomime strangling with chains.*) Someone shouts. We turn and see the fire leaping from where the crew sleeps. They try to escape the fire, but we kill them with the chains fastened to our

359

wrists, with marlin spikes, with machetes—with our bare hands. (*Each method of killing is illustrated with pantomime.*)

ACTRESS M: They are all dead now, but the fire . . . we have another fight . . . the fire! (COMPANY *runs to and fro across the stage, stops in one position.*) It sears us, it scorches our naked bodies. (COMPANY *takes agonizing postures and freeze.*) Still we try to put it out. Many fall, and we are not able to drag them from the fire . . . but we are victorious . . . but then, but then we see in the moonlight, we see the water rising. The ship sinks. (*Great confusion about the stage.*) The fire has eaten away the hull. The ship sinks. Adejola pacifies us. He tells us we must die in peace and dignity. We await death now. (COMPANY *takes positions of rest on the stage.*)

ACTRESS J: Folami and Adejola hold each other. They hold each other and dream.

COMPANY: We all dream. We dream of a land, a beautiful land, where sky, earth, water, and all living things belong to each other because they are all one. Some of us dream of holding hands and flying back to this land—to Africa. And all because strangers came to take our hospitality and then tried to take us.

COMPANY *and* SOLOIST (*sings*):
> I will arise out of the sea
> No sea will roll over me
> It's not so deep
> It cannot keep
> Nothing but this shell
> Which has always been a cell
> To hide me away from the sun
>
> I will arise out of the sea
> I will burst through the foam
> And meet the sky
> And greet the sun
> Wrap myself in a cloud
> And fly back home
>
> I will arise out of the flame
> There is no way a fire can claim
> More than this life
> What is this life?
> Nothing but a spark
> Shining in the dark
> To guide me away from the sun

COMPANY:
> No one will see me as I stand tall in the waterfall
> As a blade of grass I dance in the wind

As the root of the mangrove tree
As a trickle in the stream
My ageless soul will dream

Death is nothing but a door
To godliness
And nothing more

I will arise,
I will arise

I will arise
I will arise, etc.
(*They stand and face down right, proudly.*)

END OF ACT ONE

ACT II

(*Same as Act I. Actors come on in darkness and form diamond position with* MEN *on the outside and* WOMEN *in three
parallel lines inside the diamond. Lights come up and first line
of* WOMEN *start singing and moving to the right in unison.*)

FIRST LINE OF WOMEN (*singing and moving*):
Let me tell you 'bout slavery
And what it did to you and me.

SECOND LINE OF WOMEN (*singing and moving left while
first line continues under*):
Tell it like it is!

THIRD LINE OF WOMEN (*singing and moving to right while
first and second line continue singing under*):
They will weep from what they reap
'Cause Little Bo Peep ain't never had no sheep.

MEN (*singing and moving arms in stylized strength while*
WOMEN *continue to sing and move as stated*):
We been fighting, we been fighting, we been fighting,
For a long, long time.

ACTOR L (*sings as* COMPANY *continues individual lines and
movement*):
I will arise out of the flame
There is no way a fire can claim
More than this life
What is this life?
Nothing but a spark
Shining in the dark
To guide me away from the sun

(*Music fades momentarily then resumes: first line of the*
WOMEN, *then second line, then third line, then line of* MEN—

all as COMPANY *moves into position of a deep "V." As last chord of music fades* ACTRESS M *steps into center spot.*)

ACTRESS M: Of course all black people just love watermelon. Everybody knows that.

One day as Master John was riding through the lowlands of his 7,200-acre plantation, he noticed a little black boy—a slave of his—whose name just seemed to slip from his Southern memory. The thing that interested Master John was the fact that the little boy was squatting in the middle of the watermelon patch, hungrily eating a watermelon, juice streaming down his little brown cheeks. Master John couldn't help but find the little boy amusing. He told his pale Southern wife and they had a good laugh. He told his overseer and they had a good laugh. In fact he told all his friends and acquaintances, and they all had a good laugh.

Everybody laughed at the fact that Little Jimmy—four-and-a-half-year-old Little Jimmy who had never seen his real mother—Little Jimmy who had been fed one cup of cornmeal mush once a day since arriving at Master John's plantation three months before: everybody laughed at the fact that Little Jimmy was just about starving to death.

Who knows, Little Jimmy, you just might have started something. You just might be the reason why they say: "All black people just love watermelon." Everybody knows that.

ACTOR J (*moving into spot vacated by* ACTRESS M): Tonight we make love, but afterward Melissa don't sleep, and she will not stop trembling. I pretend to be asleep. There is a low steady knock on the door. I feel Melissa leave my arms. I hear the door close. I follow them. (COMPANY *starts low foreboding sound—as if a hurricane is in the making. The sound builds slowly under as* ACTOR J *continues.*) I take the butcher knife with me. It is very dark, but I hear voices. I move toward the voices. I hear the overseer say, "I'll have his manhood cut away. I'll have your children sold on the auction block tomorrow."

Melissa cries, but this does not stop him. He flings her to the ground. Melissa covers her eyes, but this does not stop him.

His back shines white in the moonlight. He heaves and moans over my Melissa—my Melissa. She sees me; she knows better than to scream. Quickly and smoothly, just as I have always dreamed it, I grab him by the hair . . . (*sound mounts to a peak*) pull back his head, and drag the butcher knife across his throat. The flesh parts. The blood gushes. I pull my Melissa from under him. He roles over, quivering like a slaughtered hog. (*Sound stops.*) We do not sleep. I am still

angry. Melissa is afraid. I learn that this was not the first night. I start to strangle Melissa, but I cannot.

They whip all the men, but no one knows anything. I myself am whipped on four different occasions. They know my temper, but they cannot prove anything.

Melissa is now in her last month of pregnancy. We are very afraid. We pray to our Gods. We even try praying to their Gods. For if the baby is not mine, then they will know . . . they will know.

COMPANY (*as it moves into jury–court positions. The following scene is sung—recitative style—by all actors except* JURY): MURDERER! BLACK BEAST! ANIMAL! HANG HIM! HANG HIM!

ACTOR A: HOW DOES YOUR DEFENDANT PLEAD?

ACTOR W (ATTORNEY): NOT GUILTY, YOUR HONOR.

COMPANY: NOT GUILTY. HOW CAN HE PLEAD NOT GUILTY?

ACTOR L: IT'S JUST THAT I DON'T FEEL GUILTY.

ACTOR A: YOU MAY PROCEED WITH THE QUES-TIONING.

ACTOR H: IS IT NOT TRUE THAT YOU PLANNED YOUR SAVAGE MURDERS THE FOURTH OF JULY?

ACTOR A: ANSWER THE QUESTION!

ACTOR L: THE REVOLT WAS PLANNED FOR THE FOURTH, YES.

ACTOR H: HOW DARE YOU PERVERT THE MOST SACRED DAY IN THE HISTORY OF THIS GREAT COUNTRY?

ACTOR L: IT WAS MY OWN LITTLE JOKE.

COMPANY: ANIMAL! WHY WASTE A TRIAL? HANG HIM! HANG HIM!

ACTOR H: IS IT TRUE THAT YOUR FIRST VICTIMS WERE YOUR OWN MASTER, HIS WIFE AND CHIL-DREN?

ACTOR L: YES.

ACTOR H: YOUR MASTER WAS THE GENTLEST, MOST CONSIDERATE GENTLEMAN IN THE STATE OF VIRGINIA. WHAT INSANITY DROVE YOU TO SUCH A VILE, VICIOUS, COLD-BLOODED ACT?

ACTOR L: IN MY OPINION, SIR, THERE IS NO SUCH THING AS A CONSIDERATE SLAVEMASTER.

ACTOR H: DO YOU ADMIT TO KILLING 51 INNO-CENT, GOD-FEARING WHITE MEN, WOMEN, AND CHILDREN?

ACTOR L: THAT SOUNDS ABOUT RIGHT.

ACTOR W: YOUR HONOR, MAY I SPEAK, SIR?

363

ACTOR A: YOU MAY.

ACTOR W: THOUGH MY CLIENT ADMITS TO THE AFORESTATED CRIMES, I THINK IT SHOULD BE NOTED THAT THERE WAS NOT A SINGLE INSTANCE OF RAPE . . . NOT ONE.

ACTOR L: YOU CONFUSE REVOLUTION WITH RAPE! PERHAPS IT IS BECAUSE YOU ARE SO FAMILIAR WITH RAPE.

COMPANY: HANG HIM! HANG HIM! INSOLENT NIGGER!

ACTOR A: SILENCE!

ACTOR H: YOUR HONOR, THAT THE DEFENDANT IS GUILTY IS UNCONTESTED, BUT THERE ARE TWO QUESTIONS I'D LIKE TO ASK HIM, WITH THE COURT'S PERMISSION.

ACTOR A: PERMISSION GRANTED.

ACTOR H: WHATEVER POSSESSED YOU, NAT TURNER, A SELF-EDUCATED MAN, A PREACHER, A MAN RESPECTED BY HIS OWN TO THE HIGHEST, WHATEVER POSSESSED YOU TO ATTEMPT SUCH A CRUEL, DESPICABLE VENTURE?

ACTOR L (*singing like Baptist preacher*): GOD IN-STRUCTED ME, SIR.

ACTOR J: GOD!

ACTOR L: THE SPIRIT OF THE LORD APPEARED TO ME AND SAID THE SERPENT WAS LOOSENED, AND CHRIST HAD LAID DOWN THE YOKE HE HAD BORNE FOR THE SINS OF MEN, AND THAT I SHOULD TAKE IT ON AND FIGHT AGAINST THE SERPENT.

ACTOR H: AND WHO IS THE SERPENT?

ACTOR L: WHY YOU ARE, SIR, YOU ARE!

ACTOR A: THIS IS RIDICULOUS! DOES THE DEFEND-ANT HAVE ANYTHING ELSE TO SAY?

ACTOR L: I HAVE, YOUR HONOR. I ADMIT DECLAR-ING WAR ON THE SERPENT, BUT DO MY PEOPLE HAVE TO SUFFER FOR WHAT I DID? THE THOU-SAND OR SO SOLDIERS WHO DEFEATED 71 OF US, DECAPITATED 17 AND TORTURED 20 OTHERS. DUR-ING THE MONTH OF AUGUST, YOU KILLED AT LEAST 10 NEGROES A DAY. THE SERPENT IS INDEED A SNAKE.

COMPANY: MURDERER! HANG HIM! HANG HIM!

ACTOR A: HAVE THE MEMBERS OF THE JURY REACHED THE VERDICT?

ACTOR G (*singing*): WE HAVE, YOUR HONOR. WE FIND THE DEFENDANT

COMPANY (*sings the following to a rock beat as they move from court position back to deep "V" position*):
Guilty, yeah, yeah, yeah.
Guilty, yeah, yeah, yeah.
(*Selected actors add the following.*)
I'm so glad he's guilty, don't you know, don't you know
I'm so glad he's guilty, don't you know.
(*When positions are reached,* COMPANY *punctuates end of "Nat Turner" scene with a rising chord structure of the following.*)
Oh, yeah! Oh, yeah! Oh, yeah!
ACTOR J:
Grandma took me South with her one very hot July.
I carried too much luggage for such a little guy.
"Columbia," yelled the conductor, "is far as we can go.
You'll have to take the bus from here though it's really kinda slow."

Despite all those suitcases we were the first in line,
But the driver held us back like he was waiting for a sign.
Along came a young white girl who got right on the bus.
I said, "Hey there, girl, you can't just bust in front of us."

The driver slapped me 'cross my face and said, "Boy, hush yo' mouth.
Didn't yo' grandma tell you that you is in the South."
The bus filled up with whites from the driver's seat on back.
We stood in the aisles for fifty miles, swinging from the luggage rack.
Grandma, she said nothing, just hummed a little hymn.
Me—well, I was planning how I'd get even with them.
(MEN *begin imitating sound of martial drum as* WOMEN *hum "The Battle Hymn of the Republic" under.* ACTOR M *marches back to his place in the "V" as* ACTOR A *takes the spot.*)
ACTOR A:
Abe Lincoln, a hero?
Hell no, you Negro.
Let me write the books
The way it really looks,
Not just to keep alive
That legendary jive,
But just so I can show
What you call ODODO.

Freed the slave?

365

He'd a put you in your grave
To give this country peace and unity.
It's dumb to say he gave you your liberty.

Emancipation?
So you could help secure the Nation.
He knew that you would help fight the Civil War.
That's what that fancy phony document was for.

Let's not keep alive
That legendary jive.
From 1865 to 1875
The black man's plight was cinched
Thirty-five hundred men, women, and children were
    lynched.

You want a honky hero,
You poor misguided Negro?
Then you'd better recognize,
You'd better canonize
The only one I've found
Lies a-moldering in the ground.

It ain't no mystery.
The man wrote history.
We've never left slavery—
Reconstruction has yet to be.

COMPANY (*sings aloud as they move into same diamond position formed at the beginning of this Act*):
    John Brown's body lies a-moldering in its grave . . .
    (*Music immediately dissolves into "Reconstruction Blues."*)
MEN (*singing and moving in place*):
    I got the Reconstruction blues.
    I got the Reconstruction blues.
WOMEN (*as* MEN *continue their line under,* WOMEN *sing and move in place*):
    RE-CON-STRUC-TION! RE-CON-STRUC-TION!
ACTOR G (*as* COMPANY *continues the two musical lines under,* ACTOR G *sings the following*):
    The Civil War was fought by plan,
    Had nothing to do with the rights of Man.
    The liberty they gave to me
    Forgot about my dignity.
    (*Holds last note as* COMPANY *fades singing.* ACTOR G *sings bridge in clear.*)
    When I go home, it makes me sad,
    Makes me mad, things are so bad.

ODODO

When I go home . . .
I never go home—no more.
MEN (*sing and move as before*) :
I got the Reconstruction blues.
I got the Reconstruction blues.
WOMEN (*sing and move as before*) :
RE-CON-STRUC-TION! RE-CON-STRUC-TION!
ACTOR G (*as before*) :
The Congressmen talked all day long
While bigotry kept growing strong.
I ain't too far from where I started,
Hungry, jobless, and so downhearted.
(COMPANY *fades as before.*)
When I go home, it makes me sad,
Makes me mad, things are so bad.
When I go home . . .
I never go home—no more.
MEN:
I got the Reconstruction blues.
I got the Reconstruction blues.
WOMEN:
RE-CON-STRUC-TION! RE-CON-STRUC-TION!
ACTOR G:
I left the South as soon as I could,
But things up here just ain't that good.
The only reason it's North I stay
Appearances say: "No K . . . K . . . K . . ."?
(*Music swiftly changes to theme utilized at beginning of
Act II—Let me tell you 'bout slavery—undergirded by a
strong rock beat.* MEN *boogaloo to where daishikis were hung
in Act I, don daishikis and boogaloo to automaton positions—
each actor standing perpendicular to an actress. When they
reach these positions, they become automatons and move in
circles of two like doll-machines as they sing the following.*)
COMPANY (*until each couple subscribes a complete circle*) :
Let me tell you 'bout slavery
And what it did to you and me.
ACTOR L (*moving to center spot as music fades under, but
maintains an atmosphere throughout*): Let me tell you 'bout
Luke. Luke is the one who brought all the handshakes to town,
all the shoulder grabs. Luke brought all the buttons. Luke
knows everything in the world. You walk up to Luke and you
say what's going on, Luke? Luke comes on like this: (*Demonstrates* LUKE'S *greeting, burlesque-fashion.*) That's the way
Luke comes on above 110th Street—in Harlem, ya dig? But
when Luke gets downtown? Well, I saw Luke downtown at

Joseph A. Walker

the old Madison Square Garden. Luke forgot his ticket and the officer walked up to Luke and said, "Where's your ticket, boy?" And Luke started in like this: (*Demonstrates severe stammering and stuttering.*) I-I-I-I-I-l-l-lo-los-lost . . .

I dug Luke about to get on a subway after having forgot his token. The man came up and said, "Boy, what you trying to do?" Luke started in something like this: (*Demonstrates severe stammering and stuttering again.*) I-I-I-I-I-f-fo-for-forg-forgo-forgot-m-m-my . . .

What I'm trying to say is, you got to be a man wherever you are.

(*Actors ad-lib approval as* ACTOR L *resumes his automaton position, and again* COMPANY *moves doll-machine fashion while singing.*)

COMPANY:

Let me tell you 'bout slavery

And what it did to you and me.

(COMPANY *repeats procedure between each segment.*)

ACTOR: Like the other day it was my woman's birthday, ya dig, and, well, I had a few coins in my pocket. So I thought we'd make it on over to this here new black restaurant they just opened up on Lenox Avenue. My woman is all giggles, and you know how lovable a black chick gets when she starts giggling. I mean we are cool, you understand, cool, down, together, ya dig. Anyway, my woman orders shish-ke-bob—you understand, one of them Arab dishes. Now, I order pork chops, ya dig. I always believe in being on the safe side. Colored folks can fix them some pork chops, ya dig, but they subject to mess up a good steak 'cause they fixes steak like they ain't sure the cow's dead—and they're trying to burn the rest of the life out of him, dig. Anyway, this cute little old brown waitress with the mean, I mean, mean rippling rear end finally brings us the food. Sure enough there's my pork chops looking sho' nough good, but Betty-Jean's shish-ke-bob ain't right, ya dig. So I call over rippling rear end and I say "This ain't no shish-ke-bab, baby." She say, "Yes it is, baby." And I say, "Then how come it ain't flaming on them little swords." She turns up her nose, rolls her eyes as only a sister can, and she says to me—to me—a basically evil black cat, she says, "Ain't you just like a nigger!" Well now, I stop hitting women long time ago. So I told her to call the manager. Here comes the manager. She's a dark "Negro" chick with a polkadot dress, honky white stockings, and a strawberry wig. And this untogether Sapphire tells me, "I know your game. You just trying to get outta paying." And she runs to get the bouncer. Now when this big ole funny-looking cat comes on the scene

368

I'm counting my wad, ya dig, "One hundred and twenty, one hundred and sixty." All coins I won in Kelly's poolroom Friday night. This cat knows me anyway, knows about that twenty-two automatic I carry in my jacket and the razor I carry in my shoe just for people who make errors. So the cat turns tail and leaves the Wig standing there, false eyelashes drooping to her cheekbones. What I'm running down to ya is this. The honky has taught us the bad habit of assuming. Ripple-behind assumed I was trying to get hinkty just 'cause *she* don't know what shish-ke-bob looks like. The Wig assumed I was a bum. And, do you know, I got mad. I started to snatch that red wig off of her head. I got so mad till you know what I did? I made her pay *me* the price of both meals. Yeah, baby, that honky has taught us a whole bunch of bad habits. He's taught us not to believe anything a black man has to say. He's made us our own worst enemies.

COMPANY (ACTOR A *resumes position*):
    Let me tell you 'bout slavery
    And what it did to you and me.
ACTRESS E (*moves to center spot*):
    Teachers are striking everywhere,
    But, dig it, baby, I don't care
    'Cause ain't nothing happening today—no way.
    You got to be swift!

    In school they got about every kinda rule,
    But rules are made to keep you cool,
    And cool ain't what's happening today—no way.
    You gotta be swift!

    Our teachers number about ninety-five,
    And most of them ain't nothing but jive.
    They got this one Negro cat
    Who's afraid to tell 'em where it's at,
    And he wears his hair cut so tight

    Like he's trying to hide it out of sight.
    So you know he don't know what's happening no way.
    You gotta be swift!

    They got a white teacher-cat who talks like a boot
    With Chinese beads and a Nehru suit,
    Who's got nerve enough to wear an Afro.
    If you're hip at all you got to know
    He can't know what's happening no-kinds-of-way.
    You got to be swift!

Yeah, the teachers are striking everywhere,
But, dig it, baby, I don't care
'Bout sitting around on no wooden seat
'Cause I can learn much more out in the street.
So until teachers run down some nitty-grit
All I got to say is bullshit.
I'm gonna stay swift!

COMPANY (*Singing*):
> Swift, yeah (*4 times*)
> What it means to be black
> What it means to be black.

(COMPANY *continues song until they change positions.* ACTRESS J *takes center spot.*)

He was long.
His fingers were long.
His arms were long.
He was long.
The muscles of his back were long.
From shoulder to shoulder he was long.
He was long.
His hair was black and bushy and long—
Like spruce trees on a hilltop.
He stretched all the way from the earth's center
To the top of Kilimanjaro
He stretched all the way from the valley
To the noonday sun.
He could work long.
He could play long.
He could laugh long.
He had cried so long inside
Until his tears had too long to go
To reach the outside.
It was a long time before he knew how
Long he was.
But they knew,
And they envied him long,
And they desired him long,
And all because a dark brown color
Covered his whole length
And painted the whole length of his long, long soul.

(ACTRESS J *resumes position.* ACTOR L *moves to center and sings.*)

ACTOR L:
> Big, boss, black and burly
> With an attitude

More beat than the heat of the sun
Don't allow nobody no latitude.

COMPANY (*sings*):

    Hero with an Afro
    Mojo in indigo
    Gonna overthrow
    The status quo.

ACTOR L:

    Don't allow nobody no latitude.

    Long, lean, lank and lively
      With an attitude
    So bad that the mad go glad
      Don't show nobody no gratitude.

COMPANY:

    Hero with an Afro
    Mojo in indigo
    Gonna overthrow
    The status quo.

ACTOR L:

    Don't show nobody no gratitude.

    And when he moves, everything
    In nature belongs to him
    And when he grooves, he's the king
    And nature's singing songs for him.

COMPANY:

    Hero with an Afro
    Mojo in indigo
    Gonna overthrow
    The status quo.

ACTOR L:

    Don't show nobody no gratitude.

COMPANY:

    Hero with an Afro
    Hero with an Afro
    Let me tell you 'bout slavery
    And what it did to you and me.

ACTOR G:

In my dream
Standing on the corner
A Hundred and Thirty-Fifth and Lenox
By the uptown Seventh Avenue subway
At the evening rush
With my Southern mother
(God rest her soul).
"Don't you bring home no dark girl, son,

371

You got to think about your children."
In my dream
Everything is slow motion.
Up the subway steps
Comes a sister—in slow motion
The color of peach ice cream
Ample lips, smiling,
Country red bush of natural hair.
"She's light enough, son, but she got bad hair."
I say,
"Mama, I ain't never seen hair cut or shoot nobody."
Mama say,
"If it ain't straight, it's bad, son."
I say,
"It curls up thata way 'cause it's got more life than
    honky hair, Mama."
My mama
(God rest her soul)
My mama says nothing.
Thinks.
While Mama's thinking
They're coming up the steps
From across the street
From every whicha way
In slow motion,
In all colors
One's got cheeks of maple syrup
One's got mahogany hands
One's got a dimpled chin of tapioca
One's milk-chocolate pudding
One's the red clay
One's rosewood
And teak
And walnut
And golden oak
One's a orange-brown sunrise
One's a red-brown sunset
Hair like spun steel
And mulberry bushes
And black hedges
Clustered like the treetops
All that power in mere strands of hair.
Do you hear me?
One walks on by with
Rolling eyes and rolling hips
In slow motion

And I say, "Yeah!"
A tear in Mama's eye
She says,
"I wish this were my time, son"
(God rest her soul).
Mama's fading in my dream
In slow motion
And I'm saying,
Be cool, Mama, be cool
"You just didn't know . . ."
In slow motion
"What a real black man
Feels in his soul."
In slow motion
"You just didn't know
But you were a soul sister too."

(ACTOR J *takes position in "V" as "Soul Sister" theme swells and* ACTOR L *takes center. Singer and* COMPANY *sing first two lines together.*)

ACTOR L:

>   I love a soul sister, soul sister, soul.
>   I love a soul sister, soul sister, soul.

(*Singer takes solo.*)

>   Bushy flare of natural hair,
>   It looks so fine.
>   Full-grown pair of lips to share
>   And drink my wine.
>   I can sing aloud
>   I'm so proud.

(COMPANY *and* SINGER.)

>   I love a soul sister, soul sister, soul.

(COMPANY *and* SINGER ACTOR L.)

(SINGER ACTOR L *takes solo.*)

>   It's very late so let's talk straight.
>   What went so wrong?

>   Let's activate and reinstate
>   What was so long
>   A mere pantomime
>   Of an ancient rhyme
>   To renew me and you . . .
>   Renew me and you . . .

>   Renew me and you . . .

>   Renew me and you!

Now you know that if you treat me like a king,
You will see that we can do most anything
We want to do!
(COMPANY *and* ACTOR L.)
  I love a soul sister, soul sister, soul.

  I've got no itch to make a switch
  From sister soul.

  The kind of chick who makes me click
  Is sister soul.

  Renew me and you . . .
  Renew me and you . . .
  Renew me and you . . .

  Renew me and you!
COMPANY:
  I love a soul sister
  I love a soul sister, etc.
(ACTOR L *resumes position.*)
    Let me tell you 'bout slavery
    And what it did to you and me.
ACTRESS Y (*moves to center spot*): They really don't know.
COMPANY (*quietly*): Really!
ACTRESS Y: They say they know. They think they know.
But they really don't know.
COMPANY: Really!
ACTRESS Y: I didn't know either. I felt it but I didn't know
COMPANY (*a little louder*): Really!
ACTRESS Y: I was blind.
COMPANY (*louder*): Really!
ACTRESS Y: Color-blind
COMPANY (*even louder*): Really!
ACTRESS Y: All the stars I saw were white.
COMPANY (*even louder*): Really!
ACTRESS Y: Now I see black stars.
COMPANY: Really!
ACTRESS Y: Now I know.
COMPANY: Really!
ACTRESS Y: I ain't blind no more.
COMPANY (*loudest*): Really!
ACTRESS Y (*moves to position, then turns*): Now get to that!
COMPANY (*softly*): YEAH!
(ACTRESS Y *resumes automaton position.*)
    Let me tell you 'bout slavery
    And what it did to you and me.

ACTRESS D (*moves to center*):
I am the earth and yet beyond it
I know every crevice, every speck of space, every ounce of
   warmth
Contained in the blades of grass, the black dirt, and the red
   clay
I do not have feet
I have roots which grab at the very muscles of the earth
I am so firmly rooted that if you pull me away you pull away
The earth's heart
When you look at me you must look everywhere—at the soil,
For I am there,
At the sky, for I am there, in the mountains, for I am there,
To your right and to your left, in the pit of the ocean,
Above and below, for I am truly everywhere—a child of the
   universe!

(ACTRESS E *joins* ACTRESS DD *and they sing the following in
duet.*)

> I am the earth itself
> I make so much noise
> Because there are so many joys
> Deep, deep, deep inside my heart.
>
> I am the earth itself
> I run, shout, and yell
> Because I want to tell
> The beat, beat, beat inside my heart
>
> Look at me!
> Look at my eyes!
> Look at me!
>
> The fire never dies
> Which brightens the skies
> Which pours from my eyes
> I am the earth itself . . .

COMPANY (*snaps fingers at audience*): Now . . . get to that!

(COMPANY *changes positions to two separate "V" forma-
tions which face each other as the following is sung.*)

> You gotta dig yourself
> Nyeusi, yeah
> You gotta dig yourself
> Nyeusi, yeah
> You gotta dig yourself
> Nyeusi, yeah

(ACTRESS L *and* ACTOR A *step into the spotlight.*)

ACTRESS L: It is generally accepted by most reputable white
anthropologists that if you . . .

ACTOR A: remove the hair from most higher mammals, you will find that the skin underneath is pink or white. Black skin is therefore:

COMPANY: SUPRAHUMAN!

ACTOR A: White skin?

COMPANY: SUBHUMAN!

ACTRESS L: Except for sheep, most higher mammals have straight hair. Kinky hair is therefore:

COMPANY: SUPRAHUMAN!

ACTRESS L: Straight hair?

COMPANY: SUBHUMAN!

ACTOR A: Most higher mammals, the gorilla being the prime example, have wide thin lips. Thick lips are therefore:

COMPANY: SUPRAHUMAN!

ACTOR A: Thin lips?

COMPANY: SUBHUMAN!

ACTRESS L: Of course we're not trying to imply that black people are suprahuman—which means higher in the plane of human evolution. Black people have their share of subhuman characteristics.

ACTOR A: The point is that for over three hundred years the Man has laughed at the very characteristics in the black man that his own anthropologists deem suprahuman. And merely because he didn't understand.

ACTRESS L: He has a history of laughing at that which he does not understand.

ACTOR A: Until recently, many of us accepted his spirit-sucking ignorance as truth.

COMPANY (*sings*):
> You gotta dig yourself
> Nyeusi, yeah

ACTOR G (*sings*):
> I used to think that they had something
> Something that was saying something! !
> Dig it!
>
> Now I know it was all illusion
> Something based on mass confusion!
> Dig it!
>
> TV commercials
> Better than the shows.
> Blonds have more fun
> Everybody knows.
>
> Band-Aids colored pink
> That match some people's skin.

You got to have a white knight
'Cause a black knight won't win.

Fancy toilet paper
That even runs a race.
High-rise apartments
Which have no living space.

A free education
That fills our every need,
Graduating students
Who don't know how to read.

An occupation army
That's all dressed in blue
To guard the racketeers
From the likes of me and you.

People in the suburbs
Sneaking back in town.
They hate to see the black man
Thrive on hand-me-downs.

Yeah . . .
I used to think that they had something
Something that was saying something
Dig it!

Now I know it was all illusion
Something based on mass confusion!
Dig it!

That which is black is
That which is not . . . is lifeless

What we are, not what they are, is
Beautiful
What we do, not what they do, is
Beautiful
What we feel, not what they feel, is
Beautiful

Black is beautiful.

(*Moves back to place.*)
ACTOR L (*moves center stage*): Black is the foundation!
COMPANY (*as they again take up "V" positions*): Is the way!
ACTOR L (*remains in his position*): Black is the strength!
COMPANY: Is the way!
ACTOR L: Black is the magic!

COMPANY: Is the way!

(*By this time everyone is in position.*)

ACTOR L (*goes to his position*): Black is beautiful!

COMPANY (*raises hands in black power symbol*): UHURU!
(*Swahili for "freedom."*)

ACTOR G (*moving down right*): Hey, Jack, you think there
any decent white people?

ACTOR A (*moving down left*): Yeah, Mack, it does put a
strain on your belief 'cause they have really put a hurtin' on
the black man . . .

ACTOR G: And every other non-white man.

ACTOR A: I'm digging, brother, I'm digging.

ACTOR G: Like some people complain about the murder of
six million human beings in Nazi Germany, and they are right.
That was sad.

ACTOR A: Yeah, brother, that was very sad.

ACTOR G: Course now I look at it a different way.

ACTOR A: How's that, brother?

ACTOR G: It was their own fault. They ain't had no business
thinking of themselves as white in the first place.

ACTOR A: Dig it.

WOMEN (*sing*): Six million people.

ACTOR A: Yeah, that's a lot.

ACTOR G: How many millions of blacks died by lynchings,
rapings, murderings, torturings, starvings, and diseasings?

ACTOR A: Before and after slavery.

ACTOR G: Dig it.

ACTOR A: How many have they killed in South Africa?

ACTOR G: Dig it, baby, dig it.

ACTOR A: Today.

ACTOR G: Every day, my man, every day.

ACTOR A: And how about the one hundred million who
died on the voyage from Africa?

ACTOR G: One hundred million, Jack?

ACTOR A: That's one hundred, ten hundred thousand.

COMPANY: One hundred million.

ACTOR G: That's about 94 percent more than six million,
to use whitey's favorite game, *statistics.*

COMPANY (*sings*): One hundred million young black men
and women.

ACTOR G: That's more than one half of the now current
population of America.

ACTOR A: Dig it, baby, dig it!

COMPANY (*sings*): Long-stemmed, high-busted black African women.

ACTOR G: Dig it.

COMPANY (*sings*): Long-legged, ebony-muscled, sleek black African men.

ACTOR A: ONE HUNDRED MILLION.

ACTOR G: Not to mention those blacks who were too old or too young to make the journey.

ACTOR A: Many of whom were therefore slaughtered.

COMPANY (*sings*): Not to mention them.

ACTOR G: And those who took their lives and the lives of their children rather than be taken into slavery.

COMPANY (*sings*): Not to mention them.

ACTOR G: Not to mention that they brought new diseases to Africa which killed millions.

COMPANY (*sings*): Not to mention that.

ACTOR A: And let us just positively ignore . . .

COMPANY (*sings*): Positively ignore . . .

ACTOR A: That ten million American Indians were killed in the colonization of this fair land.

COMPANY (*sings*): Ignore that, please.

ACTOR G: Ignore the diseases they introduced into this land.

COMPANY (*sings*): Ignore that too.

ACTOR G: Ignore the generations of millions of Afro-Americans whose minds, souls, spirits, and beings they killed with their special poison.

ACTOR A: I think they call it white supremacy.

ACTOR G: Or black inferiority.

COMPANY (*sings*): Good Madison Avenue, mind-bending phrases.

ACTOR A: Not to mention these things.

ACTOR G: Let's ignore it.

COMPANY (*sings*): Let's ignore everything.

ACTOR A: Forget the existence of facts.

ACTOR G: And principles.

ACTOR A: Love.

ACTOR G: Dignity.

ACTOR A: Humanity.

COMPANY (*sings*): Forget them all. They don't exist.

(*Pause.*)

ACTOR A: It was sad though.

ACTOR G: What?

ACTOR A: What they did to those people in *Nazi* Germany.

ACTOR G: Oh, yeah. Dig it.

(*They slap palms and return to place.*)

COMPANY (*moves to an inverted position of the "V" with the apex down center as they sing the following*):

       Let him be remembered
       Let him be remembered

Our brother, our beautiful brother
Though he did not receive
He really did believe in . . .
The power of love
The power of love
(*The "power of love" phrase fades under.*)
ACTOR L (*music for "Dreamer's Epitaph" fades in as he sings*):

He was much too far ahead,
Not because of what he said,
But because he could see
Through the waterfall
And the glare of the sun
Through the moonless night
And the veil of the mist

Through the keyless door
Of created insanity
And unified stupidity
He could see . . .

That we can be victorious
Over the lack of dreams within us.

He was much too far ahead,
Not because of what he said,
But because he could see

A way to rid the world
Of so-called necessary evil.

He was much too far ahead,
And that is why he's dead . . . dead . . . dead!

ACTOR G: Near the end of World War II Adam Ford began studying the Yoruban culture. As a soldier, he was particularly interested in the ancient Yoruba concept of ownership. Land was given to a family, depending upon that family's needs. Therefore, each man owned part of the state. Indeed the Yorubas had a saying, "The man who fights for what he does not own or rule is a fool." In a sense it was a mistake for Adam Ford to have read this because it ignited his inner spirit. There were only twelve black soldiers in Adam's company, and not one of them had shot his rifle since reaching Bataan six months before. They had become the ditch-diggers, the trench-diggers, the grave-diggers for the company. Several of the white soldiers in the company got a big laugh out of calling them the "nigguh digguhs." The ancient Yoru-

bas had ignited Adam's spirit. So he told the lieutenant that he would gladly risk his life for his country, but that he would not dig another ditch unless it were on a rotating basis with the white soldiers in the company. The other eleven black soldiers followed Adam's leadership. They were court-martialed. Charged with failure to obey a command during an enemy action, the punishment for which is death.

All eleven were blindfolded, and at the lieutenant's request lined up in front of eleven graves—graves they themselves had just recently dug. They were shot and buried on the spot, some of them still alive. The ancient Yorubas have a saying, "The man who fights for what he does not own or rule is a fool."

COMPANY: Ododo!

ACTOR G: In New Haven, right after the riots, on the dingy green walls of a tavern bathroom was scribbled: "What you got in Vietnam is . . .

COMPANY: Is the white man . . .

ACTOR G: Using the black man . . .

COMPANY: To fight the yellow man . . .

ACTOR G: To protect what he stole . . .

COMPANY: From the red man.

ACTOR G: The other day I asked a brother just what he felt about those "Negroes" over here who are still going around talking about nonviolence, and he said,

"If a cat's tapping on my head with a piece of wood,
brotherhood—no good."

(*Moves back to place.*)

ACTOR G (*sings*):
Oh, Malcolm!
Cry for Malcolm!
He lived the answer!
Fierce as a panther!

Love your brother, yes, yes, yes
Give one another, yes, yes, yes
Help every man, oh, yeah,
That's Ali's plan, oh, yeah.

Praise be to Ali!

But when a man tries to put his hands on you,
There ain't but one thing you should do.
Yeah, when a man insults your dignity
And plays around with your humanity,
Yeah, a man who messes with your manhood,
You better kill him,

381

Kill him,
Kill him,
Kill him good!

I say kill that man!
And that's Ali's plan.

Praise be to Ali!

Oh, Malcolm!
Cry for Malcolm!
He lived the answer!
Fierce as a panther!

Black Superman!
(*Returns to place.*)

ACTOR (*stepping forward*): A wise old man in Alabama told me, "Why, yeah, I believes in nonviolence. But the only way to have nonviolence is to git yourself a gun, and use it."
(COMPANY *begins to hum "America, the Beautiful."*)

ACTRESS D:
Sing a song of laughter,
Uncle told a lie,
And because he told it,
Uncle's going to die . . .
Turn your face to the wall,
Bite your tongue in two,
But suffer your death without consolation
Here at last is a reality you must face,
You cesspool of undigested lies,
Manufactured so fast until you have become bloated and gaseous,
Gas is what you are—hot air.
Die, hot air.
Hot air heaving from an inferno of trickery, Great white Fatherdom
And guilt
Die, hot air.
Seep from the diseased rectum of bullshit
And die.
You talk out of your ass,
Lip-service nation with laryngitis of the anus.
Don't you know nature is unconquerable,
Is to be conversed with.
Enemy of nature,
Upsetting her beautiful balance with the egotism of your

Polluting factories, and concrete and insecticides.
The earth can't breathe, the sky can't breathe,
The land chokes to death,
The land that you had to have all of
To rape the streams and castrate the trees,
Drive its rich red inhabitants into the swamps,
And glorify this mystical pure blood-red genocide in heroic
Song and legend.
Today's children know the bullshit of the Calvary and the truth of
Sitting Bull
The children know.
Don't you know humanity is unconquerable
Is to be conversed with.
Enemy of humanity,
Your *Mayflower* is a hoax,
Black prisoners of war saw it drop anchor,
Watched the scum of Europe disembark,
The thieves, the religious hypocrites,
The Founding Bastards.
The putrid air of the slave holes where one hundred million
Black men, women, and children died retching
Weeded out the weak,
Leaving you the ebony cream, the thickest black juice of Africa,
The juice of her mountains, indestructible lava of her soul.
Pathological liar, claiming not to fear this superman created
By your avarice, profaning his lush power with your
Flatulent protestations of superiority, knowing all the
Time that you die—today's children know—the flower children know
That you are obsolete.
Who cares about America, who cares about a Hollywood set
Manned by soulless technicians
Technicians with vacant eyes, with no beat, no vibration,
No glory in their rhythmless hearts.
Bloodless, you waste away still crying, "I am."
Bloodless phantom, seeking to suck nourishment from the rich
Realities of the real people, the true people
Who give you your pulse—the non-honkey, non-redneck, non-cracker people
Whose song you stole with a lie in your teeth.
Sick blue-veined shadow, reaching for the substantial
Which is not part of you

But part of the drum—
You can never ignore the drum
Rhythm created, maintained and sustains the universe.
Zombies—who cares about zombies,
Dead before you die.
Suffer your death without consolation
Here at last is a reality you must face.
March, real people, true people, beautiful people,
March through the cockroaches, the Congressionally approved rats,
March to Washington, the Capitol, the Archives,
Take turns wiping your asses on the
Declaration of Independence, the Gettysburg Address,
The Constitution, the Bill of Rights, the Civil Rights Act.
Wrap them in Old Glory and bury them in the sewer
With a twenty-one-gun salute.
Paper Nation,
You don't know, motherfucker, but
Your children know the answer.
I pledge allegiance to the flag of the United States of America
And to the Republic for which it stands, one nation, under God,
Invisible
Invisible! Motherfucker!
Sing a song of laughter,
Uncle told a lie,
And because he told it,
Uncle's going to die . . .
COMPANY:
>
> I have looked at you for centuries
> And I do not see you anymore
>
> Let me tell you about slavery
> And what it did to you and me.
> Tell it like it is.
> They will weep from what they reap
> 'Cause little Bo-Peep ain't never had no sheep
> 'Cause underneath there lurked
> A big black cat.

(MEN *chant* "Ododo" *as* WOMEN *chant* "Nyeusi" *while moving into positions for the following song.*)

> Let me tell you about slavery
> And all the truth (Ododo) it made me
> see.

COMPANY (*sings*):
> I don't want no intergration,
> Assimilation or admiration,
> I'm not hung up on miscegenation.
>
> Just leave me alone,
> Just leave me alone,
> Just leave me alone,
> Just leave me alone!
>
> Don't you dare approve of me,
> 'Cause I approve of very few,
> And I keep on thinking,
> And I keep on thinking,
> And I keep on thinking,
> That I'm gonna turn my back on you.
>
> I ignore all stigmatism.
> I reject all ostracism.
> I have always lived Black-Powerism.
>
> Just leave me alone,
> Just leave me alone,
> Just leave me alone,
> Just leave me alone!
>
> I don't need no LSD,
> Or guilty hands to set me free,
> For my destiny,
> For my destiny,
> For my destiny,
> Depends on me!
>
> I won't listen to elocution.
> We both know there's just one solution,
> And that solution is revolution.
>
> And we won't stop,
> Until the top,
> 'Cause on the top,
> There's nothing but the wind.

(COMPANY *makes musical-wind sounds as double-line position used in African proverbs is taken*—WOMEN *in front. As soon as positions are formed, the following lines are shouted as if at the sky.*)

It's a bird, it's a plane, it's . . .

ACTRESS Y (*immediate cue—rapid-fire exchange*):
We're super-strong
And we've been strong so long

ACTRESS E:
We'll outlast all of you

ACTRESS Y:
No matter what you do

ACTRESS L:
Because before we're through

ACTRESS DD:
We're gonna mess with you

ACTRESS D:
So forget about your concentration camp

ACTRESS M:
Have you ever seen a black man vamp?

ACTRESS Y:
He'll cut you ten times before your raise your lamp

WOMEN:
To see who it is.

MEN:
Without even getting his switch-blade damp.

ACTRESS J:
So look up, look out, then get off the track

ACTRESS D:
'Cause a train is coming, and that train is black.

ACTRESS E:
And it's hard to stop a train

ACTRESS L:
And they don't turn back

ACTRESS J:
Ain't nobody worried 'bout all your might

ACTRESS M:
You dealing with a cat who's out-of-sight

ACTRESS Y:
I know you gonna worry as you plan your invasion

ACTRESS DD:
But we're gonna be preparing for a festive occasion

WOMEN:
And before we enter this terrible fight,
We gonna eat ham-hocks and dance all night.

ACTOR L (*the following exchange is sung rapidly also in the style of African leader-response—as actors back into karate dance positions*): You remind him of a man.

COMPANY (*sings*): What man?

ACTOR L: A man with power.

COMPANY: What power?

ACTOR L: Power Hoodo?

COMPANY: Hoodo?

ACTOR L: You do!

COMPANY: Do what?

ACTOR L: Remind him of a man.

COMPANY: What man?

ACTOR L: A man with power.

COMPANY: A MAN WITH POWER!

ACTOR L: And it disturbs him.

COMPANY: It frightens him.

ACTOR L: That I remind him of a man—a man with power! (*Singing stops and African chant begins.*) AR SAR WANDA!

COMPANY: DID TON FA!

ACTOR L: AR SAR WANDA!

COMPANY: DID TON FA! E E E E E E E E E E E!

ACTOR L: COW PLEA—OH!

COMPANY: GEE!

ACTOR L: COW PLEA—OH!

COMPANY: GEE! (*Brief pause.*) AR HAR!

ACTOR L: AR SAR WANDA!

COMPANY: DID TON FA!

ACTOR L: AR SAR WANDA!

COMPANY: DID TON FA! E E E E E E E E E E E!

ACTOR L: COW PLEA—OH!

COMPANY: GEE!

ACTOR L: COW PLEA—OH!

COMPANY: GEE! (*Brief pause.*) AR HAR!

(*At this point the karate dance begins, with each movement punctuated with "KIA." The dance mounts to a pitch which then turns into a free-for-all. At the end of the free-for-all one actor screams, "Liars!" Entire* COMPANY *follows suit, running downstage in various directions, screaming "Lies" and "Liars" at top voice.* COMPANY *points accusing fingers at audience and whispers: "Liars," first to audience, then to every direction as if accusing the entire population of the white Western World.*)

COMPANY:

> AMERICA, LAND OF THE FREE,
> DEMOCRACY AND LIBERTY,
> IF YOU DON'T BE
> WHAT YOU CLAIM TO BE,
> WE'RE GONNA SEE
> THAT YOU DON'T BE—AT ALL!
> *ODODO!*

(ACTOR L *steps forward and with an improvised yodel-sing-chant, commands the Spirits—the* COMPANY—*of ages past to return from where they came. The* COMPANY *falls into line, becomes rigid and zombielike, begins the same other worldly sounds used in the beginning of the First Act, and walks off stage right and left.* ACTOR L *moves stage center, raises his arms and, with a final sound, brings them back to his sides as lights fade to black.*)

CURTAIN

All White Caste

(AFTER THE SEPARATION)

A SLOW-PACED ONE-ACT PLAY

by BEN CALDWELL

Ben Caldwell is a Harlem essayist-playwright-artist whose plays have been performed in Harlem, at Newark's Spirit House, and on the West Coast by the Black Arts Alliance. Five of Mr. Caldwell's works were published in the summer '68 issue of *TDR: The Riot Sale, the Job, Top Secret, Mission Accomplished,* and *The Militant Preacher.*

CHARACTERS

GUARD   A white man in his forties
SECOND GUARD   A Negro in his forties
PRISONER   A white man in his thirties

TIME: 199?
PLACE: Harlem, New York City

(*Two white men enter the living room of what appears to be a rundown tenement building. One of them has on a blue policeman's uniform. He's carrying a small leather portfolio. If possible, the* GUARD *looks and sounds like John Wayne. The second man, younger, has his hands cuffed in front of him. He has long hair and a beard. He wears a bright orange suit and green shoes, a green shirt, blue tie, a big white cap. It looks as though he dressed himself while under the effect of a blow on the head from a heavy blunt instrument. The walls of the room are cracked and peeling and in need of painting, the furniture old (old TV, old dinette, etc.) and shabby. The* GUARD *guides him to a big raggedy chair and seats him. The* GUARD *sits in a creaky wooden chair opposite him. Conspicuous is a large picture of J. E. Hoover, looking bulldog stern, hanging from the wall. The* GUARD *unlocks the cuffs and removes them.*)

GUARD: Take off your hat. This is the living room. This is where you'll stay. You and all your generation.

PRISONER: (*excited, yelling, half-rising out of his seat*): But I'm innocent! I haven't done anything to deserve this! What you've shown me so far is horrible! It's hell!

GUARD (*shocked—then like a father to an unruly child*): The doctor said you were all right! What's wrong with you? Don't make me have to restrain you again!

PRISONER: Where am I? What time is it? This "117th

Street," this "Harlem," this is not where I lived. I don't remember this. You said I was being taken to my home.

GUARD: This will be your home from now on, whether you like it or not. You are controlled and ruled by us. You weren't satisfied with the way things were. (*He gestures around the room.*) 'Course you don't remember anything like this—you didn't live like this before.

PRISONER: Before? Before what?

GUARD (*puzzled by his actions, explains*): Before the war! Before the trial! Don't you remember anything? You were a writer. A rich one too. Owned *Rampage* magazine. You remember the Third World War, don't you? You helped them during the war. We didn't win. We couldn't win without destroying the whole world. We threatened to do just that, but we couldn't really do it. That could only come of an accident same as we were. We decided it's better to have lived and lost than to end it all! So here we are. You'd be dead if that smart-ass lawyer hadn't got them to believe you were insane. Temporary insanity of a self-destructive nature. You're a war criminal. A traitor—but you got off easy. You tried to help the niggers, and now our continued existence is not so certain—in fact it's in constant jeopardy. I doubt very seriously if we'll last another six thousand years! Do you realize what might happen if those niggers make an A or H bomb? Your punishment is fitting; life imprisonment here, in a world like that we allowed them to make for themselves.

PRISONER: "Allowed?" Don't you mean forced?

GUARD: Oh, you still got some sympathy, huh? Okay, forced if you say so. You're a lucky devil! If I had my way, you'd be in chains, at least, instead of a comfortable prison like this! The state won't even allow us to call it a prison for fear of upsetting your sense of security. You're fortunate to begin your term now. The penal system has been drastically revised. During the worst part—the inquisition—you were hospitalized.

PRISONER: Hospitalized? For what? Jailed for what? I still don't understand.

(*The* PRISONER *calms some, trying to get his bearings, trying to understand what's happening.*)

GUARD: The ungrateful, distrusting niggers you tried to help beat hell out of you at one of their meetings! Later you were convicted by the court of states for aiding in the destruction of old America. All the beautiful, established institutions, the traditions—all gone. You wrote and confirmed the truth that we whites exploited niggers, etc., and that they deserved their freedom by any nonviolent means necessary. That's why your

lawyer pleaded insanity. Either you were crazy or got lost; forgetting you were only supposed to add to their confusion, not strengthen their convictions about their "rights" to freedom and justice, etc. You were in the hospital for five years. This is new America now. Beautiful new established traditions and institutions—but most similar to the old. There has to be a bottom to every top, you know. You were sentenced after you were discharged from the hospital—many others like you were executed. There would be no America, old or new, if the niggers and your kind had had their way. How long we can last now, only time will tell! Our flag is only white and blue now, no stars! I never thought I'd live to see such sorry days! Any more questions? Sympathizer!

PRISONER: If all that has happened to America, what's happened to the world? Has it changed much?

GUARD: It's about the same, 'cept there're hardly any niggers in our world—'cept by choice! Our influence and control is nowhere near as extensive as it used to be in old America. The Pentagon is now a bowling alley! Lack of niggers is why the state didn't kill all of you sympathizers—you gotta take the niggers' place. Fill their role. (*He removes a paper from his case and reads it.*) By the way, you'll be employed as a shipping clerk at the Judy Bolshevik Blouse Co., 50th and Madison, in Wallace Center. Your salary will be $55 a week, before taxes. You start Monday. Be there 8 a.m. sharp if you wanna keep a good record!

PRISONER: Fifty-five dollars! That's absurd! All of this is absurd!

GUARD: Call it what you want—there's a state-enforced limit on the amount of money you're allowed to earn—so you won't be able to do certain things, in case you still remember the power of money. Don't you remember how it was for the niggers?

But you won't have much need for money. Rent on your cell—excuse me—your apartment is only $85 a month. And every week we raffle a brand-new Cadillac. The niggers used to love 'em! We figured you might too! You will, too, as a contrast to the norm. A little luxury in the midst of all this abject poverty might prove inspiring. (*Takes another sheet of paper from case and hands it to the prisoner.*) Here's a list of ambitions you're allowed to consider. You may find something that interests you. (*Sarcastically.*) Mechanics make more money than shipping clerks or "sympathizer" writers!

PRISONER (*composure shaken again*): I don't want to be a stock clerk, or a mechanic, at any salary! I don't want to be

any of those things! No! No! I can't live like this! (*Looks around room.*) I won't!

GUARD: Aw, it's not so bad. (*Slowly.*) *It could be worse!* That's what the niggers used to say all the time. Save your money. Go to school, get a better job, after a while move into the projects—or a co-op with a terrace overlooking somebody's fire escape! Try to better yourself. (*Reassuring.*) You've got a lot to live for. There's life where there's hope. Always remember, it could be worse. Things'll get better. It takes time!

PRISONER: But I don't have to go to school to know this is not right. I'm qualified for better. I'm trained. I have a degree from Harvard . . .

GUARD: Harvard? What's that? Is that something, some place, like the nigger myth, "Timbuctoo"? Doesn't matter where you went or come from, you're still subject to the usual procedures of retardation—same as all the other sympathizers.

PRISONER: No! This is wrong! You can't do this! What gives you the right? You can't force these conditions upon me!

GUARD: Why not? Who the hell do you think you are? You're a prisoner—just as sure as the niggers were our slaves! We could call you a prisoner and treat you as one. We're considerate only because you were once a fully qualified white man. You're a war criminal! A sympathizer! You're being punished for crimes! These conditions of your punishment were determined by a duly elected body of officials. You oughta know—you voted for them, remember? Remember one Tuesday the nurse brought you a ballot and a sedative? I don't see what you got to complain about, you're living as good, if not better, than any nigger or Viet Cong ever lived! The manner of your punishment is so you'll see firsthand that the niggers didn't really have it so bad. Maybe you'll repent and ask forgiveness from those of us you caused to lose so much. The niggers' crimes of protest and resistance were unjustified and unwarranted. And certainly there was no justification for you aiding and abetting them in these crimes. They were as free as they needed to be! They won their freedom, but I bet my bottom dollar they're not as happy as they used to be! They had *some* rights: fair housing; fair employment; anti-lynch and civil rights laws; the whole bit! But no, you holier-than-thou bastards had to go and stir 'em up. You get what they had, and it's what you deserve! (*Anger.*) You goddamned, sympathizing, liberalantiestablishmentcommunistabolitionistoutsideagitatoryippiehippiebastard! You destroyed this country and now you're complaining 'cause of a little hardship! I

oughta . . . (*He's reaching for his blackjack—he spots a roach and leaps across the room to step on it. The* PRISONER, *frightened by this sudden move, cringes.*) Oh, oh, you've got problems! (*Smash.*) Roaches! They're a regular nuisance 'round here! Tell you the truth, I do kinda sympathize with you even though I hate your guts! Just between me and you, I couldn't stand to live like this! (*On several occasions, while talking, he moves stealthily about the room and pounces on a roach with a loud,* "I gotcha." *Sound of a gunshot nearby.*)

PRISONER (*concerned*): What was that? An execution?

GUARD (*reassuring*): Naw! Just another sympathizer taking the easy way out. Suicide rate is very high here. You people can't seem to cope with your problems as well as the niggers could!

PRISONER: Are there many more like me here?

GUARD: Oh, of course. This is a regular little community of white sympathizers. Place used to be called "Harlem"—used to be full of niggers. Everyone leads a pretty normal life here —normal for sympathizers, that is. Some of you are even allowed to operate small businesses—as long as they depend upon our big businesses—now that's progress compared to the way it was when we first released you sympathizers from *actual* prison!

Certain of you are allowed to contribute and participate, to a certain predetermined extent, in the mainstream of our society, if you prove you're worthy and qualified. Why there's even talk of electing a representative to Congress from among you people—you sympathizers! There's opportunity galore! It's not like you were actual prisoners! It's more like, say, a second-class citizen! For a war criminal I'd say your punishment is light. In old America they'd'a hung you! We're much more humane now.

PRISONER: You call this humane!?

GUARD: We banned the bomb, didn't we? Or don't you remember *any* of the significant events in our fearful flight toward respect for the world and humanity? If you'd acted like a normal natural white man, you wouldn't be in this predicament, goddamn you! It's hell living with such a low level of international prestige. We make transistors for Japan. The world is ruled and controlled by those damned . . .

PRISONER (*excited by this possibility*): You can't keep me in this devilish trap! I'm a white man just like you—there are no bars, no gates; suppose I just leave! Escape!

GUARD: (*slowly*): Economically impossible—among other reasons. These identifying clothes we make for you—

(*touches prisoner's garments*)—especially for you! And the means by which you would travel wouldn't allow you to go very far undetected. Cadillacs are reserved for use by sympathizers. Old Cadillacs, new Cadillacs, that's all you're allowed to drive. That's the only means of travel—you're marked just as sure as a nigger is black!

I make a guaranteed $50,000 a year in this leisurely, automated society. In this prison we allow you just enough to pay rent and feed yourself. A ticket to Brooklyn would cost a sympathizer a year's wages! You're not allowed to produce anything that would enable you to sustain yourself independent of us. And, finally, our conditioning will affect and mark your personality with easily identifiable "sympathizer" characteristics. Escape to where? Like I keep telling you—it's not so bad!

Oh, and you can also have a wife. We've got one already picked out for you, with all the right characteristics for a sympathizer's woman. She's as fine a piece of white trash as you ever did see! I had her just the other night—a real fine gal! And you'll be able to have children. (*Sound of sirens passing.*)

What did you expect? You're different. You're not a normal natural white man! All that contrary "peace–love" nonsense! See what it got you! You'd have us practicing ideals and principles so contrary to our natures we'd lose all we've gained of our natural strengths.

PRISONER (*stands, self-righteous attitude*): You're saying that because I believed *all* men are created equal and entitled to life, liberty, and the pursuit of happiness, and all that jazz, I'm being cruelly punished?

GUARD: Yeah, something like that. Other than the fact that your community is heavily policed, you're absolutely free! You can live as good as the niggers used to live. Only difference, and *this* is the punishment, in their minds they were convinced they were free—but you know the difference. You know you're not as free as you should be or could be. You know you're ruled and controlled. Most of them didn't know this—till almost too late! But you're a writer—use your imagination—imagine yourself out of this predicament.

Heyyyyy, by the way, one of your neighbors is a nigger. Called himself a "black revolutionary." He's retired here. He was a writer too! He left the country in the sixties—but he came back 'cause he couldn't live in a segregated society—all the rest of the world excluded whites from their society. After the war he believed whites—those who sympathized with his cause—were entitled to equal rights with the rest of the world.

We started to execute him but we thought it even better to allow him to live among you sympathizers. He doesn't write any more protest, he's one of the niggers-by-choice! He's the super of this building, incidentally. And the Wilkins family is still here. Great old Negro family. Keeps up all the old traditions made famous by old Uncle Roy, as we used to call him. Old Uncle Roy died at the age of 125—of a broken heart—sad that his organization's goal of integration was never achieved. He wouldn't leave with the others—even most of the members of the N-A-A—something-or-other left. Uncle Roy said he never wanted to leave all us "good white people." "Good white people," those were his exact words. (*Laughs.*) We tried to deport the old gray bastard, but he insisted he had a "constitutional right" to live with us. It was decided he couldn't do us any harm, so we let him stay. He was like an institution or something—we used to rub his head for luck every time we'd see him slowly shuffling down Milhous Lane. There's a statue of him hanging in Central Park.

Wonder what all the other niggers are doing in their part of the world? They're so damned secretive! No communications with us. No diplomatic relations. They send back, unopened, all the birth control CARE packages we send them. They don't believe we're still genuinely and sincerely concerned about them. I guess they went back to their savage existence in the jungles of Africa. (*Nostalgic reminiscence.*) I kinda miss them; all their protests and frustrations; all their poverty and Cadillacs; their illusions of progress within our system; the carefree manner they accepted our oppression and exploitation for so long; their drug addicts were so funny and profitable; their childlike joy in spite of the terror and death we so often unexpectedly visited upon them; they were such irresponsible angels! Then came that damned "Black Power" business—and you damned white sympathizers! (*Distant gunshot.*)

There goes another one! I always said you sympathizers were weaker than ordinary white men! Even the niggers finally didn't want you! Well, you might as well try to relax. You'll get used to all this. Go to the movies, or the theater. The state has produced a musical comedy based on the life of Malcolm X. Or watch TV. There're reruns of some of the great old Sullivan shows on tonight. Probably some niggers on it as niggers should be; laughing, singing, dancing, telling jokes. You still love niggers, don't you?

I like the comedians. Goddamn, those boys are funny! I really enjoy them making fun of their misery. They love to entertain at any cost and in spite of themselves. Negroes were,

basically, very happy people. I liked this little black bastard, Flip Wilson. He told this story about slavery that was so funny I almost . . . mmmmmmmmmm, you don't seem interested. I'm wasting my time trying to make you feel comfortable. You look depressed. If you feel depressed there's plenty of liquor stores around—you can hang one on and loosen up a bit. (*Laughs.*) But if you need something a little stronger just let me know. (*He mimics the actions of the heroin user.*) I'll fix you up! Know what I mean? Sure-fire relief for tensions and frustrations. (*Starts toward the door.*) You'll be seeing me kinda regular, but I won't be wearing this uniform, for your comfort's sake. I come by monthly to collect the rent, and to see if you need anything—and to see if you have anything you don't need. I'm more like a landlord than a jailer. (*Soft chuckle.*) I'll be seeing you.

PRISONER: Wait! Wait! You can't leave me!

GUARD (*looks for a moment at the seated, distressed, distraught figure of a white brother*): You have some more questions?

PRISONER (*on the verge of tears*): No! No! This can't be true! Oh, God help me!

GUARD: Aw, come on now, you know better than that! God is dead! (*Points to the picture of Hoover.*)

PRISONER (*hysterical, rising, reaching for the GUARD*): No, you can't make a prisoner of me! I won't let you! I'LL KILL YOU!

(*He lunges for the GUARD who seems strangely pleased by this action. They struggle weakly as two unarmed white men must. A big "burly" Negro wearing a policeman's uniform bursts into the room—almost doing a rhythmic shuffling dance step—blowing a whistle—white helmet on his head. He sprays something from an aerosol can on the PRISONER, stifling him, and proceeds to beat him with his fists and a club, and stomps and kicks him when he falls to the ground. All the while reciting, with sincerity and conviction,* "We must have law and order at any cost!" *The PRISONER's loud screams turn to agonized moans and groans, the white GUARD has to restrain the black GUARD from unholstering his gun and killing the PRISONER where he lies.* "Whoa! That's enough, boy!" *They pick him up and place him in the raggedy chair. The Negro crouches behind the chair as though expecting some hasty move from the semiconscious PRISONER. He unholsters his pistol, cocks it, aims at the back of the white man's head.*)

GUARD (*as he straightens his ruffled clothing*): Whew! He almost had me there! He's just like all the rest of them sym-

pathizers—a weakling. And the niggers thought something like that could help them gain their freedom!

You're Whitney's boy, aren't you? I'll have to send a message to your daddy's grave and tell him what a good boy you turned out to be! You're a credit to what remains of the Negro race—just like your daddy was.

He'll probably try to escape. You know what to do. If he doesn't try to escape, if he resigns himself to his fate, get the guitar and teach him some "blues." Be seeing you.

(*The Negro nods his head and adjusts his weight to make his crouching position more comfortable.* GUARD *exits. The Negro says loudly and hatefully to the semiconscious* PRISONER, *"Make one false move and I'll kill you, nigger!" Gradual lights out.*)

Mother and Child

A THEATER VIGNETTE

by LANGSTON HUGHES

Langston Hughes was born in Joplin, Missouri, in 1902. He died in New York City on May 22, 1967. He devoted his life to writing and lecturing on the life of black folk. In his lifetime he published thirty-six books—poetry, short stories, plays, autobiography, juveniles, and anthologies. He traveled widely in this country and abroad, and for a long time made his home in Harlem.

CAST

The characters are typical Negro women to be found in any farm community on the edge of the South. They are not well dressed, nor very well educated.

LOTTIE MUMFORD
MATTIE CRANE
LUCY DOVES
SISTER WIGGINS
CORA PERKINS
MRS. SAM JONES
SISTER JENKINS
MADAM PRESIDENT
SISTER PRIME
SISTER HOLT

(*The parlor of a small farmhouse in southern Ohio, overcrowded with old-time furniture. Springtime. Bright sunlight through the lace curtains at the windows.*

The monthly meeting of the Salvation Rock Missionary Society, a religious organization of rural colored ladies, is being held. The members are beginning to gather. SISTER WIGGINS, MATTIE CRANE, *and* CORA PERKINS *are already present. They are gossiping as usual, but today the gossip centers persistently around a single tense and fearful topic—a certain newborn child that has come to Boyd's Center. As the curtain rises, the hostess,* LOTTIE MUMFORD, *her apron still on, is answering the door. Enter* LUCY DOVES *and* MRS. SAM JONES.)

LOTTIE MUMFORD (*at the door*): Howdy, you-all! Howdy! 'Scuse my apron, Sister Jones. I'm makin' some rolls for the after-part. (*Laughs.*)

OTHER SISTERS: Howdy! Howdy-do!

LOTTIE MUMFORD: Lucy Doves, all I wants to know is, what news you got? Is you seen that chile?

399

MATTIE CRANE: Yes, is you seen it? You lives right over there by 'em.

LUCY DOVES (*bursting to talk*): Ain't nobody seen it. Ain't nobody seen it, but the midwife and the doctor. And her husband, I reckon. They say she won't let a soul come in the room.

LOTTIE MUMFORD: Ain't it awful?

LUCY DOVES: But it's still livin' cause Mollie Ranson heard it cryin'. And the woman from Downsville what attended the delivery says it's as healthy a child as she ever seed, indeed she did.

SISTER WIGGINS (*from a rocking chair*): Well, it's a shame it's here.

MATTIE CRANE: Sho' is!

SISTER WIGGINS: I been livin' in Boyd's Center for twenty-two years, at peace with these white folks, ain't had no trouble yet, till this child was born—now look at 'em. Just look what's goin' on! People actin' like a pack o' wolves.

CORA PERKINS: It's ter'ble, ter'ble.

MRS. SAM JONES (*taking off her hat*): Poor little brat! He ain't been in the world a week yet, and done caused more trouble than all the rest of us in a lifetime. I was born here, and I ain't never seen the white folks up in arms like they are today. But they don't need to think they can walk over Sam and me . . .

SISTER HOLT: Nor me!

MRS. SAM JONES (*continuing*): For we owns our land, it's bought and paid for, and we sends our children to school. Thank God, this is Ohio. It ain't Mississippi.

CORA PERKINS: Thank God!

LUCY DOVES: White folks is white folks, honey, South or North, North or South. I's lived both places and I know.

SISTER WIGGINS: Yes, but in Mississippi they'd lynched Douglass by now.

MATTIE CRANE: Where is Douglass? You-all know I don't know much about this mess. Way back yonder on that farm where I lives now, you don't get nothin' straight. Where is Douglass?

LUCY DOVES: Douglass is here! Saw him just now out in de field doin' his spring sowin' when I drive down de road, as stubborn and bold-faced as he can be. We told him he ought to leave here.

SISTER HOLT: Huh! He's a *man,* ain't he?

SISTER WIGGINS: Well, I wish he'd go on and get out, if that would help any. His brother's got more sense than he has, even

if he is a seventeen-year-old child. Clarence left here yesterday and went to Cincinnati. But their ma, poor Sister Carter, she's still tryin' to battle it out.

LOTTIE MUMFORD: She told me last night, though, she thinks she have to leave. They won't let her have no more provisions at de general store. And they ain't got their spring seed yet. And they can't pay cash for 'em.

CORA PERKINS: Po' souls.

MRS. SAM JONES: Don't need to tell me! Old man Hartman's got evil as de rest of de white folks. Didn't he tell ma husband Saturday night he'd have to pay up every cent of his back bill, or he couldn't take nothin' out of that store? And we been tradin' there for years!

LUCY DOVES: That's their way o' strikin' back at us colored folks.

MRS. SAM JONES: Yes, but Lord knows my husband ain't de father o' that child.

LUCY DOVES: Nor mine.

MRS. SAM JONES: Sam's got too much pride to go foolin' 'round any old loose white woman.

SISTER WIGGINS: Child, you can't tell about men.

MATTIE CRANE: I knowed a case once in Detroit where a colored man lived ten years with a white woman, and her husband didn't know it. He was their chauffeur.

SISTER WIGGINS: That's all right in the city, but please don't come bringing it out here to Boyd's Center where they ain't but a handful o' us colored—and we has a hard enough time as it is.

LOTTIE MUMFORD: You right! This sure has brought de hammer down on our heads. (*Jumps.*) Oh, lemme go see about my rolls! (*Exits into kitchen.*)

SISTER WIGGINS: Lawd knows we's law-biding people, ain't harmed a soul, yet some o' these white folks talkin' 'bout trying to run all de colored folks out o' de county on account o' Douglass.

SISTER HOLT: They'll never run me out!

MRS. SAM JONES: Nor me!

LUCY DOVES: Don't say what they *won't* do, 'cause they might. (*A knock and the door opens.* SISTER JENKINS *enters.*) Howdy, Sister Jenkins.

OTHERS: Howdy!

SISTER JENKINS: Good evenin'! Is you 'bout to start?

MRS. SAM JONES: Yes, de meetin due to start directly.

MATTIE CRANE: Soon as Madam President arrives. Reckon she's havin' trouble gettin' over that road from High Creek.

SISTER WIGGINS: Sit down and tell us what you's heard, Sister Jenkins.

SISTER JENKINS: About Douglass?

SISTER HOLT: Course 'bout Douglass. What else is anybody talking 'bout?

SISTER JENKINS: Well, my daughter told me Douglass' sister say they was in love.

MATTIE CRANE: Him and that white woman?

SISTER JENKINS: Yes. Douglass' sister say it's been goin' on 'fore de woman got married.

MRS. SAM JONES: Un-huh! Then why didn't he stop foolin' with her after she got married? Bad enough, colored boy foolin' 'round a unmarried white woman, let alone a married one.

SISTER JENKINS: Douglass' sister say they was in love.

SISTER WIGGINS: Well, why did she marry the *white* man, then?

MATTIE CRANE: She's white, ain't she? And who wouldn't marry a rich white man? Got his own farm, money and all, even if he were a widower with grown children gone to town. He give her everything she wanted, didn't he?

SISTER HOLT: Everything but the right thing.

MRS. SAM JONES: Well, she must not o' loved him, sneakin' 'round meetin' Douglass in de woods.

CORA PERKINS: True, true!

MATTIE CRANE: But what you reckon she went on and had that colored baby for?

SISTER WIGGINS: She must a thought it was the old man's baby.

LUCY DOVES: She don't think so now! Mattie say when the doctor left and they brought the child in to show her, she like to went blind. It were near black as me.

MATTIE CRANE: Do tell!

CORA PERKINS: And what did her husband say?

LUCY DOVES: Don't know. Don't know.

SISTER HOLT: He must a fainted.

(*Reenter* LOTTIE MUMFORD, *pulling off her apron.*)

LUCY DOVES: That old white woman lives across the crick from us said he's gonna pit her out soon's she's able to walk.

MRS. SAM JONES: Ought to put her out!

SISTER JENKINS: Maybe that's what Douglass waitin' for.

MATTIE CRANE: I heard he wants to take her away.

SISTER WIGGINS: He better take his fool self away 'fore these white folks get madder. Ain't nobody heard it was a black

baby till day before yesterday. Then it leaked out. And now de white folks are rarin' to kill Douglass!

CORA PERKINS: I sure am scared!

LOTTIE MUMFORD: And how come they all said right away it were Douglass?

LUCY DOVES: Honey, don't you know? Colored folks knowed Douglass been eyein' that woman since God knows when, and she been eyein' back at him. You ought to seed 'em when they meet in de store. Course, they didn't speak no more 'n Howdy, but their eyes followed one another 'round just like dogs.

SISTER JENKINS: They was in love, I tell you. Been in love.

MRS. SAM JONES: Mighty funny kind o' love. Everybody knows can't no good come out o' white and colored love. Everybody knows that. And Douglass ain't no child. He's twenty-six years old, ain't he? And Sister Carter sure did try to raise her three children right. You can't blame her.

SISTER WIGGINS: Blame that fool boy, that's who, and that woman. Plenty colored girls in Camden he could of courted ten miles up de road. One or two right here in Boyd's Center. I got a daughter myself.

MRS. SAM JONES: No, he had to go foolin' 'round with a white woman.

LOTTIE MUMFORD: Yes, a white woman.

MATTIE CRANE: They say he loved her, though.

LOTTIE MUMFORD: What do Douglass say, since it happened?

LUCY DOVES: He don't say nothin'. Just goes on with his plowin'.

SISTER HOLT: He's a *man,* ain't he?

MRS. SAM JONES: What could he say?

SISTER WIGGINS: Well, he needn't think he's gonna keep his young mouth shut and let de white folks take it out on us. Down yonder at de school today, my Dorabelle says they talkin' 'bout separatin' de colored from de white and makin' all de colored children go in a nigger room next term.

MRS. SAM JONES: Ain't nothin' like that ever happened in Boyd's Center long as I been here—these twenty-two years.

LUCY DOVES: White folks is mad now, child, mad clean through.

LOTTIE MUMFORD: Wonder they ain't grabbin' Douglass and lynched him.

CORA PERKINS: It's a wonder!

LUCY DOVES: And him calmly out yonder plowin' de field this afternoon.

MATTIE CRANE: He sure is brave.

SISTER HOLT: Douglass is a *man*.

SISTER WIGGINS: Woman's husband's liable to kill us.

MRS. SAM JONES: Her brother's done said he's gunnin' for him.

CORA PERKINS: They liable to burn us Negroes' houses down.

SISTER WIGGINS: Anything's liable to happen. Lawd, I'm nervous as I can be.

LUCY DOVES: You can't tell about white folks.

LOTTIE MUMFORD: I ain't nervous. I'm *scared*.

SISTER HOLT: Huh! Ain't you-all got no weapons?

CORA PERKINS: Don't say a word! It's ter'ble!

MATTIE CRANE: Why don't Sister Carter make him leave here?

MRS. SAM JONES: I wish I knew.

LOTTIE MUMFORD: She told me she were nearly crazy.

SISTER WIGGINS: And she can't get Douglass to say nothin', one way or another—if he go, or if he stay. (*A knock and the door opens. Enter* MADAM PRESIDENT *and* SISTER PRIME.) Howdy, Madam President.

OTHERS: Good evenin', Madam President.

(*The gossip does not halt.* MADAM PRESIDENT *goes to a little table and takes a small bell from her purse.*)

SISTER JENKINS: I done told you Douglass loves her.

MATTIE CRANE: He wants to see that white woman once more again, that's what he wants.

MRS. SAM JONES: A white hussy!

SISTER WIGGINS: He's foolin' with fire.

LOTTIE MUMFORD: Poor Mis' Carter. I'm sorry for his mother.

CORA PERKINS: Poor Mis' Carter.

SISTER JENKINS: Why don't you all say poor Douglass? Poor white woman? Poor child?

(*The* PRESIDENT *taps importantly on her bell, but the women continue in an undertone.*)

MATTIE CRANE: Madam President's startin' de meetin'.

SISTER PRIME: Is it a boy or girl?

LUCY DOVES: Sh-s-s! There's de bell.

SISTER WIGGINS: I hear it's a boy.

SISTER PRIME: Thank God, ain't a girl then.

MATTIE CRANE: I hope it looks like Douglass, cause Douglass a fine-looking nigger.

SISTER HOLT: And he's a *man!*

SISTER WIGGINS: He's too bold, too bold.

MRS. SAM JONES: Shame he's got us all in this mess.

CORA PERKINS: SHAME, SHAME, SHAME.

SISTER PRIME: Sh-s-s!

LOTTIE MUMFORD: Yes, indeedy!

SISTER HOLT: Mess or no mess, I got ma Winchester.

MRS. SAM JONES: They'll never run Sam and me out, neither!

MATTIE CRANE: Amen!

MADAM PRESIDENT: Sisters, can't you hear this bell?

LUCY DOVES: Sh-ss!

MADAM PRESIDENT: Madam Secretary, take your chair.

(MRS. SAM JONES *comes forward.*)

CORA PERKINS: Ter'ble, ter'ble! (*Again the bell taps.*) Sh-s-s!

MADAM PRESIDENT: The March meetin' of the Salvation Rock Ladies' Missionary Society for the Rescue o' the African Heathen is hereby called to order. Sister Holt, raise a hymn. All stand! (*As the talking continues.*) Will you-all ladies *please* be quiet? What are you talkin' 'bout back there, any-how?

LUCY DOVES: Heathens, daughter, heathens.

SISTER WIGGINS: They ain't in Africa neither!

SISTER HOLT (*singing from her chair in a deep alto voice as the others join in*):

> I shall not be,
> I shall not be moved.
> Oh, I shall not be,
> I shall not be moved.
> Like a tree that's
> Planted by the waters,
> I shall not be moved.

CURTAIN

The Breakout

by CHARLES (OYAMO) GORDON

Charles (Oyamo) Gordon is a member of the Black Theater Workshop in Harlem, New York.

THE PEOPLE

DISC JOCKEY
SLAM
FEET
FIRST HACK
SECOND HACK
THIRD HACK
REVEREND J. P. JACKSON
TIGER LIBERATOR
FIRST REPORTER
SECOND REPORTER
THIRD REPORTER
WOMAN
DOLLABILL
MALCOLM X
AUDIENCE

All the people are black except for the SECOND HACK *and the* THIRD HACK, *who are in white-face.*

PART I

(The jail. There is a suggestion of two jail cells across the corridor [street] from each other. One cell is plushly furnished and decorated like an expensive, prestige apartment. The other cell has two beds, a battered chest of drawers, and a toilet and sink. Structurally, both cells are made of brick walls and steel bars, but there are no actual bars blocking the entrances. Near the cells is a typical street sign like that on any corner in any large black urban center. There are also billboard advertisements slanted to capture the black market. There are garbage cans, litter, empty bamboo packets, wine bottles, and all the other items that we see in the so-called ghetto slums of America.

In the sparse cell are two black men. One of them dances to a heavy beat from a portable radio. He wildly dances with a life-size rag doll made from a blanket, a string mop, and a rubber ball with a painted white face. It is a replica of a white girl. The other man taps one of his very big feet as he watches. The lights are predominantly red and they revolve and flicker

407

as in a fantasy. When the first number ends, the DISC JOCKEY *announces.*)

DISC JOCKEY: Are you ready for another one? It's a WRPL double-play! Yes, indeed! See if this can't git next to ya. Number three in the top ten!

(*Another currently popular black tune blares out. It continues for a few defining bars as the* FIRST HACK [*prison guard*] *in a policeman's uniform strolls toward the cell. He motions to them to turn the music down. The lights slowly revolve to gray prison pallor, the general lighting for the play. The men answer back in loud protest. They wolf like they are not in jail but know full well they are.*)

FEET (*as he turns down the radio*): Down the radio? What da fuck fa?

SLAM: Ain't dis some shit?

FIRST HACK: Keep that racket down from now on. And don't forget to say "sir" when you talk to me.

FEET (*fidgeting*): Dis muthafucka gon come to our house, break up our party 'n shit.

SLAM (*laying the doll on his bunk*): Ah know ah ain't done a goddamn thang. Mufucka kin kiss mah black ass.

FIRST HACK (*pulls out his stick and unfastens the clasp over his gun*): You're going to get your black nigger ass *kicked* from one end of this jail to the other. Okay, wiseguys, I tried to be nice but now you better off the radio or I'll kick that fucking thing into a million fucking pieces and there won't be no more nigger music in this block. That's after I stomp the shit outta you. (SLAM *and* FEET *glare at him.*) You black boys going to do what I told you or do I have to come in there and show you? (SLAM *turns the radio off. The* HACK *begins to stroll on by.*) Now you keep it like that until I tell you differently, you hear? (*There is silence. The* HACK *stops.*) I said, "You hear?"

SLAM *and* FEET: Yeah.

HACK: WHAT?

SLAM *and* FEET (*louder*): Yessir.

HACK: That's better. You boys want something to do, lick that rag slut's cunt. (*He walks away, pigsnickering. After he is gone, the men speak.*)

FEET: Who da fuck do that hack think he is? Ah swear, Slam, dis place is like being in jail.

SLAM: Oh yeah? You mean you think you ain't in jail?

FEET: But ah mean like jail with bars 'n shit.

SLAM (*feeling the brick wall*): Feet, what da fuck you think this brick is?

FEET: Ah don't mean these tenement walls.

SLAM: You must be talking 'bout some jail ah ain't never heard of. You in jail and you talkin' 'bout you ain't in jail. Every nigga we know is in jail. Whas' wrong wit you, Feet?

FEET: Damn, nigga. Ah was just reflecting; ain't no need for you to crack.

SLAM (*low*): Some of us in this block been trying to crack these walls. (*Normal voice.*) Now here you come along and just gon reflect on this wall and make it crack open.

FEET: You crackin' again?

SLAM: Ah ain't said nothin' 'bout yo juju shit.

FEET: Den why da fuck is it on your mind, Slam, huh?

SLAM: Awww man, don't git warm. Ah ain't got nothin' against juju. You kin juju yo ass off as far as um concerned. (*Pointing at the other cell.*) See if you can't juju us one them boss cribs.

FEET: Yeah, okay, Slam.

SLAM: You ain't been in this block one month yet and I don't hardly know you, but you sho' gits hard to deal with sometimes. You know that, Feet? You mah man, square bidness, but you hard to deal with.

FEET: Das 'cause ah be minding mah own bidness.

SLAM: But you need to relax, man, you jump salty too quick.

FEET: Being in dis place keep me salty.

SLAM: Um here witchu. I don't like it either, but you can't be goin' 'round fucking with yo brothers jus' 'cause Mista Ann got you locked up. You know I be jiving when I crack on you. Just passin' time till ah git mah shit tagetha to break outta here.

FEET (*relenting*): Yeah man, ah know.

SLAM: Da only serious cracking ah do is on yo big feet.

FEET (*jiving*): Aw, kiss mah ass, nigga.

SLAM: But damn, Feet, yo' feet so big, man, no jive.

FEET (*moving toward* SLAM): And um gon put both of em dead up yo ass.

(*The lights fade to fantasy.* SLAM *and* FEET *do mock nigga battle, sparring and jumping around each other like on the corner.* FEET *dances lightly on his feet, waiting for any opening to kick or to hit.* SLAM *feigns punches to* FEET *and provides the sound effects of blows landing.*)

SLAM: Be cool now, Feet. You know um fast. BIP! Look-adere, ah almos' bus' yo jaw, nigga. Okay, keep fuckin' wid me, umo lay mah heavy shit on yo. Now check dis—BLAM!— ah jus caved in yo chest. Damn, nigga, you ain't dead yet? (FEET *scares* SLAM *with some fancy foot kicks.*) Now don't jump serious, Feet. You know I will lay you out. (FEET *traps*

SLAM *in a corner and feigns attack with well-controlled kicks.*)
Be careful, Feet; you know you might trip 'n shit. Dig, pardna,
we only playin'. (FEET *becomes more aggressive in the mock
battle.* SLAM *falls to his knees and cops a mock plea.*) Oh,
please, Feet, don't put yo giant feet on mah head. Don't kill
me, Feet. Ah'll never crack again, square bidness. Don't crush
me, Feet!

FEET: You promise not to talk about mah feet anymore?

SLAM: Ah promise not to ever again crack on yo feet.
(FEET *dances away victoriously.*) Whew! Dem feet is a
monsta!

FEET (*jumping back on* SLAM): See dere, nigga, you don't
know when to lighten up, do ya? (SLAM *grabs his rag doll
and shoves her at* FEET.)

SLAM: Ah'll give you mah white slut if you spare mah
black ass.

FEET (*with one foot on the doll's chest*): What kin yo rag
bitch do for me?

SLAM: She majored in head jobs at Vassar.

FEET: Can't ah just git some plain ole simple pussy?

SLAM: She minored in that at City College.

FEET (*flopping on his bed as the lights return to prison
pallor*): Ah can't go on, Slam. I mean, we be crackin' 'n shit,
but we know it's all dead serious.

SLAM (*getting off the floor to retrieve the doll*): Awww
man, why you always wanna jump that way? What else kin we
do? Dig it, we in jail. Them hacks fuck ova us like we dogs,
we git our ass beat if we look like we might do wrong, our
women hate us, our children don't listen to us, and da help
treat us like shit. What else kin we do now besides crack on
each other?

FEET: We kin try to break outta here. Go to Africa maybe.

SLAM: Outta here to Africa? Ain't no such place, brotha.
(*As they talk,* SLAM *removes the doll's mop wig and produces a white rubber ball that serves as the head. He plays
catch with* FEET. *They shoot at imaginary hoops, pitch at
home plates, practice throwing grenades, etc.*)

FEET: Less not start crackin' again, okay?

SLAM: Square bidness, Feet, what used to be Africa is now
southern Europe.

FEET: All right, we talked about it before—I mean like
France and England is trying to keep them African niggas
under control—but you can't say Africa don't exist by calling
it southern Europe. That don't make no sense.

SLAM: Look, Feet, you know ah admit ta bein' a dumb
nigga, but you also know um hip, right?

FEET: Right.

SLAM: Okay, ah read up on all kinds a shit.

FEET: Where you find something ta read in this place?

SLAM: Th' brother who be passin' 'round *Muhammad Speaks*.

FEET: *Muhammed Speaks?* Why ain't he never passed it to me?

SLAM: It's hard 'n a mufucka slippin' that paper 'round in this jail. You got to git up off one a dem candy bars you be gettin' at the commissary store when you lock out to the avenue.

FEET: You mean ah got to give dis nigga a candy bar to git at the truth?

SLAM: Das pretty cheap for some truth, ain't it? Or is you just cheap?

FEET: Yeah, okay, man. Whas da point?

SLAM: Well, goin' to Africa is like gettin' deeper in jail, unless you goin' over there to fight with guerrillas like in Mozambique. Jail is wherever white people run black people's lives.

FEET: But they got black governments over there, man, with armies 'n shit.

SLAM: Lookahere, nigga, if you head house nigga an da masta come to you an' say he goin' away for a while, an' you 'sposed ta run da plantation for him, whose plantation is it?

FEET: The masta's.

SLAM: Dig on it.

FEET: That sure don't leave no hope.

SLAM: Hope? Hope for what?

FEET: I gotta have someplace else to go if umo break outta jail.

SLAM: Damn, Feet, think about breakin' out first. That's what we got ta do now.

FEET: Okay, Africa is out, except for side visits to find out what's happening there.

SLAM: You sho is anxious ta git over there. Why don't you try walkin', Feet.

FEET: If ah had the power I could do it.

SLAM: Power.

FEET: Power to do what I know I can do. Ah wanna write poems and study for the priesthood.

SLAM: A black Catholic juju nigga?

FEET: Is you crackin' or is you jus dumb?

SLAM: Um crackin' cause um dumb. What you wanna study to be?

FEET: A voodoo priest, maybe in the Yoruba religion. See,

411

all ah know now is how to ask unnamed gods for favors. Mah grandma taught me that. She da one who gave me this juju ah wear around mah neck. But it might make things easier if ah knew exactly what god to ask for what. There's so much ah don't know. Ah wanna learn; that's why ah quit college.

SLAM: Oh, ah see. Well, ah'll tell ya what. Ah don't crack on anybody's religion, but, dig it, no harm intended, but ah don't think a few roots is gon crack these walls. Best thing you kin do with a root is eat it, man. It ain't got no power.

FEET: Don't say that, don't say that, 'cause you know as well as I do how much power just one root has.

SLAM: How much do it got?

FEET: If I plant just one seed under this wall and that seed sprouts, this whole wall gotta move to let that root grow. Now, that's just one root.

SLAM: Aww man, what kin ah say afta dat? Okay, pardna, roots got power. But dig it. (*Low.*) A bunch is fixing to bus' a whole wall down an' raise. If you got yo shit tagetha, you kin lay wit us.

FEET: Um down.

SLAM: Keep cool till ah let you know what's happening. I have to hip da otha brothas so they'll know where you at.

FEET: Where um at? I'm in jail wid them.

SLAM: Square bidness? You in jail, eh?

FEET: Damn, you da crackinest nigga. I bet that's how you got in here; you fell for crackin'.

SLAM: As a matta a fack, das what happened. I cracked when ah shouldna cracked.

FEET: How's dat?

SLAM: Ah cracked mah mama's legs and crawled out. Eva since then ah been in jail.

FEET: Ah guess das how we all got here.

SLAM: Das true, but you never did tell me how you got moved to this block.

FEET: It just fell on me one day, you dig? (*As* FEET *talks, the lights begin to fade into fantasy.*) Like, ah was doing mah thing out there, tryin' to survive like everybody else. Next thing ah know, the hacks was sent after me. They said ah did something wrong, and so they took me to see this dude—ah guess he was the judge, but, dig, this dude spoke a different language—ah didn't understand a word he was saying. Like, les say, he was faggot and I was a young boy who didn't know what a faggot was.

(*The lights are completely in fantasy.* SLAM *goes into a cracking thing as he plays the faggot image of the oppressor.*

FEET *couples his hands behind his back and kneels before the "bench," the dresser.*)

JUDGE (*greedily checking out* FEET): My, my, what have we here? You may get up off your knees for the time being, dear. (*Leafing through some papers as* FEET *gets up.*) Oh, I see, "A wise punk," the officer says here. Knowing *that* fact may tend to make the court more lenient if you are willing to throw yourself at my . . . ah . . . mercy.

FEET: At yo what? Climb down, dude, you know ah ain't done nothin' but cop what's mine. Um innocent, baby.

JUDGE: Your violations of the court's decadent decorum was—however delightful, baby—not at all within keeping with our ancient traditions of words. I must therefore ask you to desist from ejaculating your primitive vulgarities.

FEET: Bullshit!

JUDGE: I look upon you in contempt and subsequently find you guilty of your black crimes.

FEET: Ah ain't done nothin' but keep mah family alive.

JUDGE: You are hereby judged guilty of the following crimes:

Going into extensive debt for your house, clothes, food, and Cadillac . . .

Producing too many black children . . .

Dropping out of high school . . .

Operating a numbers establishment without legal consent . . .

Peddling without a license . . .

Thinking . . . and thinking that you are better than other Negroes in our eyes . . .

Driving without a license . . .

Sleeping with welfare mothers and being on welfare yourself . . .

Possession of dangerous narcotics such as marijuana . . .

Drinking expensive Scotch and imported wines . . .

Failure to pay your gas and electric bill for over two months . . .

Using abusive language . . .

Being consistently late for work over the years . . .

Drawing unemployment compensation for eighteen months.

Making degrading statements about your employer and about white people in general . . .

Doing skilled work without a license . . .

Trying to start a business that only benefited black people . . .

Producing inflammatory poems, essays, plays, sculptures, and paintings for black people . . .

Telling innocent Negroes that they are really the New Africans . . .

And in general for having a belligerent, antisocial, un-American attitude.

FEET: But I'm innocent, ah ain't done nothin' but keep mah family alive.

JUDGE: The court might forgive your guilt if you promise to "be nice" to the court, honey.

FEET: You suck mah black dick, muthafucka!

JUDGE (*after a high-pitched giggle-titter of delight*): The court is willing to defer sentencing until after your demand is satisfied.

FEET: MUTHAFUCKA! (*He spits at the* JUDGE's *face.*)

JUDGE: Why you miserable black masculine ingrate. You are hereby sentenced to spend your entire lifetime in prison . . . sweetie.

(*The lights begin to slowly fade back to prison pallor. The* JUDGE *laughs hysterically during the changeover.*)

FEET: My lifetime? But I'm innocent. I was just trying to take care of mah family. I ain't done nothin' wrong, nothin' wrong, nothin' wrong, innocent, innocent, innocent.

(*The lights are back at prison pallor.*)

SLAM: Yeah, dat sounds like the same meatball trip we all been on.

(*We hear* HACK's VOICE *over the loudspeaker.*)

SECOND HACK's VOICE: OKAY, OFF THE RADIOS, READY UP FOR THE COUNT AND YOU BETTER BE UP OFF YOUR ASS. BLOCK C, TIER 5, READY-UP FOR THE COUNT.

SLAM: Awwwshit, same ole bullshit. Get ready for the census taker, welfare worker, and time clock.

(*The* HACK *is heard counting as he approaches.*)

SECOND HACK: 27, 178, 769—27, 178, 770—27, 178, 771. (*Now in view, the* HACK *carries a clipboard and pencil. He is counting as he points first at* SLAM *and then at* FEET.) 27, 178, 772—27, 178, 773. Hey, niggers, why ain't your rag bitch standing up for the count?

SLAM: What da fuck you think? She ain't real.

HACK: What you say, boy?

SLAM: I said, "What da fuck you think, sir? She ain't real, sir."

FIRST HACK: Pick up that bitch so I can count her too.

SLAM: But she ain't no jail nigga, sir.

FIRST HACK: As long as you fucking her, boy, she a jail nigger until she changes her mind.

SLAM: But she a rag doll, sir.

FIRST HACK: Pick that bitch up or get your ass stomped, boy. (SLAM *picks up the headless doll.*) Where's her fucking head? (SLAM *retrieves her head and the mop wig and places them appropriately.*) That's more like it, boy. (*He goes on counting as he walks by.*) 27, 178, 774.

(*After the* FIRST HACK *has gone by,* SLAM *and* FEET *flop on their respective bunks.* SLAM *throws the doll on the floor. We can still hear the* FIRST HACK *counting as he passes other cells in the block.*)

FIRST HACK'S VOICE: 27, 178, 775—27, 178, 776—27, 178, 777 (FIRST HACK's *voice fades to silence.*)

FEET: Um ready to break out this joint now. I can't take this shit too much longer. I just can't take it!

SLAM (*looking around nervously*): Lighten up, Feet, don't blow. We got a scheme cooking. Dig, Dollabill gon drop by tonight and run down whas' happ'nin' with the plans.

FEET: Dollabill? Who's dat?

SLAM: Be cool, Feet; you'll find out tonight.

(*We hear the loud clanking of steel doors opening and closing. Then we hear feet marching.* REVEREND JACKSON *enters flanked by two hacks,* SECOND HACK *and* THIRD HACK. SECOND HACK *carries two expensive leather suitcases embroidered with the* REVEREND's *initials. The* THIRD HACK *carries fresh towels and a tray with a pitcher of icewater and a glass.* JACKSON *carries an attaché case. He is well dressed and he is treated with utmost respect and politeness by the* HACKS. *Once in his cell,* JACKSON *seats himself and removes some papers from his case. He puts on his spectacles and surveys the papers importantly.* FEET *and* SLAM *look on. The* HACKS *set down the cases and tray and "freshen up" the room a bit for* JACKSON. *When they are finished:*)

SECOND HACK: Is there anything else, Reverend Jackson?

JACKSON (*in an affected, proper or "high" English accent*): No, thank you, Guard. (*The* HACKS *start to leave.*) Oh, Guards, there is one thing you could do for me.

SECOND HACK: Yessir?

JACKSON: Please have the commissary store send up coffee and doughnuts for my press conference this evening.

SECOND HACK: Yessir.

(HACKS *start to leave again.*)

JACKSON: Oh, and one other thing, have *The New York Times* sent up. And whatever you do, get me some stronger sleeping pills for my nightmares.

SECOND HACK: Yessir. The doctor is making up stronger pills now. They're called Formula H, guaranteed to make you sleep.

JACKSON: Fine. That will be all.

(*The* HACKS *leave. We hear the steel doors closing after they are off.* SLAM *and* FEET *speculate between themselves.*)

SLAM: What in da fuck dis nigga do?

FEET: His "press conference"?

SLAM: Send up coffee and doughnuts? In jail?

FEET: Dem hacks was kissing his ass. Did you see that?

(FIRST HACK's *voice booms through the loudspeaker.*)

FIRST HACK's VOICE: STAND BY FOR COMMISSARY LOCKOUT. STAND BY FOR COMMISSARY LOCKOUT.

(FEET *and* SLAM *jump to their feet. They go into their pockets to check their money.* JACKSON *settles comfortably on his bed for a nap.*)

SLAM: It's about time. Um down to mah last candy bar.

FEET: Umo git me some paper, pencils, ten bean pies, six boxes of crackers, and a pound of cheese.

FIRST HACK's VOICE: OKAY, FALL OUT YOUR CELLS AND FORM A STRAIGHT LINE.

(SLAM *and* FEET *fall out and form a straight line facing the audience, the rest of the prisoners.*)

SLAM: You got yo dough together? Dey ain't gon waste no time waiting for you ta dig in yo pockets.

FEET: Ah got a five-dolla bill in mah hand right now.

SLAM: Five dollas? Damn, you ain't gon git all you want for that in this commissary store.

FIRST HACK's VOICE: KNOCK OFF THE BULLSHIT. PRISONERS, RIGHT, FACE, FORWARD, DOUBLE-TIME, MARCH!

(SLAM *and* FEET *double-time out of the block. The lights fade down to black. In the black we hear steel doors clanking shut again. As the house lights come up, we hear the* FIRST HACK's *voice barking at the audience.*)

FIRST HACK's VOICE: STAND BY FOR INTERMISSION LOCKOUT, NIGGERS. LOCK OUT FOR INTERMISSION. LOCKOUT FOR INTERMISSION. YOU GOT ———— MINUTES. I REPEAT. YOU GOT ———— MINUTES.

(*The same voice calls the people back from Intermission.*)

PART II

(*The lights come up as* SLAM *and* FEET *double-time back before their cells with their arms full of packages. They halt before the cell.*)

FIRST HACK's VOICE: LEFT FACE, FORWARD, MARCH!

(SLAM *and* FEET *march into their cell. Once inside, they tear into their packages.*)

FEET: Damn, this sure ain't much for five dollars.

SLAM: Ah tole you that. Next week you gon get even less for five dollars. When you a prisoner, you got to pay the prices they want.

FEET: It's gon be a hungry week for me.

SLAM: Relax, they gon give you three squares a day.

FEET: Three squares mah ass. They give us half a meal and four slices a stale, white bread for filling. That's not healthy.

SLAM: It's better than nothin'. Least it taste good.

FEET: Das 'cause they got Jamima chained in the kitchen.

SLAM: What you got to do, Feet, is always have you one bean pie after each meal. Othawise you'll starve to death.

FEET: But what about mah paper and pencils? If ah got ta spend all mah money on bean pies, how um gon write poems 'n shit?

SLAM: If you wanna write and starve, go 'head. But you'll be doin' good if you save the wrappers and write yo shit on them.

(JACKSON *begins to toss, turn, and moan in his sleep.* SLAM *and* FEET *are attentive.*)

SLAM: Don't look like them sleeping pills doin' dis mufucka any good.

FEET: He havin' a nightmare.

(JACKSON *mumbles loudly as he tosses.*)

JACKSON: Ungrateful dog—bad nigga—agitator—it ain't that way—you're exaggerating—that's not true—shut up, I tell you—you gon get hurt—we all Americans—Negroes won't follow you—no—no—NO—NO-O-O-O-O-O-o-o-o! (*He leaps up from his dreambed and tries to focus his consciousness back to reality.*)

SLAM (*to* JACKSON): Yo, brotha, you all right?

(JACKSON *is still shaking off the nightmare. He doesn't answer.* FEET *watches him carefully.*)

SLAM: Ah say, yo, brotha, you all right? You was having a bad dream.

JACKSON: Wha . . . what?

SLAM: You musta been havin' a monsta of a dream, brotha. You all right?

JACKSON (*recovered, he speaks sharply and condescendingly*): Of course, I'm all right. Sorry if I disturbed you.

SLAM (*sensing the bad vibrations*): Say, dig, brotha, ah thought ah was doin' you a favor.

JACKSON: Thank you, but there was no need for you to be alarmed. I'm quite all right, thank you.

SLAM: Yeah, well wuddin no need to jump all salty, brotha. We all in jail, you know?

JACKSON: Perhaps the latter is true, but being in jail together doesn't make us brothers.

FEET: Say what?

SLAM: Awwwwshit, one a dem. What you say yo name is?

JACKSON: I didn't say, but my full title is the Most Reverend J. P. Jackson.

SLAM (*mimicking*): Oh, I'm so sorry to have bothered you, old chap. But I thought your name was Thomas Pee.

JACKSON: I suspect that you engage in personal rancor for which I have little taste and much contempt. (*He removes his jacket and shoes, loosens his collar, and lies back down.*)

SAM (*to* FEET): Pin dis muthafucka.

FEET (*to Jackson*): Whas wrong wid you, brotha? Mah man tryin' to be friendly an' you come down on him. Now, that ain't correct, brotha; you know that.

JACKSON (*perching on his elbows*): My dear sir, let me assure you that my brothers are all located in different sections of this place and they are all professional men with college degrees. So, if you would be so kind as to desist from addressing me as your brother . . . (*He lies back down and turns over.*)

FEET: Damn!

SLAM: Dis a hopeless mufucka. Don't waste yo time.

FEET: But there's got to be some truth somewhere in him.

SLAM: Truth? The truth is dat the dude ain't correct, dass all. He think he better than the rest of us. Look at him. Got him a boss pad, git shit sent up to him, hacks kissing his ass.

FEET: But there must be some reason for all that. I mean like, he is another black man; he got to have some good in him. The truth is right before our eyes, but we just can't see it.

SLAM: Well, ah'll tellya what. Ask yo unidentified gods for the truth. How's dat?

FEET: Das a good idea, Slam. Thank you.

SLAM: Damn!

(*A brother with a long-handled push broom and a janitorial pushcart walks into the block and stops near* SLAM *and* FEET's *cell. He is dressed in some sort of uniform. He wears a beret and a medallion around his neck. He begins a sweeping operation of the area.*)

SLAM: Yo, Cat. Whas to it, brotha?

CAT: Ain't nothin happ'nin'; you got it.

SLAM: You think they ever gon let you out that solitary confinement?

CAT (*checks over his shoulder and then approaches their cell*): Shit, the Man said that we so dangerous he gon keep us segregated from everybody.

FEET: We?

CAT (*to* SLAM *as he checks out* FEET): Who dis?

SLAM: Dis mah main man Feet.

CAT (*as he does a complicated handshake greeting that somewhat bewilders* FEET): Power to the people, brotha. They calls me Cat. (*Finished with the greeting.*) "We" is the Royal Order of Tiger Liberators.

FEET: Oh yeah, ah read about yaw in *The New York Times.*

CAT: Well, don't believe what da pig say 'bout us, brotha.

FEET: Naw man, ah ain't sayin . . .

CAT: What you sayin,' brotha, is dat you read some lies about us in the chief pig newspaper. Now, if you want the truth, um ready to give that to you . . . if you can take it.

FEET: If ah can take it? Hole tight. I always want the truth so that . . .

CAT: You hole tight, brotha. The truth is always in the source, and the Royal Order of Tiger Liberators is the source of truth about the black man in the wilderness of North America. If you so down, like Slam say, ah know you wanna hear the truth, you dig?

FEET: Da dude in the paper tole the truth, cause he belong . . .

CAT: Tole the truth? Naw, brotha, you better stop an' listen fo it's too late. Nothin' personal, but you one of our deaf, dumb, and blind brothas.

FEET: Sheeet!

CAT: Brotha, ain't no need ta git drugged. Ah said it wasn't personal. Most of the niggas in dis jail is deaf, dumb, and blind. They can't help it. You so hip, why don't you listen for a change.

SLAM (*to* FEET): You might as well listen; he gon tell you anyway.

FEET: Um listening, brotha.

(*The lights begin to fade to fantasy. The Tiger Liberator shoulders the broom as if it is a rifle. He gives a rifle salute and raises his left fist in a power salute. His fist remains thus until his monologue is over.*)

CAT: We, of the Royal Order of Tiger Liberators, in recognition of the plight of all poor people, especially black people,

do hereby pledge our lives, fortunes, and sacred honor to the restoration of poor people's rights and dignities in this wilderness of North America. We also recognize and proclaim the aggressors to be the Wall Street capitalist pigs. Since the capitalist pigs constantly oppress working class black people and white people, we vow to defend our people by any means necessary, and this is to be understood as meaning the use of weapons and guerrilla warfare. In recognition of the crisis that exists today, we further hereby form this organization and will subscribe to the following rules:

1. There will be no spitting on the floor during Liberator meetings.
2. No Liberator may attack another Liberator on or off duty.
3. Fornicating with another Liberator's woman is strictly prohibited.
4. All Liberators must at all times carry a semi-automatic 30 caliber carbine and 200 rounds. If he cannot carry it, he must have it nearby.
5. All Liberators must obey his superior and show him utmost respect.
6. All Liberators must be neat, courteous, and well groomed at all times.
7. All Liberators must wear their uniforms to cell meetings.
8. No Liberator may miss more than two cell meetings a year.
9. All Liberators must show utmost respect for black women.
10. No Liberator may engage in racial slurs against any race of people.
11. All Liberators must cooperate cheerfully with our allies be they black, yellow, or white.
12. All Liberators must read Mao's *Redbook* and Marx's *Das Capital* (*nigger pronunciation*) three times a year, and he must be prepared to quote passages when asked.
13. No Liberator may eat pork chops, drive a Cadillac, or drink Scotch.
14. Any Liberator breaking any of the aforesaid rules will be punished severely.

(*The lights fade back to prison pallor.*)

FEET: Ah see where you at now.

CAT: Beautiful, brotha. Ah knew you would. You hang wit the Liberators, you'll be taken care of.

FEET: Kin yaw break us out of here?

(SLAM *looks at* FEET *tensely.*)

CAT: We gittin' to that now. If you got anything planned, you oughtta hole tight till we give you the word. We kin even git some hacks to help you.

SLAM (*hurriedly*): Das just what we doin',' holding tight till yaw git it tagether. So, like, why don't you find out what you can and let us know.

CAT: Bet.

FIRST HACK'S VOICE (*loudspeaker*): OFF ALL THE BULL-SHIT. GET YOUR BLACK ASS UP TO THE NEXT BLOCK, CAT.

CAT: Sheeet!

FIRST HACK'S VOICE: WHAT THE FUCK YOU SAY, NIG-GER?

CAT (*as he loads his cart*): Yessuh.

SLAM: Lata, Cat.

FEET: Don't forget to let us know.

CAT (*as he quickly hats*): Huh? Oh yeah. Sure thing, brother.

(*As soon as* CAT *is gone,* SLAM *turns to* FEET.)

SLAM: Damn, brotha, you almost blew. Dat muthafucka—ah don't know about him. Some of the brothers think he is the Man in disguise.

FEET: Naw, ah wasn't gon blow. Ah had this dude pinned when he first started rappin'. That article I read in *The New York Times?* It was written by the minister of defense of Royal Order of Tiger Liberators. Das why I knew he was jiving. I just wanted to see how far he'd go, das all.

SLAM: Whew! Um sho glad to hear that, Feet.

FEET: Um still layin' for this Dollabill dude you be talkin about.

SLAM: He on his way. Soon as he git here we gon hook up and leave this joint.

FEET: Well, ah wish he'd just git here so we kin git this scheme tagetha.

(*We hear the steel doors clanking. A group of four black people, three men and one woman, enter escorted by the* FIRST HACK *and the* SECOND HACK. *One man carries a camera, another a portable tape recorder, and the other two have pencils and reporters' notepads. The* FIRST HACK, *who is the last to enter, carries a serving tray with coffee and doughnuts. The* SECOND HACK *halts them in front of* REVEREND JACKSON'S *cell.*)

SECOND HACK: Wait here while I wake him for the press conference.

(*The* REPORTERS *mumble among themselves. The* SECOND HACK *enters the cell and gently wakens the tossing and turning* JACKSON. *Once up,* JACKSON *puts on his jacket, shoes, and sprinkles some water on his face. The* HACK *places the tray*

421

on the dresser and tidies up the cell a bit. While this is going ON, SLAM *cracks on the bitch.*)

SLAM (*quietly*): Psssst. Say, baby.

WOMAN (*speaks reluctantly and condescendingly*): Are you addressing me?

SLAM: Dig, baby, step over here. (*She doesn't move.*) All ah want is some information, square bidness. (*She moves a couple of steps in his direction.*) What did that nigga do to get all this good treatment?

WOMAN: You might do better to heed his example rather than ask questions about things which don't concern you.

SLAM: Damn, bitch, ah ain't ass you f'all dat.

SECOND HACK: Who gave you permission to speak to that gal?

SLAM: Ah need to ask you 'fore I can speak to mah own sista?

WOMAN: He's no brother of mine. I've never seen him before in my life. I swear it.

SECOND HACK (*to the* FIRST HACK): Sam, your buddy needs some discipline. (FIRST HACK *rushes over to Slam's cell.*)

FIRST HACK: All right, punk, step out now.

(SLAM *steps out and the* HACK *hits him in the stomach hard enough to make him double up and fall back into the cell into* FEET's *arms.*)

FIRST HACK (*as he goes back to* SECOND HACK): Disturb these people again and you'll get worse. You understand, boy?

SLAM (*in pure frustrated hatred*): Yessir.

SECOND HACK (*to* REPORTERS): Okay, you people can go in and have your press conference. Sam here will let you know when it's over.

(*The* REPORTERS *enter* JACKSON's *cell and partake of the refreshments as they listen to* JACKSON. *The* HACKS *leave.*)

JACKSON: Now that we can proceed without further distraction, let me first read a brief statement I prepared with the help of the honorable police commissioner. (REVEREND JACKSON *puts on his spectacles and clears his throat. The camera flashes. A microphone is held up.* SLAM *and* FEET *listen out of curiosity.*) Last week I was the happy recipient of the President's National Hero Medal. I was awarded the medal as a result of my successfully carrying out a dangerous and secret mission for the government of these United States. For reasons of national security I cannot reveal the explicit purpose or the nature of the mission. Nevertheless, I accepted the medal, and I accepted it on behalf of my people. And let me quickly add that my people are all those who seek

to work and live together in peace and harmony, be they white, yellow or black. I have called this press conference at the request of the President to clear up any points of contention as to where my loyalty lies. I have always believed in the United States of America and the principles of the Constitution. I believe in maintaining law and order to the last degree. Let us fill our jails with those who cannot act in accordance with the law, be they black or otherwise. I believe that white and Negro people should work together to realize the American Dream. I am adamantly opposed to those Negro extremists who advocate breaking away from the American institutions and traditions. There is no room in my heart for those who want to break out of the greatest system of democracy the world has ever seen. Finally, let me say, the Negroes' destiny is inextricably tied to the destiny of white people in America. When America suffers, I also suffer. God is colorless and he is with America. I shall accept questions, but I only ask one favor. Would the reporters kindly identify themselves and their newspapers when asking a question.

FIRST REPORTER: Luther James, the *Joliet Gazette*. Reverend Jackson, since you cannot elaborate on the mission, could you tell us what result your mission achieved?

JACKSON: I can only reply in general terms. The mission has resulted in the elimination of divisive factors in the Negro community.

SECOND REPORTER: Samuel Brinkley, the *Alcatraz Journal*. Is it true, Reverend Jackson, that working for the government has caused black extremist breakout groups to name you as their number one enemy?

JACKSON: It is true that they wish to chastise me for being loyal to the United States Government. But I'm quite secure in my surroundings, and I seldom think of danger when I'm doing a job for America. God will watch over me.

THIRD REPORTER: William Jones, *Rikers' Island Courier*. Is it true that you suffered extensive brain damage as a result of your secret mission?

JACKSON: It is true that I am receiving treatment for a cranial difficulty, but I wouldn't call it extensive brain damage, as my enemies would have everyone believe.

THIRD REPORTER: Just what is the problem, sir?

JACKSON: I have extreme difficulty sleeping.

SECOND REPORTER: You suffer from insomnia?

JACKSON: No, but I seem to have terrible nightmares.

FIRST REPORTER: What are your nightmares about, sir?

JACKSON: I cannot disclose that without revealing the nature and purpose of the mission itself.

WOMAN: Isabel Washington, *Blackwood* magazine, Johnson Detention Center, Publications Department. You mentioned you were receiving treatment for your nightmares. What kind of treatment?

JACKSON: The doctor tells me to take frequent naps, and he is presently preparing a new prescription for me called Formula H, a most powerful sedative.

WOMAN: Just one more question, sir. Actually, it's a request. As you know *Blackwood* magazine has a monthly column called "Speaking of People." In that column we publish the achievements of prominent Negroes in all fields. If it is possible, we would like to feature you in our column next month. Could you possibly write a brief sketch of your important contributions and send it to Johnson Detention Center, Publications Department?

JACKSON: I would be most delighted.

WOMAN: Oh, thank you so much, sir. Your story should inspire thousands of our young Negro men to great heights of achievements.

(FIRST HACK *returns.*)

FIRST HACK: All right, the press conference is over. You people line up outside here. (*The* REPORTERS *line up. The* HACK *hands* JACKSON *a small bottle filled with pills.*) Here's that Formula H you've been waiting for.

JACKSON: Thank you. I shall try them immediately.

FIRST HACK (*to* REPORTER): All right, move out.

(JACKSON *removes his jacket and shoes, loosens his collar, and takes a pill. He lies down. The* REPORTERS *are marched out.*)

SLAM: You kin see where dat mufucka's at now. What more truth do you need?

FEET: We still don't know what he done.

SLAM: Ah don't give a fuck right now. We breaking out this joint tonight.

FEET: Tonight?

SLAM: Tonight.

(DOLLABILL *comes on the block and heads for* SLAM *and* FEET's *cell. He constantly rattles a pair of dice, throws them up against the cell wall, etc.*)

DOLLABILL: A dolla ah git nine.

SLAM: Dollabill! Where da hell you been, nigga?

DOLLABILL: Makin' me some heavy, heavy dollas.

SLAM: We been waitin' all day.

DOLLABILL: Here I am. Ah woulda come soona 'cept some nigga tried to rough me off in L Block, but he copped out to a punk one, and ah had ta take time ta cool him out, you unnastan?

SLAM: But we 'sposed to be scheming to git out this joint.

DOLLABILL (*checking* FEET): You sho you ain't blowin'?

SLAM: Naw, dis mah man Feet. He down.

DOLLABILL (*checking up and down the block*): Dig, it's all set up. We just waiting for the right time.

FEET: The right time?

DOLLABILL: Yeah, you just can't be breaking out any time; you got to do it when the time is right.

SLAM: And when is dat?

DOLLABILL: Soon as we git all these niggas together, and git us some financing.

FEET: I think we better do it a little sooner than that.

DOLLABILL: No such thing. Can't no nigga break out by himself; he got to take his brothers with him or it's no go. And ah know for a fact that niggas ain't ready to jump off.

FEET: How can you know something like that?

DOLLABILL: 'Cause ah know every nigga in jail.

FEET: Bullshit.

SLAM: Ah don't think he jivin,' Feet.

FEET: But how he gon know every nigga in jail?

DOLLABILL: Um the freeest nigga in this jail.

FEET: How's dat?

DOLLABILL: Wherever the dolla goes, ah goes, and the dolla goes everyplace. Ah got ten dollas say ah hit five. How much you wanna cover?

FEET (*to* SLAM): You mean *he* settin' up the breakout?

SLAM: Not anymore.

DOLLABILL: Yaw some crazy niggas. Um tellin ya yaw can't break out till you git these niggas tagether and that means you got to git you some dollas tagether first, you dig?

SLAM: Why don't you raise, man?

DOLLABILL: Raise? Ah just got here.

(SLAM *and* FEET *step closer to* DOLLABILL.)

FEET: Mah man said raise.

DOLLABILL (*as he leaves*): Well, it don't seem like the dolla is here anyway.

(*After he is gone.*)

SLAM: Well, Feet, we back where we started.

FEET: Maybe not. At least now we know that we only have ourselves.

FIRST HACK'S VOICE (*loudspeaker*): STAND BY TO OFF THE LIGHTS.

SLAM: But what we gonna do now?

FEET: Right now ah just wanna find out what Reverend Jackson did. Um gon ask the gods to let me sit in on his nightmares.

SLAM (*lying down*): Yeah, well while you checkin' the sandman, umo try to dream up some way to get us outta here. Good night.

FEET: Good night.

(FEET *removes a small candle and some incense from under his bunk. He quickly sets up a makeshift altar on the floor and as he lights the candle:*)

FIRST HACK'S VOICE: OFF THE LIGHTS.

(*The lights snap off.* FEET *is mumbling homemade incantations over the burning candle. He makes various gestures reminiscent of his magician ancestors. We hear faint drums and chanting.* JACKSON *is tossing and turning and moaning in his cell. In a short while the lights begin to come up on the fantasy of* JACKSON'*s nightmare. As they come up there is a black speaker behind a small podium addressing the audience. The drums and the chanting have faded out. The candle is blown out. Both* FEET *and* JACKSON *move from their cells into this enactment of* JACKSON'*s nightmare, the reenactment of his secret mission.*)

MALCOLM X: We all agree tonight that America has a very serious problem. Not only does America have a very serious problem but our people have a very serious problem. America's problem is us. The only reason why she has a problem is that she doesn't want us here . . . What we need to do is learn to forget our differences. When we come together, we don't come together as Baptists or Methodists. You don't catch hell 'cause you're a Baptist, and you don't catch hell because you're a Methodist. You don't catch hell because you're a Democrat or a Republican. You don't catch hell because you're a Mason or an Elk. And you sure don't catch hell 'cause you're an American, 'cause if you were an American you wouldn't catch no hell. You catch hell 'cause you're a black man. You catch hell—all of us catch hell for the same reason. So, we're all black people, so-called Negroes, second-class citizens, ex-slaves . . . There were two kinds of slaves. There was the house Negro and the field Negro. The house Negro, they lived in the house with master. They dressed pretty good; they ate good 'cause they ate his food—what he left. They lived in the attic or the basement, but still they lived near the master. They loved their master more than the master loved

himself. They would give their life to save their master's house quicker than the master would . . . If the master got sick, the house Negro would say, "Whatsa matta, boss? We sick?" And if you came to the house Negro and said, "Let's run away, let's escape; let's separate; let's break out," that house Negro would look at you and say, "Man, you crazy. What you mean break out? Where is there a better house than this? Where can I wear better clothes than this? Where can I eat better food than this?" That was a house Negro. In those days he was called a house nigga. And that's what we call him today 'cause we still got some house niggas running around today . . . When I was in prison, I read an article—don't be shocked when I say I was in prison—you still in prison. That's what America means, prison. All black people in prison. When I was in prison, I read an article in *Life* magazine showing a little Chinese girl, nine years old; her father was on his hands and knees and she was pulling the trigger 'cause he was a Uncle Tom Chinaman. When they had the revolution over there, they took a whole generation of Uncle Toms—just wiped them out. And within ten years that little girl became a full-grown woman. No more Toms in China. Today it is one of the toughest, roughest, most feared countries on the earth by the white man, 'cause there are no Uncle Toms over there. Yeah, that's what happened over there. We better stop and use the Chinese example in understanding what it is we got to do right here. You all know who I am. My name is Malcolm X and I'm talking about a black revolution.

(JACKSON *leaps upon the stage.*)

JACKSON: Ungrateful, lying dog. You a bad nigga. We all Americans. We all believe in the American way. (*He draws a pistol and as he pumps shots into* MALCOLM *he shouts:*) I love America. I'm a proud American Negro. Negroes don't want to follow you. Blippity blip, blippity blip—no enemas want violence in the golden sewers. Scabalappa, ashy legs, die nappy-head nigga. Die—die—die—die . . . di-i-i-i-i-ie.

(*The lights fade to black on the last "die." Shortly the candle is relit. The rest of the play is done in candlelight plus some dark gray stage lighting.* FEET *is shaking* SLAM.)

FEET: Slam, Slam, get up, man.

SLAM: What da fuck?

FEET: Shhhhhhhh.

SLAM: You wake me up to tell me to be quiet?

FEET: I know why the hacks treat Jackson so good.

SLAM (*sitting up*): Ah was just dreaming about that.

FEET: You was? What you dream?

SLAM: It was some weird shit, but I dreamt Reverend Jackson killed Malcolm X.

FEET: Das just what happened.

SLAM: How you know?

FEET: I visited his nightmare.

SLAM: Das why that mufucka can't sleep. Fucking black bastard.

FEET: I think it's time we busted out this joint. Both of us could take off that hack. I'll put on his uniform and march us both to freedom.

SLAM: Um down, but it seem like we should get us some more brothers to help us.

FEET: Slam, right now it's only me and you. If we start, maybe the others will join. But we could die waiting for them.

SLAM: Yeah, they probably waiting for us.

FEET (*collecting his shit*): Shit, les raise.

SLAM (*gets up and pulls out his knife*): Umo take care of Brother Jackson 'fore we leave.

FEET: We ain't got no time now. Lesgo.

SLAM (*retrieving the rag doll*): Won't take but a minute. Hole tight. Ah also got a gift for Brother Jackson.

(SLAM *creeps over to* JACKSON's *cell, which is in darkness. After a few moments,* FEET *speaks.*)

FEET (*in a whisper*): Slam? Slam? Slam, come on before the hack comes.

(SLAM *returns without the rag doll.*)

FEET: What da fuck was you doin'?

SLAM: Finding a dead nigga. Ah think da mufucka O-D'd with that Formula H.

FEET (*ready to leave*): Ah knew there was some good in him.

SLAM (*collecting his shit while* FEET *looks out for the* HACK): Maybe, maybe not. That bottle was hardly touched. (*When he is ready.*) Blow out that candle. And don't forget yo juju shit.

(*The candle is blown out.*)

BLACK

Three X Love

by RON ZUBER

Ron Zuber lives and works in Detroit. He is a young poet and playwright. He worked with the Spirit of Shango Theater Company. Ronald Milner introduced Mr. Zuber to the theater.

NOTE:

The reasons for writing this script are many but none more profound than the praise that should be bestowed on the black woman. There are no words that can fully express all that should be said. Nor, as a black man, can I relate her story with the conception that she would have. I can only relate what I see that she has endured and what I feel that she has said in her silence and in her storm. I hope that I have done her justice and that those who portray any part of this performance will give the artistic ability in respect to her.

E'RON ZUBA

As the curtains open, the MALE NARRATOR *is standing at a podium downstage left. The* DRUMMER *is upstage center toward the left. The* SINGERS *are directly across from the* DRUMMER *to the right, and upstage right is a microphone across from the* MALE NARRATOR. *The* MOTHER, SISTER, *and* LOVER *will be using this position. I would like to add that the sisters who portray these characters are not limited to this position. In fact, if a mike is not needed then one shouldn't be used.*

The MALE NARRATOR, DRUMMER, *and* SINGERS *are the only ones on stage when the curtain opens. Sisters will follow cues.*

(The play starts with the DRUMMER *setting a two-four beat. At the appropriate time, the* SINGERS *join in.)*

SINGERS:

Three X Love *(Two beats in between.)* Three X Love, Three X Love. Three X *(Two beats.)* Love. Three X *(Two beats.)* Love, Three X Love. *(This continues until* MALE NARRATOR *begins.)*

MALE NARRATOR:

   Mother, sisters, lovers.
   Stop the wheels of us.
   Step in our path and STOP!
   Us from moving past you,
   Pass the apex and foundation of ourselves.
   STOP!
   And listen!
   Listen to what black emotions have to say.
   Stop and listen to your woman's silence.

SINGERS:
>Three X Love (*Two beats.*)
>Three X Love (*Two beats.*)
>Three X (*Two beats.*) Love.

MALE NARRATOR:
Mama,
From you silently or in agony
Which of what in my behalf.
Mama,
Giver of this life, this spirit.
Have endured my coming.
You have endured and adjusted your song to the beats of
Oppression.
Mama, creator of Black Love and Black Life
You have adjusted your soul to the rhythms of disappointment.
All with your strong softness.
Mother of the Black Crusader,
Crawing bewildered,
Into this world,
A marble throbbing hot in the hands of God
A world that strips love naked
Stares at her realness
Fondles it, mingles with her Godness
Then rejects it for being truth.
From you, Black Mother, unto this I have come.
With freedom in my heart and change on my mind.
I have searched in the small space that slavery has provided,
And have no rewards for your being.
I can only give love back to you,
As the evolution of man always returns to God.
For it is your love that I repeat,
Your hand upon my hand,
Your song in my voice.
As I arrived from your love,
Returning to it is the ultimate.
Exalting you as Queen of our Nation,
And the natural unifying force.
Truly you are our beginning and ending
To you . . . we owe life.

SINGERS:
>Gave you everything I had, now didn't I
>Gave you everything I had, now didn't I
>Gave you everything I had, just to make you be so glad.
>Gave you everything I had, now didn't I.

(*As the* SINGERS *are singing,* BLACK MOTHER *enters from stage right. After the song has stopped, the* DRUMMER *will roll the drums from low to high, and back to low. This will be the cue for* BLACK MOTHER.)

BLACK MOTHER:

BLACK MOTHER! The highest form of womanhood.
Knowing more joys and suffering than any other.
    (DRUMMER *picks up a slow tempo.*)
I, Black Mother.
Mother of warriors, kings.
Mother of slaves and freemen.
Mother of niggers and black men.
I, Black Mother, seek to be free.
    (*The tempo changes.*)
There must be a peace in death
For life is black sweat boiling on the fires of oppression
I know more than any other,
The weight of poverty.
More than any other,
My people's plight.

I, mother of traders,
Twisting their own souls white.
I, mother of black warriors,
Mending freedom in the dark of the night.
There must be a happiness in sorrow.
Black blue-blues is my secret song.
I have endured, I have suffered, I have waited
I have given sons and daughters to bear
America on their backs . . . FREE ME!

Free me,
Sons, sons, sons.
Free me, my abandoned man,
From the forces that are dragging me down,
Making me a whore,
Making me a fool,
Making me weaker
       The weakest,
         Wea-kling
         Under the burden of red-pro-white blues.
Black Manhood that I know I've given,
RISE.
Black Daughters, never let him cease—not a minute.

431

Black Grandchildren, do not fail your queen of creation.
> Black Life
> Black Existence

Do not fail me.

(BLACK MOTHER *steps back as the* SINGERS *begin "Freedom."* DRUMMER *starts with a slow tempo, something light.*)

SINGERS:
> Freedom for your Mama,
> Freedom for your Papa
> Freedom for your Brother
> But, no freedom for me.
> Freedom for your Mama's Mama,
> Freedom for your Papa's Papa,
> Freedom for your Brother's Brother,
> But no freedom for me.

BLACK MOTHER (*stepping forward*):

I rose in the South,
Like a young sapling.
The torment in the devil's eyes
From the devil's death-cold touch,
Half-men were born.
And from half-men came the reflection of a nigger.
A nigger wench I was called
Or
Harriet Tubman.

I was living in the foulest part of the city,
When my man shivered at responsibility.
He ran from infants black, seven an' a quarter pounds, his sons.
I spent my choicest years,
Scrubbing suburban floors on skid-row knees.
But never stopped producing men.
Marcus Garvey, the torment in the She-Devil's eyes.

I have given the best of minds.
I have given strong black men whom the forces turned into:
Junkies, hustlers, pimps
Car-washers, janitors, porters.
I gave Black Daughter to guide the spirit.
I gave brotherhood and love to place in their hearts.
Negroes! Where are my warriors?
> Where did you place them in your fantasy?
> Bring them to me, dreamers, individuals.
> Or I will send Malcolm to call them out.

The fires of Newark are warm
Against the face of Fate.

The death of my sons adds heaviness
To the heart of a mother.
She seeks only warrior men now.
All others will slowly vanish.
For I have dispatched my greatest generation.
Believers of brotherhood.
Unifiers and organizers,
Leaders and followers,
Poets and musicians and dancers
A prince and a princess
My guards and my last weapons

Fail me not, my children,
Bring nationhood to the next generation
And the one after.
For there is nothing which the spirit has withheld
Nor is there a naked space where the vastness of my love
Has left uncovered.
    (*Drums roll high to low, high to low,* BLACK MOTHER *continues.*)
BLACK MOTHER! The highest form of womanhood
                Knowing more joys and sufferings than
                                      any other.
   SINGERS:
    Gave you everything I had, now didn't I
    Gave you everything I had, now didn't I
    Gave you everything I had, just to make you be so glad.
    Gave you everything I had, now didn't I.
    (BLACK MOTHER *exits stage right. The* SINGERS *bring their song to a low moaning, and fade out as the* MALE NARRATOR *begins.*)
   MALE NARRATOR:
Black Mother prevails.
Yet, from her well-sowed seed come the young blossoms
Of her soul.
She is the mirror of all black people,
Our image staring back into our eyes.
She the results of our efforts and
The reward of our victory.
Our sister, thy brother's daughter,
Being discarded by frightened minds.
Bring her back!

If she is not loud, man is silence.
Her beauty astounds and all men respond.
She strides through the darkness of our lives

And confirms what we have not given as we
Clutch so tightly her life that we receive.
Bring her back! Brothers
Restore her to your heart, her throne.
Bring her back,
From the spaces that you forced her to wander in.
Bring her home from the days of labor, the days of sweat
That roll down her face like tears,
Down through the valley of her breasts,
Across her navel,
Down between her thighs.
Will it come!
Will it come!
Will the black man come to save her.

SINGERS (*with Female Lead*):
    Tell where can I go
    There's no place I can see
    Where to go, where to go
    Every door is closed to me
    To the left and to the right
    It's the same in every land
    There's nowhere I can go
    And it's me who should know
    Won't you please take my hand.

BLACK SISTER:
What shall become of me, my brother
What mountain can I claim,
What road can I travel without you.
Where in this prison can I go with the reassurance of
Succeeding if I'm capable of success.
Through my conformity I have no gain,
No freedom, no peace.
Where, along the cold gray walls of America, does the
Sun shine clearly,
Giving even your future a shadow.
If there is such a place take me there.
If not, make me one.

For so long, my brother
You have sat back and judged my worth.
And you froze at the realization that walks
Across your mind and made you sleep.
I am the second half of man, as he is
The other half of me. —
There has never been a life conceived from one person,

Nor will there ever be.
As the knowledge of myself towers from
Experience after experience,
Pain after pain,
Tear after love tear,
I cannot merely request that you be a man.
BUT I DEMAND IT.
Woman and boy are an uneven, unbalanced scale,
The same as man and girl,
If we are to be together in the totality of our lives
WE MUST BE EQUAL.
Yes, my brother I am your sister,
But I am the woman of your brother
And still more.
More than the figure that caresses your warm night
With softness.
More than the receiver of your giving and
The appraiser of your attainments and their value.
I am more than the listener of your solemn songs
Or the enlightener of your hipness.
I am more than the thrilled
When your ego is announcing the wealth it will conquer
And the gifts that you will bestow.

I am the mirror of your affections, baby,
And the teacher of your heart.
I am the goddess of your manhood
And the director of your love.
Me,
I,
Your woman, in and from the dust of the world. To make
A mark, or an "X" or cross for you. The sound in my
Voice is not me crying, but me requesting
MY RECOGNITION!
Have you blind eyes, my brother
Placing me in double-darkness —
Have the chains of servitude bounded your heart to hate.
Can you not feel the freedom of my love moving like a
Key into your locked soul.
Seeking all of your releases.
From the movements of your deeds and the shifting of
Your words it's hard for me to understand the image of
Man that you have blurred. Harder for you to defy my role.
Am I to celebrate the man in you or perpetuate the boy.
Am I to be your slave admitting, committing, and submitting,

Or your companion, sharing your every rapture, your every
Thought, adding to your every victory.
The time for decision is now, my brother
The time for respect is now,
In your emancipation I will rise.
In your fullness I cannot do anything but
To submit.
And you will have no question about your being
Free.

(SISTER *steps back with her head bowed and* SINGERS *go into "Respect Her, Protect Her."*)

SINGERS:

> Respect her, protect her
> Respect her, protect her
> Respect her, protect her
> Respect her, protect her.

(BLACK SISTER *exits stage right.*)

(*As* SINGERS *and the* MALE NARRATOR *begin again.*)

MALE NARRATOR:

> She could be seen as a jewel
> Sparkling colors, shaded blue,
> A nude pearl, hot in the sun
> A diamond in the rays of her
> Own reflection
> She is your woman.
> Your woman
> Rebuilding her soul on the remote
> Islands of thought.
> Rising above the streets of half-men
> Bitter in their intense disguise
> Refusing to be whole,
> Maintaining a life song,
> > In slave time,
> > A lifetime.
> Your woman,
> Quietly walking from this bitter mystery
> Claiming the remnants of bitter desires
> Changing them
> As she changes directions
> But never withholding her ever-giving gifts.
> Never disappearing from your eyes.
> Your woman
> Inspiring your efforts,
> Lighting, fulfilling your worth

To yourself, to your people.
Lingering in the meldoious slumber
As she is the first chapter of your every dream
Your woman being for you
Ever warm, ever close,
Ever giving, ever thankful,
Ever understanding, questioning always.
She turning! To the black side of her reality.
Turning to the point of your completion
Inside you with deep fullness
Where your spirits grind into each other
And become one.
She turning, can you stand it, brother.
Can you bear the stare at your lover.

(BLACK LOVER *enters from stage right. The* DRUMMER *is taking off on a solo until the* BLACK LOVER *reaches her position.*)

BLACK LOVER:
I can perceive the virtue of our mothers.
Their vibrations speeding off on the vagueness of her man.
Negatives. She speaks to the deaf.
Negatives. Disrobes her love to the blind
Negatives. She moves in the direction of silent sounds
          Spoken by the mute
I have seen their style, year after year, storm after
Storm. Day after tomorrow they will still be there
Proclaiming a manhood into each other. While the
Third image listens, invisibly.

The third image is my man moving, displaying the
Totality, his awareness, his heart.
Nothing can stop him. He is mighty.
Nothing can stop him. He is persistent.
Nothing can hold him, but the black woman that I am.

He needs not to be told of the space in the cage.
When he extends his giving, he can feel the walls rubbing
My hands as I rub his.
Just enough space for giving.
Just enough for receiving.
This is what he has provided me with.
It is for the benefit of me and my people.
I need not comfort him with a well-confirming
Lie. For he knows that the cage is a lifeless box.
Nothing grows. Everything is breaking or dying out.
My man is that force of change. For he challenges the

437

Cage, key, and the mind of the jailer. He's a freedom-
Crazy nigger, loving me for loving him.

I can perceive the distress of the Sister. Moving
From face to space and still moving. Seeking that
Someone for her completeness.
Her desperation, wanting a man to take the treasures
She is offering. But they plunder around like flies.
Ever landing on the same bullshit. Faggots, their
Minds are tighter than the ass of their pants.
Half men—loving with their needs, hating for their
      Submission to woman.
For being of truth between imposed lies.

I can perceive of my virtues. We with our balance
Complete love. Pushing together for truth. Pulling
Together for unity. We together displaying our adulthoods
With dignity, respect, and understanding. With love as
Black as a shadow, moving with our every step. The shadow
Of one spirit dancing close to the sun.

The future is a un-secure tomorrow, that no wealth or
Prestige can reserve for us. Constantly we are between
The beak and claws of a dying eagle. Unified we are
Bringing it to its knees.
My man and I
Black as we are.

MALE NARRATOR:

We were born in the fields of sorrow, crawled, walked, ran
down the road of misfortune away from the house of oppression. We have suffered the whip, the swine, and the white
image of death. We have come from one angle of poverty to
the other and retained the weight on an unbalanced scale.
Challenge our oppressor to add no more of his burden upon
us. We have moved to this point. With a love profound and a
love supreme. But still we seek the answer of our mystery.

A Medal for Willie

by WILLIAM BRANCH

William B. Branch's first playwriting effort was *A Medal for Willie*, which was produced on a shoestring at a Harlem cabaret to enthusiastic critical and audience acclaim.

Subsequently, Branch has turned out a succession of plays for theater and television. Among them are *In Splendid Error*, a historical drama about John Brown and Frederick Douglass which the Greenwich Mews Theater turned into an Off-Broadway hit; *A Wreath for Udomo*, presented on the London stage and based upon Peter Abraham's prophetic novel about the rise and fall of an African prime minister; and *Light in the Southern Sky*, an NBC television drama about the life of Mary McLeod Bethune which won for its author the Robert E. Sherwood Television Award.

CAST OF CHARACTERS

TAYLOR	CUSTOMER
MRS. JACKSON	EDITOR
LUCY MAE	REPORTER
CAPTAIN	BERNICE
MAYOR	BUDDY
SUPERINTENDENT	WHITE BOY
GENERAL	PRINCIPAL
BARBER	MR. JACKSON

A JANITOR AND A JANITRESS
A SHINEBOY
A PHOTOGRAPHER

TIME: *The early 1950's.*

SCENE: *The auditorium of the Booker T. Washington High School in Midway, a town in the South.*

(*A bare stage greets the audience as they enter the theater. Shortly before curtain time, a* JANITOR *and* JANITRESS *appear and begin to set the stage as if for an assembly. They bring on a lectern, which is placed directly down center. An American*

flag is placed next to the left proscenium wall and a United Nations banner to the right. Eight polished mahogany armchairs are brought in and placed in a straight row across the stage behind the lectern, and two large, potted palms are placed one on either side of the lectern. The JANITRESS *sweeps up a bit of last-minute debris, then turns to dusting the chairs. The* JANITOR *brings on a stepladder and, mounting it, begins to pin a large American flag to the backdrop, display fashion. At this point the houselights dim and dialogue begins onstage.*)

JANITOR (*has pinned up one corner of the flag and is endeavoring to align the opposite corner*): How's that look now, Harriet?

JANITRESS (*looks up from her dusting*): You got your end a little too high, 'pears to me. Bring it down a little.

JANITOR (*moves the corner down*): 'Bout here?

JANITRESS: No, now you got it too low. Take it up some more.

JANITOR: How's that?

JANITRESS: Jus' a little bit more. That's better. Look all right to me. You better as' Mr. Taylor, though, 'n see if that's the way he wants it.

JANITOR (*calls offstage*): Hey, Mr. Taylor!

TAYLOR (*offstage*): Yes!

JANITOR: Will you step here a minute, please?

TAYLOR: Coming!

(TAYLOR *enters. He is a pleasant-looking, well-dressed young man, and he carries a length of red-white-and-blue bunting, which he lays on the lectern.*)

JANITOR (*indicating the flag*): That look all right to you? Is it straight?

TAYLOR: That's okay, I guess. Wait a minute—bring it down just about an inch more to your right, there. Not too much. That's fine. You can go ahead and pin it now.

JANITOR: Okay, Mr. Taylor. (*He complies.*)

TAYLOR (*turns to draping the lectern with bunting*): Did you give those chairs a good wiping, Mrs. Moore? Everything spic and span?

JANITRESS: I'm finishin' 'em up right now, Mr. Taylor. Don't you worry, we'll have everything lookin' nice. (*Pauses.*) Like my grandmama used to say, "Missy"—she always called me Missy—"Missy, it don't do nobody no good to try to work up a sweat by just sittin' down worryin', worryin'. You got to get up off your butt an' use a little elbow grease!" (TAYLOR *grins.*) That's what my grandmama used to say! (*She resumes her dusting.*)

A MEDAL FOR WILLIE

TAYLOR: Your grandmama had good sense. (*He finishes with the lectern, steps back to survey his handiwork.*) There, I guess that looks proper enough. (*To* JANITOR, *who is descending the ladder.*) You can take that ladder away now, if you want to. Guess we're about set. (*He gazes about the stage.*) Looks all right. (*To* JANITRESS, *indicating chair.*) Move that last one over just a little more, will you, Mrs. Moore? That's it. Don't want them to be too crowded.

JANITOR: That all, Mr. Taylor?

TAYLOR: I think so. Have you swept down the front steps yet?

JANITOR: No, not yet.

TAYLOR: Well, better get them now. Crowd'll be gathering before long.

JANITOR: All right, sir. (*Starts to pick up ladder.*)

TAYLOR: And when you get a chance, be sure to straighten up the Principal's office, will you?

JANITOR (*makes a futile gesture*): Ain't got but two hands, Mr. Taylor. Two hands, that's all! (*Picks up ladder and exits, wagging his head and grumbling to himself.*)

TAYLOR (*to* JANITRESS): That's about enough, Mrs. Moore, they look fine.

JANITRESS: Oh—well, thank you, sir. (*Gets her things together.*) I think everything looks real nice, real nice. All this decoratin' makes me feel real sad-like. Kinda reminds me of a funeral.

TAYLOR (*smiles*): Whose funeral—yours?

JANITRESS (*sighs wistfully*): No. My grandmama's. (*Turns to go.*) See you later, Mr. Taylor! (*She exits.*)

TAYLOR (*takes a last look around. Then turns very naturally to the audience and addresses them in a friendly, personable manner*): In case you're wondering what we're doing here, we're getting the platform ready for the ceremony this afternoon. You see, this is the auditorium of the Booker T. Washington High School in Midway, a town in the South. (*Shrugs.*) A fair-sized town, I guess. Smaller than some, bigger than others. I don't need to tell you, of course, that this is a colored high school. I'm one of the teachers here. Frank L. Taylor's the name. Ordinarily, I teach general science and chemistry, and coach the football team—no basketball, we don't have a gymnasium like the white schools—but today, I'm in charge of the committee on arrangements for this afternoon's ceremony. Committee of one, I might add. We don't have a very large faculty here.

But about the program—no, it's not a regular students'

assembly as usual. The Principal gave the kids a holiday—to keep them out of the way, I suppose, since the program's open to the public and we don't have enough seats for all the students, much less for all the people who'll be turning out here today.

You see, there's going to be a memorial service and presentation ceremony here in about an hour and a half. You already know, of course, that Willie Jackson's dead. Corporal Willie Jackson, I should say, but he was still just a schoolkid last time I saw him. Played left end on the team year before last. He wasn't a bad ball-player, either. Had lots to learn, but he was a good kid who played hard with all he had. Just wanted to keep on going.

Well, anyway, he's stopped now—for good. His family got a telegram from the War Department a few weeks ago that "Corporal Willie D. Jackson, serial number so-and-so-and-so, has been killed in action in the performance of his duty, somewhere on the fighting front." It didn't seem to matter much to most folks in this town when the news got around—Willie wasn't exactly the fair-haired boy, if you get what I mean. But when the War Department announced that Willie had shown "extraordinary heroism" before he was killed and that they were awarding him a posthumous medal for bravery, well! overnight Willie became a hero! Willie's the first boy from this town, white or colored, to win a big medal this time, and people began to talk it up in a big way. Then the Pentagon in Washington announced they were going to send down a general just to present Willie's mother with the medal, and the whole town's gone crazy! The Mayor formed a Willie Jackson Day Committee and they drew up plans for a public ceremony. And since Willie'd been a student here at Booker T. before he went away to the Army, they decided to hold it here.

So now the platform's all set for the General and the Mayor and the Superintendent of Schools and Willie's family—and the Principal, of course. He's chairman of the Willie Jackson Day Committee and he'll preside during the program.

We've got quite a little while, though, before things begin here, so I'd like to suggest in the meantime you might want to look around town a bit until we're ready. There's really not so much to see—Midway's pretty much like any other town in this part of the country. Basically, there are people, and more people, some like you, some like me, some like the folks down the street, or up on the hill, some like those across town. As a matter of fact, you might start your tour by going across town to look in at number 217 Railroad Place, the third house from

the corner. It isn't exactly a fashionable neighborhood, but there are some folks down there you'll want to meet . . . (*During the last few lines the lights fade to blackout.*)

Scene 1

(*Lights come up on just an area of the stage to the right of the lectern and in front of the chairs, revealing* MRS. JACKSON *seated at a table while her daughter,* LUCY MAE, *applies a hot pressing comb to her hair. The table is spread with newspaper, upon which stands a small mirror, a hot plate, a box of hairpins, and a jar of "Dixie Peach" pomade.* MRS. JACKSON *is in her slip and has a towel around her shoulders. She is still fairly young, though hard work and lack of care have left her tired and wilted.* LUCY MAE *is wrapped in a nondescript bathrobe and wears bedroom slippers. Her fresh hairdo is protected by a hairnet. She is fifteen.*)

MRS. JACKSON: Ouch, baby, be careful! You came a little too close that time.

LUCY: I'm sorry, Mama, but you got to hold still. How do you think I'm goin' to get through if you keep movin' your head around?

MRS. JACKSON: I'm doing the best I can, Lucy Mae. (*Sighs.*) What time is it?

LUCY: It's something to one. We got plenty of time. They won't be here to pick us up before two.

MRS. JACKSON: I know. (*Wearily.*) Lord, I wish it were over already.

LUCY: Don't say that, Mama! Why, this is a day we can be proud of all the rest of our lives. It's not like it's going to be a funeral, Mama. We're not supposed to be sad.

MRS. JACKSON (*slowly*): No, it ain't a funeral, exactly. Don't guess Willie had a funeral.

LUCY: Oh, they always have something. They always read over them before they—I mean, before—

MRS. JACKSON: Go ahead and say it, Lucy Mae. Before they bury 'em. Ain't no use in us tryin' to make Willie ain't dead and buried. We all got to die sometime.

LUCY: It still seems kinda—kinda funny, Mama.

MRS. JACKSON: What?

LUCY: About Willie. I keep thinking he's still just away with the Army. I just can't get used to thinking he's not coming back—ever.

MRS. JACKSON (*quietly, half to herself*): I know, Lucy Mae baby. I get that way too, sometimes. I hear a step—somebody

443

comin' up the street—and I get real quiet-like and listen, just hopin' to hear 'em turn in the yard and come up the steps. I know in my head it can't be Willie. But I listen just the same. Guess it'll be a long time before I stop listenin'. (*Turns.*) Better heat up that iron some more, honey.

LUCY: Okay. (*Places the iron on the hot plate.*) Aren't you awfully proud of Willie, Mama? Winnin' a medal and all? I always knew Willie'd do something someday, 'spite of the way Daddy used to call him no-count.

MRS. JACKSON: Your daddy didn't understand Willie.

LUCY (*going on*): All the kids at school are just so thrilled. They even point me out when I walk down the halls. "There goes Willie Jackson's sister," I can hear them whispering! And all the teachers are so nice. And the Principal too, Mr. Torrence. He got up in assembly that day and made the announcement about the ceremony and all, and he said we should all be very proud because Willie was a product of our own school.

MRS. JACKSON: Yes, child, I know, but I guess you done 'bout forgot the times I had to get off from work and go up there to beg Mr. Torrence to let Willie back in school. I guess Mr. Torrence has 'bout forgot it by now, too.

LUCY: That's nothing, Mama. You know Willie just didn't like school. He never got along with any of the teachers except for the football coach. And he wasn't learning anything.

MRS. JACKSON: They sent him to school in the Army, Lucy Mae. They taught him all about machine guns and fightin' and how to kill and they didn't have no trouble. Why couldn't they take a little patience with him in school, 'stead of puttin' him out in the street where he could get into trouble.

LUCY: But, Mama, you know Willie just couldn't stay out of trouble.

MRS. JACKSON: What you mean?

LUCY: Well, what about the time he and them boys broke into that grocery store and stole some beer? If it wasn't for Daddy's boss-man down at the icehouse, they'd have put Willie in jail.

MRS. JACKSON: Willie wasn't no angel, honey. I know that. And I never stuck up for him when he was wrong. I whipped him myself for doin' that—wouldn't let your father touch him —he'd a killed him. But if Willie'd been in school that day 'stead of bein' put out in the street, he'd never got into that trouble.

LUCY: Maybe so, Mama.

MRS. JACKSON: I couldn't blame him much when he quit. I

tried to get him to go back, but he said he was gonna get him a job and work awhile.

LUCY (*scoffs*): Humph! Shining shoes at that barber shop wasn't much of a job, was it, Mama?

MRS. JACKSON: No, but it was all he could get. He did right well with it, too, considerin', till he got girls on his mind.

LUCY: I know who, Mama! Bernice Myers! Willie was *crazy* about her!

MRS. JACKSON (*smiles*): I know. I met her. She was a right nice girl. Willie sure 'nough wanted a real job then. I bet he was even thinkin' about gettin' married. (*Her smile fades.*) But he couldn't find no better job. So he got tired and went ahead and joined the Army.

LUCY (*resumes her hair-fixing*): Hold still now, Mama. I guess Willie just kinda took to the Army with his rough ways and all.

MRS. JACKSON: You been listenin' to your father again, Lucy Mae. Willie wudn't all that rough. You remember that little wall-thing he made me in his shop class? The one that's hangin' in the corner in the front room with the little flowerpot on it?

LUCY: Uh-huh. That's a whatnot.

MRS. JACKSON: A what?

LUCY: A whatnot. That's what you call it.

MRS. JACKSON: Yeah? Well, *whatever* it is, it's beautiful! It took a lotsa time and lovin' care to make that. Willie wudn't rough. He was a little stubborn sometimes when somebody was botherin' him, but he wudn't rough.

LUCY: Well, anyhow, we can all be very proud of Willie, now, Mama, can't we?

MRS. JACKSON: Yes, baby. Only I been proud of him all along.

LUCY: Everbody's gonna be at the ceremony today, Mama. Just everybody! And for the first time at a public meeting in Midway, the seating's going to be unsegregated. Anybody can sit anywhere they want, no matter whether they're white or colored. That's makin' history!

MRS. JACKSON (*patiently*): Yes, Lucy Mae.

LUCY: And they're going to name the new colored park after Willie, too! When they get it built, that is.

MRS. JACKSON: Yes, Lucy Mae. And after two years already of notin' but promisin', you better make that *"if"* they gets it built.

LUCY (*undaunted*): And you and me and Daddy's going to

sit right up on the platform right along with the Mayor and the Superintendent and the General from Washington—!

MRS. JACKSON: Yes, Lucy Mae.

LUCY: And they're going to present you with Willie's medal! Oh, Mama, won't you be just thrilled?!!!

MRS. JACKSON (*slowly, with great feeling*): Yes, Lucy Mae, I'll be thrilled, I guess. It's all very nice what everybody's doin' and I'm proud, very proud. Only—where was everybody when Willie was alive? Where was they when your father and me was strugglin' to feed him and put clothes on his back and bring him up decent? Where was everybody when he needed help in school, but they put him out instead 'cause they "didn't have time to fool with him." An' where was they when he was walkin' the street lookin' for work? It's all very nice to give him a program he can't come to, and a medal he can't wear, an' name a park after him they ain't built yet. But all this can't help Willie now! It ain't doin' him no good. (*She blows her nose into the towel and wipes at the corner of her eyes.*) That's 'bout enough, baby. My hair ain't been like nothin' ever since I been bendin' over them hot stoves in the white folks' kitchens. I don't guess you can do much with it now. I'll finish fixin' it. You go and see if your father's through with the wash tub and go get your bath.

LUCY (*near tears*): Mama—!

MRS. JACKSON: Go on now, Lucy Mae baby. We won't want to keep the Mayor and the Superintendent and the General waitin', now do we? We all want to be on time. (*Pats her arm.*) Go on now, go get your bath. (LUCY *starts off, pausing for a last glance of concern at her mother before she exits.* MRS. JACKSON *stands looking after her for a moment, then her hands reach up to touch her hair as the lights black out.*)

Scene 2

(*Lights come up on the upper left area to reveal the* CAPTAIN, *the* MAYOR, *and the* SUPERINTENDENT. *They are standing, facing off left. There is the sound of an airplane's engines idling, and the men hold on to their hats as the prop-wash flaps their clothes. The* CAPTAIN *is a young, snappy Air Force officer. The* MAYOR *is middle-aged, suspicious, and the* SUPERINTENDENT *has seen his best decades.*)

CAPTAIN (*shouting over the roar of motors*): They're taxing up now. He ought to be getting out in a minute.

MAYOR (*straining forward for a glimpse*): That's not the *Sacred Cow,* is it?

CAPTAIN: No. One like it, though. For the General's personal use.

SUPERINTENDENT: Huh! Never catch me in one of them things. Not even if I was a general. No, sir, give me the cavalry any time. Why, in the Spanish-American War——

CAPTAIN (*cutting in*): They're opening the door! Watch. (*Pause.*) There he is! That's him climbing out now. See?

MAYOR: Oh, yes. Oh, yes! (*Clears his throat.*) Well, I guess I'd better be prepared to say a few words of welcome, don't you think? Ah—how do you go about addressing a general, Captain? I ain't never met one of them before.

CAPTAIN: Don't worry. Just call him "General." That's his title.

SUPERINTENDENT: I saw General Pershing once. Ol' Blackjack, they called him. Gave him that name during the Spanish-American War, 'cause he was in command of a bunch of niggers. (*Blandly.*) Don't know how he ever got to be a general after that!

CAPTAIN: Here he comes! (*Calls.*) Right over this way, General Atkins! (*Beckons.*) General—(*Snaps into a smart salute. The* GENERAL *enters, carrying his trench coat over his arm and a briefcase in his hand. He returns the salute.*)

GENERAL: Good afternoon, Captain.

CAPTAIN: Afternoon, sir! (*The sound of the motors have died away by now and they no longer have to shout.*) Captain Alvin Berger, at your service, sir.

GENERAL (*stretches out his hand*): Glad to know you, Berger.

CAPTAIN: Did you have a nice trip, sir?

GENERAL: Oh, pretty fair, pretty fair. Strong crosswinds over the Alleghenies, but no trouble.

CAPTAIN: I'm glad, sir. May I take your things, sir? (*The* GENERAL *hands his coat and thanks him. They turn to the others.*) Sir, I'd like you to meet His Honor, the Mayor of Midway. Mayor Bleecher, General Atkins.

GENERAL (*extends hand*): Glad to make your acquaintance, Mayor Bleecher.

MAYOR (*pumping his hand*): General Atkins, sir, on behalf of the people of our fair city, I want to welcome you to Midway. Now, I know you're a very busy man up there in Washington these days, and we all think it's mighty nice, mighty nice, indeed, for you to take up your valuable time to come down here for something like this. Welcome, General Atkins! (*Pumps harder.*)

GENERAL (*finally retrieving his hand*): Er—thank you,

MAYOR. (*The* SUPERINTENDENT *presses forward.*)

CAPTAIN: Oh—and this is the Superintendent of Schools in Midway, Mr. Clemmons.

SUPERINTENDENT: I'm most happy to meet you, General. And, er—in my capacity as Superintendent of the Public Schools, I want to add a special welcome on behalf of the teachers and students of our model school system. Of course, the school we're going to this afternoon isn't so much, you understand, but if you get a chance later, I'd like to take you over to one of the white schools and show you through. All the very latest modern equipment, spacious sunlit classrooms, fully equipped gymnasium and swimming pool—you'll be delighted, sir!

GENERAL: Thank you kindly, Mr.—Mr.—

SUPERINTENDENT (*beaming*): Clemmons, sir, Cyrus P. Clemmons. Direct descendant of Major Clay Clemmons of the Third Cavalry, Army of the Confederacy!

GENERAL: Oh, yes, Mr. Clemmons. Thank you both for your kindness and hospitality, but I'm afraid I'll be a little rushed for time. Now—ah, Captain, I trust you have transportation into town?

MAYOR: Don't worry about a thing, General Atkins. That's all arranged. My car is right over there and I'll drive you in myself.

GENERAL: Well—

MAYOR: We will adjourn first to the official residence where the wife will serve us a little, ah—shall I say, liquid refreshment—and we'll be in plenty of time to make the ceremony.

GENERAL: All right, Mayor, I accept your invitation. If it's not too much trouble, that is.

MAYOR: Oh, that's quite all right, General, old boy. And if I can possibly be of any further assistance, you know, such as speech-writin' and all that, don't hesitate at all to speak right up.

GENERAL (*with a tolerant smile*): Well, I don't think that will be necessary, Mayor. I have here the official citation and the medal and a résumé on Corporal Jackson, and from there I think I'll be able to manage very well.

MAYOR (*nervously*): Why, of course, of course you can, sir. Only—well, you know how we are down here, General. Being a Southern town, we're all like one big family, you see, and I thought maybe a friendly suggestion or two as to the tone of your remarks might—er, might add to the effectiveness of the proceedings.

GENERAL: Why, what do you mean, Mayor?

MAYOR: Well, we'd kinda like to be sure that you are properly aware that, er—Well, we think highly of our Negras down here, and we want to show 'em all the credit they're due. But then, of course, too, we pretty much like things the way they are here in our little city, and it wouldn't do if—er, we encouraged the Negras too much. We want 'em to be proud of Willie Jackson—sure, all of us are! But we don't want any trouble out of 'em for gettin' to feel too good about it. In other words, General Atkins, we have to kind of pat 'em on the wool a bit one minute, you know, and then make sure the next they don't get any fancy ideas about gettin' out of their place, what with all this talk about fightin' for freedom and democracy and all.

CAPTAIN (*who has been growing increasingly uncomfortable during the preceding speech, blurts out*): If you don't mind, General, sir, I'd like to say a word here! (*To the* MAYOR, *who is astonished.*) I'm from the Bronx in New York and I went to school with plenty of colored fellows, and they were all right! Well—good, bad, and indifferent, like anybody! And when I hear somebody like you talk like that about a whole race of human beings, it just——

GENERAL (*interrupts*): All right, that will do.

CAPTAIN (*stops short for a moment, then blurts out again*): You don't seem to realize that——

GENERAL (*sternly*): I said that will do, Captain! I'll handle this! (*Pause. The* GENERAL *turns to the* MAYOR *as if to speak, then imposingly turns back to the* CAPTAIN *with weighted words.*) What did you say your name was, Captain?

CAPTAIN (*his face flushes as he realizes what the* GENERAL *has in mind. Then defiantly*): Berger, sir! Captain Alvin M. Berger.

GENERAL (*coolly*): I see. (*He turns to the others.*) Gentlemen, I can understand your concern about these matters and I assure you there is no cause for alarm. You see, before I went to West Point, I was born and bred in the cottonfields of South Carolina!

MAYOR (*grins and extends his hand*): Well! Well, then! Welcome back to the South, General. Welcome home!

GENERAL: Thank you, Mayor. (*Turns.*) Shall we go, Captain?

CAPTAIN (*darkly*): Yes, sir. Right this way, sir. (*They start for stage right. Blackout.*)

Scene 3

(*Discovered down right:* BARBER, CUSTOMER *in barber chair, and* SHINEBOY *with his box, working on* CUSTOMER'*s shoes. The* BARBER *is tall, lean, and home-towny. The* CUSTOMER *is stout and well dressed. As the lights come up, the two are roaring with laughter.*)

BARBER (*laughing*): You don't mean it?

CUSTOMER: I swear to God, Ed! I had to pull on my pants in a hurry and run down the hall after her, throw a bathrobe around her and bring her back 'fore she woke up the whole damn hotel! (*He cackles.*) *Jesus Christ,* what a party!

BARBER (*still chuckling*): I should say so.

CUSTOMER: And you should have seen this babe, Ed. She was about five foot six, real red hair, and built like the battleship *Missouri!* (*He makes an appropriate gesture with cupped hands.*) And boy, she sure knew what to do!

BARBER: Is that a fact?

CUSTOMER: I didn't mind tippin' her ten dollars extra. It was worth it. Every goddamn bit of it! Yes, sir, believe me, that was the best damn convention I ever went to! (*The* BARBER *busies himself with the haircut. After a pause the* CUSTOMER *notices the* SHINEBOY, *who is polishing away with his cloth.*) That's about enough on that shoe, boy. You want to wear right through to the skin? (*The* SHINEBOY *glances up quickly, then proceeds to work on the other shoe.*) See you got another new boy, Ed. What happened to the last one? Steal something and run away?

BARBER: No, no—nothin' like that. Up and joined the Navy 'fore they drafted him.

CUSTOMER: Joined the Navy, eh? Well, good for him. Keep him outta trouble for a while. All these young bucks 'round here oughta be in service. (*To* SHINEBOY.) When you goin' to the Army, boy? (*The* SHINEBOY *looks up quickly, then resumes his work.*)

BARBER: He's not old enough yet. Only fourteen.

CUSTOMER: Well, he looks plenty big to me. You know my boy got his notice the other day.

BARBER: That right? Well, now. When does he have to go?

CUSTOMER: Early next month, it says. But we been tryin' to get him out of it. Talked to Charlie Wilkins over at the draft board this mornin'.

BARBER: That right? What did Charlie say?

CUSTOMER: He said he'd see what he can do to get him one of them college deferments.

BARBER: But I though your boy flun—I mean, quit college?

CUSTOMER (*unabashed*): You was right the first time. (*He cackles.*) But now he wants to go back. Gonna enter State next semester. Long as he keeps a "D" average he won't have to go to the Army.

BARBER: Oh, is that the way it works?

CUSTOMER: 'Course, he'll have to take one of them college deferment tests they got out now. But Charlie says he can pass that easy. Said to send him over to the draft board meetin' Monday night and he'd fix it up with the board.

BARBER: Well, now, is that a fact?

CUSTOMER: When he got his notice, it got poor Martha all upset. She's nervous anyhow, you know. She was so worried she didn't know what to do. Can't blame her much either. This war ain't like the last one. That was bad enough. But the way they been killin' up our boys over there is somethin' awful.

BARBER: Guess you heard about Willie Jackson, ain't you?

CUSTOMER: No. Who's he?

BARBER: Oh, I forgot. You been away conventionin'. (*The* CUSTOMER *cackles.*) It's in all the papers, though. Willie Jackson, colored boy that got killed over there. He's a big hero now. They're giving his folks a medal this afternoon over at the colored high school. A general's comin' in from Washington, special, to present it.

CUSTOMER: You don't say?

BARBER: That's right. And you know one thing? That boy used to shine shoes for me right here in this barber shop!

CUSTOMER: Is that so?

BARBER (*proudly*): Sure is. I was pretty flabbergasted when I heard. Even been thinkin' 'bout gettin' a gold star and pastin' it in the window. Don't you remember Willie? Tall boy. Used to work here 'bout a year ago.

CUSTOMER: I don't know, Ed. All these young bucks look alike to me.

BARBER: Well, everybody's mighty proud. Mighty proud. Went over there and made a name for himself. Hear they're gonna build a new park, for colored, and name it after him.

CUSTOMER: Oh, yeah?

BARBER: I think it's pretty nice, myself. I been thinkin' I oughta close up this afternoon, put on my coat, and go on over to the ceremony. Never seen a general before. And Willie used to work right here in this shop. Yes, sir. I think it's mighty nice. (*The* SHINEBOY *finishes and exits right.*)

CUSTOMER (*glumly*): What'd he do to win a medal, Ed?

BARBER: Well, seems he held a mountain pass open for two

hours, all by himself, with just a machine gun, while his company was makin' a withdrawal. Say he got hit four or five times, but he just kept on firin' away till all his buddies was safe. Then he died 'fore they could get him to a medical aid station. Real brave boy, Willie!

CUSTOMER (*impatiently*): Well, I wish they had some more of 'em like him over there, 'stead of callin' up my boy. He's just a kid, only twenty. Don't know nothin' 'bout no wars.

BARBER (*raising his eyebrows*): Willie was only eighteen. Don't guess he knew much 'bout 'em either.

CUSTOMER (*annoyed*): I know, Ed, but that's different. My boy's goin' back to college. Gonna make somethin' out of himself one of these days, if I have to whale the hell out of him to make him take his lessons. I don't think he'll have any trouble, though, knowin' he'll have to go to the Army if he doesn't. I been plannin' on takin' him on under me at the plant 'ventually, and let him gradually take over like, till I get ready to retire. But I think he's still too young right now. (*Clears his throat.*) "John H. Mason and Sons, Hardware and Appliance Manufacturers." How's that sound to you, Ed?

BARBER: Oh—fine. Just fine. Too bad Willie Jackson didn't get to go to college somewhere. They say his folks is pretty poor. He was a bright boy, though. Too bad he had to get killed.

CUSTOMER: Yeah, too bad. Well, if I can count on Charlie Wilkins, my boy won't have to go. I'll get him back in school and that'll keep him out for a while at least. If that don't work, I'll put him on out at the plant. We're makin' spare parts for the government again, you know. That'll make him an essential worker. I know he won't like the idea of goin' to work on the line like a common, ordinary laborer, but he'll stand it if it keeps him out of the Army. He's real sensitive, my boy is. Kinda delicate, too. Takes after his mother that way. The Army ain't no place for a boy like him. 'Specially the way they're killin' up them boys over there.

BARBER (*quietly*): No, maybe not. Guess they need some more boys like Willie Jackson. Guess he didn't mind fightin' and dyin' while some others who could pay the price sat up in college or made money in war plants.

CUSTOMER (*sits stiffly for a moment, then slowly turns around in the chair*): Ed, are you tryin' to be funny? What's all this crap about Willie Jackson? Willie Jackson? All right, so he's a hero—everybody's "mighty proud!" They're gonna give him a medal. He was a "brave boy." That still don't cut hogs with me! I'm talkin' 'bout *my* boy, John H. Mason, *Jr.!*

To hell with this Willie Jackson! He ain't nothin' to me but another nigger dead!

BARBER (*is momentarily taken aback, then reaches out to remove the cloth from around the* CUSTOMER): Well, now, Mr. Mason, I guess I'm about through. You can step down, now. (*He does so.*) That'll be seventy-five cents for the haircut, ten cents for the shine. And, er—when did you say your boy comes up before the draft board?

CUSTOMER: Next Monday night. Why?

BARBER: Oh, nothin'. Nothin' at all. Just wanted to make sure of the date. You see, I'm on that draft board, too, and I wouldn't want to miss an important meetin'. (*Shakes out the cloth with a snap.*) Next! Next, please!

(*Blackout.*)

Scene 4

(*The lights comes up on* EDITOR *seated at desk down left. He wears a green eyeshade and his shirt sleeves are rolled to the elbow. He puffs away at a cigar as he bends over papers on his desk, proofreading with a red pencil. There is a sharp rap.*)

EDITOR (*without looking up*): Come in!

(*A young* REPORTER *enters from off left.*)

REPORTER: You wanted to see me, Chief?

EDITOR: Yeah, got an assignment for you, Logan. Something special.

REPORTER: Special, eh? Okay, shoot. (*He takes out pad and pencil and perches on a corner of the desk.*)

EDITOR (*leans back in his chair*): I want you to get over to the Booker T. Washington High School and cover a ceremony. They're presenting Willie Jackson's mother with his medal. General Atkins flew in from the Pentagon a little while ago to make the presentation. Take a camera with you and get some pictures.

REPORTER: Okay, Chief.

EDITOR: And now listen. I want you to give me a good story. Human interest and all that sort of stuff. Talk to the Jackson woman and find out how she feels. Get some quotes. You might talk to Mayor Bleecher and see what he has to say. (*Makes a wry face.*) No, on second thought, for God's sake don't! We ain't quite that hard up for quotes.

REPORTER: What else, Chief?

EDITOR: And make sure you get the text of the General's speech.

REPORTER: Sure thing.

EDITOR (*rises and begins to pace*): I want you to build it up. You know, a real sob story with a patriotic theme. How this teen-age little colored boy from the darkytown slums went over there and fought and died for this country, his native land, to preserve the American way of life and give the lie to these subversives who continually try to stir up trouble between the races by all this harping on inequality. You know what I mean.

REPORTER: Gotcha, Chief.

EDITOR: And how his admiring hometown pauses today to pay homage to this brave young martyr, and to his proud little mother—Emma, I think her name is, Emma. You might even call her Mrs. Jackson in this story, Logan.

REPORTER (*hesitating*): You—you mean that, Chief? I thought it was strict policy to—

EDITOR: Well, be a precedent, giving darkies titles like white people, but I don't guess anybody'll mind, just this once.

REPORTER: Anything you say, Chief.

EDITOR: Now, I picked you special for this job, Logan, because you're my best feature man. Make this story good and I'll run it on the front page.

REPORTER (*craftily*): Front page, eh? Say, you know, Chief, this sounds like it oughta be worth a by-line.

EDITOR: By-line, by-line!—What the hell is this, everybody wants a by-line! Just you make this a good story and don't worry about no by-line.

REPORTER: Well, after all, Chief—

EDITOR: You young J-school Pulitzer Prizes give me a pain in the ass! Give you a pencil and teach you the alphabet and you think you're William Randolph Hearst! God rest his soul! Okay, you can have your by-line! Hope you hang yourself with it.

REPORTER (*grins*): Thanks, Chief.

EDITOR: Now. As I was saying, I'm running this on the front page. Maybe I can get the Associated Press to pick it up, flash it all over the country. And that's not all. I'll wire the story to a friend of mine up at the Voice of America—he's always looking for stuff like this. If they use it, you might even add a bonus to your by-line.

REPORTER: Hey! That would be great, Chief. Just great!

EDITOR: All right then! Get outta here and bring me a story. Get some good pictures, too. The General and the Jackson woman, get 'em shakin' hands if you can. They always shake hands with the darkies at things like these. Might even get a shot of the crowd. They tell me they're gonna let 'em sit any-

where they want to today. Guess they have to, though, it being a colored school. Well, you got your assignment, "Walter Winchell"! Now, get the hell outta here!

REPORTER: Yes, sir, Chief! (*Dashes off.*)

EDITOR (*stands calling after him*): And bring me back a good story!

(*Blackout.*)

Scene 5

(*As the lights come up again, down right,* BERNICE *and* BUDDY *enter.* BERNICE *is a girl of eighteen, dressed in her Sunday best.* BUDDY *is thirteen or so, wears a "Hi-Y" tee-shirt. They pause just after entering and look to their right and left, as if at a street corner. Then* BUDDY *starts for stage left.*)

BERNICE (*pulling him back*): Wait for the light, Buddy!

BUDDY: Aw, ain't no cars comin'.

BERNICE: Maybe not, but you know the way they zoom up and down this highway. Besides, do you want to be arrested for jaywalking?

BUDDY: Ain't no cops around, neither.

BERNICE: Well, just the same. (*Turns to him.*) You don't have to walk me any farther, Buddy. The bus stops right across the street. I just wanted somebody to come with me through those woods. Honestly, I wish we lived farther in town. I just hate coming down that road, even in the daytime. You never know what's liable to jump out at you from behind a tree.

BUDDY: Aw, you're just a scareycat, Bernice. Who'd want to bother you?

BERNICE (*tosses her head*): Well, if that's all you think of your big sister—

BUDDY (*shrugs*): You're okay, I guess. For a girl.

BERNICE (*smiles and playfully musses his hair*): What's the matter with girls, Buddy? Don't you like girls?

BUDDY (*pushing her hand away*): Aw, they're so awful silly sometimes. Like in the movies. You go to the show to see a good cowboy pit-cher, an' just when things is gettin' good an' the Montana Kid is hot on the trail of the Dalton gang, then 'long comes some old crazy girl wantin' to be huggin' and kissin' on him, and talkin' about gettin' married and all that love stuff! (*Complains.*) Messin' up a perfectly good pit-cher!

BERNICE (*laughs*): Why, Buddy, there's nothing wrong with that. You'll want to get married yourself someday.

BUDDY: No, I won't either! That's sissy stuff.

BERNICE (*smiles*): Just wait until you're a little older.

You'll be glad to eat those words. (*Turns away and poses, patting her hair.*) What would you say if I got married one of these days, Buddy?

BUDDY: Aw, you ain't gonna get married, either. You were talkin' about runnin' away and marryin' that Willie Jackson once. I heard you and him talkin' one night out on the front porch.

BERNICE (*surprised*): Buddy! You didn't tell Mama and Papa, did you?

BUDDY: Nah, I didn't tell nobody. I knew you wasn't goin' to run away with him. What's Papa been sendin' you to business school for if you gonna jump up and marry somebody like Willie Jackson?

BERNICE: What have you got against Willie? He was a wonderful guy! He was a wonderful guy! You just don't know.

BUDDY: Oh yeah? That Jackson was a bad one. Always gettin' into trouble.

BERNICE: He was not!

BUDDY: He got put out of school, didn't he?

BERNICE: But it wasn't his fault!

BUDDY: An' he was runnin' around with them boys that got put in jail for all them holdups!

BERNICE: That was after Willie went to the Army. He didn't have nothing to do with any holdups!

BUDDY: But he would have if he'd been here.

BERNICE: He would not! You don't know, Buddy, you're just—(*Turns away.*) Oh, what are we standing up here arguing about Willie for now. He's dead and I'm on my way to his memorial service. Besides, Willie and me broke up a long time ago—just before he joined the Army. He said he couldn't ask me to be a soldier's wife and he couldn't make enough money out here. So he signed up and went away to war—and got killed! (*Her voice breaks.*)

BUDDY: What's the matter with you?

BERNICE: I don't know. I—I just can't help it, that's all. Oh, why did he have to get killed. I told him I'd wait for him if he wanted me to!

BUDDY: What you cryin' about? It wasn't your fault. (*Looks around.*) Hey! Stop that! You're out in the street!

BERNICE: I don't care. (*Takes out a handkerchief.*) It's been all balled up inside of me ever since I heard. Willie was such a swell guy. Why'd he have to die?

BUDDY (*shakes her arm*): Come on, Bernice. Cut it out! You're gonna miss your bus and be late for the program. (*Insistently.*) Bernice!

BERNICE (*begins to dry her eyes*): All right, Buddy. I'm sorry. I—I don't know what's the matter with me. Oh, I'll bet my face looks a sight! (*Digs in her pocketbook for a mirror.*)

BUDDY (*admiringly*): You look okay. You always look okay. You're my sister, ain't you?

BERNICE (*gives him a hug*): Thanks, Buddy. You're a darling.

BUDDY (*pulling away*): Aw, quit huggin' me. Women!

BERNICE: Thanks for walking me over, Buddy. I'll see if I can't get a ride back home after the service. You don't have to meet me. Tell Mama not to worry.

BUDDY: Okay. So long.

BERNICE: 'Bye, Buddy.

(BUDDY *turns and exits the way they came.* BERNICE *looks carefully up and down the street—then crosses to right. There is a "Bus Stop" sign at right where she halts. She looks to the left as if watching for a bus, then takes out her compact and touches up her makeup. Behind her is a waiting-bench, upon which a man sits, legs crossed, reading a newspaper which blocks his face. Shortly, he stirs, closes the paper to turn a page, and looks up to see* BERNICE *in front of him. He is a* WHITE BOY *in his early twenties, wears slacks and an open-collared shirt. He turns to his paper again, then thinks better of it. He folds up his paper and rises, slowly. He pauses before speaking, looking about first to be sure no one is watching.*)

WHITE BOY (*awkwardly*): Care to sit down, er—miss?

(BERNICE *looks around, startled, then quickly turns back front without answering.*)

WHITE BOY (*coming forward*): I said, care to sit down, miss?

(BERNICE *ignores him, puts her compact away, and peers up the street for the bus.*)

WHITE BOY: Well, you might at least say yes or no.

BERNICE (*turns to look at him indignantly, then looks away*): No, thank you!

WHITE BOY: Why not? Bus won't be here for another eight minutes yet.

BERNICE (*turns toward him again*): You know that bench is for white folks only!

WHITE BOY: So what? You can sit down if you want to. Ain't nobody goin' to say nothin'. I won't let 'em.

BERNICE: No, thank you. I'd rather stand up. (*She looks off for the bus.*)

WHITE BOY: Okay, if that's the way you want it. Ain't no harm in askin', is there? (*No answer.*) You live around here?

457

(*No answer.*) I ain't never seen you out this way before. I live over in the Greenwood section. You just comin' from work over there or somethin'?

BERNICE (*her cheeks burning*): Do I look like somebody's maid to you?

WHITE BOY (*embarrassed*): Well, no, but—(*Almost angrily.*) Well, I don't know!

BERNICE: Well, now you do. No, I don't work for anybody in Greenwood!

WHITE BOY (*defensively*): Okay! Okay! You don't have to bite my head off about it. (*He pauses, then slowly walks around behind her, looking her up and down.*) You're pretty dressed up, ain't you? Goin' to church or somethin'?

BERNICE (*controlling herself*): Today is *not Sunday!*

WHITE BOY (*moves closer, speaking almost over her shoulder*): Well, where you goin', then? To meet your boyfriend?

BERNICE (*whirls around*): Look, if you don't mind. I'd rather you didn't say anything to me. Anything at all!

WHITE BOY (*taken aback*): Well, what's the matter? I ain't said nothin'. Did I say somethin'? All I did was offer you a seat, polite-like.

BERNICE: Well, thank you, very much, but I want to stand up!

WHITE BOY: Okay! Okay! (*Walks back around her slowly.*) Don't know what you're so touchy about. I ain't poison. (*He stops, pauses, then trying a new approach, he turns to her and offers his hand.*) My name's Johnny. John H. Mason, Jr. My father owns the hardware plant out on Old Tree Road. (BERNICE *ignores him. His hand drops, along with his pretense of politeness.*) I don't know what you got to be so stuck-up about. I'm just trying to be friendly!

BERNICE: Well, just keep your friendliness for your friends! I'm not one of them.

WHITE BOY: You don't have to holler at me!

BERNICE: And you don't have to say anything to me! Anything at all!

WHITE BOY (*gives a hitch to his belt*): If I didn't know better, I'd think you were trying to be sassy.

BERNICE: All right! So I'm sassy! All I want you to do is leave me alone! That's all you white boys think, that you got a right to approach any colored girl you see, anytime, anywhere, and we're supposed to be tickled to death! Well, I'm not laughing, white boy! I'm not tickled at all! And I'm not scared of you either. So you can go back and sit on your lily-white bench and read your paper, 'cause I don't want any parts of any white trash like you!

WHITE BOY (*at first surprised, then snarls*): Why, you black bitch! (*He slaps her hard. She drops her pocketbook.*) Call me white trash, will you? Who do you think you are anyway? That'll learn you some respect when white folks speak to you! (*At this,* BERNICE *snaps out of her initial shock, and with a little cry of rage and indignation, she flies at him, flailing with her little fists. He adroitly grabs both her wrists and holds her while she struggles.*)

WHITE BOY (*laughs*): Well, if you ain't a spirited little wench! You better look out now, 'fore you hurt yourself. (*He forces her hands behind her so that his arms are about her waist, still holding her wrists. He pulls her to him and laughs again.*) You know, I kinda like you. Now, if you was to gimme a little kiss, I might forgit what you said just now. How 'bout it, huh? Just like you do for your boyfriend. Hold still a minute and I—(*He tries to kiss her. With a great effort she frees one hand and tries to push him away, beating and slapping at his neck and shoulders. He finds her lips and kisses her while she struggles desperately. Finally, she scratches his cheek with her nails. He breaks loose, pushing her from him.*)

WHITE BOY: God *damn!* (*He puts his fingers to his cheek and examines them to make sure the scratch hasn't drawn blood. Then he turns to her, grinning sheepishly.*) Hey, you really are a wild one, ain't you? (*She stares back at him in disgust and hatred, her bosom heaving with rage as she rubs her sore wrists. He begins, stops and, with an eager taunting, he takes a step toward her with hands upraised and feints as if to strike her. Involuntarily, she flinches. He laughs again, then gives a hitch to his belt.*) You little fool, you. I'd a been good to you. I'd a given you money—bought you clothes. Anything you want! (*He pauses, then points off left.*) Here comes your bus—miss. (*He turns and strolls brazenly off right, still chuckling to himself.* BERNICE *stands in silent indignation for a moment, her hair and clothes disheveled, her hat askew. She looks down at herself helplessly, then gradually gives way to tears, sinking slowly to her knees on the bench, head bowed, hands to her face.*)

BERNICE (*sobs*): Oh, Willie—Willie—Willie . . . (*She sobs uncontrollably as the lights black out.*)

Scene 6

(*The lights come up half-strength over the entire stage to suggest that we are looking through the drawn curtain at what takes place on the platform. From left enter the* PRINCIPAL *and*

TAYLOR. *They march on stiffly and the* PRINCIPAL *looks around, inspecting the arrangements. He is a fat, pretentious little man, who struts erratically, as if pulled by a puppeteer's strings.*)

PRINCIPAL (*gazing about*): Uh-huh. Uh-huh. Looks pretty fair, I suppose. (*He straightens a chair which is an inch or two out of line.*) Yes. Good job. Good job, Taylor.

TAYLOR: Thank you, Mr. Torrence.

PRINCIPAL (*walks to front center and pretends to peer through a crack in the curtains.*) Filling up pretty rapidly out there, isn't it?

TAYLOR: Yes, sir. There'll soon be standing room only.

PRINCIPAL (*turns back*): Well, I think everything's about ready. Don't think I've forgotten anything. As principal of the school and chairman of the committee, I've had quite a load in preparing for this, Taylor.

TAYLOR: Yes, I know you have.

PRINCIPAL: And I want you to know I appreciate your help. I couldn't do it all alone, you know.

TAYLOR: No. Of course not, Mr. Torrence.

PRINCIPAL: But at last everything is ready and the hour has come. (*Sighs.*) You know, Taylor, today is a real triumph for us. There's national attention focused on Booker T. The press, the radio, the television . . . They'll all be carrying stories of today's affair. They'll be hearing about Booker T. Washington High School all over the country.

TAYLOR: Yes, I suppose so.

PRINCIPAL: And, in view of my various capacities, I suppose they'll just have to mention me, won't they? (*He smiles eagerly, waiting for confirmation.*)

TAYLOR (*without enthusiasm*): I don't see how they can get around it.

PRINCIPAL: Not that I'm at all interested in the publicity, you understand. After all, this is primarily to honor *him*. Great sacrifice that boy made. One of *my* boys—a Booker T. boy. (*Sighs.*) You don't know how much I love this place, Taylor, really I do. When I think back over my years as a teacher and then as principal of Booker T., of how I've slaved away and put up with all sorts of discouragement and abuse at the hands of my own people as well as the other folks . . . I've given this place the best years of my life, for all the little appreciation I'm ever shown around here.

TAYLOR: Well, I wouldn't say that, Mr. Torrence.

PRINCIPAL: Oh, you just don't know, Taylor. You're still comparatively new here. You haven't lived in this town as

long as I have and you don't know what's been going on, what I've had to face all this time. Oh, I know sometimes perhaps I'm a little too strict on the students, faculty as well, but if they could only see it's for their own good! They don't have to go down to City Hall like I do and practically fall on my knees and beg for every little piece of equipment, every book, every chair, every dollar that goes into this school. They don't know how I've had to humiliate myself before the board, how I've been laughed at, cursed at, called "boy"! I'm telling you, Taylor, mine hasn't been an easy job. Not for one instant.

TAYLOR (*sympathetically*): No—no, I guess it hasn't.

PRINCIPAL: I don't usually confide in any of the teachers here. They're against me, most of 'em. Oh, I know they all laugh and grin in my face and say, "Yes, Mr. Torrence," but I know them. They'd try to get rid of me in a minute if they could. They go around behind my back calling me an "Uncle Tom" and "handkerchief head" and "white folks' nigger" and turning the kids and parents against me.

TAYLOR (*impatient that he is a captive audience to all this*): Mr. Torrence, do we have to—

PRINCIPAL: Oh, I know it. Nobody has to tell me. I always keep my eyes and ears open. I know which ones are doing it, too! I know them all. And I could fire every one of them to-morrow if I wanted to! But I've got a school to run and I try to run it the best I can, even if I have to put up with teachers who aren't loyal to their principal. But, Taylor, my boy (*puts his hand on* TAYLOR's *shoulder*), I've been watching you ever since you came to us fresh from college two years ago. Maybe you think I haven't noticed, but you've been doing a good job. A fine job, and I know all about it.

TAYLOR (*glancing uncomfortably at the* PRINCIPAL's *hand*): I'm not so sure I understand you, Mr. Torrence. I mind my own business and try to do my job as best I can.

PRINCIPAL: You do. You do. You're one of the best teachers we've ever had—and best liked, too. You know how to get along, and that's important. Very important.

TAYLOR: What are you getting at, Mr. Torrence?

PRINCIPAL: Just this, Taylor. (*He clears his throat in preparation.*) How'd you like to take my place as principal of Booker T. next year? (*Grins and holds up his hand.*) Don't say anything now, anything at all! I can't be definite about it myself yet. But if everything goes along as planned, I'll be leaving this place after this year. You see, the State's getting worried to death about all these Supreme Court rulings about equalizing education between white and colored in the South.

They've spent millions trying to make sure that Negroes don't ever enter the white schools, and now they're scared the government is liable to make them do away with Jim Crow school systems altogether—and you know they don't want that to happen! They may sound rebel yells and make speeches about never giving up segregation and all, but if the government ever really gets after them, they'll have to comply and they know it!

TAYLOR: I know all that, Mr. Torrence. But where do you come in?

PRINCIPAL: That's what I'm getting to. Now the State's going to create a new position. A big position and I'm in line for the post. It's State Supervisor of Negro Schools. How's that sound?

TAYLOR: All right, I suppose, but what will you do?

PRINCIPAL: As State Supervisor of Negro Schools, I'm supposed to travel around and make speeches and all—a general public relations thing, you know—pointing out how progress is being made and keeping down criticisms. I'll consult with Negro leaders throughout the country and advise them to go slow, that gradual improvements will be made if they keep their mouths shut. You see, it's a snap! Ten thousand a year plus expenses. (*Chortles in delight.*) And when I leave for the new job, Taylor, my boy, I've decided my mantle as principal of Booker T. shall fall on your shoulders. So congratulations! And not a word about this to anybody, now, until it happens. You see—

TAYLOR (*has been quietly growing angrier by the second*): Mr. Torrence!

PRINCIPAL (*unaware*): Er—yes, Taylor. What is it?

TAYLOR (*stands silent for a moment, controlling himself. Then glances at his wristwatch*): Willie Jackson's family is waiting in your office. Shall I bring them to the stage now?

PRINCIPAL: Oh, yes, the Jackson crowd. I'd almost forgotten. Yes, you can bring them in now if you want to. (TAYLOR *turns and starts toward right.*) And be sure to inform me the minute the Superintendent and his party arrive. I want to greet them personally at the door. These things are important, you know.

TAYLOR (*stops short, looking offstage*): I'm afraid you're a bit too late for that, Mr. Torrence. (*Points.*) Here they are right now.

PRINCIPAL: What? Oh, er—well, well, come in, gentlemen! (*He turns on his widest grin.*) Come in, sirs, come in! I wasn't aware that you had arrived as yet. Here, let me take your hats! Yes, suh! Yes, suh! (TAYLOR *stands looking at him in disgust as the lights black out.*)

Scene 7

(When the lights come up again, full strength this time, the ceremony is in progress. Seated stage right to the left are: TAYLOR, MRS. JACKSON, MR. JACKSON *(whom we have not seen before; he is large, quiet, and self-conscious),* LUCY MAE, *the* PRINCIPAL, *the* GENERAL *and the* MAYOR. *The* JACKSONS *are all in their Sunday best now and* MRS. JACKSON *wears a corsage. The last seat is vacant, as the* SUPERINTENDENT *is at the lectern addressing the audience.)*

SUPERINTENDENT *(as the lights come up)*: And I say to you, ladies and gentlemen, that the public school system of Midway is pr-roud to have had a hand, to have played its part in developing the fine boy whose sacred memory we are honoring here today. It is from these hallowed halls of learning and wisdom, from the very fine and able staff—headed by Lester here—that this brave young boy, out there somewhere on the battlefield, must have drawn courage and inspiration, to have thrown caution to the winds, faced the dastardly foe with guns blazing, and sacrificed his young life that his fellow American soldiers might safely pass over and complete their heroic advance. Yes, my friends, it was the principles of loyalty and self-sacrifice and service that Willie Jackson learned right here at this great Booker T. Washington High School that buoyed him up and gave him the strength to carry on in the face of withering fire of the enemy.

And so I say to you again, I am very pr-roud to be here this afternoon, to take part and add my feeble voice to this great tribute to one of our brave boys. And I want to say to this brave little mother sitting here, and the father and sister of our fallen warrior, that we of the public school system mean to keep faith with our departed friend. We pledge ourselves to continue in our great tradition of the American way of education, to instill in the boys and girls not only the necessary facts and figures of book learnin' but also the very vital and necessary attitude and spirit—the kind of spirit we are honorin' Willie Jackson for, here today. *(He gazes skyward in an attitude of reverence.)* Willie—rest easy, boy. We won't let you down. We're goin' to keep on fightin' the gallant fight here on the home front, to preserve those sacred principles of the American way that you laid down your sweet young life defending. Rest easy, boy. We'll keep the faith. *We're gonna keep things just the way you left 'em!*

(As he concludes his speech, a PHOTOGRAPHER *appears at the front of the audience and explodes his flashbulb at the* SUPERINTENDENT, *who artfully waggles an upraised finger,*

463

acutely aware that this is his big moment. As he returns to his seat, those on the platform applaud—all, that is, except MRS. JACKSON *who sits tightly with head bowed.* TAYLOR *applauds hesitantly as if it were expected of him;* LUCY MAE *naïvely;* MR. JACKSON *thickly, and the others with enthusiasm. The* PRINCIPAL, *of course, is on his feet clapping away for dear life. Offstage, the other members of the company add to the effect with applause and whistles.*)

PRINCIPAL (*at the lectern as the applause subsides*): I want to thank Superintendent Clemmons for those inspiring remarks. It has been my grateful privilege to have served under Dr. Clemmons for many wonderful years and he has long been an inspiration and an example to me as I go about my daily task of trying to administer to the educational needs of my people. Many a time when I was discouraged and heartsick, I found solace in Dr. Clemmons, who lifted my spirits with a word or two of timely advice and gave me the courage to go forward. And so I'm particularly happy that Dr. Clemmons could take this time out to bring us these words of courage and inspiration. (*He turns and nods, grinning, to the* SUPERINTENDENT, *who beams in acknowledgment.*)

And now—(*He rustles his notes and adjusts a pair of glasses.*) And, now, as we draw near the climax of our program, I'd like to introduce, or rather, present to you one who needs no introduction, who will in turn introduce our military guest of honor. (*Reads now from his notes.*) "For the past eighteen years, the people of Midway have been fortunate in having in their midst and in their City Hall, a man whose record of integrity and faithful public service has been his own best recommendation for continued reelection to the mayoralty. He has been the friend and champion of all, regardless of race, creed, or color. He has been firm, impartial, and just in all his dealings. He is one of the finest and best-loved sons of Midway, a Mayor of whom we are all justly proud, a man we are happy to know as a *friend.*" Therefore, it is now my great pleasure . . . and privilege to present to you, His Honor, the Mayor of Midway, Mayor Stephen Farley Bleecher!

(*Applause as before. The* SUPERINTENDENT *rises and the others follow, excepting* MRS. JACKSON. *After bowing and nodding to the applause, the* MAYOR *holds up his hands for order. The others resume their seats.*)

MAYOR: Thank you! Thank you! Thank you, my dear friends, for this very touching demonstration. It has been my pleasure and privilege to serve you all for many years as Mayor of this great town. And may I say, I love this town

and all its people, black as well as white. And whenever I'm called upon to do my bit on behalf of any of its citizens, then you can bet that I'm awfully happy to be able to be of service. So this morning I affixed my signature to this document, which I have before me now. I'm gonna read it to you because I think it's one of the most important documents I've signed in my entire eighteen years as Mayor. (*He takes out glasses and adjusts them.*) It reads as follows:

The eleventh day of March in the year of Our Lord, nineteen hundred and fifty-one.

To all men who come by these present, greetings!

Whereas Willie D. Jackson, Negro, a citizen of the town of Midway and a soldier in the Armed Forces of the United States of America, did lay down his life in the performance of his duty, and

Whereas, he distinguished himself by certain acts of unselfish heroism before he surrendered the last full measure of devotion,

Whereas, on this day is to be presented to him, posthumously (*The* MAYOR *reads it* "*post-humorously.*") a token of his country's reward for his demonstration of heroism,

Then, now do I, therefore, Stephen Farley Bleecher, duly elected Mayor of the town of Midway and last sworn into office on July 17, 1949, hereby proclaim this day as Willie Jackson Day, and direct that it be observed with proper public and private manifestation of tribute to its gallant son.

(Signed) Stephen Farley Bleecher,
Mayor.

(*There is applause.*) Thank you. Thank you. Now, this is a very important document to all of us here, white as well as colored, so I'm turning a copy over to Lester here, to frame and put on display in the library room here in Booker T. Washington High School. (*More applause. The* PHOTOGRAPHER *pops up to take a picture as the* MAYOR *hands the* PRINCIPAL *the document.*)

Now, in addition, I want to announce right here that the Board of Public Works at its meeting last Thursday night voted unanimously to name the proposed new park, to be built west of Midway Creek, as the Willie D. Jackson Memorial Park for Negroes. (*More applause.*)

Now, 'course it may be a little while yet before the town budget can afford it, but sooner or later we're gonna get

around to providing a park for you colored friends, just like we got the Midway Municipal Park for the whites.

And now—now, it is my duty to present to you a most distinguished figure. Traveling by plane all the way from Washington, D. C., just to be with us for this program. We ain't always happy to see people from Washington down this way, I might say. Sometimes they turn out to be meanin' to tell us how to take care of our own backyard and we ain't so friendly about that. We're all just one great big family down here, and we like to iron out our family difficulties the best we can in our own way. May take us a little while, sometimes, but we always manage to keep things runnin' smoothly on our own hook without anybody from Washington or up North comin' down here tryin' to change things. Willie Jackson gave his life over there defendin' our free and democratic privilege to settle things for ourselves. And Willie was a boy from right here in the South, and if it's good enough for him to go way over there and die for, then it oughta be good enough for us to live in peaceful-like, and get along like we been a-doin! (*At this point, the* SUPERINTENDENT *half-rises from his chair, clapping his hands broadly, as if to lead the audience in applause. His claps peter out, however, when no one else follows him, and he resumes his seat in an embarrassed fluster.*)

'Course, I don't suppose I really have to say all this, because our guest from Washington today is a true gentleman of the Old South himself, right out of the cottonfields of South Carolina. General Atkins grew up and went to school there, and then he went to West Point where he won his commission as an officer in the United States Army. Since then, he has distinguished himself with the Army in two world wars, and I'm sure will soon be doin' so in the third. Ladies and gentlemen, I have the honor of presentin' to you, Lieutenant-General Percival R. Atkins from the Pentagon in Washington! General Atkins.

(*Long and loud applause, with the principals on the platform standing. The* GENERAL *acknowledges the applause, raising his hand aloft as the* PHOTOGRAPHER *takes his picture. He arranges his papers on the lectern, the applause subsides, and the* GENERAL *begins.*)

GENERAL: Mr. Mayor, Mr. Superintendent, the bereaved family of Corporal Jackson, ladies and gentlemen. It is at once my pleasure and my extreme regret that I am with you this afternoon. My pleasure because it gives me a chance, an altogether too rare chance, to visit for a few hours a section of my beloved Southland. It is my pleasure because I can feel a

genuine rejuvenation as I am back once again among my people of the South, and to be reassured that the dear old Southland I knew and loved and grew up in as a child is still the same, old, happy place that I remember. A few things have met with change, of course, as is inevitable in our flourishing land. But, as Mayor Bleecher so aptly put it, these changes are being made by the South itself and in its own way, and require no interference from outside the family. And the basic grand old traditions of gracious old Dixie are, and will continue to be, the same.

And so in this vein I am very happy to visit with you this afternoon, and to participate in this family meeting. But then it is my deep regret that I come to you under quite these circumstances, with their overtones of tragedy in the death of our young honoree. I do not long dwell in melancholy, however, over the death of one who served so nobly, for I glory in the honor that is mine in serving as the official courier of our great country in tendering to Corporal Jackson's family and friends the thanks and appreciation of a grateful and admiring nation.

(*Grimly.*) We are engaged today in a struggle which tests the very vitals of the people of our great nation. The question is whether we shall be free to continue on in our great national heritage of the American way of life, or whether we must allow the alien ideologies of an imperialistic power to devour our country and our heritage. This bitter struggle requires of us the stamina and the courage and the loyalty of every citizen of this land. We may not all be called upon to make the supreme sacrifice that Corporal Jackson so willingly made, in order to protect the freedoms which are ours. But the inspiration and the example of Corporal Jackson ought to fire every heart and soul with a burning zeal to meet the test and weather the storm. Our homes, our children, our traditions, our industries, and our very existence in the world as a free and independent nation lie at stake. But I have little doubt that, as evidenced in the heroism of Midway's Willie Jackson, we Americans are going to meet the challenge and emerge victorious! (*Applause.*) And, therefore, it is with delight that I come to you today to convey the posthumous reward of our government to one of its great heroes. I have before me the official citation by the War Department which I shall read to you at this time: (*He reads.*)

The War Department, Washington, D. C.
The President of the United States takes pride in present-

ing the Distinguished Service Cross posthumously to Corporal Willie D. Jackson for service as set forth in the
following citation:

For extraordinary heroism in protecting the withdrawal of
his platoon during an action on the afternoon of January
21st, 1951. Heedless of his own personal safety, he manned
a machine gun in an exposed position overlooking a mountain pass to cover the retreat of his unit. Disregarding a
withering enemy barrage and firing so rapidly that the gun
metal burned his hands, he remained at his post for over
two hours, suffering five separate bullet wounds in the process, until mortally wounded by mortar shell fragments. His
exceptional fortitude and self-sacrificing concern for others
were in keeping with the highest traditions of the United
States Army. He gallantly gave his life for his country.

(*Applause.*) *The* GENERAL *beckons for* MRS. JACKSON *to step
forward.* TAYLOR *and the* PRINCIPAL *assist her to the lectern
and the others rise. The applause subsides and a hush falls as
the* GENERAL *takes the medal from a small box.*)

And, now, with the authority vested in me by my commission as Lieutenant-General in the United States Army, I hereby
present you, Mrs. Emma Jackson, with the Distinguished Service Cross awarded to your son as official recognition by his
country of his noble sacrifice. May you ever cherish this precious token and the high esteem of the nation which goes with
it.

(*He pins the medal on* MRS. JACKSON's *lapel, then steps
back and salutes smartly. Long and loud applause. The* PHO-
TOGRAPHER *takes several pictures. The* MAYOR, *the* SUPERIN-
TENDENT, *and the* PRINCIPAL *crowd in to get in the shots.* MRS.
JACKSON *wipes away a tear at the corner of her eye. The*
PRINCIPAL *takes* MRS. JACKSON's *arm and steers her to the
lectern to face the audience. He places a paper on the lectern
and, nodding and grinning, indicates to her that she is to read
it. He steps back. The applause has abated and the* GENERAL
*stands to the side, waiting for her to begin. She casts a final
look back at her husband, who sits like stone, and at her
daughter, who gives a broad smile of encouragement. She
turns back to the lectern and begins to read, slowly and
timidly.*)

MRS. JACKSON (*looking at each in turn*): M-Mish-tuh General, Mis-tuh Mayor, Mis-tuh Sup'rintendent, Mis-tuh Principal, ladies and gentlemen. I'm very happy to be here and to
'cept this beautiful medal for—for my son, Willie. Willie was

a—a fine son, an'—(*She breaks off reading and speaks breath-lessly as if to a person unseen.*) Yes . . . yes, you was a fine boy, son. A fine—son. I—(*She catches herself and goes back to the speech.*) Willie was a fine boy, and if—if he could be here with us today, I am sure he would be very proud to know that his sac—sac—sacrifice (*She finally gets it right.*) was not in vain. (*Again off the track.*) Not—in vain. Or was it, son? Was it? Did it really mean anything to 'em, Willie? (*Behind her, on the platform, there have been uneasy glances. Now the* PRINCIPAL *half-rises from his seat. But* MRS. JACKSON *has found herself again.*) I—I mean—(*She is breathing heavily. She pauses to wipe her brow with a handkerchief, then continues.*) I want to thank you-all for this medal—on behalf of Willie, an'—an' (*She stops again and shakes her head slowly from side to side.*) No, Willie. I just can't do it, son! (*She looks up quietly and announces.*) I can't read this speech. (*There are ad-libs of surprise. The* PRINCIPAL *rushes forward.*)

PRINCIPAL: What's the matter? What's the matter—? (*Lowering his voice to a whisper.*) It's all written out there for you. All you have to do is read it—just like it is. Just like you read it for me a while ago, remember?

MRS. JACKSON: I'm sorry.

PRINCIPAL (*desperately*): Please, Mrs. Jackson. We've got to get on with the program!

MRS. JACKSON: I said I can't read that speech.

PRINCIPAL (*takes up the paper*): Let me see it. Something wrong with the typing? I typed it out myself—

MRS. JACKSON (*eyeing him*): Yes, I know you did. That's just why I can't read it.

PRINCIPAL: B—b—but I don't understand—!

MRS. JACKSON (*with emotion*): Don't you! No. I don't guess you do. You'll never understand, will you? None of you all. (*Her glance takes in the* GENERAL *and his cohorts who stand watching in bewilderment. Then she turns and starts for her seat, with head bowed. There are ad-libs of consternation from the others, breaking off when* MRS. JACKSON *halts suddenly. With all eyes on her, she turns again in the direction of the officials, defiance in her gaze. Her hand comes up to finger the medal on her lapel. Then, looking down at it, she hastily unpins the medal and comes forward, extending it in her hand.*) Here! (*The* PRINCIPAL *retreats in apprehension, leaving the* GENERAL *directly before her.*) Yes, here! You take it— General. Take it back! (*There are ad-libs of amazement.*)

GENERAL (*holds up his hands in dismay*): But—but I can't do that!

MRS. JACKSON: Why not? You brung it down here, didn't you? Well, now you can take it back!

GENERAL: Why, I—my dear woman, don't you understand? It must be the excitement. (*Explains patiently, as if to a child.*) Now, Mrs. Jackson, this is your son's medal. Willie's. He won it. He deserved it. Since he's dead, it belongs to you. I just presented it to you on behalf of your government. (*In desperation as she fails to respond.*) You *can't* give it back!

MRS. JACKSON: Why?

GENERAL (*he is nearly purple*): Be—because it just isn't done, that's all. Why, I never heard of anything like this! (*He looks at the* MAYOR *and company and they echo him.*)

MRS. JACKSON (*extending the medal again*): Take it back. Please!

GENERAL (*backs away and almost explodes*): But—but, why? WHY? (*The others chorus,* "Why.")

MRS. JACKSON: Why? (*The others,* "Yes, why?") All right, then. I'll tell you why. You asked me. Now I'm gonna tell you. (*She begins quietly and builds in intensity, a tower of strength and emotion.*) I didn't want to go through with this program an' all, to begin with. But standin' here just now, readin' off them words, I knew I just can't! I can't be that much of a hypocrite, not even for Willie. You-all 'spect me to 'cept this medal and read that speech you had all ready for me, say, "Thank you kindly, suhs," and then go home an' be happy about the whole thing. But I can't! I can't go through with this —this big LIE. (*The others are shocked.*) Yes, I said lie. What has all your fine talk ever meant to Willie? He walked around this town nearly all his young life and nobody cared. You jim-crowed him and shunned him and you shoved him off in a corner. You gave him a third-rate schoolin' and when he wasn't quiet like a mouse, you put him out in the street. You looked down on him and you kept him down 'cause he was black and poor and didn't know no better than to believe that was the way things is supposed to be!

Yes, my Willie was dumb in a lotta ways. He didn't know nothin' 'bout no i-de-lol-ogies or whatever' you calls it. He wasn't fightin' 'cause he hated anybody. He joined the Army 'cause he couldn't get a decent job here. Willie thought if he did what they told him in the Army and didn't get in no trouble, maybe someday he could come back home and walk down the street and *be* somebody. Willie tried so hard, he got himself killed. But he didn't know. 'Cause even while you-all's here supposed to be honorin' Willie, you keep talkin' 'bout keepin' things the way they is. Willie didn't want things to stay

the way they is. 'Cause it always meant he come out holdin' the short end of the stick—the Jim Crow end, the poor folks' end.

That's why this is all such a big lie. You-all here ain't really honorin' Willie. You here tryin' to tell yourself that you been *right* all along—that the way you been doin' things is perfeckly okay, 'cause you can get boys like Willie to go out and fight and die for you and never know the difference. And you tryin' to use me and my dead boy's memory to make out like everybody's all satisfied here in the land of the free, that we's all "one big happy family" who's just tickled to death with the American Way!

Well, I don't know nothin' 'bout no other kinda way. I ain't never been on no trips to Europe or Russia or China or any of them places that I hears the man talk about on the radio, and I don't know what they does anywhere else. But I do know a whole lot 'bout right here from my whole life of experience. And I say I don't like everything the way it is! And it's high time—way past time—that a lot more changes were made! So that folks like my boy and your boy will have the same chance as anybody else to grow up and enjoy life and live like decent folks without no holdbacks 'cause they're colored.

Yes, Willie's dead and gone now, and I'm proud he was brave and helped save somebody else 'fore he got killed. But I can't help thinkin' Willie died fightin' in the wrong place. (*Quietly intense.*) *Willie shoulda had that machine gun over here!*

So you can take this medal back on up to Washington and tell 'em I don't want it! Take it back. Pin it on your own shirt! Give it to the ones who keeps this big lie goin' and send boys like my Willie all over the world to die for some kinda freedom and democracy they always gets the leavin' of! You done a pretty good job. You had folks fooled a long time with all this honey-talk, an' you even had me readin' off your words for you. But I done woke up! I knows what you're tryin' to do and I ain't gonna let you do it to me no more! Here! Take it back!

(*She hurls the medal at the* GENERAL. *He ducks in terror and the medal sails over his head and offstage somewhere where it falls to the floor with an empty clatter.* MRS. JACKSON *turns defiantly and marches off right, her head held high now, tall and proud.* LUCY MAE *runs after her, crying,* "Wait for me, Mama!" MR. JACKSON *gives a fearful glance or two about him, then takes a deep breath and follows.* TAYLOR *stands gazing*

471

after them, and a quiet smile appears on his face. The others stand in silent horror for a moment, then all begin to speak at once.)

OTHERS: This is outrageous! The nerve of her throwing that thing at me! Why, the ungrateful little—! Like I always say, give 'em an inch and they'll take a mile! What'll I tell Washington! I never heard of anything like this! She can't do this!

PRINCIPAL (*mopping his brow and turning from one to the other as they speak*): Gentlemen, this is terrible—terrible! I—I—I must apologize! She must have been out of her mind! She must have been drunk—You know how it is with those lower-class Negroes! Oh, this is terrible! (*Puts his hand to his chest.*) Oh!—my heart! (*He slumps down into a chair as the lights black out.*)

Epilogue

(*Discovered:* TAYLOR *leaning against the proscenium, as the* JANITOR *and the* JANITRESS *go about, striking the stage. They move slowly and silently almost as if in a dream, and begin to cart away the chairs, the lectern, and the flags. Mounting his stepladder, the* JANITOR *takes down the large display flag which has overlooked the proceedings throughout the play.*)

TAYLOR (*after a pause, to the audience*): Well, it's all over now. The General's up in his personal plane, winging his way back to Washington to file a full report on the afternoon, together with his vehement recommendation that they should stop awarding medals to Negroes. The Mayor and the Superintendent have reached their homes and are still fuming indignantly. The Mayor's wife has stepped out to get some milk to soothe His Honor's ulcers. The Jackson family are quietly eating their supper of pigs' feet and potato salad. And the Principal, Mr. Torrence, is home in bed under a doctor's care.

And me, I'm still here seeing that the place gets back in shape for school tomorrow. We'll need the auditorium for chapel first thing in the morning, for our daily pledge of allegiance to the flag. (*Pause.*) You know, I wouldn't be surprised if today wasn't the beginning of some big changes. In any event, we're not likely to forget today for a long time in Midway—Willie Jackson Day.

JANITRESS (*has approached* TAYLOR *with something in her hand*): Excuse me, Mr. Taylor, but what shall I do with this? (*She hands* TAYLOR *the medal.*) I found it on the floor back there. Is it worth anything?

TAYLOR (*looks the medal over*): Well, I'm not sure, Mrs. Moore. (*Muses.*) This bit of ribbon and metal—scant exchange for a young life. Yet, I wonder if someday we *could* present it . . . selflessly, without false fanfare or measured motive . . . a symbol, instead, of a pledge at long last fulfilled. It won't be quick and it won't be easy. (*Turns to include both* JANITRESS *and the audience.*) But, what do you say—shall we try it? Shall we? Shall we make this medal *worthy* of Willie—? (*He holds aloft the medal as the curtain falls.*)

Ladies in Waiting

by PETER DeANDA

Born and raised in Pittsburgh, Pa., Peter DeAnda makes his living as a professional actor. The play included in this volume marks his publishing debut, but his works have been seen in part or in toto. *Ladies in Waiting* was produced by Lonne Elder at the Negro Ensemble Company during the summer of 1968, and scenes from his play *Sweetbread* have been produced on Broadway and on television. He is now collaborating on the script for a Broadway musical entitled *Cyrus*. Mr. DeAnda has spent the last ten years of his life on the stage portraying characters from other playwrights' imaginations. He now hopes that he may change that status a little. Though he has no aims, or even desires, to quit the stage, he does "harbor a wish to see more of *my* thoughts than can be shown by making a character of the white man's design."

ACT I

Scene 1

(*Third tier, a women's prison somewhere. There is wire netting separating the* MATRON's *post from the cell block area. The set is neatly divided in half by this partition and the action takes place on both sides of it. We see three sets of double bunks with footlockers on one side and, on the other, a desk, a chair and prison guard's paraphernalia. There are small signs of femininity about the cell such as a curtain over the cell window and a doily on the desk. These are the only touches of outside life we will see. There are no signs of life as the play begins.*

The lights come up and we hear electrically operated doors clang open and then clang shut from somewhere offstage. Three women in medium-brown-colored prison dresses enter the MATRON's *area and stop in front of the netting. They are motionless and silent. There is a long pause before the* MATRON *enters the room. She is buxom and stern-appearing. The* MATRON *comes up to the netting and unlocks the door. Silently, the girls enter and, one by one, stand at the foot of their beds. Again a long pause as the* MATRON *closes and locks the door and then walks over to her desk and riffles through some papers there. Satisfied, she looks up and over to the girls and nods her head.*)

AGRIPPA (*she is nearest the netting*): Well, it's about time. First she marches us all the way up here and then she wants to play bad.

MATRON: Awright, Agrippa, knock it off.

AGRIPPA: Sure, Mama. Where's it at? You got me in here with these two old bags I wouldn't touch with a ten-foot pole.

CARMEN: Watch who you call a bag, sister. That's your problem, not mine. You the old bag. That's the reason you're the way you are. A man wouldn't put his hands on you.

AGRIPPA: What's wrong there, Carmen? Mad 'cause I wouldn't turn you on?

CARMEN: Aw, bitch, why don't you just keep quiet. You so mad 'cause you got to diddle yourself all night. I saw you trying to creep over to old Lolly last night. Didn't have no luck, did you?

AGRIPPA: Just keep your mouth shut, girl. I'll come over there and hit you one!

CARMEN: Why don't you?

MATRON: I'm going to come in there and hit both of you one. Knock it off!

AGRIPPA: Look who's talkin'. Shit, Mama, you out there servin' out your time just like us. Only thing is: you got to do it in eight-hour shifts.

MATRON: You want to go down, Agrippa?

AGRIPPA: Not downstairs I don't.

(CARMEN *and* AGRIPPA *laugh together.*)

LOLLY: I wonder what my babies are doin' right now. Poor things. They don't know how to take care of themselves.

AGRIPPA: Now, why you worrin' about them damn cats, Lolly? You wasn't home often enough while you was out to do 'em any good so why you cryin' about 'em now?

LOLLY: I did too. Them cats was always cryin' for me. They used to lick at me like I was somethin' good to eat when I come home to 'em.

AGRIPPA: If you had about five more they probably woulda ate you. What the hell did you want with twenty-eight cats, Lolly? They musta stunk somethin' awful.

LOLLY: I never noticed no smell. The ASPCA man came aroun' an' tole me—that I'd have to get rid of my babies. But I fooled him, I did.

CARMEN: What'd you do, Lolly?

LOLLY: I just said I would take care of it an' the next time he come aroun' there wasn't a cat in sight. I went out an' bought a mess of fish and just threw it out in the alley down the way. You can bet that there wasn't one of my babies in sight.

AGRIPPA: That man shoulda come aroun' more often. Them

pussies ate good for the first time in their lives.

LOLLY: Oh, keep quiet!

(*A buzzer sounds near the* MATRON'*s desk. She stands.*)

MATRON: You girls are going to have some company for a while.

AGRIPPA: You didn't tell us no one was comin'. It's too crowded in here as it is.

MATRON: I didn't want it preying on your mind, Agrippa. You got six places in there, not three.

AGRIPPA: Yeah. But there's only walkin' room for us.

CARMEN: Stop complaining, Agrippa. She just might be your style.

(*The buzzer sounds twice and the girls go to the netting, curious. We hear the doors clang open and a voice say:* "She's yours." *The doors clang shut again. A young girl enters. White, pretty, and demure.*)

AGRIPPA: My, my, my.

CARMEN: Stop drooling at the mouth, girl.

LOLLY: Ain't she a pretty one?

AGRIPPA: Yes, she is, ain't she?

MATRON: Awright, knock it off! (*Pause.*) Lana Kaufmann? (*No answer or acknowledgment from the girl.*) I asked you a question, speak up!

LANA: Ah—yes.

MATRON: It's yes, m'am.

AGRIPPA: Now ain't Mama bad?

CARMEN: Sure is. (*Gruff, imitating.*) "It's yes, m'am." Spit an' polish an' all that. She musta been in the Army.

AGRIPPA: Yeah. Regular Army, Male Division.

(*The* MATRON *reaches over and grabs a long police billy. She whacks the netting once, very hard. The girls jump back, intimidated.*)

MATRON: Just keep it quiet or the next time it won't be the netting. (*To the girl.*) Well?

LANA: Ah—yes, m'am.

MATRON: What's your time?

LANA: M'am?

MATRON: Your time? Your sentence?

LANA: The judge gave us thirty days, m'am.

MATRON: Who's us?

LANA: All of the pickets, m'am.

MATRON: You one of them peace marchers?

LANA: No. I mean, I have done that.

MATRON: Well, what were you picketing, girl?

LANA: This prison, m'am.

(LOLLY *laughs shrilly and loud.*)

MATRON (*she ignores* LOLLY): Oh, I see. You don't like the way we do things here, hey?

LANA: No, m'am, I don't.

MATRON: Well, that's just too bad. Come here. (LANA *steps forward but stops a couple paces before the* MATRON.) I said: Come here. (LANA *moves but too slowly. The* MATRON *grabs her arm and jerks her forcibly close to her.*) Raise your arms.

LANA: M'am?

MATRON: Your arms! (*The* MATRON *reaches out and hurls the girl's arms up by inserting her arms under hers and knocking them upward.*)

LANA: Ow!

MATRON: Hurt, didn't it? From now on when I speak, you better be listening. (*The* MATRON *begins frisking her. She does this roughly but quite firmly and definitely. Her hands touch every part of her body.*)

LANA: They did that downstairs.

MATRON (*still frisking her*): That's downstairs. I'm not going to get cut because someone downstairs didn't know what they were doing. You had an internal?

LANA: A what, m'am?

MATRON: Did one of the boys downstairs put his two fingers in your cookie jar?

LANA: Yes, m'am.

MATRON: Well, I don't have to, then. Someone like you they'd be pretty thorough with.

LANA: Yes, m'am, they were.

MATRON: Just speak when you're spoken to. (*She goes to her desk and pulls out paper and pen.*) Sign this. (*She gives her the pen.* LANA *starts to read it.*) Don't read, sign.

LANA: But I don't know what I'm signing.

MATRON: That's the point. Sign. (*The* MATRON *looks at her menacingly.* LANA *signs.*) Awright, you're clean. (*She opens the gate.*) Get in. (LANA *walks forward but stops before the entrance. The* MATRON *waits a moment and then pushes her through the opening and into the enclosure.*) Take any empty. You'll find what you need in your locker.

(*The* MATRON *walks back to her desk and sits down. She is unmindful of the girls.* LANA *looks around the cell fearfully and she cries.*)

LOLLY: Ain't no need to cry, honey. You'll be out of here in thirty days. I been here three months already.

CARMEN: Aw, leave the girl alone, Lolly. You need a good washin' when you first come in here. I cried too.

AGRIPPA: That was so many times and so many years ago, I don't know how you remember what you did. Lolly's right, girl. There ain't no use in cryin'. You can do thirty standin' on your head.

LANA: I shouldn't be here. I didn't do anything.

AGRIPPA: Me neither.

CARMEN (*laughs*): Sure, we all didn't do anything. Did we, Lolly?

LOLLY: That's right. I didn't do a thing.

AGRIPPA: Yeah. Lolly just poured a gallon of gasoline over her old man an' struck a match to him. That ain't nothin'.

LOLLY: If the judge knew him like I knew him he woulda said the same. I didn't do nothin' but the righteous thing.

AGRIPPA: That's righteous, all right. Seein' as how he was goin' to hell anyway, you just gave him a little samplin' of things to come.

LOLLY: The good Lord come an' tole me I was doin' the right thing. He tole me to destroy my devil, to fight fire with fire.

AGRIPPA: Yeah, Lolly. Girl, what you doin' in here with us? They generally stick us all together.

LANA: It's all a prison, isn't it?

AGRIPPA: That's what they say. Why don't you take that bunk over there? You can be right close to me.

CARMEN: Agrippa's gettin' in her bid early.

AGRIPPA: You watch out for that one, girl. She's got a nasty mouth.

LANA: My name's Lana, Agrippa.

AGRIPPA: That's pretty. That's Carmen over there with her mouth open and this is Lolly. She's crazy with God and cats.

LOLLY: Don't talk vain about the Lord, hussy. He's watching you.

AGRIPPA: What for? Where am I goin'?

LOLLY: To hell.

AGRIPPA: Now that ain't nice. Lana, you gonna take this bunk?

LANA: Yes, why not?

CARMEN: Oh, oh.

(*Agrippa makes a nasty face at* CARMEN *which* LANA *doesn't see.* LANA *goes to the bunk and unrolls the mattress.*)

AGRIPPA: Here, let me help you. (*She goes over and begins to help her.*)

LANA: You needn't.

CARMEN: She's goin' to, anyway.

AGRIPPA: You gotta make the bed nice and tight or Big Mama out there won't let you sleep in it. If she can't bounce her one and only quarter on it, then you gotta sleep on the floor that night. (*They are making the bed.*) Now, down here is your locker. You'll find some hard soap an' some oversized drawers. Don't complain or you won't get any. An' it gets kinda cold in here at night.

CARMEN: Not if Agrippa can help it, honey.

LANA: What did you say, Carmen?

AGRIPPA: She didn't say nothin'. That's just her way, Lana. She talks to herself, sometimes. That's right, honey. Pull it tight. You do that real good. You been in the slammers before?

LANA: Have I been where before?

CARMEN: The joint, Lana. The jug, jail, the slammers. They call it that because of them big iron doors slamming shut behind you all the time.

LANA: Oh. No. I was a counselor at camp for a few summers. We had to keep our bunks tight too.

AGRIPPA: Why? Would they make you sleep on the floor?

LANA (*she laughs*): No. Maybe you would have to run a few laps around the baseball field, or police the area.

CARMEN: The only police you gonna see around here is that big fat one out there.

(*They finish making the bunk and* LANA *sits in the chair and drops her head to the small desk that is in front of it. She cries again.* AGRIPPA *comes up behind her and begins to stroke her hair.*)

AGRIPPA: That's right, baby. You just cry your heart out. Agrippa's right here.

LOLLY: You just pray to God to make you a good girl after this. He'll hear you. He'll make you walk that straight walk an' talk that good talk. Yes, He will, child.

LANA: I didn't do anything! We were picketing this jail and the cops came and told us we were on the wrong side of the street.

CARMEN: That ain't no reason to go to jail, honey. You sure you didn't do something else?

LANA: He told us to move and we wouldn't. Then he said we were all under arrest. The judge said that we could not break laws and disobey the police and expect any leniency from his court. He gave us all thirty days.

CARMEN: Honey, where I'm from when the law says move,

you move. If you don't, you liable to wind up in a hospital prison, or worse.

LANA: But we're trying to change that. That's one of the reasons we were out there.

CARMEN: Well, now you're in here an' you ain't gotta worry about it no more.

AGRIPPA: Aw, cool it, would you? Can't you tell she's upset? Don't you fret none over her nasty mouth, Lana. She ain't nothin' but a fifty-cent trick.

CARMEN: You once offered me two dollars, Agrippa.

AGRIPPA: I'ma bop you right in your mouth, girl.

CARMEN: Shit.

AGRIPPA: What'd I say! (AGRIPPA *jumps at* CARMEN *and slaps her across the mouth. They tussle and the* MATRON *gets up quietly and unlocks the gate.*)

MATRON (*she yells*): ONE! (*They stop and stand at attention.*) Two.

(*The two look at each other for a moment and* CARMEN *walks forward. She comes up to the* MATRON *and stops in front of her. The* MATRON *has the stick which she quite deliberately and with much force jabs end-first into the girl's lower abdomen.* CARMEN *falls over, clutching herself. She is mute.* LANA *screams and rushes over to her.*)

LANA: This is a woman! Are you mad?

MATRON: Stand up, Kaufmann.

(*The* MATRON *doesn't say any more. She waits for* LANA *to comply. She doesn't, looking after* CARMEN. *The* MATRON *yanks* LANA *up by her hair and methodically inflicts the same punishment on her as she did with* CARMEN. *The girls lay side by side as the lights go out to end Scene 1.*)

Scene 2

(*The lights come up to silhouette the cell and its occupants. There is another* MATRON *on duty. She is asleep. The four cellmates are in bed and we hear the sound of weeping.*)

AGRIPPA (*softly*): Hey, hey. Lana?

LANA (*within her sobs*): Yes.

AGRIPPA: Shh! Keep it down. We got ol' Maxie on duty now. She works two jobs. She sleeps on this one. She won't wake up, but keep it down anyway.

LANA: Why, Agrippa, why?

AGRIPPA: Honey, you don't know this place. That was nice you takin' up for Carmen that way. But I coulda told you what

was gonna happen. Ol' Mama's a bastard. You lucky you didn't get it across your head. When she hits you, no one says nothin'. You do that an' you get it again.

LANA: How's Carmen?

AGRIPPA: Now ain't you somethin'. You got it worse than she did an' you frettin' over her. Ain't you somethin'. How much you weigh, girl?

LANA: Ninety-five pounds. Why?

AGRIPPA: When she jugged you with that stick I coulda swore I saw it come out the other side. (LANA *laughs*.) Now, that's better. You sobbin' like you was wasn't doin' neither of us any good.

LANA: Did it bother you?

AGRIPPA: Sure it did. I felt like droppin' a few tears myself. You the first child I ever saw cry in their sleep. It was pretty though. Your cheeks was glistenin' like a young baby's.

LANA: Agrippa, you're not as hard as you seem.

AGRIPPA: Don't you believe that, honey.

LANA: Agrippa?

AGRIPPA: Yeah, honey?

LANA: Why did you fight with Carmen? Was it because of me?

AGRIPPA: Sort of.

LANA: Do—do you like women?

AGRIPPA: What do you mean?

LANA: You know. Like, do you like women in that way?

AGRIPPA: What are you talkin' about, Lana? What way?

LANA: The way Carmen implied. That's why you hit her, isn't it?

AGRIPPA: I hit her 'cause she had designs on you. That's why.

LANA: No, Agrippa. I'm not that young. It's you, not her.

AGRIPPA: No, I guess you ain't all that young if you saw all that about me. Yeah, I like women.

LANA: Why?

AGRIPPA: "Why?" she asks me. Honey, I don't know why. Maybe I was born with too many of them male things in me.

LANA: Hormones.

AGRIPPA: Yeah, them things. Lana, you like women?

LANA (*she laughs*): No, Agrippa, I don't.

AGRIPPA: Damn the luck.

LANA: Do you always joke about yourself?

AGRIPPA: Lana honey, I got fourteen more years to put in here. If I took myself serious all the time, I'd blow my cool. Where you from?

LANA: Forest Hills.

AGRIPPA: What'd your people say about you goin' to the slammers?

LANA: My father thinks it's wonderful.

AGRIPPA: What's so wonderful about it? Baby, this ain't no fun. Tell him he's crazy as a coot.

LANA: I'll tell him. He believes in the rights of man and each man—should have his due share of life. I suppose I'm here because I believe the same thing.

AGRIPPA: Oh hell, you two is communists.

LANA: No, we're not.

AGRIPPA: I remember down home when people like you come from up North and tried to organize the colored folk. Boy, did my folk go through some head-whippings over you communists. I better stay away from you, girl. First thing you know you'll be organizing us and all of us'll be receiving organized head-whippin's. No, no.

LANA: I won't try to organize you. I promise.

AGRIPPA: Promise?

LANA: Yes. But you have to promise something too.

AGRIPPA: What's that?

LANA: I don't like girls, remember? Promise you won't bother me that way.

AGRIPPA: Now that's a hard one. I'll promise. But if I fuck up every once in a while, don't hold it against me. You're a pretty girl, Lana.

LANA: I'll remember that when I bathe.

AGRIPPA: Yeah. Don't you go tantalizing me, now.

(*From one of the other bunks we hear a mumble which grows into audible sounds. It is* LOLLY. *She is softly singing a prayer.*)

LOLLY:

One of these days I'm gonna take a vacation.
Cool my heels in—that shimmering water.
An' I ain't gonna worry no more.

LANA: She has a lovely voice.

AGRIPPA: Only when she's sleep, honey. Don't get her started in the day. She sounds like one of them cats wailing then.

LOLLY (*she speaks in her sleep*):

If we tell, gently, gently
All that we shall one day have to tell,
Who then will hear our voices without laughter,
Sad complaining voices of beggars
Who indeed will hear them without laughter?*

* From the poem "Vanity," by Birago Diop of Senegal.

AGRIPPA: She's either singing or tellin' poetry. Hey, Carmen!

LANA: Let her sleep.

AGRIPPA: She ain't sleep. Carmen's over there waiting for us to get into somethin' so she can watch. That girl's pretty strange. Ain't that so, Carmen?

CARMEN: You better cool it, Agrippa. I ain't but two seconds off your behind as it is.

LANA: Have you been awake all the while?

CARMEN: My stomach's too sore to let me sleep. And ol' Lolly over here been mumbling all the while. Thanks, Lana honey, for stickin' up for me. But you a idiot. Don't they teach you folks that you ain't supposed to mess with the Man?

LANA: You're also a man, Carmen.

CARMEN: What do you mean?

LANA: I don't mean that. I mean that you are also somebody. Somebody not to be afraid of the Man.

CARMEN: Hell, I ain't afraid of nobody.

LANA: Then why do you let them treat you like you are?

CARMEN: We're in jail, honey. We ain't out in the street. I did something wrong an' they caught me at it. I have to take my punishment until my time is up.

LANA: Your punishment doesn't include that brutality. You should try to have her punished for doing that to you. We can both sign a complaint. I'll—

AGRIPPA: I thought you promised not to organize us.

LANA: That's not organizing. It's merely complaining about brutality. Every person has a right to complain.

AGRIPPA: Baby, you don't do that in the big apple. We complain together and all they're goin' to do is split us up into different tiers and beat the hell out of us anyway. Like Carmen said: "We're in jail."

LANA: But—

AGRIPPA: No, honey.

CARMEN: She's right, Lana. I ain't signing no complaint. Is Maxie gone?

AGRIPPA (*she looks over to the* MATRON): Forever.

(CARMEN *gets out of her bed and lifts the end of her bunk. She undoes the bottom of one of the posts and retrieves something.*)

CARMEN (*to* LANA): You smoke?

LANA: Mentholated.

CARMEN: Well, sister, we ain't got no Salems. (*She throws her one of the cigarettes she has. It is a reefer.*)

LANA: I'm sorry. But I don't smoke this.

CARMEN: Give it to Agrippa.

LANA (*she does*): Aren't you afraid you're goin' to get caught?

AGRIPPA: Maxie ain't got two jobs. She got two and a half.

LANA: You mean she brings that to you?

AGRIPPA: That's smart. She sleeps and we smoke the gangster.

LANA: But you're in jail!

CARMEN: Can you think of a better place to smoke? Light that, Agrippa. I hear there's some good quality floating around town.

(AGRIPPA *strikes a match guardedly. She lights up and inhales deeply. She hands it to* CARMEN.)

AGRIPPA: You oughta try it, Lana. Relaxes you and makes the nights go faster.

LANA: It stinks. Aren't you afraid for the smell?

CARMEN: The best thing about a cell is that it's kept well ventilated. No heat and cold as hell. The air comes in and goes right back out.

AGRIPPA: It tastes good. Good head quality. Soft and mellow like real good wine. Hey, Carmen?

CARMEN: Yeah, like real good wine. I should be up at Jimmy's now listenin' to some real good sounds and all curled up in that black nigger's arms. Whew! He can make me feel fine.

AGRIPPA: The only time he makes you feel fine is after he goes upside your head when you don't bring enough of that green stuff to him.

CARMEN: That's all right. But he sure knows how to make a woman feel good when he's in the right mood.

AGRIPPA: Pass me that reefer.

(CARMEN *does.*)

LANA: Are you really a—prostitute?

AGRIPPA: You don't think she's in here for givin' it away, do you?

CARMEN: Yeah, baby. I hook for my bread.

LANA: How is that? I mean, how does it feel to do that? All those men, different ones all the time.

CARMEN: It can be fun, Lana. Some of the Johns are real good people. I remember once I picked up this fat, white-haired gent and me an' him had a ball. We went up to Harlem and took in Small's and Well's an' a few other of them places. Then we checked into the hotel an' went to bed. He didn't touch me all night. All he wanted to do was for me to stroke his head while he laid on my breast. Just like a little boy. He

gave me two hundred dollars the next mornin'. The next time we met he gave me ninety days.

LANA: He was a judge?

CARMEN: Yep. This sure is some good reefer. I get some real sick ones at times. At times. Hah! I get more of them than I do the others. They have you do all kinds of things to 'em an' for 'em.

LANA: Like what?

CARMEN: I don't think I have to tell you. You just think of anything that ain't good an' natural an' that's it. I want to dance. Dance with me, Agrippa.

AGRIPPA: Sure, honey. (*She looks to* LANA.) Don't worry none, Lana. We do this all the time. She likes the way I lead. She tells me that I dance better than most men. That ain't all I do better than men, but she won't go for it.

(AGRIPPA *takes* CARMEN *in her arms and they begin to do a slow dance. In their long cotton gowns the effect is striking and mesmerizing. They dance as if it is to the most beautiful music in the world. As they dance,* CARMEN *begins to speak lazily and softly.*)

CARMEN: Jimmy, why do you treat me so bad? I want to be good to you, baby, I really do. But you make me so bad. I didn't want to cheat on you, but you make me do those things. When I come home all I want you to do is hold me in your arms and kiss my lips, my eyes, my shoulders. But you like to beat me too much, Jimmy. I can't get nothin' but five-dollar tricks sometimes when you beat me so bad. I didn't mean to give him none, Jimmy. But you said you'd meet me. You didn't show up, Jimmy baby, you didn't show up. He wasn't good like you, nobody could be good like you, Jimmy. Let's go home, Jimmy. Let's go home. (*She drops her head to* AGRIPPA'*s shoulder.*)

AGRIPPA: Sure, baby, we'll go home. Come on, we're at the door now. That's right, step up, step up. (AGRIPPA *is leading her over to* CARMEN'*s bed.* LANA *is paralyzed, believing she is witnessing* CARMEN'*s seduction.*) That's right, baby. Get in bed. Yeah, that's right. Close your eyes. I'll kiss you good night and you sleep it off. Softly now. (AGRIPPA *kisses her on the lips. She stands and comes back to her own bed.*) Don't worry, Lana. That happens all the time. She can't smoke no reefer. You know what she is? A big baby, that's what. Jimmy's her mother, brother, sister, and father all rolled up into one. Too bad he's a no-good pimp.

LANA: But she let you kiss her.

AGRIPPA: Before your month's up you may be letting me

kiss you too. Don't look at me like that. She was no more aware of what I was doin' than the man in the moon. But don't you let her know I kissed her. I gotta get my kicks someway, don't I?

LANA: You're sweet, Agrippa.

AGRIPPA: Yeah, like somebody's poppa bear. Have some reefer. (LANA *doesn't answer.*) All right. Then don't have some reefer. (*She pads back over and lifts the corner of* CARMEN's *bed. She redeposits the marijuana in its hiding place. She pads back and climbs into bed.*) Good night, honey.

(*The lights go out to end Scene 2.*)

Scene 3

(*It is early daylight. The three older women are up and about as* LANA *sleeps. An alarm sounds; loudly and long.* LANA *awakes and stretches.*)

AGRIPPA: Get out of that bed, honey. Big Mama'll be down on you like white on rice if she catches you in there after the bell.

LANA: I thought I was at home. (*She gets up and stretches.*)

CARMEN: That's where you are for twenty-nine more days.

LANA: When do we eat?

AGRIPPA: Soon as we clean this cell. We're runnin' late now. You better hurry along, baby.

LANA: You're all ready.

LOLLY: You was restin' so quiet and peaceful-like, we let you sleep on a bit.

LANA: That's just like my mother. I'm always late for school because she says I look like an angel when I'm sleeping. She still thinks I'm a little girl.

AGRIPPA: You go to school, honey?

LANA: Yes, I go to Hofstra College.

CARMEN: A college girl! Ain't we sportin' it?

AGRIPPA: What do you take, honey?

LANA: Humanities. I'm a junior.

CARMEN: I thought girls couldn't be juniors. I'm my daddy's oldest, but my brother Willie is called Junior.

LANA: No, that just denotes how far along you are in your studies.

AGRIPPA: What's that make me in here? A freshman? I got twenty years and I ain't done but six.

LANA: That's a long time. What did you do, Agrippa?

(AGRIPPA *doesn't answer her.*)

CARMEN: She don't like to talk about it, Lana. And you'd do better not to ask.

(*There is silence as they go about their chores.* LOLLY *sings a spiritual as she cleans. Her voice is scratchy and not so pleasant as the night before.*)

AGRIPPA: Why don't you stop all that caterwauling, Lolly? It ain't bad enough that we gotta listen to you all the night, now you gotta start first thing in the morning.

LANA: You sing well, Lolly. Did you study?

LOLLY: No, child. I been singing since the day I was born. My man was like Agrippa there. He didn't like my singing neither.

AGRIPPA: Well, he sure don't have to worry about that no more. (*She looks at the netting.*) Cool it.

(*The* MATRON *has stood up and walks to the netting. She unlocks the gate.*)

MATRON: Awright, ladies. Stand by. (*The girls go and stand at the foot of their bunks.* LANA *follows their example. The* MATRON *comes in and goes first to* LOLLY. *She looks her and her bunk over.*) Well, Lolly, you keep yourself and your area real good. Whenever you get out of here I could use a good daymaid. You should of just used a straight razor on your old man. Intent to kill carries a lighter sentence.

LOLLY: Yes, m'am.

MATRON: Go stand at the desk. (*This indicates her approval of* LOLLY's *area. She moves on to* CARMEN. *Looking her over.*) That's just like a whore. Can keep herself looking neat and trim, but can't do a damn thing around the house. Carmen, your area is sloppy; straighten it out. You do ten around the yard today.

CARMEN: Yes, m'am.

MATRON: Keep you in shape for the trade. (*She moves on.*) Here's the little do-gooder. Still up to protecting others? Speak when you're spoken to.

LANA: Yes, m'am.

MATRON: You didn't hear the question.

LANA: Uh, no m'am.

MATRON: That's better. (*She takes out a quarter and bounces it on* LANA's *bed.*) Around here we forget about little things like protest and picketing. When you get out you can start your good works all over again, but in here you mind your manners. Got that?

LANA: Yes, m'am.

MATRON: You make a bed real well. (*She moves on to* AGRIPPA.) Good morning, Agrippa. Sleep well?

AGRIPPA: Like a log, Mama.

MATRON: Move on.

(CARMEN *finishes her area and they all file singly to the desk area. The* MATRON *comes out and pushes a buzzer. The doors clang and open and they all file out. The doors clang shut as the lights go out. The lights come back up as they file in.*)

MATRON: All in.

(*They march on into the cell. It is early evening. They have spent the day at their chores and work assignments and all show signs of fatigue.*)

CARMEN: I can't do that no more. Outside all I do is lay on my back and in here all they want to do is lay on it. I'm bushed.

AGRIPPA: Cut out your beefin', woman. You ain't got but sixty more to do. They got me makin' them damn uniforms all day an' I keep stickin' them needles into my fingers. By the time I get out of here I'm gonna look like I got sponges for hands. What'd they have you doin' today, girls?

LANA: They've got me on maintenance with Carmen. We must have scrubbed twenty miles of corridors today. My hands look awful.

AGRIPPA: They always stick you short-termers on the mops. Me an' Lolly are on rehabilitation. I guess they figger bull-dykes should make good tailors.

LANA: I don't like that word.

CARMEN: Why not? She is, ain't she?

LANA: I suppose so.

AGRIPPA: Hell, I like it. Bull for the man in me and dyke for stemmin' the tide of frustrated womenfolk.

LANA: Doesn't being that way make you unhappy?

AGRIPPA: The only thing that makes me unhappy is when I don't get none. Who wants to play some cards? (*No one answers so she sets up the desk to play solitaire. She begins playing.*) You know, my mama once caught me in bed with my brother. She didn't beat him, but she beat the shit out of me. Told me that I was woman, the devil's temptress, and that I tempted him with the fruit of my womb. She didn't believe me when I told her he raped me. Hurt something awful. I ain't touched a man since.

CARMEN: I'll make up for your part.

AGRIPPA: You probably done that a thousand times over already, sweetie. You got a boyfriend, Lana?

LANA: No.

AGRIPPA: I guess not. A girl pretty as you don't need no steady. You probably got 'em lined up smellin' at you.

LANA: Not really.

489

CARMEN: You mean you ain't got even one boyfriend?

LANA: No.

AGRIPPA: Now, you ain't gonna stand there an' tell us you ain't had no lovin'?

LANA: I've never been to bed with a boy, if that's what you mean.

CARMEN: Well, as I live and breathe. A sure-enough virgin. You hear that, Agrippa?

AGRIPPA: Yes, I did. I ain't never been around a grown-up virgin before. Come over here, girl. (LANA *is bemused and walks over to her.* AGRIPPA *looks her over.*) That's enough. I just wanted to see you up close.

(LANA *walks back to where she was before.*)

CARMEN: How come you're still a virgin?

LANA: I don't know. I suppose I haven't found anyone I liked well enough.

CARMEN: You just ain't been around the right kind of men. Where I'm from, if a girl ain't been done in by the time she's fourteen she's thought of as either queer or crazy. I think I was eleven years old when I was busted wide open. And it didn't hurt a lick.

AGRIPPA: Didn't expect it did. Damn it. I'm goin' to beat these cards yet.

(LANA *takes her stockings off and goes to the washbasin to wash them out.*)

CARMEN: Right now I'd be eatin' supper with one of my best payin' customers. We'd be at the Copper Rail sucking on some pigs' feet or pickin' at some fried chicken. Lana, don't you scrub them things too hard now. They'll come apart right in your hands. That one's from down home too. He told me I remind him of his nigger woman back there.

LANA: Does he say that to you?

CARMEN: Sure. I seen a picture of her. I do look like her a bit.

LANA: No, I mean does he use that word when he's speaking of his woman?

CARMEN: You talkin' about "nigger woman"? Shee, that ain't nothin', Lana. You should hear what he says when we're makin' it. Always has me tellin' him how much better he is than a black man. "I'm good, ain't I, girl, real good?" That's all he says most of the time. "I'm good, better than your nigger man, ain't it?" If he paid attention to what he was doin', an' stop all that talkin', maybe he could be better than other men.

LOLLY: You should pray to the Lord to deliver you from

all your sins. You oughta get down on your knees and beg His forgiveness, sinner. He watches you, He sees you at your evil workings. You gotta make repentance at Judgment Day. There ain't no way you can get away, there ain't no hidin' place on Judgment Day.

CARMEN: That's what they tell me. Lolly, you tell the good Lord that if He pays my rent every month and puts some dollars in my pocket, I'll repent. But not a day before. An' you tell Him that peep freaks gotta pay extra to watch.

(LOLLY *falls to her knees and begins to pray.*)

LOLLY: Forgive her, O Lord, for she knows not what she does. The sinner is ignorant of her wrongs, but she will repent before Judgment Day is at hand.

CARMEN: Pray, girl, pray. Say one for old Agrippa over there. She can use it.

LOLLY: Blasphemy is of the wicked. God came down and destroyed Sodom for its wicked and un-God-fearing ways. Heed the words of the Bible, sinner, and mend your errant ways.

CARMEN: I'm heedin' the words of that judge when he said: "Ninety days."

AGRIPPA: Oh, leave her alone, Carmen.

LOLLY (*she stands and rushes over to* AGRIPPA): My prayers are bein' used in your behalf also, woman. You defile the very use of your creation. First God created man, then He created woman. Each to serve each other's needs. Your ways are unnatural and not meant to be. Renounce your foolish deeds and come back unto the way of the Lord!

AGRIPPA: Awright now, Lolly.

LOLLY: The Lord said: "Come unto me, my children." He sent his Son down unto the face of the earth to brave the wrath and evil barbs of the unbelievers and was crucified to save mankind. God is most holy. Repent and be saved!

LANA: Agrippa, she doesn't know what she's doing. What's wrong with her?

AGRIPPA: I know, Lana. She gets like this every now and then. Lolly, why don't you go over and lie down? It'll do you good.

LOLLY: The Lord said: "Don't be deterred. Let not your path be changed." Repent, sinners! Pray with me for your deliverance! (LOLLY *grabs* AGRIPPA *and tries to pull her to her knees. They both fall in a heap.*)

AGRIPPA: Awright now! Carmen, get Mama!

(LOLLY *is tussling with* AGRIPPA *and wailing some sort of unintelligible gibberish.* AGRIPPA *is trying to hold her arms*

without hurting her. The MATRON *unlocks the gate and comes up to them. She helps separate them.*)

MATRON: Awright, Lolly! That's enough! Stop it! (*She shakes her.*)

AGRIPPA: I think she needs a little shower, Mama.

MATRON: Come on, Lolly. We gotta go down. (*She begins to lead her off.*)

LOLLY (*she is seemingly sensible again and begins to fight her off*): I don't want to go down, I don't want to go down! I'm awright, I'm fine! See, I'm fine. Don't take me down! Agrippa, don't let 'em take me down there! I'm fine, I tell you! See, look, I'll sing you a song. (*She begins to sing a loud and untuneful spiritual.*)

MATRON (*as she struggles*): Agrippa, come out and push the buzzer. Come on, Lolly. (AGRIPPA *comes out and pushes the buzzer. She buzzes one long and two short twice in quick succession. She has done this before, or she has seen it done. The doors clang open and* TWO MATRONS *rush in.*) Get this one. (*She hands* LOLLY *over to them and they rush her out. The doors clang shut again.* AGRIPPA *looks at the* MATRON *and shrugs her shoulders before walking back to her cell. The* MATRON *sits and resumes reading or whatever.*)

LANA: What will they do to her?

AGRIPPA: They're just goin' to take her down and give her a long, cold shower. She'll come out of it okay.

LANA: She's disturbed.

AGRIPPA: Bellevue had her, but they said she was perfectly normal and could stand trial. (*She shrugs.*) What you gonna do?

LANA: But she should be someplace where they can help her.

CARMEN: What you gonna do?

AGRIPPA: There ain't nothin' can be done about it, Lana. She blows like that about once a month. That was the second time in less than a week. She may be really crackin' now.

LANA: Is she dangerous?

AGRIPPA: About as dangerous as a fly. Annoyin' but that's about all. They'll bring her back up in a hour or so. Mama, it's about coffee time, ain't it? (*The* MATRON *reaches down into her drawer and takes out a pot of coffee. The pot is electric. She plugs it in after preparing the works.*) I hope you drink coffee?

LANA: Why yes, I do.

AGRIPPA: Since you ain't got no other vices, I thought coffee might be a little strong for you.

LANA: I've got my vices.

AGRIPPA: I'm still tryin' to figger how you got in here. Didn't the judge see the same person I'm seein'?

LANA: I believe it's my father he saw, not me. My father was before him at least twenty times during the McCarthy hearings. My father was always being arrested for doing the same kind of things I'm in here for. When he sentenced me, his eyes were directly staring at my father.

CARMEN: I don't understand you kids. What do you care what they do to us in here? We're wrong, ain't we?

LANA: Maybe. But you're human and should be treated as such. My father once told me that if we take the attitude that people who commit crimes against society are less than people, then we who think we are better are less than they and we should treat ourselves accordingly.

CARMEN: You lost me there. When I'm out on that street makin' my bread, I know I'm wrong, and if the Man catches me in the wrong, I take the consequences.

LANA: And you should. But only to the degree which the law says. It says that you are to serve ninety days, you serve ninety days. It doesn't say that you are also to get poked in the stomach.

AGRIPPA: Mind your mouth, Lana. How's that coffee comin', Mama?

MATRON: It's ready. Bring your cups.

(*They bring cups up to the netting. The* MATRON *opens the gate and they all come forward while she pours the coffee.* AGRIPPA *sits in the* MATRON's *chair and throws her legs up on the desk.*)

AGRIPPA: Boy, that big behind of yours sure makes this chair feel good.

MATRON: Awright, take the feet down, Agrippa. Don't take advantage of my hospitality.

AGRIPPA (*she does*): I wouldn't think of it, Mama. Now, why don't you tell Lana and Carmen there that you're sorry? Hittin' them poor girls in their bellies like that? (*The* MATRON *continues sipping her coffee and doesn't reply.*) Aw, c'mon now. We're all gonna be here together for a while. Why don't you tell 'em that you won't let that happen again?

MATRON: As long as I'm in charge of this section, I run it the way I see fit.

AGRIPPA: Sure, you're the boss. But you ain't gotta be bad about it. We can all get along together just fine, now can't we? (*The* MATRON *doesn't answer.* AGRIPPA *grabs her by the wrist and pulls her over the desk.*) Now, can't we? (*She exerts more force.*) See, you ain't all that bad, Mama.

MATRON: Let go of my arm!

AGRIPPA: Tell the girls you're sorry for what you did.

MATRON: Agrippa, let go!

AGRIPPA: What you gonna say? (*She applies more pressure.*)

MATRON: All right! All right! I—I apologize.

AGRIPPA: You won't do that no more, will you? Will you?

MATRON: No, no, no more! Agrippa, you're breaking my arm.

(AGRIPPA *releases her. The* MATRON *goes toward the buzzer.*)

AGRIPPA: I don't think you'd better do that. (*The* MATRON *stops. They both stare at each other quite intently until the* MATRON *backs down. They go back to sipping their coffee.*) You make some mighty lousy coffee, Mama. Lana, you'd think after sittin' out here for all these years, she woulda learned how, huh? (LANA *doesn't say anything.*) You know, Mama used to be a schoolteacher in a all-girl's school. They had her resign when she took to layin' her ruler down a little too hard and a little too much on those little ladies' behinds. Ain't that right, Mama? You see, Lana, Mama's funny that way. She likes to hurt people. (*There is silence from the trio.*) Mama, we don't like bein' hurt.

MATRON: I don't see where it should concern you.

AGRIPPA: It didn't before yesterday. You coulda whipped ol' Carmen there until the cows came home for all I give a damn. She gets paid for it. But you shouldn't have done that to little Kaufmann here. I didn't like that.

MATRON: You'll get yours, Agrippa. Don't get too smart.

AGRIPPA: I won't. Just watch where you lay that stick from now on. (*There is silence. They continue drinking their coffees.*) I used to be in this little cubbyhole all by myself. Just me and Mama there. We had us a grand old time, didn't we, Mama? (*She doesn't answer.*) Yeah, me an' Mama had us a grand old time together. Remember, Mama?

MATRON: All right, Agrippa. Keep it quiet.

AGRIPPA: Just mind your manners, Mama, from now on.

CARMEN: You get around, don't you, girl?

(AGRIPPA *ignores her. The doors offstage clang open and clang shut.* LOLLY *enters slowly. She has a scarf tied around her head, covering her hair. She walks as if she is drugged to the open cell door and stops for a moment before it. She waits a moment as if it is closed and then enters as if someone has opened it. She goes to her bunk and then sits on her locker.*)

AGRIPPA: Tell her to lie down, Mama.

MATRON: On your bunks, girls.

(LOLLY *goes to her bunk and lies down. The lights dim and go out to end this scene.*)

Scene 4

(*It is night. The girls are again in their nightshifts.* MAXIE *is on duty. She is asleep.*)

CARMEN: This is a hell of a way to spend your birthday.

LANA: Is it, really? Happy Birthday, Carmen.

AGRIPPA: Yeah. Many happy returns. Which you will have.

CARMEN: Naw, they ain't gettin' me back in here. I got a angle I thought up. I'ma do like the high-class white tricks do, get me a answerin' service an' work out of one joint. The Johns wanna see me they gotta call up an' leave a message, take me out on the town an' get their value received for one hundred dollars. One turn a night from now on.

AGRIPPA: Carmen, ain't nobody gonna give you one hundred dollars, so stop runnin' off at the mouth. If you get more'n five dollars for a trick now, you must be givin' out green stamps.

CARMEN: That's all you know. I got Johns who want me to give up the gig, want me to go home with 'em. That's how good I am.

LANA: Are they serious about it?

AGRIPPA: You heard of words said in the "heat of anger," ain't you, Lana? Well, you better get hip to things said in-between the sheets. When you finally do give in to some young stallion you better know the difference in fact an' fiction. If it's good they'll lie to you, if it's bad they won't say nothin'.

CARMEN: Don't let her scare you off, Lana. Whether they lie to you or not, there ain't nothin' like it. I ain't never thought about takin' any of my tricks up on what they say. But they seem to mean it.

LANA: How is Lolly?

CARMEN: She's sleepin'.

LANA: She seemed to be in a trance when she came back.

CARMEN: She's always like that.

LANA: No. She was acting different than usual. She didn't say one word.

CARMEN: There ain't nothin' wrong with her. She just misses her cats.

LANA: She shouldn't be here.

AGRIPPA: That woman does get to be strong as a bull when she goes into one of them things. She damn near broke my

495

arm. I just hope she don't have one while I'm sleepin'. She could choke me to death.

CARMEN: I don't see what you worryin' about. I sleep right next to her.

AGRIPPA: That's a thought. I think I'll sneak over there an' do you in one night an' Lolly cops the trial.

CARMEN: You would too. I'ma ask for a transfer in the mornin'.

AGRIPPA: Yeah, why don't you do that? This place could stand a little fresh air.

CARMEN: Shee! I don't know what you're talkin' about, girl. I use the best perfumes.

AGRIPPA: Sure do. But I think you'd find that it'd work a lot better if you bathed before applyin'.

CARMEN: The only reason you're in the shower room so much is so you can get that freakish nature of yours off. My doctor told me city water is bad for my skin.

AGRIPPA: I guess he told you that while he was givin' you a shot of penicillin.

CARMEN: I'm clean, woman. All of my tricks come back to me. So don't you say nothin'.

AGRIPPA: I ain't. I ain't one of your tricks.

LANA: Carmen! Let's have a party. It's your birthday. We should be celebrating. My mother made me some cookies. Help me pull the desk out. (LANA *begins to pull out the desk to the center of the cell. No one moves to help her.*) Come on! (CARMEN *and* AGRIPPA *look at each other.*) Well, are we going to have a party or not?

(CARMEN *and* AGRIPPA *are affected by* LANA'S *mood. They shrug their shoulders and move to help her.*)

AGRIPPA: Girl, I guess you don't know where we are.

LANA (*after they get the desk out into the middle of the floor*): We need something to brighten it up. I suppose we could use a sheet. (*She mulls it over.*)

CARMEN: I got something.

LANA: Well, get it.

(CARMEN *goes to her locker and from it takes a bright green slip. She holds it up.*)

LANA: Marvelous!

CARMEN: They let me keep it, but they won't let me wear it.

(LANA *takes it and spreads it over the desktop. She goes to her locker and gets the cookies.*)

LANA: I don't have any candles.

AGRIPPA: Yeah, we do. (*She goes over and gets a pack of matches from under her pillow.*) How old are you, girl?

(CARMEN *hesitates.* AGRIPPA *goes back and gets another pack.*)
I ain't got no more.

CARMEN: You only needed one.

LANA: Okay. (*She tears off the paper matches and begins placing them in the cookies.*) Tell me when to stop, Carmen. (*She places at least twenty and looks up.*)

CARMEN (*she looks at* AGRIPPA): You can go on a couple more.

(LANA *places five more and stops without asking.*)

LANA: We should have something else.

AGRIPPA: What do you want? Ice cream?

LANA: That's impossible. But it would be nice.

(AGRIPPA *pauses for a moment and then walks over to her locker. She takes from it a miniature bottle of Scotch.*)

AGRIPPA: I copped this from my sister. I was savin' it for my seventh anniversary.

LANA: That will do just fine. Thank you, Agrippa.

AGRIPPA: I figger I gotta get along with her at least once in awhile.

(*The three of them form a circle of sorts around the desk.*)

LANA: Lolly should be here to wish Carmen Happy Birthday.

AGRIPPA: I don't know now. You better leave her be.

CARMEN: She's liable to start preachin' again.

LANA: I'm going to wake her.

AGRIPPA: All right. You been warned.

(LANA *goes to* LOLLY. *She wakes her gently.*)

LANA: Lolly, we're having a party. We want you to come.

LOLLY: A party, child? Where? I'm invited? I ain't been to a party in forty years. You sure I'm invited?

LANA: You're one of the hostesses. It's a birthday party for Carmen.

LOLLY: I ain't givin' no party for no whore! You tell her she ain't invited!

LANA: It's her birthday, Lolly. When yours comes she's going to give one for you. Please come. Carmen says she won't unless you're there.

LOLLY: Did she say that?

LANA: Yes.

LOLLY: Well, I gotta be there, ain't I? It ain't no party 'less ol' Lolly's there.

LANA: Good. (LANA *rushes back over to the group.* LOLLY *gets up and straightens out her shift.*) Lolly's coming to the party.

AGRIPPA: You invited her.

LANA: Shh!

LOLLY (*as she comes over*): My, those are pretty. We was goin' to give you a surprise party but we thought you wouldn't like that.

LANA: Yes, we were. Weren't we, Agrippa?

AGRIPPA: Yeah, yeah. That's right. We sure were.

LANA: Let's all light the candles for Carmen. (*The three take matches and light the other matches on the cake.*) C'mon, Carmen. Make a wish and blow.

LOLLY: No. We gotta sing "Happy Birthday" to her first.

AGRIPPA: Aw, c'mon now!

LANA: Lolly's right. It's no party without the song.

AGRIPPA: Awright. But if we wake up the whole jail, don't look at me.

LANA: Lolly, you lead it off.

(LOLLY *begins the song: "Happy Birthday" in her "ugly voice." The two others join in. They complete it and look to* CARMEN.)

LANA: Make your wish, Carmen.

(CARMEN *looks at them and then closes her eyes for a moment. She opens her eyes and blows very hard at the "candles." They all go out.*)

LOLLY: Your wish is goin' to come true.

LANA: I wish you happiness, Carmen.

AGRIPPA: Yeah, be happy, girl.

LANA: I'm sorry we don't have anything to give you.

LOLLY: Yes we do. We got somethin'. (LOLLY *goes to her locker and takes from it a carving of a cat. She hands it to* CARMEN.) That's from me, Lana, and Agrippa. Ain't she pretty?

CARMEN: I don't like no damn—

LANA: It's beautiful, isn't it, Agrippa?

AGRIPPA: Yeah, it sure is. Ain't it, Carmen? (*She glares at her.*)

CARMEN: Yeah, yes, it is pretty. Thank you, girls. I'm gonna put this right where I can see it. (CARMEN *goes to her bunk and places the carving where* LOLLY *can see it but she can't.*) Now let's pour the wine.

LOLLY: Wine? We got us some wine?

AGRIPPA: No, Lolly. Tough luck. We ain't got no wine. It's just a symbol of the amount we should have. (*She holds up the bottle.*) Ain't no sense in gettin' out the cups. (*She undoes the top and hands the bottle to* CARMEN.) Kill the poison. (CARMEN *takes a quick swig and hands it to* AGRIPPA. *She takes a*

quick swig and hands it to LOLLY. LOLLY *drains it with one long swallow.*) Hey! Save some for Lana!

LANA: It doesn't matter. I just wanted to wet my lips.

LOLLY: There's enough to do that with. Here. (LANA *wets her lips with the dregs.*) That sure tastes like some more.

AGRIPPA: Yeah. But that's all it does: Tastes like. It ain't.

LOLLY: Ain't you gonna pass the cookies?

LANA: You're supposed to do the honors, Carmen.

CARMEN: Your mama makes some mean cookies, Lana.

LANA: You don't like it?

CARMEN: It's delicious. Could stand some more sugar, though.

LANA: Mother's on a diet. Everyone suffers.

(*They settle down.*)

AGRIPPA: You're sweet to do that, girl.

LANA: To do what?

AGRIPPA: Throwing this big bash for Carmen. It's probably the first one she's had since she became a whore. You always treat people you don't know this nice?

LANA: People I don't know and people I do know are all the same.

AGRIPPA: That ain't gotta be so.

LANA: No. But I can think that way.

CARMEN: Lana, you want any reefer?

AGRIPPA: No reefer tonight. You ain't supposed to serve marijuana at no birthday party.

CARMEN: You ain't?

AGRIPPA: No, you ain't.

CARMEN: I wish we had something to do. In here the party stops when it starts.

AGRIPPA: You ever try conversation?

CARMEN: What fun is talkin'? I want to do somethin'.

LANA: You should try it, Carmen. That's what we do at home, my mother, my father, and I. We go on for hours.

CARMEN: What do you talk about?

LANA: Oh, all sorts of things.

CARMEN: All Jimmy talks to me about is the money. After we settle that, we go straight to bed. I think I like goin' to bed more than sittin' around talkin' about nothin'.

LANA: My father tells me about the time when he and his friends were in Spain fighting fascism. And I tell him about what I'm doing in school or the sit-in's. He sat-in with us one time, but the student leaders said he was too old. They said he gave us a bad image.

LOLLY: You got good people, Lana.

LANA: I think so. Father always tells me to recite a poem when I become too angry to think. He says it's to temper the mettle. I think it does too.

AGRIPPA: How's it go?

LANA: It's by William Blake. He was an English poet. It goes:

> To Mercy, Pity, Peace, and Love,
>   All pray in their distress,
> And to these virtues of delight
>   Return their thankfulness.
>
> For Mercy, Pity, Peace, and Love,
>   Is God, our Father dear;
> And Mercy, Pity, Peace, and Love,
>   Is man, His child and care.
>
> For Mercy has a human heart;
>   Pity, a human face;
> And Love, the human form divine;
>   And Peace, the human dress.
>
> Then every man of every clime,
>   That prays in his distress,
> Prays to the human form divine:
>   Love, Mercy, Pity, Peace.
>
> And all must love the human form,
>   In heathen, Turk, or Jew.
> Where Mercy, Love, and Pity dwell,
>   There God is dwelling too.

AGRIPPA: Your old man taught you that? (LANA *nods yes.*) He gotta be a swinging cat. (*She yawns.*) I think I'll call it one. You people better too. You got a early day. (AGRIPPA *crawls under her covers and falls asleep.*)

CARMEN: That was a pretty poem, Lana. I used to like poetry when I was in school. I used to write some too.

LANA: You did? Do you remember any of it?

CARMEN: Yeah!—I mean—no. I don't remember none of it. I had to quit when I got pregnant.

LANA: When did you quit?

CARMEN: In the sixth grade. My baby died when it was born.

LANA: I'm sorry.

CARMEN: I wouldn't of known what to do with it noway.

He'd be almost tall as me now. I ain't but twenty-seven. I think I better go to bed now. Night, honey. (*She goes to her bed and crawls in.*)

LOLLY: Did I sing good, child?

LANA: Like an angel, Lolly.

LOLLY: I used to be head of the sisters' choir at my church. I used to sing real good.

LANA: You could still be the head of the choir, Lolly.

LOLLY: No, child. I like my wine too much. Ol' Lolly can't hit them high notes like I used to. The only time I sound good is when I'm dead asleep.

LANA: You know that you sing in your sleep?

LOLLY: My old man told me often enough for me to know. He told me that I sing when I'm sleepin' like I used to when I was in the choir.

LANA: He knew you then?

LOLLY: He was the deacon.

LANA: Oh.

LOLLY: I sure enjoyed givin' that party. I shoulda fried some chicken for my guests. You wait till the next time, though. Ol' Lolly gonna have everythin'. Greens an' dumplin's, an' hot bread. All the fixin's. You just wait, honey. Nobody's gonna sell ol' Lolly short. You just wait. (LOLLY *goes to her bunk and crawls in.* LANA *is left alone.*)

END OF ACT I

ACT II

Scene 1

(*Bright morning. The girls are up and finishing the morning's chores. We watch as they do this and await the* MATRON'*s inspection. Two other* MATRONS *enter the outer area. The* MATRON *stands and unlocks the gate. She steps inside.*)

MATRON: All right! Big one coming. (*The girls stand at their bunks. The* MATRON *comes to the end bunk and the other two women follow her. This is* LOLLY'*s area.*) Dump your locker, Lolly. (LOLLY *does immediately what she is told. She lifts the locker and dumps its contents on the floor. The* MATRON *examines it.*) No candy, Lolly.

LOLLY: I didn't know I had it, m'am. My brother musta slipped it in my package last time he came.

MATRON: See me. Lift the bunk. (LOLLY *lifts the end of her bunk. The* MATRON *puts her finger in the post-hole. She finds*

nothing and repeats the process on the other three corners.
LANA *appears visibly nervous. The* MATRON *finds nothing and moves to* LANA's *area.*) Dump it.

LANA: M'am?

(*The* MATRON *upends* LANA's *locker and strews her things over the cell floor. She sifts through the stuff with her foot.*)

MATRON: Lift it. (LANA *lifts the end of her bunk. The* MATRON *goes through her exploratory probings as before. She finds nothing. She goes through the desk. She finishes and moves to* CARMEN's *area.*) Dump it. (CARMEN *does. The* MATRON *finds nothing.*) Lift it. (CARMEN *is scared. She hesitates and lifts the opposite end of her bunk. The* MATRON *probes three corners before reaching the one where* CARMEN *has hidden her cache. The* MATRON *probes and comes up with nothing. She moves to* AGRIPPA's *area and repeats the process. She finds nothing.*)

AGRIPPA: Find it?

(*The* MATRON *doesn't reply. She is angry and walks out of the cell. The* MATRONS *follow her out and leave the stage proper.* CARMEN *falls to her knees and heaves dry sobs.*)

LANA: But you had—

AGRIPPA: I been here too long now to let them go catching me in the wrong. Shut up, Carmen. I should of let her catch you with your pants down. I thought about it, but that would of kept you here for another year. I couldn't take you that long.

LANA: But when did you—

AGRIPPA: You know, Maxie gotta watch her back too. She told me two days ago that the ox was gonna spring a surprise. I got up early this morning and got rid of the incriminatin' evidence.

LANA: The Matron's after you, Agrippa.

AGRIPPA: When she catches me in the wrong she got every right to stick it to me. Until then—she can hate me all she likes. Let's clean this mess up.

(*They fall to straightening up their areas.*)

LANA: I wouldn't want to go through that again. My knees were knocking like crazy. I was sure she was going to find something.

AGRIPPA: I was gettin' a kick outta watchin' ol' Carmen there. That girl turned pure white. Hey, Carmen! Why'd you start from the other end? Thinkin' it might disappear by the time you got to it? Boy, girl, you was scratchin'.

CARMEN: That ain't funny. Why didn't you tell us somethin'? I coulda got two years for holdin'.

AGRIPPA: Serves you right. I didn't know you was holdin'

so much. You know, Lana, I found almost a ounce of stuff in that girl's bed. I think I'll charge you half for savin' your life.

CARMEN: You can have it all. I got a little over two months to do an' I don't feature doin' no more than that.

AGRIPPA: You ain't gotta worry. She ain't gonna catch me with my drawers down. Mama's mind works too slow.

LANA: She's out to get you, Agrippa.

AGRIPPA: No sweat. (*They go on cleaning their areas. The* MATRON *comes back in and glares at* AGRIPPA. *She sits at her desk.*) You know, I once knew a man "went huntin'." He was a funny little man. Whenever he went huntin' he would always come home empty-handed. Year after year he would go out into the woods an' year after year he would come home without a thing to show for his troubles. So this went on for I don't know how many years an' one day one of his friends asked him: "Every year you go out with your gun and every year you come back with nothing. Why's that? Are you hunting something special?" The funny little man looked at his friend in surprise and then shot his own brains out. You see, the funny little man wasn't hunting anything. He had forgotten there was a purpose involved in going out huntin'. It had become another bad habit. (*The* MATRON *is chewing a nail.*) Like chewing your fingernails. (*The* MATRON *rushes to the gate.*)

MATRON: I'll get you, Agrippa. I'll get you. You're gonna make your slip and I'm gonna get you. Don't you worry about it!

AGRIPPA: Okay, Mama, I won't. With a little time off for good behavior you got about ten years to do the catching. Don't wind up like the funny little man though, Mama.

(AGRIPPA *laughs as the* MATRON *walks back to her desk. There is a moment of silence as they straighten up their areas.*)

CARMEN: The day I step out of here I'm gonna rent me a suite of rooms in the finest hotel and just lay up and luxuriate in a big fine bed. Soft linen sheets with just me in 'em.

AGRIPPA: That costs money, girl. You sure ain't been makin' much in here.

CARMEN: I got me a stash.

AGRIPPA: You been holdin' out on your pimp? That ain't ethical, Carmen.

CARMEN: Shee! My last boyfriend taught me one fine lesson: Look out for yourself. You know what that bastard did? I was bringing him five, six hundred a week; every last penny I made. I got real bad sick an' I couldn't work, not a bit. You think he'd look after me? His Cadillac run out of gas an' he

503

didn't have a dime to put into it. That man made me get up out of my sick-bed an' try to hustle. Sick as I was, I was down on the corner tryin' to earn a dollar for that sonofabitch. I passed out. There was this cop I knew; we used to do each other favors. He took me home. You know what my lover did? He didn't say nothin' when he saw the fuzz, but soon as the man left he beat me when he found out I didn't bring him no money. The next mornin' he took all my clothes an' hocked 'em. He didn't come back either. Just left me there. I coulda died if it wasn't for the rent-man. He come for his rent after two days an' found me there. He thought I was dead. The City came an' got me an' they kept me in the hospital for over two months. You call my stash "holdin' out." I call it "self-preservation."

LANA: After all that, you still do the same job?

CARMEN: It's a livin', Lana. I like my luxury. You tell me where else I could make the *money* to support my habits.

AGRIPPA: Lana, it's like the money that them rich, white divorcees get from their ex-old men. When you're used to the good life it's kinda hard to give it up. The courts call it: "The manner to which one has become accustomed." In other words: Once a whore, always a whore.

CARMEN: That's about right. But a well-paid one.

(*They finish their areas.*)

AGRIPPA: Hey, Mama! When we gonna eat?

MATRON: You're a little late for that. Breakfast is over.

AGRIPPA: It's against the rules to keep us from eatin'. We ain't in solitary.

MATRON: No, you ain't. In solitary you get staples. In here you ain't gonna get nothin'.

AGRIPPA: It's against the rules.

MATRON: Tell it to the administrator. She's in the next building. And just how you gonna do that? She administers from her little office over there, she don't ever see this one. So you tell it to her, Agrippa.

LANA: But that's not right. We didn't do anything. How can you do this? We didn't break any rules.

MATRON: None that I caught you at. If I found something it woulda meant some more time for you. But since I can't get you legal, I'm gonna get you illegal. You don't go out today—at all.

LANA: But we've got to work. You've got to let us out to do our jobs.

MATRON: I ain't got to do anything. Your work is my prerogative. If I don't take you out of here it means I got use for

you inside. And you know what? Tomorrow's Sunday. That's your off-day, ain't it?

AGRIPPA: You sure one evil bitch, ain't you?

MATRON: Evil is as evil does, Agrippa. (*She laughs and heads back to her desk.*)

AGRIPPA: It's just me you want, Mama. Why don't you let the others eat? (*She doesn't answer.*) Well, I hope y'all ain't too hungry. Now, ain't that just like a bitch?

LANA: She's a sadist.

CARMEN: What's that?

LANA: She likes to hurt.

AGRIPPA: That's what I told you before. The slammers likes her kind. I bet they got a testin' room just like them old dungeons in them old castles. With racks an' iron maidens an' all them things. The first time you don't make your victim scream you fail the test.

MATRON: No, we don't, Agrippa. But I wish we did. You'd be my first to work on.

AGRIPPA: Aw, go play with yourself, Mama.

MATRON: When your stomach starts achin' for something to fill it then you'll wish you hadn't played with me.

AGRIPPA: We'll see.

(*There is silence.*)

LOLLY: I gotta eat. I got bleedin' ulcers. I gotta eat or I'm gonna hurt somethin' awful. Agrippa, tell her you're sorry, that you didn't mean nothin'. Tell M'am you're sorry.

AGRIPPA: Sorry for what? I didn't do a thing. I'm sorry about your ulcers, girl. But Mama ain't takin' no apologies. She's just mean.

LOLLY (*runs to the netting*): M'am, I didn't do nothin'. You gotta let me eat. I didn't do nothin'. Agrippa didn't mean to make you mad. See, I bet she wants to tell how sorry she is. Don't you, Agrippa? Tell the Matron how sorry you is. Tell her, 'Grippa.

(AGRIPPA *doesn't answer.*)

MATRON: Go back to your area, Lolly.

LOLLY: M'am, I got a bad stomach. The doctor tole me I got ulcers. I can't treat my stomach bad. I'm on a special diet, m'am. You gotta let me eat. I have to eat, m'am.

MATRON: Back to your area, Lolly.

LOLLY: M'am, I'm beggin' you: Let me eat. My stomach's gonna hurt somethin' awful if you don't let me eat. (*She grasps the netting.*) You gotta let me eat!

(*The* MATRON *comes around her desk with the billy.*)

MATRON: Back to your area.

LOLLY: Let me eat! I gotta eat!

(*The* MATRON *swings the billy against* LOLLY's *fingers. First one hand, then the other.*)

AGRIPPA: Watch out, Lolly!

(LOLLY *screams out but doesn't release her grip on the netting. The* MATRON *hits her hands again.* LOLLY *lets go and slumps to the floor. She is conscious.*)

LANA (*she runs to her*): Oh, Lolly, Lolly. (*She looks at the* MATRON.) You beast, you inhuman beast!

LOLLY: I gotta eat, I gotta eat. The doctor says I gotta eat. My belly.

(*The* MATRON *smirks and goes back to her desk.* AGRIPPA *and* LANA *help* LOLLY *to her feet and walk her back to her area. They seat her on the footlocker.*)

AGRIPPA: Lemme see those fingers, Lolly. Straighten 'em out. C'mon, open 'em up.

LOLLY: They hurt.

AGRIPPA: I know they hurt. Open 'em. (LOLLY *doesn't.* AGRIPPA *takes her hands one at a time and pries them open.* LOLLY *screams, then whimpers.*) I don't know. They're all swollen. (AGRIPPA *examines her fingers one at a time.*) That big one feels like it might be broken. How's that feel, Lolly? (*She does something with the finger.*)

LOLLY: It hurts. That's how it feels. Stop that. Dear Jesus, dear Jesus.

(AGRIPPA *turns to the* MATRON.)

AGRIPPA: I think you done broke one of her fingers. She gotta see the doctor. We gotta take her to the infirmary.

MATRON: She'll live.

LANA: Her right index finger is broken. You can't leave it untreated. She has to see a doctor.

MATRON: There ain't no doctor on the weekends. She can wait till Monday. What's a little sore finger? She'll live. Now keep it down.

LANA: Isn't there a nurse on duty? Take her to see the nurse. Her finger can become infected. Haven't you a heart?

MATRON: No. Now pipe down before I break your ass.

LANA: Agrippa, what are we going to do?

AGRIPPA: I don't know. Let me see that finger. (*She examines the finger.*) Lolly, what's that on your bunk? (LOLLY *turns her head to see. As she does* AGRIPPA *yanks her finger.* LOLLY *screams and falls into* LANA's *arms. She is semiconscious.*) I think I straightened out that bone a little. At least it won't hurt as much. She can soak it in the basin. (*A pause.*) Aw, shit.

LANA: What's wrong?

AGRIPPA: I was just wonderin' where do her kind come from. The big bitch.

LANA: Sometimes I can understand hatred when I meet up with her type. (*She and* AGRIPPA *put* LOLLY *into her bunk. There is silence as they move around the cell doing odd bits of nothing; straightening their bunks; staring out the window.*) What are you in here for, Agrippa?

AGRIPPA: To serve time.

LANA: That's not an answer.

AGRIPPA: So what? What do you care? You gonna serve your thirty days, get out, an' go about your business. So what's it to you what I'm doin' in here?

LANA: There is something good in you that makes me wonder what you could have done that was so wrong.

AGRIPPA: I chewed up and ate a little girl who asked too many questions.

LANA: For asking questions or for supplying answers?

AGRIPPA: Both. Now leave me alone now.

LANA: Does she mean what she says?

AGRIPPA: You saw her use that stick. What do you think? I hope you ate well last night.

(LANA *doesn't reply. They all go and sit on their bunks. Silence for a long while.*)

CARMEN: Naw, they ain't gettin' me in here no more. I have learned my lesson.

LANA: Are you going to quit?

CARMEN: I didn't say that. I just said that I ain't comin' back to the slammers.

AGRIPPA: When quota time comes up and the cops need a bust, you gonna go to jail just like always.

CARMEN: Not if you know the right people, you ain't. Grease the right palms an' you in like Flynn.

AGRIPPA: How much is that gonna cost you?

CARMEN: It's kinda steep but Jimmy's just gonna have to learn how to budget himself from now on. He can buy his shoes at the cancellation shop. They got the same brand an' no one can tell the difference where they went wrong. I know this John who gets his clothes wholesale from this Jew store an' they look better than Jimmy's. He can go there.

AGRIPPA: Jimmy ain't goin' for no secondhand car. What you gonna do about that?

CARMEN: Jimmy don't drive. He never goes out of Harlem so he don't need no car.

AGRIPPA: Well, pimps do come an' pimps do go. A non-Cadillac-ownin' pimp. Pray tell!

CARMEN: He's a good man. You know he sponsors a boys' sports team in Harlem? That's right. Baseball, football, and basketball. Buys them their uniforms an' everything. His team won the community championship triple crown last year too. You shoulda seen the party we threw for them. I come in my shorty mink an' this green satin dress an' Jimmy was sporty. Like one of the kids. They sure love that man. There ain't a one of them ever been in the slammers.

AGRIPPA: Well now, Carmen's got herself a big-time philanthropist.

CARMEN: What's that?

LANA: She means you have a very good man.

CARMEN: That's right. An' you'd better believe it too. You know, his daddy was a big man up in Harlem before he died. He used to own his own business. Jimmy told me how he used to walk around with him an' how the people would come up to his daddy an' shake his hand an' say: "How you doin', Mr. Jake?" An' his daddy would slip 'em all a five or a ten because that's how they told him they was needy. He died an' Jimmy got all his debts. Jimmy ain't never been much of a businessman.

AGRIPPA: He seems to be doin' all right now.

CARMEN: Oh, why don't you just stop bein' smart.

LANA: That's nice what he's doing for the kids.

CARMEN: Thank you, Lana. At least someone knows a good man when they see one.

(LOLLY *begins to move and groan in her bunk.*)

LANA: She's coming around.

AGRIPPA: Maybe I should go upside her head. Cool her down before she starts in again.

LANA: No. Let her be. I'll see to her. (*She goes over to* LOLLY's *bunk.*) How are you, Lolly?

(LOLLY *doesn't sit up but remains prone.*)

LOLLY: I hurt. Inside an' out. My stomach's on fire, Lana. It's just like when I had that trouble that brung me in here. My stomach was hurtin' so they had to take me to the clinic. They told me that I hurt myself bad by drinkin' so much of that bad wine. They told me I bleed inside.

LANA: I'll try to get you something. (*She starts to leave.*)

LOLLY: No. You stay away from that woman. She's evil. She's Satan's daughter. She'll do you bad. I'ma be all right.

LANA (*pause*): Okay. Do you want some water for your finger? Maybe I can get some salt and put it in the water. (*She*

508

doesn't wait for a reply. She goes to the sink and fills a cup with warm water. She then walks over to the netting.) M'am, do you have any salt? (*The* MATRON *is reading and doesn't answer.*) Pardon me, m'am. Do you have any salt? I need it to put in the water for Lolly's finger.

MATRON (*looks up*): Still playing the Good Samaritan, hey? (*She gets up.*) Sure I got some salt. (*She reaches down and gets the salt.*) Where do you want it?

LANA: I want to put it in this water. (*She extends the cup. The* MATRON *comes around her desk and up to the netting.*)

MATRON: In the water, hey? (*The* MATRON *takes the salt cellar and hurls some of its contents through the netting and into* LANA'*s eyes.* LANA *drops the cup and grabs her eyes.*) There! You like to cry for the niggers? Now you can cry for real. (*She laughs.*)

(AGRIPPA *and* LOLLY *run up to* LANA *and move her over to the sink.*)

AGRIPPA: Aw, girl. You done it again. Didn't Lolly tell you to stay away from that bitch? (*She swabs her eyes.*) Stings, don't it?

LANA: I'm all right. Get the cup and see to Lolly's finger.

AGRIPPA: There you go. Lookin' out after other people when you need it yourself. Lolly can fix it herself. Go on, Lolly. Get the cup. (AGRIPPA *continues swabbing* LANA'*s eyes.* LOLLY *picks up the cup and comes over and fills it with warm water. She goes back to her bunk and sits.*)

LANA: There must be a way to get word out of here.

AGRIPPA: Nope. There ain't.

LANA: What about tonight? There's Maxie. She's your friend. She can help us.

AGRIPPA: Maxie ain't my friend. Money is Maxie's friend.

LANA: I can give her money. I'll have my father—

AGRIPPA: Maxie ain't workin' this weekend.

LANA: Well, what about her replacement? We can talk to her, can't we?

AGRIPPA: Big Mama is her replacement. They switch off whenever they want a long weekend.

LANA: Oh Agrippa, what are we going to do?

AGRIPPA: Watch yourself an' wait, chicken. How's your eyes now?

LANA: I'm all right. How's Lolly doing?

AGRIPPA: See for yourself.

(LOLLY *is sitting soaking her finger and humming a tune. She is keening with the tune.*)

LANA: Yes. I guess she's all right.

CARMEN: Anybody got a cigarette?

AGRIPPA: There's some on my bed.

(CARMEN *gets up to get them.*)

MATRON: No smoking.

CARMEN: What do you mean? We can't smoke neither?

MATRON: You heard me.

CARMEN: Well, that's just too bad. (CARMEN *goes over and gets a cigarette. She lights it.*)

MATRON: What'd I tell you? (*She gets up and grabs the billy.*)

CARMEN: I'm gonna smoke this cigarette whether you like it or not.

(*The* MATRON *comes up to the door with her keys.*)

AGRIPPA: I don't think you better open that gate, m'am.

MATRON: I'll come in there and beat you all to your knees.

(AGRIPPA *snatches her blanket up from the bunk and wraps it around her arm.*)

AGRIPPA: Get yourself a blanket, Carmen. (CARMEN *does.* LANA *stands transfixed.*) Now open the door if you must. But I'll tell you: if I get the best of you it's gonna be your ass. Now, c'mon. (CARMEN *and* AGRIPPA *challenge the* MATRON. *She stands at the gate, deciding. She backs down.*) Why don't you call downstairs? Yeah, you do that. You got us locked up in here, but it looks like we got you locked up out there. Don't it? (*She laughs.*) See that, Lana? She's scared. She don't want no part of us little colored girls. We'll eat in due time. Just tighten your belt. Gimme one of them cigarettes, Carmen.

(CARMEN *does. They put down their blankets.*)

CARMEN: I had enough. I just had enough.

Scene 2

(*The women are about the cell in varying places and positions. They are humming softly the tune of "We Shall Overcome."*)

MATRON: Yeah, you will. When I say so. You might as well put on your nightshifts. You ain't goin' nowhere.

AGRIPPA: That's so.

LANA: How are you feeling, Lolly? How's the finger?

LOLLY: Throbbing up to beat the devil. But it ain't nothin'. I done worse to my hands just pickin' cotton. Don't you worry none, child.

(*The ladies get up and start undressing to put on their shifts. The activity is slow and casual, taking plenty of time.* LANA *assists* LOLLY *into her shift.*)

AGRIPPA: I never took a peek at all of us here in these grandma cottons before but we sure do look silly. Like a insane asylum or somethin'.

CARMEN: Why not? You sure gotta be insane to be in here. Umm! They sure don't do nothin' for a good-lookin' woman. I like my silk and Dacron.

LANA: Why not all-silk?

CARMEN: No, honey. That all-silk feels like a man who ain't never done a lick of work in his life. You ever touch a man's skin who just done pampered and oiled himself all his life? (*She grimaces.*) Silk gives me that same feelin'.

(LANA *whirls around the cell.*)

LANA: I must look like the judge who sentenced me. (*She makes a stern face. As judge.*) Miss Lana Kaufmann. I now do sentence you to the term of thirty days. (*She pretends she is the judge.* CARMEN *walks up to the desk* LANA *is sitting at. She has a contrite look on her face.*) What do you plead?

CARMEN (*she shuffles her feet and puts on her most winning smile*): Not guilty, Your Honor.

LANA: The disposition of the arresting officer states that you had propositioned him for the purpose of engaging in the sex act for a fee to be paid to you. That is prostitution, is it not?

CARMEN: No, Your Honor. Proposition is not the act. Now if the officer is willing to say that we engaged in the act and then he paid me and then he arrested me, that's fine. Then I'm a prostitute.

LANA: Are you?

CARMEN: Sure I am, Your Honor. But he paid me for goods received. I think my rightful tag should be businesswoman. Why, I'd love to pay taxes to the government.

LANA: Spoken like a good American.

CARMEN: I'd even get me a Good Housekeepin' Seal of Approval, take out ads in *Time* an' *Life* magazines.

LANA: Keep up the economy.

CARMEN: Sure, Your Honor. An' I'd even get me one of them Madison Avenue places to handle my advertising.

LANA: I can suggest one. My son has started an agency. He would be most willing to see to your trade. Let's say a spread in *Life:* two pages, facing one another. Subtle. A photo layout of a perfectly appointed boudoir—

CARMEN: A what?

LANA: Bedroom. A hint of mystery. Maybe a peignoir draped casually over the bed.

CARMEN: No model?

LANA: No. This must be subtle. The copy? (*She thinks.*) Ah! Like this: "A place he always feels welcome." Or "We try harder."

CARMEN: That's a good one.

LANA: I've got a million of 'em! Then we would branch out into television. Maybe sponsor a show.

CARMEN: Like *Bonanza*?

LANA: Yes! Then we could diversify: go into toiletries, design. All the related fields. You could be vice-president in charge of—What would you be good at?

CARMEN: Good at? Hey, Judge, ain't you forgettin'? I started this business.

LANA: You did? Well, we will just have to do something about that, won't we? What's the charge? Treason? Give her one hundred and ninety-nine years.

CARMEN: Treason? What did I do?

LANA: Interference with good, old American ingenuity, that's what. For trying to stop the age of progress. This is the land of free enterprise with the accent on enter—you can't stand there and block the path of a completely new field of endeavor. This is America! Guilty as charged!

CARMEN (*meekly*): Prostitution?

LANA: Treason!

(*They break up laughing. After a while they compose themselves.* LANA *stays at the desk.*)

AGRIPPA: You two is silly as children.

LANA (*as* LANA): We're none of us that ancient. You've got to laugh sometimes.

AGRIPPA: Sure you do, honey. Take your mind off your belly.

LANA: Why don't you play? You can afford to laugh also. I know. Let's continue the game. You be the judge and I'll stand trial.

AGRIPPA: I don't feel like playin'. Go on, now.

LANA: Come on, Agrippa. Don't be a spoilsport. (*She grabs her hand and pulls her around to her side of the desk. She sits her in the chair.*) Carmen, Agrippa shall now set sentence. Since we all know that we're guilty, why say she'll decide our fate? I plead innocent.

AGRIPPA (*in a bored fashion*): Until proven guilty. Which shall pass. Who's gonna serve as your defense?

CARMEN: I don't know too much about the case, Your Honor, but I'll take it.

LANA: But—

AGRIPPA: Approved. What's the charge?

LANA: Trespassing.

CARMEN: Not obeyin' the law.

LANA: One of the laws.

AGRIPPA: Which one was that?

LANA: Trespassing.

CARMEN: One law, one God. That's what the Good Book says.

AGRIPPA: Good point. Charge stands: Disobeying the law.

LANA: The good counsel makes it appear that she is not on my side but serves for the state.

AGRIPPA: True.

CARMEN: True.

LANA: But who will serve as impartial observer to my trial?

AGRIPPA: I hereby appoint Lolly to that place. Lolly, raise your right hand. (LOLLY *is asleep*.) Good. You are sworn. Now, will the defendant take the stand. How do you plead to this charge?

LANA: Innocent.

AGRIPPA: Why?

LANA: Because I am.

AGRIPPA: Explain.

LANA: I was with a group of people who have a common aim to destroy anything that is wrong. And we were told to disperse when we had gathered to picket or bring notice to a disgrace.

AGRIPPA: Who were you tellin'?

LANA: Other people.

AGRIPPA: Don't you think other people know?

LANA: Most other people haven't been inside such places that we picket.

AGRIPPA: Why not?

LANA: Well, we picket places like jails, hospitals, and Army posts. Most people aren't given to being inside any of these places. They must be told what is wrong with them.

CARMEN: I want to change the charge, Your Honor. Insanity by choice.

AGRIPPA: Maybe.

LANA: It is the condition of the jail we're concerned about. If the person jailed has done something which calls for his removal from law-abiding society then, by all means, do so. But his place of separation should not be too much different in character from the society from which he came. Hospitalization should be sanitary, helpful, and exactly a home away from home. The Army is to protect us from our enemies, to deter, to protect our shores. It should not be a mercenary force that

invades others' homelands. Most of all, it should not be used to further political ambition.

CARMEN: I want to go home an' get my law books, Your Honor. The defendant done threw in some mumbo-jumbo that her counsel don't understand.

AGRIPPA: This is a closed trial. No one is allowed to enter or leave by decree.

CARMEN: We plead guilty to all charges and specifications, Your Honor.

AGRIPPA: Guilty!

LANA: Yes, I am guilty. But I would like the opportunity to explain my position.

CARMEN: Sister, you'd do best to try an' cop a plea.

AGRIPPA: Go right ahead. You're still guilty.

LANA: Yes, Your Honor. Since the vast majority of our society does not spend any of its life inside prison walls, therefore it cannot be aware of what may or may not be wrong with prison life. Ignorance has always made a very effective shield for those who like the uninvolved and uncomplicated life. I see no wrong in what our group is trying to do. It just seems that society doesn't like truth and makes of us who try to help it—makes of us, criminals, prohibitionists, nuts—

CARMEN: That's so.

LANA: But that is not so!

AGRIPPA: Well, baby—

LANA: No, let me finish! What about our armies? There are many troubles in the world today. Poor nations, new nations, warmongering nations. One group of people killing off another group of people because their beliefs are different. The United States sending troops into the Congo because of some whites being held hostage by some blacks. The United States withholding troops from Indonesia because we don't interfere in another country's internal troubles. Especially if the trouble is communist and democracy is winning. What about the democratic process right here in this land? What about black people clamoring for the simple things of life? What about the Appalachian whites doing the same? What about those things? Politicians disgust me. They have taken a word—politics—and fashioned it into a way of life. It's no longer man is—it's become political dictate. It's no longer what is right. But what will my constituents think? Will it make me President? Ah, Judge. Yes, I'm guilty. But guilty of what? Dreaming? Of wanting love to be the element that governs people? A friend of mine returned from Vietnam. He left a good friend there.

His friend was a poet—he composed his own epitaph. Do you want to hear his epitaph, Your Honor? It's two life-stories.

AGRIPPA: If counsel has no objections?

CARMEN: Defendant is guilty. I have no objections, Your Honor.

AGRIPPA: Defendant has two minutes for summary.

LANA: He found the poem when he went through his friend's bloody clothing. It goes like this—

> One house, a summer cottage. One main street,
> a private beach.
> McPherson, Alice—Mother. Father unknown.
> City welfare patient #21765. Given name: John.
> One school, piano teacher. One tree,
> a backyard.
> McPherson, Johnny (Mac the Knife). Gang leader.
> Black Dragons. Police File 78653-1.
> One college, English major. One car,
> credit card.
> McPherson, John No Middle Initial. Draftee
> Serial #135 22 2588.
> One job, pregnant wife. One life,
> many bills.
> McPherson, J. Serial #135 22 2588.
> Vietnam Casualty 2743.

(*There is a long pause as she finishes.* AGRIPPA *pounds the desk with her fist.*)

AGRIPPA: Order! Order! Order in the court! Guilty! Guilty as charged. We find the defendant guilty of disobeying the law of the land. The defendant tried to prey on the sympathies of the court but she will find no mercy here. Guilty as charged. And I'm through with kids' games.

(AGRIPPA *gets up and goes to the sink. She pours herself a glass of water and drinks it.* CARMEN *goes to her bunk.* LANA *remains before the desk.*)

MATRON: That was interesting. Why don't you monkeys go on? That was very entertaining.

LANA: Oh, shut up.

MATRON: Hungry? (*She smirks.*)

LANA: Monday will be here soon enough. I'm going to sue you, beast. You're going to see the other side of that netting.

MATRON: We'll see what we'll see. I think I'm going to have me some coffee and donuts. How about it? Want some? Leave the niggers an' come on over with me.

AGRIPPA: Go on, Lana. Feed yourself. We'll eat sooner or later.

LANA: No, thank you. You may give me something for Lolly.

MATRON: Sure I will. (*She laughs.*) Let me see—what do I want? Plain, powdered, or glazed? Maybe all three. (*She reaches into her desk drawer and takes out a large box of assorted donuts. She lays out the three different kinds before her. She smacks her lips. The lights dim to end this scene.*)

Scene 3

(*Night. The women are in varying positions as before. Maybe* AGRIPPA *is in her bunk lying atop the coverings,* LANA *is at the desk, reading.* CARMEN *is restless. She prowls.* LOLLY *is asleep.*)

CARMEN: Man, my stomach is hollering to beat the band. Feed me, feed me, please feed me! That's what it's saying.

AGRIPPA: At least it's saying something. Mine done just disappeared on me. You there, stomach? Don't you run away on me now. I might be needing you.

LANA: Carmen, look at Lolly. Is she all right?

CARMEN: She's fine. As long as you're sleepin' food don't make no never mind. I wish I could fall asleep an' wake up Monday mornin'.

LANA: She'll wake up soon. Your stomach tells you to after awhile.

AGRIPPA: How do you know that? Forest Hills ain't no place to go wantin'.

LANA: On the sit-in's we would sometimes go thirty-six hours without eating. Our stomachs would shrink so that the first time we got anything to eat, we couldn't. Lolly's been asleep over eight hours now. She's not a young woman. She should eat regularly.

AGRIPPA: Keep your voice down. You'll wake her up. Girl, you worry, worry, worry. Lolly's been through ten times this trouble. She's gonna outlive us all.

LANA: Maybe. But she doesn't have to suffer all the while she lives.

AGRIPPA: You care too much, baby.

LANA: There's no such thing. How can you say that?

AGRIPPA: Baby, what kind of old man do you got? Didn't he teach you that you gotta stop caring somewhere? Didn't he tell you that sometimes you gotta walk away from love? You care too much the only one who's gonna get hurt is you.

LANA: I haven't been hurt.

AGRIPPA: Not yet, you ain't. This afternoon you was cryin' your heart out about all the things that bug you. Do you think you can make all those wrong things right?

LANA: I don't know. I can try. I don't have to stop caring because I can't make them right. How do you know if you don't try?

AGRIPPA: Try real hard once an' get hurt. You'll stop. You'll see.

LANA: Is that what you did? Tried once and it didn't work? Is that why the big cynic?

AGRIPPA (*turns over, away from her*): Aw, let me go to sleep.

LANA: Confrontations bug you, don't they? Agrippa, you've been in this cell for over six years. What do you think about? Or do you think at all?

AGRIPPA: Leave me alone, girl.

LANA: No. I want to know. What do you think about when you are alone with yourself? Maybe late at night when you can't sleep? What is it you think about? Maybe about the time when you could have cared longer? Maybe about the time when you should have tried harder? What do you think about? Tell me.

AGRIPPA: I don't think. How do you suppose I ain't gone off my nut all these years? I don't think.

LANA: I don't believe that. What about the thing that brought you here? I don't think that something worth twenty years of your life could lack importance.

CARMEN: You better leave her alone, Lana.

LANA: Carmen, you seem to know what she's in here for. What was it?

CARMEN: No, girl.

AGRIPPA: Lana, leave things as they are. You turn over a rock you gonna get ugly things to look at.

LANA: Nothing is that ugly. When I look at you I always seem to get an image of a big Buddha. Centuries old and weathered. Hiding many secrets and knowing many things. Inscrutable but not invulnerable. There's a chink in your armor and you know about it. How do you hide that chink from your enemies, Agrippa?

AGRIPPA: By hitting first. Now leave me alone before I do.

(*She settles. There is no more to say.* LOLLY *starts turning and tossing. She moans.*)

CARMEN: Oh, oh. Here comes trouble.

LANA: She's no trouble. How are you, Lolly? How do you feel?

LOLLY: Lana, Lana honey. I'm sick. Bad sick. My stomach's like a big ball of fire. Pray for me, baby. Pray for me.

LANA: I'll pray even though you'll be all right. It will go away. Think about something else.

LOLLY: That's what I been doin'. But all I see is ham-hocks an' greens, chitterlin's an' greens, fried chicken an' greens. I tried thinkin' about the church an' the choir, but all I got was the dear Lord Jesus with a handful of hot bread. My belly is on fire, Lana.

LANA: I'll see what I can do, Lolly. (*She stands abruptly. She walks to the netting.*)

LANA: M'am. I'd like some of those donuts.

MATRON: You would, would you? For who?

LANA: For me. I'm starving. I can't wait anymore.

MATRON: Well, now. Your belly had to tell you what color you are, huh?

LANA: I know what color I am, m'am. I'd like some of your coffee and donuts. May I?

MATRON: You ain't gotta say that. Get close by the gate. Real close. I don't want them niggers rushing me. That's right. (LANA *moves to the side of the opening. The* MATRON *opens the gate and reaches in and pulls* LANA *out quickly. She slams and locks the gate.*) The water's hot. Pour yourself some. The donuts are in the drawer. (LANA *goes over to the desk and gets out the donuts. She pours herself some coffee. She sips the coffee.*) You know how many black bitches we got in this prison? It's four to one. We try to keep you separated. You know what you're doin' in here?

LANA: No, m'am.

MATRON: You ain't gotta call me that. The matrons got you labeled a white nigger. That's what we call you peace marchers.

LANA: Not anymore, m'am.

MATRON: My name's Betty.

LANA: Okay, Betty.

MATRON: That's better. I thought for a while there you was gonna give me some big trouble. You know, them bitches in there can't bother me. No one looks out after them. But if you told some bigwig out in the street what I did, I could be in real big trouble.

LANA: I wouldn't do that, Betty. You're like me.

(AGRIPPA *and the others are looking on. They are not surprised though.*)

MATRON: You know, Agrippa got eyes for you.

LANA: She tried to do something last night.

MATRON: She did? What was that?

LANA: I wouldn't let her touch me.

MATRON: Why not?

LANA: I don't know. The thought of those black hands touching me gave me the willies.

MATRON: Yeah, that'll do it. You got some real pretty skin. How old are you?

LANA: Twenty.

MATRON: That's awfully young. Why don't you sit down? Use my chair.

LANA: Thank you.

MATRON: You don't have to thank me. (LANA *sits. The* MATRON *comes up behind her and touches her hair.* LANA *does not move.*) You remember when Agrippa was tellin' you about how I like to take care of you people?

LANA: Yes.

MATRON: I do like to take care of my people. You got about a month to go. It can be hard on you. It doesn't have to be.

LANA: It doesn't?

MATRON: No. Not if you think right.

LANA: I'm willing to.

MATRON: You sure have got soft skin. (*She is touching the back of her neck.*)

LANA: You have gentle hands, Betty.

MATRON: I've been told that.

LANA: You seem very gentle now.

MATRON: I try to separate my job from my personal life. Can I kiss you there? (*She indicates her neck.* LANA *does not reply. The* MATRON *kisses her gently on the back of the neck. She kisses her more when she feels that* LANA *will go along with it. She becomes like a bull in sight of a cow. She moves quickly, wanting.* LANA *pulls away.*)

LANA: Wait!

MATRON: What? What? Don't lead me on now, girl.

LANA: You are so rough. I'm here. I won't run away. We have all night.

MATRON: Yeah. I guess so. I been looking at you for three days. You look so good. I want to kiss you for real.

LANA: Do.

(*The* MATRON *moves over to her and embraces her, kissing her full on the mouth. The kiss is a long one.* LANA *reaches out with her free hand and picks up the billy. She holds it out behind her. The* MATRON *releases her and steps back. She smiles.* LANA *brings the billy around hard, hitting her on the*

side of the neck. The blow only stuns her. LANA *has to swing again. We see that it takes great effort for her to hit a person. But she forces herself to do it again. The* MATRON *falls to her knees, half-conscious.* LANA *grabs the keys and runs to the gate. She unlocks it.* AGRIPPA *and* CARMEN *rush out and pinion the* MATRON. LANA *is shaking, crying and gripping the netting.*)

AGRIPPA: Lolly! Come on out of there! Quick!

(LOLLY *gets up and comes out of the cell.*)

LOLLY: Oh. What you done? What'd you do, 'Grippa? We gonna die, now.

AGRIPPA: You're gonna die anyway. Move out of the way.

(*They drag the* MATRON *into the cell. They drop her on the floor. They come out and* AGRIPPA *takes the keys from* LANA's *limp hand. She pries* LANA's *fingers from the netting and pulls her over to the chair. She sits her down.*)

LANA: Agrippa, Agrippa. I had to do that, I didn't want to hit her.

AGRIPPA: You didn't do it hard enough. Now stop that bawlin'. Here, wipe your eyes. (*She hands her a napkin or tissue from the desk.*) Let's see what we got. (*She looks into the drawer and takes out the coffee, the donuts, and some fruit.*) Old Mama's a pig. Ain't that good for us.

CARMEN: How do you like your coffee, your majesty? (*She is talking to* LANA.)

LANA: I don't want anything.

AGRIPPA: Strong and black. You are too much, girl.

LANA: Make Lolly something. She needs it.

(LOLLY *is stuffing herself with the donuts and munching on an apple.*)

CARMEN: Lolly's seein' to herself.

LANA: How can one human being treat another like that? I couldn't stand it any longer! She's a human being, doesn't she know that? Doesn't she know that, Agrippa?

AGRIPPA: I don't think so, baby. So, now rest yourself. You done enough for three people. Have some coffee.

LANA: I feel so ashamed.

CARMEN: Feel proud, Lana. Feel proud.

LANA: I let her kiss me. She kissed me like a man.

AGRIPPA: I felt jealous. For a while there I thought you meant it.

LANA: I had to. I had to make her believe me. You didn't believe me, did you?

AGRIPPA: Yeah, baby. I did.

LANA: Oh Agrippa, I wouldn't. I couldn't. I couldn't be that kind of person.

520

AGRIPPA: What? My kind of person?

LANA: No! I mean the kind of person who doesn't care. That kind of person. (*She points into the cell.*)

AGRIPPA: You forget. That's my kind of person.

LANA: I don't believe that, Agrippa.

AGRIPPA: What do I have to do to make you believe it?

LANA: Tell me.

AGRIPPA: What? Tell you about how much I don't care? You want to hear that? It ain't for pretty young ears.

LANA: Try them.

AGRIPPA: I wanted the chair but they don't give out with light sentences anymore. The judge told me that he wished he could give me the chair. He wished! I wished! You wanta know what I did? I didn't care, Lana. She was like you—young, pretty—an' I loved her. Loved her more than anything in the whole world. I used to work for these rich, white folk down South. They had a daughter. We used to talk way late at night, talk about everything. About how we gonna run away together and live like princesses in a castle. You know, I was the one who corrupted her, made her like me. She probably woulda found somebody if I had left her alone. When I come up to New York I wasn't here more than three months before she come knockin' on my door. She left college to come knockin' on my door. Said she couldn't live without me. We did live like fairy princesses. We used to lay up in the bed an' tell each other stories. Funny stories, sad stories, happy stories an' then no stories at all. I loved that child. Then I thought she found somebody else. She started stayin' away, comin' home late. Her lipstick would be smeared an' her clothes wouldn't be together. I was like a jealous husband. I used to look through her purse, smell at her underwear. Look for strands of hair. I found some too. It was nappy hair. But not like mine. We had our periods about the same time of the month so we used to use the same box of napkins; she wasn't usin' any. My love had gone an' got herself pregnant. Ain't that a bitch! I thought she was all mine. But some—man—had got to her. Some man had come an' taken my love away from me. I took to beatin' her. Like Carmen's pimp beats her. I used to beat her an' ask—Who is it? Who is the black son-ovabitch! I'll kill him! I will, I'll kill him! She never would say one word. An' I hurt her. I hurt her bad. Then her stomach started swellin'. I would help her take a bath an' I would see that awful swellin' in her belly and I would hate it. I used to wake up in the middle of the night and watch it move. I would put my hand on it an' try to push it down, try to push it out. I

pushed so hard that she used to wake up screamin'. She thought the baby done hurt her. That baby had hurt me. Then I had to find her a doctor. That was a sight. Me an' my love walkin' to the baby doctor like husband and wife. I told her to tell the doctor that the baby was a bastard. She gave my name as hers. Mrs. Agrippa Johnson. It got so I couldn't take it no more. I started walkin' around the bed late at night. Watching her. Watching that belly move. Then, one day, I just picked up a knife and did it. I did it an' I did it an' I did it. She was lookin' at me when I did it. Her big green eyes were lookin' at me. You know somethin'? Her eyes had love in them. Even as I stabbed they were lovin' me, tellin' me "I love you." When the cops come an' took me away I wasn't even cryin'. I wasn't even sad. She didn't die right away. My lawyer brought me a letter from her. You know what she said? She told me that she knew I wouldn't understand what she had done but she had to do it. She told me how she searched all over the city for some man who looked like me, who thought like me, who talked like me. She said she found him and she fell in love with him. Not because of him but because he was Agrippa. She said she wanted to give me something we couldn't give each other. A child. She wanted to give me a child. Something we could love together as it grew with us. I didn't care, Lana. My love got pregnant and all I cared about was my hurt feelings. I should of cared for her, nursed her, helped her through the pregnancy. But no, ol' Agrippa didn't care. Ol' Agrippa's love was a selfish —love. An' that judge wanted to give me the chair. I wish he had.

LANA: I'm sorry.

AGRIPPA: Don't be sorry, Lana. I didn't care about you either. I was just tryin' to figger out some way to get you into my bed. When you was cryin' your heart out in there about the things you feel about—I didn't care. I just wanted to hold you in my arms. Girl, how do you do it? How do you care so much?

LANA: I never think about it.

(*The* MATRON *gets up. She is a bit shaky.*)

CARMEN: Here comes the Ox.

MATRON: What did you do? What am I—

AGRIPPA: You are in the slammers, m'am. Your eyes was bigger than your stomach.

MATRON: Agrippa, you better let me out of here. You know what will happen if you don't.

AGRIPPA: I don't believe so, Mama. In about six hours it will be breakfast time. What you're gonna do is just come out

of there then an' walk us down to the food. We gotta see about Lolly's finger too. It'll hold till mornin'. Let's just say she tripped while she was goin' through one of her tantrums, what say to that?

MATRON: I'm going to report you all when I get out of here.

AGRIPPA: I don't think so. You gotta come through us to get out of here. We're goin' with you when you do. An' Lolly, get ready to scream blue murder when we go out that door in the mornin'. Lana gets out of here in a couple weeks or so. She just might go talkin' to those bigwigs you spoke of. Huh, Lana?

LANA: I'm going to do that anyway.

AGRIPPA: No, don't do nothin' like that. Just hold it over her head. It'd be more effective that way.

LANA: If you say so.

AGRIPPA: I say so. Care for some coffee, Mama?

MATRON: Yeah.

AGRIPPA: Coffee for Mama, Carmen. With lots of sugar.

LANA: How do you feel, Lolly?

LOLLY: Oh, just fine. Just fine. (*She swallows another piece of donut.* LANA *smiles. The lights dim and go down to end this scene.*)

Scene 4

(*Some weeks later. The day of* LANA's *release. It is early morning. The women are up. They are all in their prison dresses.*)

LOLLY: Big day a'comin'. Lana's goin' home today.

CARMEN: Now, Lana, remember what I told you: Lenox an' 116th. He'll be on the northeast corner. An' if you see him with somebody else, that's all right too. He gotta make a dollar some way, don't he?

LANA: Yes, Carmen.

AGRIPPA: It won't be workin', that's for sure.

LANA: Leave her alone, Agrippa.

AGRIPPA: Aw, she knows I'm just teasin'. You ready to go home?

LANA: No. I think I'll ask for an extension. Think they'll give me one?

AGRIPPA: Not if Big Mama can help it, they won't.

(*The* MATRON *comes up to the gate. She opens it.*)

MATRON: Stand by! (*The women shuffle over to their bunks. Inspection. She goes through the routine. She gets to* LANA.) You make a bunk real well. What do you plan to picket next?

LANA: I don't know, m'am.

MATRON: Stay away from here, would you?

LANA: Maybe.

MATRON: What was that?

LANA: M'am.

(*The* MATRON *goes to* AGRIPPA's *area.*)

MATRON: Good mornin', Agrippa.

AGRIPPA: G'mornin', Mama.

MATRON: Come with me, Kaufmann.

LANA: Yes, m'am. (LANA *follows the* MATRON *out to her desk. The* MATRON *pushes the buzzer. The doors clang open.* LANA *looks behind her. She smiles and walks out the doors.*)

MATRON: Well, now it's just the four of us again.

AGRIPPA: Yeah, Mama.

MATRON: One of these days, Agrippa, one of these days.

AGRIPPA: Yeah, Mama. One of these days.

(*The lights go down to . . .*)

END OF PLAY

Black Cycle

by MARTIE CHARLES

Martie Charles is a member of the Black Theater Workshop in Harlem, New York. She acts and writes for the New Lafayette Theater Company.

THE PEOPLE

VERA: *"Every time they see me I'm sharp."*
Beautician, well-developed, dark, feminine woman in her late thirties.

JEANNIE: *"Mah mother is too much, I wish I could get away."*
Vera's daughter, sixteen, attractive, with a figure which shows that she will be as well developed as her mother.

MARAY: *"I couldn't do nothin' like that to mah customer much less mah fren."*
Beautician who rents a booth from Vera. Middle-aged, sympathetic.

SADIE: *"Whas suppose to happen to mah family."*
Wiry, big-voiced feminine black woman, Jerome's wife, mother of six.

CAROLYN: *"I be sick a lot an' I ain't got no clothes."*
Sadie's daughter, sixteen, Jeannie's best friend, pregnant, very aware.

CALVIN: *"Hold still, lil' girl, everything's gonna be all right."*
Slim, quiet-talking young hustler, twenty.

FLORIDA: *"I took you off the streets."*
Tall, husky, quiet-talking authoritative banker man.

JEROME: *"Thas all you gettin,' now git the fuck out mah face."*
Slender, nervous movements, Sadie's husband, numbers runner, middle forties.

All of the players are black.

All inquiries concerning production rights to this play should be addressed to:
Whitman Mayo,
New Lafayette Theater Agency
2349 Seventh Avenue
New York, N.Y. 10030

Martie Charles

INVOCATION

When the sun come up, I'm gonna be white
When the sun come up, I'm gonna be white
'Cause a black face 'round heah, ain't
No man's delight.

Spirits of black womanhood, surround me
Spirits of black womanhood, surround me
Spirits of black womanhood, be with me.

Fill every pore of my being with a knowledge of who I am
Be with me
Peel my brain
Remove the layers of white thought, white talk
Gouge out that inner eye, implanted in my mind oh so long
   ago by
The devil beasts . . .
Root out that evil inner eye, programmed to destroy
   blackness
That has programmed me to destroy myself
That has created in me the desire to be pale and colorless
As were those who tore us from our homeland
Used our bodies as receptacles, sucklers, fodder,
Fodder in the building of their nation
Upon the blood . . . bones . . . and flesh of our men . . .
Murdered . . . murdered . . . multilated . . .
Foh us . . .
In the heat of the many rape-filled nights
O Spirits of Black Womanhood, surround me, be with me,
   enter me
And cast out the accursed inner eye
That leaves me never satisfied with my blackness
An ever-straining imitation
Ignorant of my man, of his desires, of his world
As he would have it.

Spirits of Black Womanhood, cast out this curse,
Fill every pore of my being with a knowledge of who I am.
SISTER MARTIE CHARLES

ACT I

(*There are two small booths for each beautician. A large plate-glass window faces the street and forms one partition for the first booth. A waist-high divider forms the other wall and*
526

separates it from the second booth. At the end of the plate-glass window is the entrance to the shop. A small love seat-type couch is in front of the window. Each booth contains a high stool, a swivel chair, a countertop table, and a large mirror. A door leading to the storage closet is at the end of the second booth. A small basin and chair are downstage left of the second booth.

The invocation should be said by one female voice in total blackness. She can be accompanied by drums. Following the invocation, the music from the radio in the shop is heard. The lights go up on the shop.

At rise, VERA *and* MARAY *are in the shop. They are wearing white uniforms.* VERA *occupies the first booth.*

They are both rolling wigs. The radio is tuned in to a black station and the latest music is playing. VERA *stops her work, stands, goes to the window and looks out.* VERA *places her hands behind her back (where most women feel strain) as if to relieve it of the strain of sitting for a long period of time.*

VERA looks at her watch, starts to return to her work. The phone on the wall above the divider rings. MARAY *looks up to see if* VERA *is answering.*

VERA: Paradise . . . (*Pause.*) Hey, baby . . . (*Pause.*) Yeah, Jeannie school havin' a big affair tonight an' I want you to drive us there. In the shop! Florida, ain't nothin wrong with that Caddy. (*Pause.*) Treats it better'en you do me . . . (*Pause followed by laughter.*) You suppose to . . . iss a machine, I ain't. (*Pause.*) Eight o'clock. We not goin' there in no damned taxi, I told you iss a big thing an' I wanna do it right . . . (*Pause.*) No! you be here seven thirty . . . Okay. We can talk about that later, Florida . . . Um hmmm, mmmmm, okay. (*Hangs up.*) Go down there in a taxi. Man must be out his mind.

(*The radio plays throughout* VERA's *phone conversation. After she hangs up, the four o'clock news is announced. The news item should be a meaningful up-to-date statement concerning something that black people should be aware of. The first statement by the announcer should be brief and to the point.*)

VERA: Sho don't wanna hear that. Jeannie gotta do better'en this. She was suppose to git here early.

MARAY: You gone be able to do her hair?

VERA: I don't know the way this time's runnin'. An' I still don't have nothin' to wear since I gained all this weight.

MARAY: You don't look like you picked up none.

VERA: You cain't tell in this uniform. (*Hits her hips.*)

527

Probably have to buy somethin' offa Calvin real quick if he come by.

MARAY: Why you wait till the last minute to find you somethin' to wear?

VERA: I have a green suit I was gon wear. Bought it offa Calvin two weeks ago. Went to try it on last night and couldn't git in it.

MARAY: Iss dressy, huh?

VERA: Imma dress up. Wouldn't be caught 'round them people no other way. Every time they see me I'm sharp.

MARAY: Wearin' that mink Florida gave you?

VERA: You know I am. If Jeannie don't get here soon I really won't have time to do her hair. And bad as it is I know iss gone need somethin' done to it.

MARAY: Where iss gone be?

VERA: Hilton.

MARAY (*sound of admiration*): Why on a Monday night?

VERA: I oun't know.

MARAY: You payin'?

VERA: Fifty dollars.

MARAY: Fifty dollars???

VERA: Um hmm. Twenty-five dollars a ticket.

MARAY: Damn, Vera.

VERA: Thas right. Twenty-five dollars a ticket, an' my child gonna be there just like them white kids in her class. 'Cause you know what they gone say if she don't show, an' I'm tryin' to git her started off right.

MARAY: I wouldn't give a damn what they say. I couldn't pay that kinda money foh no dinner.

VERA: Thas not all to it, you know! She suppose to be gittin' a special award tonight.

MARAY: Foh what?

VERA (*using her hands to emphasize what she is saying*): Makin' the highest mark average they say of all the kids in her grade.

MARAY: She didn't.

VERA: Yes, she did. Got a letter from the dean last week. Did better'en all them white kids.

MARAY: She beginnin' to feel different about the school?

VERA: She don't say too much no more, so I guess she willin' to give it a try. (VERA *returns to the window and looks out onto the street.*) Jeannie gotta do better'en this. (*Two beats.*) There go Sadie, probably lookin' foh Jerry.

MARAY: She was in here this mornin askin' 'bout her new wig.

VERA: *New* wig?? She betta pay me for the ole one thas on her head.

MARAY: Your money be a long time comin' if she payin' you outta what Jerry give her.

VERA: I don't care what she do it outta, long as I git mah money.

MARAY: That wig she wearin' now look terrible. You seen it?

VERA: Sadie don't take care uh nothin' she got and never did. An I been knowin' her a while.

MARAY: She said y'all grew up together.

VERA: Uh hmm. Right 'round here. (VERA *takes out a little black book and thumbs through it.*) She still owe me fifty dollars.

MARAY: Owe you? How much it cost?

VERA: Seventy-five.

MARAY (*unbelieving*): Sadie payin' you seventy-five dollars foh that wig she wearin'??

VERA: Thas a hunnert-dollar wig I let her have. (MARAY *makes a disapproving sound.* JEANNIE *enters and sits on the customer bench.*)

JEANNIE: Olafia!

MARAY: Oh what?

JEANNIE: Olafia!

VERA: Somethin' new they done taught her in school. Whas that, French?

JEANNIE: Yoruba.

VERA: Yoruba??

JEANNIE: One of the African languages!

VERA: African!!

MARAY: Now thas nice, how it go again??

VERA: You was suppose to be here at two o'clock.

JEANNIE: I got somethin' to tell you, Vera.

VERA: Come over here so I can git started on your head.

JEANNIE: Vera!

VERA: Tell me while you sittin' over here. I still gotta try an' git me somethin' to wear after I do your hair.

JEANNIE: None uh the black kids is goin' tonight.

VERA: Not goin'?!!? To the dinner at the Hilton??

MARAY: What you say?!?

JEANNIE: Thas right. We decided we just won't show tonight.

VERA: What you talkin' 'bout, girl!?!

JEANNIE: I'm not goin' to that scholarship dinner tonight, none uh us are goin', so don't worry 'bout my hair.

MARAY: Ain't that somethin'.

VERA: Who's us?

JEANNIE: I told you. The black students.

VERA: Why not?

JEANNIE: We don't like what's goin' down for tonight.

VERA: What??

JEANNIE: We don't like somethin' the dean's doin'.

VERA: Y'all don't like some . . . *Whas that!!*

JEANNIE: He plannin' on parading all the black kids up on stage so people at the dinner can give more money for scholarships.

MARAY: Oh no!

JEANNIE: Thas right. He gonna put us on stage and start talkin' 'bout how bad we was in our old school and how we was bad 'cause we was so poor and how the school gave us a chance to be somethin' by lettin' us in, and how the people at the dinner should give more money to help other unfortunates like us.

MARAY: An' you say they doin' this to all the black children, Jeannie?

JEANNIE: Well no, just those who on scholarship.

VERA: Oh! I *thought* somethin' was wrong with that. What they doin' to them kids ain't got nothin' to do with you, honey. You ain't on no scholarship.

JEANNIE: I knew you'd say that. I said none uh the black students is goin'. Vera, that means me too.

VERA: You just said they was doin' this to the kids who on scholarship.

JEANNIE: We all stayin' home, those who got scholarships an' those who don't.

MARAY: These kids is really steppin' out there.

VERA (*pats the back of the chair*): I don't wanna hear no more 'bout that, Jeannie.

JEANNIE: You don't need to worry 'bout mah hair, Vera. Imma start doin' it mahself.

VERA: You haven't been doin' it. Look at it now.

JEANNIE: Thas 'cause I didn't like the way you fixed it in the first place.

VERA: I be too embarrassed to have them white girls at school see me with mah hair lookin' like that.

JEANNIE: Well you know! different strokes for different folks.

VERA: Don't git smart with me, Jeannie!!

(JEANNIE *picks up a magazine and thumbs through it.*)

JEANNIE: Well, I don't care 'bout no white girls.

VERA: You should. (*Takes out irons and prepares for hair-straightening.*) Y'all don't like somethin' the dean's doin'! Them people been runnin' Walden Academy all this time with no help from niggas, you know what I mean, an' they finally let a few niggas in foh free. God knows why! An' soon's they gits they foot in the door they turn 'round and try to bite the hand thas feedin' them. Tellin' them people how to run they school.

JEANNIE: Nobody tryin' to tell 'em how to run the school, Vera.

VERA: Thas all they doin', tryin' to tell the people how to run they school.

MARAY: How many uh us in that school, Jeannie?

JEANNIE: 'Bout fifty an' most uh them is on scholarship.

MARAY: All fifty stayin' home?

JEANNIE: No, but most of us are.

MARAY: Uh huh. Them with some sense is goin' to the dinner!

JEANNIE: We just got some black people that still not together.

MARAY: You done said somethin' there!

VERA: Black, black, black, thas all I hear out of your mouth. Time was anybody call you black you start to cry or git mad one.

JEANNIE: Thas 'cause I believed all that stuff you was tellin' me.

VERA: Anything I told you 'bout niggas 'round here is true, you betta believe it, 'cause I grew up with 'em an' still deals with 'em every day. An' I loves mah people good as the next one but I don't be lettin' 'em hold me back.

JEANNIE: Hold you back??

VERA: Thas right. Like they tryin' to do to you. They know you ain't on no scholarship, so why they askin' you to stay home, iss 'cause niggas always gotta pull one another down.

(MARAY *shakes her head, disagreeing.*)

JEANNIE: Well, I tole you I didn't wanna go to no private school in the first place. I wanted to stay with my frens at Franklin.

VERA: Half them at Franklin'll end up in the street. (*Two-beat pause.*) Carolyn's pregnant now. (JEANNIE *ignores the statement and continues to look through the magazine.*) You hear what I said?

JEANNIE: I already know. Barbara tole me.

VERA: Where you see her?

JEANNIE: At school, she got a scholarship.

VERA: *Barbara* got a scholarship to Walden!

JEANNIE: Uh huh.

VERA: Lawd!!

JEANNIE: Lotta kids from Franklin on scholarship at Walden.

VERA: No wonda the people havin' so much trouble.

JEANNIE: Thas why I can't go tonight.

VERA: You don't have the same problem as them kids. I'm payin' foh whatever you git at that school.

JEANNIE: Vera, them people don't treat me no betta 'cause you payin'. I'm still black. Thas why we stayin' away, we not gonna help 'em do what they do to us.

MARAY: God knows iss time.

VERA: Oh we goin' all right, matter fact, I won't wash your hair 'cause iss too late. I'll just touch up the edges.

JEANNIE: You can go if you want to, I'm stayin' home.

VERA: Now lemme tell you one thing, I done paid fifty dollars for them tickets an' we goin'.

MARAY: Jeannie, suppose the other kids change they minds.

JEANNIE: They not gonna do nothin' like that, an' even if they did, thas hip, wouldn't make no difference to me.

VERA: I wasn't gonna say nothin' to you 'bout it. Was gone let it be a surprise. But you gittin' a special award tonight foh makin' the highest average of all the kids on your grade an' you know I'm not gonna miss that.

JEANNIE: How you know about it?

VERA: I got a letter from the dean. You knew?

JEANNIE: Yeah!

VERA: Why you didn't tell me?

JEANNIE: I used to do the same thing at Franklin . . .

VERA: This ain't *Franklin!*

JEANNIE: An you never made no big thing over it. They couldn't git you out to none uh the meetin's.

VERA: I took you outta there an' put you in Walden where them good marks can pay off 'cause you makin' them 'round the right people, an' you do me like that.

JEANNIE: With you the right people is always the white people.

VERA: So they puttin' your lil' frens from Franklin up on the stage so's they can tell everybody how bad they was before they came to Walden. Well iss true! They is bad. All them kids in Franklin is bad. Thas another reason I took you outta there, an' why I'm payin' foh you to be where you are. Cause if you want what somebody else got, an' you ain't got no

money then you do what they want you to do to git what they got. (*Turns to* MARAY *for approval of what she is saying to* JEANNIE.) You know what I mean. So your lil' frens gotta go through that foh one night if they wanna keep on goin' to the school foh free. Thas the way it is. An' what you kids don't understand is you gotta take the bitta with the sweet.

JEANNIE: They got more white kids on scholarship than black an' none uh them have to go up on stage. Why's that?

MARAY: She got a point there, Vera!

VERA: I oun't know. I ain't tryin' to tell them people how to run they school. All I know is they cain't do nothin' to you 'cause I'm payin' foh you.

JEANNIE: But Vera, if iss not right what they doin' to us, and they don't be doin' these things to their kids, shouldn't we do somethin' about it?

VERA: No! You not on no scholarship so you got nothin' to do with it, just like them white kids.

JEANNIE: I'm black.

VERA: You sho are! Just like yah damned daddy!! So like I say, you stay out it, you got nothin' to do with it.

JEANNIE: It was mah idea foh us to stay home.

VERA: Yoh idea! You hear this, Maray??

MARAY: Why, Jeannie??

JEANNIE: We had to do somethin'. We couldn't let 'em git away with it.

VERA: Girl! The people ain't doin' nothin' to you but tryin' to give you uh award foh doin' good in school.

JEANNIE: Nothin' but a piece uh paper.

VERA: Iss more'en that to me!

JEANNIE: Don't mean nothin' if I gotta walk all over mah frens to git it!

MARAY (*shakes her head in agreement*): Ummmm hmmmm.

VERA: Well, it mean somethin' to me! To sit up there in that hotel, with all them other parents an' see you walkin' up to git your award. It may be nothin' but a piece uh paper to you but ain't nobody else gettin' it. You doin' better'en all they kids an' Imma see you git that paper! You owe me that foh payin' yoh way.

JEANNIE: Payin', payin', payin', Vera, I'm not talkin' 'bout no money!

VERA: Yes you is! Yes you is. You just don't know it but thas all you talkin' 'bout. *Money!* Thas why your lil' frens goin' through what they goin' through 'cause they ain't got enough *money* to pay they own way.

JEANNIE: Well, all I know is I cain't make that scene. Not when mah brothers an' sisters is hurtin'.

MARAY: Vera, maybe you oughta lissen to what she got to say.

VERA: She betta lissen to me! What about your mama?! What about me, don't I count?

JEANNIE: You mah sister too, Vera, but you just don't understand.

VERA: I ain't none uh yoh damned sista! I'm yoh mother an' you not gone cheat me outta this night.

JEANNIE: Cheat you!??! Goin' to the dinner. Thas all you wanna do, huh? Is go to the white people's scholarship dinner and sit up there with them in yoh dusty fur. You don't care nothin' 'bout me, 'bout what I feel. You don't care nothin' 'bout us. I can really see that.

VERA: You don't see nothin'. But *me* in this shop makin' money so you don't have to go through the kinda changes I went through when I was your age. Do you see that!? Can you understand that!? Makin' money foh you so you don't have to be out there like me. Seein' more'en I was suppose to. (*Stops, catches her breath.*) Just bring yoh lil' ass ova here an' sit down! An' don't you say shit to me 'bout no goddamned Afro, you hear!

(JEANNIE *stands and moves to the side of the bench.* VERA *moves toward her.* MARAY *stands.* CALVIN *enters with suits in a plastic bag.*)

CALVIN: Some nice suits.

VERA: Just the man I'm lookin' for. What sizes you got?

CALVIN: Tens an' twelves.

VERA: Lemme see a twelve. You ain't got no fourteens?

CALVIN: Not now.

VERA: Gimme the twelve, lemme try it on. (CALVIN *takes the suit out and hands it to* VERA. *She holds it up, examining it. To* JEANNIE.) Imma git back to you in a minute. (VERA *takes the suit and goes to the storage closet to try it on.*)

CALVIN (*to* MARAY): How 'bout you, mama?

MARAY: No, baby. I ain't got no money today.

CALVIN (*moves over to* JEANNIE, *looks at her. She is thumbing through a magazine*): What about you, sista?

JEANNIE: I don't believe in buyin' stuff that's stolen from the homes of black people.

CALVIN: I don't know what the fuck you talkin' 'bout!

MARAY: Now Calvin, that ain't necessary.

CALVIN: Mah shit come straight from the Man's factory.

JEANNIE: I'm not interested.

CALVIN: Why you ain't say that in the first place. 'Stead uh rappin' 'bout what you don't believe in. (*Silence.* CALVIN *studies her for a while.*) Ain't you Vera's lil' girl?

JEANNIE: I'm her daughter.

CALVIN: Yeah. Thas what I said. (*Long pause.*) Her lil' girl. (JEANNIE, *uncomfortable under* CALVIN'*s gaze, gets up, goes to window.*) Yeah. I got some stuff *I know* you look good in.

MARAY: Well, Calvin, maybe Vera's the one you oughta talk to 'bout that.

CALVIN: Yeah. I'll bring it around. Maybe your mama'll hook you up.

JEANNIE: Like I said, I'm not interested.

CALVIN: Some boss vines, baby. Change your mind once you see 'em.

(VERA *comes out. The skirt of the suit is much too tight across the behind. The jacket is short.*)

VERA: How it look y'all? (VERA *walks out, rolling her hips sensuously.*)

CALVIN: Look good to me.

VERA: I know iss a lil' too tight across here.

JEANNIE: A little!

CALVIN: Look good to me!

JEANNIE: It's too tight and it's too short!!

CALVIN: Look good to . . .

VERA: Yeah, I know, Calvin. It look good to you. What you think, Maray?

MARAY: You need to try on a fourteen so you could know which one fit the best.

VERA: He say he ain't got none. (*Looks at* CALVIN.)

CALVIN: Thas right.

VERA: I need me somethin' foh tonight. I really like this. Iss nice. (*Looks at her behind in the mirror.*) I could git away wid it foh tonight. 'Cause mah stole come up to here. You know, Maray.

MARAY (*studies* VERA *in the tight suit, then looks down, continuing to do what she was doing before.*) I guess so, Vera.

VERA: How much it cost??

CALVIN: Forty.

VERA: Oh, no, baby! I ain't got that kinda money.

CALVIN: Thas a ninety-dollar suit, mama.

VERA: I ain't got that kinda money to pay on somethin' that don't even fit good.

CALVIN: Gimme the suit if you not gonna take it, baby. I gotta split.

(VERA *looks at herself in the mirror again, spreads her hands across her behind. And then slowly walks back to the storage closet.* SADIE *comes to the door.*)

SADIE: Calvin. You seen Jerome?

CALVIN: No.

SADIE: If you run up on his ass, tell him I'm lookin' foh him.

JEANNIE: Hello, Miss Sadie.

SADIE: Hello, Jeannie. How you doin'? Ain't seen you in a while.

CALVIN: *Miss* Sadie!! Ain't this some shit.

SADIE: Nigga leave that chile alone an' let her show some respect foh her elders. You keep callin' me Miss Sadie, honey. Don't pay this mothafucker no mind.

JEANNIE: How's Carolyn doin'?

SADIE: She okay. When you comin' by??

JEANNIE: Soon.

SADIE: How you like your new school?

JEANNIE: It's okay.

SADIE: Where your mama??

JEANNIE: In the back, tryin' on a suit.

SADIE: Oh yeah! She got mah wig, Maray?

MARAY: I oun't know, Sadie. You betta ask Vera 'bout that.

SADIE: Uh huh. I be back.

JEANNIE: Carolyn home now?

SADIE: Yeah. See y'all later. (SADIE *exits.*)

JEANNIE: Maray, tell Vera I be right back.

CALVIN: See you around, Vera's lil' girl.

(JEANNIE *looks at* CALVIN, *then exits.* VERA *comes out with the suit.*)

VERA: Didn't I hear Sadie's mouth out here??

MARAY: She was askin' 'bout her new wig.

VERA: If she give me some uh the money she owe me, I can git this suit. (*Holding it up, looking at it.*) I really like it, Calvin, leave it here. Come back foh your money 'round seven thirty, quarter to eight. I'll have it. (CALVIN *puts a fixed look on* VERA *for two or three beats.*) Whas the matter, baby?? You know I'm good foh it!!

(CALVIN *turns and exits.*)

MARAY: Look like Calvin takin' a likin' to Jeannie.

VERA: Whaaaaaaaaaaaaaaat?! I wish he would. Put Florida on his ass!! Jeannie ain't foh none uh these niggas 'round here.

MARAY: Maybe thas what she need, Vera, a lil' boyfren.

VERA: If she play her hand right, she find everything she

need right there at Walden Academy. Where she go? To the store?

MARAY: Just said she'd be right back.

VERA: Maybe she went around to mah mother's. (*She moves to the phone, picks it up.*)

MARAY: Give her time. She just left.

VERA: I just wanna make sure she not with them frens she was talkin' 'bout. (*Puts the phone down.*)

MARAY: Even if she was, you couldn't do nothin' 'bout it.

VERA: For a suppose-to-be-smart girl, Jeannie can make some dumb moves.

MARAY: She gotta do what she think is right.

VERA: What she think is right!!?? Do you know how much money I'm payin' foh her to go to that school?

MARAY: If the black kids say they stickin' together, what else she gon do?

VERA: Soon's I git her off to a good start here *they* come. *They* don't like somethin' the dean's doin'. She don't have to be in that shit.

MARAY: How you know? You not there.

VERA: If I was. Lawd if I was, and I had the opportunity she got. (*Shakes her head at the thought of it.*) You can believe I wouldn't be no beautician today. An' I damn sure wouldn't have time foh no niggas. You hear me?

MARAY: I hear yah.

VERA: Sheeet. I be somewhere makin' it. I be somewhere wheelin' an' dealin'. Lawd, I know if that was me I have me a white boy fren by now. (*Pause.*) An' I love mah people good as the next one. But I don't be lettin' 'em hold me back from nothin'!!

(*Blackness on the shop and lights up on a small kitchen table.* CAROLYN, *who is about five months pregnant, is sitting at the table drinking soda and listening to the radio. The bell rings, she rises to answer the door.* JEANNIE *enters.*)

CAROLYN: Hey, girl.

JEANNIE: Hi. (*The girls greet each other warmly. They laugh excessively, the sounds of the laughter on the verge of tears. They stand away from one another,* JEANNIE *looking at* CAROLYN's *stomach with fascination.*) Can I touch it?

CAROLYN: Go 'head. (JEANNIE *slowly places her hand on* CAROLYN's *stomach, then withdraws her hand quickly.*) Whas the matter?

JEANNIE: Somethin' moved.

CAROLYN: Fool. Thas the baby.

JEANNIE: The baby?

CAROLYN: Com'on, les sit down. I was suppose to be gettin' dinner ready, but I don't feel good, can't keep nothin' on mah stomach. Want some soda?

JEANNIE: Yeah. You don't have to git up. I'll git the glass. Les see if I remember where they are. (*Locates the glass, returns to the table, pours soda.*) Where all the kids?

CAROLYN: Downstairs.

JEANNIE: Your mother come in the shop?

CAROLYN: Oh yeah. She was lookin' foh daddy or a new wig?

JEANNIE: She was doin' both.

CAROLYN: He didn't leave her no money. David class suppose to go on a trip but he couldn't go. Mama didn't have no money to give him.

JEANNIE: Your lil' brother David?

CAROLYN: Um hmmm.

JEANNIE: How he doin'? (CAROLYN *shrugs her shoulders.* JEANNIE *notices* CAROLYN's *hair, gets up, touches it.*) When you started wearin' uh Afro?

CAROLYN: Couple uh months.

JEANNIE: Imma start doin' mine. Vera talkin' 'bout if I go to school with mah hair like that they won't understand, and think Imma start some trouble.

CAROLYN: How you like it there?

JEANNIE: Iss terrible. I know you glad you don't have to go no more.

CAROLYN: I'm goin' to a special school.

JEANNIE: Foh girls who havin' babies?

CAROLYN: Uh huh.

JEANNIE: I didn't know they had schools like that.

CAROLYN: Iss somethin' new. I didn't wanna go but Mama made me. Talkin' 'bout just 'cause you havin' a baby don't mean the world gotta stop, go learn how to take care of it.

JEANNIE: How you like it?

CAROLYN: Iss okay. Somethin' like regular school except I don't go all day, just in the mornin'. I don't see you too much no more.

JEANNIE: Since we moved from my grandmother's an' my mother put me in this school I don't see anybody.

CAROLYN: Some uh the kids from Franklin go to your school.

JEANNIE: Yeah I know. They tole me you was havin' a baby.

CAROLYN: Oh yeah.

JEANNIE: I was surprised. Barbara come runnin' up to me

an' said, you know Carolyn's havin' a baby. I said, Whaaaaa-aaaaaat? I couldn't believe it.

(*The two girls laugh again on the edge of tears.*)

CAROLYN: Why?

JEANNIE: I oun't know.

(*A period of silence. They drink soda.*)

JEANNIE: How it feel havin' a baby?

CAROLYN: I be sick a lot. An' I ain't got no clothes.

JEANNIE: You gittin' married?

CAROLYN: I oun't know.

JEANNIE: It's Vincent baby??

CAROLYN: Uh huh.

JEANNIE: Y'all been makin' it foh a long time.

CAROLYN: Yeah. He gittin' uh apartment foh us to stay. He say he take care uh me an' the baby but he not ready to git married right now.

(JEANNIE *pauses, thinking how to ask the next question.*)

JEANNIE: I wonder what it's like when you do it.

CAROLYN: You never did it?? (JEANNIE *shakes her head negative.*) It's goooooooooooooooooood.

JEANNIE: Yeah???

CAROLYN: Uh huh. You don't go with nobody?

JEANNIE: Noooooo. (*Pause.*) Mah mother is too much.

CAROLYN: Yeah??

JEANNIE: Yeah. I wish I could git away. She don't understand nothin' thas goin' down. Got me goin' to school with all these white people. Most uh the brothers is diggin' on the white chicks. When there's somethin' at school we don't have nobody to take us or even dance with 'cept them white boys an' they too soft foh me.

CAROLYN: Y'all gotta dance with white boys?? How they dance?

JEANNIE: You know how they dance.

(*The two girls laugh.*)

JEANNIE: Iss nothin' like Franklin. It's really horrible and Vera thinks it's the best thing that could ever happen to me. They havin' a scholarship dinner tonight, and some of us said we not gonna show. They not gonna stand us up on stage while they beggin' foh money, and Vera talkin' 'bout I ain't got nothin' to do with it 'cause she payin' foh me. She don't know they don't treat me no betta 'cause she payin'. Matter of fact they treat me worse 'cause they think I think I'm as good as them 'cause I'm payin'. Shit, I don't think nothin' like that, I know I'm betta.

539

CAROLYN: Dig it.

JEANNIE: I tried to tell her all that an' she still talkin' 'bout we goin' to it.

CAROLYN: She makin' you go?

JEANNIE: Yeah.

CAROLYN: Well, dig it. Why don't you split. Don't show at the shop neither.

JEANNIE: What?

CAROLYN: Split till it's over. That way she cain't make you go.

JEANNIE: She be worried. (CAROLYN *looks at* JEANNIE *as if to say,* "Well what the fuck you care?") Where should I stay?

CAROLYN: I got someplace you could stay.

JEANNIE: I don't know about that.

CAROLYN: The only way to git people to stop fuckin' with you is to go where they cain't git to you.

JEANNIE: But I ain't never done nothin' like that to Vera before. Splittin'.

CAROLYN: Thas why they don't pay no attention to what we be tellin' 'em. We don't do nothin' to really let them know where we at!

(*Blackness on the kitchen. Lights up on the shop.* VERA *is seated in the swivel chair, dressed in the green suit over which she is wearing a mink stole.* FLORIDA *leans on the window with his back to her.*)

FLORIDA: What you gon do, baby?

VERA (*her head resting on her chin, stares into space at times, rocking rhythmically in her anger*): I oun't know. What time is it?

FLORIDA (*checks his watch*): Nine thirty. What time it suppose to start?

VERA (*staring vacantly, not really talking to* FLORIDA, *but into the air*): Eight.

FLORIDA: Still gonna try to make it? Them kinda things don't start on time. (VERA *doesn't respond.*) Lemme run you on down there an' see whas happenin'. If it's too late, come on back.

VERA: I cain't go in there by myself!

FLORIDA: Why not?

VERA: Jeannie's suppose to be there. They givin' her an award tonight.

FLORIDA: If she don't wanna go, she don't wanna go, baby. You know thas why she didn't show. You pick it up foh her.

VERA: I don't wanna hear that shit!

FLORIDA (*sits on the bench and looks at* VERA): You know, baby, she kinda remind me of you when you was that age.

VERA: When I was her age I was out in the streets an' had been there awhile. I don't mean foh that to happen to Jeannie.

FLORIDA: Maybe thas somethin' you cain't do nothin' about. Your mama couldn't do nothin' with you.

VERA: 'Cause she ain't had nothin'. I had to git it foh myself, and I found out early you git it where you can, however you can.

FLORIDA: I took you off the streets.

VERA: I remember Florida, an' you was good to me too.

FLORIDA: You still split on me.

VERA: It was time.

FLORIDA: Thought you'd gotten all you could. (VERA *is silent. Stands up.*) Imma make it, baby. (*He moves toward the door.*) Don't be too hard on her.

JEANNIE (*stands in the doorway*): Hello, Florida.

FLORIDA: Where you been, girl? (*Turns to* VERA.) Talk to you later, baby. (*Exits.*)

(VERA *doesn't move. Her eyes, full of anger and hatred, are fixed on* JEANNIE.)

JEANNIE (*moves slowly toward* VERA): I uh, uh want to talk to you, Vera. (VERA *continues to stare.*) I tried to tell you this afternoon where I was at. I want you to understand how I feel.

VERA: Where you been?

JEANNIE: With some frens.

VERA: Them same ones you was talking about today??

JEANNIE: Yeah!

VERA (*stares for a two-beat pause*): Come here. (JEANNIE *looks suspicious. Soft voice.*) Come here. (JEANNIE *stands in front of her.* VERA *looks at her, in a lightning move jumps up and socks* JEANNIE *with her fist which knocks the girl up against the waist-high divider.* JEANNIE *stands holding her face, looks at her mother, then runs out of the shop.*) Jeannie! Jeannie! Jeaaaannnieeee!!! Bring yoh lil' ass back in here. You hear me? Jeannie!!

(*Blackness. End of Act I*)

ACT II

(CAROLYN *and* JEANNIE *are seated on a small couch in the living room of* CALVIN's *apartment.*)

CAROLYN: You goin' back?

JEANNIE (*holding the side of her face*): I don't know. Vincent gonna mind me stayin' in y'all apartment?

CAROLYN: It still belong to his brother. We not ready to take it over.

JEANNIE: I didn't know Vincent had a brother.

CAROLYN: Thas 'cause he be in jail so much.

JEANNIE: I can't stay here if he gonna be here.

CAROLYN: He livin' with somebody somewhere else, he just come here once in a while. (*Looks at* JEANNIE.) You betta put some ice on it.

JEANNIE: I guess she really hate me.

CAROLYN: You should uh split foh the whole night.

JEANNIE: I didn't want her to worry. I wanted her to understand.

CAROLYN: You betta understand what you up against. (CALVIN *enters and stands behind the couch.* CAROLYN *hears him and turns.*) Hey now, Calvin. What you doin' here?

(CALVIN *tries to figure out who's next to* CAROLYN. *He goes around to the front.*)

CALVIN: Vera's lil' girl. (*He moves closer, removes her hand from her face.*) Damn baby! What happened to yoh face??

(*Blackness on* CALVIN'*s apartment and lights up on the shop.* SADIE *is seated on the customer's bench reading a newspaper. A cart of clothes is beside her.* VERA *is seated in the swivel chair. She flexes her hand every now and then. It is ten o'clock the following day.*)

SADIE: Them mothafuckers still messin' with the moon. All I need is a lil' uh the money they be usin' to go way the hell out there in space.

VERA: You wouldn't know what to do with it!

SADIE: Who wouldn't. First thing I probably do is fix up mah place.

VERA: First thing you oughta do is move.

SADIE: Why!? If I had me enough money I stay right here an' be happy. Whas wrong wid your hand?

VERA: Sprained it.

SADIE: Soak it in some warm water.

MARAY (*enters*): You in early.

VERA: I stayed 'round to mah mother's last night.

MARAY: How was the dinner?

VERA: Tell you 'bout it later.

SADIE: What dinner?

MARAY: Jeannie's school had a big dinner at the Hilton an' she got an award foh makin' the highest average in her class.

SADIE: Is that right. She use to do the same thing at Franklin. Carolyn say Jeannie was the smartest thing in the school.

VERA: If you wanna know what to do with money, Sadie, you watch the kinda people that sens they kids to that school.

SADIE: Sheet, Vera. They the same mothafuckers what sendin' all mah money up to the moon. They don't know a goddamned thing.

VERA: I mean it, Sadie. You watch them people, they even act a certain way.

SADIE: Yeah. Like a bunch uh pigs, an' I know 'cause I was a maid in they houses foh many a year.

VERA: Well I ain't never been nobody's maid, so I don't know 'bout all that.

SADIE: Florida was takin' care uh you.

VERA: I do know they act different.

SADIE: Thas why you sendin' your daughter 'round them, so she could act different too?!

VERA: No! Uh uh! I know what you tryin' to say, Sadie. I ain't tryin' to make Jeannie be white or act white. I'm just tryin' to give her a chance by starting her in the right direction, which is somethin' most niggas don't do.

SADIE: You full uh shit! You ain't doin' nothin' but messin' up that chile's mind.

VERA: I admit it'll take her a lil' time to understand what I'm doin' foh her. If mah mother could uh done foh me what I'm doin' foh her I be somethin' today.

SADIE: Oh you ain't nothin'!?

VERA: You know what I mean, Sadie! Startin' our kids off right is somethin' a lot uh us just don't take the time to do. I got customers comin' in here every day with somethin' to say 'bout they kids in trouble. This one on dope, that one pregnant, the other one in jail. It don't make no sense. Thas why I took her outta Franklin and moved from around here. She cain't be nothin' 'round people like that.

SADIE: So you put her 'round the white people. Humph! How she like it?

VERA: Like I say. It'll take her a lil' time to git use to it.

SADIE: She stopped by to see Carolyn yesterday.

VERA: Jeannie was to your house? What time?

MARAY: Oh thas where she went. She musta stayed a long time 'cause she hadn't got back when I left. I know y'all musta been late gettin' there.

SADIE: She ain't stay too long 'cause when I got home she was gone. Which remind me y'all got any work Carolyn can

543

do down here? She need somethin' to help her pass the time. She goin' to school in the mornin', but she got the whole afternoon an' evenin' free.

VERA: I thought they put you out if you was havin' a baby.

SADIE: I found me a school thas foh pregnant girls. Like I tole her, just 'cause you havin' a baby don't mean the world gots to stop. Go learn how to take care of it 'cause I sure ain't. I done had mines.

MARAY: I got some wigs I need set. I can't pay too much.

SADIE: Thas okay. Be a way foh her to make a lil' change an' help her to pass the time.

MARAY: Maybe she could come in once in a while an' help me wid my shampooin'.

VERA (*annoyed*): Maray, you ain't got *that* many customers. You could do your own shampooin'. Have that girl in here reachin' an stretchin' over people.

MARAY (*struck by* VERA's *attitude*): Not for a couple uh months yet.

VERA: You could send them wigs right on up to her so's she don't have to be goin' up and down stairs.

MARAY: I like foh her to work right here so's I can see what she doin'.

SADIE: You betta let her work here les you want them wigs to look like the one thas on mah head. 'Cause them kids uh mines sure'll git to 'em.

VERA: What I tell you yesterday?

SADIE: What you tell her?

VERA: That you don't take care uh nothin' you got an' never did.

SADIE: Oh y'all was talkin' 'bout me huh?

MARAY: No, 'bout your wig.

SADIE: Yeah, this shit do look bad. An' I got me a dance to go to on Sattiday. Where mah new wig?

VERA: When you payin' me foh the ole one?

SADIE: What you mean? I paid you foh this.

VERA: No, you didn't, Sadie.

SADIE: Don't tell me, Vera. I paid you foh this wig. (VERA *opens the drawer and takes out her black book.*) Whas that?

VERA: A book I'm startin' to keep foh niggas who forgets how much they owe.

SADIE: Oh you into that kinda shit now, huh? Ain't this a bitch. This woman out her mind keepin' books on people an' shit. I don't give a fuck what yoh book say, I know I paid you foh this shit you sold me.

VERA: You ain't give me but twenty-five dollars.

SADIE: Thas right. Like I told you, I paid you.

VERA: You still owe me fifty.

SADIE: How much do the mothafucker cost??

VERA: You know I told you I was lettin' you have this hunnert-dollar wig foh seventy-five.

SADIE: You ain't told me no shit like that. In the first place I cain't afford no seventy-five-dollar wig. In the second place, even if I could, this shit whas on mah head ain't worth no seventy-five dollars.

VERA: Thas why I don't like to deal with no niggas, you hear me.

SADIE: Well, you got yoh shop in the wrong block. Look at this shit, Maray. (*Snatches it off her head.*) Bald as a monkey's ass an' I ain't had it but three months an' she talkin' some shit 'bout seventy-five dollars!?

VERA: Wasn't like that when you bought it.

SADIE: You wouldn't believe we been knowin' each other ever since we was ten an' . . .

VERA: I ain't hear all this out yoh mouth when you walked out the shop with it on yoh head.

SADIE: An' she pullin' this kinda shit one me.

VERA: Everybody gotta make a livin'.

SADIE: You ain't got to kill me while you doin' it! Lemme git on to the laundromat. (*She moves to the door with her clothes.*) Vera, Imma give you some more money on this thing. (*Puts her wig on.*) But I be goddamned if Imma pay you any seventy-five dollars 'cause you an' me both know you just full uh shit. And if was anybody else but you, you can be sure I kick they ass foh tryin' to pull that kinda shit on me! (*Exits.*)

MARAY: Vera, I don't see how you could do it. I couldn't do nothin' like that to mah customer much less mah fren.

VERA (*turns and looks at* MARAY): Thas why you still here rentin' from me an' don't own a goddamned thing!

(*Blackness on the shop and lights up on* CALVIN's *apartment.* JEANNIE *is seated on the couch listening to Yusef Lateef's "Trouble in Mind."* CALVIN *enters, crosses behind the couch, goes to the room offstage.*)

CALVIN (*offstage*): Where's Carolyn?

JEANNIE: I didn't hear you. She comin' over later.

CALVIN: You talk to Vera??

JEANNIE: No.

CALVIN: You eat??

JEANNIE: Uh huh.

CALVIN: What?

JEANNIE: I went out and got some fish an' potatoes.

CALVIN: There's food in the box. Can't you cook, girl?

JEANNIE: A little.

CALVIN: A little, huh? (*Comes out with woman's lounge robe on his arm, African style.*) You like this? (*He holds it up.*)

JEANNIE: It's pretty.

CALVIN: Yeh. I picked it up foh one uh mah customers. She's about your size. Do me a favor, baby, an' try it on.

JEANNIE: Why??

CALVIN: I wanna see if it'll fit her. If it's her size.

JEANNIE: All you gotta do is look at the tag on the neck.

CALVIN: Yeah. But I wanna see how it looks.

JEANNIE: No, I don't think so.

CALVIN: This ain't come outta no black people's house, if thas what you worried about.

JEANNIE: I know, it came straight from the Man's factory.

CALVIN: Yeah. Well??? (JEANNIE *shakes her head negative.*) Whas wrong?? (JEANNIE *doesn't answer.* CALVIN *drops the robe in her lap.*) Here, baby, go in there an' put it on foh me. (*He sits, becomes busy with his shoes, socks, etc.* JEANNIE *looks at* CALVIN *and then slowly rises, goes to the room offstage.* CALVIN *changes the records. Lowers the lights. He returns to the couch, lights a joint, smokes.* JEANNIE *comes out and stands at the entrance to the room.*) Um hmm. Yeah. Come here. (JEANNIE *doesn't move.*) Come here, girl. (JEANNIE *moves a little nearer.*) Damn, baby, I ain't gonna bite you. (JEANNIE *walks and stands in front of him.*) Ummmm hmmm? Turn around. (JEANNIE *turns around stiffly.*) Don't you know how to, you know—(JEANNIE *raises her arms and turns slowly.*) Yeah. Walk over there. (JEANNIE *walks quickly to the other end.*) Slow down. Um hmm, yeah, okay. I think she oughta like that. What you think?

JEANNIE: Uh huh. (*She starts to the other room.*)

CALVIN: Where you goin'?

JEANNIE: To take it off.

CALVIN: Wait a minute, I wanna talk to you. Come here. (JEANNIE *walks over to the couch. He pulls her down next to him.*) You goin' back home?

JEANNIE: I don't know.

CALVIN: What you gonna do?

JEANNIE: I don't know yet.

CALVIN: You betta start thinkin' about it, baby. Vera probably got the pigs out lookin' for you now. You betta decide on what you gonna do. Goin' back or cuttin' loose.

(*They sit and listen to the sounds, not speaking for a long period.*)

JEANNIE: I'll git a job.

CALVIN: How old are you, baby?

JEANNIE: Sixteen.

CALVIN: You ever work before?

JEANNIE: No.

CALVIN: Your mom's somethin' else, I wonda what she think she was gettin' you ready foh. I really like to know whas goin' on in her mind. (*They listen to the music.*) How's your face?

JEANNIE: Still sore.

CALVIN: You been puttin' ice on it?

JEANNIE: Um hmm, it went down some.

CALVIN: Lemme see. (*Holds her chin with one hand, turns her face to the side.*) Damn, baby, what she hit you with, baby? Her fist? (CALVIN *kisses her cheek, her eyes, her ear.* JEANNIE *tries to move.*) Hold still, lil' girl. Everything's gonna be all right.

(*Blackness on* CALVIN'*s apartment and lights up on the shop.* MARAY *has a customer seated under a heat cap.* VERA *sits in the swivel chair staring into space. The radio is playing and news is being broadcast.*)

MARAY: Thought you didn't like the news.

VERA: What? (*The phone rings. She jumps to answer it.* MARAY *watches her.*) Paradise . . . No, Mama. I'll call you when I do. (*Hangs up.*)

(SADIE *enters with a cart of just-washed clothes. The radio announces four o'clock.*)

SADIE: Jerry been in here yet?

VERA: No.

SADIE: How your hand?

VERA: Okay.

SADIE: Betta soak it like I tole you.

MARAY: What happened to your hand, Vera?

VERA: I sprained it.

MARAY: At the dinner?

VERA: No. Sadie, when you see Jerry, tell him I got a couple uh numbers I wanna do somethin' with.

SADIE: When I see that mothafucker won't be no time to deliver no messages. I ain't seen no kinda money out that man. I mean I am really tired uh his shit.

VERA: You always sayin' that. I don't see you goin' no-where.

SADIE: Where I'm goin' with six kids? 'Sides I ain't like you.

547

You walked out on your man foh . . . (SADIE *sees* JEROME *passing in front of the window.*) Jerry, Jerry. (JEROME *continues to walk.*) Now you know that man hear me. 'Scuse me a minute y'all. (SADIE *steps out into the street.*) Jeeerome! Jeerome!

JEROME: What you want, Sadie!?

SADIE: Some money, man.

JEROME: You gotta wait, baby. Florida's around, I gotta take care uh some business.

SADIE: I don't give a fuck who around. I want mah money. I got six uh yoh kids to feed and ain't nothin' in that house.

JEROME: I told you to wait. Now stop fuckin' with me. (*He walks away.*)

SADIE: You always got somethin' to spen on that bitch in 1422. But when it come to me an' your kids you ain't never got nothin'! (JEROME *continues to walk, ignoring her.* SADIE *runs after him.*) Lemme see what's in your fucken pockets. (JEROME *turns and pushes* SADIE *away from him.*) You gon have to beat mah ass out here today, Jerry.

JEROME: You keep fuckin' wid me out here and Imma do just that.

SADIE: I ain't goin' back in that house with no money. You ain't got to turn it all in to Florida.

(*All of the women in the shop are watching the fight.* VERA *stands in the doorway.*)

VERA: All right, goddamnit! You niggas move on down a couple uh doors with that shit, you breakin' up mah store.

SADIE: Fuck yoh store, bitch. (JERRY *has moved offstage.* SADIE *turns to continue, sees that he is gone, runs off after him.*) Jerry! That mothafucker!

(CAROLYN *enters, stands near the door of the shop and watches her* PARENTS.)

VERA: Maray. You see Carolyn. Looka that. Watching her mother carryin' on like that in the street.

(MARAY *moves to the door, sees* CAROLYN. *Sound of slap is heard.*)

JEROME: Didn't I tell you to stop fuckin' wid me!

SADIE (*hollers*): Ow, Jerry. Don't do that!

MARAY (*to* CAROLYN): Carolyn. Why don't you come in here and sit down.

JEROME (*slaps* SADIE): Told you I had some business to take care of.

SADIE (*crying sounds*): Why it gotta be like this all the time?

CAROLYN: I'm all right.

SADIE: Why you cain't do right.

JEROME: Here, bitch.

SADIE: That ain't enough, Jerry!

JEROME: Thas all you gettin', now git the fuck out mah face!

SADIE: This ain't enough, Jerry. I got food to buy. I owe Vera some money, I need to git me somethin' foh the dance on Sattiday. Jerry— (*Calls after him.* SADIE *reappears on stage, exhausted. She walks toward the shop and sees* CAROLYN.) Carolyn. Go in there an' talk to Maray. She got some wigs she want you to set. (CAROLYN *turns and walks away.*) Carolyn! (SADIE *enters the shop and notices that* MARAY's *customer is looking at her.*) What the fuck you lookin' at!

VERA: All right, now, Sadie.

MARAY: Now that ain't necessary, Sadie.

(SADIE *places five dollars on* VERA's *counter.*)

VERA: Whas this?? Five dollars.

SADIE: You don't expect me to give you all.

VERA: I couldn't go through that kinda shit to git money out a man.

SADIE: Thas cause you ain't never had to do it. And you ain't got no six kids.

VERA: Go to work. Take care uh yourself.

SADIE: Whas suppose to happen to mah family?

VERA: Be better'en what you goin' through now to feed 'em. Carolyn was standin' right there watchin' y'all. I saw her walk away from you.

SADIE: She'll cool out.

(FLORIDA *enters and walks over to the partition that divides the two booths.*)

FLORIDA: What you mean jammin' mah man up in the street like that, Sadie?

SADIE: A nigga that do right don't git jammed up!

FLORIDA: You betta check yourself, woman.

VERA (*nervous*): What you doin' round here so early? (*She begins to flex her hand.*)

FLORIDA: See how you doin'.

VERA: I'm makin' it.

FLORIDA: How's Jeannie? (VERA *looks at him.*) Talked to her grandmother. You found her yet?

SADIE: Found her?

VERA: No.

FLORIDA: What you doin' in this shop?!

VERA: I'm waitin' to hear from her, Florida.

SADIE: Where is she, Vera?

549

VERA: Ask yoh daughter. She was the last one to see her.

SADIE: What you talkin' 'bout?

VERA: This ain't right, Florida.

MARAY: Vera? What happened?

SADIE: You know what happened, Maray. She got tired uh Vera's shit.

VERA: I don't appreciate you puttin' mah business in the street like this.

FLORIDA: Was Jeannie with Carolyn, Sadie?

SADIE: Yeah but that was early in the afternoon, and she didn't stay long 'cause when I got upstairs she was gone.

FLORIDA: You ask Carolyn what they talk about?

SADIE: That school Vera got Jeannie in. She say Jeannie tole her she hate it but Vera think iss the best thing could happen to her.

(FLORIDA *looks at* VERA *who has been nursing her hand throughout the conversation.*)

FLORIDA: Whas wrong wid your hand?

VERA (*weakly*): I sprained it.

(FLORIDA *and* VERA *look at one another.* VERA *looks away.*)

FLORIDA: How?

VERA (*weakly*): I don't see what you got to do with it, Florida.

FLORIDA: You *know* what I got to do wid it, baby.

MARAY: How long she been gone? Vera! How long the girl been gone?

VERA: Since last night.

MARAY: You call the pohlees?

VERA: No.

MARAY: How you know that girl ain out in the street dead somewhere!

SADIE: You see how Vera was sittin' in here actin' like everythin' was everythin'.

VERA: She probably stayin' with one uh them frens uh hers.

FLORIDA: When you gettin' on the phone to find out?

VERA: I don't have they numbers, Florida.

FLORIDA: Where can you get 'em?

VERA: From the school. But she probably be back when she ready.

SADIE: Vera don't want them white people at the school to know Jeannie split on her. That girl could rot out there an it'd be all right long as they don't know 'bout it.

VERA: Stay outta mah business, Sadie!

SADIE: I knew you wasn't doin' nothin' but confusin' that chile.

MARAY: So y'all didn't git to go to the big dinner, after all.

SADIE: An' thas 'cause you confuse yourself. Always been that way.

MARAY: She say you didn't really care nothin' 'bout how she felt.

SADIE: Sittin' there like nothin' was wrong an' the girl out in the streets all night. And you ain't told nobody and ain't doin' nothin' to find her, I wonda whas goin' on in yoh mind, Vera. (*Lateef's "Trouble in Mind" plays softly.*) Takin' her outta Franklin, where everybody knew her.

VERA: What was you tryin' to prove, Florida?

FLORIDA: Tryin' to find Jeannie, baby.

SADIE: Carolyn say Jeannie really hate it there.

MARAY: Vera, all she wanted to do was stick with the other black kids.

SADIE: Puttin' her in some strange white school so she could act different.

VERA: Thas right. So she don't end up like Carolyn.

SADIE: Carolyn's a lot better off en your child.

VERA: You think so. I rather foh her to be dead than end up like Carolyn.

SADIE: Imma act like you ain't said that.

VERA: I don't expect you to understand nothin' I was tryin' to do foh mah child. I don't expect you to understand my tryin' to give her a life thas different.

SADIE: You really want your child to be different from you.

VERA: Damn right I do! Different from me, from you, from Carolyn, from Florida, from Maray, from all uh us. (*Indicating the audience.*)

SADIE: Humph. (*Looks off.*)

VERA: I know what you thinkin', Sadie. I know whas on your mind. After all the money an' all the time I spent on her, I ain't got no further with Jeannie than you did with Carolyn. But I'd do it again, and again, and again even. 'Cause I rather foh her to turn up dead than to end up like Carolyn, repeatin' mah life all over. 'Cause if it cain't be no different foh her than it was foh me, no sense in her livin'.

SADIE: Well I guess she daid then. 'Cause damn sure ain't nothin' different 'bout her now. She out there in the streets like you and me when we was that age. You dig. An' you betta hope she find a man's good to her as Florida was to you.

BLACKNESS

Strictly Matrimony

A COMEDY IN ONE ACT
by ERROL HILL

Errol Hill, who was born in Trinidad, West Indies, is professor of drama at Dartmouth College, Hanover, New Hampshire. Trained at the Royal Academy of Dramatic Art in London, England, and at the Yale School of Drama, Mr. Hill functions as actor, director, playwright, as well as teacher and scholar. His West Indian folk musical, *Man Better Man*, was produced by the Negro Ensemble Company in 1969 while he was appearing as Othello and directing *The Royal Hunt of the Sun* with the Dartmouth Summer Repertory Company. His book on the theatrical elements of the Trinidad carnival is soon to be published.

CHARACTERS

MANNY BONAPARTE, a strapping laborer
BELLA, his common-law wife
SLICK, Bella's half-brother, who lives by his wits
LADY POLLY LOVE-MUGGINS, a socialite
THE REVEREND TIMOTHY SHRIMP, a clergyman

SCENE: Manny's house in the Jamaican countryside.

Scene 1

(*The house in which* MANNY BONAPARTE *and his common-law wife,* BELLA, *live is a one-room cottage in the Jamaican countryside. This single room serves as living, dining, and sleeping quarters, and although the furniture is necessarily crowded in, the room presents an appearance of cosy tidiness. One section, cut off by a folding screen, is used as a bedroom and holds a four-poster bed whose canopy spreads a starched white sheet across that part of the board ceiling. A curtain stretched between the screen and the wall covers the entrance to the bedroom. Over the top of the screen are thrown certain items of a workingman's attire: dirty shirt, trousers, and vest.*

The furniture in the visible part of the room is strong and roughly made. Down close to the audience are two straight-back chairs, a rocker, and a center table with a vase of flowers.

553

*On the wall are a mirror and some passe-partout pictures of
the family and friends. This serves as the sitting room. Immediately above this is a dining table and two chairs, a wire safe,
a washstand and, on the back wall, a shelf from which hang
cups, pots, and pans. This is the dining area. The table is laid
for one.*

Sunday morning. The village church bell clangs noisily.
BELLA *is on the back doorstep bending over a coal pot preparing breakfast. She is an honest, hard-working type, endowed
with an amplitude of feminine virtues which she happily sur-
renders to her man. At the moment, she is busily fanning the
coals and singing a hymn. Her lucid notes wrestle with the
nerve-racking clangor of the church bells. And, as if these
were not enough to disturb the peace of Sunday morning, the
duet is joined by the heavy snoring of* MANNY *who is asleep
behind the screen.*

BELLA *sets out breakfast on table. It consists of a large
flour bake, run-down mackerel, and a mug of cocoa. She goes
to the curtained opening and calls into the bedroom.*)

BELLA: Manny! Wake up, wake up, boy. Day break long.

MANNY (*off*): Eh . . . oh . . . what time it is there?

BELLA: Time to get up. Nine gone.

MANNY (*off*): Gone! Why you didn't call me before?

BELLA: You always say don't rouse you when you sleeping.

(MANNY *appears around the curtain. He is not quite awake
and speaks drowsily.*)

MANNY: But how come the clock didn't alarm this morning? You mean I going late for work again!

BELLA: Late for work! What wrong with you, boy, you
stale drunk? Is Sunday morning.

MANNY: Sunday! Yes, in truth. Well, what the hell you
disturb my sleep for? I tired tell you when Sunday come . . .

BELLA: Tea ready. I don't want it get cold. (*She gets a
duster, begins to wipe off the furniture, singing meanwhile.*)

MANNY: I going back and catch my second nap. You could
hot over the tea later. (*He retires.* BELLA *sings more loudly.*)
Bella, what for you keeping so much noise in my head? (*She
persists.* MANNY *reenters the room.*) You gone crazy or what?
I ask you again: What you shouting so for?

BELLA: Big Sunday morning you want to sleep till sun-high.

MANNY: When else I going sleep then. "Six days thou shall
labor and rest the seventh." I breaking my back Monday till
Saturday from sun up to nightfall. When I going sleep late if
not Sunday.

BELLA: Your tea getting cold. You better eat it. I don't have no time to warm it over.

MANNY: No time to warm it over? But what wrong with you this morning, Bella? First thing, you stir before cock-crow. Big Sunday, you don't even stay abed to pass a little time with me. Next thing, you make the tea before sleep well leave my eye and you start harassing me to eat it. And third to begin with, you singing in my ears as if judgment come and St. Peter ask you to wake the dead. What wrong with you?

(*While he speaks,* BELLA *pours water into the washbasin, gets a towel from the bedroom and puts it on his arm, then continues dusting.* MANNY *shrugs his shoulders and goes to wash up. He keeps glancing at* BELLA, *who is vigorously tidying the room.*)

MANNY: You feed the fowls?

BELLA: Yes. One of Rosa chickens dead.

MANNY: You milk the goat?

BELLA: Yes. I think is time you fix the piece of fencing.

MANNY: But why she so brisk-brisk today? (*He draws on his trousers.* BELLA *pulls out a chair at the dining table for him. He sits.*) You eat already?

BELLA: No. I had a cup of coffee.

MANNY: Where your plate then?

BELLA: I will eat what you leave.

MANNY: None of that. When Sunday come I like my wife to sit down beside me at table. If we poor self we could still behave like decent people. Sunday is the one day of the week we have together.

BELLA: Hmph! (*She sits.* MANNY *fetches a plate, cup, and spoon for her. They begin to eat.*)

MANNY: I like Sunday breakfast. No hustlement. And I like how you does prepare my meal good.

BELLA: I glad.

MANNY: You's a good woman, Bella. If is no lie you have your little contrariness. A man couldn't ask for nothing better. (*He slaps her fondly on her buttocks.*)

BELLA: So you say.

MANNY: I mean it. You know, work ain't sweet and when I out there on the wharf lifting old load and that foulmouth foreman bawling out his liver string after me, I does feel sometimes to throw up the whole caboodle and go away to England or someplace. Then I remember you. I remember how on a Sunday we does sit down peaceful-like and talk together and eat good food and thing. And I decide to stick my grind. It worth it.

BELLA: That's good.

MANNY: Eat some more, nuh? You finish already?

BELLA: Yes. What about you?

MANNY: I done too. My stomach feel a little upside-down after last night.

BELLA (*begins to clear table*): Well, take a bath and tidy yourself while I wash up the things.

MANNY (*sits on rocker*): Come over here, nuh.

BELLA: What you want?

MANNY: Draw nearer. I ain't going bite you.

BELLA (*up to him*): Yes? (MANNY *makes a sudden lunge and pulls her down on his lap, laughing. He begins to fondle and kiss her as she struggles.*) Oh shucks, man, you going ramfle up my hair and my clothes!

MANNY: What I care about clothes. You shouldn't have on none. Come, give me a little love-up, girl.

BELLA: Take time, take time with me, I say. I busy bad this morning.

MANNY: You too busy to kiss me? What is this at all? (*He kisses her flush on the lips.*) After all, we is man and wife.

BELLA: I not your wife.

MANNY: Eh?

BELLA: I say I is not your wife.

MANNY: Well who wife you is, then? Gombo Li-Li?

BELLA: I is your concubine.

MANNY: My how much?

BELLA: Your concubine. Look it up in the Bible what you always quoting. It write down there in black and white. You like to talk decency but you ain't talk the right thing yet.

MANNY: What you telling me at all?

BELLA: I saying that I not your lawful wife.

MANNY (*pushes her off and gets up*): And what you bringing that up for now, sudden-like?

BELLA: Yes, you don't want to hear the truth, because you know you wrong.

MANNY: Know I wrong? Woman, what fool-fool thing you talking?

BELLA: I talking plain as day. If you don't like the song, is up to you to change the tune.

MANNY: Talk straight, girl. Come out from behind the pretty-pretty word and talk straight.

BELLA: You don't want to hear the word mention, but I will mention it: Matrimony.

MANNY: Look, Bella, is Sunday morning. The Lord give us

this day to rest and relax. Don't disturb it with no marriage talk. Is years we living together ...

BELLA: Living in sin.

MANNY: All right—in sin. We born in sin. So the Book say. We in it already and we might as well stay there so longst we happy.

BELLA: My eyes was close. Now they open.

MANNY: Okay, open them. Only don't see no marriage contract write up on the wall. You know what I think about that already.

BELLA: Time going. I have to clear the table.

MANNY: Pass me a cigarette there and ask Jamesy if he finish with the newspaper.

BELLA: And I think you hadst better tidy yourself before you loll off. In case anybody come.

MANNY (*gets cigarette himself and settles down in rocker*): Anybody like who? You expecting company?

BELLA: You never know who to drop in after church. (*She brings him bath towel and soap.*)

MANNY (*laughing*): All right, missis, I know you have some sort of surprise cook up for me. But tell me who you expecting, nuh? I hope is not your half-brother, Slick. The last time he come here all the silvers vanish like smoke.

BELLA: Slick never thief nothing. (*She takes the garments off the screen and folds them up.*)

MANNY: I didn't say he thief, nuh? But I think the knives and forks get up off the table and walk down the road after him. Slick must be had magnet in his pocket.

BELLA: He borrow them for an "At Home" and somebody misplace them. He promise to pay us back when he working.

MANNY: That is when cock have teeth.

BELLA: Well, he working now.

MANNY: How you know that? Slick come by here since last time? (*A silence.*) Answer me, Bella.

BELLA: Give the boy a break, nuh? Because he get in a little scrape once you always charging him.

MANNY: What he come here for?

BELLA: Slick get a work in the district. He come to tell me.

MANNY: You check all the things. I miss a gray pants three days now.

BELLA: Is I send it to the laundry. Give the boy a break! He get a respectable work with the white people and he coming to make a visit this morning after church with important company. So I begging you please to behave yourself and don't disgrace me.

MANNY: Well, Slick take up religion now. When the devil start going to church, zip up your pocket quick-sharp.

BELLA: Come off the boy back, nuh!

MANNY: All right. I ain't going pass on him till he try. But so help me, this time he better walk good. As he slip, he slide with me.

BELLA: Go on and bathe. Church nearly over.

(MANNY *goes out through the back door.* BELLA *resumes her tidying. A face shows at the window. It is* SLICK.)

SLICK: Pss . . . pss . . . Bella!

BELLA: Hey! Is you Slick?

SLICK: Eh-heh. Where Manny?

BELLA: Bathing.

SLICK: Is all right to come in?

BELLA: Yes, man. But watch your step with him.

(SLICK *enters through the front door. He is handsomely decked out in a neat-fitting parson-gray suit and a gray felt hat. He holds a briefcase under his arm.*)

BELLA: Church over already? Where the white lady?

SLICK: She coming later with the parson-feller. I couldn't take no more of that sermon. The man is a mamapoule. He ain't long come out from England. If you hear the stupidness pop out his mouth. He must be think because people black they ignorant, nuh? All you take tea yet?

BELLA: Just finish. You want some?

SLICK: Tumble a sandwich on me. And something to wash it down with.

BELLA: I make bake this morning.

SLICK: All going the same place. (BELLA *prepares a tray for* SLICK. *He picks a flower from the vase and places it in his buttonhole.*) This work I doing well hard, you know. No rest, not even on Sunday. Look me, dress up to kill, like I going to Grace Kelly wedding, nine o'clock in the hot morning sun when I should be coasting an old sleep.

BELLA: Anyhow you looking well sharp.

SLICK: Is Lady Love-Muggins give me this outfit. How you like it? The tie is my own. I think she catch a fall for the old style, you know. Me with my sweet talk and nice ways and the old Alan Ladd smile.

BELLA: You ain't playing you like yourself, nuh, Slick! (*She hands him the tray.*)

SLICK: That look good. I had was to hustle off to church this morning before I finish eat good. And I was damn near late too. The parson-man talk out all the food in my belly. (*He begins to eat.*)

BELLA: Before Manny come back inside, you better prime me up what to say.

SLICK: You tell him anything yet?

BELLA: I drop a few spratt, but he ain't biting. His face set against this marriage business like is jail self.

SLICK: Don't fret. Polly going fix him up good-good.

BELLA: Who Polly that?

SLICK: Lady Love-Muggins. Between you, me and the bed-post, I does call her Polly sometimes—in private. She have a likeness for spades.

BELLA: Boy, you too rude. (*They smile together understandingly.*) Tell me again how you does convince people to do this thing, nuh?

SLICK: Charm, Bella, just charm. And after I hypnotize them I hit them couple few smart words, you know, like how the cost of living going up and withouten you married, nobody don't respect you; you is a conks . . . a conks . . .

BELLA: Concubine.

SLICK: Yes, something so. But mostly, is charm.

(MANNY *comes in, half-dressed. He pauses at the back door and looks steadily at* SLICK *who returns his look with uneasiness.* MANNY *bursts out laughing and comes forward.*)

MANNY: Hey, Slick boy, you look as if is the last supper you eating. What happen, friend?

SLICK (*much relieved*): How you do, Manny.

MANNY: I there, man. Sit down and finish eat. I hear you working now. You bring the money for the silvers and them what you thief . . . I mean, lost? (*He puts on a shirt and tie during the scene.* BELLA *removes the tray and goes behind the screen to change her dress.*)

SLICK: I land this job only last week. But I promise you as soon . . .

MANNY: Slick, your promise same like Moses and the promised land. It never reach. Where you working?

SLICK (*begins to feel more at home. He pulls out a cigar and lights up*): I employ with the S.P.P.W.R.

MANNY: Tonnerre!! What it mean in English?

SLICK: The full name is the Society for the Protection and Preservation of Women's Rights.

MANNY: God almighty!

BELLA (*off*): It spread all over the world. Slick belong to a branch here that run by a social lady name Lady Polly Love-Muggins.

MANNY: You really climbing high this time. Take care you fall, boy.

SLICK: Easy-cai, man. Don't frighten for Slick. Look, nuh, is after ten. All you ain't ready yet? (*He goes to window and looks out.*)

MANNY: Ready for what?

SLICK: Bella didn't tell you?

BELLA (*coming out*): Slick invite the new parson and Lady Love-Muggins to come and meet us after prayers.

MANNY: Oh-ho! And you bound to make so much fuss about that?

SLICK: See them coming down the road now! I best hadst give all you a few ideas how to behave in social company.

BELLA: Listen good, Manny. We don't want to shame weself in front the white people and them.

MANNY: Nobody ain't ask them to come here. What you exciting-up yourself for?

SLICK: All right now. When her ladyship reach, everybody must stand up and you must say: "Honored to meet you, my lady." Don't stick out your hand until she put out hers; and, if you want, Bella, to make a good impression, you could drop a little curtsy, like this. (*He demonstrates awkwardly,* BELLA *following him.*) And you, Manny, you should . . .

MANNY: Look, saga-boy, maybe this house ain't no palace, but I is king in it. If Lady Love-bird don't like it here, she could fly back where she come from.

BELLA: Behave yourself, nuh, boy!

(LADY POLLY'*s voice is heard off. She speaks rapidly and unceasingly, in a high-pitched, near-falsetto and penetrating voice, punctuating her flow of language with occasional burbles of laughter. She is a tall, well-proportioned woman with striking blond hair framing a handsome, if masculine, face. Her manner is authoritative and slightly condescending, with a trace of vulgarity. She is talking now to the* REVEREND TIMOTHY SHRIMP *as they come through the Bonapartes' front gate.*)

LADY POLLY (*off*): And so, my dear Reverend, I would strongly advise you to consider giving up this outmoded theological jargon and come straight to the point. Who wants to be a soldier of the Lord? What does it mean? There's too much war in the world altogether. Talk about everyday problems, if you see what I mean . . . (SLICK *opens the front door and stands there like a commissionaire.* BELLA *and* MANNY *rise.* LADY POLLY *sweeps in.*) Oh, how do you do? I'm so pleased to meet you both. (*She takes their hands.*) Mr. Bonaparte, isn't it, and Miss er . . . Miss er . . . Of course, we understand, don't we? (*She emits a ripple of laughter.*) Bonaparte, such a lovely name, so romantic, so vigorous, so full of history. I

always think, don't you, what a pity he was so diminutive. I mean Napoleon, of course. I like tall, well-built men. You, Mr. Bonaparte, you couldn't be more admirably suited to the name. What a splendid torso you have, if you don't mind my mentioning it. Robust and er . . . virile, no doubt. Well, let's be seated, shall we? You sit there, Mrs. Bona . . . I mean, Miss . . . well, my dear, what shall we call you?

MANNY: She name Bella.

BELLA: But in the village I goes by the name of Miss Bonaparte.

LADY POLLY: Yes, well we'll call you Bella—for the present. It's much simpler. You sit over there, Mr. Bonaparte can sit here beside me. Crawford, you'd better sit on my other side. Now we're all set. Oh, Mr. Shrimp!

(SHRIMP *has been hovering half-in and half-out of the front door. He is a little man, middle-aged, quite out of his depth in this environment, terrified of* LADY POLLY, *and longing for the seclusion of his rural English parsonage.*)

LADY POLLY: Come along in and find a seat, Mr. Shrimp. I suppose it's necessary to have a representative of the church here? Now we're all set. Ah, by the way, I imagine you know Mr. Shrimp? He's the new minister. Mr. Shrimp, Mr. and Mrs. er . . . I mean, Mr. Bonaparte and his er . . . Well now, I daresay that Mr. Crawford told you I represent the S.P.P.W.R., a worldwide organization whose sacred duty it is to protect and preserve the rights of women everywhere. I'm president of the local branch and I'm sure our Mr. Crawford prepared you for . . .

MANNY (*lugubriously cutting in to assert his headship*): Excuse me, missis, I not too sure what all this is about, but my mind tell me . . .

LADY POLLY: What your mind tells you, Mr. Bonaparte, is really of no interest to us here, I think? Yours is a passive role in this affair. You must listen and when the appropriate time comes, act. (*She pats his hand affectionately and adds.*) You big, strong man. (*A burble of laughter.*) As I was saying, the purpose of our visit is to enlighten you on the moral, social, and economic dangers of the sort of relationship you have both condoned for some years now, I believe? (*The question, requiring no confirmation, is directed at* SLICK. *He nods assent.*) This relationship, I regret to say, though very prevalent in this country, is indefensible on social, ethical, or legal grounds, and can lead only to untold complications and unhappiness. That is why the S.P.P.W.R. is doing all it can to remove this blemish on the good name of Jamaican women.

561

And remove it we shall in this village, and throughout the island, with the aid of people like Mr. Crawford here and Mr. Shrimp . . . Mr. Shrimp! (SHRIMP *is dozing away in a corner. He starts up guiltily.*) Really, Mr. Shrimp, didn't you sleep well last night or were you otherwise engaged—at your age too. Hmph! Well, as I was saying, socially, Mr. Bonaparte, your mate is an outcast unless she can carry your full name.

MANNY: I don't stop her using it.

LADY POLLY: That's not the point. She has no legal right to it. We hardly know how to address her. It's embarrassing, to say the least. You can't be invited out together, she is, in a way, deprived of playing her full role as a leader in the social life of the village. This is bound to make her dissatisfied and unhappy.

MANNY: Bella and me been living together happy for six years and we never had no trouble till all you come and put this marriage talk in her head. That ain't true, Bella?

LADY POLLY: Ah, but think what you've been missing all these years, both of you. Now we turn to the legal side of the matter. Mr. Crawford, will you . . . ?

SLICK (*takes out a notebook from his briefcase and makes a show of consulting it*): Well, yes, as I was saying, the legal side. For instance, to begin with, living in conks . . . conks . . .

LADY POLLY: . . . Living in concubinage means that the woman is not entitled by law to anything that her husband possesses and, in case of death, she has no claim to his estate. She has no security, her so-called husband can walk out on her at any time, and where there are children, the responsibility is entirely hers. For though the law can compel a man to contribute toward the upkeep of his offspring, it is incumbent on the mother to prove who the father is; and that's not easy nowadays. (*A tinkle of laughter.*) All this is very complicated, of course, and I don't expect you, Mr. Bonaparte, to understand the intricacies of the law. I merely cite a few instances to show you how much you stand to lose by persisting in this sham liaison.

MANNY: Nothing sham about it. If Bella and me like it so, I don't see why all you have to interfere.

LADY POLLY: But we don't live unto ourselves. There are others to consider. And now, here is where Mr. Shrimp comes in. He will explain the attitude of the church in this matter.

SHRIMP (*his big moment has come. He rises, clears his throat, and prepares to deliver his sermon*): It is written: "He that covereth his sins shall not prosper." Though we're all

of us sinners, in the sight of God, it behooves each and every one of us to search our hearts . . .

LADY POLLY: Yes . . . I really think, Mr. Shrimp, we can defer this heart-searching to another occasion? Sometime, perhaps, when you can conveniently probe with Mr. Bonaparte and his er . . . wife? In camera? Good. Now we have one or two small details to settle and then you can sign the documents. First of all, in case you're worried about the finances. Let me reassure you that all expenses of the wedding will be borne by my Society. The ring will come from America, the shoes from Italy, the hat from Paris. The wives of twelve different countries will be contributing to your wedding. The bride's dress, of course, will have to be made here, but we have received the most exquisite silk from China only last week. I'd better have your measurements right away. (*She produces a measuring tape from her handbag and hands it to* SLICK. *He passes it on to* SHRIMP *and signals to him that he must take* BELLA's *measurements.*) Isn't it exciting to think of all those wonderful people all over the world who are interested in your welfare, Mr. Bonaparte? I'm afraid we have no provision for the husbands, but if you need it, I'm sure I could rustle up something suitable for you to wear. (*She glances over his figure admiringly.*) Really, it's most exciting. We shall have the usual VIP's in attendance and lay on a chicken mayonnaise dinner . . .

(*The company is now divided in two groups,* LADY POLLY *and* MANNY *seated on one side. She continues to talk interminably and he tries hard to keep his temper. On the other side are* BELLA, *being measured by* SHRIMP, *and* SLICK, *who is writing down the measurements.* SHRIMP *is obviously embarrassed by* BELLA's *nearness and circles round her trying to avoid coming in too close contact.*)

SLICK: Length?

SHRIMP: Forty-seven.

LADY POLLY: You realize, of course, that you two will be the first couple in the village to benefit from our current S.P.P.W.R. campaign. We hope that with your precedent, scores of others in similar unfortunate circumstances will come forward to declare for upright and decent living. I want to surpass our record in Bogles where twenty-seven couples were married together—a mass wedding and a great day for the sanctity of Jamaican womanhood. I remember the address given by the Custos of the Parish when he said: "You will feel the difference tomorrow morning"—he was speaking to the new brides—"you will feel the difference when instead

of saying, 'Anyone see Mass Joe?,' you will stick out your chest and ask, 'Where is my husband?'" (*She burbles a laugh.*)

SLICK: Waist?

SHRIMP: Thirty-eight.

LADY POLLY: Now I must have your full names for this form. You will be er . . . "Bella Crawford," I suppose, and er . . . yours, Mr. . . . ?

BELLA: My title is Carrington, not Crawford. You see, Slick and me is half-brother and sister. Same mother but not same father.

LADY POLLY: I see. Perhaps one day soon we can look into that situation too. And Mr. Bonaparte?

BELLA: My husband name "Manny." "Manny Bonaparte."

LADY POLLY (*writing*): Manny Bonaparte.

SLICK: Hips?

SHRIMP: Forty-two.

LADY POLLY: Well, those are very pretty names, but I really don't think the abbreviations improve them. I should like to have your full names.

BELLA: But Bella is my right name, my lady.

LADY POLLY: Dear child, surely you weren't christened "Bella"—and if you were, that was an oversight. Now let me see: "Annabel Carrington" and er . . . er . . . "Emanuel Bonaparte." That's much better. They would sound so much more impressive in the newspaper report—I always write one myself —something like this: "After long years of faithful and devoted er . . . companionship"—we have to choose our words carefully—"wedding bells have at last pealed for Annabel Carrington and Emanuel Bonaparte of Havendale. Preceded by flowergirls and bridesmaids, the bride, in radiant attire provided by the wives of twelve nations, entered the church to the strains of the Bridal Chorus from Wagner's *Lohengrin*" —we'll get the Police Band to play for us. "This was the first of what is expected to be a cavalcade of nuptial ceremonies in the village, sponsored by the S.P.P.W.R. of which Lady Polly Love-Muggins is president." I always include my name at the end to make sure the report is printed on the social page.

SLICK: Bust? (*A brief silence.*) Bust? (SHRIMP *is struggling futilely to encircle* BELLA. MANNY'*s anger, which has been slowly mounting, now erupts.*)

MANNY: No, by God! No! No! NO!!

BELLA: No what?

MANNY: There ain't going be no wedding. You hear what I say? I not having no pappyshow wedding. Who you think I

is? Dressing up in a monkey suit and parading myself and my woman like a couple of blasted chimpanzees! I say no! We not in no circus.

SHRIMP: Mr. Bonaparte! Please moderate your language. In front of Lady Love-Muggins, too!

MANNY: You shut your mamapoule mouth! Mad Benjy by the street corner got more sense than you. This is my house and if I want to damn and blast I going damn and blast in front of Missis Queen self!

BELLA: But Manny, how you could get on so? Where your breeding?

MANNY: You going taste breeding when I down hand in your skin. You is the ringleader in this plot to deceive me, you and that lousing half-brother you have there. (SLICK *melts into his chair.*) But I warning all of you. I's a peaceful, pacific, law-abiding man and I don't want no trouble. Don't make the blood fly up in my head or, bejeez, is the grave for all you and the gallows for me.

LADY POLLY: But, Mr. Bonaparte, nobody wants to harm you. We're here to help you really, you and Annabel.

MANNY: I didn't ask for no help. With all due respects, Lady, if you would mind your business and I mind mine, we wouldn't cross each other path. You don't know the ways of woman as I know them. You don't have no experience of how our people does get on. Me and Bella living nice together, we love one another, and we content to stay as we is. She free to walk through one door, and I free to walk through the other. That is how we accustom living and I don't see why all you should come with your high-and-mighty ideas and interfere in what don't concern you.

BELLA: But, Manny, we not living right!

MANNY: Look, I done say my piece. I not having no wedding. No bells ringing and no band playing. If you want Yankee ring, buy one in the store. If you want chicken dinner, I have fowls in the yard. I not letting no woman tie me up like a crab because next day they break off your gundy and drop you in hot water. And another thing, your name is Bella where I concern. Now I going down the road by George to fire one, and I want my house nice and quiet and peaceful— like how it was before these marriage-mongers come—by the time I reach back. Is Sunday morning. (*He stomps out angrily.*)

SLICK: Well, Lady Polly, you can't say I didn't warn you. The man is a mad bull when his temper raise.

SHRIMP: I did what I could to calm him down.

BELLA (*crying*) : I know Manny would've blow up. I know all the time he would never agree to this thing. What we going do now?

LADY POLLY: Do? Why nothing, of course. Just carry on with our plans as if nothing happened to disrupt them. I've come across this kind of behavior more than once. In fact, I should've been surprised if Mr. Bonaparte, who is every inch the caveman, didn't act like one. I expected much more violence. Never mind, my dear, I have ways and means of getting round him. Don't worry, you'll have your wedding bells sooner than you think, and a full military band too. The S.P.P.W.R. is not easily balked; we won't let you down, I assure you. (*She rises.*) Well good-bye Annabel. You'll hear from us. Get these papers signed, Mr. Crawford, and have them processed in the usual way. You've got all the measurements?

SLICK: Bust? (SHRIMP *snatches up the tape measure and leaps back to his task.*)

The curtain falls
followed immediately during the blackout by wedding
bells and the strains of the "Wedding March."

Scene 2

A Mime

It is another Sunday morning, a month later. The room is the same, but simple rusticity has given way to the new and gaudy. The furniture is now of the Morris style, heavy and vulgar, crowding the room even more than before, with cushions covered in a loud flowered print material. The wall pictures display screen stars, the curtains and drapes are also brightly colored. The atmosphere has changed from modest cosiness to cheap gaudiness.

The room is empty. MANNY *enters from the backyard. He holds a sick chicken in one hand and a paper bag of chick feed in the other. He finds a small cardboard box, deposits the chicken in it and places the box on the table, then pours in some feed. He looks at the coal pot at the door on which he is trying to prepare breakfast. The fire is dying out. He bends down and blows into the arch to fan the coals but succeeds only in covering his face with ash and smoke. He coughs and splutters, crosses to the washstand, but there is no water in the basin or pitcher. He glares at the bedroom and yells:* "Bella! Bella!" *There is no reply.*

MANNY *wipes his face in a towel and proceeds to lay out*

dishes for breakfast. He picks up the teapot from the fire and burns his fingers. He drops it back and plunges his fingers in the flower bowl to cool them in the water. A rose thorn sticks him. He seizes the roses and throws them on the floor. He sits down to eat. An insistent bleating comes from the yard. He stops and listens. The bleating continues. He yells again: "Bella!" *No response. The goat appears in the doorway.* MANNY *takes it out to feed it.*

BELLA *enters from the bedroom, drawing on her housecoat. She has changed. She is legal mistress in her own house and has acquired the airs befitting a mistress. She is in silk pajamas, a Chinese kimono, and gay slippers. She stretches lazily, looks around for a hairbrush which* MANNY *has left on the table. She fetches this and stands before a wall mirror, brushing and putting her hair in paper bows.*

MANNY *returns and sits at table eating and glowering at* BELLA. *She ignores him, begins to hum a calypso tune:* "Mama, Look a Boo-Boo." *Once or twice he thinks of having it out with her, but changes his mind and restrains himself. Each time he makes to rise,* BELLA *senses his intention and begins to hum louder, thereby asserting her authority.* MANNY *pushes away his plate in disgust, gets up, crosses to washbasin, takes up empty pitcher, and goes outside to fetch water.*

BELLA *puts away the hairbush, pins, etc., gets towel and soap, and waits for* MANNY *to return. He comes in with filled pitcher which she promptly takes from him and begins to wash her hands and face.* MANNY *crosses to window, picking up roses from the floor. He throws them through the window.* BELLA *moves to dining table, pours a cup of cocoa, brings cup and saucer down to rocker, sits, puts cup on center table, takes up a bottle of nail varnish and begins to touch up her nails, still la-la-ing a calypso tune.* MANNY *turns sharply on her, attempts to speak, changes his mind again, sits in a chair facing* BELLA. *He lights a cigarette.* BELLA *continues to polish, sip her cocoa, and hum. A pause.*

A knock at the front door. MANNY *looks at* BELLA, *she looks at him. She puts down the nail polish, smoothes her housecoat and waits. A visitor, perhaps, after church. The knock is repeated.* MANNY *goes to answer it. It is only the newspaper boy.* MANNY *turns back into the room with the paper. As he crosses* BELLA *she holds out her hand for the paper. He hesitates a moment, then hands it over. Without once looking up at him, she extracts the comic section, puts it on her lap, and hands him the rest of the paper. He stands there fuming.*

BELLA *drains her cup of cocoa, holds out the empty cup*

and saucer for MANNY *to put away. This is the last straw. With a mighty sweep he knocks the dishes away.* BELLA *rises majestically—there is an echo of* LADY POLLY *in her movement—looks him up and down, and marches into the bedroom with her comic sheets.* MANNY *is a monument of controlled rage. He begins, very slowly and deliberately, to rip the newspaper into pieces and drop them on the floor.*

Curtain
followed immediately by a gay
passage from the "Wedding March."

Scene 3

(*The room as in Scene 2. Sunday morning, a week later.* MANNY *is packing his things. A battered suitcase is open on the table and two carton boxes are on the chairs. He folds and puts away a few garments, takes up a pair of heavy workingman's boots and pauses, wondering where to put them.* SLICK *appears at the window.*)

SLICK: Hey Manny, you get my message? (MANNY *ignores him.*) I ask Jamesy to tell you I want to see you—important-like. (MANNY *dumps the boots in the suitcase and continues packing.*) I could come inside? I have a piece of news to your benefit. (*He leaves the window and enters by the front door. He is dressed in a gay sports shirt and colored gabardine trousers. He approaches* MANNY *tentatively.*) You packing?

MANNY: No. I playing dolly-house.

SLICK: Where Bella?

MANNY: What you want with her?

SLICK: Nothing, nothing. But she ain't here?

MANNY: She gone traipsing off to one of them Women's Rally. What you have to tell me?

SLICK: You leaving Bella?

MANNY: Mind your damn business.

SLICK: I have a piece of news give you.

MANNY: Well, spill it then and stop dancing me around.

SLICK: I want to know how matters stand first.

MANNY: Look, Slick, you done capsize my life already. Is only because I was mook enough to agree to it that I ain't beat out your brains yet. But don't try your luck too far. If you don't have nothing to say, hoist yourself out my house quick-sharp.

SLICK: Man, I come here in your interest and you getting on like a Russian! Like you don't trust me.

MANNY: You dead right.

SLICK: Okay, if is so you want it . . . (*He moves to the door and stops.*) You don't want to hear the ballad.

MANNY: How come you not at the Rally this morning, Slick?

SLICK: I don't have to go every time, man.

MANNY (*approaches* SLICK *menacingly*): Come clean, Slick. I could see the lie forming up behind your eyes. Where your monkey clothes?

SLICK: The truth is, Manny, I let go the work.

MANNY: You mean they fire you?

SLICK: Fire who? Is I walk out. It was getting kind of dull —you know how—so much woman all about, however you turn you bounce up with one. And when you talk about talk! My ears didn't stop buzzing two weeks solid! Look, I going tell you something, eh. When nighttime come, instead of coasting a nice limn with a brownskin as mate, I beating a bottle hard with the boys behind Joe bar. And why? Because I sick-sick hearing woman-talk. I too young for that, boy.

MANNY: You working now?

SLICK: I taking a rest after all the hustlement.

MANNY: That is why you hanging round here. You come to see what you could pick up? (*He collars* SLICK.) You expect soon I will walk out my house in disgust the way Bella getting on, and you will take over. You louse!

SLICK: No, Manny, no! You charging me wrong!

MANNY: What for you come here this morning!! Talk sharp, my patience running out!

SLICK: Is a lawyer friend I have. He say he could get your marriage annul if you want.

MANNY: Annul? What you mean?

SLICK: Break up, squash, like how you was before.

MANNY: How he could do that?

SLICK: Some legal mixup in the business. I ain't too well understand the ins and outs. But he's a good lawyer. You could trust him.

MANNY: How soon he could fix me up?

SLICK: He say in a week or two.

MANNY: What he name?

SLICK: He tell me don't mention his name to nobody—you know how it is—being as the business not strictly aboveboard.

MANNY: I suppose he want a pound and a crown for that?

SLICK: He's a good lawyer, you know, and seeing that he taking a big risk, you will have to compensate him good.

MANNY: How much?

SLICK: I tell him how you's my family and all that, so he willing to cut down the price for you.

MANNY: Jeeze-and-ages! How much? You don't understand English?

SLICK: Fifty pounds.

MANNY: Fifty what? Where in France I going get that kind of money.

SLICK: That is what he charge at first, but I beat him down to thirty. And too beside, you could pay him off by degrees. He tell me bring anything you have as a bind.

MANNY (*collaring* SLICK *again*): You ain't lying? You ain't trying to bamboozle me again? Because if you do, so help me . . .

SLICK: No, Manny, no! I could really fix you up!

MANNY: You could?

SLICK: I mean the lawyer-feller. Jeezu-web, man, and we is family? I wouldn't fool you.

MANNY: Slick, if you could do this thing for me you's a real friend. I don't want to leave Bella, but I can't go on no longer in this tanglement. From the time she get married, Bella change. Like the ring take away all her born sense. Every striking day is something new. First thing, she make me buy up a whole new set of furniture and put me in debt. Me who never owe the chinee shop for a pound of rice, I owing the joinershop, the shoemaker, and the store. Next thing, she can't do no more housework; she don't want the neighbors see her milking the goat or cleaning out the fowl coop; if Emily get a kimono, she want one too; Doris wearing sack, she want one too, and all day and night the woman flying out the house like she mad going to rally and social and soiree. And on top of that, if I call her Bella, she ignore me. Is Annabel or Emanuel, otherwise nothing doing. You think any God-fearing man would stomach that stupidness?

SLICK: Is a hard life.

MANNY: Not she alone what turn, you know. The whole village gone crazy with this society living. George throw out Agnes last week. Harry and Emily in noise every living day. Is you I blame for the whole commess. You and that nosy white woman.

SLICK: Manny, boy, I agree is my fault and I trying my best to equalize matters. Leave it to papa. Me and my lawyer-friend going straighten you out. How much you have on you?

MANNY (*takes a cloth bag from his grip*): I have eleven, no twelve pounds save up here. I could give you five as an advance.

SLICK: You better make it eight. We don't want the lawyer-man to turn down the case.

MANNY: All right. Here. (*He hands over the money.*) Tell him don't waste no time. The sooner the better.

SLICK: Eh-heh. You smart. (*He moves to the door.*) Well, I better peel off now. I have to make my rounds.

MANNY: Stay and take a drink, nuh, man? I feel better already.

SLICK: Next time. We going pick up. (*He opens the door, makes to leave but jumps back inside and closes the door again.*) Is Lady Polly. She coming in here.

MANNY: What the hell she want now?

SLICK: I going out the back way. I don't want her see me.

MANNY (*suspicious now, he forcibly restrains* SLICK): No, stay here. We going see what she want.

(SLICK *drifts disconsolately into a corner as* LADY POLLY *knocks at the door and enters peremptorily without waiting to be admitted.*)

LADY POLLY: Good morning, Mr. Bonaparte, I . . . (*She sees* SLICK *and pauses melodramatically, then decides it is better to ignore him completely.*) I'm sorry to have to visit you unceremoniously like this, but it's rather urgent and I'm pressed for time. The point is—and I very much regret to say this—there has been a slight miscarriage in the arrangements made for your wedding some weeks ago. I've only now discovered that it was not conducted strictly er . . . shall we say, according to the book. It happens that certain important documents were mislaid and not registered . . . (*She glares at* SLICK.) . . . and other legal requirements were overlooked at the time. It's all our fault, of course, the S.P.P.W.R. assumes full responsibility, but it does mean we shall have to repeat the ceremony—merely a formality. Of course, on this occasion we shall do it quietly. No sense in making a fuss about it a second time. Now if you will just sign these documents . . . ?

MANNY: You mean to say—I not really married to Bella?

(SLICK *tries to edge his way toward the door.* MANNY, *realizing he has been tricked, attempts to forestall him. During the following scene with* LADY POLLY, *they play a private game of cat-and-mouse.*)

LADY POLLY: Well, you are and you aren't. In the eyes of the church, you most certainly are. But legally . . .

MANNY: Legally?

LADY POLLY: I'm afraid not. I know this must upset you terribly . . .

MANNY: Oh, yes, mum. It upset me a lot!

LADY POLLY: And I don't mind telling you, Mr. Bonaparte, because I know you will understand and be discreet about it, a certain member of our staff, who is also, I regret to say, a member of your family, misled us dreadfully, deceived us in fact, that he had got the signatures and complied with all the regulations. It was with horror that I discovered otherwise and it has caused the S.P.P.W.R. a great deal of embarrassment in the village and in official circles. Needless to say, disciplinary action has been taken against that member and he is no longer in our employ. However, that is past history now. We are trying to repair the damage at the earliest possible moment, so if you would just sign . . . ?

MANNY: Just leave the papers there, mum. I'll be happy to sign them for you. Just leave them there.

LADY POLLY: Very well. And get Annabel to sign too. I've filled them up myself. I will have the forms picked up tomorrow and taken to the record office. Now if you'll excuse me, I have several other calls to make. Good morning! (*She leaves.*)

MANNY (*pounces on* SLICK *who cowers behind a piece of furniture*): You damn worthless scamp! So you know a lawyer who could fix things, eh? Give me my money back, you bloody thief!

SLICK (*returning the money*): Look the raise, Manny. I was only joking you. Don't take it serious, I beg you.

MANNY: Boy, I should blade your skin with my poui. But I let you off this time. But look my trouble, nuh? (*He laughs uproariously.*) So you fire the job because you fed up. Ho-ho-ho! How come you forget to take in the marriage papers?

SLICK: I was running a booze that weekend and as the liquor fly in my head the work fly out. I can't tell what the France happen to the forms and them.

MANNY: Thank your stars, boy, thank your stars and sing hallelujah! I could tell you now. I had every intention when all this finish to bathe you with licks. Because you was at the back of everything. Anyhow, let that pass. Reach a grog there and come fire one.

SLICK: Let me hear that tune again. Is my favorite.

MANNY (*chanting*):

Fire one, I say, fire one,
Take a shot before life done,
Warm up the wet and cool down the sun,
So fire one.

SLICK (*gets a bottle of rum and glasses. He pours the*

drinks): I didn't tell you what really cause the old mass between me and Polly. Pardner, after the first novelty wear off, I didn't have no more uses for her. She run kind of stale, you understand. Them kind of people ain't have no zip. Anyhow, one morning she get a great idea in her head. Whaddap! She come out with how it ain't look decent to have me in the setup as a single man, so much women all around, and how is high time I get married, and she think some old fowl name Josephine would make me a good wife. Well I never hear that in forty-four years! Me, Slick, who ain't even cut my eyeteeth good—look, my mother's features still on me, the woman want to come blight my future with wedding ring. And come see the Josephine! She been down here since the days of Methuselah! (*He makes a grimace.*) I sure is spite Polly want to spite me. Boy, is then the old man decide to bail out fast. Never me in woman affair again, boy.

MANNY: But you know the woman well bold-face. She have the brass to come back here, after what I done pass through, and talk about . . . (*Mimicking* LADY POLLY.) . . . "I know this must upset you terrible, but we trying to repair the damage . . ."

SLICK (*joining in the fun*): And "if you will just sign here, Mr. Bonaparte, and get Annabel to sign too . . ."

MANNY: Annabel! Annabel my eye. Now we going see who is man.

SLICK: What you going do?

MANNY: Just watch me. (*Very deliberately he sets about disarranging the room. He throws pieces of clothing over the screen and on the chairs, spills food on the table, scatters a newspaper about the floor.* SLICK *helps himself to another rum and recites.*)

SLICK:

> I am monarch of all I survey,
> My right there is none to dispute,
> From the center all round to the sea,
> I am lord of the fowl and the brute.

I remember that poetry from third standard. Hey, Manny, I just think up a master plan. Listen. How about me and you starting up a society too. We could charge shilling-a-week subscription and we could call it the S.S.S.P.P.W.R.

MANNY: What the devil name is that?

SLICK: The Society for the Suppression of the Society for the Preservation and Protection of Women's Rights. What you saying? Every man-jack would join up. Is a good idea.

MANNY: Eh-heh. Is a good idea.

(SLICK *laughs uproariously and pours more drinks.* MANNY *rises quickly and takes up his poui-stick.*)

MANNY: Ss . . . hh! She coming.

(BELLA *enters. She is outrageously overdressed with gloves and hat. She closes the door and hesitates, looking from* MANNY *to* SLICK *and back to* MANNY. *Finally, she approaches him slowly.*)

BELLA: Emanuel, I hear . . .

MANNY: Manny!

BELLA: Manny, I hear that . . .

MANNY: Good. Say it again. Say my name again let me hear.

BELLA: Manny.

MANNY: And you. What your name is again? (*A pause.*) Tell me, I forget it. What your name is?

BELLA: Bella.

MANNY: Good. Now, Bella, take off them society gloves and don't let me see you wearing them again. Hands make for work, not for show. (*She removes her hat and gloves.*) And I find the house looking kind of dirty. You ain't find so? Clean it up give me please, and wipe off the table, and wash out the basin. When you finish, go outside and feed the fowls and the goat. And I think I would like my food ready by one o'clock sharp. If you don't mind?

(BELLA *turns away, a pitiful figure of submission. She fetches an apron, puts it on, gets the broom and duster and begins to clean up.* MANNY *sits brooding.* SLICK *pours another drink and tries to cheer him up.*)

SLICK: That's the way, Manny, that's the way. "I am monarch of all I survey . . ."

MANNY: You get to hell out of here. Out off, I say! (*He hurls* SLICK *out by the scruff of his neck.*) A no-good louse! I don't want to see him round here again. I done with him— for good.

(MANNY *watches* BELLA *as she moves about her chores sadly. He relents. He collects the scattered newspaper, puts away the rum and glasses, begins to unpack his clothes from the suitcase.* BELLA *stops and looks at him. He looks at her. They reach for each other.*)

FINAL CURTAIN

Star of the Morning

SCENES IN THE LIFE OF BERT WILLIAMS

by LOFTEN MITCHELL

Music and Lyrics by Louis Mitchell and Romare Bearden

Loften Mitchell, a native and current resident of Harlem, was born in 1919, the oldest son of Willia Spaulding Mitchell and Ulysses Mitchell.

During his boyhood in the 1930's he wrote sketches and acted for local Harlem drama groups, namely the Progressive Dramatizers and the Rose McClendon Players. After serving in the Navy during World War Two, he went to Columbia University Graduate School and studied playwriting under John Gassner.

His plays *The Cellar* and *The Bancroft Dynasty* were performed in the Harlem area. *A Land Beyond the River* (1957) was shown at the Greenwich Mews, then on tour. In 1958 Mitchell won a Guggenheim Award for creative writing in the drama. His other plays include: the musical, *Ballad for Bimshire* (1963); *Ballad of the Winter Soldiers,* written with John Oliver Killens (1964); *Star of the Morning* (1965); *Tell Pharaoh* (1967), and *The Afro-Philadelphian* (1970). His book, *Black Drama,* was published in 1966.

CHARACTERS

    BERT WILLIAMS
    OLIVER JACKSON
    JACK RIDGE
    GEORGE WALKER
    THEATER MANAGER
    LOTTIE THOMPSON
    JESSE SHIPP
    ADA
    HATTIE
    MR. DUDLEY
    CHARLIE
    ABRAHAM ERLANGER
    BELLE BLAZER
    MEMBERS OF THE ENSEMBLE

SETTING

The play is written to be performed on a ramped stage with the use of lights to assure fluidity of movement and continuity. At the rear of the stage is a large cyclorama that,

depending upon the scene, is lighted accordingly. Four major parts make up the total setting: one large piece extends from extreme right and another from extreme left. These may meet in center and form a playing area above the lower stage level. These pieces may also be used separately for individual scenes. There should be a pair of steps leading to the upper level. Chairs and table, placed as needed, make up the fourth group of objects.

The onstage action described in the play takes place in center. The wing areas are at extreme right and extreme left.

The entire action of the play takes place during the latter part of the nineteenth century and the early part of the twentieth century.

ACT 1

Scene 1

(*The scene is a San Francisco honky-tonk. The time is late one night in the year 1895.*

The lights fade in slowly on this dark, smoke-filled, dimly lit, crowded place. At the extreme right is a small room with a table and chair. The honky-tonk literally splashes across the remainder of the playing area. The entrance from the street is upstage, left.

A crowd of white patrons sit at the tables, drinking noisily. Loud voices, laughter, and beer-spilling predominate. JACK RIDGE, *the proprietor, a short, plump, middle-aged, pleasant white man, stands upstage near the door.*

BERT WILLIAMS *enters, walks through the small room out into the center of the honky-tonk. He has a banjo under his arm.* BERT *is nineteen years old, but he seems much older than his years. He is tall, well developed, quiet, reserved, somewhat reticent and a trifle supercilious, but not without humor. He is what is known as fair-skinned and wavy-haired, neatly dressed in a dark suit.*

BERT *plucks the banjo. There is a moment of silence from the crowd. He then plays a few bars of a sugary, sentimental calypso-like melody. The crowd becomes restless.*)

A MAN: What the hell is this?

A WOMAN: Come on, boy. Get hot! Get hot!

A MAN: Get something, damn it!

(*The others echo these remarks.* BERT *freezes, bites his lips, sticks his banjo under his arm, turns and walks into the small room. He puts banjo on the table and sits, silently.* OLIVER JACKSON, *a tall, stocky, elderly Negro, well over sixty-*

five, steps into the back room. Despite his age, he is an agile man with movements much like those of a dancer. He goes directly to BERT.)

OLIVER: What's wrong, Bert?

BERT: They—want something I can't give them.

OLIVER: I been saying it like a parrot: If you ain't got no beat, you liable to get beat.

BERT:

> When life is full of cloud and rain,
> And I am filled with naught but pain—

(OLIVER *starts to say something, stops.* RIDGE, *in the meantime, has stepped into center stage. He holds up his hands to the noisy crowd.*)

RIDGE: Folks! Folks! Oliver Jackson says this boy's gonna be great! You got to give him a chance—

A MAN: Gimme a drink! I don't wanta hear from you or him!

(*A roar of agreement from the crowd. Their voices drown out* RIDGE. GEORGE WALKER *steps inside the doorway. He is a small, thin, ragged black man, just about twenty years old. He is an active, quick-thinking young man with little formal training but with keen native intelligence. He goes directly to* RIDGE.)

GEORGE: Mister, I'm hungry. I need a job and— (*More noise.*) Mister, I can stop 'em.

RIDGE: Who the hell are you?

GEORGE: Nash Walker. George Nash Walker. I sing and dance some. (*He cuts a few steps.*)

RIDGE: Well, start! (*Calling out.*) Williams!

OLIVER: Ridge's calling you. You get out there and ring that banjo!

RIDGE (*as* OLIVER *practically pushes* BERT *forward*): Play for this boy—George Walker.

(BERT *confers with* GEORGE. *Now* GEORGE *steps into center stage, smiles. The crowd looks at him, then sits, silently, as* BERT *accompanies him on the* BANJO. *He sings.*)

GEORGE:

And when it rains, the rain is a refrain
Right on that beat from Golden Gate to Maine—
Who can explain it?
It's vain to disdain it,
So hear me while I explain it:

Follow the beat whenever you hear it!
Follow the beat—listen and get with it.

I repeat: Folks, always follow the beat!
Follow the beat whenever you feel it—
Follow the beat—no one can conceal it.
I repeat: Folks, neatly follow the beat!
Da Da Da Dee Dum—one, two, three, four! Once more!
Da Da Da Dee Dum—you have felt it before!
Follow the beat—listen and get with it—
I repeat: Be discreet, lift your feet,
Life's complete!
Folks, always follow the beat!

(*By the end of the song, the crowd is applauding.* A MAN *yells.*)

MAN: Yeah! Dance, black boy!

(BERT *slaps the banjo angrily with open palm, then glares at the* MAN. OLIVER *rushes to* BERT.)

OLIVER: Now, don't go getting all touch-us.

GEORGE: No. 'Cause I'm hungry.

(BERT *controls himself; then pour his anger into his playing. The music becomes furious and driving.* GEORGE *dances until he becomes weak and tired.* OLIVER *steps forward and joins him. They perform a number of intricate steps as* BERT *accompanies them. Now,* OLIVER *takes* GEORGE *by the arm and they dance off into the small room.* BERT *follows them. The crowd is applauding, wildly.* BERT *takes* GEORGE's *arm, leads him back into the honky-tonk. He bows as does* GEORGE, *then they return to the small room.* GEORGE *slumps into chair.* OLIVER *pats* GEORGE *on the back, then goes offstage.*)

BERT: Excellent! Excellent!

GEORGE: Thanks.

(*In the meantime the crowd is beginning to leave the place.* RIDGE *is at the doorway, bidding people good night.* OLIVER *steps back into the small room with a tray of food. He places this before* GEORGE. *There are four cups of coffee on this tray.*)

OLIVER: Look what the cook left.

(GEORGE *begins to eat, savagely.* OLIVER *gives* BERT *a cup of coffee, takes one for himself and gives one to* RIDGE *as the last of the crowd leaves.*)

RIDGE: You got a job, Walker! Three dollars a week. Start tomorrow night.

GEORGE: Thanks, mister. Thanks—

RIDGE (*with coffee*): That the only clothes you got?

GEORGE: Yes, sir. They was good, but riding the rails ain't no good for a suit or the body that's in one . . .

RIDGE: You got to show up looking decent. (GEORGE *continues eating.* RIDGE *smiles.*) Be careful you don't eat the plate.

GEORGE: I won't. This sure is good of you.

OLIVER: Oh, Mr. Ridge is good. Long as I been working here, I never was scared of fire, 'cause 1 knowed if my place burned down, he'd let me sleep in his stable.

(BERT *laughs.* RIDGE *looks at him, turns to* OLIVER.)

RIDGE: Oliver, I'll bet your master was glad when slavery ended.

OLIVER: He sure was, 'cause that lye I was putting in his coffee was eating his insides out. (RIDGE *nearly spits coffee on himself.* OLIVER *asks, innocently.*) Something wrong, Mr. Ridge?

RIDGE: No. Nothing. I just remembered—I've got to close up the rest of the place. (*And he rushes out.*)

GEORGE: Nice man.

OLIVER: Yeah, but sometimes you got to straighten him. First night I walk in here, he says to me, says: "Boy, you mighty old for night work." I says: "I ain't too old to muzzle you, puppy dog!"

BERT: You told him—that???

OLIVER: Well—it's what I woulda told him if I'd a got a chance. Play with a puppy and he'll mistake you for a pole. (*Then.*) Time to move on.

BERT: Thanks for everything, Mr. Jackson, And good luck to you and the Touring Minstrels.

GEORGE (*impressed*): You going with *them?*

OLIVER: They sent for me. Train tickets and all. (*Holds up tickets.*)

GEORGE: That what train tickets look like?

OLIVER: Yeah. They call it success when you can ride in style. Right now I'm rich with the smell of success.

GEORGE (*looks at his clothing*): I ain't sure that's success you smelling right now.

BERT: Mr. Jackson, if they need anyone else—

OLIVER: Not you.

BERT: But, you told me—

OLIVER: That you got talent. I sure did. But you got something else, too. You think you a man in a house where they and some of us think we boys.

GEORGE: That's what I been called all my days.

OLIVER: Ain't no success in going with minstrels nohow. Back there when I was a slave, it was, though. You know what minstrels was, boy? We did 'em on the plantation to poke fun

579

at Old Master. We got that house Negro to stand up and say: "Gentlemen, be seated!" Then we'd line up with Tams and Bones as the end men.

BERT: Tams and Bones?

OLIVER: That was the instruments they played. You think we could afford pianos? (*Remembering and reenacting.*) We used to take off on that house Negro 'cause he was the Master up and down. (*Imitating Tams.*) Tams would say: "Mistah Stafford, do darkies go to heaven?" (*Moves over, imitates Bones.*) Old Bones would say: "Yes, suh, Mistah Stafford, do us darkies go to heaven?" (*Moves back, imitates the house Negro.*) House Negro would say: "Now, why would you darkies be going to heaven? That's for white folks!" (*Imitates Tams.*) Tams would say: "We just wanted to know who opens them Pearly Gates for white folks to get inside!" (BERT *and* GEORGE *roar with laughter at his antics.* OLIVER *stops now and becomes serious.*) That's how it *was.* Then white folks come from up North and copied what we was doing. They made me a fool and now I got to go out here and make money laughing at me!

BERT: Mr. Jackson—

OLIVER: Ain't no success no kinda way. You-all ever see greens growin'?

BERT: Greens?

OLIVER: Collard greens. They come up, bunched together. Some get tall and you got to pull up the small ones. Nighttimes we slaves used to sit on the cabin floor, rubbing our backs 'cause they ached from pulling up small greens. One real old slave, a preaching man, always talked about how much smarter it'd be if we planted different so all the greens could grow tall. I didn't know what he meant, so one night he took me outdoors and pointed up to the stars, the bright stars, and showed me how they could all shine together 'cause the Good Lord had planted them right. (*Then.*) That's what success is, boys: Planting right. (OLIVER *turns, quickly, goes out.*)

GEORGE: Lord Jesus! Colored folks ain't even happy when they oughta be!

BERT: No one is happy in America, but everyone pretends he is.

GEORGE: Watch that stuff! I'm an American.

BERT: Yes. I know. You get enough to eat?

GEORGE: I ain't never got enough to eat or wear in all my life. (*Quickly.*) What I had's all right for now, thanks.

BERT: I don't mean to be forward. I have an old suit. My mother can cut it down for you.

GEORGE: Sa-ay, thanks. We gonna be friends, after all.

BERT: Why shouldn't we?

GEORGE: I thought you was real proper. Where you from?

BERT: Antigua. British West Indies.

GEORGE: An—what??? That sounds further'n Kansas.

BERT: It is.

GEORGE: Hope it ain't no worse.

BERT: It was nice—till my father took sick. We moved here for his health.

GEORGE: You could say I come here for mine, too. And I aim to stay.

BERT: I don't. Someday I'll return and buy our old house. Then I'll sit there on that mountainside and figure out why I'm here.

GEORGE (*curiously*): You don't know why you here? I'm here 'cause this man's gonna pay me three dollars a week!

BERT: For that matter I'm here because I couldn't afford Leland Stanford University. Without formal training there are only menial jobs for us.

GEORGE: You doing something high-class 'round here now?

BERT: No. I'm singing, mimicking, playing the banjo. Temporarily. (*Then, animated.*) But, when I speak of being here, I mean *really* being here. On this earth. John Stuart Mill said man's in an early stage of development. He hoped for the day we could ease our burdens and pursue intellectual things—

GEORGE: Say—you not only talk funny, but what you say is funny.

BERT (*stops suddenly, picks up banjo*): I live 15 Chestnut. You may come by in the morning for the suit.

GEORGE: Wait a minute! I hurt your feelings. (BERT *shakes his head.*) I did, too. Don't be mad.

BERT: Why must you Americans insult a man, then tell him how to react to it?

GEORGE: I'm sorry. I oughtn't a done that. But, you treated me like I'm real dumb and—

BERT: I did not say you are dumb. You have good basic intelligence—

GEORGE: You signifying on me, man? I know what base means.

BERT: I am not going to stay here and argue with you.

GEORGE: Please don't go! (*He is subdued.* BERT *looks at him.*) Oh, I am dumb! Real dumb to be 'way out here, hungry.

581

(*Walks away, sits.*) It wasn't supposed to be like this. Told Mama I was gonna make us rich—that I was gonna buy me a new suit of clothes for every day I went raggedy—which is a heap of days. Never gonna do it off'n three dollars a week.

BERT (*goes to him, awkwardly, trying to console him*): Now, look—this is temporary. An early stage of development. Later—the train ride. (GEORGE *stares at him.*) You think I'm —silly?

GEORGE: I think you smart as hell! (*Suddenly, on his feet.*) We oughta team up! We can do big things! You be my straight man and— (*Stops.*) Only, you look funnier'n me.

BERT: What's funny about me?

GEORGE: That awkward way of yourn. We'll put some burnt cork on you and—

BERT: No, sir.

GEORGE: And we'll take you to a Baptist church where you can learn to talk right.

BERT: I'm an Anglican.

GEORGE: What the hell is that?

BERT: The Church of England. They call it the Episcopal Church here.

GEORGE: Never mind all that. Do they shout?

BERT: Hardly.

GEORGE: Don't say "hardly." Say "No, suh, indeed."

BERT: "No, suh, indeed."

GEORGE: Quit interrupting! (*Paces, excitedly.*) We gonna stay here awhile and get known. I'm gonna pester every booking agent 'round here till they know Williams and Walker is hotter'n fire. We gonna get booked into theaters so fancy that folks will have to wear their Sunday clothes to get inside to see us! (BERT *toys with banjo.*) You ain't even listening!

BERT: I am. I play the banjo when I'm thinking.

GEORGE: Where was I?

BERT: We just played to folks in their Sunday clothes.

GEORGE: And we're getting ten dollars a week. (*Taps, emphatically.* BERT *hits banjo.*) Then, fifteen! (*Taps again. Another note.*) Twenty-five! (*Another tap. Another note.*) Fifty dollars a week—apiece! (GEORGE *taps, then sails into the air.* BERT *looks at him, tucks banjo under his arm.*) Folks gonna know us in Chicago, New York, England—*and* Europe.

BERT: We travel quickly.

GEORGE: We gonna make so much money we won't have time to spend it.

BERT (*ringing the banjo*): Talk on! We'll find a way!

(*They shake hands, smiling.* RIDGE *steps back into the room.*)

RIDGE: Well, boys—time to call it a night.

BERT: You know, if you studied the human anatomy, you'd discover a remarkable difference between a boy and a man. (RIDGE *looks at him.* GEORGE *grabs* BERT's *arm, cautioning him. Slowly, a grin appears on* BERT's *face—an all-too-patient, understanding grin. He lapses into a singsong, rhythmic pattern.*)

Yas, suh, boss. Ah didn't mean to be cross—

Lawd, shut my mouf 'bout dis sad nation

So Ah can be shut off from dis trial and tribulation!

(GEORGE *and* BERT *lock arms and start out, almost strutting.* RIDGE *looks after them, puzzled. He shrugs his shoulders, turns and blows out the lamp. The lights fade as the music rises.*)

Scene 2

(*A Milwaukee theater. One month later.*

The lights fade in on a scrim. On it we see a theater marquee. It reads: "Milwaukee Theater: Four Big Acts: Belle Blazer. The Strutting Jugglers. Dandy and Candy, dance stylists. Williams and Walker Comedy Team."

LOTTIE THOMPSON *and* JESSE SHIPP *enter and look at the marquee.* LOTTIE *is a pleasant, attractive, well-groomed young lady with an air that is decidedly nontheatrical. She is honest, straightforward, utterly lacking in grand gestures and poses.*

JESSE *is a tall, thin, intelligent young Negro, smartly dressed in the style of the period.* LOTTIE *points to the marquee.*)

LOTTIE: Here they are, Jesse. Williams and Walker.

JESSE: Oliver Jackson said catch their act. He didn't say what we'd have to go through to catch them. Talent-hunting is damned expensive!

LOTTIE: If these are our men, it'll all be worthwhile. Let's go—

(*They move into the shadows. The lights come up in center stage. Framing this center area we find two vaudeville cards: "Milwaukee Theater: Williams and Walker Comedy Team."*

The THEATER MANAGER, *a tall white man, stands in what represents the theater wings beside an old trunk.* GEORGE *and* BERT *march into the center area. Both have rolls of bills and they count.*)

583

GEORGE: Ten. Twenty. Thirty. Forty. Fifty. One hundred! Count yours.

BERT (*counting*): One—

GEORGE: One what??? (*Snatches bill from* BERT.) Where the hell did you get that one-dollar bill? (*Rips it to shreds.*) Man, as long as you know me, don't you ever be caught with no damn one-dollar bill!

BERT (*picking up pieces*): You shouldn't a done that. (*Singing.*)

> When all my luck has turned out bad
> And I am weary, blue and sad,
> The only friend I's ever had
> Was my last dollar!
> Now, I ain't never been low-down—
> I's been the honest man in town,
> But when I'm broke I never frown
> At my last dollar!
> But what you ain't got, you can't get.
> I ain't paid nothin' on no debt
> 'Cause all I gets is sympathy
> From all the folks who asks 'bout me.
> When I'm feelin' down and out
> And I am just about give out,
> There ain't no one to fight my bout
> But my last dollar!

(*He has picked up the pieces of the torn dollar. Now he counts out his other money, sticks this in his pocket, tips his hat to* GEORGE *and shuffles from the stage.* GEORGE *follows him out into the wing area. The* THEATER MANAGER's *face registers his disapproval.* GEORGE *bends, picks up one end of the trunk.* BERT *picks up the other end. The* MANAGER *places a bill in* GEORGE's *hand.* BERT *and* GEORGE *leave with the trunk. The* MANAGER *looks after them, shakes his head.*

The vaudeville cards flip. They now read: "Belle Blazer, Song Stylist." An attractive white woman appears in center stage and we hear applause from the audience. She sings.)

BELLE (*singing*):

They call it love, and from birth until we die,
I'll love him so and I know that I know why.
Though love's a game for fools, they claim,
Played by none who have won.
They call it love, no other word will do.
I'll love him so and I know he loves me, too.
The world's a stage for clown and sage,
And love's the play to be done.

When he smiles, my heart leaps
Though I tell it to be still.
All the while my soul keeps measuring my every thrill.
They call it love, no other word will do—
I'll love him so, though our days of joy are few—
It's all the same in any game,
They'll always call it love!

(*As the song ends, the lights fade.* LOTTIE *and* JESSE *are in the wing area. They approach the* THEATER MANAGER.)

JESSE: We're looking for Williams and Walker.

MANAGER: They've gone. I sent them away to keep them from going to jail.

LOTTIE: To jail. For what?

MANAGER: For robbing people of their damn money, their damn time, and their God damned patience!

(*The lights fade out quickly.*)

Scene 3

(*The scene is a freight car. Late night of that same day.*

This scene is played on the lower level. The train's sliding door is to the ramp. It is partially open and occasional light from the countryside homes slips through the doorway opening. BERT *is sitting, trying to read a book by the slivers of light.* GEORGE *is on the floor nearby, trying to sleep.*

The train whistle blows. Light streams into the freight car and into GEORGE's *eyes. He jumps up, goes to the door and slams it shut.*)

GEORGE: How can you be reading at a time like this?

BERT: I can't now. You blocked out the light.

(*The train sweeps around a curve.* GEORGE *is thrown halfway across the car.* BERT *reaches up and grabs him, preventing his falling.*)

GEORGE: Good Lord!

BERT: We turned a curve. Are you all right?

GEORGE: Yeah. Thanks. (*He sits.*)

BERT: In the West Indies they speak of America's luxurious train service. Apparently not enough West Indians have ridden trains here.

GEORGE: Not this kind in this way. What was that man's name? Oliver Jackson?

BERT: Yes.

GEORGE: He said, walk together and we gonna find some train tickets. We been walking together, all right—from one job to the next!

BERT: We didn't walk in Omaha.

GEORGE: No. Them white folks run hell outa us.

BERT: I didn't think we were any worse than the other performers.

GEORGE: The audience did.

BERT (*as* GEORGE *stretches out again*): George—I've been thinking: There may be something wrong with our act. We've worked exactly two weeks in the last two months.

GEORGE: I can count.

BERT: I didn't say you couldn't.

GEORGE: You mighta been thinking it. (*Then.*) Our act ain't funny, that's what's wrong. Them folks got notions 'bout what's funny and when you get out there, acting all proper-like, we end up not eating proper—and riding freight cars!

BERT: George—our people's faces are black, beautiful. I will not ridicule them by wearing burnt cork.

GEORGE: Others do it. And they work regularly.

BERT: My father's plantation workers worked regularly, too. And no one knew their names. My father depended upon me to remember each worker. He didn't want to pay the same man twice. (*He laughs.* GEORGE *gives a mocking laugh.*)

GEORGE: I could laugh, too, if I wasn't weak from not eating.

BERT: Listen—Man gets smaller each year. When he came out of darkness, he saw a ray of light and thought he was the center of things. Along came Galileo, Newton, Copernicus. Man found this earth's a tiny part of a large universe—and he's a speck of dust.

GEORGE: This speck here is so hungry his stomach is playing tag with his backbone.

BERT: A man has only his identity. He's a fool to lose it behind a false face. (*Then.*) Art must represent truth. I've been reading of Ahmed Baba and the learned men of Timbuctoo, of Pietro who captained one of Columbus's ships, of Crispus Attucks and Salem Poor and Toussaint and Douglass and Banneker.

GEORGE: Who the hell are they?

BERT: Great black men whose lives we should portray on the stage. That's why we should be in the theater—to tell their truths, not lies about their ancestors!

GEORGE: Will we eat if we do?

BERT (*exasperated*): Avarice will be the death of you Americans!

GEORGE: I wish I had the energy to pronounce words like that.

BERT: Avarice—

GEORGE: Does that mean eating?

BERT: Listen—we'll eat when we get to Chicago.

GEORGE: With what??

BERT: I don't know. Something will turn up. Meantime, we should give serious consideration to putting on stage the truthful history of the black man in this hemisphere—

GEORGE (*annoyed*): Ohhhh!

BERT: What's wrong, George?

GEORGE: There's nothing wrong! Nothing! (*Angrily.*) What you think? We been fired in Los Angeles and Omaha and Milwaukee—and you ask me what's wrong? It don't bother you, does it? No—'cause you can read a book or fly off into the clouds. Well, man, I can't do it 'cause I got to make something and fast! You hear me? I got to get so big in this business that that there theater in Lawrence, Kansas, will beg me, beg me to come home and play there. I got to be so big I'll be able to tell them: No! No, *Mister* George Walker ain't playing there 'cause when I was shining shoes outside your door, you wouldn't let me in! I got to tell 'em: You made my mother cry—made her cry 'cause I asked her to take me to that theater and she had to tell me: "Son, we can't go in them places!" (*Then.*) Oh, what'm I wasting words on you for? Read your book!

BERT: George—don't talk like that. Don't get discouraged. Remember: This is the early stage of development. Later— the real train ride. (*The whistle blows. He goes, opens the sliding door and light seeps in.*) That's Chicago, George. A big city! Look out there at the dawn breaking over the lake. The waves are rolling into the city, but the city's standing there, rising up like a mighty mountain, not moving. It looks like we're riding in on the lake waves and the dawn. And nothing's going to stop us—not even that mountain of a city! We're going to make it here, George! We're going to make it! (*He stands there, swerving just a little as the train whistle shrieks loudly. His feet are planted firmly now. The music rises and the lights fade out.*)

Scene 4

(*The Chicago Theater. Two days later.*

The lights fade in on a marquee which shows the theater name and headliners. Included we find "Ada and Hattie: Dance Team" and "Williams and Walker Comedy Team."

LOTTIE THOMPSON *and* JESSE SHIPPS *appear beneath the marquee.* LOTTIE *takes some money from her pocketbook.*)

LOTTIE: I'll pay this time, Jesse.

JESSE: Wait. Don't pay. Let's wait in the alley and meet them as they're being bounced.

LOTTIE: Don't be silly. They're going to hit it big someday, Jesse.

JESSE: I hope it's soon. I'm going broke following them around.

(*They move off into the darkness. Now the lights come up and we see* ADA *and* HATTIE, *two attractive black women, performing a dance routine in center stage. They are framed by vaudeville cards which identify them by name. At the extreme right we see the wing area where* MR. DUDLEY, *manager, stands, watching* ADA *and* HATTIE. *This large, fat, middle-aged white man chews on his cigar approvingly as the dancers conclude their number and move off into the wing area.* GEORGE *steps into the wing area, preparing to go on stage. He meets* ADA *and* HATTIE *as they dance off.* GEORGE *looks at* ADA.)

GEORGE: Yum-yum-yum! You can play the same bill with me any day!

HATTIE: Lord! Who hired you? You know the Man ain't letting more than two of us work one place at the same time!

DUDLEY: Hey, you, Walker! You hired to do a show back here or out there?

GEORGE: Oh! Yes, sir!

(*And he rushes toward the onstage area.* ADA *looks after him, draws a deep breath.*)

ADA: He's cute!

HATTIE (*grabs her arm*): Come on, starry eyes! He's after your job, not your loving!

(*She pulls* ADA *completely offstage. The music has now become low and mournful. The vaudeville cards flip and we see: "Chicago Theater: Williams and Walker Comedy Team."* BERT *enters from stage right, neatly dressed, banjo in hand.* GEORGE *enters from stage left. In center stage they pass without seeing each other. This action is obviously designed to create laughter by suggesting that both men are so dark-complexioned that they cannot be seen. It fails because* BERT *is without blackface. Both men leave the stage, then return with lamps. They meet in center stage, hold up the lamps to each other's faces, then there is recognition.*)

GEORGE: Hey, man!

BERT: Hey, yourself! I didn't know that was you. I sure am

glad to see you. I wanted to ask you: Who was that lady I saw you with last night?

GEORGE: That wasn't no lady. That was my mother-in-law! (*Both men laugh.* DUDLEY *bites his cigar in disgust.*)

BERT: Boy, you is a mess!

GEORGE: Listen, I got a deal for you. The only reason I'm letting you in on this is 'cause we is friends, see—?

BERT: I done seen so many deals that I closes my eyes when one comes along. This house I just bought is right by a cemetery. Coming home the other night, I saw a ghost. Ummm—I run so fast my feet never touched the ground. About a mile away, I set down to rest some. I looked around and the ghost was right beside me. The ghost says: "That was some purty running. Purtiest piece of running I ever saw." I says: "Yeah? Well, you wait till I catch my breath and you gonna see some more!" (*The drum "punctuates" this remark.* DUDLEY *groans and nearly swallows his cigar.*)

GEORGE: But, listen—this deal of mine means money!

BERT (*playing banjo and singing*):
Money is the root of all evil
No matter where you happen to go.

GEORGE (*singing*):
But nobody pays any objection
To the root—now, ain't that so?

BERT:
You know how it is with money—
How it makes you feel at ease—
The world puts on a big, broad smile

GEORGE:
And your friends am thick as bees!

BERT:
But, oh, when your money is running low,
And you clinging to a solitary dime—
Your creditors are num'rous and your friends are few

GEORGE:
Oh! That's the awful time!

BOTH:
That am the time—oh, that am the time
When it's all going out and nothing's coming in!
That's the time when the troubles begin:
Money getting low, people say: I told you so!
And you can't borrow a penny from any of your kin,
And it's all going out and nothing's coming in!

589

BERT:
Had my share of this world's trials—
Nobody knows how hard I has tried
To keep my little boat from sinking
And to battle with the tide!
GEORGE:
You know when you've got money
You can easy keep afloat—
The stream is smooth and all your friends
Tries to help you to row your boat.
BERT:
But, oh, when your money is running low,
And the stream gets rough,
And things look mighty blue,
You look around for help and find
GEORGE:
Each of your friends is paddling his own canoe!
BERT:
That am the time! Oh, that am the time!
BOTH:
When it's all going out and nothing's coming in!
That am the time when the troubles begin—
Money getting low, people say: I told you so!
And you can't borrow a penny from any of your kin,
And it's all going out and nothing's coming in!
(*They face each other and dance the Cakewalk. They move off into the wing area.* DUDLEY *is obviously annoyed. He gives* GEORGE *a bill.*)

DUDLEY: That's your carfare. Get outa here before the audience catches you!

BERT: What's wrong?

DUDLEY: What's wrong??? Damn it, I coulda hired *any* two comedians to do *that.*

GEORGE: Come on, Bert.

BERT: Wait. We were hired and—

DUDLEY: Now you're fired.

BERT: You have to give us our pay.

DUDLEY: I'll give you hell! Get your black asses outa my theater!

BERT: Why, you parasitic paranoid—!

GEORGE (*rushing between them, pushing* BERT *offstage*): Man, come on! You wants start a riot???

(DUDLEY *puzzles a moment and he is about to start after them when* ADA *and* HATTIE *reappear. He turns on them.*)

DUDLEY: Ada—Hattie. What the hell does parasitic para-
590

something mean? (*The girls look at each other, then shrug.*) I think that son of a bitch might've insulted me! After all I did for him! (*He bites on cigar. The lights fade.*)

Scene 5

(*The scene is a small room in a Chicago boarding house. An hour later. The room is small and cluttered. There is a closet door, center, rear, the suggestion of a window opening onto a balcony at extreme left, a balcony rail. In the room there are chairs, a table an armchair, and the old trunk.*

A knock is heard offstage as the lights fade in, then.)

A WOMAN'S VOICE: Mr. Williams! Mr. Walker! (*No answer.*) They ain't in, folks.

(*Footsteps are heard, moving away. A moment later the closet door is opened.* BERT *is in the closet on hands and knees.* GEORGE *is on* BERT'S *back.* GEORGE *jumps off and into the room.* BERT *follows, stretching his limbs.*)

GEORGE: She got the law after us! Over a couple days' rent! Come on! Let's get outa here. (*He takes one end of the trunk and* BERT *takes the other. They start for the door, then stop.*) Wait! We can't go out that way! (*They drop the trunk with a thud.*) Shhh! Fool!

BERT (*sitting on trunk*): Someday I hope we'll be able to pay a landlady and not have to slip this thing out.

GEORGE: Yeah . . . You said things would be better in Chicago.

BERT: "A dark man shall see dark days." Who said that?

GEORGE: Probably you. (*Sits on the other end of trunk.*) This trunk gets heavier and heavier. What you got in there?

BERT: Your stuff's in there, too.

GEORGE: A few suits wouldn't make that much difference.

BERT: The price of those suits would've paid our rent.

GEORGE: You spent as much on books as I did on clothes.

BERT: A book is something you can keep forever.

GEORGE: Yeah? Well, you let your behind get cold and see which does you the most good, a book or a suit.

BERT: At times your utilitarianism is misdirected.

GEORGE: You got words like that in them books? No wonder they so big! (*Suddenly.*) What you do with them books? (BERT *avoids his look. Realization strikes* GEORGE *who closes his eyes, points to trunk.*) No! Don't tell me! (BERT *shrugs.*) Now, listen— (*And he jumps up, stops, then.*) Wait! I got an idea! We can go out the window—

BERT: With the trunk?

GEORGE: No. With just the books. We can take 'em, sell 'em, and pay our rent.

BERT: No, indeed!

GEORGE: You got any better ideas?

BERT: Yes. Let's pawn your clothes.

GEORGE: Man, you gone crazy? You put my clothes in the pawn shop and you gonna put me in there, too! (*Then.*) These clothes is new! Some of them books is old as hell. You said yourself one was wrote three thousand years ago—the one by Harry Bottle.

BERT (*corrects him, sharply*): *Aristotle!*

GEORGE: Whatever his name was! Anyway, everybody's read a book that old.

BERT: You haven't!

GEORGE: Stop changing the subject! What the hell good are them books?

BERT: They keep me in harmony. (GEORGE *looks at him.*) Especially after trying days among people.

GEORGE: You stuck-up, stubborn West Indian fool! No wonder we can't get no place! You keep holding us back!

BERT: I???

GEORGE: Yes, you! You won't wear burnt cork! You won't do nothing but act hinkty! That manager in Omaha told me I ain't gonna get no place 'cause of you. You think you something!

BERT: Don't echo the attitude of your arrogant whites.

GEORGE: *My* arrogant whites? I didn't invent them, you know. (*Then.*) Yours any better? And don't tell me yes, either! Your pa went and built up that fine rum-exporting business, then his white relatives come in to help him out. And they helped him right outa his business! (*Angrily.*) I get sick and tired of folks complaining about this country!

BERT: It's the people, not the country.

GEORGE: What's the difference between my white folks and yourn?

BERT: The British knife with subtlety. (*Then.*) What are we arguing about?

GEORGE: I don't know. You started it.

BERT: I did not. American whites started it.

GEORGE: I ain't talking about them. To hell with them!

BERT: That's wrong, too.

GEORGE: Then, to hell with you *and* them! I mean it, too! Just try seeing how far you can get without me! Go ahead! (BERT *rises, reaches into trunk to remove his books.*) Never mind! I'll get *my* things out. Your folks brung this trunk here from the island and I sure don't want it! (*Getting his things.*)

Looks like Noah brought it here on his Ark! (*He pulls out his suit, shoes, socks, shirts, stacks these in his arms. A shirt drops to the floor,* BERT *reaches for it.* GEORGE *shouts.*) Leave it alone! That's my good shirt! (*He starts to pick it up and as he does, he spills the other things.* BERT *again starts to help him and* GEORGE *snaps.*) I don't need your help!

(GEORGE *finally gets all the pieces in his arms, then stands there.* BERT *reaches into the trunk, gets out a pair of shoes, holds them out to* GEORGE. GEORGE *reaches for the shoes and as he does, he drops the whole stack of clothing.* BERT *laughs.* GEORGE *is furious. He starts to pick up things and this time* BERT *gets down and helps him. Now, they stand there, both with their arms full. They look at each other and* GEORGE *smiles, feebly.*)

BERT: Put this damn stuff back in the trunk! (*They are both smiling. They put the stuff back into the trunk.* BERT *shuts the lid, tries to lock it and snags his fingers.*) Owww! (*He sticks his finger in his mouth.* GEORGE *takes handkerchief, goes to him.*)

GEORGE: Lemme see it.

BERT (*as* GEORGE *wraps finger*): That's your lace handkerchief.

GEORGE: The devil with it!

BERT: Thanks.

(*They sit back down on the trunk.* BERT *turns, looks at* GEORGE. *They both smile.* BERT *places an arm around* GEORGE's *shoulder.*)

GEORGE: We got to get that lock fixed!

BERT: Yeah. (*Suddenly* GEORGE *jumps up.*) You have another idea?

GEORGE: Yes! One of us oughta go down and try sweet-talking that landlady while the other one slips the trunk outa the window. Then we can meet outside. (*Charitably.*) I'll move the trunk.

BERT: It's pretty heavy. Besides, you talk faster than I do.

GEORGE: Well—if you insist. Meet you outside in five minutes.

BERT: How will I get outside?

GEORGE: Jump. (*And he goes out.* BERT *now begins to move the trunk toward the window. It is heavy. He pulls it to window, reaches for one end, starts lifting it so he can get behind the other end and push it out the window. He has it in the right position when we hear* GEORGE's *voice.*) Bert! Bert! Wait—

BERT (*as* GEORGE *dashes in*): Man, you're supposed to be outside!

GEORGE: No! We're staying here!

BERT: George, did you promise the landlady you'd marry her?

GEORGE: No. Of course not.

BERT: Then you must've promised her I'd marry her. (*And he starts trying to push the trunk.* GEORGE *grabs his arm.*)

GEORGE: Man, will you wait? She called us 'cause Jesse Shipp and Lottie Thompson was here to see us. (BERT *looks at him.*) You heard me. I said Lottie Thompson, the concert pianist. And Jesse Shipp, the producer-director-writer-singer and everything else—the man who knows folks so big they use five-dollar bills to light their cigars with.

BERT: Someone's playing a joke on us. Help me with this trunk.

GEORGE: Will you listen? We're on her good side now.

BERT: Wait'll she finds out this was a fake.

GEORGE (*struggles with* BERT *who struggles with trunk*): Will you stop a minute? Here's Jesse Shipp's card—saying that they'll be stopping back this way soon.

BERT: They can't come here and find the place like this!

(*They look around, then launch into the furious business of cleaning the room. In rapid-fire tempo the trunk is put back into its place, the chairs are properly placed, and* BERT *has swept the floor.* GEORGE *holds up the armchair and* BERT *sweeps the trash under it. The men now flop into chairs and try to catch their breaths.*)

BERT: We should be reading when they arrive.

GEORGE: They'll think we're putting on airs. Let's play Smut.

BERT: They'll think we're gamblers.

GEORGE: Not the way we play!

(*They sit at table.* BERT *deals cards.* GEORGE *promptly beats him.* BERT *reaches for the lamp as* GEORGE *laughs. We hear a woman's voice.*)

WOMAN: Mr. Walker! Mr. Williams!

(GEORGE *goes, admits* JESSE SHIPP *and* LOTTIE THOMPSON.)

JESSE: Good evening. I'm—

GEORGE: Jesse Shipp. And this is Miss Thompson.

LOTTIE: Yes. Good evening.

GEORGE: Come in, please. I'm George Walker. And this is Bert Williams.

LOTTIE: Are we interrupting?

BERT: No. We were just playing Smut—

GEORGE: That's poker without money. The loser puts lamp soot on his face. You just saved him. (BERT *has moved arm-*

chair for LOTTIE *to sit in.* GEORGE *reaches over, pulls his coat, gestures toward trash they have swept under it.* BERT *puts chair back, quickly.*) We—we don't think that's chair's comfortable enough for you.

LOTTIE: Oh, I'm sure it's all right. (*And she crosses and sits in chair.*)

JESSE: Oliver Jackson told us—

BERT: Mr. Jackson!

JESSE: Yes. He told us to be sure and catch your act. We did today.

BERT: Yes. (*Looking at* LOTTIE.) You sat in the first row balcony. Right side.

LOTTIE: Ye-es.

BERT: I glanced that way. You also saw us in Milwaukee.

GEORGE (*to* BERT): Keep your mind on your work and we might keep a job.

JESSE: We're here on business. Lottie—

LOTTIE: Yes. In this growing country every town and hamlet will have a theater by the year 1900.

GEORGE: Yeah, but will we play in them?

LOTTIE: *How* will we play in them is the question. The Irish will be the drunks, the Jews the money-lenders, the Italians the fools. You know what that means for us:

(*In dialect.*)

"Poor black me is just old Black Joe—

The white man is boss, the whole show!"

BERT: Say, you have a wonderful ear! Of course, your subject matter—

JESSE: That's why we're here. To bring truth to the theater—

BERT (*to* LOTTIE): I love mimicry! Back home I used to study the birds and—

JESSE: Miss Thompson and I have been attacking this obliquely—doing ragtime and classics.

BERT (*continues, to* LOTTIE): I would copy their gestures and—

JESSE: Mr. Williams!

BERT: Oh! Yes?

JESSE: We're attacking minstrels head-on. I'm producing an all-colored show on Broadway, then in England. I want you two to star in it.

GEORGE (*as he and* BERT *exchange looks*): Slap me. I wanta see if I'm awake. (BERT *raises his hand.*) No. Never mind!

JESSE: Interested?

GEORGE: Well—we ain't talked about money yet.

JESSE: That'll be your decision. You'll be producers, too.

GEORGE: Bert, maybe you better slap me after all. (*Then.*)
Now, wait a minute. This is all fine and we appreciate the
compliment, but we can't produce our rent, let alone a show.

JESSE: No one's asking you for a dime.

LOTTIE: This is no quick decision. We scouted a hundred
people before deciding on you two.

JESSE: We book you into Koster and Bial's in New York,
along with Oliver. We'll team you with Ada and Hattie.

GEORGE: Forget Hattie. I'll team with Ada.

JESSE: Please let me finish! You do a long sketch there.
In a week's time the script's worked out, the money's raised—
and you're paid and headlined!

BERT: Sounds good!

GEORGE: Too good! What's the catch?

JESSE: There may be one: Williams must wear burnt cork.

BERT: Why?

JESSE: Everything else is going for you. Voice. Gestures.
In Lottie's words: You have the hands of an artist.

BERT: Why burnt cork?

LOTTIE: Because—because you're not like we're expected
to be.

GEORGE: Told you to forget that Anglican stuff in a Baptist
world!

BERT: I thought you were breaking with minstrels.

JESSE: We will.

BERT: Slowly, I suppose. (GEORGE *nudges him.*) Stop
elbowing me!

JESSE: Mr. Williams, theater is *business*.

BERT: I happen to know that.

JESSE: Sentiment is for audiences. And they're not going
to finance your personal revolutions. In fact, you're naïve if
you think we *want* a revolution. We're struggling for the right
to be mediocre.

BERT: So far you're a blazing success.

JESSE: You could be, too. A success, I mean.

BERT: Yes. In the parade of indistinguishable comedians.

JESSE: The cork washes off, you know.

LOTTIE: Jesse!

BERT (*facing him*): Maybe it does, Mr. Jesse Shipp. But
can it be washed out of my mind, out of the minds of people
who'll say: That's what he is, what they all are! (*Then.*) No,
thank you. I'll starve first. (*He turns, goes out onto the balcony. An annoyed* LOTTIE *faces* JESSE.)

LOTTIE: Jesse, for God's sake! If our future depends upon your tact, we'll die young deaths in the poorhouse.

JESSE: I swear to God, when I leave here I'm going to the zoo and stick my head in the lion's cage. And I'll bet he'll be gentler with me than you folks.

LOTTIE: Take some bicarbonate of soda along for the lion! (*She goes out toward the balcony area.* GEORGE *starts to follow, stops, faces* JESSE.)

GEORGE: Mr. Shipp, I'm sorry. Look—my partner doesn't handle business matters. Let's you and me talk.

JESSE: Yeah. Let's go down to the corner bar.

GEORGE: Well, I—er—don't drink after five o'clock. Not good for me.

JESSE: Oh. I was going to buy you a couple.

GEORGE: Well, in that case—rather than disappoint you, I'll forget my health. Let's go.

(*They start out.* JESSE *stops, makes a gesture toward* LOTTIE *who is on the balcony with* BERT. *The lights fade in this area.*)

Scene 6

(*The balcony area, just outside the window of the room. Immediately following the previous scene.*

As the lights come up in this area we see BERT *standing alone, leaning against the building. He toys with his banjo, then sings. During the course of the song* LOTTIE *appears behind him on the balcony.*)

BERT (*singing*):

  I left my home on an island shore
  Where sailfish played all day long.
  I came a-knocking at the stranger's door
  With my funny smile and my brand-new song.

  I left my home on a tropic isle
  Where sky and sea kissed the sand—
  Though through my tears I am compelled to smile,
  There's a sadness I cannot understand!

  Dreams haven't always come true!
  I suppose I've always understood
  That the sun hasn't shone as it should!
  If it could!
  Dreams haven't always come true!

I left my home with a dream to try
To climb the mountains and sky,
And now I find there's a tear in my eye
For my memories cannot ever die!

LOTTIE: Beautiful. You wrote that?

BERT: Once. In the wild dream it could be used in a show about us. Not one *he'd* produce.

LOTTIE: Jesse's excitable—but nice. He'll love your song. And use it someday.

BERT: I'll be dead by then.

LOTTIE: I don't believe you believe that.

BERT:
"Full many a flower is born to blush unseen
And waste its sweetness on the desert air."

LOTTIE: Gray's *Elegy*. Poetic masochism.

BERT: Eh-eh!

LOTTIE: "A city on a hill must be seen." I like that better. It was my father's favorite sermon.

BERT: He was a minister?

LOTTIE: A great one!

BERT: I didn't say he wasn't.

LOTTIE: Forgive me. I'm defensive about our men. They're shoved into the shadows of that city.

BERT (*impulsively*): I like you! You're brilliant and beautiful!

LOTTIE: Thank you. I like you, too.

(*He starts to reach for her hand, stops, turns away.*)

BERT: I forgot: you're working on me.

LOTTIE: I'm what?

BERT (*imitating the gesture* JESSE *made to her*): I don't miss anything, Miss Thompson. The flight of a bird. A wisp of smoke. A gesture to a lady. I might use them someday.

LOTTIE: To make that someday a reality. That's what interests me.

BERT: Enough to ask a man to wear a false face.

LOTTIE: Face? Is that all you see, Mr. Williams? Can't you talk from the inside—or are you afraid to show what's really there?

(*She moves away from him, annoyed, steps to the balcony rail. He smiles at her outburst. Suddenly, she whirls around, dizzily, then tries to move from the rail. Her hand flies up to her head as she starts to collapse. He rushes to her side, grabs hold of her.*)

BERT: Miss Thompson! Miss Thompson! (*He stands there, holding her. Now he leads her back into the room as the lights come up in that area.*)

Scene 7

(*Inside the room.* BERT *assists* LOTTIE *into the room, takes her to a seat, and sits beside her.*)

BERT: Miss Thompson—can I get you something?

LOTTIE: No. I'll—be—all right.

BERT: I'll get you some water.

LOTTIE: Please. Just let me sit like this a minute.

BERT (*his arm around her*): You sit like this as long as you want to . . . (*Her head is on his shoulder.*) Feel better?

LOTTIE (*disengaging herself*): Yes. Thank you.

BERT: You certainly have marvelous recuperative powers! (*Tries to embrace her again.*) Are you sure you're all right?

LOTTIE (*avoiding his embrace*): Positive.

BERT: I looked around and you were—

LOTTIE: I know. I know. I feel silly.

BERT: You people here punish yourselves for being different.

LOTTIE: Don't people everywhere?

BERT: I like to think they don't back home. What happened?

LOTTIE: Nothing.

BERT: Something *did* happen. Suddenly the direct business woman became very feminine. (*Insistently.*) Miss Thompson, why does height make you dizzy?

LOTTIE: You'll laugh at me.

BERT: I won't. I hate people who laugh at others. (*He takes her hand. She looks at him, then seemingly beyond him.*)

LOTTIE: We had an apple tree in our backyard. Tall, almost touching the sky. When I was a girl I thought its peak was the top of the world. Sometimes in my dreams I'd climb the tree, then reach up and touch the tip of a star—and it would lift me out over the town and people would point at me and say: "There she is! She stands for something!" . . . When I was ten I decided to climb the tree. At the top I reached for that star. I crashed to the ground. I was near death for two months.

BERT: Good Lord!

LOTTIE: After that, a flight of stairs frightened me. Papa said it was a warning: Beware of the top of the world. He was right. When I overstep myself, it always happens.

BERT: No. It happens to others. I've had that same dream—of the highest Antigua mountain, of climbing it, but never reaching the top—because I was always alone. (*Then.*) I wish we were there together.

LOTTIE: We will be someday. (*He holds her hand.*) We've

599

brought you a way back to your island.

BERT: You're working on me. I know it. But I love it! (*Singing, impulsively.*)

> I'm glad I'm gone from that island shore
> Where sky and sea kissed the sand—
> Now through my tears I am compelled to smile—
> There's a gladness I cannot understand!

LOTTIE (*as music carries under*): Mr. Williams, don't wallow in tears. No one gets to a mountaintop climbing alone.

(*He walks away in thought, sits at card table, lights cigarette, toys with the cards.*)

BERT: America is one place where everything is done in excess—and quickly.

(*He plays cards, somewhat mechanically. He spreads out a dummy hand, takes a card from the dummy, then plays a winning card from his own hand. He reaches into the dummy and carefully, deliberately, chooses the wrong card.*

LOTTIE *now stands over him. She reaches and takes the wrong card that he has played. She puts it back in the dummy hand, then she selects the right and winning card. He looks up at her. She smiles, takes the lamp, pushes it toward him.*)

LOTTIE: You have your first citizenship papers.

(BERT *smiles, ruefully, takes the lamp and starts to apply lamp soot to his face. A smile appears on her lips. The music rises and the lights fade out.*)

Scene 8

(*The scene is Koster and Bial's, New York City. A month later.*

When the lights fade in we see JESSE *and* OLIVER *in the wing area with* LOTTIE. *They are watching* GEORGE, ADA *and* HATTIE *in the onstage area. Vaudeville cards frame them, reading: "Williams and Walker Company."* GEORGE *talks over music.*)

GEORGE:

> I'm a summer breeze on a cold, cold night—
> I'm a girdle holding a figure tight—
> I'm the key to a winekeeper's cellar,
> I'd have been the Queen of Sheba's feller!
> I'm the scent to a skunk,
> I'm the dough lent a drunk,
> And if you want to know what's next:

(*Lively music. He sings.*)

> I'm absolutely, positively, I'm most acutely unperplexed

'Cause I'm the key to sex!

The critics doubt that I'm good,
It's understood their heads are wood,
For they don't rate me as they should,
For positively I'm the most!
I'm real sure of all that I've got.
I have much more than I have not—
My lot is Johnny-on-the-Spot,
For positively I'm the most!
I hold the upper hand in each situation,
Have the answer to all aggravation,
Nature will allow just one like me per nation!
I own the key to Paree—
Its women are my cup of tea!
In fact, the world's in love with me,
For positively I'm the most —
For positively I'm the most!

(GEORGE *and the girls perform a dance routine.* GEORGE *then breaks into his famous strutting routine and the girls join him. As the routine continues* LOTTIE *steps into the wing area, carrying a telegram.*)

LOTTIE: Telegram, Jesse.

JESSE (*opens it, reads*): Look, Lottie! Look!

(*She reads it. They embrace, happily.*)

OLIVER: Jesse, you gone crazy? You better unhand that girl 'fore Bert sees you!

JESSE: Here it is! Here it is!

OLIVER: Jesse—you lost your mind?

JESSE: Listen! Our agent— (*Trying to read.*) "You open —you—"

LOTTIE (*reads for him as his voice trembles*): "You open Majestic Theater Broadway in six weeks, then England. Can you do it?"

OLIVER: Can we do it? (*Jumping up and down.*) We made it! We made it! We had to go through Third Avenue burlesque houses and outhouses, but we made it! (*Starts toward onstage area.*) George! George!

JESSE (*recovers, grabs him*): Where the hell you going?

OLIVER: Out there to give George something to strut about!

JESSE: Fool! Come back here! (*He practically tackles* OLIVER *as the lights fade out quickly.*)

Scene 9

(*The Majestic Theater. Six weeks later.*

The lights fade in on the playing area. GEORGE, ADA, *and* HATTIE *continue their strutting routine from the previous scene.* OLIVER *has joined them.* LOTTIE *and* JESSE *remain in the wing area, watching.*

BERT *wanders into the playing area, in blackface. He attempts to join the dance routine. He is ridiculously awkward and both feet slide out from under him. He lands on his backside in vaudeville fashion.* GEORGE, ADA, HATTIE, *and* OLIVER *dance off. The music becomes low and mournful.*)

BERT (*singing*):

> I'm a Jonah man, I'm a Jonah man
> And no matter how much right I do
> It always comes out wrong.
> I sing the bluest song.
> I'm a Jonah man.
>
> I'm a Jonah man, I'm a Jonah man
> Who's 'bout left the belly of the whale,
> When almost gettin' out
> I falls back in and shout:
> I'm a Jonah man.
>
> I tries a little bit of this,
> I tries a little bit of that.
> There ain't a thing that I has missed.
> I give my underwear and hat.
> I reach a helping hand to all,
> The more I reach, the lower I fall.
>
> I'm a Jonah man, I'm a Jonah man
> Who's lost about all a man can lose,
> The blues I'd never choose
> But caught the Jonah blues.
> I'm a Jonah man.

(*He sits there.* GEORGE, ADA, HATTIE, *and* OLIVER *strut by him, ignoring him. Now* BERT *pulls out a roll of bills from his pocket. The four stop, abruptly, and their stops are accentuated by drumbeats.* BERT *pulls out another roll.* GEORGE *dances forward, offers* BERT *his hand.* OLIVER *dances forward, offers* BERT *his hand.* ADA *whirls around, suggestively, beckoning to* BERT. HATTIE *dances a few more suggestive steps.* BERT *shakes his head, starts putting the money back into his pocket.*)

BERT (*singing*):

You're in the right church but you're going to the wrong
   pew—

You're on the right street but you don't know what to do.

You're in the Lord's house but you don't know 'bout the
    right score.
You're in the right church, still you don't know what
    to do.
If you plays with fate,
You'll be dealt with straight.
You can't expect to win
If you play with sin.

You're in the right church but you're going to the wrong
    pew—
That's all.
That's all!

(He places all the money back into his pockets, turns, tips his hat, then walks off. The lights fade in that area and they come up in the wings. LOTTIE *embraces* BERT.)*

LOTTIE: Honey! You remembered all the words to the song this time!

BERT: Couldn't miss. I had the lyrics written on my gloves. *(Holds up his white gloves. She laughs, then hugs him impulsively.)* Look out! You'll get this cork on you.

LOTTIE: I don't care, I don't care.

BERT: I do. I'll remove it during intermission and propose to you in style.

LOTTIE: I'll take you any way I can get you.

BERT: You deserve me at my best, not in this stuff. It eats into my skin.

LOTTIE: You eat into my heart!

BERT *(kissing her)*: Lottie—Lottie—

(They remain in an embrace as the music rises. The lights fade out completely.)

Scene 10

(Buckingham Palace. London, England. A few years later.

Across the backdrop, etched in lights, we see the Tower of London. The lights now fade in on the wing area where ADA, HATTIE, GEORGE, JESSE, BERT, *and* LOTTIE *stand, watching* OLIVER *perform a soft-shoe tap routine in the onstage area.* JESSE *holds a script in his hand. The others are in costume, waiting to go on.)*

LOTTIE: That man gets younger every year.

BERT: Oliver? Yes!

JESSE: You climax sixty years of knocking around with a Command Performance and you'll find the Fountain of Youth, too!

ADA: I still can't believe it! Me! Playing before the King of England! And all *these* English *men!* They look at a woman and undress her at the same time.

GEORGE: They better not look at *you.*

ADA: I'm not letting England go to my head, dear.

HATTIE: It wouldn't be going any place if it did.

ADA: Hattie, shut up!

HATTIE: Don't you—

JESSE: Both of you shut up! Every day for two straight years I've had to listen to your mouths! Stop for tonight. (*Then, as* OLIVER *completes his number.*) Cue 112—

(*A spotlight is on* OLIVER *in the onstage area. We hear a blues number as he sings.*)

OLIVER (*singing*):

We have a young man who's in a low-down jam!
We have a young man who's in a low-down jam!
He's stole a vase. His fate's not worth a damn!

(*Now another light comes up on* BERT *who is sitting behind bars.* GEORGE *stands on the other side of the bars, talking to* BERT. *The light on* OLIVER *is down.*)

GEORGE: Now, you went and done it! I brought you all the way here to Abyssinia and you got to wind up in jail! For stealing a vase! Man, I done took you outa the country, but I sure can't take the country outa you!

BERT: I sure wish you could take me outa this country fast!

GEORGE: Oh, keep still! You know the punishment for what you done? They gonna cut off your hand! What you gonna look like with one hand and a nub?

BERT (*finally*): Oh, I'll put a hook on it!

GEORGE: Lord, how much can a man stand? I brung you over here where you can get some culture and refinement and you go walking through all this culture, looking like some *vulture!* I even take you swimming, half-hoping you gonna drown, but the water takes one look at you and it begins to frown! And it backs up to your knees! You just one great big worriation to me. Like a bad penny, always turning up when you oughta be turning down! (*Music. He sings.*)

You like a bad, bad ole penny—
It's time for me to toss you away,
But when I do, you'll just roll back one day!
You like a bad, bad ole penny—
I can't see how you're worth one cent,
And don't tell me you're going to repent!
Bad, bad ole penny—
Bad, bad ole penny!

You do disgrace poor Mr. Lincoln's face!
Yes, you're a bad, bad ole penny—
You're counterfeit and who wants you,
And when you fall you can't seem to ring true!
You good-for-nothing ole penny,
Now since I can't give you away,
Must I be stuck with you each weary day?
Bad, bad ole penny!
Bad, bad ole penny!
You do disgrace poor Mr. Lincoln's face!

BERT (*singing*):
Now, listen, George Walker, don't say that to me!
Now, listen, George Walker, don't say that to me!
'Cause if you do, we is bound to disagree!
My friends treat me like a old pair of shoes.
You kicks me 'round and does me like you choose!

GEORGE (*singing*):
Bad, bad ole penny—
Bad, bad ole penny!
You do disgrace poor Mr. Lincoln's face!

(*The music carries under.* CHARLIE, *a young Negro actor, steps into the scene, dressed as the* EMPEROR. *He goes to throne that has appeared in center stage. Two* GUARDS *remove* BERT *from behind the bars and bring him before the* EMPEROR. GEORGE *gets out of there.* BERT *kneels before the* EMPEROR. OLIVER *steps forward as the music continues.*)

OLIVER:
Say, listen, young man, you're in a low-down mess!
Say, listen, young man, you're in a low-down mess!
You stole a vase—you ain't 'bout to be blessed!
You've done a few things since you've been in our midst.
You've done a few things since you've been in our midst,
So we've compiled and we've a lil' old list!

(*He produces the list. The little old list turns out to be fifteen feet long. Music carries under.*)

BERT: Your Honor—I mean, Your Majesty—I know you got the sentence all writ, but ain't no sense giving it to me 'cause I can't read it. (*He laughs nervously. No one joins him. He stifles his laugh, then.*) I can't read 'cause when I was a young'un old schoolhouse was six miles away. I couldn't walk that fur 'cause I didn't have no shoes to walk in. Besides, I hadda work in the fields and raise crops for my ma and my six brothers . . . Your Majesty, I just don't unnerstand the ways of the folks back home, let alone over here. And I done the wrong thing. But I ain't never seen a vase as purty as

that one. (*Looks at his hand.*) Don't know how I'm gonna eat with one hand and a nub. 'Course, I ain't always had something to eat so I reckon it won't matter much if I ain't got nothing to eat with . . . When I was borned hard luck was flying 'round my head and it lit smack on me, and there it's stayed. But, I ain't never meant to do no wrong. I ain't never done nothing to nobody no time— (*Music. He sings.*)

I ain't never done nothing to nobody—
I ain't never got nothing from nobody no time,
And until I get something from somebody sometime,
I don't intend to do nothing to nobody no time!

When life is full of cloud and rain
And I am filled with naught but pain,
Who soothes my aching, bumping brain,
Umm—nobody—no time.

I had a steak some time ago,
With sauce I sprinkled it over—
Who said that was tabasco sauce?
Nobody—umm—Nobody!

When I was in that recent railroad wreck
And I thought I cashed in my last check,
Who pulled that engine from 'round my neck?
Who? Umm—Nobody!

I ain't never done nothing to nobody no time,
I ain't never got nothing from nobody no time
And until I get something from somebody sometime,
I don't intend to do nothing for nobody no time!

CHARLIE (as the music breaks): You'll be told the judgment by the ringing of our great bell. If it rings four times, you'll be pardoned. If it rings only three times, you'll have your right hand cut off—up to here!

(*He indicates the shoulder, then gets up and leaves the stage.* BERT *stands there.*)

I ain't never done nothing to nobody—
    (*The bell rings.*)
I ain't never got nothing from nobody no time—
    (*The bell rings again.*)
And until I get something from somebody sometime
I don't intend to do nothing for nobody no time!

(*The bell rings a third time.* BERT *opens his mouth, but the words will not come. He gasps through the song, his hand in mid-air. He tries to move it, but he cannot. He sinks to his knees. Suddenly, the bell rings a fourth time. He becomes*

GEORGE: What did I do wrong?

BERT: It would take me all year to tell you! (*And he follows* LOTTIE *off.*)

ADA: Honey—even I know that you don't ask married women when they're having children. Or—for that matter —single women either. (*She goes.* GEORGE *stands there, puzzled. Then, suddenly he realizes that* LOTTIE *cannot have children. He kicks himself on the shin as* JESSE *appears.*)

GEORGE: Jesse, what in the hell is wrong with me?

JESSE: Ask me when I'm on a ten-year vacation! Where's Bert? (GEORGE *points.*) Abraham Erlanger sure wants him. He left him this note.

GEORGE: He ain't left nothing for me.

JESSE: He didn't get to be a smart producer by accident. (*They start moving across the stage together, both laughing. Suddenly,* GEORGE *stops, catches his chest.*) George—what is it?

GEORGE (*draws a deep breath, then*): Nothing. This damn indigestion.

JESSE: You've complained all week. I think we'd better get back to the States so we can all vacation a while.

(*The lights have come up in the dressing room where* LOTTIE *sits beside* BERT.)

LOTTIE: I'm all right, Bert. It was just that I was soaring and the crash of reality hurt.

BERT: Having children isn't the only thing in life.

LOTTIE: It isn't if you're not a woman

BERT: Honey, we'll have millions of children. Audiences, audiences and more audiences. (*He holds her close.* GEORGE *and* JESSE *step into the scene.*)

GEORGE: Excuse us—for a lot of things.

JESSE: Here. (*And he gives* BERT *a note.*)

BERT: Thanks . . . Erlanger wants to see me tonight. (*Then.*) In Antigua a rich man left his estate to a barefoot orphan. Everybody on the island suddenly wanted to adopt the boy, but the boy kept right on walking around barefoot.

GEORGE: Why?

BERT: So he could stick out his foot and tell folks to kiss it. (GEORGE *and* BERT *laugh.*)

JESSE: Man, don't you tell Erlanger to ki s your foot. His syndicate controls theater.

BERT: It doesn't control the Williams and Walker Company.

GEORGE: Right! And if he comes in here I'll tell him: "Don't you send us no more notes without fancy paper and envelopes."

hysterically joyful, but he is unable to speak or sing. He simply gestures, wildly. The music breaks. He stands, speechless, as the lights fade.)

Scene 11

(The backstage area. Immediately following the previous scene. LOTTIE, ADA, *and company stand there, reveling in the applause we hear from the previous scene.* BERT *and* GEORGE *step into the wing area.* LOTTIE *rushes into* BERT'*s arms.* ADA *hugs* GEORGE.*)*

GEORGE: I tuned 'em up for you, Ada baby!

ADA: You make beautiful music.

GEORGE: Wait'll after the show when I get my whole orchestra to swinging for you!

ADA: I'll dance to your music any day. *(She kisses him.* LOTTIE *gives* BERT *a towel.)*

LOTTIE: After two years I know. The cork eats into your skin.

BERT: Thanks, honey. *(He wipes his face. The others, with the exception of* GEORGE *and* ADA, *leave.)*

GEORGE: Ada, with this behind us we're going places. Even gonna do Shakespeare, with me playing Bologna.

BERT: Polonius!

GEORGE: Yeah. That's the man! He talks for pages and pages—and dies right onstage. *(Stops.)* Say, what act does he die in? I seem to remember a whole lot of talking *after* he dies. What act do you die in?

BERT: The last one.

GEORGE: We'll get Alex Rogers and Jesse to do a little rewriting.

LOTTIE: On Shakespeare?

GEORGE: He won't say anything about it.

BERT: Man, that's like rewriting the Bible!

GEORGE: I've seen some preachers do just that! *(*BERT *laughs, waves at him, then turns back, embraces* LOTTIE, *who is also laughing.)* Ada—look! They married all this time and still honeymooning!

ADA: I don't want to ask you when we're going to start—

GEORGE: Hey, when y'all gonna start collecting diapers instead of books? *(As* LOTTIE *practically freezes.)* What's wrong, Lottie?

LOTTIE: Nothing. Nothing at all. *(She turns, starts off.)*

GEORGE: Lottie—

BERT *(steps in front of him)*: The only reason I don't stick my fist in your big mouth is fear of hydrophobia.

King!" (ERLANGER *laughs.*) I'm just glad it happened to a liberal head of state, not, say to the governor of Alabama or Georgia.

ERLANGER: It's happened to me. My first hit and I'm in the box office. A lady demands four front-row seats. She tells me: "I'm a personal friend of Abraham Erlanger, America's greatest producer." I give her four tickets and tell her: "This is on me." It's during intermission that I realize: I never saw the woman before in my life. (*Then.*) I'd like a word with you, Mr. Williams.

BERT: Please speak freely. We're all one family here.

(*But* LOTTIE, JESSE *and* GEORGE *leave.* BERT *gestures for them to remain.*)

ERLANGER: I'll be brief: I'm a man with a mission.

BERT: A mission?

ERLANGER: Yes. There's no Bible under my arm, but the spirit's in my heart. The spirit of theater, of projecting images through art.

BERT: We're not at odds.

ERLANGER: We will be in a minute. Theater in America is fairy tales. Unreal.

BERT: You produce theater there.

ERLANGER: As a means to an end. The Wright brothers took an airplane over North Carolina. Flew twenty-four and a half miles in little over half an hour. Soon you can fly from New York to Philadelphia, from New York to Jackson, Mississippi.

BERT: Who wants to fly to Mississippi?

ERLANGER: You missed the point. In a shrinking world, organization rules. Railroad, coal, steel, oil. Organized! My syndicate's bringing that to theater.

BERT: For whose sake?

ERLANGER: The theater's. Because I love it, want it to mean more than Cinderella tales, want it to speak directly to human beings. I intend to put it back on the right track. I told you I have a mission.

BERT: Napoleon Bonaparte wanted a United States of Europe.

ERLANGER: I resent that!

BERT: The shoe pinches. West Indians say: Beware of those helping others, for in the end they help themselves.

ERLANGER: You're in the West Indies and I'm in America, even now, standing on British soil. Later for polemics. I want you in my company to become the first featured Negro performer in an all-white company.

BERT: And he'll tell you—(*Imitates the way he believes* ERLANGER *would speak.*) "Mister George Walker, we don't even send notes to whee-eet dolka on fancy paper."

GEORGE: Oh, sorry, boss! I shoulda sanded. I got special shoes for sanding so's I can be called "Mister." (*Freezes.*) Damn it! (*Holds up suspenders.*) I been sanding so much I busted my ten cents suspenders!

(BERT *and* JESSE *are laughing at* GEORGE's *antics. A knock is heard.* LOTTIE *crosses, admits* ABRAHAM ERLANGER, *a medium-sized, pleasant-faced white man of middle years.* GEORGE *does not see him and continues speaking directly to* BERT.)

GEORGE: Look here, Mr. Erlanger. Sanding is expensive!

LOTTIE: Yes?

ERLANGER: I'm Abraham Erlanger.

GEORGE (*to* BERT): I know who you are, so don't be interrupting me. It's got so a colored man can't even get a sentence finished.

LOTTIE: George, this is Abraham Erlanger.

(*Her words reach* GEORGE's *ears. He freezes, one hand in the air, then he brings it down slowly, pretending he was flexing a muscle.* JESSE *and* BERT *also become aware of the visitor.*)

GEORGE: Oh. How do you do, Mr. Erlanger?

BERT: Mr. Erlanger. I'm Bert Williams. Mrs. Williams. Mr. Walker. Mr. Shipp.

ERLANGER: How do you do? I'm interrupting a—a rehearsal?

LOTTIE: No.

GEORGE (*quickly*): Yes! . . . For a new skit. We call it "How to Sand, Man, Without Holding the Bag."

ERLANGER: What's that?

BERT (*glares at* GEORGE, *then*): A family joke. You don't do a Command Performance every day and it's made us giddy. I light two cigarettes at one time. Mr. Walker gets delirious and Mr. Shipp irascible.

ERLANGER: Success has a way of going to the head.

BERT: We started off this morning with Mr. Shipp setting up the stage. A short man in a red vest kept coming around, asking how thir   were going. The third time he appeared, Mr. Shipp expl   d and told him in direct American terms what is wrong v h England, its people, and its customs. The man smiled and walked away. Tonight when the band played "God Save the King," Mr. Shipp peeped out through the curtains and he saw the red-vested man. "My God!" he yelled. "Is that the King? I was expecting the King to look like a

609

BERT: Why ?

ERLANGER: Because artistically, financially, and theatrically, it's worthwhile.

BERT: And my company?

ERLANGER: I won't believe you're so naïve. Companies like this will evaporate like water vapor over a desert.

BERT: Man, you've got nerve!

ERLANGER: Just sense. Know something? Every Jewish section in New York has a theater company like yours, saying what should be said. In fifty years you can count on one hand the Jewish theaters left.

BERT: Hell, if you think that of Jews—

ERLANGER: You *are* naïve! In fifty years someone's going to assume Jews—and maybe Negroes—are humans—and even forget to persecute them. Then—how many Jews will speak Yiddish? How many Negroes will have dialects?

BERT: I don't have to wait fifty years to be human. I'm doing a Command Performance.

ERLANGER: On the shore. I want to put you in the mainstream.

BERT: There's muck in the mainstream.

ERLANGER: We'll pump life from these small companies into it and clean it out. You'll need me as I need you.

BERT: What're you telling me? That I can be the greatest violinist in the world, but I'm second fiddle until you recognize me?

ERLANGER: You're doing a show now about Emperor Menelik of Abyssinia. Three people in the audience may know his name—

BERT: He's part of our history.

ERLANGER: Four people in the audience, then. If five people know, then you're in trouble. When Western society lets a people keep their identity, those people are in trouble. Ask the Jews! The Star of David was on every ghetto lock. (*Then.*) Enough polemics. I'm offering you real recognition. Meantime, you live. In first-rate hotels. Fine theaters. Audiences in mink applauding you. I'm giving you the chance to fly upward among the stars, the bright stars—

BERT (*intrigued, but slowly shakes head*): No. I'd be riding freight elevators in those hotels—with the applause still ringing in my ears.

ERLANGER: Think of the opportunity—

BERT: Excuse me, Mr. Erlanger.

ERLANGER: Mr. Williams—

BERT: I said: Excuse me!

ERLANGER (*looks at him, then*): Good evening, Mr. Williams. (*He goes out.* BERT *stands there as* LOTTIE, JESSE, *and* GEORGE *reenter.*)

JESSE: Man! That was Abraham Erlanger!

BERT: If I had some island foo-foo dust, I'd sprinkle it after him!

JESSE: You might need him someday.

BERT: For what? To fly to Mississippi?

GEORGE: Come on, Jesse. Let's check on the company.

BERT: What the hell's wrong with you two?

LOTTIE: They're trying to tell you you bungled. I think so, too.

BERT: I thought you'd understand. With him I'm chained to burnt cork the rest of my days. Here—there's a way out.

LOTTIE: If we live. He wasn't optimistic.

BERT: Talk straight! First it was wear cork for a while. Now, it's listen to him—

LOTTIE: The cork got you close to the mountainside.

BERT: And we're near the top. Just a few more steps—

(OLIVER *bursts into the room.* HATTIE, ADA, *and* CHARLIE *follow him.*)

OLIVER: Bert! I've got to talk to you!

HATTIE: We've got to talk to you. Right now, too!

ADA: Folks say you're joining Erlanger.

BERT: No, no, no—

HATTIE: Damn it, soon as we get a table, they come and take our bread and butter!

ADA: And break up our family. That's what this is—a family. And I've got to leave home all over again. A good home this time.

CHARLIE: After all of this glory I've got to go back to running elevators and hoping for a part here and there—

BERT: Wait a minute—

HATTIE: Honey, in this business all you got is hope and you sure God can't take that in a store and buy a thing with it!

BERT: Will you wait a minute??? (*Then.*) I am not joining Erlanger. This is my company.

HATTIE: For how long?

BERT: Forever! We're going on from tonight—to do real theater, not the typical colored show they expect from us.

OLIVER: So—ain't we still colored?

CHARLIE: Oliver, this is important. Don't interrupt.

OLIVER: Boy, don't you tell me what to do and what not to do.

CHARLIE: When you're interfering with my career, I will.

OLIVER: Your career? Manure!

CHARLIE: What??? . . . Now, look, Bert, George, Jesse. Ideals kept me with this company. I'm not really a musical type. (*To* OLIVER.) I don't want to tell you what type you are!

OLIVER: One sure thing: You ain't big enough to erase my type! (*To* BERT.) Bert, these folks looking for theirselves. I'm looking out for you 'cause I know you. You and me—we colored and we like it. We come from something and I don't wanta see it wasted away. And that's what's gonna happen if you get up with Erlanger.

CHARLIE: Exactly what are you talking about?

OLIVER: Lord, these young Negroes don't know what I mean. How can I expect white folks to know? (*He turns and walks out.*)

ADA: Uh-uh! Can't colored folks do nothing without arguing?

HATTIE: Let 'em argue. What you want 'em to do? Pass?

ADA: Who's trying to pass?

HATTIE: I didn't say *you* was!

ADA: You better not!

GEORGE: Good Lord! What'd you all have for supper? Ground-up razor blades with acid for appetizers? We got enough headaches without adding ulcers to them!

(*The others become silent, then suddenly* LOTTIE *breaks into tears.*)

HATTIE: Oh, Lord!

ADA: George, what's happening to us? We ain't this kind of company.

BERT (*goes to her*): Lottie, honey, what is it?

(*They are standing, now, apart from the others who are in the shadows.*)

LOTTIE: I'm sorry. I can't stand any more arguments.

BERT: Don't, honey. That damn Erlanger's upset everybody.

LOTTIE: It's not really—him. It's something more. Maybe me. (*Quietly.*) Ever since I told you about my fall—about not having children—you've acted strange.

BERT: Nonsense!

LOTTIE: No! I feel it, you hear me—feel it in every part of my body, in my very soul. You hold me close and our heartbeats thump in broken rhythms. The rhythm of yours keeps saying: "She robbed me! She robbed me!"

BERT: I won't listen to any more of this!

LOTTIE: You will listen! Listen to my heartbeat for once. It's telling you that what I have tried to bring you is love— love to inspire you toward greatness. And all my love has done is send us both to hell!

BERT: Lottie, stop it!

LOTTIE: You don't want to see it, but I have to! I'm not able to leave you anything but theater to carry your name through the years. You'll always want a company like this so you can play Papa to it. Or you'll need books, or audiences, or parties and people to hide you from the reality of our lonely lives. And things will get worse. When you're not working, you'll be reading, or dreaming, and you'll have less and less to say to me. Then—one day there'll be another woman.

BERT: To hell with this damn foolishness!

LOTTIE: I'm looking directly at rows of lonely nights, of pillows rain-soaked with tears—

BERT: Lottie, I love you—but this is no time to be acting like a woman. I have a show on my hands!

LOTTIE: I am a woman! I can't hide behind makeup and stage techniques.

(*He reaches to touch her. She trembles, afraid, hurt. His shoulders sag. He draws a deep breath.* OLIVER *reenters.*)

BERT: What the hell do you all want from me? Everybody wants me to be something else! (*Angrily.*) Jesus, God! Something powerful and evil is in every sound and sight, in theater lights and in people's eyes! I wish to God I didn't have a heart and mind!

OLIVER (*steps forward*): Easy, boy. Easy. You going on— in another minute.

BERT: What for? What the hell for?

OLIVER: 'Cause you got to, that's all. Now, get ready.

GEORGE: Yeah. Get ready.

(BERT *whirls around, angrily, begins dabbing his face with burnt cork. The music rises. The company lines up, somewhat mechanically.* BERT *now joins them and they start out, singing, half-heartedly.*)

COMPANY:

> Ohhh—keep your eye on a star
> And you'll find your way
> Where your troubles are few
> If only you
> Don't let your dreams go astray!

(*They file out toward stage area as the lights fade.*)

Scene 12

(*The scene is onstage. Immediately following. The lights come up as the company moves into the area.*)

GEORGE (*singing*):

    I rode the rails to Kansas City
    Without a dime or a word of pity,
    My soul was sagging,
    My body dragging,
    But I kept looking for the Golden City!

COMPANY:

    Ohhh—keep your eye on a star
    And you'll find your way
    If only you
    Don't let your dreams go astray!

JESSE:

    I had a song I knew folks would sing,
    I kicked around doing any old thing—
    But I kept in mind that wonderful day
    When I'd wind up on the Great White Way!

COMPANY:

    Ohh, keep your eye on a star
    And you'll find your way
    To that glorious state
    That chance of fate
    No matter what comes your way!

LOTTIE:

    My life has had its ups and downs
    With hasty meals in nameless towns,
    But on the stage my life has its appeal,
    It burns with quite a different kind of zeal!

COMPANY:

    You can't go wrong when there's a song—
    You can't deny
    With head held high
    You'll follow one star
    And find that there are
    Wonders still to try!

BERT:

    I've been a minstrel all my life
    And just one thing through all this strife
    Has filled my heart where all the meanings are—
    I've kept my eye on a star!

COMPANY:

    Oh, keep your eye on a star

No matter what they say,
And so hopefully dream,
You will seem
To turn the night into day!
So, keep your eye on a star!

(GEORGE *moves into center now and he begins to lead the group.*)

GEORGE:

Oh, keep your eye on a star
And you'll find your way—
Where—where—where—

(*His voice begins to drone and he becomes thick-lipped, struggling and shaking as he sings. The company looks at him, not knowing whether or not he is clowning.* GEORGE *begins to tremble, violently, then starts for the offstage area. He barely reaches the wings when he sinks to the floor.* BERT *rushes to him as the others crowd around.*)

LOTTIE (*over* GEORGE): Get a doctor—quick!

ADA: Is he—?

LOTTIE: No. Call for a doctor!

(CHARLIE *rushes out.* JESSE *points to onstage area, indicating* ADA *and* HATTIE *should go. They do so, reluctantly.*)

BERT: George! George!

LOTTIE: He's going to be all right. I'm sure of it.

BERT: He's got to be! (*Then.*) George, you can't get sick now! You can't die! We're making it, partner. We're making it! (GEORGE *is still.* BERT *looks up at* LOTTIE. *She is crying and so are the others. He throws up both arms and shouts.*) Almighty God! What do you want from us? What? All we want to do is our work! Is there something wrong with that? Answer me, God! Is there something wrong with that??

(LOTTIE *reaches for him, holds him close. The music rises and the lights fade out.*)

CURTAIN

END OF ACT I

ACT II

Scene 1

(*A New York theater. 1909.*

A light fades in gradually on LOTTIE. *She stands in the wing area of the theater, her face turned upward.*)

LOTTIE: Oh, God! I sometimes think that devastating natural forces make mockery of the petty ills of man. Don't

let George Walker's stroke cripple him and our company! Stop this nightmarish hurricane from roaring into the calm of our dream . . . Forgive us for not understanding the earlier warnings—the Jim Crow laws being passed, the race riots, the assaults upon us by press and public. We felt the rain, but we had to believe the sun would come out! . . . And this night—let there be light, for too many hopes and dreams of others are here with us. Let us not write their epitaphs here tonight. Let us fly forward, their banners flying, soaring above the night and setting the darkness on fire!

(*The lights now slowly fade in around her and we see a section of the wings of a New York theater.* JESSE *is standing looking off toward the action that is out of view.* OLIVER *stands beside him. We hear the sound of dancing feet.* LOT-TIE *remains, standing alone, apart from the others.* OLIVER *calls to her.*)

OLIVER: Lottie . . . (*She does not move.*) Lottie—

LOTTIE: Oh! Yes?

OLIVER: Jesse said stand by. Two minutes.

(HATTIE *charges in from the onstage area. Faint applause is heard.*)

HATTIE: Damn it! I have to keep looking out there to make sure somebody is in the house! Told you to put this show off till George got well!

JESSE: We couldn't afford to. It's that simple.

HATTIE: Go out there and find out what the word "bad" means. And, Lord, just a few years ago I was walking 'round England with my neck hurting from holding my head up so high!

LOTTIE: Don't be discouraged. You're an old pro, Hattie.

HATTIE: I ain't that old.

LOTTIE: I didn't mean in age.

HATTIE: When I die of old age, you make sure your insurance is paid up. (*Then.*) Blame your husband for this jam! They sure letting him know who owns the fruit and the jars!

LOTTIE: My husband has made no jam.

HATTIE: Now I'll tell something you're old enough to know: You can't fly up in Abraham Erlanger's face and get away with it. You got to make deals with folks like that and then you get financing and big audiences—

LOTTIE: But you said before—

HATTIE: I don't care what I said! What I'm telling you now is: We are in hot water and we ain't taking baths!

OLIVER: All right, Hattie! Cut, Lottie—

ADA (*entering from onstage area*): Good luck, Lottie. You're going to need it.

(ADA *and* HATTIE *go off.* LOTTIE *goes in the opposite direction. Now we hear the music and a sugary, sentimental ballad.*)

OLIVER: Ten laughs all night. I counted 'em.

JESSE: Stop counting and start praying.

(BERT *steps into the area, unseen by them. He stands apart.*)

BERT: This one moment must redeem all the rest. There was a star burning a hole in the night. We reached for it, and the world turned over and crippled us. We've got to keep reaching, reaching—

LOTTIE (*in the playing area, singing*):
When shadows darken your day
No need to give your dreams away,
The shadows will go and you'll learn to know
That laughter follows after tears.
Sometimes a song is the way
To see you through a troubled day—
With heart on your sleeve, you'll learn to believe
That laughter follows after tears.
We'll go along as the old Pied Piper went
And sing his song to the smiling innocence of merriment!
We'll take the world by the hand
And find our promised wonderland
Where fear disappears and love fills the years
Where laughter follows after tears!
Where laughter follows after tears!

(*The lights fade out as she concludes the song.*)

Scene 2

(*The scene is the theater. The next morning. The set is being struck.* OLIVER *and* JESSE *are unhooking flats and moving them off.* GEORGE *is sitting on the old trunk in center stage, reading over stacks of morning newspapers.* GEORGE *has a cane near him which he uses for support.*)

GEORGE: Damn! (*Puts down paper, takes another, scans it.*) Another damn! (*Puts this down, picks up another, then.*) Gawd damn! (*Reading.*) "The Negro musical comedy plot is running thin."

JESSE: We read the reviews. I hope you don't think we're striking this set so we can play games.

GEORGE: They got a smash hit down the block and its two inches thinner than wet tissue paper.

(OLIVER: That ain't *our* show. We liable to need this flat, Jesse?

JESSE: I told you, Oliver: There's no next show.

OLIVER: You-all are the giving-up-est folks I ever saw! If you'd been slaves, you never woulda got free! You'da given up walking the Underground Railroad 'cause you didn't have the proper shoes to wear!

JESSE: You put up the money and we'll produce another.

OLIVER: Me? Boy, you gone crazy? I ain't gonna enterprise you *and* advise you. (*He takes the flat and starts out.* ERLANGER *enters.*)

ERLANGER: Good morning, Mr. Walker. Mr. Shipp.

JESSE: Good morning.

GEORGE: I hope yours is good.

ERLANGER: It's not. I read the reviews. I'm sorry.

GEORGE: For years I been wondering what they use to make printer's ink. Now I know: Blood. *My* blood.

ERLANGER: I'm looking for Mr. Williams.

GEORGE: He ain't around.

JESSE: Mrs. Williams is upstairs packing. I'll get her. (*And he leaves.*)

ERLANGER: Actors look for me. I don't look for them.

GEORGE: The man you looking for ain't just an actor.

ERLANGER: I know. That's why I'm here. Where is he?

GEORGE: Walking. Which he does when he's hurt. After these reviews, he's liable to be trying to walk New York Bay.

LOTTIE (*enters*): Yes, Mr. Erlanger?

ERLANGER: Mrs. Williams, I'm very sorry. I came to help. The news is out that your husband lost six weeks of summer bookings with the reviews. I'm here to offer him work.

LOTTIE: I'll tell him.

ERLANGER: I had a role written into my new Follies for him the moment I heard Mr. Walker was sick.

LOTTIE: You were that certain?

ERLANGER: Of only one thing: Your husband is a compulsive artist who must work. And I'm the key to his working.

LOTTIE: You needn't gloat. We know your syndicate and the price of not cooperating with it. You forced Mrs. Fiske to play in second-rate theaters and the great Sarah Bernhardt to appear in a tent. And we know where that leaves us: outside.

ERLANGER: It does. I'm not proud of the record.

LOTTIE: You helped write it.

ERLANGER: I had to help write it!

GEORGE: Why?

ERLANGER: (*angrily*): Who in the hell are you to question *me?* (*Then.*) I can read the contempt in your eyes. You think my life is luxury next to yours. Maybe. Maybe not. People don't just look for a pound of my flesh but for my neck. I'm made into a businessman when I want to create beauty and a good life. I have to wander when I want to stay home. (*Bitterly.*) I don't give a God damn about the syndicate, but I've got to have it to be in theater. (*Then.*) I—I talk too much. I don't have to apologize to you for being human.

LOTTIE: No. You don't.

ERLANGER: I hope you mean it. I'm talking to you because I think you're like me: American. Practical. Ready to ride the tide but feeling the undercurrents to change the stream. Will you tell your husband that on that basis he has a job in my new show?

LOTTIE: I'll tell him.

ERLANGER: Thank you. Thank you so much. (*He goes out.*)

GEORGE: Lord! To sell Bert on that one you're gonna need God, Buddha, Allah, and a few voodoo tricks at the same time.

LOTTIE: I talked him into the burnt cork. Reality's going to have to help out. I'll finish packing.

(*She goes.* GEORGE *sits there on the trunk.* JESSE *enters, starts to remove other pieces of scenery.* GEORGE *rises to help.* BERT *enters.*)

BERT: Who said: "Death is an empty theater"?

JESSE: I don't know. He had a point.

GEORGE: You got all your things?

BERT: All that I want.

GEORGE (*as* BERT *sits on trunk, lights cigarette*): You'll get other jobs, Bert. You're a star.

BERT: At night. This is the morning and stars don't shine then.

GEORGE: Some do.

(HATTIE *enters with her bag. She is followed by* ADA, CHARLIE, *then* LOTTIE. OLIVER, *in the meantime, has joined* JESSE *in helping to remove things.*)

HATTIE: The keys, Jesse—

JESSE: Put them on the table out there.

HATTIE: Somebody said maybe you'll rewrite the script. We'll get Erlanger and the syndicate to book it on the road. (*Before anyone can say a word.*) It's a great idea. Know what else I think? My part needs a bit more—er—uh—develop-

ment. Needs to be doing *something*. I thought that before, but I didn't want to second-guess you.

JESSE: That was considerate.

HATTIE: You know me. When you're ready for the road, just get in touch—

CHARLIE: Same here. Especially if you have a part for a good elevator boy.

ADA: I'll be available, too, although I'll be doing some vaudeville gigs in the meantime. I just got a brand-new four-room apartment in Harlem and the rent's thirty-four dollars a month. So you know I've got to work! (*She turns, abruptly goes out before she breaks into tears.*)

GEORGE (*following her*): Ada—Ada—

(CHARLIE *and* HATTIE *leave.* BERT *crushes cigarette.*)

BERT: Jesse—

JESSE: No. It takes three things to do a show: money, money, and more money. Those kids will hear the alarm clock soon. Not every star shines in the morning. I'll finish my work.

BERT: Jesse. Where'll you go?

JESSE: Uptown. A hundred thousand Negroes in New York now. Lots of them moving to Harlem. I'll go there. Maybe they'll be needing a theater. (*Smiling.*) There's no airplane linking Broadway to Harlem yet.

BERT: Erlanger said there'll soon be one to Philadelphia.

JESSE: It's a longer distance from Harlem to Broadway than it is from Philadelphia to New York. (*Then.*) Those days, those dreams. Burned out. Gone.

BERT: No. They're here now in this empty theater and I can almost touch them!

JESSE: Only the truth is here. The organized control the theater, the audience, the backers. If we could afford to do a show, we'd have no place to put it. Either we go off to a place they haven't reached—or some of us may join them.

BERT: What do you mean?

JESSE: I mean, you have responsibilities and no dream of yours can change them. (*He goes.* BERT *sits on trunk.* LOTTIE *has been standing, listening. She moves down, sits beside him.*)

LOTTIE: Jesse's excitable. Ignore him. (*Then.*) I found the bills you hid in Aristotle's *Poetics*.

BERT: I thought the old boy might have bright ideas of how to pay them.

LOTTIE: Don't make jokes.

BERT: It's time to laugh or cry a river full of tears.

LOTTIE: Abraham Erlanger was here—to offer you a part in his new show.

(GEORGE *enters, stands, listening.*)

BERT: I can't go begging to that man.

GEORGE: What else you gonna do? Hang around an empty theater? Look, man, you got no job now.

BERT: I know that.

GEORGE: I just wanted to make sure you did. Call him.

BERT: We'll go into that tomorrow.

GEORGE: What's wrong with today? Hell, I'll call him— (*Starts out.*)

BERT: Will you wait?

GEORGE: Man, look at what's happening! Swallow your pride or go back to the honky-tonks! I wanta see the hopes from Kansas City and San Francisco live on. I wanta see just a little bit of the millennium 'fore I die.

LOTTIE: George, leave him alone. It's not his fault, it's mine—mine for not being able to support him when he needs me.

BERT: Lottie, stop trying to make me over.

GEORGE: Damn it, don't bark at her 'cause you scared of me!

BERT: I'm only afraid of myself. God, I don't understand life here under this heel where you're a coward if you run and a brave man if you turn the other cheek!

LOTTIE: It's time you tried.

BERT: I have tried. From the seventh grade on. Their insults ripped my ears. Their stones bruised me. Then, I almost caught their leader—caught him and beat him half to death. That's when I decided to stay away from them—because I don't want to be a murderer! (*Then.*) And you—you're pushing me back to that class. Well, I can't stand being alone out there with them, holding my breath every minute, waiting— waiting for their insults. I can't stand walking into places, waiting for a silence full of slurs!

LOTTIE: Are you suggesting that I like it? Are you?

BERT: Shut up a minute!

LOTTIE: Not when you're rattling like an idiot!

BERT: Shut the hell up, I said! You damn American Negroes spout streams of stagnant words. You've talked yourselves into buying a bill of goods that says anything all-black is wrong, inferior. You've got to get white approval to take a deep breath—even when that approval is cutting your insides, killing you! (*Then.*) And, oh, Lord, if I sign with Erlanger there'll be oceans of words. You'll call me a deserter.

You'll swear I'm doing things for Erlanger that I argued against doing in our shows. You'll want to picket the place every night I play. When I sign and go to the barber shop, they won't keep me there for hours telling them stories. I'll get fast service! (*Then.*) Damn it, I won't take this. I'm going back to Antigua.

LOTTIE (*her voice becomes low, threatening, with a strange undercurrent*): Do you remember Antigua? Really remember it?

BERT: Of course I do.

LOTTIE: I mean the Antigua your mother told me about . . . What happened to your father when he lost his business? He went to work, unloading ships, didn't he?

BERT: Yes.

LOTTIE: Then there was the sun—gentle in the morning, slashing at high noon, lashing his body like a whip. What happened to him when your mother lit the lamp at night?

BERT: Nothing. Nothing.

LOTTIE: Something did happen!

BERT: He thought it was the sun!

LOTTIE (*moving in now suddenly, for the kill*): Yes! And he cried for her to put it out. He shouted: "God, never let my son know this place exists!" (*Then.*) It's a false dream. There is no Antigua and no mountaintop. There's no hiding place now. Here and everywhere. There are only streets, modern streets, and we're trying to crawl from their gutters. That's the way it's been written for us and I can't play it any other way!

BERT (*flops on trunk*): What's wanted from me in this life? All I ever wanted was to do my work, to please troubled people, then go home and read my books. (*Then.*) There was an Antigua once. I was six years old and my granny lay on her death bed. I used to climb the stairs to her dark room. Light seeped in through the curtains and you could see the pain gnawing at her face. I hated pain, especially for what it did to her! Then—I had an idea. I began imitating the birds she could no longer see, the crawfish, the clouds. And a smile broke out on her sick face. The day of her death she told me: "You don't know how much joy you brought me." (*Slowly.*) That's why I went into this business—to bring joy, not pain to myself nor to others. Well, I picked the wrong damn business!

GEORGE: I—I'll go—take Ada home. (*And he goes out.* BERT *remains sitting on the trunk.* LOTTIE *goes to him.*)

LOTTIE: Forgive me, Bert. (*He looks up at her.*) For trying

623

to make you over. The moment I saw you, I knew you were the answer to our prayers for leaders. I saw something pushing you toward greatness, telling you to say: "I have not coveted. I have been coveted. I have not killed. I have been killed. I cannot destroy because I've been sent to redeem."

BERT: You thought that of me?

LOTTIE: Yes.

BERT: Why?

LOTTIE: Because I loved you—love you now.

BERT: I love you, too, Lottie. (*They embrace.*) Lottie—

LOTTIE: Yes, Bert?

BERT: You're shuddering.

LOTTIE: I'm cold.

BERT (*holding her close*): That better?

LOTTIE: Yes. (*Then.*) I feel—like—our wedding night. When I was undressed.

BERT: I remember. You were embarrassed.

LOTTIE: At first. Then, suddenly, I was free of weights bogging me down. I pulled a feather from the pillow and flung it into the air. It floated and I floated with it.

BERT: I remember, Lottie. I remember. And suddenly—I can fly again, fly upward, and nothing is big enough to stop me.

(*They are sitting there on the trunk.* JESSE *and* OLIVER *enter.*)

JESSE: That flat, Oliver—(OLIVER *removes flat.*) This is good-bye, folks.

LOTTIE: Good-bye, Jesse. (*She embraces him.*)

JESSE (*as* OLIVER *reenters*): See Erlanger, Bert. You'll do him good. I'll be rooting for you.

BERT: Thanks, Jesse. Good-bye, Mr. Jackson.

OLIVER: Bert, I'll be praying for you.

BERT: Thank you. That's good to know.

OLIVER: Praying you don't feel what I felt one time. After the war we settled on some land where nothing growed. Me and a bunch of young'uns got up and left. Years later, when I was doing pretty well, I passed through the old place. The folks I'd left behind asked me if we wouldn'ta all been better off if we who left had stayed on. They made me cry.

BERT: I don't feel too good right now.

LOTTIE: Well, we're not farming now. Come on, Bert. (*She has him by the arm and she starts leading him off.* JESSE *turns to* OLIVER.)

JESSE: We'll move that trunk now.

(OLIVER's *shoulders sag. He turns, pulls the trunk offstage.*

It is the only thing left on stage. JESSE *takes one last look at the empty stage, draws a deep breath, then goes out as the lights fade.*)

Scene 3

(*A New York theater. Later that week.*

The lights fade in on a bare stage. ERLANGER *sits in a chair, watching* ADA *and* HATTIE *singing and dancing to a lively period tune.*)

ADA *and* HATTIE (*singing*):

> I see laughter in the distance,
> He's holding both his sides
> And then the chances are
> He's cried a tear besides—
> Oh, isn't it exciting, delighting, and inviting
> If you pretend!
> I could suggest the best of Old Broadway—
> I could propose repose in San Jose—
> Oh, isn't it exciting, delighting, and inviting
> If you pretend!

(*They go into a dance routine as* BERT *enters. He stands, watching them. When the dance ends,* BERT *and* ERLANGER *applaud.*)

BERT: Excellent!

ERLANGER: Beyond excellent!

ADA: Thank you.

ERLANGER: No. Thank *you!* I'll get in touch with you shortly.

HATTIE: Thank you very much, Mr. Erlanger. And Bert.

ADA: Yes, thanks again. And 'bye now.

(*The girls go out.* ERLANGER *calls a* "Good-bye" *after them, then turns to* BERT.)

ERLANGER: It was good of you to recommend them. They're talented. Spirited. Full of freshness! (*Dancing sprightly.*)
Isn't it exciting, delighting and inviting—
    (*Steps.*)
They take the gray out of your hair.
    (*Again, imitating their steps.*)
If you pretend!

BERT: You like them!

ERLANGER: Oh, yes!

BERT: You plan to use them?

ERLANGER (*stops dancing*): Er—uh. Sit down a minute, Mr. Williams. (BERT *sits.*) You and I—we understand things

625

so well that sometimes we don't understand. It never dawned on me before that I can only hire one Negro.

BERT: I hired many.

ERLANGER: Don't sound holier-than-thou. How many times did I read where you complained because the public wouldn't accept love scenes in your shows? (*Then.*) I can't hire them. I can only hire you. Even that caused problems. I had a role written into this show for you. The cast threatened to strike.

BERT: It's no sin to be colored, but it sure is an inconvenience.

ERLANGER: I started to fire them all, but some of my backers threatened me, too. It was negotiate or lose out. I never lose.

BERT: What're you talking about?

ERLANGER: This: I told the cast you'd do a set of monologues in this show. On stage. Alone. They agreed to that.

BERT: As long as I'm not mixing with them, it's all right. (ERLANGER *nods.*) You know, that's exactly what I wanted, too. Only now it's not—simply because it's what they want.

ERLANGER: This really wasn't directed at you. They're afraid. It would've been the same if I'd hired any star. With you—a little more so. (*Then.*) The whole thing's temporary, anyway. The most inconsistent thing in existence is emotion in the theater.

BERT: I'm glad you're able to take a long view.

ERLANGER: I've had to. What do you say?

BERT: What can I say? It's been said for me.

ERLANGER: That means???

BERT: When I was captured in our show, *Abyssinia,* there was a way out—

ERLANGER: What does that mean?

BERT: I wish I were back in *Abyssinia* again . . . (*He stands there, fighting back the tears as he realizes he is about to be forever trapped. He turns, abruptly, goes out, leaving* ERLANGER *alone. Music rises as the lights fade out.*)

Scene 4

(*The scene is Harlem. Later, that night.*

The lights come up on a scrim and suggested here is a Harlem street. At the extreme right we see a store front. Painted across the window is "Ralph's Rib-House." Next to this, center, is a marquee over a door. The marquee reads: "Al's Alley." Next to this, stage left, is an apartment building.

BERT *walks along the street, obviously under the influence of alcohol. He stops in front of Al's Alley.*

Music is heard, loud, brassy. The lights behind the scrim come up and we see the inside of Al's Alley. It is a dimly lit place with brass railings circling an elevated dance floor. Couples move off the dance floor to the tables at ringside. OLIVER JACKSON *stands at ringside. He waves to* BERT.

The drummer goes into a fast break, then OLIVER *races into the center of the floor.*)

OLIVER: Yes, indeedy, folks! Yes, indeedy! I am pleased to meet and greet you here tonight in good old Harlemtown where things are done up a solid brown . . . But, before we start spinning our propellers and taking off, I wanta tell you the great Bert Williams just walked in the door. Stand up, Bert, and take a bow! Bert! (BERT *stands. There is applause.*) Man! Come on up here and share a stage with me! (BERT *starts for the stage.*) You-all don't know it, but Bert's going to work for Abraham Erlanger on Broadway!

BERT (*on stage by now*): Thank you, Oliver Jackson. Thank you, folks! I'm like the old preacher who wandered into the whiskey still. He said: "I know I ain't supposed to be here, but I sure am glad I am here!" (*Noisy laughter.*) Seriously, folks—I had to come home tonight, not just because my friends are here, but because this is one place where insults don't bounce off your ears all day long.

OLIVER: Tell us a story, Bert!

FROM AUDIENCE: Yeah! Come on, man!

BERT: Are we all Negroes here? (OLIVER *tries to signal that there are whites in the house, but the audience is laughing now and* BERT *continues.*) Maybe you all heard about my Uncle Ben. He was a big, black preacher and he was always going off to preach folks sermons. One night he's walking down the road and it come-est to storm something terrible. Uncle Ben stopped off at a farmhouse and asked the owner to let him stay overnight. The man said: "Rev, I ain't got no room, but that whole house up yonder on the hill is empty. You can stay there all night. But I'm gonna tell you something: That house is haunted!" Uncle Ben said: "Ain't no haunts gon bother me whilst I'm reading my Scripture Book here!" (*Stops.*) Wait a minute now! (*To the band.*) Let's hear some spooky music back there, boys! (*The band plays a couple of eerie notes.* BERT *holds up his hands.*) That's enough! I just wanted to make sure somebody was listening! (*Noisy laughter from crowd.*) Well, Uncle Ben went on up the road and into the house and he made hisself a big fire. He set in the rocking

chair, reading and rocking, rocking and reading. The wind howled and the rain beat down on the rooftop. A little white cat come down the chimney, washed his paws in the ashes, then sat down beside of Uncle Ben's left leg. Uncle Ben rocked and he read out loud: "In the sixth chapter in the seventh verse—" And another cat, the size of a bulldog, come down the chimney. This was a Angora cat and he washed his face right in the fire, then he set down side of Uncle Ben's right leg. Angora cat licked his lip and he says to the first cat, says: "When we gwyne begin on him?"

The first cat says: "We can't do nothing till Martin gets here." Uncle Ben read his Scripture Book: "In the fifth chapter, in the sixth verse—" And another white cat come down the chimney. This one was the size of a Newfoundland dog. He washed his face and paws in the fire, chawed on some live coals, then spat out blazes. He licked his lips and said: "Shall we commence on him now or shall we wait till Martin gets here?"

The other two cats shook their heads and said: "We can't do nothing till Martin comes." Uncle Ben closed his Scripture Book and started running out, shouting: "When Martin comes, you tell him I was here, but I done gone!"

(*The drummer punctuates the ending of this story with a crash of cymbals. The crowd applauds.* BERT *returns to his table, shaking hands around, then grabs a glass and gulps its contents.* OLIVER *steps back into spotlight.*)

OLIVER: I'll betcha Uncle Ben run right to Harlem. That's what lots of us did. (*He turns now, signals to band. It plays a number with a blues, calypso, work-song base—a three-part number that describes the people who settled Harlem and their aspirations. The refrain to that number of theirs is a smashing up-tempo number, sung feverishly, in exultation over the founding of a new community.*)

OLIVER (*singing*):

I had the blues downtown and I had to move uptown—
I had the blues downtown and I had to move uptown—
It was so hard down there that my world went 'round and
    'round!
I said: "Listen here, world, don't you treat me that-a-way."
I said: "Listen here, world, don't you treat me that-a-way."
World said: "Son, you better go someplace where you can
    stay!"
Harlem, Harlem—that's the place for me!
Harlem, Harlem—where a man is free!
Harlem, Harlem—way, way, way uptown!

Harlem, Harlem—home for black and brown!
Nobody making you walk a chalk line,
Nobody telling you you ain't fine as wine,
From late Saturday evening to Monday morn
You find out exactly how you oughta been born!
Harlem, Harlem—that's the place for me!
Harlem, Harlem—where I've got to be.
Harlem, Harlem—show the world the way
Harlem, Harlem—how it oughta stay!

HATTIE (*appears. The blues again*):
I tilled the soil in the old, old romantic South,
I tilled the soil in the old, old romantic South,
But I couldn't get a piece of bread to stick in my mouth!
I told my mama: "I got to leave this land of bliss!"
I told my mama: "I got to leave this land of bliss!"
I'm headin' north, Mama, to face that snowman's kiss!"

HATTIE *and* OLIVER:
Harlem, Harlem—that's the place for me!
Harlem, Harlem—where I've got to be!
Harlem, Harlem—you're the world on a stage,
Harlem, Harlem—let them make you its sage!

ADA (*appears. A calypso note*):
They got blue skies and deep brown eyes
All over the Caribbean—
They got lots of cries and plenty sighs
For it's no real millennium!
You cut that cane and you know pain,
And at you the boss-man hollers,
But he keeps those Yankee dollars!

HATTIE, ADA, *and* OLIVER:
Harlem, Harlem—a world for all to see—
Harlem, Harlem—where folks are truly free!

(*They continue with a rousing, special vocal arrangement, then they break into a series of torrid dance steps. The music is loud and furious.* BERT *continues drinking, wildly, and pounding the table, rhythmically. The crowd joins in the singing and dancing.* BERT *turns and staggers out as the number continues to a rousing climax. The lights fade out.*)

Scene 5

(*The scene is the Williams home. Later, that same night.*
GEORGE *is sitting in a chair. He rises, starts to pace, then stops as he hears* BERT's *voice.* LOTTIE *enters.*)

BERT'S VOICE:

> Harlem—Harlem—that's the place for me.
> Harlem—Harlem—where a man is free!

(*He enters, sees them, stops, tries to get his bearing.*)

LOTTIE: Honey—

GEORGE: Man! We been waiting for you!

BERT: I made a stop.

GEORGE: So I smell.

LOTTIE: How did it go?

BERT: It went. Tell you about it—tomorrow.

GEORGE: Don't play in the low-key, man. We ain't British. We get excited.

LOTTIE: The doctor said no excitement, George.

GEORGE: The doctor's best friend ain't making history! This could pull a man back from the graveyard. We got a foot in the door now and we gonna all walk through it. Told Ada today I'm marrying her and supporting her by managing you.

BERT: Will you two stop it? (*Steadying himself.*) What would you say if I told you—there's no contract—that the actors wanted me to work by myself. That I walked out—

GEORGE (*clutches cane as his lips form the word "No." He shakes his head*): I—I wouldn't believe it. I'd believe you— joking. (*Fumbles for watch.*) Getting late. I got to go. Near morning time—and I ain't got time for jokes. (*He turns, goes, quickly.* LOTTIE *draws a breath, then speaks in low, hushed tones.*)

LOTTIE: I don't believe it, either. I have a husband. Bert Williams.

BERT: I am your husband. Bert Williams.

LOTTIE: He is man's dignity. Gentle. Sometimes moody. Always understanding.

BERT: I am understanding.

LOTTIE: My husband angers quickly. His heart's big. Injustices hurt him. But he's brilliant. If something like this happened, he'd stay on and show them Bert Williams is more important than any of them. He'd never get in the dirt with them.

BERT: Lottie, I am he—your husband, Bert Williams.

LOTTIE (*crying out*): Liar! You're not! You're not! You've killed him! You're a murderer and you killed my husband!

BERT: Lottie—

LOTTIE (*as he reaches for her*): Don't put your hands on me! I'm a minister's daughter, raised in the church, to love one man till death. Death has robbed me of Bert Williams.

BERT: It hasn't!

LOTTIE: I believe in the Resurrection and the Life. Will he come back?

BERT: Lottie, are you out of your mind?

LOTTIE: I wish I were. The lost mind knows no pain. And I know pain, do you hear me? I know pain—

BERT: Lottie!

(*She starts out. He tries to follow, stumbles, drunkenly, falls to the floor.*)

LOTTIE: Stay away from me, stranger. My husband—he's dead.

BERT: He's not dead!

LOTTIE: He's not here, not here! I won't believe he's here! (*She goes. He sits on the floor, shaking his head, trying to sober himself.*)

BERT: I am Bert Williams. Yes. Comedian. Tragedian. Star-gazer. Trail-blazer. Wisdom's tool. And complete fool! That's who the hell I am! Nobody! (*Then.*) Man, what're you doing talking to yourself? (*Bitterly.*) You've got to talk to yourself! You've driven your wife out of her mind. You're in the trap you've always tried to avoid. You've got no place to go. (*Angrily.*) You need somebody, Bert Williams. A lot of some-bodies. You need your own private union! (*Rises, paces floor.*) Well, organize your own! Isn't that what you always said? (*He goes to cabinet, gets a bottle and drinks from it. Now he lines up four chairs in a row.*) The Bert Williams Union is now officially organized! (*Bangs table.*) The union will now come to order. The question on the floor is: Should Bert Williams strike and stay out of Erlanger's show? I recognize Member Number One.

BERT (*goes, sits in first chair and speaks as first member*): Mr. Chairman, Mr. Chairman! Why is there a Bert Williams Union? Can't he belong to one with others? Everyone belongs to something!

(*Suddenly.*)

Yes! Yes! I belong to my wife—

(*Then.*)

It's your job to make people know, to show them you belong.

BERT (*goes to second chair, speaks as second member*): Belonging to something didn't make the other actors want to work with you. They had no other choice.

(*Then.*)

Now, look, gentlemen; don't send this man along a blocked road toward a mountaintop. For—there are no mountaintops here nor in Antigua. They've been shorn, made into shifting

631

plateaus. Let this man stay in the back alleys with yesterday's laughter.

BERT (*moves to third chair, as third member*): Mr. Chairman, I've listened patiently to these other two members and I submit that these gentlemen are—to put it euphemistically—negativistic . . . I submit a third approach—a gradual one. (*Raises his hand.*) Please! Let me finish! (*Then.*) In the eighteenth century Edmund Burke said: "Public calamity is a mighty leveler" . . . And Williams faces a calamity. But to what will he be leveled? What is the middle ground in this leveling process? (*Quickly.*) It is not Williams's! It is theirs who say: "What is European is civilized. What is not is uncivilized . . . Gentlemen, I state categorically that neither the Bert Williams Union nor its allies can bring a readjustment. Let's accept this bone and thank God for it!

BERT (*moves to fourth chair, as fourth member*): Now, I been listening to you all and I don't know what you wants from this here boy. Bert, son, you got to put your trust in the Lord, then you got to give Him a little bit of help yourself. He didn't mean for you to listen to no Uncle Toms, no matter how fancy they talks. He give us a job to do and you carrying His banner. It's mighty heavy, too. It'd be a heap easier for you to put it down. The Lord don't want no scared chickens carrying it. Ain't many folks fit and if you gonna stop and worry about it being heavy, you ain't fit, either!

BERT (*returns to chairman's seat*): It has been stated in effect that Bert Williams does not now belong to anything—and that he can't belong!

(*Suddenly, bangs table with his fists.*)

But I do! I do! And I always will! (*Angrily he knocks over chairs, one by one.*) You lie, damn you! You all lie! I do belong! I belong to the world and the world will know it! Shut up! Shut up! I won't listen to you! (*He has knocked over all the chairs by now and he stands there, panting. Slowly now, he straightens up and he calls*): Lottie— (*Then.*) Lottie Thompson Williams!

LOTTIE (*in doorway*): You called me.

BERT: I have found your husband. (*Then.*) Lottie, I'm going to shove everything down their throats. I'm going to make them sorry for what they tried to do! (*Calling out.*) You out there in the night and in the stars, listen to me! I'm going to walk here on this earth and breathe like other men! You're going to hear my footsteps thundering through the darkness you've tried to wrap around me! Do you hear me out there in the darkness? Do you hear me?

(LOTTIE *has rushed into his arms. They cling together as the lights fade and the music rises.*)

Scene 6

(*The lights fade in on a theater marquee which indicates it is opening night of the Follies. A* WHITE GIRL *and* BOY *are singing and dancing.*)

GIRL (*singing*):

There's a reason you and I are here—
Why of all the flowers you can see
You should pick a lonely rose like me,
Love ain't nobody's fool!

There's a reason you and I are here,
Why the apple tempted even Eve,
Why I need a man I can believe,
Love ain't nobody's fool!

Although every child begins to feel
All kinds of things when he's in school,
It's only life that can reveal:
Love ain't no one's fool!

There's a reason you and I are here,
Why the moon could never leave the sky,
And it's love that knows the reason why,
Love ain't nobody's fool!

BOY:

There's a reason you and I are here—
Why Delilah cut off Samson's hair,
Why old Jezebel was not a square—
Love ain't nobody's fool!

GIRL:

There's a reason you and I are here—
Why a young man's fancy turns in spring,
Why the nightingale finds songs to sing:
Love ain't nobody's fool!

BOY:

Old Sol, it is said, found him a wife
Who taught him 'bout love's golden rule—

GIRL:

Which only shows that all through life

BOTH:

Love ain't no one's fool!

(*As the number concludes, they dance off. Now there is a single spotlight on the curtain.* BERT's *gloved hand slips through it. Now he steps into center stage.*)

BERT: Welcome to opening night of the Follies, folks. In case you-all wondering what I'm doing here, they didn't have no place for me backstage so they sent me out here whilst the girls are changing their costumes. (*He turns, steps back between the curtains. Suddenly, he comes charging out, falling down in vaudeville style. We hear a crash of cymbals. He leans on his elbow as he speaks to the audience.*) The girls ain't finished dressing yet. (*Rises.*) My luck is running about like Bill Johnson's. Y'all know who Bill Johnson was—? (*Music. He sings.*)

Bill Johnson was a dud—
He joined the Darktown Poker Club
And cursed the day they tell him he could join—
When he held Queens, they held Kings
And each night he would contribute all his coin—
So he said: "I'm gonna play 'em tight tonight,
No bobtail flesh gonna make me bite,
And when I go in, my hand will be a peach!
You see this brand-new pistol?
I had it polished just today—
I want you to follow these rules
Hereafter when you play:
Keep your hands above the table when you dealing,
     please—
And I don't want to see no cards between your knees,
And stop dealing from the bottom 'cause it looks too rough:
When you playing poker, five cards is enough!
We ain't gonna play this game according to Hoyle.
We gonna play this game according to *me!*

(*The music carries under. He sits in a chair and performs his Poker Game Pantomime. He deals imaginary cards. Five times around he deals, then puts down the imaginary deck. The drum punctuates these gestures. He picks up his cards and glances at his imaginary companions. Now he puts down his hand and deals the extra cards. He is pleased to give out three cards, curious when a player draws two, and filled with misgiving when someone draws one. In the end he draws two for himself and we can see that these are just the cards he needs. Some lively betting starts. He becomes so confident that soon his whole stack of chips is in the pot. Now comes the moment for the call. He prepares to rake in his winnings. But there is a turn of events! He cranes his neck and looks.*)

He has lost! His face and body become that of the saddest man in the world. He gets up, starts away, sadly, his shoulders slumped. The music rises as he walks from the stage.

Applause is heard over. He returns with a towel, bows to audience, then begins to wipe the burnt cork from his face.)

BERT: Thank you. And now—a song I wrote. One that's a little different from those you associate with my work. (*Music. He sings.*)

Excuse me, but there's something in my eye,
Yet somehow I see things clearly today—
The dreams that I dreamed beneath that tropic sky
Have come true in life's tragic way, as poets say.
The way has been long—my life's been a troubled brew.
I've learned that the song that's saddest is sweetest, too.
Excuse me, but there's something in my eye,
And somehow I've known this feeling before—
Our laughter, it seems, is closest to a cry,
And through years and tears I've found love's forever
    more—
Excuse me, but there's something in my eye!
(*He walks from stage into* LOTTIE'S *arms as lights fade.*)

Scene 7

(*The lights are up in* BERT'S *dressing room.* LOTTIE *and* BERT *step into the dressing room as* GEORGE, ADA, JESSE, *and* OLIVER *burst into the place. The stage literally explodes with energy and enthusiasm—with the exception of* OLIVER *who stands off to one side in silence.*)

JESSE: Congratulations!

GEORGE: Yeah, man!

ADA: You were nearly as good as you were in our shows!

GEORGE (*nudging* ADA): Man, tomorrow's reviews are gonna look like Erlanger's press agent wrote them. They'll call you an overnight success. Nobody knows how many nights a man stays up to become an overnight success. (*Then.*) I'm so happy I'm gonna let you beat me at Smut!

BERT: I've done nothing. What're they saying uptown? I expected them to picket the show.

ADA: They were scared to.

BERT: Because it had the stamp of white approval.

LOTTIE: Honey, don't be caustic.

BERT: I may be naïve, but I'm not stupid.

OLIVER: That old slave, Bert, who pointed up to the stars and showed how the Lord had planted them right—he said:

"Even the little ones—they different from the big collards that grow while the little ones die. The big collards get holes eaten in 'em by worms." Seemed like he was talking silly then, but that's what he said. (*Then.*) You a big collard, Bert, not a star.

(OLIVER *turns and goes out. The others stand, looking after him.*)

GEORGE: Well, damn!

LOTTIE: Forget him, Bert. Time's passed him by and now he's trying to play philosopher. A fancy way of showing envy.

BERT: I wish it were that, Lottie.

(ERLANGER *rushes into the room, bubbling with enthusiasm.*)

ERLANGER: Mr. Williams! Mr. Williams—the cast just met with me! They asked me to put back into the show the scenes between you and the others! (*Laughing.*) What did I tell you about the inconsistency of emotions in the theater?

BERT: The worms are biting.

ERLANGER: What's that?

BERT: They were so sure I'd jump at the opportunity! What the hell do they think I am?

ERLANGER: Truthfully—they don't know what to think. One called you—The funniest man I ever saw, the saddest man I ever knew.

BERT: Tell them all to go to hell!

LOTTIE: Bert, please don't!

BERT: I will! I will!

LOTTIE: Not now. Not now.

BERT: How long, then? Even a dog bites back when he's kicked!

LOTTIE: Don't— (*Her hand flies to her head. She reels a bit.* BERT *starts toward her, then stops, suddenly, stands firmly.*)

BERT: Step on over and fall, honey. I'm not picking you up this time.

GEORGE: Lottie— (*And he is at her side, attempting to support her. He looks at* BERT.) Man!!!

LOTTIE (*suddenly moves out of* GEORGE's *arms, resolutely determined. To* BERT): The time's run out for overstepping. When you do, you need someone strong enough to support you.

BERT: I don't like that!

LOTTIE: That's too damn bad!

ERLANGER: Excuse me. I have to go—

LOTTIE: You have to go nowhere. Just stay and listen!

(*To* BERT.) You've cried an ocean, but you don't know what in hell it's all about! You came here with something! You knew your parents and your grandparents. Some of us were lucky to know *one* parent! (*Angrily.*) It was no accident, either! It was planned from the day a bunch of sniveling, starving European rogues raped African royalty and enslaved it. They placed rogues and thieves and serfs over a people that they wouldn't have been allowed to speak to in another land. These rogues and thieves and serfs had no status and they had to achieve it by denying status to black people. The Europeans were not men and they had to prove they were men by killing, looting, stealing and raping! (*Then.*) What do you think George Washington's great-grandfather was? A sailor! And Washington himself would have been poor white trash if he hadn't inherited thirty slaves from his father! And God knows the number of slaves Washington himself fathered! What do you think Patrick Henry was when he cried: "Give me liberty or give me death!"? He was the owner of twenty-three slaves!

BERT: Lottie, wait—

LOTTIE: You wait! And shut up a minute! I've read a few books myself and I've had some thoughts you haven't had! (*Then.*) The one thing these Europeans knew was that to destroy a people they had to destroy men. They learned it over sixteen centuries from the kings your Shakespeare idolized! They knew it when they reached Plymouth Rock and made love to animals while killing off the Indians! They knew it when they sold black men away from their families. And they knew it after slavery time when black men had to wander off from home to earn a pittance. They know it, still, for they kill black men who are men! (*Fiercely.*) Well, who in the hell was left to keep the family together? Black women! We had to work in the fields with our babies at our sides. We had to wash and cook and clean for ourselves and for white folks. And who was beside us late at night when we wanted a gentle touch, a kind word? Who was there to protect us from the night noises and the night riders? Nobody! We *had* to over-step our bounds, to be more than women—to be maneuverers. It wasn't our fault, but you weren't around. You American Negroes were going off someplace and you West Indians were standing around, criticizing! (*Annoyed.*) This white man— he will give you nothing! Oh, he'll smile and give you a few dollars to fly up in his face, to pout and rave and rant at him. He'll give you a few dollars for that and he won't feel guilty worth a damn because he'll have cleansed his soul. And he'll

go out and kill and make millions and keep on doing that while you're letting off steam! . . . Do you think I like pushing you down the road to heartache, trying to get a little bit of something in a land of nothing? Do you think I like holding out hope in the midst of hopelessness? Well, I don't like it, but what else can I do? (*Sinks into chair, annoyed. Tears stream down her cheeks.* BERT *goes to her.*) We didn't want to be the poor cousins begging for a corner in a land we built! We didn't want to be reduced to that . . .

BERT: Lottie, Lottie—I'm glad you told me. Glad because now I know what I have to do. (*He holds her close. She stops crying. Now he releases her, gently, then stands, facing* ERLANGER.) Mr. Erlanger, I was going to send the cast a message—something subtle—about waiting till Martin came. I couldn't wait because you've always made me run from Martin. I was going to leave your show and it would've had to close because I, Bert Williams, made your show. And that would've been my revenge—putting them out of work. (*Suddenly.*) Only I'm not going to do it! I'm not because now I know what they are! They're lost children here on this shifting plateau called America. This plateau has cut down the mountains all across the sea and its sickness is imposed on foreign lands. I know now that no mountain can be built here. But I'm an artist and I intend to kick up so much dirt that maybe a small hill might appear. Yes, I'm an artist and I can't resist standing here, trying to be remembered as Somebody, not Nobody—of trying to be remembered beyond the walls of time and I'll build my own mountain for the world to see! (*Then.*) And tell them not to cry for me. Cry for the children —the lost children. They'll look at me and see two thirds of the world as clowns. When they have to face those people they call darkies and chinks and brown beasts, they won't know how to deal with them. Every laugh at me and every abuse is a nail in white America's coffin! (BERT *stands there with just a trace of a smile on his face.*)

ERLANGER: Yes. Yes, I'll tell them. Time for me to go back— (*And he goes out, quickly.*)

GEORGE (*to* BERT): You stuck-up, stubborn West Indian fool! You still being Anglican in a Baptist world! And damn if I ain't hoping you'll convert even me! (*He goes out, followed by* JESSE *and* ADA. BERT *and* LOTTIE *stand alone. He moves down to her.*)

BERT: No tears, Lottie. Never.

LOTTIE: Never.

BERT: Even after death.

LOTTIE: Even then.

BERT: For there's one consolation for that star shining over the big collards, seeing it eaten by worms. The consolation is the star will be there, morning and night, long after the collards have been eaten by worms and people. (*Then.*) Let's go home and have a drink to that.

LOTTIE: Let's just go home and have a drink.

(*He puts his arm around her and they start out together as the lights fade out. The music rises through the darkness.*)

CURTAIN

THE END

Toe Jam *

by ELAINE JACKSON

Elaine Jackson is a graduate of Wayne State University. She is an actress now working and writing on the West Coast.

CAST OF CHARACTERS

XENITH GRAHAM: Attractive girl of about twenty-one years
ALICE GRAHAM: Xenith's sister, about sixteen years old
MOTHER: The mother of Alice and Xenith, attractive, middle-aged
MARTIN: A friend of XENITH, about twenty-eight years old
ANNIE: Upstairs neighbor, fat, middle-aged
FIRST MAN ⎫
SECOND MAN ⎬ Bar patrons
THIRD MAN ⎭

The other bar patrons are optional, as they can be merely suggested.

ACT I

Scene 1

(*Scene opens on the apartment living room of a Negro family in a metropolitan city in a Negro section. There is a six-place rectangular table down left, with one straight-back chair on the lengthwise far side, facing the audience. There is an old-fashioned, high-backed rocking chair sitting center stage. A telephone on a small stand is visible down right. A large picture window faces the audience from upstage, and near it is a floor-type three-way mirror. A portion of a small bedroom can be seen down left, and the rest of the room is modestly and haphazardly furnished. There are two exits: the front door, up left of the picture window, and one down left, below the bedroom.*
When the scene opens, XENITH *is seated at the table in a deeply contemplative mood . . . trancelike. Suddenly she breaks out in a woeful crying.*)
XENITH (*angrily*): Mother *told* us never to go out alone (*Pause.*) but you did it anyway. I didn't want to have to come home alone—so I didn't go. Forgive me, Alice. I never got a chance to show you how much I loved you . . . but I did love

---

* TOE JAM, as it is commonly called, is that sticky, stinky stuff that collects between the toes and toenails of *dirty feet*.

you, really. (*Pause.*) I *wanted* to be there, Alice. I wanted to be there . . . I wanted to, I wanted to, I wanted to, I wanted to . . . I wanted to be there so much . . . because, it was the last time we could be together—but I felt like . . . I felt like . . . since we couldn't leave together . . . you were going someplace alone . . . we wouldn't be able to come back together. I didn't go. You were the only sister I ever knew—and I never really got to know you. I didn't go . . . But I could see you anyway—I could see you lying there . . . as though you could speak to me, but as though you no longer cared to—like you were all snug and secure in some place that I could never understand. I told a whole lot of lies on you, Alice— (*crying*) and Mother believed 'em—but I didn't mean to hurt you, honest . . . I never dreamed that you would leave me when you were only (*overcome*) sixteen years old! MY GOD, ALICE! ALICE—

MOTHER (*shouting from the kitchen*): Xenith, stop that noise and call your sister in for dinner.

XENITH: God damn! Mother—? Mother—?—I hope you know what you've just done! I-just-hope-you-know!

MOTHER (*still from the kitchen*): Can you hear me? Call Alice, and both of you eat dinner.

XENITH (*quiet, resigned*): Why couldn't you have waited, Ma? Why do you have to be so crude, huh? (*Her mother is unable to hear her and she is aware of this.*) Just five more seconds, that's all. Just *five* seconds—couldn't you wait just five funky seconds? No, huh? I had it going perfect—perfect! —and you interrupted me . . . for dumb dinner!

(MOTHER *comes through the living room, on her way to the bedroom, in a rush.*)

MOTHER: I don't intend to tell you but *once* to do something, Xenith. Get your sister and eat. (MOTHER *enters bedroom.* XENITH *slumps over to window up left and opens sash, sits on sill, sticks head out of window, and looking up, gives a "Tarzan" call.*)

XENITH: Aaahhaahooohaahaaaa! (XENITH *pauses, sulking. Waits. Repeats call.*) Aaahhaahooohaahaaaa! (*Another pause and finally an echo of the Tarzan call from her sister on an upper floor of the apartment building.*)

ALICE: Aaahhaahoohaahaaaa!

XENITH (*still shouting, hands cupped over mouth*): Moth-herr saaay come hooome for din-nerr!

ALICE (*acknowledging with call*): Aaahhaahoohaahaaaa!

XENITH (*to mother*): She's coming. (*Pause.*) I'll never be able to get it again, Ma. It's a damn dirty shame what you did.

(*Pause. She begins walking aimlessly around room, repeating snatches of thoughts from her opening monologue.*) Alice? Alice? You know I loved you. (*Picks up notebook and writes.*) Alice? . . . Ah, Shhh—hoot! (*Throws notebook on table and crosses in front of three-way mirror, changes voice and scribbles in her hand.*) "Miss Graham, the editors of my magazine have asked me to get your own opinion as to why you failed to get the Pulitzer Prize for this year's most outstanding play?" —Well, frankly, I know the exact cause. "Oh? Well, our readers would be more than delighted to know."—Well . . . you see, I got a *very* important call that upset me . . . right in the midst of my most successful moment and . . . the moment was lost . . . lost forever. "Oh, I'm so sorry to hear of your disaster . . ." That's quite all right. Lovely—It's only *every* day that one gets called to dinner! Heee-heheheeeheee. (*She turns, starts rummaging through a drawer in the table.*) Where's that poem I was gonna put in the first act? Damn it! Where is it! (*Crosses her arms disgustedly.*) If I've lost it . . . I might as well forget the whole thing. (*Discovers it.*) Well, I was gonna say . . .

ALICE (*enters hopping on one foot*): I sliced my big toe on the stairs—get me some bandages, Xenith . . .

XENITH: That's what you get for going around in this filthy building barefoot. Stop bleeding! You're dripping blood all over everything. You need to wash 'em so we can find out which toe is hurt . . .

ALICE: Come on, Xenith. I'm not playing around . . .

XENITH (*goes into bedroom*): Ma, Alice stubbed her toe. Where's the bandages?

MOTHER: Under the bed. I gotta go. Can't be late at the hospital anymore. (*They both come out of the bedroom.*) I want both of you to be in bed when I get in this morning. You think you have a field day when I work evenings. Good night. (*Starts to leave.*) Lock this door, Xenith. (*Leaves.*)

XENITH (*bandaging ALICE's toe from shoebox full of medicines*): Okay, Ma. (*Rummaging through shoebox.*) I ought to put some turpentine on it and let it burn your ass off. Maybe next time you'll remember to wear some shoes. There's some of everything known to the medical world in this box . . . (*Reads.*) Look, Alice, dog mange! Who's that for? When did we ever have a dog? Fish food! What's that doin' in the medicine box?

ALICE: Owww! Fool! What are you trying to do? Terrorize ma' toe?

XENITH: I would think you'd be getting a little bit mature by now, Alice . . . just a *little* bit.

ALICE: If I was growing ten feet tall every five minutes, you wouldn't know about it. You'd be too busy checking out what's happening on *Brr-oadway* to see my show. (*Pause.*) For your information, old lady, I've got a date . . . tonight!

XENITH (*calmly*): With whom?

ALICE: Charles.

XENITH: That old dude? Mother'll swing you through hell for even talking to that trash. Girl, you starting off where most people finish up.

ALICE: There's no finer person anywhere than Charles.

XENITH: Yeah. Well, I'll be frank with you. There's no worse lookin' person than Charles either. He's older than Ma. He looks like the last thought I'd have before committing suicide.

ALICE: You and Ma are just alike. You can't tell a book by its cover.

XENITH: That's one book that very few people would ever want to study.

ALICE: I don't see any difference between him and that bum Martin that you hang around with.

XENITH: Martin is a friend, not a date. That makes a whole lot of difference, baby . . . let me tell you . . .

ALICE: Well, we are going out tonight . . . and you can tell Mother if you want to.

XENITH: You think I'd tell Ma? You must be crazy. She'd beat my tail for even *telling* her such a thing.

ALICE: We'll be back before she gets home at two. Can I wear your black dress with the straight skirt?

XENITH: You touch anything of mine and this whole block will know your story.

ALICE: Well, what'll I wear?

XENITH: If you're going out with Charles, what you have on is fine.

ALICE: Ah come *on*—(*Knock at the door.*) Somebody's at the door. Damn! He can't be here this early. (ALICE *starts rushing toward bedroom as* XENITH *goes to the door.*)

XENITH: Who is it?

ANNIE: Me, Annie. Can I use you-all's phone?

XENITH (*opens door*): Hi.

ANNIE: Hi. Mother gone to work already?

ALICE: Hi. How ya doing?

ANNIE: Oh fine, honey. How you?

ALICE: Oh, decent, decent. Excuse me. (*Goes into bed-room.*)

XENITH: Help yourself to the phone.

(ANNIE *begins searching through a little phone book for her party while* XENITH *picks up her poem.*)

ANNIE: Enter any more beauty contests lately, Xenith?

XENITH: Uh, uh. I've got something better going for me now.

ANNIE: You know, me and ma boyfriend, Quinton, went down to the Lodge last week to see you come across the stage, but we never saw you.

XENITH: Yea. Well, the girls started ratting on which ones of us was padded, and they made us depad . . . so I just came home.

ANNIE: Aw, Xenith . . . as pretty as you are, you didn't have to worry about that.

XENITH: Yea. Well, I had put 36 down on the questionnaire and I didn't want them to know I lied. So . . . anyway, like I said, I got something much better going anyway.

ANNIE: Now I *knew* I had Mattie's number in here. (*Pause.*) I guess not. I got to tell her about the party Quinton's giving this weekend. (*Dials Information.*) What'cha got going for you now, Xenith?

XENITH: Aaahaahahaaa. Don't tell nobody. Especially Ma. (*Pause.*) I'm gonna pull the crime of the century if this works, Annie. See—nobody's ever let me play the role I want to play, even if I got the chance . . . So—I'm gonna write my own play.

ANNIE: Hello? Information? You give me the number of my girl friend, Mattie Mae? (*Pause.*) Naw. Her last name is Doodle. Mattie Mae Doodle. (*Pause.*) Doodle! Spell it!? (*To* XENITH.) Dumb heifer! (*Back into telephone.*) Doodle, Operator! *D* like in . . . Dumb! *O* like in . . . Out-Rageous, *D* like in . . . in . . . damn it, *Dog!* (*Pause.*) Hello, Operator? Hello, Operator! Hello! (*Slams down phone.*) Hell!

XENITH: I'll get it for you. (*Gets out phone book.*)

ANNIE: Thanks, darling . . . So you gonna write a play, huh?

XENITH: Not *a* play, Annie . . . *The* play. It's never been done before, but I decided all I gotta do is write about my neighborhood and I got a play that's a "real" play—right? (*Pause.*) Her first name is Mattie?

ANNIE: Yes.

XENITH: On Tulsa Street?

ANNIE: Yeah. That's her.

XENITH: I'll dial for you. (*Goes to phone.*)

645

ANNIE: Yeah. I guess you can't go wrong if you write about real people.

XENITH: That's what I figure. I mean, I been living here all my life—so I ought to know what's happening. Right?

ANNIE: Yeah. You got a point there.

XENITH: It's ringing. Here. (*Hands her the phone.*) You wanna hear how it starts off?

ANNIE: Oh, shore, honey.

XENITH: See I'm writing the story about this girl named Veronica, which means "true image." Get it? "True image?" I'm writing the role so I can play it—so you know it's out-of-sight.

ANNIE: Hello, Mattie? Annie. Yeah, girl, I went through some hellava changes to get you. What'cha doin'? Yeah, well look, Quint's giving a little get-together Saturday night. Yeah. At his place. Am *I* gonna be there? Girl—I'm gonna put on ma dancin' shoes, ma loose girdle, ma floppy bra—and some clean draws—I'm gonna be out with *ma* crowd Saturday. You better believe I'm gonna ball into the wee smalls—heeheehaa. Listen, Mattie—I gotta tell you 'bout what happened on the bus yesterday. I was sittin' up near the driver and I started smelling this odor, you know. It got so bad, I was about to ask myself did I need a . . . Yeah! Heehehahaa! Anyway, the odor got so bad, I went into my purse to get a napkin to hold over my nose—and guess what? I had done forgot all about this egg sandwich I had put in my purse for lunch yesterday— boy, was that something—Heehaaha! Yeah. I'll wait. (*To* XENITH.) She had to go to the bathroom. Now what was you saying about this girl in your play?

XENITH: Well, see, it's about this girl who lives in the heart of the slums and vice, but who is untouched and untainted by all the dirt around her. Like, in the first scene, she is reading poetry. Let me read you the poem—tell me what you think about it.

ANNIE (*back into the phone*): Yeah, Mattie. If I'd known you was gonna be gone that long—I'd a sent you a laxative.

XENITH (*reading poem*):
Traces of lavender
Glittered in the sunlit ray that fell upon the rarity . . .

ANNIE: You a goofy heifer, Mattie. You know you don't have to bring your own stuff to the party. Quint ain't cheap.

XENITH:
A fragrance frightening
Yet filled with exciting deviations, devoured the imme-
    diate . . .

ANNIE: . . . Did Irene marry *who?* Honey, did the fox get the grapes?—Well, all right then.

XENITH:
Trembling, yet irresistibly
Drawn, I fell upon the spot and trancelike, died . . .

ANNIE: Yeah. Well, look, baby—I got to go. Yeah. See you Saturday. 'Bye now. (*Hangs up.*)

XENITH:
The sensuous senselessness
Of my awakening, swallowed my sophistication . . .
That's all I got right now.

ANNIE: Well, it really sounds good, Xenith baby. You keep on that way—you'll make it.

XENITH: You really like it?

ANNIE: Well, you know I don't know too much about poetry—all I can do is tell you how it sounds to me—and it sounds real good. (*Telephone rings.*)

ALICE (*from the bedroom*): I'll get it.

XENITH (*picks up telephone*): Hello. Yes. Just a moment. Alice!

ALICE: Told you I'd get it.

XENITH: Yeah. You gonna get it all right.

ALICE (*on phone*): Hello. Yes. Okay, five minutes. (*Hangs up.*)

ANNIE: Well, I'll see you two. Let me know when your play is finished, Xenith.

XENITH: Okay, Annie. And look, if you hear of any happenings, let me know where, so I can write them into my play.

ANNIE: Okay, darling. I'm going on back upstairs, but I'll tell you right now, if you'd spend a half hour up in my place, you'd have yo'self a play. 'Cause when me and Quinton gets to . . . playin' around . . . Heeehehheehee! Well, if you need me—don't wait to call on me . . . never fear—Annie's here! See you-all.

XENITH: 'Bye.

ALICE: Ba-aaiiee! (*Rushes out of bedroom.*) Don't lock it, Xenith. I gotta go. Wait till she gets upstairs.

XENITH: If Mother asks me—I'm gonna tell her exactly where you are.

ALICE: I told you I'd be back before she got here. 'Bye! (*Exits.*)

XENITH (*locks door and rushes over to her notebook and pencil; writes*): Never fear—Annie's here. Haahaaaeiehaaa-haaha. (*Very excited. Sings.*) I got it. I got it. Everybody, I got it. Ain't nobody got it, but *I* got it. An' I'm gon keep it, too.

(*She continues singing and begins a cancan and soft-shoe mock dance.*) "How you gonna keep 'em down on the farm, After they've seen Par-EEE!" Heehehahaahaahaa. (*She affects English accent.*) "Miss Graham, we are veddy, veddy proud to present you with the Pulitzer Prize for this year's most outstanding play." Owwwoww, you've given me such a surprise. Really, it didn't take much on my part . . . But I wanna thank ya, gentlemen . . . Thank ya, thank ya, thank ya . . . Yeeaaaga Yeeyaayooyaahyaya Yumum . . . (*This is chanted and danced in Zulu fashion.*)

Scene 2

(*Same scene, one week later, in the morning.* XENITH *is in the three-way mirror wearing a sexy formal gown. She is posing and eating an apple. She occasionally writes in her notebook lying on the table.*)

XENITH: Gentlemen of the press, PLE-ase! One at a time! I can't speak to you all at one time.

ALICE (*entering with school books from bedroom*): Who you supposed to be this morning?

XENITH: Don't disturb me, I'm concentrating.

ALICE: I hate to tell you what you look like—(*To audience.*) an ass.

XENITH: Are you going to school or not?

ALICE: Why don't you get a look of your own instead of copying everybody? I know a look you could get that would really be original—when you first get up every morning. (*Laughs.*)

XENITH: You don't want me to tell Ma something, do you?

ALICE: 'Bye! (*Goes over to phone and dials.*) Hello? Alice. Decent, love, decent. Guess what? (*Speaks softer.*) The ship came in today. (*Laughs softly.*) Yeah. See you later, after Ma goes to work? Okay. 'Bye-bye. (*To* XENITH, *after looking at her still posing.*) You better be yourself before you be by yourself! (*Laughs and leaves, slamming door.*)

XENITH: That old dog made me forget what I was thinking about. (*Knock at the door. Goes to the door.*) Who is it? Who *is* it?

MARTIN: Martin.

XENITH (*delightedly opening door*): Martin, luv—Where you *been?*

MARTIN: Downstairs. I have to come up in order to see you, 'cause you don't *never* come down.

XENITH: Well, I been workin' on a few things, you know

. . . and anyway, Ma supervises me when I come down where you stay.

MARTIN: Your ma supervises you no matter where you go, sweetheart. Your ma is the next best thing to Sherlock Holmes I *ever* saw. Your ma is the *only* person I hide from. I don't even hide from the law like I hide from her.

XENITH (*motions silently offstage left to indicate* MOTHER *is there*): There's no way in the world that you can guess what I'm doing, Martin.

MARTIN (*looks at her gown for a few minutes*): You're going to a formal breakfast.

XENITH: You funny. Seriously, Martin—I got something so beautiful about to happen that I can't sleep at night for thinking about it.

MARTIN: Don't tell me—now I know what it is . . .

XENITH: Naw you don't.

MARTIN: Yep. If it's that beautiful it must be that you gon finally make it down to my pad so I can . . . show you some new aspects of life.

XENITH: Awwoohahhahaha, I knew you didn't know.

MARTIN: Okay, baby, spit it all out—what is it?

XENITH: I'm writing my own play, Martin. (*No response from* MARTIN.) I got it all figured out. (*Pause.*) Listen, everything goes in cycles, huh? So—that being the case, the movies goes in cycles, too. Remember three years ago, the Orient was what was happening? There were about *ten* Oriental flicks on top. Then the fashion magazines made the slant-eye the "look," you know. Now England is reigning. The Mod mob is "in." Well, I figure the damn cycle is gonna swing south next—Latin America? They've already covered Sweden—so, there ain't too many places left before they *got* to come home to me. Heee-haahehahaa.

MARTIN: Uh, do that again, sweetheart.

XENITH: The law of averages. All I got to do is get sweet lil' ole me ready—and you better believe I'm gon be ready. I'm gonna get me a real tough photographer, like tough Martin, to get me in all the magazines—make me the "in" look and . . . these sweet, big, juicy lips will be the new lip-line for 19 . . . diddley-bop! (*She puckers them.*) And this precious nose will be imitated from coast to coast . . . *I'll* be what's happening. How 'bout that?

MARTIN: Lovely—you're already what's happening. All you have to do is "be"! (*He grabs her affectionately.*)

XENITH: Well, look, Martin, what they did with that bogue-looking child from Oklahoma. She didn't have a thing going

for her—with her old ugly self—so they said the "plain, nothing look" was "in" . . . I ain't kidding you.

MARTIN: Why you have to go way up there to be an oddity, when you can stay down here and be a queen?

XENITH: 'Cause I'm already odd. Everywhere I go, all kinds of people, "Is you fo' real? Is you Oriental? Is you Greek? Is you . . . *Is* you!" I might as well get paid for being rare. (MARTIN *laughs.*) And, listen, I got an out-of-sight plan for making sure it's a hit. All I gotta do is get some friends stashed on several bus lines and have them carry a paperback version of the play for about a week—everyone will think it's a best seller that they been missing. I'll bet you, within a week, one third of the bus riders will be carrying that book. They gon naturally assume it's pornographic. Heeehehehaa. I'll get the royalties from my play *plus* my acting salary. With that kind of money I don't have to depend on nobody. Heehehehahaaa. You ride the bus? Ain't that too much? (*She starts dancing and running around at a feverish pitch.*) Yeeaaaga Yeeyaayoo-yaahyaya Yumum.

(MARTIN *seats himself in the straight-back chair. He has been watching her antics unmoved.*)

MARTIN: You know, I've been trying to figure out if you're extremely "hip" or extremely naïve—I just figured it out.

XENITH: It's gotta work—it's gotta work!

MARTIN: Baby, you're too beautiful, too beautiful! I'm gonna tell everybody I know that it's one helluva play coming out. (*Runs his hand over his head.*) You think my hairline'll ever make it "in"?

XENITH: Hahahaahaahaaaheehaha!

MARTIN: Seriously, baby, I'm with you all the way. I'm with anybody that's driving. You know what I mean?

XENITH (*begins a spontaneous, playful kissing of* MARTIN): Ooh! Oh, Martin. You sweet thing (*kiss*), you lover (*kiss*), you chocolate drop (*kiss*), you . . . you . . . you . . . (*Kiss, kiss, kiss.*)

MARTIN (*calmly*): Don't start writing no check that you can't cash, baby.

XENITH: Heeheehaha. Oh, Martin we gotta start taking thousands of pictures to start distributing to the magazines. I'll have one key picture with a dark, murky look . . . you know, like the one you did down by the dock of that little boy . . . you know, the one I liked? Oh, goddamn! Martin, don't say you gonna do it and then don't do it. Lord, help me! They're crying for new plays and the epitome of the play-world is about to descend. Oh, Mother!

MARTIN: Uh, since I'm gonna have a hand in this masterpiece could I have a little rundown on what it's about?

XENITH: Okay. What kind of plays are going right now?

MARTIN: I hope it's not the same kind of manure they're passing off for photography nowadays.

XENITH: Abstracts. You know, *Mess* that's almost written in a foreign language. You know why folks did Mess now? Because they've lost touch with real humanity. Instead of concentrating on humans now, they concentrate on colors, sounds, lines, no-colors . . . *bunk!* See, they've lost contact with humanity so they're hopped up on Mess 'cause it don't have to have no sense to it. Now, what I'm gonna write about is gonna be the new commercial gig. The "for real" stuff. Like what happens every day around here. See, there's this girl, Veronica, and that stands for "true image," . . . I looked it up. True image. (MARTIN *nods.*) Anyway she lives *here*—in what's *really* happening—and she remains untouched by her environment. You know what I mean? Every day she gets propositioned; upstairs, an old dude runs a still, there's a knifing a day practically in her front yard, and she associates with it all . . . but it doesn't reach her true nature. She doesn't change.

MARTIN: Yeah.

XENITH: What'd you say?

MARTIN: Where'd you find this girl?

XENITH (*pointing to her head, comically*): She came right out of upstairs, here. When the play opens, she is reciting some poetry—and all around her . . . her mother and her relatives are acting in their natural, uninhibited environmental way—so there is immediate contrast.

MARTIN: I got the picture, sweetheart. What time you got?

XENITH: What'd you say?

MARTIN: What time is it?

XENITH (*goes over to the upstage picture window and looks at the time on the store front*): Eleven fifteen. You gotta go?

MARTIN: Yeah. I gotta run over some material with Carl. (*He gets up.*)

XENITH: When are we gonna take the pictures?

MARTIN: Anytime you can manage to get out of this house . . .

XENITH: Listen, how 'bout one evening after Ma goes to work?

MARTIN: Okay, I'll set up the studio. Let me know when.

XENITH: Can you set it up here after Ma leaves? (*Pause.*) Sometimes she calls back to see if I'm here.

MARTIN (*looks at her questioningly, but does not say the obvious*): Yes, m'am.

XENITH: I'll have all my outfits ready. I gotta look versatile. I knew it was gonna work, Martin. Because of people like you. (*He starts to leave.*) Hey! Guess what else? I'm gonna go down on Flame Street and write it like it *is!*

MARTIN (*at door. He pauses and looks at her*): When you go—be sure to take your shoes off.

XENITH: Oh, baby, you know I'm gonna dress the part.

MARTIN: That's not what I meant. But you work it out, baby.

XENITH: Please don't forget about the pictures, Martin. I'll call you.

MARTIN: I'll have no problems with my end of the project, you still have a lot to work on for your end, though. Come down and visit us peons when you can.

XENITH: Shhh—I'll be ready with everything for the session. 'Bye. (MARTIN *motions good-bye and leaves. She goes back to the mirror and poses.*) Darling! What'll I do with all these flowers for my opening performance? Ahhahhahahaaa-heehaha. Oh! More! Over there! I say—

MOTHER (*enters in nightgown*): Did someone come in?

XENITH (*pause*): Just Martin.

MOTHER: What did he want?

XENITH: Nothing. Just said hello.

MOTHER: I told you not to have that bum hanging around. If you can't have any decent-class friends, then just do without friends. (*Notices her dress.*) At it again, huh?

XENITH: At what?

MOTHER: You must have thought I was joking when I told you that your days of play-acting were over. Take that dress off and get down to business.

XENITH: What are you talking about?

MOTHER: I mean it, Xenith. You can put all that movie jive behind you. It's time for you to get a man and get married. I don't know what happened between you and Kenneth, but I can tell you this—if he asks you to marry him, you better give him the right answer or you'll really be having some hard times.

XENITH (*fiercely*): Ma, I'm sick of you telling me to marry somebody—anybody. Just because Kenneth's *father* is a doctor doesn't mean he's worth a damn! Sick of it! Do you hear me —sick . . . of your telling me . . .

MOTHER: I'm not going to *tell* you again, Xenith. This is the last time I'm gonna tell you—next time I'm gonna take some

different action. I've tried talking nice to you—you know you don't have a father anymore, you know if you hang around like you are now—running from one alley-hole to another for this stage stuff, you'll be as big a tramp as these other girls around here—I'm not going to see you end up like that—I worked too hard to put you out of their reach—now you're old enough so that it won't be long before you won't be so free with your laughter . . . when the stars won't be something you wish on, but . . . and your body will be giving you pain instead of pleasure . . . I mean it. You get that nonsense out of your head—

XENITH: Why can't you see things like Daddy? He always said my life was my own to do with as I wanted to—even if I wanted to mess it up. 'Cause he always said you only get one life—and not to let anybody whose life was already over to try to live yours.

MOTHER: You shut up bringing up that rotten, loafing dreamer. His whole life was a *dream*. You just stop trying to make him into some kind of saint. (XENITH *moves violently down to the table and is so overcome that she doesn't speak or move, but picks up a sheet of paper and is silently ripping it.*) I know you've got some new scheme going—but I've had enough. Get it out of your system right this minute. Take that dress off and start thinking about your future—your *real* future. (*Pause.*) You can hear me or not, I'm warning you. (*Pause.*) I'm going back to bed. I have to be at work by four. (*Pause.*) When your sister gets in, you can warm up the roast for dinner. (*She goes into the bedroom.*)

(XENITH *sits silently, still tearing paper. She has fashioned a "stick" doll out of the paper.*)

XENITH (*holding doll up*): Hur-ry, hur-ry, hur-ry—get your exact replicas of the famous Mother Doll here! These dolls do *not* walk, talk, think, or cry. They *do* eat and sleep. They grow fat and ugly in no time. Notice the fine workmanship in reproducing the exact hair and feet and skinny legs of these dolls. The Mother Doll can also be used to place a Voodoo Curse on *anybody*—they are guaranteed to scare and ruin—Hur-ry, hur-ry . . . Yaaa Yeee Yaah Yaaa Yemyaakyooh.

ACT II

Scene 1

(*Scene same as Act I. One month later. Afternoon.*)

ALICE (*making a phone call*): Charles? (*Lovingly.*) Hi. (*Giggles, whispers.*) I-love-you-Charles. (*Giggles.*) The ship?

No. It's still behind schedule. I did take 'em. No, I'm not worried. (*Giggles.*) I-love-you-Charles. What? No, nothing happened. I took 'em just like you said. Charles? I-love-you-all-over. (*Giggles.*) Yes, I'm still drinking that stuff . . . (XENITH *enters carrying packages.*) Uh, oh. Gotta hang up, 'bye! Yes, yes . . . I remember . . . two in the morning. (*She assumes a casual air.*) Yeah. Well, I'll see you later. I got homework to do. 'Bye.

XENITH: Where's Ma?

ALICE: She's gone to work. She's working a split-shift today.

XENITH: Wanna see what I got? (XENITH *goes into the bedroom and changes into a tacky-looking, bare, skimpy dress. She passes several outfits out to* ALICE *from the bedroom as she explains them while she is dressing.*) This is for when I go down to the Temple. (*Hands her a severe-looking black and white dress and a hat.*) I think that looks kinda holy, don't you?

ALICE: It sure does. (*She holds outfit up, puts on hat, and mimes* XENITH *in the mirror.*)

XENITH (*still dressing in bedroom*): And this . . . (*passes* ALICE *some Levi's, a tee-shirt, sunglasses, and dirty tennis shoes*) . . . this is gonna be my outfit when I go down to the Nostredamous.

ALICE (*gingerly and comically assesses these articles and assumes a beatnik pose*): I hope you didn't *pay* for this junk. The welfare *gives* it away.

XENITH: Do you know, they actually sell tennis shoes with that beat-up look and they cost more than new-looking ones? I can wear the same church dress when I go to the Russell Street Baptist Church. (*She emerges from the bedroom wearing cocktail dress.*) See. (*She poses.*) Heeehahahaaaheee. They're for my play. This is what I'm going down to Daddy's in. I gotta look like I belong there or the folks won't be "for real" while I'm around. See, I'm gonna be taking notes on the sly.

ALICE: You already got some dresses that look like that in your closet.

XENITH: You wouldn't know life if it smacked you across your silly head.

ALICE: If this is what it's all about (*refers to the clothes*), then I can go down to the five-and-dime and get a real run-down.

XENITH (*still posing*): I can also make the Step and Stomp in this outfit.

ALICE: Girl, you need a checkup!

(XENITH *goes over to* ALICE, *takes her finger, blows on it as if she were blowing up a balloon; she then ties it neatly and precisely, and mimes watching* ALICE *float in the air.*)

XENITH (*looking at her very studiously*): You ever had your neck chopped off?

ALICE (*her attitude has become more serious*): Speaking of checkups, you wouldn't happen to know of a decent doctor, would you?

XENITH (*engrossed in her treasures*): Nope. Why'd you want to know?

ALICE: I don't know. I might want a checkup one day. (*Laughs. Pause.*) Oh, Xenith, you know Gloria? Well, I'll bet you'll never guess what happened to her.

XENITH: What Gloria?

ALICE: My friend at school named Gloria.

XENITH: I don't know any Gloria.

ALICE: I thought you met her once. (*Pause.*) Well, anyway this child is pregnant . . . and you never would have thought it of her . . . I mean, she's so quiet and nice-acting.

XENITH (*still engrossed*): Yeah . . .

ALICE: But let me tell you the rest of it. She's been going around taking quinine and castor oil and hot tea and hot wine and all kinds of ugly pills trying to get rid of it. I told her she was only going to mess up her guts and maybe mess up the baby. Don't you think so? (*Pause.*) Right?

XENITH: How should I know?

ALICE: Yeah. Well, I don't know myself—I was just giving her my own opinion. I say, the best thing is for her to go on and have it, regardless of the consequences—Right?

XENITH: Why you ask me about something I don't know *anything* about? I DON'T KNOW! Now stop asking me—I'm busy. (*She makes a short, inaudible phone call.*)

ALICE (*affronted, nastily mimicking*): You wouldn't know life if it smacked you in your silly head . . . but *me,* well, dearie, let me tell you, I am the *tree* of life! (*Long pause while* ALICE *sits staring into space and* XENITH *puts on fanciful airs with her new clothes.*) Well, I gotta go anyway. Uh, I may not be in till late Friday night—in case Ma looks for me.

XENITH: Friday's the night when I check these places out— so I won't be here myself.

ALICE: Hokey-dokey—ah gots ter go . . . stay decent! Baahaaeeii . . . (ALICE *stops and looks in the three-way mirror before she leaves.*)

XENITH (*sings*): "Next time you see me, things won't be the same . . ." (*Slips red dress over her other dress as* ALICE

655

leaves. XENITH *starts practicing a "hip" walk and "cool" talk in front of the mirror.*) Hey, Daddy! What's happenin'? (*Struts around.*) Cool, Daddy, cool. Are you fo' real? (MARTIN *enters through the door* ALICE *has left open. He is carrying camera equipment. He stops and watches* XENITH *in her antics.*) Whatcha' got on your hip, ma man? (*Struts around burlesque-style.*) Ain't got no money, honey—don't get no funny . . . (MARTIN *bursts out laughing.* XENITH *is surprised.*) You ole dog! What you doin' spying on me. (*She laughs.*) Well . . . I was just getting ready for Friday night.

MARTIN: I think your main problem is whether or not Friday night is gonna be ready for you.

XENITH: I'm really going, Martin . . . all by myself.

MARTIN: I think I just missed the most original pictures. (*He is setting up his equipment for the picture-taking session.*) Damn! I could've stood out in the hallway and made a fortune off those poses you just went through.

XENITH: Hey, listen! Mother's working funny hours today. She's working a swing-shift. She left this morning before Alice went to school, but she always stays downtown until she goes back to work. So she won't be in until tonight; and we don't have to worry about Alice, either. That's why I called you for today—we can really work out because ain't nobody gon be around.

MARTIN: I brought some background scenery—this one looks like an outdoors scene. (*He unrolls a large painted scene and attaches it to the upstage wall facing the audience. He continues setting up his materials.*) Oh, I found a little something that I thought might be a little pertinent to your trip down on Flame Street. I cut it out of my brother's old biology book. (*He unfolds a paper.*) I thought this might help you with your play—it reminded me of Flame Street and my street, and the whole West Side here. (*Reads.*) "In the Benthic part of the ocean, that is the deepest part, the ocean bottoms are covered with a fine mud called ooze. This ooze is made up of dust which settles on the surface of the ocean and sinks slowly to the bottom. At this level, plants do not grow, because light reaches only into the shallow parts of the ocean. At the deepest known point in the ocean, pressure reaches about six tons. At this level, also, there are several fish that depend solely upon food matter that filters down from the upper regions. In order to devour this food, they have developed disproportionately large teeth which enable them to have a much better chance of capturing the pieces of food as they go past. These ferocious little fish live in a dark cold world. Scarcity of food

stunts their growth to about four inches or less. The Lino-phryne Arborifer and the Angler Fish attract their prey with a light that grows from their head. It is important for these fish that they not miss any morsel of food, for at these depths, they are unable to swim far from the level they are accustomed to for fear of bursting. For instance, the Dragon Fish would burst if brought to the surface. A slight increase or decrease in pressure from descending or ascending would result in explosion of the fish."

I was thinking how much the Benthic part of the ocean and Flame Street have in common. Our folks don't miss nothing that filters down through here if its sellable, edible, or spendable . . . and they can pick you just as clean as that fish with the fierce teeth . . . just with their eyes.

XENITH: That was beautiful, Martin . . . just beautiful! How come you know everything? That's great! (*She rushes to the table for pencil and paper. Pause—writing.*) How do you spell Benthic?

MARTIN (*goes over and pushes pencil out of her hand*): Don't write it down. Think about it. Remember it on Friday. (*He ushers her into a chair against a bare pale-colored wall.*) Let's get some face-shots first.

XENITH: But it was so beautiful, Martin. So true. I need it in my play.

MARTIN (*peering into camera*): Hold it, baby! Hold it right there! Lovely, lovely! Okay. Let's get some soft, romantic-type shots. Now look right at the camera and think of the finest-looking cat you can imagine. He's coming at you from a distance and he's your main man. He's beginning to run because he can't wait to get to you, and your eyes are lighting up with all the love you hold for him. Wet your lips. Leave your mouth open in anticipation. That's it, baby! That's it. Uh, uh, wait! You lost that look in your eyes. If you're having trouble picturing him—you can look at me.

XENITH: Shh—oot!

MARTIN: You got it! You got it now, baby! Oh, yes! Yes! Okay. A couple of more like this. (*He continues taking different shots. Still peering into the camera.*) What do *you* want to be?

XENITH (*still posing*): What? What do you mean?

MARTIN: I know what all those people that you play at want to be . . . but what do *you* want to be? (*He turns the chair with its back facing the camera and indicates for* XENITH *to straddle it. She poses coyly and sexily in this position.*) Hold

it right there, baby! Beautiful! (*She continues to strike different poses while casually speaking.*)

XENITH: Nothing. There's nothing I want to be. I'm some of everything and everybody and I equal nothing by myself. There's *nothing* I want to be. (*Pause.*) Except maybe T-Bird. Quinton's black cat. Nothing affects her.

MARTIN: Pull your chin up a little higher. Higher. Righ—t there! Okay. Now pull that one piece of hair over your left eye. Yea!

XENITH: You can pull her tail and she might bristle her fur a little, but then goes right back to being the same old T-Bird. You remember when they had that explosion at the plant about a year ago? T-Bird saw it. She saw everything that everybody else saw. T-Bird saw it all . . . all those amputated limbs and the blood splattered everywhere . . . just like all those fellows did who went into shock from the sight of it. Remember Pete? He'll never be the same. T-Bird didn't go into shock.

MARTIN (*laughing hard*): Ha, ha, ha, ha—and I used to think you were a cool "hippie"—baby, that cat turned completely white. Quinton was all over the streets telling how they paid him to use the cat on TV to show how it had turned from jet-black to stone white.

XENITH (*jumping out of the chair*): Don't tell me a lie. Don't tell me a lie! (XENITH *hits* MARTIN *brutally. He grabs her as she starts crying.*) The cat did? The cat did? (*Pause.*) Everything gets changed, Martin . . . *everything?*

MARTIN: That's right, baby . . . everything. Except maybe a few things that are afraid to come out of their dark prison shells . . . (*Pause.*) What outfits are you ready to photograph next? We'll use the outdoors scene.

XENITH (*she slowly removes the red dress and reveals a cheesecake-type outfit underneath—a brief sports outfit or a bikini. She distractedly stands in front of the backdrop*): And the minute the light hits them . . . they change into something else . . .

MARTIN: Yea . . . like you. (*Pause. He goes over to her to indicate a pose.*)

XENITH: Like me? How?

MARTIN: The minute you leave this dark cell you've been sheltered in and the minute you take your shoes off and let the dirt get between your toes—instead of trampling on it with your shoes on—then you're gonna change too . . . and you'll be so different . . .

XENITH: I'm *not* gonna change, Martin. I can walk in all the dirt there is . . . and I can still stay the same . . . all I have to do is wash my feet . . .

MARTIN: And then you'll forget what they felt and smelled like when they were dirty.

XENITH: I didn't change when Daddy died . . . but I can remember his death. Alice changed. She started acting more . . . older. Mother changed too, she became more tired-looking and acting, but I didn't change. When it was cold, Daddy used to let me crawl under the blankets with him to get warm, and we'd both holler, "Cold sheet tonight" and then we'd both "crack up." Then he'd say, "Xenith, I don't think the old man's gonna be around in the morning. If I live through this night, it'll be a miracle." And then I'd say, and I'd still be laughing, "Aw, Daddy, stop playing around." (*Laughs.*) Then he'd say, "What'cha gonna do, Xenith, when Daddy's gone?" Then I'd say, "Shut up, SHUT UP!" Then I'd put my hands over my ears and jump out of bed, and shout real loud, so I couldn't hear what he was saying, "Chung, yemma yaaa, Eaaah chung chang chaaa eeeh." Then I'd run to my room and slam the door and jump on the bed, crying . . . You shoulda seen how I'd carry on . . . I'd just cry and shout and cuss . . . but, what was so funny . . . what was so funny was when he really died. I didn't change. I just stood there looking at myself look at him . . .

MARTIN: Maybe you should've changed then—

XENITH: Maybe you should swing through hell!

MARTIN: That's a good place for you to start . . .

(MOTHER *has entered during this. She has been staring unbelievingly at them.*)

MOTHER: You get the hell outa here! Come sneaking around here putting that con man's mouth on my daughter— You get out!

MARTIN: Wait a minute, Mrs. Graham . . . why you got to shout at me? All you got to do is nod in that direction . . . I'll leave.

XENITH (*frightened*): God damn, Ma! Martin just stopped in to see how I was doing.

MOTHER: I'm gonna tell you right now, Martin. Xenith has a boyfriend. A *good* boyfriend. He can do more for her than any of you bums. His father's a doctor. You're not going to ruin her chances with him.

XENITH: Shhh-hh . . .

MOTHER (*hollering at her*): And I *mean* that! Get in your

room and change your clothes! (XENITH *pauses half-fearfully, half-angrily. She finally walks off hesitantly.*)

MARTIN (*facing* MOTHER *with a dark, studied look*): What do you have against me?

MOTHER: I don't have anything against you—'cause there's nothing to you. Why should I waste my time considering something that ain't *nothing.*

MARTIN (*starts moving downstage left*): When you say I'm nothing—do you mean you can't see me, or what you see equals nothing . . .

MOTHER: You know what I mean, Martin—I'm not even gon waste my breath talking to a no-good *nothing*—nothing, trying to be something by clinging to something . . .

MARTIN: You mean, Xenith? (*Pause. He starts pacing.*) Yeah, I know what you mean, Mrs. Graham. And you know I know—but you got a few things wrong . . . Whatever I am is *not* no good! I'm beautiful and I'm good! Now I can either tell you about it or show you . . . see? (*Opens his sport jacket.*) Everything about me is good! (*Starts parading like a peacock.*) All six and three-quarter feet of me is *good!* It's a whole lot of people know I'm good!—and if you want me to—I'll be glad to show you how good I am! Let me tell you something, lady! What I am, you are too. And that, love, is why you hate me so. (MOTHER *starts*, MARTIN *goes to her and grabs her.*) Yeah —I'm nothing . . . but so are you. That's why you know so well what I am. Now, I'm admitting what I am, but you won't admit your story. I wonder if that makes me a better *nothing* than you, huh? (*Brutally.*) I'M YOU, NAKED! You and me are attracted to each other because we're mirror images of one another . . . and lady, you're clinging to Xenith just like I am —'cause she looks like a prettier picture of us than we do, doesn't she? I'm gon tell you the *truth!* Better yet, let me show it to you. (*Drags her to mirror.*) See! See how we look alike? Can't tell us apart, can you? Repelling, isn't it? Who? Me or you? (*Shouts.*) ME or YOU!? (*Kisses her.*) What do they call it when you kiss yourself? I like me. You must like me—is that your story, Mrs. Graham? (*Struts again.*) Lord, look at me— I'm beautiful! (*Holds out his arm.*) You ever see a prettier shade of black than this? Huh? And check these teeth—they're out-of-sight! (*Mockingly.*) The better to eat you with, my dear. HAAAhaaahaahaha! (*Struts.*) You know, if you eat vanilla ice cream all the time—you'll never know what chocolate tastes like. Hahaahahaahaaa. Lord, I'm beautiful and good!

MOTHER: Fool! I'm gon get the law!

MARTIN: The law! You mean my comrades? They ain't gon bother me—they my friends. Yes they are. They always got their arm around me. Heeheeehehe. Shoot! They know me by name. First name, mind you. That's how well they know me. Now, if you give 'em *my* name—they ain't gon even come, They gon say, "Oh, Martin? We know him, lady. He's nice, but no-good—unless he's gone contrary to his nature and killed somebody. What street you live on? Lady, this is the police department, not the friends of 18th Street. Now look, if you don't like the way your boyfriend's acting—give him a drink and settle his nerves. What! He's been shooting a gun off at you? Well, what do you want us to do? Stop calling us, lady, or next time we'll pick you up on a harassment of the police department act." How do you expect the cops to come over on 18th when they got their whole force over there protecting Lake Drive? You know, of course, they have a beautiful girls' school over there and the police force has to supervise their coming and going. No one is allowed to enter the grounds without a special permit—and so forth. What you say? How come the poor girls on 18th have cars lined up accosting them with not one cop in sight? Well, honey, didn't you know that *all* the girls on 18th are prostitutes and not nice and clean and *"good"* like those girls on Lake Drive? Now that's a fact! Xenith herself told me she gets accosted on the average of about five times a day—but there don't never be a cop around . . . Oh, I'm wrong. I'm wrong! One of the guys that approached her the other day was a cop . . . Sorry!

MOTHER (*grabs knife from the table with her free hand*): Get your filthy con-man hands off me before I run you through and lay you out for good!

MARTIN (*swings his camera up into position as though taking her picture*): Hey! That's a good one! Hold it! Let me get this picture of the "good" and the "beautiful" in all its glory! (*He walks over to her and gently lowers the knife behind her back.*) I'm leaving, love. (*He kisses her.*)—And when Xenith comes back, you tell her she just missed a good thing! (*He leaves.*)

(*Lights dim out. A soft light comes up on the telephone.* ALICE *is making a hasty phone call.*)·

ALICE: Charles? Charles, it's me. (*Pause.*) Charles, what's gonna happen? (*Pause.*) The ship hasn't released its cargo! The ship still hasn't come in—after all that . . . after all that, Charles. Yes. Okay. I'm not gonna get upset. Okay. Yes, I

661

remember . . . Friday . . . on Tracy . . Meet you at the restaurant . . When? Yes, I got it. (*She hangs up slowly.*) 'Bye, Charles.

Scene 2

(*Scene same. One hour later.* MOTHER *is seated at the table in a pseudo-calm air. She remains thus for a short time. She looks up and calls* XENITH, *still forcing a calmness.*)

MOTHER: Xenith? Xenith baby, come here. I want to talk to you. (XENITH *enters slowly, suspiciously.*) Baby, sit down, I want to talk to you. (XENITH *sits sullenly in rocker.*) Xenith —? (*A long pause.*) You know I want to see you happy. And sweetheart, I don't care *what* you do, but I just want you to do it after you marry somebody.

XENITH: Mother, what I want to do, I got to be free to do it. Martin didn't come here like my boyfriend . . . he came like a friend . . . Naw, but he ain't *good* enough for *my* friend. (*She gets up and goes toward* MOTHER.)

MOTHER (*draws* XENITH *close to her*): Xenith, I worked every kind of job there was so that I could raise you above these snotty-nosed brats that you grew up with. Not one of them has three quarters of the education or class that I gave you . . . and if I didn't have it for you—I *got* it for you. You didn't shed a tear from the day that you were born that I wasn't there to wipe it away for you. (*Laughs.*) The first day I brought you home from the hospital, your father said, "That gal don't have a *chance* to wet the way you change her every thirty minutes." And . . . to make sure that you wouldn't have to suffer in the mud of the world, I made your father buy that tall fence to put around the backyard, when we were living over on Canon Street . . . so that you and Alice could play outside, untouched by the garbage in the block. Alice was always trying to climb out, but not you . . . you were content. Now the whole neighborhood has their eye on you—you gotta show them that I didn't sacrifice in vain. I been more than good to you. I let you try everything in the world—even though I knew you'd fail because you're not hard enough for the world, Xenith. But I sacrificed everything to let you follow every whim you ever had. I let you try every school, every contest . . . it's time for you to change . . . what other mother would give her whole life for her daughter—

XENITH: But you've been *living* my life too, Ma. You tell me that you only do these things to spare me the dirty work. Well, how do I know that they're dirty? Just because you tell

me? The doctors and the newspapers tell me that "junk" is not good for you. Just because they *tell* me it's no good, doesn't mean it might not be good for *me*. I have to smoke it first to find out for myself if it's any good for me.

MOTHER (*upset*): I told you, I don't care *what* you do—go to hell if you want to . . . *after* you get married. No young girl can afford to go too long without being married . . . and still be considered decent. All these dogs that you grew up with are either on the corner or . . .

XENITH: Ma, why you got to call them dogs? They're not dogs just because they happen to be uneducated, or because they dress bad, or even because they're on the corner—that don't make them dogs.

MOTHER: Name me two that legally have a Mrs. attached to their names.

XENITH: I told you, Ma—I don't want to leech on to some dude that has already earned . . . (*Sighs.*) I want to get it myself. I want it to be mine—'cause I worked, 'cause I planned, maneuvered, dreamed it up *myself*.

MOTHER: You can still do that.

XENITH: What'd you say?

MOTHER: You can still do all that after you marry. Do you think Kenneth would be anything but glad to let his wife diddle around in the theater. He'd be glad to see you with some activities.

XENITH: But that's just it, Ma. I don't want to "diddle" around on the stage. It's *all* the way—which no dumb ass like Kenneth is going to understand—or I don't want to go at all.

MOTHER: If you marry Kenneth, you can do all that . . . you can do it better. You won't have to . . .

XENITH: No, Mother. I'm trying to tell you, it won't be the same. That's just it. If I marry him—half the work will be missing.

MOTHER: You mean the dirty work.

XENITH: Whatever it is, I want to know it on my own . . . not because someone painted over the dirt on it so that I couldn't see it.

MOTHER (*suddenly shouting*): You damn fool—I'm not going to sit here pleading with you. I'm *telling* you—you're going to do as I say!

XENITH: No, no, no, no, no, no, no. I'll die first!

MOTHER: Yes, you will—'cause I'll kill you before I let you ruin my name and yours by running after some foolish dream.

XENITH (*screaming*): It's no dream—and you can kill me

663

now . . . 'cause I won't marry Kenneth and I'll do what I want to—it's my damn life!

(*After this high pitch,* XENITH *subsides into a tired, hard-breathing, after-a-hard-fight calm. Her* MOTHER, *too, becomes quiet and resigned.*)

MOTHER: Well, then I guess there's no reason for me to continue to hang around. All I've worked for is turning against me.

(XENITH *has seated herself in the rocker. She stares, cold and indifferent, at her mother.* MOTHER *goes into the bedroom and brings out the box full of medicine. She dumps the box on the floor, and bottles, pills, etc., clatter and roll on the floor.*)

MOTHER: Let's see . . . (*Reads.*) "Forty aspirin per box . . . " (*Looks at* XENITH.) That ought to take me where I'm going . . . (*Turns bottle up and makes gasping, gurgling noises as she swallows some.* XENITH *bites her nails, but is still cold and indifferent in her attitude.*) Lysol! That gets rid of germs, doesn't it? (*She tosses some down—gasps—holds her chest—throws the bottle down.*)

XENITH: Ha! I know you're just—

MOTHER: What's this? (*Reads.*) "Oily nail-polish remover —helps prevent dryness—keep away from heat or flame." It ought to explode inside of *me!* (*She turns the bottle up to her lips. She is on her knees, downstage left. She slowly pours the rest of the nail-polish remover from the bottle onto the floor, trancelike. She speaks to the flowing liquid as she watches it spill out.*) Oh, you disappear as easily as all the years I've wasted.

XENITH: Aaeheehaaa ha ha ha . . . you're really good, Ma . . . really good . . .

MOTHER: Here is that shellac I brought you to preserve that basket you made in school . . . remember? Here it is . . . after all these years. (*She puts it to her lips. She begins breathing hard and gasping.*) Oooh, my stomach . . . my stomach . . . burns so bad . . .

XENITH: Aahahaha, Mother, I ought to give you the award for the best actress! (MOTHER *no longer makes any sounds. She slowly sinks onto the floor. Silence.* XENITH *still rocks in chair. Silence. Finally* XENITH *jumps up and screams.*) MA-AAA!!?

SCENE ENDS

Scene 3

(*Friday evening. Lights dim up on telephone area.* ALICE *dials.*)

ALICE: Charles? What happened? I waited there for you from three o'clock until now. What? But . . . but can't you take off sick? Yes, I know you told me how your boss is . . . but . . . (*Pause.*) You've got it all set up for tonight? Yes. Just a minute. (*She gets pencil and paper.*) What's his name? (*Writes.*) Yes . . . Yes . . . I got it. (*She lights a cigarette and smokes it furtively and nervously.*) Yes, I can go, I guess. You'll pick me up? Okay. No, I'm not gonna be afraid. Yes. I know you'd be there if you could . . . you already told me about that. I just thought . . . maybe . . . Okay. Yes. (*Hesitantly.*) Yes . . . I . . . I love you too. (*Starts to hang up.*) CHARLES! *Please* be there to pick me up! (ALICE *hangs up slowly. Crushes out cigarette and stands motionless, near tears. Lights dim out and up full on the apartment.* XENITH *is sitting dazedly rocking in chair. There is a knock at the door.* ANNIE *enters.*)

ANNIE (*uncertainly*): Honey, I got to use you-all's phone to call the TV repairman. That damn Quinton's been staying at my place ever since his landlady's kicked him out . . . and now that he done fucked up my TV—*now* he ready to go. I'm gon put that man in the wind if he don't get hisself together. (*There is an uncomfortable silence as neither one of the girls responds.* ALICE *slowly walks off toward the kitchen area.*) Ain't no sense in you two makin' yourselves sick, honey . . . your mother's gon be all right. Now, I was standing right there when the doctor told you she would be all right in no time. You-all's the one needs to be in bed, the way you-all's carrin' on. (*Starts looking through phone book.*) Honey? What I look under for TV's?

(XENITH *gets up and indifferently looks through phone book.*)

ANNIE (*uncomfortably*): How your play coming, honey?

XENITH: Which TV repair you want?

ANNIE: Oh, Lord! It's a whole lot of 'em, huh?

XENITH: Um, hum. You want one on this side of town?

ANNIE: Yeah. That's good. (XENITH *continues looking.*) So your play comin' along fine, huh?

XENITH (*still looking in telephone book*): I gotta finish it in a week.

ANNIE: What'cha mean?

XENITH: I have exactly one week to try to live my own life. Now that's really *funny,* isn't it? You think I can write a play in one week? I got to. Mother has consented to allow me one week to try to finish my play. After that, I made a pact with her that I would marry Kenneth.

ANNIE: Honey, marriage ain't so bad—especially if the joker got some money. You'll grow to it . . .

XENITH: I got to write my play, Annie. It's my only salvation, or else I have to descend into a death with Kenneth. I told Ma I'd marry if she'd let me work on my play for another week. I told her that—but I don't think I could ever really marry him. I've thought about it. I've tried to think that I could . . . but I can just feel his wet clammy hands on me . . . I can just see myself carrying a butcher knife to bed and stabbing him every time he stabbed me. The thought of him makes me nauseated. I really don't think I could do it. I mean, if I could do that—I could get out on the corner. So I guess my play better come off . . . 'cause Mother says this is my last time . . . and hers too.

ANNIE: You don't want no man, honey?

XENITH: Oh, yeah, Annie. There's nothing wrong with me . . . he just can't be Kenneth or any putrid, dead flower like Kenneth. That's all . . . And I wanna marry when and if *I* want to marry . . .

ANNIE: I just remembered . . . Mattie had these people fix her TV a while back. I'm gonna call her and ask her what their number is. You find that number for me, baby, instead? (XENITH *looks it up and dials. She gives* ANNIE *the phone and goes into the bedroom.*) Mattie? Listen, girl. Quinton been staying over to my place and he acting a big fool. Yeah, girl. You know how he always talking about how I ain't cultured? Well, when he come in the other night, I was watchin' this old movie on TV about Christmas. They was playin' this real se-dittyfied version of "Silent Night," you know, with bells and jive. So, Quinton comes in and I says, very refined, "Honey, I'm sure you recognize the tune, with all your cultured background." You know what that loudmouthed cuss said? He goes over and turns it off, talkin' 'bout, "If it had a little *soul* to it, it might be sayin' something." Then he started singing (*She imitates his singing.*), "Merry Xmas, bab—beee . . ." Heeehaahaahaa. Yeah. In't he dumb? Heehaahaa. Listen, what I called you about . . . 'member you had your TV fixed a while back? What? Yeah, I'll wait! (*Pause. To herself.*) Doggone! Every *time* she talks to me, she gets the "runs." Damn! (*Finally.*) Listen, child . . . when the last time you been for a medical checkup? Heeehaahaa. (*Looks at watch and jumps up.*) Girl, I got to go—Quinton'll be back soon and I ain't fixed nothing for dinner. What? Oh, yeah. What's the number? (*Writes.*) How do you spell that? Yeah. Yeah. Okay. I got it. 'Bye. See you later. (*Rushes out.*) 'Bye, Xenith—got to go.

(XENITH *enters wearing the tacky cocktail dress and stops at the table, picking up notebook and pencil. She looks them over and goes over to the mirror and poses for a short time. She starts for the front door as the scene ends.*)

ACT III

Scene 1

(*These next scenes are short, rapid scenes in which rock 'n' roll music is blaring, glasses are clinking, cigarette smoke is dense, and there is a suggestion of a crowded throng of people dancing, shouting, and cursing in dimmed, sensuous lights. In each scene,* XENITH *is seen sitting alone at a table downstage right, sipping on a drink and very self-consciously smoking, sometimes laughing, and writing in her notebook. There should be an almost ritualistic, hypnotic, mechanical dance quality inherent in these scenes. After the end of each quick scene, there is a tableau of the last action before the next scene fades in—except for the very last scene when* MARTIN *enters. The lighting on* XENITH *is not a spotlight, but the other people are seen as shadows in comparison to her.*

In the first scene, XENITH *is sitting and drumming the table in time to the music, occasionally sipping her drink and writing in her notebook. She sits thus for several minutes and finally taps one of the male patrons as he goes past her table.*)

XENITH: What time is it?

(*There is a tableau as their forms are silhouetted and the lights fade and come up on a comparable scene in a different club. The situation of the above scene is repeated and* XENITH *stops another male patron as he goes past her table.*)

XENITH: Do you have a light?

(*Another tableau as the lights fade out and up on a new nightclub scene. She once more sits and writes, laughing occasionally. She tries harder to be more natural in her surroundings, laughing harder, responding more to the music, but very self-conscious. Suddenly a male patron spies her. He is huge in size and dressed in a glaringly bright-colored suit. When he sees* XENITH *he lets out an ear-shattering wolf-howl that makes* XENITH *react with a start, but that is ignored by the other patrons.*)

MAN: OW—OOH, OWWW—MAMA! Get thee to a nunnery—thy beauty is too much for "us's." (XENITH *just smiles self-consciously.*) If you not in your lady-bag, baby . . . let's make it! (*He holds out his arms to dance.*)

(*At this point,* MARTIN *enters as if from nowhere. He mo-*

tions the man away, sits down at XENITH's *table, motions to the waitress, orders drinks. He does not speak. When the drinks arrive, he shoves one to* XENITH. *She sips, looking at him in consternation. He indicates she is to drink it all. She does. He then pushes his glass to her. She is looking at him almost with a fear at his strangeness. She drinks the second glass. When she finishes, he pulls her roughly up into his arms.)*

MARTIN: *Now*, baby. There gon be some changes goin' on. You can't come down here playing in the mud without getting dirty.

(They dance and seem to fade in and out of the crowd. Occasionally XENITH *emerges from the crowd and returns to the table downstage right to toss down a drink. Her speech becomes progressively slurred and brutal. Her dancing becomes less inhibited and frankly suggestive. She laughs a lot and can be heard above the crowd. Intermittently she can be heard shouting to her partners:* "Hey, lover, you *real* good!" "AWWW-W *DO* IT!" "Hang on to it!" "Sock it to 'em!" "Do it like it *is*," *etc.* MARTIN *seems to have disappeared while* XENITH *cavorts with numerous partners. He later appears downstage left, motionless and expressionless, watching her.* XENITH *finally crashes through the crowd on the shoulders of one of her dancing partners. He places her, breathless, laughing, and excited, on the top of the table downstage right. The crowd surrounds her, clapping and laughing. She continues dancing and laughing. One of her former dancing partners is overcome and goes up and strokes and caresses her legs while she is dancing.)*

MAN: Baby, where you been hiding? You a whaler from way back!

XENITH *(stops suddenly, looking at him fiercely and drunkenly)*: Who you think you talkin' to? Listen, son of a bitch, you think you big stuff 'cause I talk to you? You think you feel big? Well, let me tell you something . . . ! See, I know all about you . . . *(Someone in the crowd laughs,* XENITH *turns swiftly.)* And you too, pimp! . . .

MAN *(angry)*: Look, woman, you better get cool before I forget that you *supposed* to be a woman!

XENITH *(continuing)*: Let me tell you all just one goddamn thing . . . *(A few members of the crowd begin to disperse and ignore her.)* I been *playin'* with you jokers! I been actin', see! While you-all was for real, I was just ACTIN'! Haaahaahaha.

SOUNDS FROM THE CROWD:
Show business is getting better every day . . .

If you been actin', sister . . . you put them other actors to shame!

Hold on, everybody. We on *Candid Camera.*

If I'd a known we was bein' entertained, I'd a paid for admission.

XENITH (*above the crowd*): I *was* actin'! You thought I was for real? Haaahahahahaa! I was just playin'! I was just playin'! Heeeheeheeha! I was . . . just . . . playin'. (*Begins to cry hysterically.*) It's not *ME!* It's not *ME!* NO! NO! NO! NO, no, nono . . . it's not me . . . it's not me . . .

(MARTIN *watches her impassively and finally walks over and lifts her off the table as the scene ends.*)

Scene 2

(MARTIN *enters the* GRAHAM *apartment carrying* XENITH *who is crying and covering her eyes with her hands. Her clothing and hair are disheveled.* MARTIN *puts her down and she stumbles over to the table and crawls onto it, huddling in one sobbing lump, hiding her face.*)

XENITH: I don't want to see any more! I don't want to see any more! I don't want to see any more! I don't want to . . . I don't want to . . . I don't want to . . . I don't want to see ANYTHING, Martin! (*She looks up at* MARTIN *who has remained upstage near the door.*) It *was* me, Martin. I *was* me. I did change, Martin. I did change. (*Pause.*) But I want to change back. (*She looks at him searchingly.*) Why, Martin? Why?

MARTIN: Why? Well . . . You take the crowd over at Daddy's . . . nobody thinks of them as *real.* As human beings —so they play their part. They were just playing . . . and since their show might close any day—they want to make sure they don't leave any scenes out . . . that's why they are constantly making the scene. The cops don't think they're real, the storekeepers don't think they're real . . . (*Pause.*) *You* don't think they're real . . . so they just puttin' on a show for you. They only get real sometimes when they're alone . . . when they don't have an audience. (*Pause.*) Just like you don't think I'm real.

XENITH (*surprised*): What do you mean? I know you better than . . .

MARTIN: Naw, you don't, baby. You didn't know me years ago when I used to watch you and Alice behind your fence when we lived over on Canon Street . . . before the expressway

moved us. You didn't know how I used to climb up on the roof of my house just to watch you play in your backyard. You didn't know how I used to stand outside your house just to watch your mother take you to school . . . how I used to break into Sam's liquor store to take your old man a pint—so he would talk to me . . . and so he would sometimes mention you. I got tons of pictures of you that you don't even know I took. It's like I was an undeveloped negative, sweetheart. You don't even know that I'm not your friend, Xenith—your mother knows it . . . even Alice knows it. I was just playing my part. The funny thing is . . . I always wanted to see if you were real. (*He walks slowly over to her and towers over her at the table.*) Is there gonna be a love scene in your play? (*He begins kissing her slowly on the neck and ears.*) How are you gonna write about it? (*Pause.*) Now I *know* this girl, what's her name? Veronica? Veronica can't keep her shoes on in the love scene. (*Takes off* XENITH'*s shoes. Kisses her, slowly sinking onto the table as the lights fade.*)

(*Lights come up on* XENITH *sitting alone in the rocking chair with her shoes back on. Presently her sister enters.* ALICE *is walking stiff and rigid; both hands are clutching her sweater, which she has pulled down taunt over her abdomen. She walks downstage in front of* XENITH *and crumbles to the floor. Distant rock 'n' roll music is heard.* XENITH *looks at her dazedly and makes no motion.* ALICE *has a bitter expression on her face.*)

ALICE: Damn butcher! (*As if shouting to someone.*) BUTCH—ERRR! (*Howling, she looks up at* XENITH *who has not stirred.*) And you know what that damn pukey pimp, Charles, had the nerve to say to me when I came out? (*Burlesques his words.*) "Ship in yet?" . . . I said (*screaming*) HELL, YES, IT'S IN! . . . and it's not ever gonna sail again— not for you, brother! You'll never set foot on deck again—you damn dog! (*Crying.*) Oh, Xenith, Xenith, it hurt so bad— (ALICE *grabs* XENITH'*s leg and clings to it, rocking back and forth with the rhythm of the chair and the rock 'n' roll rhythm.* XENITH *does not move.* ALICE *looks up at her searchingly.*) You know what I kept thinking about all the time? Funny . . . I wasn't thinking about the pain. I kept thinking about when I die, someone might dig up my grave and everything would be decayed except the "bag" . . . the baby "bag" . . . with this scar, grinning in mockery, from one end of it to the other . . . the bag wouldn't decay, just so the whole world would know . . . (*Looks at* XENITH, *who is still motionless.*) LOOK AT ME! (*Still no response from* XENITH.) Maybe I

have to stand in the mirror in order for you to see me! (*Crawls to mirror, screaming.*) Can you see me now! Can you see me now! XENITH! XEE—NITH! (XENITH *begins to stir and reaches toward her feet.*) What are you doing? (*Screaming and crying.*) What are you doing, Xee—nith?

XENITH: I'm taking off my shoes. I've never walked around the house barefoot.

(*Scene ends with the loud thud of* XENITH's *shoes as she tosses them away, and the lights and the strains of the rock 'n' roll music enclose them in their environment.*)

END

Black Drama
Anthology